BRITAIN AND ARGENTINA
IN THE
NINETEENTH CENTURY

Oxford University Press, Amen House, London E.C.4

GLASGOW NEW YORK TORONTO MELBOURNE WELLINGTON
BOMBAY CALCUTTA MADRAS KARACHI KUALA LUMPUR
CAPE TOWN IBADAN NAIROBI ACCRA

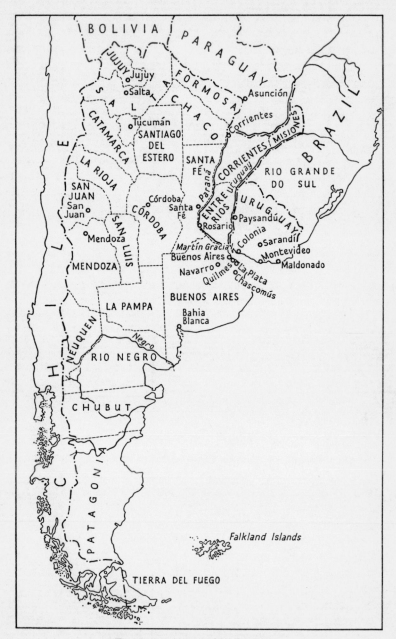

FIG. 1. Argentina and its Provinces

BRITAIN AND ARGENTINA

IN THE
NINETEENTH
CENTURY

BY

H. S. FERNS

OXFORD
AT THE CLARENDON PRESS
1960

TO THE MEMORY OF
MY FRIEND
EGERTON HERBERT NORMAN

PREFACE

MORE than half a century ago Alfred Marshall suggested to a group of his students that someone among them should devote himself to studying the growth of the British connexion with the Argentine Republic. One of that group, Dr. C. R. Fay, made the same suggestion in 1938, and persuaded me of the importance and interest of such a study. Although I have turned aside from the subject frequently and for long periods during the past twenty years and more, I have never regretted Dr. Fay's advice. Studied over a sufficiently long span of time, Anglo-Argentine relations constitute a case history touching many problems of great contemporary interest.

It is a well-known fact that by 1914 Argentina as a place of British investment and trade was comparable with Australia and Canada, and was exceeded in importance only by the United States and India. Until World War II few communities were more important to the British people—whether investors or consumers—than the Argentine Republic. An account of the conditions under which this development of business activity took place is the subject-matter of this book.

The papers of the Foreign Office constitute a continuously recorded and reasonably uniform body of information covering the entire period, from the British invasions to the resolution of the Baring Crisis, during which the character of the Anglo-Argentine connexion was formed. Supplemented by information drawn from private papers and the papers of the Admiralty, the War Office, the Board of Trade, and the Companies Registration Office, the Foreign Office files are the principal source of this study. They contain a vast variety of information of an economic and social as well as a political character. They have the merit of being focused upon the most general and critical problems of the intercourse between the two communities. For the most part they are the work of trained and often very acute observers.

I have, of course, relied upon and am indebted to the work of scholars and journalists who have concerned themselves with Argentina and Anglo-Argentine relations. It has been my method, however, to avoid theorizing, model-building, and using the conclusions and reflections of others in order that, by submission to the authority of my sources, I might discover something about the conditions under which in this instance economic development did or did not take place. The only general conclusion I have come to is neither novel nor surprising. It would appear from this study that economic growth is not something which occurs by itself, but is dependent at every stage upon political decisions and organization and more remotely upon the faith and values of the community.

The sources which I have used have influenced the presentation of the material. During the time when political decision-making was a predominant feature of Anglo-Argentine intercourse, a dramatic narrative springs at once from the sources, and one is concerned with individuals of distinctive character. Once political stability was in some measure achieved and the foundations of economic development laid, the impersonal, faceless character of business activity supervenes. Hence the character of this book, which commences with men and ends with processes.

I wish to acknowledge gratefully the generous assistance I have been given in my work by the Leverhulme Trust and the University of Birmingham. No less important to me has been the kind encouragement and help of my family and friends, and particularly Mr. D. M. Joslin, Dr. Jorge Sabato, Mrs. Barbara Smith, Mrs. Virginia McDonald, and my wife, Maureen Ferns.

H. S. F.

The University
Birmingham
1960

CONTENTS

LIST OF MAPS

ABBREVIATIONS

A.P.	British Museum, Additional Manuscripts, Aberdeen Papers
C.R.O.	Bush House, Documents of the Companies Registration Office
D.H.A.	*Documentos para la Historia Argentina* (Buenos Aires, various dates)
H.A.H.R.	*Hispanic American Historical Review*
B.P.	Public Archives of Canada, Baring Papers
F.O.	Public Record Office, Foreign Office Papers
Adm.	„ „ „ Admiralty Papers
W.O.	„ „ „ War Office Papers
B.T.	„ „ „ Board of Trade Papers

The first reference to other works gives the author, full title, and place and date of publication. Thereafter reference is made to the author and a short title.

INTRODUCTION

TODAY Buenos Aires is one of the great cities on the rim of the Atlantic Ocean. If there is an Atlantic community, Buenos Aires is one of its chief centres. Only London and New York exceed Buenos Aires as places of population, commerce, industry, and finance and as foci of railway, water, shipping, and air-line systems. Only Rio de Janeiro, São Paulo, and Philadelphia are comparable. The place of Buenos Aires and the Argentine Republic in the Atlantic world of colonization, trade, and investment was not always of the comparative consequence which has been its character during the past century. If we look back two centuries to a time before the revolution which separated the American empires of Spain and Britain from their motherlands, we see quite a different order of relationships. The great metropolises of the Atlantic were on the European side of the ocean. Buenos Aires and its hinterland were not as populous nor as important as the interior province of Córdoba, and nearly four times as many people lived and worked in the mountains of Alto Peru as there were in the community by the sea.[1]

The North Atlantic triangle has been the subject of much study and speculation. But there are also triangles whose lines cross the Equator and find their apexes in the Orinoco, Brazil, and the River Plate. This last triangle is no less interesting and important than the others. Its creation and development involved problems of politics which were unique in their character and yet contained elements of generality which are readily recognizable in our world of militant new nationalities. Anglo-Argentine intercourse is particularly interesting because, born of political revolution, its growth and maturity depended upon the strictest mutual respect and independence on the plane of politics, while on the plane of economics it involved a complex and delicate interdependence.

Like the United States, Canada, and Australia, Argentina

[1] J. Alvarez, *Estudio sobre las guerras civiles Argentinas* (Buenos Aires, 1914), p. 19. Estimated population in the mid-century: Buenos Aires province 130,000; Córdoba 200,000; Alto Peru 500,000.

was one of the significant frontiers of British business enterprise during the century before World War I. Initially, as the revolution against Spain drew to a close in the early 1820's, Argentina excited interest as a new Eldorado in Liverpool and London, and attracted both people and capital. A long period of disillusionment supervened. As the age of the gauchos and *caudillos* passed away in the 1860's, hope revived. British money and men began again to seek opportunities in the Argentine Republic. The tide of men and women from Britain and Ireland never flowed as strongly to Argentina as it did to the United States and the British dominions, but capital and the business men and technicians, who converted money into productive plant, flowed to the River Plate with almost torrential force in the 1880's. Then came the great Baring Crisis of the 1890's, an event of endless interest to those seeking to discover the secrets of the economics and politics of international investment. After a long pause for readjustment, a new tide of British trade and investment began to flow during the Boer War. Here this book terminates, for with this revival a new phase of Anglo-Argentine relations commenced; the phase of maturity and old age, which came to an end with the régime of General Perón.

The development of Argentina as a frontier of British business enterprise is a phenomenon of the nineteenth century: a factor in its industrial and commercial expansion and in the improvement of British real income. Before the Napoleonic Wars, British intercourse with the River Plate existed within the framework of a very old system of rivalry and co-operation between England and Spain, which came into being following the Anglo-Spanish stalemate reached at the end of Elizabeth I's reign. This system was based upon the Anglo-Spanish Treaty of 1604, and it endured and developed amid many vicissitudes and even war for nearly a century and a half.[1] Between the termination of the Asiento Treaty in 1750 and the outbreak of revolution in Latin America the Anglo-Spanish connexion was characterized by tension and change, and it is during this last phase that the demand for direct intercourse between Britain and the River Plate emerged.

This last phase coincided with a period of economic develop-

---

[1] This phase was first set forth clearly by J. O. McLachlan, *Trade and Peace with Old Spain, 1667–1750* (Cambridge, 1940.

ment in both Great Britain and Spain. The improvement in industrial techniques, the perfection of commercial organization, and the accumulation of abundant financial resources in Great Britain were, of course, far more dramatic than anything which happened in Spain, but the revival of Spanish industry, the widespread interest in economic questions, and the determination on the part of the Spanish Government to consider economic problems seriously and freshly cannot be neglected as factors in the new tension which began to mount steadily after the termination of the Asiento Treaty. The Spanish Empire created by the Emperor Charles V and by Philip II has been loosely described as a prime example of a mercantilist economic structure, but in this particular it could not have been compared with the British or French Empires. The Spanish Empire, as it existed before the economic and administrative reforms of Charles III, was ill designed as a market area capable of stimulating Spanish industry and providing Spanish industrial producers with an exclusive market for their wares. Likewise Spain itself was never a protected market for colonial wares in the way in which France and Britain were favoured markets for the produce of their overseas colonies. Spanish economic policy from first to last was preoccupied with the production and acquisition of bullion, and with the maintenance of an exclusive monopoly in this field beneficial to the Crown of Castile and to a narrow commercial interest in Seville and Cadiz. Extremely strict and exclusive in the matter of bullion marketing and extremely lax and haphazard in the matter of industry and commerce generally, Spanish economic controls, until the reforms of Charles III, had a dual effect neither half of which was beneficial to the general industry and commerce of Spain itself. On the one hand, the treaties with foreign powers, which gave foreign merchants a recognized place in the commerce of Seville and Cadiz, opened a channel by which French, English, and Dutch manufactures found their way to the Indies both legally and illegally; on the other hand, the restriction of trade narrowly to two ports in Spain and three in the Americas, the high costs of transport, and the opportunities for charging monopoly prices provided an inevitable measure of protection for colonial handicraftsmen. In no respect was Spanish America more like medieval Europe than in its local self-sufficiency and in the abundance and variety of its handicraftsmen working with primitive techniques to supply the few wants of people living lives of extreme simplicity and poverty. Not a few of the political problems which confronted European mercantile interests when once the power of Spain was broken stemmed directly from the existence of local economic interests fiercely determined to employ their liberty to protect themselves from foreign competition.

The tension of the final phase of Anglo-Spanish imperial rivalry can be attributed to two general classes of factors. On the British side there was growing discontent with the limited commercial opportunities provided by the treaty arrangements which canalized Anglo-Spanish trade through Seville and Cadiz and a growing impatience with the risks and uncertainties connected with the contraband trade. On the Spanish side there was growing determination to expel foreign economic influence and to utilize the Spanish Empire for the benefit of Spanish interests, or in other words, to create a mercantilist empire *à la* Colbert at a time when more liberal conceptions of commercial and industrial regulation were beginning to take root in Great Britain.

Charles III ascended the Spanish throne in 1759 at the moment when British arms were emerging triumphant in North America and in Asia. In order to redress the balance of power and in the hope of destroying once and for all the trade treaties with Britain[1] he entered into a *pacte de famille* with France, and in 1762 declared war on Great Britain. The result was unfortunate. He failed to get rid of the trade treaties, and he lost Minorca and Florida. French power disappeared in North America. England and Spain stood face to face, the two most powerful claimants to the control of the western hemisphere. Both powers considered a final collision inevitable, and began to prepare for it accordingly.

It would be painting a false and oversimplified picture of the final phase of Anglo-Spanish imperial tensions to emphasize too much its purely political character and to seek in the diplomatists' concern for the balance of power an explanation

---

[1] This element in the decision of Charles III has been noted by A. Christelow, 'Great Britain and the Trades from Cadiz and Lisbon to Spanish America and Brazil', *H.A.H.R.* xxvii, 1947, p. 10.

of the events which followed the Peace of Paris in 1763. Both Britain and Spain were rapidly outgrowing the old relationship based upon an antiquated system of commercial intercourse. The expansion of industrial production in Great Britain had changed the emphasis of British policy so that broader markets were more the object than assured sources of colonial supplies. The British were beginning to realize what their French competitors already knew,[1] namely, that superior British skill in supplying mass markets at low prices, superior market intelligence, greater financial resources, better packaging, and more standardized and consistent quality of goods were rendering Britain independent of traditional mercantilist organization. Rapid turnover rather than high profits on an assured but small volume of trade was becoming the object of commercial policy, and direct contact with markets more important than an elaborate system of factories and mercantile establishments based on treaties. British industrial strength and the character of British goods no longer needed British subjects in Spain to sell them, as one British Consul-General remarked,[2] and the simple system of selling on consignment was becoming a possibility.

British Ambassadors to the court of Charles III were instructed to regard the protection and expansion of British commerce as 'the principal object of [their] attention'.[3] They encountered little sympathy in Madrid. One of Charles III's first actions after his accession was to order an inquiry into the economic life of his Empire, and the main thesis of the report presented to him in 1761 was that 'by far the worst offenders of all in the contraband trade (which is the root of so many disorders in Your Majesty's dominions) are the English'.[4] Judging by all that followed, this report and its arguments became the basis of Spanish policy. It became the object of the state to reduce the opportunities of foreigners to accumulate capital in the Spanish Empire by commercial operations and

---

[1] Ibid., p. 18, for an appreciation of British competitive strength by the French Consul-General in Spain.
[2] Ibid.
[3] Ibid., p. 26.
[4] Archivo General de Indias, Indiferente General, 146–1–10, quoted in A. Christelow, 'Contraband Trade between Jamaica and the Spanish Main, and the Free Port Act of 1766', *H.A.H.R.* xxii, 1942, p. 313.

to increase the opportunities of Spaniards; to reduce the number of points at which opportunities existed for illegal trading between foreigners and Spanish subjects; and to increase the number of channels by which Spaniards could trade with one another. The economic policies of Charles III involved a combination of freedom and protection: of the economic freedom of which the Spanish economists talked so frequently in the eighteenth century and of the restrictions and state-directed enterprise so much within the tradition of Spanish government.

In 1762 a Spanish force seized Colonia do Sacramento on the River Plate from the Portuguese with the object of stopping up this gap through which contraband trade flowed so abundantly into the Audiencias of Buenos Aires and Charcas. Too badly defeated elsewhere Charles was not able to retain this conquest at the peace conference, but the determination to protect the Spanish commercial system more completely remained. The French Ambassador in Madrid observed that the British paid Charles's customs officers better than Charles himself, and that that accounted for the flourishing condition of British trade. Administrative reforms were undertaken with a view principally to stopping the illegal export of bullion so that it might be available for use by Spanish merchants in the Far Eastern trade and for the development of Manila as a commercial centre. In 1767 a shipload of cinnamon imported directly from Manila enabled Spanish merchants to undercut their British and Dutch competitors by 67 per cent., and the prospect of Spanish expansion in the Far East provoked Shelburne to declare that 'the restrictions laid upon England and Holland by those treaties in regard to trade in Spanish America must, of course, cease, as they were originally a compensation for the exclusion of Spain and her dominions in general from the commerce of the East Indies . . .'.[1] The same year the Spanish Government prohibited the importation into Spain of a range of textiles important in the colonial trade, and this, too, provoked strong British criticism.

In the presence of such Spanish policies the British Government and British mercantile interests reacted with characteristic ambivalence. British Ambassadors in Madrid may have

---

[1] F.O. 94/180, Shelburne to Gray, 16 Aug. 1768, quoted in Christelow, *H.A.H.R.* xxvii, 1947, p. 23.

been ordered to report on Spanish military and naval activities, but there is little evidence of a premeditated effort on the part of the British to assault and destroy the Spanish Empire by main force. Some attention was paid to the purely political aspects of the problem of Spain, but much more was devoted to strengthening the means for direct commercial penetration of the Spanish dominions. In 1766 Parliament legislated to establish several free ports in the West Indies where foreign vessels including Spanish ships could congregate, discharge cargoes of foreign colonial produce, and load cargoes of merchandise and slaves of British origin.[1] In 1765 Commodore Byron was sent to the Falkland Islands, and, in spite of the presence of the French, a British settlement was established two years later. This was another centre for contraband trade, or so the Spaniards thought; for in 1770 they dispatched an expedition which seized the islands only to discover that their French ally was not yet prepared to plunge into another war with Britain. And so the following year the Falkland Islands were restored to Britain just as Colonia do Sacramento had been restored to Portugal previously.

The establishment of free ports and the development of offshore bases around the Spanish Empire was one manœuvre. Of greater value economically both for its own sake and for finding a way into the Spanish dominions overseas was the intimate Anglo-Portuguese connexion. By treaty right an important range of British manufactures, and particularly textiles, entered Portugal and Portuguese possessions overseas. In Brazil British merchants enjoyed greater security for doing business than anywhere except in the British dominions themselves. The Brazil trade was the means by which Britain secured a substantial proportion of the bullion required for trade in the Far East, and was the avenue by which British manufactures found their way to Buenos Aires, Paraguay, and Peru.[2] But with Portugal, Britain experienced difficulties during the ascendancy of the Marquis of Pombal from 1750 onward. Pombal anticipated Charles III by some years in his energetic action directed to economic regeneration, and in this he collided with British interests. He arrested British naval officers for

[1] F. Armytage, *The Free Port System in the British West Indies* (London, 1953).
[2] Christelow, *H.A.H.R.* xxvii, 1947, p. 5.

contravening the regulations governing the bullion trade, and they threw his police into Lisbon harbour. He set up Portuguese trading companies with exclusive charters damaging to British merchants. Such measures hurt Britain, but there were limits beyond which Pombal could not afford to go. Portugal required British political support both at home and abroad. She was encouraged and enabled to expand the territory of Brazil. At the Peace of Paris, Colonia do Sacramento was restored to Portugal. She was assisted to defend herself against Spain at home. On balance the long-standing security of the British commercial opportunities inside the Portuguese Empire was not seriously disturbed, and the channels which Portugal provided for trade with the Spanish Empire remained intact.

If Spain had been more determined than France to settle accounts with Britain in 1770, when she seized the Falkland Islands, by the time of the American Revolution Charles III had become less enthusiastic or, perhaps, more subtle. Spain like France welcomed the prospect of dissension inside the British Empire, but the Spaniards were slow, where the French were quick, in their direct practical reaction. Several elements account for this. Firstly, a great administrative and economic reorganization of the Empire was finally coming to the point of implementation. Secondly, Britain's embarrassment afforded an opportunity for dealing with Portuguese encroachments on the eastern bank of the River Plate, for it was learned in Madrid that the British Cabinet refused further to support Pombal in his 'forward' policy in Brazil. Finally, there was the Spanish aristocratic abhorrence of rebellion even among Protestants, which caused Charles's minister, Floridablanca, to view with reserve an event so laden with horror as revolution in the Americas.

Simultaneously with the establishment of a vast new administrative unit, the Viceroyalty of the Río de la Plata, in 1776 a fleet was dispatched to deal with Portuguese encroachments. Colonia do Sacramento once again was seized. Spanish influence in Lisbon secured the dismissal of Pombal, and in 1777 by the terms of the Treaty of San Ildefonso both Colonia and the Paraguayan Missions were acknowledged as Spanish possessions. In 1778 the new commercial regulations of the Empire were proclaimed, freeing Spanish wines, agricultural products, and manufactures of all duties and opening a free trade between Buenos Aires and the Spanish ports in Europe. Only in June 1779, after long trying to play the role of mediator between Britain and her revolted colonies, did the Spanish Crown consider it safe and advantageous to declare war on Great Britain.

Spanish successes were impressive. Although the Spanish forces failed to take Gibraltar, they captured Minorca, Florida, and the Bahamas. They drove the British out of their fortified logwood camps in Honduras. But, if the war appeared to justify the political, diplomatic, and administrative policies of Charles III, it served also to reveal how far already the patient, pedestrian British policy of economic penetration had gone in at least one part of the Spanish dominions. The strict and absolute prohibition of commercial intercourse between Britain and Spain proclaimed upon the outbreak of war in 1779 caused the Viceroy of the Rió de la Plata, Juan José de Vértiz y Salcedo, to inform the Crown that 'the ruin of commerce in these ports because of the war with Great Britain has stopped trading in the European necessities which they provide; and without trade the money which ought to be remitted [to you does not exist]'.[1] The Crown was obliged to contradict the essentials of its own policy by issuing decrees permitting trade with Brazil, whereupon the customs revenues began to revive.

The war also revealed significantly that internal disorder in the colonies was not confined to the British Empire in America. In 1780 there was an Indian revolt in the Peruvian highlands under the leadership of Tupac Amarú, a descendant of the Inca. This revolt was put down and its leaders were executed, but it revealed a political tendency as dangerous to the Spanish Crown as anything the British Crown had encountered in the thirteen colonies; for a number of respectable and well-established Creoles in Alto Peru displayed a marked reluctance to assist the Crown against the rebels and a readiness to exploit the discontent of the lower orders of society for the purpose of embarrassing the Government. In Mendoza in the Viceroyalty of Buenos Aires the portrait of Charles III was publicly burned and the victories of the Indians were applauded.[2] Meanwhile, in the Viceroyalty of New Granada the *'comuneros'* revolted

[1] *D.H.A.*, v, p. cii.
[2] J. Lynch, *Spanish Colonial Administration, 1783–1810* (London, 1958), p. 263.

against the Government, and, by threatening Bogotá with violence, compelled the Government to modify its revenue system. Like the Indians of Peru the Creoles of New Granada were suppressed, but the Crown of Spain had encountered in both the northern and central parts of South America a political opposition greater than it had ever experienced since the first conquest and colonization.

From the close of the American Revolutionary War until the outbreak of the revolution in Spanish America in 1810 the tide of change mounted steadily within the established order of Anglo-Spanish relations. Increasingly, the traditional modes of this intercourse revealed themselves as inadequate to the political and economic transformation developing around the rim of the Atlantic Ocean.

On the British side the policy of economic encroachment through a clandestine trade was reaching the limits of its possibilities. As early as 1763 there had been evidence that the flow of British goods to Spanish America was in excess of the demand in this market.[1] Crises of this kind were a recurring phenomenon which suggested that the obstacles to further British commercial expansion were not so much the Laws of the Indies, which could be evaded, as the laws of economics which could not; for the poverty of the Spanish colonial markets, the low level of productivity, the local self-sufficiency, the static and hierarchical character of social relations, and the profound conservatism and spirit of resignation fostered by the Church were more potent than laws in determining the real size and elasticity of the market for British goods. The point was being approached by the time of the French Revolution where commercial expansion required not the reform of the customs laws of Spain, but the reformation of society.

On the British side, too, the crisis of eighteenth-century imperialism was compelling a profound and painful reconsideration of policy. As the eighteenth century progressed to its end, and political revolutions shook society on both sides of the Atlantic, it was becoming slowly evident that the traditional alternative to economic encroachment, conquest by main force, was ceasing to offer a practical solution to problems of expansion. Shaken by revolution in the thirteen colonies, Britain lost

[1] Christelow, *H.A.H.R.* xxii, 1942, p. 329.

territory to Spain during the American War, but when revolution began to spread to France's remaining empire in the West Indies this did not prove to Britain an opportunity for the acquisition of new territories. Between 1794 and 1796 the British Government conducted a great military campaign in the West Indies to put down revolution and to extend her overseas dominions. The cost was unbearable. More British troops were lost in three years in the West Indies than in the whole Peninsular War,[1] and Britain had nothing to show for the effort except devastation and chaos not only in the French islands but in her own possessions. When the attack was extended to Spanish territory, after Spain had changed from the British to the French side in the Revolutionary Wars, rather better results were achieved. Trinidad was captured at the cost of only one casualty, but the commander on the spot, Sir Ralph Abercromby, drew the conclusion not that further conquests would be easy if undertaken against Spain, but that British policy should be directed to arousing the subjects of Spain to revolution against a decadent and incompetent ruling class. Abercromby believed that a new, liberal order in the colonies would afford Britain an opportunity to conduct nine-tenths of the commerce of Spanish America.[2]

The notion entertained in Britain that the local interests of the inhabitants of the Spanish colonies divided them from their Government was a very ancient one dating from the days of Hawkins,[3] and it had some substance. It was not until after the American Revolution, however, that it came to be taken seriously as one foundation of British policy. During the Anglo-Spanish tension in 1790 over the rights of each nation on the north-west Pacific coast of North America it was represented to Pitt that the Spanish colonies were a 'mine ready charged' for an explosion to which Pitt had only to apply a match in the shape of arms for the revolutionaries. Pitt interviewed Francisco Miranda, the renegade Spanish officer and preacher of revolution, in February 1790, and put him on the British payroll

---

[1] J. W. Fortescue, *A History of the British Army* (London, 1906), iv, p. 496.

[2] Ibid., p. 540, and *Correspondence, Despatches and other Papers of Viscount Castlereagh* (London, 1851), vii, pp. 269 ff., for a memorandum by Abercromby.

[3] I. A. Wright (ed.), *Spanish Documents concerning English Voyages to the Caribbean 1527–1568, selected from the Archives of the Indies at Seville* (Hakluyt Society, London, 1929), Introduction.

until the Nootka Sound crisis was resolved.[1] From this time
forward plans to promote revolution in the Spanish overseas
dominions were periodically considered by the leading British
politicians, but much blood and treasure were spent and many
follies were perpetrated before the clear and simple line of
Castlereagh and Canning was evolved, and the transition
effected from the policies of eighteenth-century imperialism to
the policies of liberal support for revolutionary change.

In spite of an imposing and orderly structure which in theory
and on paper provided for the government of the several orders
of mankind and ensured their well-being in their appropriate
stations both in the here and the hereafter, the Spanish Empire
was ill designed to resist the new threat. Any Spanish statesman,
whether he was as able and hard-working as Charles III or as
empty and time-serving as Godoy, was faced with an insoluble
dilemma in the presence of changes of the magnitude of those
developing in the last half of the eighteenth century. The theory
of Spanish government assumed the supreme worth of a static
condition and in its practice made change and adjustment
extremely difficult. It was rationally apprehended that changes
were required to meet the challenge of British expansion, but
what the mind recognized the heart could not embrace.
Charles III's conception of change consisted too much of
adding to the administrative machinery of the state. In that
area of his Empire where his reforms really involved a change,
i.e. in the Viceroyalty of Buenos Aires, the growth he thus
stimulated only served to render more objectionable the improved administrative machinery he designed. The new administrative instruments with which he endowed his dominions
became the means of creating divisions within the top strata of
the hierarchy of government and at the same time became the
focal points of the tensions created by the progress he had
invited.[2] The weakness of any monolithic, catholic structure
is incapacity for adjustment arising out of its harmonious
adaptation of means to unchanging ends, and no better illus-
tration of this theoretical truth is provided by history than the
Spanish Empire.

To attribute to the political character of Spain and to its

---

[1] W. S. Robertson, *The Life of Miranda* (Chapel Hill, 1929), i, pp. 97–102.
[2] Lynch, *Spanish Colonial Administration*, pp. 279 ff.

domination by an aristocratic monarchy and a dogmatic Church all the difficulties and weaknesses of the Spanish Empire on the eve of its demise is, however, an over-simplification. Nature not man determined some of the essentials of the life of the Spanish Empire. When the Spaniards came to America and established themselves there during the first half of the sixteenth century they soon learned that the riches of the Indies consisted in people and not treasure. *Sin Indios no hay Indias.* A mountain of silver in Mexico was nothing without people to dig it out and carry it to the sea; nor was a humid rain forest a source of wealth without men and women to cut down the trees and plant sugar canes. Peninsular Spain was poor in people, and became steadily poorer during the course of the seventeenth and part of the eighteenth centuries. The gentle and innocent cannibals of the Caribbean were unable to survive the rigours of their contact with the Spaniards, and the supply of people was thus further diminished. The only concentrations of people civilized enough and tough enough to survive the invasion of the Spaniards lived in the interior highlands of Mexico and Peru shut away from the sea by rugged mountains familiar enough to the Spaniards, but, like the mountains of Spain, obstacles to travel and the easy and cheap flow of men and goods back and forth in commerce. There were good economic reasons why the Spanish Empire from first to last produced principally one staple of international trade, bullion; for, of all commodities, bullion by reason of its value in relation to its weight was able to bear the high costs of transport from the remote centres of production in the Americas to the markets of Europe and the Far East.

Very little of the old Spanish Empire from the Rio Grande to Tierra del Fuego is capable of economic exploitation for the purposes of an international economy without heavy investments of capital and an advanced technology. Even today this part of the world is not as economically well developed as North America, Europe, or Australia, and the difficulties of development in the pre-industrial age were formidable indeed. Even if the Laws of the Indies had never existed to limit the scope of the international division of labour and the part of the Spanish Empire therein, the facts of soil, climate, and terrain would have compelled—as they did compel—the development of numerous and highly localized centres of production organized around a simple handicraft and agricultural division of labour. The Spanish Empire on the eve of its dissolution resembled the Roman Empire more than the contemporary British or French Empires. Indeed, the Roman Empire possessed a more solid and various economic foundation than the Spanish Empire.

Although the conquistadors of the sixteenth century could attract the capital and had the administrative and political talents necessary to solve the first problems of development in regions so challenging to human ingenuity, the Spain which continued to possess the Americas was ill adapted socially, politically, and intellectually to continue that development. The men and corporations who ruled the Americas viewed their possessions as assets which nourished their bodies, provided their pleasures, and insured their eternal salvation. They did not regard their assets as producing something which should be reinvested to produce more wealth. No contrast could be more sharp than that which existed between the conceptions and practice of public finance in Spain and Britain. The Viceroyalty of Buenos Aires, for example, alway sproduced a surplus beneficial to the Spanish Crown and to its officials. No colony every produced revenue beneficial to the British Government. If anything the British colonies were financial liabilities to the British Government. But they were commercial assets to the British people. In Britain itself the debts of the Government were the assets of its subjects. Not so in Spain, and not so in the Spanish colonies. The social surpluses of the Spanish Empire were absorbed by the Crown, the Church, and its aristocracy to build their palaces, their cathedrals, and their cities and to nourish their armies, their priests, and their politicians. When Charles III reformed the institutions of the Viceroyalty of Buenos Aires, his intendants were instructed to foster economic development, and all they succeeded in doing was building better public buildings and providing better social services.[1] In Britain and its colonies the ornaments of society were by-products provided after the owners of capital had absorbed the social surpluses and reinvested them. The Spanish Empire, which needed more capital for development than the

---

[1] Lynch, *Spanish Colonial Administration*, p. 285.

British Empire, received less. There is a real and a fundamental distinction between a social organism devoted in its main purposes to capital accumulation and one devoted to pre-capitalist purposes, and this distinction was the essential one between Spain and Britain when the Spanish Empire fell and Britain subtly assisted it to fall.

FIG. 2. The Atlantic Setting.

I

THE POLITICAL EQUATION
DISCOVERED

THE history of Anglo-Argentine relations begins on 8 June
1806 when a British fleet of warships and troop transports appeared in the River Plate. The assault upon the
Viceroyalty of the Río de la Plata which followed is in many
respects the most important event in Argentine history. In that
armed conflict not only was the authority of the Spanish
Crown overthrown but the Argentine Republic was born.
When the Viceroy Sobremonte fled before the British troops,
the Spanish monarchy in America began to die; when the
forces under Santiago de Liniers and Juan Martín de Pueyrredón compelled the British invaders to surrender, the republic as
a living institution was conceived.

These momentous convulsions in South America owed their
initiation not to the carefully premeditated policy of a government nor to the long-debated plans of a revolutionary committee but to the impulse and imagination of a single man,
Commodore Sir Home Popham of the Royal Navy. The historian of the British Army, Sir John Fortescue, has lamented the
circumstances which prevented the inhabitants of Buenos Aires
from hanging Popham 'as he deserved',[1] but, merited though
this judgement may be, this extraordinary man was in many
ways an exemplar of the age in which he lived and the nation
to which he belonged: in the variety of his talents, the abundance of his energy, and the largeness of his political imagination
and experience. Home Riggs Popham was the twenty-first child
of the British Consul at Tetuan. From his father he inherited
nothing except intelligence and a philoprogenitive tendency
which yielded him a large family whose provisioning was one
of his constant problems and excuses.[2] Educated at Westminster
School he entered the Navy after one year at Cambridge. As

[1] Fortescue, A History of the British Army, v, p. 372.
[2] Adm. 1/58, Popham to Stirling, 10 Dec. 1806.

a naval officer he displayed a number of talents, all of a high
order. While still very young he conducted a survey of the coast
of south-west Africa. He developed and refined the Navy's
system of visual signalling with flags and semaphores.[1] He was
one of the first naval men to calculate longitude accurately
with a chronometer. He surveyed the coast of Penang and
executed some feats of navigation for the China Fleet of the
East India Company considered so valuable that the Governor-
General and Court of Directors voted him a gold cup. He
surveyed the mouth of the Hooghly River, and laid out the
dockyards there. For his work as a surveyor, astronomer, and
navigator he was elected a Fellow of the Royal Society. He
enjoyed also a considerable reputation as a director of combined
operations to the extent that even Sir John Fortescue was con-
strained to admire his capacity for co-operation with the Army.

To his technical talents Popham joined a capacity for diplomacy and politics. He negotiated trade treaties with the Arab
princes at Yeddah. He conducted negotiations at the Russian
Court, where he so won favour that the Tsar knighted him and
the Tsarina presented him with a diamond ring. While on half
pay he made a large fortune trading in China, lost part of it
when one of his cargoes was seized as contraband by British
cruisers, and regained part of it by skilful political agitation and
acute legal action. He was tried by court martial for corrupt
practice in the repair of one of H.M. ships, but agitated against
his conviction with such effect that a Select Committee of
the House of Commons vindicated his character and censured
Admiral Lord St. Vincent for attempting to victimize a subordinate. After his court martial on account of his unauthorized
attack on Buenos Aires, he was soon restored to duty, and was
shortly a colleague of the future Duke of Wellington in negotiating the surrender of the Danish fleet. Before he died prematurely of ill health from service in the West Indies, Popham
had been promoted to the rank of Rear-Admiral and knighted
in the Order of the Bath.

Although much of Popham's career was extraordinary, the
most astonishing episode of all was his attempt to conquer the
Viceroyalty of the Río de la Plata. If we are to believe his own
account, it would appear that he planned an operation involving

[1] *Manual of Seamanship* (London, 1951), i, p. 243.

the conquest of half a continent in the space of twenty-four hours. The idea of doing so took rather longer to mature. In 1804 Popham had been concerned with Viscount Melville in one of the frequent meditations of the British Cabinet on the subject of how to blow up the Spanish Empire. In a memorandum addressed to Melville in October of that year Popham summed up his ideas on both the advantages of seizing South America and the mode of procedure.

The idea of conquering South America [he wrote] is totally out of the question, but the possibility of gaining all its prominent points, alienating it from its present European Connections, fixing on some Military position, and enjoying all its Commercial advantages can be reduced to a fair calculation, if not a certain operation; The Nerve and Spirit which such an Enterprize would give to this Country if successful are incalculable. The riches that it would bring in, the new Sources that it would open for our Manufactures and Navigation, both from Europe and Terra Firma, and from Asia to the Pacifick, are equally incalculable, and the popularity and stability that it would give any Government that undertook it, may be estimated from the preceding propositions . . . .[1]

At the time when Popham thus addressed himself to Melville, the British Government was still very much in the grip of the notion that Napoleon could be countered best by seizing as many strong points as possible outside Europe and that, by expanding the British Empire, the threat of Napoleon's power could somehow be met. The ghost of the elder Pitt still governed, prompting the British leaders to believe that France could be safely left to her rivals on the continent of Europe while Britain picked up the possessions of France and her allies overseas.

Popham's ideas about South America thus suited very well the disposition of one powerful school of British strategists. That this was not taken up with more enthusiasm was due only to the fear that action against Spain in America might further harden the connexion of Spain and France in Europe. 'The idea of liberating South America is certainly not a new one to me', Lord Pelham had written in a paper for Cabinet consideration, '. . . But I am not prepared to say that we should engage in an enterprise that may accelerate [our exclusion from Europe] by

[1] Adm. 1/58, Popham to Melville, 14 Oct. 1804, enclosed with Popham to the Admiralty, 30 Apr. 1806.

throwing Spain still more into the hands of France.'[1] The idea
of liberating or invading Spain's colonies overseas thus existed
side by side with the inhibitions to its realization, and so the
matter stood when Popham was appointed to command the
squadron convoying the troops dispatched to seize Cape Town
from the Dutch.

If Cape Town, why not Buenos Aires and Montevideo? This
is how Popham seems to have reasoned. The defeat of the
Franco-Spanish fleet at Trafalgar in 1805 had given the Royal
Navy a greater freedom of operation and reduced the need
for wariness and a heavy concentration of forces in European waters. There is no evidence, however, that the British
Government reasoned as Popham did, or that it wished to take
any large advantage of its new opportunities. When he was
obliged to defend himself for his actions, Popham could produce no evidence later than his memorandum to Melville of
October 1804 to suggest that any responsible adviser of the
British Crown had even thought about, let alone ordered, an
attack on the Viceroyalty of the Río de la Plata. Popham himself appears to have considered seizing Montevideo and Buenos
Aires before ever he sailed for the Cape. If he did not discuss
the project with his superiors in the Admiralty or with members
of the British Government, he appears, however, to have discussed it with mercantile friends. A certain 'Mr. Wilson, an
eminent Merchant of the City of London', for example, assured
him 'before he left town' that Montevideo was defenceless and
one thousand men could capture the colony of Buenos Aires.[2]

The operation against the Cape turned out in a way which
stimulated Popham to attempt his favourite project. The
passage south was an easy one with no losses. The forces of
the Batavian Republic offered no serious resistance when the
British landed. There were few casualties. Because he left the
Dutch flag flying over the fort, the British commander was able
to lure into the harbour a French frigate loaded with British
prisoners of war. These released prisoners served to reinforce
the number of troops available. Furthermore, a shortage of supplies due to a drought or, perhaps, a withholding of provisions

---

[1] Castlereagh, *Correspondence*, vii, p. 286. Pelham's opinion was given in Sept.
1801, but it was as much a valid view in 1804 as it had been for many years before
he set it down.   [2] Adm. 1/58, Popham to the Admiralty, 30 Apr. 1806.

by the farmers in the colony suggested the wisdom of looking elsewhere for food for the garrison. On 9 April 1806 Popham wrote to the Admiralty to say that he planned to cruise on the coast of South America in the hope of securing a supply of flour. Because the breeze was insufficient for him to clear the harbour, he went back ashore the next day. According to his own account, Popham then received information which persuaded him to conquer or liberate Buenos Aires. The twenty-four hours which elapsed between the time Popham went ashore on the 11th and the moment when Sir David Baird, the commander of the land forces at the Cape, issued his orders to Colonel William Carr Beresford on the 12th would appear to have been the time when it was planned to conquer the Vice-royalty of the Río de la Plata. If such be so, this is perhaps the first occasion in recorded history when so extensive an operation as conquering half a continent was undertaken in so short a time as a day and a night.

The 71st Regiment of Foot began to go aboard the transports at once. In all there were 36 officers, 922 men, 60 women, and 40 children embarked including, as well as the 71st Regiment, a small detachment of artillery and a few dismounted dragoons. In his last letter to the Admiralty before setting sail Popham expressed the hope that his action would be 'considered by their Lordships as far preferable to the alternative of allowing the Squadron I have the honour to command to moulder away its natural energy, by wintering in False Bay, and eventually become paralyzed after remaining so long as it has done in a state of cold defensive inactivity'.[1] *Toujours l'attaque.*

On the 14th Popham's force of five ships of war and five transports cleared the Cape, bearing for St. Helena. In squally weather they lost sight of the transport *Ocean*. At St. Helena they reassembled, and received a considerable reinforcement of infantry, artillery, and marines, which nearly doubled the men available for action. Popham seems to have employed some of his time between the Cape and St. Helena in reflecting upon the magnitude of what he was undertaking and the enormity of his offence in acting without instructions; for he dispatched from St. Helena an extensive apologia for his actions, an appeal for at least two more regiments of reinforcements, and a general

[1] Adm. 1/58, Popham to the Admiralty, 13 Apr. 1806.

plan of the politico-military strategy he proposed to employ.
On 1 June he sailed from St. Helena predicting that he would
make the passage to the River Plate in a week. On the 8th his
fleet appeared off Montevideo. The stage was set for the realization of all Popham's plans.

What were they? Before he left St. Helena, Popham begged
the Lords of the Admiralty to believe that his 'Project [had]
not arisen from any sudden Impulse, or the immediate desire
of gratifying an adventurous Spirit . . .'.[1] This was indeed the
case. Popham was no naval bravo. He had a good knowledge
of the politics behind his adventure and shrewd notions of what
might be the consequences of his action in economic as well as
military terms. He appreciated, although he never resolved, the
contradiction between conquest and liberation, and he had a
clear understanding that political manœuvre was more important than military power in achieving his objective. 'There can
be no idea', he told his superiors in London, 'of moving a Man
into the Country, the Object will be to gain that by Negotiation and the offer of a liberal Trade, and make Monte Video
as strong as possible until more re-inforcements arrive from
Europe . . .'.[2]

From Popham's memorandum prepared for Melville in 1804
and from his dispatches in 1806 there emerges an analysis of
the problem of overthrowing Spanish power in the Viceroyalty
of the Río de la Plata which is rational, comprehensive, and, in
its judgement of eventualities if not of immediacies, accurate.
Popham was persuaded that there existed in the Viceroyalty
differences of interest between the Government and its supporters and a portion of the commercial and landowning classes,
and that the latter would welcome a policy of free trade. He
believed in a confused way that the community in Buenos Aires
was potentially revolutionary and that his action against the
Spanish Government would lead to independence. Popham
was more clear on this subject after the event than before.[3]
There is no evidence that, when he had an opportunity to do
so, he insisted upon a declaration of their independence of
Spain *and Britain* as an indispensable condition for the success
of his action.

---

[1] Adm. 1/58, Popham to the Admiralty, 30 Apr. 1806.
[2] Ibid.   [3] Adm. 1/58, Popham to Stirling, 6 Dec. 1806.

Popham also assumed that the Spanish forces in the Vice-royalty were weak; that no naval resistance would be offered; that the fortress of Montevideo was in a crumbling condition, and that the land forces were inconsiderable.

Popham's analysis of the importance of Buenos Aires was chiefly commercial and economic. Buenos Aires is, he argued, 'the best commercial situation in South America', and 'so centrically situated as to be within 60 or 70 days sail of all the considerable trading countries with which we have any inter-course'.[1] He asserted that it gave access to a market for British manufactures numbering several million customers and that the region would supply hides and tallow, bullion, flour, meat, cocoa, copper, wool, and hemp. To direct its trade towards Britain and away from neutrals would be to strike a serious blow at the French and to confer a corresponding advantage upon Great Britain. Popham reinforced his general commercial argu-ments with a particular argument covering the advantages to the British forces at the Cape of having the supplies of Buenos Aires available to them.

Popham depended for his information upon a variety of sources, some of dubious value. On the political side he made much of the assertions of General Miranda, who had preached revolution in the Spanish colonies not to the Creoles of South America but to the crowned heads and revolutionary commit-tees of Europe. That Miranda had succeeded in persuading Catherine the Great of the possibility of revolution in Caracas was no proof of Creole unrest. Popham's other authorities were only slightly better informed and no less interested than he. To his last dispatches from the Cape Popham appended a 'pro-found secret' communication he had had from an American ship's captain, who described the people of Buenos Aires and Montevideo as 'so ridden by their Government . . . that if the Trade is thrown open all the Inhabitants would willingly acquiesce and keep the place for the British Nation without Troops . . .'.[2] In 1806 the world had yet had small experience of Americans who see in every government not modelled on American principles a tyranny from which their subjects long

---

[1] Adm. 1/58, Popham to the Admiralty, 9 July 1806.
[2] Adm. 1/58, J. Wain to Popham, 28 Mar. 1806, enclosed with Popham to the Admiralty, 13 Apr. 1806.

to be free, and Popham may, perhaps, be pardoned on this account, but Captain Wain's intelligence was no more particular and precise than any which Miranda had employed in peddling revolution. Popham's other informants were hardly impressive: an English ship's carpenter who had lived in Montevideo for eleven months, who told of a small garrison and crumbling fortifications, and an English customs-house interpreter from Buenos Aires, who told Popham what he wanted in any case to hear.

'We have', wrote Popham, 'many other similar Testimonies of . . . military weakness and . . . political Disaffection.'[1] These came from British merchants. They were not necessarily untrue, but they were incomplete and the result of observation by politically inexperienced people. Merchants trading to South America knew only the coast ports, and only a small segment of the population even in these ports. Undoubtedly they encountered in their operations people who were discontented with Spanish commercial regulations and were quite willing to see the end of Spanish rule. But judgements based on such experience left out of account the interests and disposition of the people living in the interior of the continent, and for this reason the easy generalizations of British merchants, on which Popham set so much stock, were an unsatisfactory guide, as events were to demonstrate, either to the course or character of political developments in South America. It is interesting to note that Sir Arthur Wellesley with no experience of South America, writing before his experience in Spain, was able to predict more accurately than Popham or his mercantile friends the real source of political difficulties for Britain in Spanish America. The priests, he argued, will be anti-British, and they will act as inciting agents of Spanish power.[2] But Sir Arthur Wellesley was an Irish landlord as well as a soldier and politician.

A judgement of Sir Home Popham in this particular episode presents many difficulties. His adventure failed, and it failed because without exception the assumptions upon which he based his action were wrong. But they were wrong only in a very particular sense and wrong only in the years 1806 and 1807. Popham *did* strike a blow at Spanish power in the Americas, the

---

[1] Adm. 1/58, Popham to the Admiralty, 30 Apr. 1806.
[2] W.O. 1/161, Memorandum by Sir Arthur Wellesley, 10 Dec. 1806.

consequences of which were greater and historically more significant than anything Drake ever did after the defeat of the Armada;
or Penn or Anson. Popham's general assertions were correct:
the Spanish monarchy in America and particularly in Buenos
Aires was feebly founded. Powerful interest groups in the Viceroyalty of the Río de la Plata were seeking larger opportunities
to trade. Political independence was a viable aspiration. Buenos
Aires was commercially and economically of great importance.

Left to himself Popham might very well have carried the day,
for he was a man of large understanding, quick perception, and
readiness to change his ideas and modes of action in the
presence of difficulties. Although he enjoyed the wide freedom
of action customarily accorded to British commanders at that
time and although he took a far wider freedom than even custom and administrative practice allowed, Popham was still tied
to the ponderous machine of government which limited his
political initiative. Before he left the Cape he had allowed himself to become so tied that he was never able to act logically
upon his larger assumptions nor was he able to exercise to the
full his undoubted political genius.

In attacking Buenos Aires he was obliged to receive the consent and support of his immediately senior officer at the Cape,
General Sir David Baird, who possessed the troops indispensable to the operation. Baird appears to have known nothing
about the Río de la Plata except that there was located a
strong point of an enemy state the possession of which might
strengthen his position at the Cape and improve his supplies.
In persuading Baird to consent to the attack on the Río de la
Plata and to supply the necessary troops Popham appears to
have refrained from the presentation of arguments about politics and limited himself to the military aspects of the case. Baird
was a man little disposed to listen to political discussion of any
kind and particularly to discussion having revolutionary implications. When Baird consented to the operation he issued
instructions, and so as to ensure that these instructions were
obeyed he raised the commander of the land forces to a rank
equivalent to that of Popham in order, it would appear, that no
claim to local seniority would give Popham freedom to behave
as he pleased. Colonel Beresford of the 71st Regiment was made
a Brigadier, and as such enjoyed authority equal to that of

Popham. The fatal defect in this arrangement so far as it concerned Popham was the fact that Beresford was bound by the
orders of Baird and that these orders were very specific on the
basic question of the political objectives of the operation. Beresford was instructed to establish himself as lieutenant-governor
'in and over the several Spanish Settlements at Río de la
Plata, which may submit to His Majesty's Arms, and to draw
as such, the same salary and allowances, as may have been
enjoyed by the Spanish Governor'. This excluded the possibility
of proclaiming the independence of the community in Buenos
Aires, and Beresford's first act after surrender made plain, by
requiring from the inhabitants an oath of allegiance to King
George III, that conquest not liberation was the purpose of the invasion. Popham lamented this action, but he lamented after he was
driven from Buenos Aires and not before he sailed from the Cape.

Popham had declared his first objective to be the seizure of
Montevideo. Although he did not explain immediately why he
abandoned this intention, he subsequently informed his successor that shortly after entering the River Plate he encountered
bad weather. Reconnaissance revealed that the walls of Montevideo were not in a crumbling condition. On the contrary they
were in good repair and were defended by artillery in a condition to fire. Beresford did not possess a train of heavy artillery.
Furthermore, the shore was of such a character that ships
carrying heavy guns could not come in close enough, except on
the rare occasions of very high water, seriously to breach the
walls with fire from the sea[1]. Sir John Fortescue has asserted
that Popham abandoned the seizure of Montevideo simply
because there was more prize money to be found in Buenos
Aires, but this seems to be an unjust judgement. Montevideo
could not be taken. There were good military reasons for by-
passing the city and for proceeding up the river to Buenos
Aires, the real heart of the Viceroyalty.

Montevideo, with its mountain, its harbour, and its fortress
standing guard, was a strong point presenting a familiar enough
challenge to a soldier. Buenos Aires wore a different aspect:
indistinct on the straight shore line, a flat city sunk in flat land
showing only four domes and spires to announce its importance.
The river constituted one defence, for the shore was flat and

[1] Adm. 1/58, Popham to Stirling, 6 Dec. 1806.

shallow, and ships were obliged to anchor at a great distance from dry land. A fortress intended as a defence of the city provided a residence for the Government, but from its platforms artillery could neither clear the river of an enemy nor protect the inhabitants from a landward assault. Buenos Aires was a place where men worked, lounged, traded, and prayed. It was the heart and brain but not the strong arm and clenched fist of the Viceroyalty—or so it seemed.

Popham and Beresford were not, however, prepared to take the capture of Buenos Aires for granted. Plainly the city would have to be taken from the landward side rather than from the river, and to do this speed and surprise were required. This was a situation congenial to the talents of the Commodore. A swift landing operation was planned. On 25 June at Quilmes eight miles down river from the city, a force of slightly more than 1,600 were put ashore quickly and without opposition: the 71st Regiment, artillery, dismounted dragoons, Royal Marines, and sailors from the fleet. At the crossing of the Riachuelo between the landing-place and the city, Beresford's troops encountered a feeble show of force, which they brushed aside without loss to themselves, and on the 27th, forty-eight hours after commencing to come ashore, Beresford's troops received the surrender of Buenos Aires. Their casualties were one man killed and twelve wounded.

This sudden conquest of the second largest Spanish city in South America requires some explanation. The Spanish Viceroy, the Marquis of Sobremonte, has found few historians willing to defend his conduct or even to explain it. When he heard of the British ships in the river, he seems to have assumed on good grounds that they could do the Viceroyalty no damage, for so small a force could not take Montevideo, and if they could not do this, they could do nothing. Sobremonte seems never to have considered a landing at Buenos Aires a serious possibility. He made no preparations of any description. When the news was brought to him on the evening of the 24th that the British fleet was moving into position to land a force, he was with his family at the theatre celebrating the betrothal of his daughter. The news flabbergasted him. He left the theatre with his family and his aides, and prepared to flee into the interior taking with him the bullion in the treasury. His action epitomized

the Spanish regime in America. Marvellously organized, monolithic, devoted to accumulating treasure, having achieved the
ideal of 'no politics' dear to the hearts of administrators, the
Spanish Viceroyalty was ill equipped for sudden action or to
summon the people to join with the Government in resisting
an enemy who somehow had defied the prescribed rules governing the defence of His Most Catholic Majesty's dominions.

By the morning of 28 June the British flag was flying from
the fortress of Buenos Aires. Now came the testing time for
Popham. Was he as skilful a politician as he was a naval commander? Beresford freely acknowledged that he needed political
instruction—he had asked for direction from London before
leaving St. Helena—and he was willing in the circumstances to
leave all political decisions to Popham and to devote himself to
the task, formidable enough in itself, of maintaining his military
organization.[1] With Popham, therefore, the main task of political decision rested. He was now in physical possession of a city
numbering between 45,000 and 70,000 inhabitants,[2] the heaviest
concentration of people and wealth in the Viceroyalty and the
community where, if anywhere, could best be found the people
most willing to try new courses of political action.

This being so, one might have supposed that the departure
of the Spanish authorities and the surrender of their armed
forces in Buenos Aires would have left the field free for the anti-
Spanish party. But it did not. In fact the flight of the Viceroy,
the Marquis of Sobremonte, strengthened politically the partisans of Peninsular Spain and gave them their last opportunity
to consolidate their position; for the presence of the British
forces in the role of conquerors enabled the Spanish to appeal
for a unity of the people against the invaders. By the terms of
his instructions Beresford was bound to establish the authority
of the British Crown, and by the terms of the capitulation the
municipal authorities and all those in public office were obliged
to take the oath of allegiance to His Britannic Majesty. Thus,
by the very instrument which ended the Spanish power, the
creation of a Creole power was denied.

---

[1] Adm. 1/58, Popham to the Admiralty, 8 July 1806.

[2] The population of Buenos Aires at this time is not certain, and various figures
are given. Moreno, who was among other things an economic calculator, estimated
60,000 in 1806. In *D.H.A.* x, p. 23, Ravignani estimated 41,642 in 1810 based on
lists of householders and exclusive of 6,372 slaves.

Popham seems to have sensed the element of disaster in this first political act after the cessation of hostilities. As soon as the salute indicating possession of the city was fired he went ashore in order, as he said, to lose 'no time in tracing the population of this City, and estimating as near as possible the actual and probable disposition of the Inhabitants'. What he found was not reassuring. 'The Persons who presented themselves . . . were generally speaking English merchants who had been trading here under neutral Colours and consequently very likely to flatter us with the most favourable view of the Subject.'[1] In fact only fifty-eight persons apart from those obliged to take the oath of allegiance came forward to do so, and they secretly.[2] When finally the British forces withdrew from the River Plate, Lieutenant-General Whitelocke observed that 'nothing can more strongly mark the inimical disposition of the Country towards us, than the circumstance of there being *only two* individuals of any respectability, who hav[e] sacrificed their Spanish connections and prospects . . .'.[3]

Having assured their sovereignty, the British commanders were prepared to be liberal. Both Popham and Beresford seem to have trusted greatly in a simple-minded economic interpretation of politics mitigated only by an equally simple-minded notion that ecclesiastical authorities, if suitably guaranteed, will automatically support any Caesar who appears. Beresford's proclamation of 29 June 1806 was intended to impress upon the minds of the people 'the Honor, Generosity and Humanity of the British Character'.[4] Freedom of religion and free trade 'similar to that enjoyed by all others of His Majesty's Colonies' were either guaranteed or promised. Furthermore, all purchases by the British force would be at moderate prices fixed by the *cabildo* or municipal government.

With the promise of such rigid protection to the established Religion of the Country, and the exercise of its Civil Laws, the Major-General trusts that all good Citizens will unite with him in their exertion to keep the Town quiet and peaceable as they may now enjoy a free Trade and all the advantages of commercial intercourse

[1] Adm. 1/58, Popham to the Admiralty, 8 July 1806.
[2] J. Street, *British Influence in the Independence of the River Plate Provinces* (Ph.D. thesis in the Library of Cambridge University, 1950), p. 34.
[3] W.O. 1/162, Whitelocke to Castlereagh, 10 Sept. 1807.
[4] W.O. 1/161, Beresford to Castlereagh, 11 July 1806.

with Great Britain where no oppression exists, and which he under-
stands has been the only thing wanting by the rich provinces of
Buenos Ayres, and the Inhabitants of South America in general to
make it the most prosperous Country in the World.[1]

Unfortunately for Popham and Beresford the community of
Buenos Aires was made up of individuals and groups who
viewed salvation and prosperity not as something generally to
be enjoyed by the whole society, but as a particular condition
connected with themselves and their place in the community.
These individuals and groups quickly began to form an alliance
to serve their own several objectives. We can discern in this
alliance three distinct elements: the Peninsular Spanish commercial interest, whose most articulate and determined spokesman was Martín de Álzaga, a Spanish merchant; the Spanish
service interest, whose most able exponent was a captain in the
Spanish navy, Santiago de Liniers, a Frenchman married into
a Creole mercantile family; and the Creole mercantile and
farming interest, whose most energetic leader was Juan Martín de
Pueyrredón. These three interests in fact comprised for all practical
and immediate purposes the political community of Buenos Aires.

It has been frequently alleged that one of the supreme defects
of the Spanish government of the Americas consisted in the
political inexperience to which it condemned the people. If this
is so, some at least of the inhabitants of Buenos Aires learned
their basic political lessons with astonishing rapidity, and
demonstrated a superiority of skill over Popham and Beresford
in a very short space of time. While the British leaders were
endeavouring to reassure the population by guaranteeing them
the possession of their coasting vessels, Pueyrredón, operating
from the safety of the pampas, boldly accused the British of
planning a social war, alleging that the intention of the invasion
was to liberate the slaves. No move could have better ensured
at this time the solidarity of the 'persons of respectability'.
Beresford, of course, had no such intention in mind, and in
answer to this charge willingly surrendered a political weapon
which the Spaniards and Creoles were quite willing to use both
against foreigners and against one another. Beresford announced
that 'the Inhabitants might command the protection of His
Majesty's Government against the insults of their Slaves . . .

[1] Adm. 1/58, Popham to the Admiralty, 8 July 1806.

and that the Military principles of the General were too high
to enter into any Negotiation with the Indians, who must
traditionally remember the extreme cruelty of their first
Invaders'.[1] Even Popham had too many scruples, or rather
social prejudices, to play the kind of game at which Pueyrredón
showed himself so adept.

The bungling of this issue was only a particular instance of
the general absence of political manœuvrability which stemmed
from Baird's orders to Beresford and from the unwillingness or
inability of Popham and Beresford to stimulate the social and
political disorder necessary to break up the opposition forming
against them. Beresford in his innocence and Popham in his
confusion assumed that a political change in the Río de la
Plata advantageous to Great Britain could be made without
altering in any way the society and the balance of political
forces in the Viceroyalty; that a change of sovereign by force of
arms followed by a few words of good will and a small amount
of economic tinkering necessary to achieve the object of British
commercial policy were all that the case required. Perhaps
there were some precedents for this view drawn from British
experience in Canada after the Seven Years War and in South
Africa contemporaneously, but the course of politics in the Far
East during nearly a century, the lessons of the French and
American Revolutions, and the contemporaneous tragedy in
the West Indies all pointed to new factors—or, perhaps, the
revival of very old and more permanent factors—in the development of politics everywhere.

The promotion of a political movement against the British
could only have meaning and effect in the circumstances of
1806 if it was capable of translation into military terms. This
Liniers, Pueyrredón, and Álzaga were able to achieve, and it is
this achievement which revolutionized the community of the
Viceroyalty and opened the way for the political and social
transformation of this part of the Spanish Empire.

The Spanish armed forces were small in number and badly
trained. The social and physical environment rendered desertion easy, and Spanish laws against desertion were much less
severe than those which governed the British Army. According
to Lieutenant-General Whitelocke the circumstances of service

[1] Adm. 1/58, Popham to the Admiralty, 25 Aug. 1806.

in the Río de la Plata were such 'that two years generally completed the ruin of a regiment from Old Spain'.[1] The poor showing made by the Spanish troops before Buenos Aires and again during the siege of Montevideo constituted the telling proof of the failure or inability of the Spanish Crown to maintain one essential instrument of its sovereignty. A successful resistance to British arms, therefore, required the construction of a military force different from that which the British had so easily dispersed.

The rapid constitution of this new force is evidence of the extraordinary vitality of the Buenos Airean community and the political capacity, courage, and imagination of its leading personalities. Three principal elements constitute this force. The first element consisted of gaucho light cavalry bearing little resemblance to a European cavalry formation. The men were drawn from the class of *chacareros*, or small farmers, and the cowboys and hunters of the pampas. Their mounts were drawn from the small, wild, and multitudinous horses of the plains. Their arms were few and primitive; their organization simple. Both Liniers, the Spanish commander, and the British officers spoke of their leaders as chiefs, and indeed this designation was accurate, for the gaucho cavalry were more akin to Indian formations than to a European army. The gauchos under their chiefs were incapable of resisting British troops at close quarters. Indeed, on 1 August 1806 Beresford defeated such a force under Pueyrredón at Perdriel outside Buenos Aires and captured all their artillery; but, dispersed over the immensity of the pampas, these troops made any penetration of the interior impossible and effectively cut off all supplies from Buenos Aires and Montevideo. Describing the final march of the British army under Whitelocke from the Ensenada de Barragón to Buenos Aires in July 1807, Major-General Leveson Gower told how 'we were constantly surrounded by a Cloud of Light Cavalry, never more distant than musquet shot from us, and indeed my aide de camp was made prisoner carrying my orders between two of the Brigades, and another Staff Officer attached to me stabbed within three hundred yards of the Flank of the Line. Without Cavalry it was impossible to get rid of these people.'[2]

[1] W.O. 1/162, Whitelocke to Windham, 23 July 1807.
[2] W.O. 1/162, Leveson Gower to Windham, 9 July 1807.

Admittedly the British forces from first to last were insufficiently provided with cavalry, but even this lack cannot explain the superiority of the Buenos Airean forces. European cavalry soldiers were too heavily equipped to mount the ponies of the pampas, and European cavalry mounts were too big and required too much fodder to subsist in the plains, at least in winter. A gaucho depended not on one horse but upon as many as twenty to move about, for each customarily possessed a *tropilla* or small herd of wild or nearly wild horses, which fed themselves and were never required to work beyond the limits of their food supplies.

The gauchos constituted a *levée en masse*. They were not altogether devoid of military experience, however, and all were natural horsemen. Among them were many with experience of Indian fighting. The viceregal authority maintained a force of colonial soldiers called *Blandengues* who acted as frontier guards and police. Beresford believed that this force would never be used against him,[1] but his refusal to stir up the Indians ensured that it would be, and it was. Thus, Pueyrredón was able to raise a mass of primitive mounted soldiers with an infusion of experienced Indian fighters. Their numbers and their adaptation to the peculiarities of their environment rendered them superior to the well-trained and well-equipped cavalry of a European nation and capable of tying down European infantry to their places of disembarkation.

The second element in the armament of Buenos Aires was the disciplined troops of Spain re-formed and reinvigorated by Captain Santiago de Liniers. In all they amounted to nearly 2,000 men, and their equipment was reasonably comparable with that of the British. Indeed in the matter of gunpowder they appear to have had a superiority. Liniers mobilized his forces at Montevideo and Colonia, marched them up river, and crossed the river at night on 3 August, evading Popham's patrols. There was nothing in their behaviour to suggest that alone they would have given any better account of themselves than the force which Beresford dispersed before Buenos Aires in June. But they were emboldened by the third element in the armament called into being by the leaders of the resistance to Britain.

[1] W.O. 1/161, Beresford to Castlereagh, 16 July 1806.

This consisted of an urban guerrilla force organized in Buenos Aires under Beresford's nose. Its effectiveness derived from a combination of architecture and politics. Buenos Aires, like other Spanish colonial towns, was laid out on the pattern of a Roman camp, its streets severely at right angles to one another. The brick and plaster houses presented a flat exterior wall on the street, broken by few doors and windows. The roofs were flat and surrounded by a parapet affording excellent cover from musket fire and a place of comparative safety for anyone armed with a pistol or a gun or even provided only with brick-bats and stones. A city arranged as Buenos Aires was could only be reduced by heavy, sustained artillery fire even though it was not technically a fortified town. Each of its streets could become a canyon of death for infantry soldiers, provided, of course, that the inhabitants were determined to use each of their houses as a strong point.

And this the citizens of Buenos Aires were willing to do. There can be no more telling commentary on the political miscalculation of Popham than the way in which the inhabitants of Buenos Aires failed even to remain neutral. Both the *Cabildo* and the Church, which remained outwardly so reassuring, worked to organize the householders in the business of resistance. On 16 July Beresford wrote to tell the Secretary of State for War how 'the satisfaction of the People' was daily increasing, and he appears to have been completely misled by an address of loyalty which he received from a body of the Roman clergy.[1] A few days later he seems to have begun worrying, for he had persuaded Popham to dispatch his fastest ship, the *Narcissus*, to England to plead for reinforcements. Popham himself could not find the men in his fleet sufficient to do all there was to do in gathering supplies, getting water, and maintaining patrols. Meanwhile a rising was being secretly organized.

On 10 August Liniers and his forces appeared before the town. Beresford had been unable to sally forth to give battle outside the city because of heavy rains and the fact that the roads were impassable to artillery and infantry. The Spanish forces, however, were moving well away from the roads. In these circumstances he thought of retiring to a place of embarkation, but Liniers commenced his assault quickly from all

[1] W.O. 1/161, Beresford to Castlereagh, 16 July 1806.

sides, and Beresford was obliged to take up a position in front of the Fort in the midst of the city. Against the regular Spanish forces he had some success, and captured three of their guns, but the firing from the roof tops became so heavy that Beresford raised the white flag after losing 165 men.

Liniers consented to parley. He agreed in a very liberal spirit to permit the embarkation of the British troops in exchange for the Spanish prisoners of war held by the British. At this stage the transformed political character of the Viceroyalty began to manifest itself. Liniers was not wholly in command of the variegated force which had come into being. The gauchos who had suffered severe casualties at the hands of the more disciplined British forces were swarming in the streets, and the white flag seemed to them a signal not to cease firing but to increase the butchery. Beresford told Liniers he would recommence firing if Liniers could not control his forces. This Liniers succeeded in doing, but before evening it became evident that he could not carry out his undertaking to exchange prisoners, and permit the embarkation of the British forces. Instead, the agreement was broken, and Beresford and his army were compelled to march into captivity in the interior of the country.

The events which we have described, the decisions which were taken by Popham, Baird, and Beresford, and the mistakes which they made from April until August 1806 were not known to the British Government. Popham's dispatches from the Cape and from St. Helena telling of his resolution to attack Buenos Aires were not received at the Admiralty until 24 June. No official word of the initial success of the expedition was received until 13 September. When Popham had left London in August 1805 to take up his command at the Cape the last Ministry of Pitt was still in power, and, although Melville, whose friend he was, had been forced out of office, Popham had some expectation of sympathy for his actions. While he was in South Africa Pitt had died, and a new Ministry of new men had taken over. This Ministry received his dispatches and could reasonably have been expected to view his proceedings with a somewhat different attitude than their predecessors.

At first it looked as if the change of Ministry implied a change in the policy governing Britain's strategy and tactics *vis à vis*

Napoleon. Fox, the leading personality in the new Ministry, was, however, bent not on fighting Napoleon more effectively than Pitt had done, but on making peace. Popham's actions were viewed, therefore, not in the light of an offence against a conception of strategy but as a breach of discipline. On 28 July Popham was ordered home, and directed to transfer his command to Rear-Admiral Stirling.[1] When the news of his first success was received, however, the Lords of the Admiralty began to revise their views. The Secretary of the Board was instructed to 'acquaint him that although their Lordships have judged it necessary to mark their Disappointment of a measure of such importance being undertaken without the sanction of H.M. Government . . . they nevertheless are pleased to express their entire approbation of the judicious, able and spirited conduct of himself, and of the Officers, Seamen and Marines employed under his Orders'.[2]

In this change of mind Popham himself had something of a hand. After the capture of Buenos Aires he addressed himself not only to the Admiralty in official dispatches but to the merchants and manufacturers of Britain in a public, circular letter. 'When the news of his success arrived, the strong objections to his plan were drowned in the universal joy at the fortunate result of his operations.'[3] Lord Grenville, the Prime Minister, had grave doubts about the wisdom of opening yet another theatre of war and spreading the inadequate British Army yet more thinly over the face of the world, but the majority of his ministerial colleagues, anxious to conciliate the mercantile and manufacturing interest,[4] and, still uncritical of the disastrous aspects of Pitt's policies, received the news from the River Plate as a portent of new and larger triumphs. Nothing less than the conquest of South America was envisaged. Within a space of weeks Windham, the Secretary of State for War, had expeditions in preparation to reinforce Beresford, to conquer Chile, and to seize Mexico. Even Lord Grenville was caught up in the delirium of enthusiasm for conquering the

---

[1] Adm. 2/1364, Admiralty to Popham, 28 July 1806.
[2] Adm. 1/58, A note for the Secretary, 25 Sept., appended to Popham to the Admiralty, 8 July 1806. Whether this expression of approval was ever sent is not clear.
[3] *Annual Register*, 1806 (London, 1808), p. 237.
[4] R. Holland, *Memoirs of the Whig Party* (London, 1854), ii, p. 112.

Spanish Empire, and he gave his personal attention to a mad plan for a pincers action against the Viceroyalty of New Spain. On 9 October Major-General Sir Samuel Auchmuty sailed from Falmouth with a force of 6,300 men to reinforce Beresford. In order to prepare the way for economic penetration, retroactive legislation was passed extinguishing the privileges of the South Sea Company and compensating them for their losses,[1] and, thus, opening the anticipated new empire to free trade.

In projecting a vast intensification of military activity across the Atlantic, the Government not only reinforced their troops in the River Plate but they reinforced the political mistakes of their commanders. Popham had been conscious of the mistakes he either made voluntarily or was obliged to make by the nature of Baird's orders to Beresford. The instructions now liberally handed out to the new officers assigned to lead the several contingents emphasized every political error made already, and ensured that nothing could ever be done to repair the damage already caused by attempting to transfer the sovereignty of the Viceroyalty from the Spanish to the British Crown. In the orders addressed to Beresford on 21 September 1806 the Secretary of State for War specifically stated that nothing must be done to alter social relations in Buenos Aires and that the real reason why Britain had hitherto refrained from invading South America was the fear of insurrection. Beresford was instructed to 'continue as much as possible to each class of inhabitants the same rights and functions they have heretofore enjoyed and exercised, preserving throughout the forms of the ancient Government . . .'.[2] The idea of conquest, which Beresford had endeavoured to underplay, he was now instructed to emphasize, for he must let the inhabitants of Buenos Aires 'judge of the reluctance with which [His Majesty] will relinquish possessions likely to prove so highly beneficial to the interests of his kingdoms. And upon these facts and views they must be left to regulate their conduct'.[3]

After the capitulation of Beresford in August, Popham received a detachment of reinforcements from the Cape. With

[1] D. B. Goebel, 'British Trade to the Spanish Colonies, 1796–1823', *American Historical Review*, 1937–8, vol. xliii, pp. 307–8.
[2] W.O. 1/161, Secretary of State to Beresford, 21 Sept. 1806.
[3] Ibid.

these he captured Maldonado and the island of Goretti, which provided a safe anchorage. When Sir Samuel Auchmuty's force arrived in January 1807 siege was laid to Montevideo and it was captured. When the news arrived in Britain of Beresford's capitulation a fresh decision was taken in London to abandon the conquest of Chile, to direct Craufurd's forces to the River Plate, to add some reinforcements, to appoint a new general officer, and to undertake 'the reduction of the Province of Buenos Ayres under the authority of His Majesty'.[1]

The instructions given to the new Commander-in-Chief in the River Plate, Lieutenant-General John Whitelocke, represented the final distillation of the wisdom of the British Government with respect to the colonies of Spain. He was instructed to use 'the most earnest endeavors . . . to conciliate the goodwill of the Inhabitants' by respecting their religion and their property, and by liberating their commerce. Like his predecessors he was forbidden to stir up revolution or to make any changes other 'than that which must necessarily arise from the substitution of His Majesty's Authority for that of the King of Spain'. But he was advised to employ Creoles in the government rather than Peninsular Spaniards. On the other hand, 'all those who were principally instrumental in promoting or executing the Insurrection against General Beresford, should be carefully removed, and either sent to Europe, or placed in some situation where their machinations may be no longer dangerous'. Finally Whitelocke was instructed 'on another point of great Delicacy and Importance, namely, the Language to be held in answer to any Enquiries on the part of the Inhabitants respecting their future Situation at a Peace'. He was ordered to answer such inquiries by saying 'that His Majesty will not surrender, but with great reluctance, Possessions to which he attaches so much value, and would, in no case, consent to such a Surrender, without providing for the security of those, who, from the Attachment shewn to His Majesty, might be fearful of having rendered themselves obnoxious to the displeasure of their former Government'.[2]

With one last burst of optimism Whitelocke was accorded permission to raise native troops so long as he preserved economy in expenditure.

[1] W.O. 1/162, Instructions to Whitelocke, 5 Mar. 1807.   [2] Ibid.

A favourite political idea of self-confident and self-satisfied nations is the belief that, provided their armed might is sufficient to put down all their enemies, a substantial body of mankind will flock to their standard anxious to enjoy the blessings of civilization once they are sure of protection from tyranny. Beresford entertained this ill-founded prejudice, and he employed it to reconcile the fact that none of the inhabitants of Buenos Aires supported British power with the naturally understood first principle that all right-minded people want to be British. In Whitelocke's instructions this prejudice was endorsed by the British Cabinet. He was encouraged to believe the myth, already emptied of any content it might once have had, that the colonial subjects of Spain would welcome the British as liberators and that a love of liberty is in reality a species of opportunism which prompts people to support the sovereign who can win the most battles.

An appreciation of Lieutenant-General Whitelocke presents many difficulties. The wisdom of the act which brought him before a court martial, where he was cashiered with every mark of ignominy, has been abundantly proved by the events of history; and yet he was a bad general officer who failed as a military leader and deserved his conviction on the grounds of incompetence. It may be argued that, in agreeing to evacuate the River Plate, Whitelocke's incompetence was the foundation of his wisdom and that by an accident of history he appears wiser than he really was. But such an argument would be unjust. The political decision which General Whitelocke made in the afternoon of 7 July 1807, when he agreed to evacuate the Viceroyalty of Buenos Aires, was not a sudden inspiration born of despair and failure, for he recognized, before he ever landed his troops at the Ensenada de Barragón below Buenos Aires, that he was undertaking a politically impossible, or nearly impossible, task. Whitelocke emerges from his dispatches and from his conduct at his court martial as a very intelligent and perceptive man; indeed, too intelligent for success; for he saw too many possibilities in situations confronting him. If he was too intelligent, he was also too lacking in self-confidence ever to succeed as a general officer with independent authority. This want of confidence in his own judgement betrayed itself in several ways: in his willingness to change his plans on the advice of others no better and often less well informed than himself; in his inclination to court the good will of the ranks and to stand arrogantly apart from officers who were his social equals; in his willingness to defer to the opinions, while expressing dislike and even hatred for them, of assistants whose appointment he attributed to political influence. Perhaps a modern psychologist would find in Whitelocke a fit subject for his science, and in the ambiguities surrounding his paternity[1] an explanation for Whitelocke's symptoms of a fatal sense of insecurity.

When he landed at Montevideo in May, Whitelocke had the candour to tell the Secretary of State for War that no opinion was possible 'upon what is to be looked for in this Country in point of sentiment and cooperation till Buenos Ayres is in our hands . . .'. But he did not anticipate an outpouring of enthusiasm for liberty. On the contrary, he declared that

the national character has assuredly derived no benefit from our first operations under the guidance of Sir Home Popham. The whole system appears to have been galling to the Inhabitants, and instead of an impression favorable to Great Britain, I am persuaded that it will be difficult ever to do away with the idea that individual interests influenced the whole of those proceedings, and not any great national object![2]

It was characteristic of Whitelocke to see clearly not only big difficulties such as these but little difficulties of equal importance. As he strolled through the streets of Montevideo he pointed at the flat-faced, flat-roofed houses with their parapet around the top and declared to Brigadier Craufurd that 'he would never expose his troops to so unfair a trial as a fight in the streets of a large town like Buenos Ayres, composed entirely of such houses'.[3] Unfortunately it was also one of his characteristics to forget his best insights and exclude them from last-minute plans made at the behest of others; for in his attack on Buenos Aires he consented to a plan of operations directly contradictory to his knowledge of the insuperable obstacle presented by the physical structure of the city.

[1] The *Dictionary of National Biography* is not very straightforward on this subject. After his court martial the fact that Whitelocke was not shot was popularly attributed to his illegitimate connexion with an exalted family.

[2] W.O. 1/162, Whitelocke to Windham, 20 June, 1807.

[3] Fortescue, *A History of the British Army*, v, p. 412.

From the outset Whitelocke was fated to make a succession of mistakes, none of them in themselves fatal, but all of them contributing to an impression of military incompetence. He had decided that if he could not deliver his attack in June he would delay until September in order to avoid the winter rains of July and August. He allowed himself to be persuaded that a shortage of supplies made imperative an attack as soon as possible, and so he ordered the commencement of operations on 24 June. More than 11,000 British troops had accumulated in the River Plate, and of these he directed more than 7,000 at Buenos Aires. On 28 June they began to disembark at the Ensenada de Barragón thirty-six miles below the city. The rains had already done their work, for the army came off the sea into an ocean of mud and swamp. By the time they reached high ground their strength had been wasted, a good part of their supplies spoiled, and their rations lost or rendered useless by the insufficiency of horses broken to pulling wagons or carrying packs.

Although the men suffered near-starvation on the march and were exhausted by Whitelocke's impatient desire to find shelter from the rains, nothing fatal to the expedition happened during the six days which were required to bring the army into a position for an assault. Suddenly at this stage Whitelocke was afflicted with one of his fits of doubting which caused him to ask his second-in-command for his views and, on the strength of them, to abandon completely his own sensible plans. These had involved some serious political disadvantages which Whitelocke acknowledged, but from a purely military point of view they were the only possible action in the circumstances. Briefly summarized, his plan was simply to march around the town to the river's edge north of the city and there to establish contact with the ships standing off shore in deep water, to land heavy guns, and to blow the city flat, house by house and street by street, so that no cover would be afforded for sharpshooters and guerrillas. Once the houses were flattened an assault would be delivered on the Fort if the Spaniards were still willing to fight.

Whitelocke, however, saw several other possibilities and was sensitive to other considerations. His instructions called upon him to conciliate the population, and he began to feel a bombardment 'might occasion an indiscriminate loss of life, ruin the

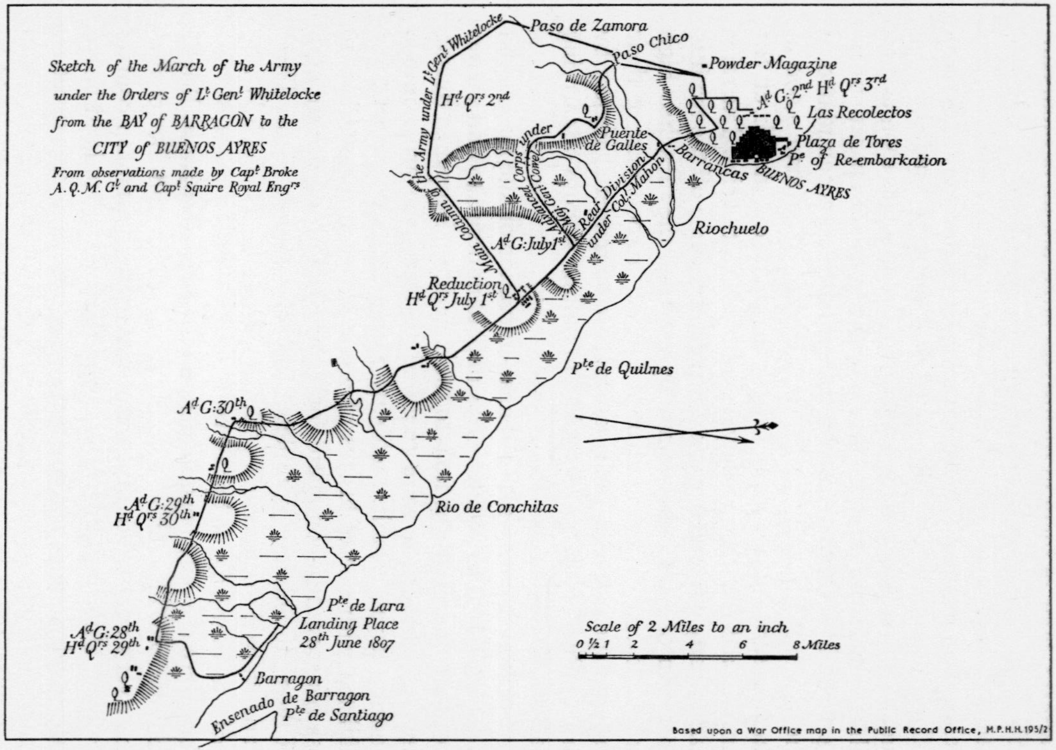

Sketch of the March of the Army
under the Orders of Lt Genl Whitelocke
from the BAY of BARRAGON to the
CITY of BUENOS AYRES
From observations made by Capt Broke
A.Q.M. Gr and Capt Squire Royal Engrs

Powder Magazine
Ad Gr 2nd Hd Qrs 3rd
Las Recolectos
Plaza de Tores
Pe of Re-embarkation
BUENOS AYRES
Barrancas
Riochuelo
Paso de Zamora
Poso Chico
Puente de Gales
The Army under Lt Genl Whitelocke
Hd Qrs 2nd
under Brig Genl Craufurd
Right Division
Light Corps
Pe de Quilmes
Main Column of the Army
Ad Gr July 1st
Reduction
Hd Qrs July 1st
Rio de Conchitas
Ad G 30th
Ad G 29th
Hd Qrs 30th
Pe de Lara
Landing Place
28th June 1807
Ad G 28th
Hd Qrs 29th
Barragon
Ensenado de Barragon
Pe de Santiago

Scale of 2 Miles to an inch
0 ½ 1   2   4   6   8 Miles

Based upon a War Office map in the Public Record Office, M.P.H.H.1957/2

FIG. 3.

Town, and irritate the people'.[1] Furthermore, a bombardment would take days, and were not the rains setting in? Whitelocke turned these and other possibilities over in his mind, and then threw himself upon his second-in-command, Leveson Gower, whom he hated and who hated him. The art of leadership consists in being able to distinguish the essential from the non-essential and in doing the essential. This faculty Whitelocke lacked.

Leveson Gower's plan like Whitelocke's was simple, but it had the additional defect of being foolish. Gower proposed to march thirteen parties of troops through the streets without firing until they reached the houses by the river and there to occupy the roofs and await orders for an assault on the Fort. Gower's plan depended upon two assumptions: that the discipline and training of the troops was of such a high order that they would advance steadily under fire without answering and that the fire of the enemy would be insufficient to stop them. The first assumption was correct. Under withering fire from concealed positions the British files did not falter and steadily advanced to their destinations. The second assumption, however, was incorrect or nearly so. The Spanish fire was extremely heavy and the casualties caused were in fact the reason why finally the British General agreed to capitulate.

Whitelocke accepted Leveson Gower's plan. On the morning of 5 July 1806 the assault was delivered. Twenty-four hours later half of the British assault force were casualties: 401 dead, 649 wounded, 1,924 prisoners.

The nature of the fire to which the Troops were exposed was violent in the extreme. Grape Shot at the corners of all the Streets, musketry, hand grenades, Bricks and Stones from the tops of all the houses. Every householder with his Negroes defended his dwelling, each of which was in itself a Fortress; and it is not too much to say, that the whole male population of Buenos Ayres was employed in its defence.[2]

The British position was, however, far from hopeless from a narrowly military point of view. Over 1,000 Spaniards were prisoners. Thirty guns had been captured. The troops were in possession of strong defensible positions on the right, left, and

[1] W.O. 1/162, Whitelocke to Windham, 10 July 1807.
[2] Ibid.

centre, and Liniers's forces were penned up in the Fort and buildings in the centre of the town. In the river was the British fleet possessed of heavy guns, which, if landed, could be used to blow the Spanish defences flat. It was evident to the troops themselves, as it became evident to the subsequent court martial, that a general officer with more determination and more self-confidence (or perhaps with less brains and imagination) could, at the stage of proceedings reached on 6 July, have turned defeat into victory by the swift and energetic blows which he had the means to deliver.

But the entire enterprise had gone rotten in Whitelocke's heart. Before the assault he had communicated with General Liniers. Writing to the Spanish General on 4 July he invited him to surrender. 'I beg you will do me the justice', he wrote, 'to impute to the principles of humanity only, the information I give you of my arrival.'[1] Liniers, too, was willing to communicate with Whitelocke. He told the British General that nothing in his situation required him to surrender, and that he had 'more than sufficient means to resist all the efforts which Your Excellency can make to conquer me'. And he was determined to have the best of the contest over principles of humanity. 'The duties of Humanity', he wrote, 'of which Your Excellency speaks will I conceive be more wounded by Your Excellency who is the Aggressor than by me.'[2]

Early in the morning of 6 July 1807, when the first flush of the attack had failed, Liniers again wrote to Whitelocke. In this letter he displayed his astonishing powers both as a politician and a soldier; a power to grasp whole situations and to act, which, if he had been privileged to exercise them in a larger theatre than the River Plate, would have earned him the reputation of a great captain and a great statesman. Sensing the despondency of Whitelocke and realizing his own weaknesses and strength, Liniers proposed that Whitelocke evacuate the River Plate completely in return for the freedom of all prisoners of war including those taken when Beresford capitulated a year earlier. He frankly told Whitelocke that he had an incomplete control of his own forces, and that a savage slaughter of prisoners might very well accompany renewed hostilities.

[1] W.O. 1/162, Whitelocke to Liniers, 4 July 1807.
[2] W.O. 1/162, Liniers to Whitelocke, 4 July 1807.

Whitelocke rejected the proposal at first, but it obviously had its attractions, for he suggested a truce of twenty-four hours. Then he rode with his second-in-command to the Plaza de Toros where Auchmuty was established for a further assault. Whitelocke, Auchmuty, and Leveson Gower talked together for a space of time. They had no heart to proceed. Auchmuty was a brave and able soldier, but he agreed to quit. Leveson Gower, ever full of excuses and designs, agreed to quit. By noon Whitelocke reached a decision which ended an historical epoch in Anglo-Spanish relations. He ordered Leveson Gower to go to Liniers with an agreement to evacuate the River Plate. On only one point did he hold out for better terms. Would Liniers extend the time allowed for British merchants to sell their goods in the markets of Buenos Aires? Liniers returned a negative to this last request. Whitelocke accepted it. 'Reflecting of how little advantage would be the possession of a Country the Inhabitants of which were so absolutely hostile, I resolved to forego the advantages which the bravery of the troops had obtained, and acceded to the annexed treaty which I trust will meet with the approbation of His Majesty.'[1] In the afternoon the firing died away, and the next day, 7 July 1807, a formal agreement was signed.

The end of the affair revealed its character more clearly than the beginning. One loyal and fuming subject wrote to Castlereagh from his neo-classical dwelling in Bloomsbury about the 'incorrigible robbers' who had opposed the British in South America. 'There is not a Person I have met with', wrote a certain Thomas Hall, 'who can bear to hear of that capitulation with temper; everyone considers it as a disgrace to the Nation, and nothing can rectify the mistake, but that of sending out another fleet and Troops to take and keep possession of Monte Video *at least*.'[2]

Frustrated mercantile greed garbed in the mantle of patriotism commonly passes for wisdom. Fortunately for Britain the recipient of Thomas Hall's letter had a mind untrained solely to economic concerns and a vision raised a little above the level of the counting house. Viscount Castlereagh was capable of a sufficiently detached view to ask what really were the interests

[1] W.O. 1/162, Whitelocke to Windham, 10 July 1807.
[2] W.O. 1/162, Thomas Hall to Castlereagh, 30 Sept. 1807.

of Britain in South America and how did these interests relate to the general interests of the nation in the circumstances created by Napoleon.

Castlereagh had replaced Windham as Secretary of State for War in March 1807, when the Grenville Ministry was dismissed by the King. Out of office he had been a harsh critic of the War Office and particularly of its recruiting methods. The smallness of the Army in relation to the political problems presented by Napoleon was his principal concern. Although he considered carefully the method of increasing the intake of men into the Army, he saw also that the use to which the Army was being put required attention. Any army was bound to be ineffective if scattered in small bodies around the shores of every ocean in the world. Castlereagh was coming slowly to the conclusion that one aspect of a solution of the size of the Army was a greater degree of concentration achieved by the liquidation of some at least of the overseas enterprises so light-heartedly undertaken and so popularly supported.

When Castlereagh took office as Secretary of State for War, one of his first actions was the preparation of a 'Memorandum for the Cabinet, relative to South America' dated Downing Street, 1 May 1807.[1] It is a long document written in Castlereagh's characteristic manner: laborious, sometimes obscure, full of pros and cons, and wanting in striking generalizations capable of focusing sentiment and opinion. Upon study there emerges from it Castlereagh's character and his marvellous political understanding. He saw the problem in terms of action and interest. He ignored 'popularity . . . and the disposition of the commercial interest', and treated with contempt the inclination of his predecessor to base policy on anything so unsatisfactory. Finally, there shines forth his willingness to make up his mind, to act upon his decision, and to stand by it regardless of pressure, clamour, and cost to himself.

Having argued painfully over the whole question, Castlereagh concluded clearly enough that 'he certainly [did] entertain a very *strong persuasion* that the policy upon which we are now acting will be productive of little commercial or political benefit, and must be felt as a great waste of our military means'.[2]

[1] Castlereagh, *Correspondence*, vii, pp. 314 ff.
[2] Ibid., p. 324.

Underlying Castlereagh's whole approach was the assumption that for her commercial and political advantage Britain must seek to re-establish the freedom of communication with the continent of Europe denied her by Napoleon. All means must be directed to this end. If, however, this end could not be achieved, 'if we are to carve out a separate existence for ourselves, and to seek to replace those channels of commerce which may be interrupted or shut against us, by opening others less exposed to French power, new and greater efforts must be made'.[1] At any one time Britain could, Castlereagh argued, work towards only one of alternative ends; not both. The first objective was the most important, and therefore its achievement must be sought first.

Surveying events in the River Plate up to the time of Whitelocke's departure to take up his command, Castlereagh concluded that the reasons for the British difficulties were political not military. The root cause of this difficulty was the failure of the British commanders and later the British Government to proclaim the independence of the Viceroyalty. This failure was the opportunity of the Spanish Government. 'The principal officers of the Spanish Government . . . found the population of Buenos Ayres, thus disappointed in their expectations, ready to co-operate in our expulsion. . . . It is not wonderful that the people of all classes should look with great jealousy to the circumstances under which we come amongst them . . .'[2]

Castlereagh argued that, this being so, the Cabinet would have to discover

whether some principle of acting more consonant to the sentiments and interests of the people of South America cannot be taken up, which, whilst it shall not involve us in any system of measures, which, on grounds of political morality, ought to be avoided, may relieve us from the hopeless task of conquering this extensive country, against the temper of its population.[3]

Having regard for strictly commercial considerations, Castlereagh thought that

it may even be doubtful whether the silent and imperceptible operation of our illicit commercial intercourse with that portion of the world during the war would not be more operative and beneficial,

[1] Ibid., p. 321.   [2] Ibid., pp. 317, 319.   [3] Ibid., p. 319.

if we approached it only as traders, than when, by approaching it as enemies, a new energy is given to the local government, which may probably enable them the better to enforce the prohibitory regulations against our commerce.[1]

Clearly, Castlereagh had a better appreciation of the economic foundations of politics than the merchants of the City of London who presented Popham with a jewelled sword as a tribute to his prowess and a compensation for his reprimand by a court martial. Indeed, Castlereagh viewed South America as a matter of British economic interest exclusively and not as a sphere where British political influence should be exerted. 'The particular interest which we should be understood alone to propose to ourselves should be the depriving our enemy of one of his chief resources, and the opening to our manufactures the markets of that great Continent.'[2]

Castlereagh was opposed to deliberate incitement to revolution, for 'in endeavouring to promote and combine the happiness of the people with the extension of our own commerce, we might, in destroying a bad government, leave them without any government at all'.[3] No note of caution was ever more abundantly justified by events.

While Castlereagh enjoined caution in using the weapon of revolutionary incitement, he did not exclude the possibility that Napoleon might so fasten himself upon Spain that Britain would be obliged to work for the dismemberment of the Spanish Empire. In that event Britain must have a clear policy in place of the confused policy with which Grenville and Windham had saddled the Government. 'In looking to any scheme for liberating South America', he argued, 'it seems indispensable that we should not present ourselves in any other light than as auxiliaries and protectors.'[4]

Castlereagh's memorandum of May 1807 is the original basis of a century and a half of British policy in South America. It was not easily arrived at, nor was it a sudden inspiration born in Castlereagh's mind. He had gone laboriously and critically over a vast body of documents embodying the confused and confusing conclusions come to by men like Sir Ralph Abercromby who had witnessed the death of thousands of British

---

[1] Castlereagh, *Correspondence*, vii, p. 320.   [2] Ibid., p. 321.
[3] Ibid., p. 320.   [4] Ibid., p. 321.

soldiers in the service of ideas and plans which the movement of politics and the economy had rendered obsolete. What he might have done had General Whitelocke landed heavy guns on 6 July 1807, instead of agreeing to Liniers' terms, we can only guess. Whitelocke as well as Castlereagh made British policy in South America, and for this Whitelocke was cashiered and his name read out as an example of unsoldierly conduct before all the regiments of the British Army. But Castlereagh was right, and Whitelocke's action ensured that he could never go wrong.

There remains only one comment to make and one aspect of British policy during the year 1806–7 to explain. All the leading British personalities concerned in the River Plate adventure strongly stressed the economic factors in the enterprise. Unquestionably there existed in the Viceroyalty of Buenos Aires a powerful and growing interest sympathetic to the notion of commercial freedom and antagonistic to the Spanish system of commercial regulation and discrimination against non-Spanish markets and mercantile enterprise. Events were to demonstrate how strong and decisive this interest was. Why, then, did not the promise of commercial liberation prove a trump card for the British to play? Why did not the powerful free-trade interest in Buenos Aires come down on the side of British intervention?

The reasons are very complex. At this stage we can only refer to those which may be described as British. Neither Popham and Beresford, in the first instance, nor the British Government, in the second instance, had offered the community of Buenos Aires commercial freedom. They offered a freer admission into a larger market, but they never offered anything which did not afford commercial advantage to Britain. The opportunity to make a free commercial choice was no more granted than an opportunity to make a free political choice. Freedom of political choice implies freedom of commercial choice, and the reverse is also true. It would be attributing too much to the calculating propensity of the people of Buenos Aires to suggest that their actions were governed by such thoughts and were decided by reading Beresford's proclamation of 18 July 1806, fixing import duties at 10 per cent. on British goods and 15 per cent. on non-British goods.[1] But the citizens

---

[1] Printed in *D.H.A.* vii, p. 339. Also mentioned in W.O. 1/161, Beresford to Castlereagh, 11 July 1806.

E

of Buenos Aires understood very clearly the economic as well
as the spiritual meaning of political independence, and in the
short space of six weeks the business class of the city had an
ample opportunity to learn.

When the Viceroy, Sobremonte, fled from Buenos Aires he
took with him the state treasure amounting to more than one
million dollars in bullion. A party of British dragoons was sent
in hot pursuit, and the *Cabildo* of Buenos Aires, with its eyes
fixed equally on this prize, offered to assist the British force in
this operation. But the Creoles were never permitted to share
in this enterprise, for the viceregal treasure was taken at Luján
on the road to the interior and $1,086,208 was shipped at once
aboard H.M.S. *Narcissus* as a prize of war.[1] Private stocks of
bullion disappeared, and, within a week of the occupation,
Popham was obliged to record that there was a scarcity of currency and an abundance of goods in Buenos Aires.[2]

Having seized the bullion supply, Popham was determined
not to permit the merchants of Buenos Aires to make good this
loss by the free operation of the market. As the Spanish currency disappeared the exchange began to move against Britain.
The dollar had exchanged ordinarily at 4*s.* 6*d.*, but it started at
once to rise. Popham decided never to let it rise beyond 5*s.*

It is proper that I should acquaint their Lordships [he wrote]
that in consequence of hearing that it was probable, that very little
Money would be offered, and that at an exorbitant Exchange, I
consulted with the General on the Subject for the purpose of keeping
the exchange at the par of Five Shillings the Dollar or under, and
we agreed that in case the Merchants offered their Money at a
higher rate, that we would direct the Treasurer and Prize Commissioners to issue at five Shillings the Dollar, and to retain in consequence a sufficient supply for the exigencies of the Service, by
which means the Dollar never would be higher, and might be
lower. This Resolution was immediately made Publick and no
Tenders will be received above Five Shillings.[3]

Such actions as these made a mockery of the professed liberality of Beresford's pronouncements about the purchase of supplies at prices fixed by the *Cabildo*, the sanctity of property and
the freedom of trade. Indeed, Popham's professed economic

[1] Adm. 1/58, Popham to the Admiralty, 8 July 1806, and W.O. 1/161, 16 July
1806.   [2] Adm. 1/58, Popham to the Admiralty, 9 July 1806.
[3] Adm. 1/58, Popham to the Admiralty, 13 July 1806.

liberalism never went very deep, nor was it based upon the confidence that in a genuinely free market British products and mercantile enterprise would show to the advantage of the nation. Here and there in his dispatches we can discern more than a trace of the old Adam of mercantilist politico-economic methods. 'The transfer also of th[e] carrying trade to our own Ships will I trust be considered a sort of two fold Advantage', he suggested to the Admiralty.[1] He glanced covetously at the slave trade so beneficial to the fat Portuguese, and he thought that what had previously found its way to Europe through Lisbon and Cadiz would now 'find their way to London'. One might almost suppose that Popham had designedly struck a blow at the Portuguese mercantile community when he told of the advantages he had created for British commerce.

The British mercantile community appears to have been even less enthusiastic about commercial freedom than Popham and Beresford. The spirit of the Seven Years War was far from dead in their hearts. At the very moment when the British Empire in the River Plate was preparing to expire from the ardours experienced in its birth, Castlereagh wrote to Whitelocke:

It appears by a letter of the 20th of March from Brigadier General Sir Samuel Auchmuty that he thought it expedient to open the Port of Monte Video to neutrals for wine and spirits for Eight months. Of the Necessity for this Measure, of which the British Merchants much complain, it is difficult at this distance to form a Judgement. I am however to recommend that this Indulgence be not extended, and if you are in possession of Buenos Ayres, there will not probably be any necessity of extending it to that Port. As the speculations of the British merchants seem to deserve every Encouragement, I am to desire you will attend to their Interests as far as in your Power consistently with the Instructions and orders you have received.[2]

Conquest by liberals, thus, appears to differ not at all from conquest. Castlereagh's failing was his incapacity to deceive himself or others about the meaning and outcome of conquest. If this failing earned him the sneers of a Shelley or a Byron, it made him a better servant of the State, for the Spaniards and the Creoles of Buenos Aires knew as well as he did what was the real character of the enterprise set on foot by Popham.

[1] Adm. 1/58, Popham to the Admiralty, 9 July 1806.
[2] W.O. 1/162, Castlereagh to Whitelocke, 8 June 1807.

II

REVOLUTION IN THE RIVER PLATE

SIR HOME POPHAM was not as much a fool nor as complete a failure as the events of 1806–7 might lead one to suppose. When he suggested that the community in Buenos Aires was ripe for change, he was correct. The blow which he struck at the Viceroyalty *did* bring to an end the power of Spain and the commercial monopoly which was one of its distinguishing consequences. Judged in the light of subsequent history the train of events which he set in motion *did* open to Great Britain a number of progressively increasing economic and commercial opportunities. In our first chapter we have discussed the folly of Sir Home Popham; in this we propose to examine the grounds of his wisdom.

In the period between the American Revolution and the deposition of Ferdinand VII by Napoleon the community of which Buenos Aires was the metropolis grew more rapidly than any part of the Spanish dominions. Population, commerce, and production all increased from two to fivefold. The amenities of Buenos Aires noticeably improved. The streets began to be paved and lighted. More children commenced attending school, and more youths the universities at Córdoba and Chuquisaca and the older establishments in Spain. A newspaper was founded in 1801. The law governing and prohibiting the importation and publication of books was increasingly more honoured in the breach than in the observance. Raynal, Rousseau, Mably, and Adam Smith were read and freely discussed. The theatre began to flourish, and one enlightened Viceroy removed a priest from his pulpit when he urged women not to attend this profane institution. Hospitals were built, and vaccination was as widely practised in Buenos Aires as in any community in the world. '. . . all values are altered', wrote a memorialist in 1804. 'The beginning and origin of this change is nothing less than the increase in population, the great influx of people into the territories, the great abundance and luxury at the table, the noticeable increase in practitioners of the arts and crafts.'[1]

The advantages of Buenos Aires as an habitation for man and as a centre of commerce and industry spring easily to mind. A vast and smoothly flowing river penetrates into a continent. South and west and north stretch seemingly endless plains covered with an immensely rich and thick layer of life-giving soil. The rainfall is adequate and the climate mild. Even the fauna were more useful than otherwise to man. But the humid pampas of Argentina presented formidable obstacles to the establishment of flourishing colonies. Empty prairies wherever they are found have offered an almost insuperable challenge to men and to communities lacking great resources of capital and technical accomplishments. The relative absence of trees and stones, which in some circumstances might be described as an advantage in the development of agriculture, meant an absence of building materials and a progressive scarcity of fuel. The great rivers provided a means of transport but the empty plains beyond the rivers were difficult to move across for economic purposes in the pre-railway age. To the Spaniards of the six-teenth and seventeenth centuries the pampas of the Río de la Plata presented a more intractable problem than seemingly more difficult countries such as Mexico, Peru, Chile, or Para-guay.[2] Indeed, from the point of view of the first settlers Para-guay with its dense forests of wonderful and various trees was a fruitful paradise compared with the barren pampas.

The Spanish Empire was founded upon people. Its centres of authority, profit, and power were the areas where civilized and semi-civilized Indians congregated in large numbers and where they lived a settled and productive existence. Such Indians were not to be found on the pampas. The Querandies, the Puelcheans, and the Araucanians were Stone Age hunters at a level of cultural development which made their incorporation into a civilized society difficult or impossible. They were few in number and hard to catch. The *encomienda* system failed miser-ably in Buenos Aires. The original colonists had been granted sixty-four *encomiendas*, but after twenty years of trying to make

[1] *D.H.A.* iv, p. 9.
[2] Luis Roque Gondra, *Historia económica de la Republica Argentina* (Buenos Aires, 1943), p. 66.

the system work not a single Indian *de servicio* existed in Buenos Aires and its neighbourhood.[1] The want of Indians explains well enough the poverty and unimpressive character of early Buenos Aires.

The community which came into being on the banks of the River Plate was a slow growth, and its social composition and economic character differed noticeably from those of other Spanish colonies. In seeking to discern its character one must make a distinction between Buenos Aires as a commercial centre and Buenos Aires as a producer of goods. As a port of entry from Europe and as a commercial centre, it differed from other Spanish American ports such as Vera Cruz, Havana, Cartagena, and Porto Bello in no significant way except that it did not possess an immediately adjacent market area. But this could have equally been said of Porto Bello which was only the Atlantic point for the transhipment of goods to Peru. As such a point Buenos Aires had certain advantages over Porto Bello. Goods imported through Buenos Aires could compete to advantage in the Peruvian market with goods imported through Porto Bello and transhipped from Panama to Callao. For reasons of defence and of interest the *Casa de Contratación* had endeavoured to limit trade to Porto Bello, but with so little success that customs houses were established at Córdoba in 1622 to dam the flow of goods entering from Buenos Aires. Whether this measure succeeded in sterilizing in any degree the commercial potentialities of Buenos Aires it would be difficult to say, but it is significant that so early in the colonial history the advantageous location of Buenos Aires as an international commercial centre was attracting the attention of authority as a threat to the *status quo*.

The most potent factor in the progress of Buenos Aires, which we can first discern in the eighteenth century, was the development of production on the pampas themselves. It is true that eventually the mining regions of Alto Peru were drawn within the commercial as well as political and administrative orbit of Buenos Aires, but the most important first step in the direction of this triumph was the creation of trade in a staple commodity produced within the immediate control of the mercantile

[1] A. F. Zimmerman, 'The Land Policy of Argentina, with Particular Reference to the Conquest of the Southern Pampas', *H.A.H.R.* xxv, 1945, p. 3.

community of the city itself. This staple was hides. Although the first Spanish colonists had failed to establish a community of the type existing elsewhere in the main centres of Spanish power in the Americas, they had inadvertently sown the seeds of what became in the course of time the main constituents of the prosperity of the River Plate. They brought with them horses, cattle, and men. All of these had multiplied on the rich lands of the pampas. During the sixteenth century great herds of wild horses and cattle grew up on the southern pampas, and in the course of the seventeenth century spread east of the Río Paraná.[1]

In the case of the men they had mingled with the Indians to produce a new race of *mestizos*, the celebrated gauchos of the pampas. These men were nearly as savage as the Indians whom they displaced in the vicinity of the great rivers, but they were nominally Christian and they lacked a tribal organization which was such an important element in preserving the defensive power of the Indians. The gauchos were men well adapted to their environment: incomparable horsemen, skilful hunters of cattle, and fierce but poorly organized fighters. Like the Indians they were not easily tamed, but unlike the Indians they were connected economically, politically, and religiously with the Spaniards and Creoles settled in the towns and their environs. They became the means by which the townsmen developed a staple trade based upon production in the hinterland of the colonial metropolis.

The characteristic productive unit of mid-nineteenth-century Argentina, the estancia, did not come into being during the early phase of pastoral production. After the failure of the *encomienda* system and its suppression the Spanish Crown began to grant land in the form of *peonías* consisting of a town lot plus 100 acres outside the town and *caballerías* consisting of a larger town lot plus 500 acres in the camp. This system of land granting attracted a small number of persons who constituted a class of *chacareros* or subsistence farmers, supplying the city markets with cereals and fruits. Beyond the limits of the *tierra de pan llevar* lay the pampas where the substance of the colony's wealth and power could be found. There the gauchos hunted cattle, lived off their carcasses, made furniture of their bones for their houses and their miserable huts, fashioned clothing from their

---

[1] E. A. Coni, *Contribución a la historia del gaucho* (Buenos Aires, 1937), p. 9.

hides, and, by selling hides, provided Buenos Aires with an export staple and themselves with their few wants: cloth, iron and steel implements, mate, and tobacco.

The structure of the primitive productive apparatus on the pampas down to the late years of the eighteenth century is not clearly understood or easily described. The Crown of Spain granted large tracts of land in the open camp to individuals, but extensive landed estates could only exist in theory because in practice there was no one to work them. A landed estate anywhere is land and people in a certain social relationship with each other; in Buenos Aires in colonial times the second constituent was wanting. In 1721 there were only thirteen estancias in the entire Banda Oriental, and the average number of workers on each was three peons.[1] The Jesuits founded a large estancia named La Vaca in the same region and equipped it with a mill, bake ovens, and an orchard, but in 1738 they were working it with 169 imported slaves. Even after the pastoral industry was well along the road to its modern development shortly before the separation from Spain there were only 327 landowners among a total population of 17,000 in Buenos Aires, and of these only 141 lived outside the city.[2] The evidence seems to suggest one negative element in the description of the early pastoral industry, viz. that it was not organized on the basis of wage labour, nor of a serf or slave economy nor of a tribute system such as the *encomienda*. The sad nostalgic myths of gaucho freedom which pervade both the folk songs of the gaucho and their sophisticated derivatives seem to have had some substance as a description of the gaucho's condition in times past. The great abundance of cattle, the immensity of the pampas, the smallness of the market, and the few wants of the gaucho produced a relaxed social atmosphere in which it would be difficult to discern a dominant class. The organizers of production for the market were the merchants and merchant-*estancieros*, but they obtained hides from several sources: from the Indians by barter, from the free gauchos by barter and money purchases, and by organizing great slaughters at which they paid the participating gauchos so much a head for each beast killed and so much a hide staked out to dry in the

---

[1] *Contribución a la historia del gaucho*, p. 24.
[2] Zimmerman, *H.A.H.R.* xxv, 1945, p. 5.

sun.[1] The gaucho, however, did not depend upon a money wage for his existence nor upon the possession of a piece of land, nor was he obliged to engage in sustained labour for a master.

The abundance of the country and the effect of this upon the social discipline to which Europeans were accustomed were matters of common observation well into the nineteenth century. 'The people of this Country', declared Major-General Leveson Gower, 'have been totally misrepresented. They are slothful to the last degree, and obtain food at so easy a rate that they will not labour.'[2] Whitelocke observed the solvent effect of the social environment upon the British Army. One hundred and seventy men of the 71st Regiment had deserted and 'the more the soldiers became acquainted with the plenty the Country affords, and the easy means of acquiring it, the greater . . . the evil'.[3] Twenty years later Sir Francis Bond Head, the manager of a mining syndicate, observed the same phenomenon. 'In Cornwall', he wrote, 'the miners are subjected to a code of most admirable local regulations, which encourage competition and industry, and leave the idle to starve:—in South America, the miners are away from the force of all these regulations, and a high, fixed salary, with cheap wines and provisions, discourage competition and labour.'[4] Even without 'high fixed salaries', neither the gaucho nor the European immigrant readily laboured in accordance with European conceptions of that activity.[5]

The state of nature which existed on the pampas during the sixteenth and seventeenth centuries was not altogether static, for certain events suggest the shape of things which were to come in the late eighteenth and nineteenth centuries. The multiplication of the herds of cattle and horses transformed the Indians and increased their numbers and the range of their

---

[1] Felix de Azara, *Memoria rural del Rio de la Plata* (Madrid, 1847), quoted in Gondra, *Historia económica*, p. 273.

[2] W.O. 1/162, Leveson Gower to Windham, 9 July 1807.

[3] W.O. 1/162, Whitelocke to Windham, 23 July 1807.

[4] F. Bond Head, *Rough Notes taken during some rapid Journeys across the Pampas and among the Andes* (London, 1826), p. 152.

[5] W. MacCann, *Two Thousand Miles' Ride through the Argentine Provinces* (London, 1853), 2 vols., is very emphatic about the shortage of labour and the unwillingness of gauchos to work. See also V. Martin de Moussy, *Description géographique et statistique de la Confédération Argentine* (Paris, 1860–1), ii, p. 113, and W. Parish, *Buenos Ayres and the Provinces of the Río de la Plata* (London, 1852), p. 298.

operations.[1] They appear to have been the first to engage in systematic slaughtering of cattle for commercial purposes.[2] But the market was small and irregular before the Asiento contract of 1716 which established an English trading factory in Buenos Aires. Coni estimates that the export of hides averaged only about 20,000 annually before this date, although in some years twice this number were exported.

Even in these circumstances the Spaniards and Creoles of Buenos Aires endeavoured to mark out private rights in the herds. Brands were registered and rights to slaughter and to sell hides were granted by the town authorities, but the system cannot be said to have been effective. The right to slaughter could be bought for the equivalent of a few pounds, and a census of 1713 revealed that there were only 18,500 cattle in private ownership on seventeen *estancias* in the jurisdiction of Buenos Aires.[3] In the main, production in this early epoch was almost completely dominated by hunters both Indian and gaucho. Some attempts were made to protect the herds by prohibiting slaughtering in certain years, for example, in 1700, 1709, and 1715, but again these prohibitions do not seem to have had any noticeable effect.

The expansion of the market for hides which followed upon the establishment of the South Sea Company's factory and the establishment of the Portuguese base at Colonia do Sacramento on the north shore of the River Plate did not affect the hunting economy for many years. Exports rose to 75,000 hides annually, until 1725, but fell during the next quarter of a century. In 1721 we hear of the *Cabildo* of Buenos Aires complaining about the activities of *gauchos vagabondos*, and of quarrels between the *Cabildo* of Buenos Aires and the Santa Fecino gauchos about the right to slaughter cattle in the Banda Oriental. On one occasion the *Cabildo* allied itself with the Indians in an endeavour to exclude the Córdobans from the slaughtering. All these events were but shadows of the future, however, and until roughly 1750 the free hunters had the upper hand on the pampas.

Contemporaneously the demand for hides began to increase. Leather at this time was a prime industrial raw material of much greater relative importance than it is nowadays. Before

---

[1] E. A. Coni, *Historia de las vaquerías del Río de la Plata* (Madrid, 1930), p. 57.
[2] Ibid., p. 44.   [3] Ibid., p. 17.

the age of rubber, elastic metals, and plastic surfacing agents, leather was widely used for a variety of purposes. In Brazil the wealthy slept in leather beds. In Europe carriages were sprung on leather springs. Fire engines were equipped with leather hoses and leather buckets. For three-quarters of a century, steam-engines were fitted with leather coupling and sealing devices. The growing armies of Europe were enormous con- sumers of leather. When exactly Europe as a whole became a leather-deficit area, it is difficult to ascertain. It was not until 1800 that the British Parliament passed a Flaying Act designed to relax craft restrictions and to promote the more economical use of hides, but the fact remains that, whatever their place of origin, hides could find an increasing market after the turn of the mid-eighteenth century.

The export of hides from the River Plate rose to an unusual average of approximately 150,000 between 1750 and 1778, and, after the opening of Buenos Aires to free, legal intercourse with the ports of Peninsular Spain in that year, exports rose rapidly to 800,000 annually by the end of the American Revolutionary War and at one point before the end of the century amounted to 1,400,000 in a year.[1] This expansion of exports represented a revolution and involved a burden which could not be borne by the commercial-hunting economy of the early state of nature. That economy was extremely wasteful. A cow was killed to make a meal of its tongue. Young bulls, heifers, and young cows were killed indiscriminately without regard to the effect upon reproduction. Needless to say no attention was paid to breeding.

We have noticed the early efforts made to control slaughter- ing and to organize production on the basis of private property. After 1750 serious efforts were made to end the commercial- hunting system and to establish a commercial-pastoral industry. Between 1771 and 1775 the *Cabildo* of Buenos Aires, which expressed the views of the merchants and *estancieros*, complained to the Governor about the slaughter of young bulls, heifers, and young cows, and as a result a system of breeding licences was introduced, which, if the *estancieros* had been able to enforce

---

[1] P. Ezcurra, 'Ganadería y Agricultura', *La Nación* (Buenos Aires, 25 May 1910), cited in R. Levene, *A History of Argentina*, translated by W. S. Robertson (Chapel Hill, 1937), p. 117.

their terms, would have been a first step in the direction of rationalized and managed production.[1] Thereafter, a number of political and administrative devices were adopted to strengthen the landlords' control over pastoral production and marketing and to terminate the anarchic and indiscriminate use of resources which characterized the state of nature. A system of registered cattle brands was introduced and the sale of unbranded hides was forbidden.[2] In 1792 the establishment of a junta or guild of *estancieros* was authorized by the Viceroy.[3] Contemporaneously with these developments the corps of gaucho soldiers, the *Blandengues*, was organized to guard the frontiers against the increasing Indian raids and to serve as a rural police force. Thus, the Indians who acknowledged no authority and the *gauchos vagabondos* who evaded it were increasingly menaced by administrative and political agencies designed to bring them into subjection or to eliminate them. After the overthrow of the Viceroy and the triumph of native merchants and landlords a complete system of controlling people was established. The decree of 30 August 1815 divided all plainsmen into owners of property and servants. All who were not declared property owners by a justice of the peace were declared servants and required to carry a passport signed by their employer and stamped by a justice of the peace every three months. Those not possessing a valid passport were declared outlaws and upon apprehension were condemned to five years military service.[4] This edifice of control was completed by the Law of 17 July 1823, which made it illegal to hire a peon who did not possess a police certificate.

These officially conceived and controlled devices for ordering the social relations of production were directed to the elimination of the free individual or band living off the resources of the pampas. In the establishment of the discipline of the estancia itself the gauchos provided from their own ranks the means of control. Personal prowess as a horseman and artistry with the knife, the bolas, and the lasso was much esteemed among the plainsmen. One savage could thus be set to catch the others and to dominate them. The gaucho *capataz* became the agent

---

[1] J. A. Pillado, *Origenes del ganado argentino* (Buenos Aires, 1909), p. 11.
[2] *D.H.A.* iv, p. 36.   [3] Ibid., p. 140.
[4] Alvarez, *Estudio sobre las guerras civiles argentinas*, p. 99.

by which the *estanciero* controlled his peons. Sarmiento described the *capataz* as one who

needs a will of iron for his task, a character resolute to the pitch of rashness to restrain the audacity and turbulence of those land free-booters, whom he has to master and rule in the desert courses. At the least sign of insubordination, the *capataz* seizes his iron whip handle and deals to the insolent blows that cause wounds and bruises. If resistance continues, rather than appeal to pistols he leaps from his horse, knife in hand, and quickly re-establishes his authority by the superior skill he shows in handling this weapon.[1]

The Robertson brothers have described how order and discipline were established on estancias in Corrientes during the anarchy and disorder of the revolutionary period. A certain gaucho, Don Pedro Campbell, was hired by one of the Robertsons 'to cut the camp'.

No small difficulty was experienced at first in bringing back all the peons or Gauchos to their old habits of labour and subordination [Robertson wrote], so completely had they been demoralized by the lawless life which, as Artigueno soldiers, many of them had led. But high wages, regularly paid, worked wonders. In many parts, indeed, the bolder and more reckless of these men would now and then show an inclination to upset the good work which was going forward. But Campbell's sway was omnipotent, and he reduced the worst of them to submission and obedience. His physical strength, his undaunted, if not ferocious, courage when roused, his dexterity with his knife, and his ever ready appeal to that, or his gleaming sabre, cowed all spirits less daring than his own, and left him undisputed master of the field.[2]

Robertson added that this 'method of reading the riot act was so effective that the country, as if by magic, started into industrious life and mercantile activity'.

The long process of transformation of the economy of the River Plate and its hinterland from a commercial-hunting to a commercial-pastoral economy based upon the privately owned and controlled estancia worked with wage labour generated a mounting political tension in the community. From the moment when Pueyrredón roused the country against the British until the presidency of General Roca, the gauchos were an ever-present factor in Argentine politics. Whether he was esteemed

[1] D. F. Sarmiento, *Vida de Facundo Quiroga* (Santiago de Chile, 1851), p. 31.
[2] J. P. and W. P. Robertson, *Letters on South America* (London, 1843), i, p. 178.

as the ideal man in the manner of General Rosas or execrated as the symbol of barbarism in the manner of President Sarmiento, the gaucho was never a man to be left out of account. The gauchos supplied the energy of Argentine political life during a large part of the nineteenth century, and they frequently set the limits to what the state and the other classes of the community could do. Except for a short period when Artigas dominated the Banda Oriental, the gauchos can never be described as controlling the community, but, as the closest student of the gaucho social phenomenon has said: 'From Rivadavia to Mitre, the most difficult task of men in the government was the establishment of authority, discipline, and class distinction (*jerarquía*) among the rural population, especially the most gaucho-like, that is to say, the most pastoral part of the litoral regions.'[1]

The political tensions associated with the development of the pastoral industry did not dominate the scene in Buenos Aires at the time when Popham invaded the Viceroyalty. Some explanation must be offered for the fact that, until the disorders set in train by the British invasion, the transformation of the economy of Buenos Aires was on the whole orderly and rational. Something must be attributed to the enlightened and responsive policies of the viceregal government, which was anything but the oppressive and incompetent tyranny depicted in British and Argentine popular propaganda. More must be attributed to the balance of social and economic forces which existed within the Viceroyalty and which was upset both by the British invasions and by the subsequent separation from Spain. Pastoral production was important in the economy of the Viceroyalty, but it was not the sole factor in the commercial prosperity of Buenos Aires, nor was it alone responsible for the growth of the city.

Before the establishment of the Viceroyalty in 1776, and even before Charles III commenced in 1764 to liberate the commerce of his dominions, the commercial connexion of Buenos Aires with the mining and agricultural areas of the interior was considerable and profitable. According to the British Minister in Lisbon in 1761 the fleet from Rio de Janeiro brought back 'besides the 10,000,000 cruzadas [*sic*] in gold brought back by the River Fleet, there are 4,000,000 cruzadas in silver, the

[1] Coni, *Historia del gaucho*, p. 77.

produce of the trade at Nova Colonia in the river of Plate. This silver the Government has ordered to be conveyed with the greatest secrecy not to give umbrage to the court of Spain'.[1] If this report is correct far more bullion was flowing eastward from Alto Peru to the River Plate than along the official channels westward to Callao and the Pacific. Coni, indeed, has calculated that silver exports through Buenos Aires averaged 1,600,000 pesos annually between 1748 and 1753 and that silver exports were worth at least seven times those of hides.[2]

When Charles III established the Viceroyalty of Buenos Aires in 1776 he brought within its jurisdiction the mines at Potosí, and thus made legal a trade which had been illegal until that time. Furthermore, he liberated the trade between the Viceroyalty and Chile and with the islands of the West Indies. In removing the obstacles to internal trade he brought into the community the centres of handicraft industry in Córdoba and Mendoza. This was not all gain from one point of view, for the free importation of Spanish wines injured the *vignerons* of the Andean provinces,[3] but what may have hurt certain interests in the interior was none the less beneficial to the commercial houses in Buenos Aires. The effects of the freeing of trade and the establishment of the Viceroyalty were, thus, twofold: they strengthened and broadened the base of the commercial interest in Buenos Aires and they created in the community as a whole a balance of interests which it had lacked legally before 1766, and which it soon lost after the separation from Spain and the internal upheavals of the revolutionary period.

This balance of interests was dynamic and delicate, for the rate of economic growth, measured by all previous standards, was very great and the intellectual ferment in the community unparalleled hitherto. Whether the political authorities were equal to the movement of society was an open question. The reforms of Charles III, the establishment of the Viceroyalty, and the expulsion of the Portuguese from the Banda Oriental had both stimulated economic development and reconciled all articulate interests to the Spanish Crown, but the very success

---

[1] State Papers, Foreign, Portugal, 89/54, Hay to Pitt, 29 June 1761, quoted in Christelow, *H.A.H.R.* xxvii, 1947, p. 5.

[2] Coni, *Vaquerías*, p. 42.   [3] Lynch, *Spanish Colonial Administration*, p. 286.

of the Viceroyalty served only to conceal what was really happening economically. The self-centred economy of early colonial times had come to an end, and the dependence of Buenos Aires upon a transoceanic commercial and economic connexion had become of fundamental importance to all the leading interests of the city. The position of the Crown of Spain had come to depend upon the degree to which it could protect and extend the opportunities of this transoceanic intercourse, for the dominant elements in Buenos Aires—the people who possessed wealth, organizing ability, and the will to action—were now enmeshed in the international economy from which they could not and many did not wish to extricate themselves. When the Spanish Crown went to war with Britain in 1796 the illusion of a free but exclusively Spanish commercial system was shattered. The British blockade reduced exports from Buenos Aires from 5,470,000 pesos in value in 1796 to 335,000 pesos in 1797.[1] The Spanish Government responded to this disaster with a decree permitting trade with neutrals and in neutral ships, a reluctant acknowledgement that there were no alternatives but transoceanic trade for the city of Buenos Aires, but that there were alternatives to trade exclusively with Spain and the Spanish overseas dominions.

The troubles of the Spanish Crown in Europe thus revealed the radical character of the changes wrought by economic development, but at the same time they intensified the disturbance of the balance of forces within the Viceroyalty. Until the deposition of Ferdinand VII by Napoleon in 1808 the Viceroyalty was juridically and constitutionally a direct dependency of the Crown and not an integral part of Spain or a colonial possession of the Peninsular community. The Junta of Seville and the Cortes which pretended to the power of government in 1810 wiped out this independence and proclaimed Spain and the overseas dominions one and indivisible. Under the government of the Crown Peninsular Spaniards had been accorded certain privileges in the overseas dominions, particularly in the matter of office-holding, and the laws governing commerce were, of course, designed to make Spain the centre of the imperial economy, but the Crown did maintain by its administrative devices a remarkable independence of particular interests,

[1] *D.H.A.*, v, p. 107.

a notable example of which was provided by the reforms of Charles III. During the ascendancy of the liberal elements after 1808, the interests of the Peninsular commercial class gained an influence which they never enjoyed under the absolute government of the Bourbons, and this influence was directed in the case of the Viceroyalty of Buenos Aires to limiting commercial opportunities for the benefit of Peninsular interests. 'The Sovereign did not confer upon Your Excellency the high dignity of Viceroy of these provinces in order to watch over the interest of the merchants of Cadiz but over ours', Mariano Moreno told the last Spanish Viceroy in 1810.[1]

This was a neat summary of the conflict created by the divergence between the Creole interest in Buenos Aires and the Peninsular interest centred in Seville and Cadiz. When the *Cabildo Abierto* of Buenos Aires deposed the Viceroy on 25 May 1810, and set up a Junta to govern in the name of Ferdinand VII, they asserted at one and the same time a conservative political doctrine and a radical economic policy aimed at the overthrow of one of the elements in the economy which limited the connexion of the River Plate with the world market. The immediate economic consequences of the political act of 25 May were an earnest of the rising power of several local interests. Within three days the prohibition on trade with foreigners was removed. Within a fortnight export duties on hides and tallow were reduced from 50 per cent. to $7\frac{1}{2}$ per cent., and within six weeks the prohibition on the export of bullion was eliminated.

These measures served for the time being to satisfy the local cattle and commercial interests. The reaction by the Cortes and the Spanish liberals was anything but sympathetic. 'No disposition exists here', Wellesley wrote from Cadiz in July 1812, 'to make any commercial concessions, even for the important object of tranquillizing America.'[2] In Buenos Aires they only provided an excuse for a further relaxation of commercial controls. The Junta of the *Cabildo Abierto* which had deposed Cisneros had continued to levy heavy duties on foreign goods. The principal British staple, cotton goods, paid 54 per cent. and some articles were dutiable at rates as high as 120 per cent.

[1] M. Moreno, 'Representación . . . de los hacendados', printed in *Doctrina democrática* (Buenos Aires, 1915), p. 68.　　[2] Castlereagh, *Correspondence*, viii, p. 269.

When this Junta was replaced in 1813 by a more revolutionary Triumvirate import duties were reduced to a flat 25 per cent. *ad valorem* with some exceptional items rated at 35 per cent. and 50 per cent. and some others such as mining equipment and firearms on a free list.[1]

The progressive crumbling of the traditional economic controls and the shattering of traditional social relations which accompanied the development of the political revolution exposed all the long-established interests of the Viceroyalty to the forces of international competition. Textiles from Britain, sugar from Brazil, flour from the United States, wine and spirits from Europe and the Caribbean flowed into the markets in Buenos Aires, undercutting local producers. Manuel Belgrano, the advocate of economic reform, had called attention in the 1790's both to the backward techniques of agriculture in Buenos Aires and to the obstacles to progress presented by price fixing and regulation,[2] but he could not have foreseen that a regime of free international competition was to become a factor in the destruction of cereal production in his native country. The liberal revolutionary, Rivadavia, who prompted the Triumvirate of 1813 to proclaim the end of slavery, could not have foreseen that his favourite vision of capital investment in mining enterprises would come to nothing for, among other things, the want of a labour force.

Under the government and protection of the Spanish Crown the colonial communities in the Viceroyalty of Buenos Aires had learned to produce a variety of goods and services, perhaps not as cheaply or as abundantly as Englishmen or Americans or Brazilians or Frenchmen could produce corresponding commodities. Under the revolutionary governments which followed they were more and more obliged either to revert to a regime of rigid commercial exclusion, as the Paraguayan community under Francia did, or turn to the production of those commodities which, having regard to their labour supplies and the state of its discipline and willingness to work, they could sell competitively in the world market. In these circumstances the pastoral industry came to overshadow all other interests and to build its fortunes and to increase its power upon the ruins of the old economy.

[1] *Registro Oficial de la República Argentina* (Buenos Aires, 1879), 590, i, p. 241.
[2] Gondra, *Historia económica*, pp. 265–7.

III

THE ESTABLISHMENT OF THE BRITISH INTEREST IN THE RIVER PLATE

EARLY in September 1807 the last British transports sailed from the River Plate bearing away the British soldiers, merchants, artisans, and adventurers whose evacuation from the Viceroyalty was the essential condition of Whitelocke's capitulation. But this was not the end; only a fresh beginning. During the year 1806–7, while the British forces held either Buenos Aires or Montevideo or both, British merchants had sold goods valued at more than £1,000,000,[1] in the River Plate and its hinterland. Now that direct access was denied, goods continued to flow to Rio de Janeiro and spill over through contraband channels into the Río de la Plata.[2] Viceroy Liniers was well disposed towards increased foreign commerce and turned a somewhat blind eye to this spill-over process. Indeed, his tenderness towards the clandestine trade seems to have been one of the factors in the bitter quarrel between him and Martín de Álzaga, the leader of the Peninsular Spaniards. When, following the grievous news of Ferdinand VII's deposition, Álzaga attempted a *coup d'état*, Liniers not only sent Álzaga into exile in Patagonia, but impaired the privileges of the Spanish merchants by admitting British merchants to trade under special licences. Robert Staples, a British merchant who participated in this trade, reported later to the Foreign Office that between November 1808 and November 1809 thirty-one British

---

[1] W.O. 1/162, Auchmuty to Windham, 11 May 1807; and R. A. Humphreys, editor, *British Consular Reports on the Trade and Politics of Latin America, 1824–1826* (Camden Society, Third Series, vol. lxiii, London, 1940), p. 349.

[2] F.O. 72/157, *Narrative of the Late Events in Buenos Aires*, by Robert Staples sent to the Foreign Office and dated 22 June 1812. Staples was a representative of Montgomery, Staples & Company of Belfast, and he was resident in Buenos Aires during the revolution of May 1810. He appears to have resided there for a period of time prior to this event.

vessels arrived at Buenos Aires and ten at Montevideo, bearing cargoes valued at £1,133,000 and £1,653,000 respectively.[1]

On the foundation of this trade a British community began to grow up in Buenos Aires. On the eve of the revolution there were believed to be 124 British subjects in the Viceroyalty, whose capital assets were estimated at a total value of between £750,000 and £1,000,000.[2] The presence of this community and its trading activities became one of the focal points of political tension contributing to the revolution. The Spanish merchants would have liked to see the British expelled completely, but the need of the Government for revenue and of the pastoral interest for markets obliged the Viceroy to pursue a liberal course. In time of war, when the normal channels of trade with Spain were interrupted or altogether cut, there was nothing extraordinary in such a modification of the trade laws. Admiral Cisneros, who was appointed to succeed Liniers as Viceroy in 1809, was instructed to preserve the exclusive rights of the Spanish merchants, but in response to the pressure of local circumstances he permitted, as his predecessor had done, a legal trade by the British merchants. They were taught, however, that their presence was only temporary. Their activities were hedged around with many restrictions designed to preserve the position of the Spanish and native merchants. British merchants could not, for example, acquire property in the Viceroyalty. They could not establish business enterprises. Cargoes could only be sold to publicly known Spanish merchants. British sailors could not even unload British ships. All ships' papers had to be deposited with the public authorities until the sailing time for the vessels.[3]

The object of these regulations was to ensure the temporary character of the British connexion and to prevent the establishment of a permanent interest competing with, and, perhaps, replacing the existing mercantile groups. The Spanish merchants were determined, as it were, to confine the British to their ships and to limit them to the business of supplying the Spaniards with imports and providing them with a means of disposing of exports. In the circumstances British enterprise

---

[1] F.O. 72/157, Staples to the Foreign Office, 21 June 1810.
[2] Humphreys, *Consular Reports*, p. 26, note 2, and p. 32, note 1.
[3] Street, *British Influence*, p. 128.

was entirely speculative, and there was no assurance that a venture, however profitable, could be repeated, or that any investment could be made in anything but the cargoes brought to the shore-line and taken thence.

Once the revolution against Spain and the Spanish monarchy began to develop, these limitations upon the penetration of British enterprise were progressively removed. Each stage in the dismantling of the carefully organized structure of the Spanish Catholic monarchy in the Río de la Plata witnessed an enlargement of the liberty and opportunity of British merchants, industrial organizers, craftsmen, shopkeepers, speculators, and investors. This enlargement continued until a point was reached where a local, not a Peninsular Spanish, reaction set in and illiberal tendencies once more asserted themselves. In the meantime, the local political and legal conditions for the firm establishment of British enterprise came into being, and, although some of these positions were lost as the revolution turned out of its liberal course, the revolution itself gave life to foreign business activity which never died and which was one of the indestructible consequences of the revolution.

Locally the revolution was set in motion, as we have suggested, by the British invasion. Overseas it was generated by the blows struck at the Spanish monarchy by Napoleon Bonaparte and by the Spanish resurgence against Napoleonic imperialism. The behaviour of Sobremonte, the Spanish Viceroy, in the presence of the British invasion had gravely compromised the Spanish Crown, but the initiative in organizing the defeat and expulsion of the British forces had been taken in considerable measure by Spaniards and men clearly attached to the Spanish imperial connexion. Martín de Álzaga, the chief alcalde, was a Spanish merchant strongly opposed to any course of action which might prejudice the exclusive mercantilist system of the Spanish Crown. Santiago de Liniers, though a Frenchman by race, was a regular officer in the Spanish service. The deposition of Sobremonte was, therefore, the work of men who questioned in no way the legal, moral, and political authority of the Spanish Crown. The Spanish Crown itself confirmed Liniers in the office of Viceroy, to which he had in fact been elevated by the local initiative of the military Junta created to organize the fight against Britain. In spite of the

fundamental commotion in the vitals of Argentine society produced by the invasions, the formal structure of the Viceroyalty
remained intact, and we can suppose that it might well have
been preserved had it not been for the abdication of Charles
IV, the deposition of Ferdinand VII, and the seizure of the
Spanish throne by Napoleon and its transfer to his brother Joseph.

This event was announced in Buenos Aires by the Marquis
de Sassenay, an emissary of Napoleon, who disembarked on
13 August 1808 bearing dispatches from the Emperor. These dispatches were opened in the presence of a Junta. Unfortunately
for himself in these circumstances, Liniers was a Frenchman.
Already the object of antipathy on account of his liberal views
on trade, Liniers was now deeply suspect in the eyes of 'true'
Spaniards like Martín de Álzaga and the Governor of Montevideo, Xavier de Elío. None the less, Liniers turned Sassenay
away without hesitation, and, in accordance with the undoubted sentiment in Buenos Aires, he proclaimed Ferdinand
VII king. He took the oath of allegiance to him as the legitimate
sovereign in the Viceroyalty and in Castile, Aragon, Leon, and
all the possessions of the House of Bourbon. This was not
enough. The 'true' Spaniards clamoured for a Junta to rule in
the name of Ferdinand and they shouted the slogan 'Down with
the Frenchman Liniers!'

Thus, the revolution was initiated by the Spaniards themselves. Liniers resisted them and maintained his authority, but
the Spanish party carried their agitation overseas, where the
central Junta in Cadiz, set up to rule in the name of Ferdinand
and to resist the imposition of Joseph by the French, listened
with a sympathetic ear. The central Junta was more imperialist
than the monarchy. In the name of liberty they had already
proclaimed the colonies to be integral parts of Spain and they
proposed that they be represented in the Cortes which was to be
summoned. The central Junta was determined to make the Río
de la Plata more Spanish, not less so. When the emissaries of
the Spanish party in Buenos Aires told them of Liniers's race
and his many crimes of a liberal character, they agreed to his
replacement by Admiral Baltasar Hidalgo de Cisneros, who
had fought at Trafalgar.

Liniers accepted his deposition, and the anti-Spanish party,
rapidly coming into being in Buenos Aires, accepted Cisneros.

But, they appear to have decided, two could play at the game of calling for a Junta to rule in the name of Ferdinand VII. Now, the liberal or Creole or anti-Spanish party (the names describe aspects of their composition and objectives) began to prepare for a Junta. Cisneros, however, headed them off by making concessions on the subject of commercial intercourse with the British. At the same time, he acted swiftly and brutally in putting down and punishing attempts in the interior to transfer authority from formally appointed officers to locally self-appointed Juntas or to town *cabildos* which in the ordinary circumstances of Viceregal government had only limited municipal functions.

In Buenos Aires the political lines tended to be drawn in accordance with interest and connexion. The landed and producer interest together with some commercial and professional men and many of the Creole military formations created at the time of the British invasions tended to be liberal and revolutionary. The official class and main mercantile groups with Spanish connexions tended to support the Viceregal power as it existed in the person of Cisneros. By the time of Cisneros's arrival in Buenos Aires in the winter of 1809, the weight of local interest favourable to a revolutionary course was greater than the weight favourable to the preservation of the old order. Wealth and established enterprise in Buenos Aires were conservative, but the new interests connected with and dependent on foreign mercantile activity, the new-born class of Creole officers and soldiers, and the inarticulate lower orders of gauchos, slaves, and wage workers had begun to look to and long for a new condition of things. Some talked of transferring power to the old, established *Cabildo* of Buenos Aires;[1] others to talk of something yet unknown, a transfer to an elected assembly. All were united in wanting an authority locally created.

On 13 May 1810 an English ship brought news of the collapse of the Junta of Seville, the last centre of organized authority resisting the French in Peninsular Spain. The authority of Ferdinand VII was now a pure abstraction; something in the hearts of the besieged in Saragossa and of the guerrillas along the roads from Bayonne. Cisneros sought to conceal for a time

[1] J. Lynch, 'Intendants and Cabildos in the Viceroyalty of La Plata', *H.A.H.R.* xxxv, 1955, p. 337.

the news that there was now no government in Spain, but the Creole leaders acted swiftly. The officers and soldiers moved into position around the Fort in Buenos Aires. The people shouted in the streets. Cisneros complained that the best people were excluded from the *Cabildo Abierto* called to consider the new order. Perhaps so; for the ordered, rational hierarchy maintained by the Crown of Spain was in dissolution. The last Spanish Viceroy quit. A Junta took his place on 25 May 1810 to govern, as Cisneros had done, in the name of Ferdinand VII.

There was no doubt about the British response to these events. The British men-of-war in the river were decked out in bunting. A salute of cannon was fired to welcome the revolution. Captain Fabian of H.M.S. *Mutine* made a lively public speech about freedom and about the joy which the revolution evoked in British hearts.[1] In July a committee of British merchants waited on the Junta to complain about the excessive customs duties, amounting to 54 per cent., levied on the main staple of their trade, cotton goods.[2] The Junta were sympathetic and agreed to recognize the committee as representative of British interests and to guarantee to British merchants the equal protection of the laws.[3]

The establishment of the Junta in place of the Viceroy was only the political prologue to a more fundamental revolution in the institutions and social structure of the community. This commenced in September 1811, when the Triumvirate displaced the Junta as the governing authority. During the period of the Junta, the partisans of the old order, established in Alto Peru, successfully resisted the efforts of the revolutionary authorities in Buenos Aires to extend their authority to the interior. At Huaqui in June 1811 a Spanish force defeated a force from Buenos Aires. Meanwhile the Portuguese monarchy in exile in Brazil was taking advantage of the revolutionary confusion to extend its authority over the Banda Oriental and Montevideo. As a result of these harassing disappointments, the more determined revolutionaries displaced the Junta. The Triumvirate consisted of one member drawn from the old Junta, Paso; Chiclana, a passionate opponent of Spanish authority; and Sarratea, a revolutionary soldier. The secretary was Bernardino

---

[1] Street, *British Influence*, p. 133.   [2] *Gaceta de Buenos Ayres*, 19 July 1810.
[3] R. Puiggros, *Historia económica del Río de la Plata* (Buenos Aires, 1945), p. 62.

de Rivadavia, the man who more than any other Argentinian of his day understood the meaning of revolution in terms of constitutional and economic change.

The revolutionary changes initiated by the Triumvirate created the conditions which made possible eventually a more settled and secure life for British interests. Export and import duties were reduced and some abolished. The immigration of foreigners was invited. The Courts were reformed and a separation between the organs of administration and judicature, unknown under the Spanish system of government, was established. The slave trade was forbidden. Secular schools were established. Liberty of the press was proclaimed. The Army was strengthened by the establishment of a general staff, and revolutionary discipline was enforced by the ruthless suppression of a mutiny over the abolition of a symbol of the old order, the soldier's queue. Finally, and this was of immense importance to the security and reputation of the British in Buenos Aires, a truce between the revolutionary forces and the Portuguese in the Banda Oriental was arranged by a British mediator, Lieutenant-Colonel John Rademaker of the Royal Engineers.

The Triumvirate of 1811 was shortly overthrown by the two leading military personalities lately come from Europe to organize the Army: José de San Martín and Carlos de Alvear.[1] But the revolution rolled forward. An Assembly was summoned. In January 1813 this Assembly declared itself to be the sovereign authority, although it did not proclaim independence of the Spanish Crown. Judicial torture together with the Inquisition were abolished. Forced Indian labour was made illegal. The entailment of estates was abolished. Ecclesiastical authority outside the bounds of Church affairs was suppressed. All children born in the territories under the authority of the Assembly were declared henceforth free. Foreign merchants were no longer obliged to consign their goods to native merchants, and the market became in fact free. Thus amidst blood, conspiracy, popular clamour, and military campaigns a liberal social order was born and the conditions for wider and more secure enterprise were established.

Had the revolution come to an end at the stage reached late

---

[1] It was reported to the Foreign Office that they were French agents, but this opinion was soon altered. F.O. 72/157, Castilla to Staples, 13 Aug. 1812.

in 1813, the British community in Argentina would have had few problems, and, indeed, British business enterprise and British immigrants might well have found in the new-born state conditions as congenial to their expansion and settlement as they discovered in the United States after the establishment of the Constitution. This was not to be. The problem of securing independence from the Spanish monarchy was no simple matter; for the revolution, which had come so easily in Buenos Aires, made little or no headway in the oldest, richest, and best established bastion of Spanish power in South America, Peru. Once Ferdinand VII was restored to his throne in Madrid, he soon discovered in that part of America ample grounds for hoping that his authority might be re-established in all his several dominions. The revolutionaries in Buenos Aires soon discovered that beating the King of Spain was a serious business, requiring the expenditure of much energy and money; the mobilization of great resources of men and materials; and the employment of much political and social ingenuity.

The necessities imposed upon the revolutionary Government by the task of beating the Spaniards further transformed society in the Río de la Plata, and, in the transformation, destroyed part of the liberal, economic, and political structure which it was the object of the early revolutionaries to create. In the struggle against the Spanish Crown the revolutionary leaders of Buenos Aires were politically obliged to generate a social revolt subversive to the order and ideas which the civilized urban society of Buenos Aires required for its existence, or at least, its predominance. Militarily they were obliged to create armies equipped and disciplined after the European fashion and to reinforce these with gaucho levies. Economically they were obliged to impose heavy burdens on the community partly in the form of taxes and partly in the form of an inflated currency at the very time when social disorder, the abolition of slavery, and the conscription of the scanty manpower of the community into the armies were impairing an already small and relatively inefficient labour force. Thus the fight against Spain created both the disposition towards and the means of fighting civil wars once the Spanish threat was pushed farther and farther away from the Río de la Plata proper.

A balance of forces developed in the Argentine community

between 1813 and 1820 which for two generations or more impaired the condition of *laisser-faire* created during the first phase of revolution. The gaucho cavalry under their *caudillos* became the foundation of provincial regimes expressing and protecting local interests: ranching interests, vignerons, handicraftsmen, and merchants. For a variety of reasons these provincial regimes were unfriendly to foreign enterprise and even to foreign merchandise, and by foreign they as often as not meant the enterprise and goods of the *porteños* of Buenos Aires. Buenos Aires itself possessed the inclination and the means of creating an army and an administrative apparatus on the European pattern, but without the co-operation and goodwill of the gauchos and the rural and provincial interests these could never function. Attempts to impose the rule of Buenos Aires, employing the army to support a centralized administrative apparatus, repeatedly failed. Even in the Province of Buenos Aires itself, the rural landholding interests employed the gaucho militia and gaucho retainers to ensure their dominance in the community and their capacity to deal with the mercantile and financial interests of the metropolis.

The achievement of a balance of forces among the contending interests created by the revolution and the war against Spain was a slow and painful process. Stability was never quickly achieved or long maintained. The geography of the country, the character of the people, and the circumstances of this phase of their history prevented the emergence of any one group strong enough to impose its will upon the whole community. In a turbulent community such as Argentina was for nearly half a century following the revolution, Britons who came to the River Plate found more opportunity than they could ever have done had the Spanish monarchy continued to rule as it had done for generations, but they also encountered a variety of difficulties stemming from the divergences and antitheses within Argentina itself, which determined the character of British enterprise, the social composition of the British community, and the scene of its activity.

The capacity of the British mercantile class for close organization, which has so often in foreign countries been both its greatest strength and weakness, soon manifested itself in Buenos

Aires. In 1811 the British Commercial Rooms were established
as a centre of commercial intelligence and sociability. Creoles
and 'foreigners' were excluded from its amenities, and it was
not until 1829 that a spirit of liberality provoked a reorganization which admitted Creoles to membership. Whatever may
have been the consequences in the long run of this close co-
operation, there can be little doubt that during this formative
period the capacity of the British to co-operate together and to
consider not only the day-to-day details of business but the
larger and more perplexing questions of politics was a source of
immense strength.

Indeed, an ability to make their needs known to political
leaders was indispensable to their survival. The River Plate
interest in London and the English mercantile interest in
Buenos Aires quickly became a force in the politics of the two
capitals working steadily towards a legal and diplomatic connexion between the British Government and the revolutionary
authorities.

The circumstances of high politics prevented formal political
intercourse for more than a decade, but this did not affect the
growth of the British community there. By the time the first
registration of British subjects was undertaken by the Consul-
General in January 1824 the tiny community of 1809 had
grown to 1,355 persons.[1] By 1831 this number had risen to
4,072 and, in addition, the Consul-General believed that a
thousand or more British subjects were unregistered.[2] The core
of the colony and its leaders were the merchants. Of the 4,072
registered in 1831, 1,422 were women and children. Merchants
and their clerks numbered only 466 of the 2,650 persons earning
incomes, but their wealth and influence were out of all proportion to their numbers; 193 were shopkeepers. Surprisingly, the
largest group numerically were artisans; 1,245 were listed as
master mechanics, carpenters, bricklayers, and labourers. In
this early period there was some expectation and hope that this
body of artisans and labourers would be vastly reinforced by
immigration and that Argentina might become predominantly

[1] F.O. 6/3, Parish to Canning, 25 Apr. 1824: M. G. Mulhall, *The English in
South America* (Buenos Aires, 1878), estimated the British community at 3,500 in
1823.

[2] W. Parish, *Buenos Ayres and the Provinces of the Río de la Plata* (London, 1839 ed.),
p. 394.

peopled, as Rivadavia intended, by 'familias industriosas . . . de cualquiera punta de Europa, en especial de las naciones del Norte'.[1]

This was not to be. During the century or more which followed skilled workers from the British Isles—bank clerks, locomotive drivers, telegraphers, engineers, draftsmen, stonemasons, stockmen—went to Argentina, often in considerable numbers, to fill gaps in the labour force created by lack of native experience or the rapidity of economic development, but these men never migrated in sufficient numbers or penetrated sufficiently deeply into the community to transform its character significantly. Indeed, by the 1830's the British community in Argentina was proportionately larger in numbers than it was ever to be, and its social composition was thus early established: predominantly city folk, many of Scottish origin, skilled in some craft or profession, mainly middle class, or occupying a special place in the community as well-paid wage workers. And the British community was mainly Protestant. The only exception was provided by the Irish shepherds who came to the River Plate in the 1830's and 1840's. These tended to mingle with the Creole community, but the main body of the British tended always to maintain its connexions with the homeland. Its members aimed at retiring to Britain to live on their fortunes or their pensions according to the calling they had followed, the work they had done, and the success of their speculative dealings.

In the two revolutionary decades following the collapse of the Spanish power in Buenos Aires, the opportunities of a fluid society attracted wanderers from all the quarters of the world. One would have expected many individual Englishmen and Scotsmen to be numbered among them. In other countries, and at other times, British workmen and traders came, settled, and were absorbed into the communities where individual inclination or circumstance had decided them to rest. Such, for example, was the case during the history of the United States until World War I, and earlier examples on a less impressive scale can be found in the Russia of Peter the Great or in Sweden or in Holland. In the case of Argentina, however, the coming and the remaining of the British requires some explanation. Although they came as individuals they soon discovered

[1] *D.H.A.* xiv, p. 52.

that group consciousness and finally the assistance of state power were necessary for the establishment of the conditions required for their life and work. Experience had demonstrated and reason had proved to Castlereagh that political power could provide no foundation for British activity in the River Plate, nor could it create the opportunity for British subjects to live and work there. And yet, within a few years of the revolution of 1810, it became evident that Englishmen and Scotsmen could not simply cross the Atlantic and disappear into Argentine society, as they might into the society of Philadelphia or New York, so that their native land and the power of the British Crown became for them but a memory, sweet or bitter according to the circumstances which persuaded them to depart, but in any case a matter of no especial significance. No. The British who came to Argentina found a half-way house in which they did not rely for their security and way of life upon the exercise of political authority by the British Crown, nor yet solely upon the will or whim of the local political authorities. More than the spirit of revelry prompted the British merchants gathered at dinner on Saint Andrew's Day, 1825, to greet with wild delirium the news of the signature of the Anglo-Argentine Treaty of Friendship, Commerce, and Navigation. More than a love of horseplay induced them to demonstrate their joy by hurling their glasses out of the windows of their dining-hall in order to express more adequately their feelings by drinking directly from the bottle.[1]

Once the British Crown had ceased to exercise direct political power in Buenos Aires and once the power of the Spanish Crown was broken, the survival and growth of the British community in Argentina depended upon its commercial capacity. The primary constituent of this capacity was low manufacturing cost; the second was abundance of commercial capital; and the third was commercial experience and connexions.

The decline in the price of imports and the rise in the price of the main export staples—hides and bullion—was a phenomenon which antedated the revolution, and can be discerned as a prominent factor in the economic progress of the Río de la Plata from the reforms of Charles III onward. Iron, for

---

[1] N. L. Kay Shuttleworth, *A Life of Sir Woodbine Parish* (London, 1910), quoting Parish to Planta, 22 Dec. 1825, p. 292.

example, fell in price from 15 to 7·50 pesos per quintal in the decade before the French Revolution; steel from 55 to 15 pesos per quintal; and brandy from 60 to 24 pesos.[1] Hides, on the other hand, advanced in price shortly after the liberation of trade from 5 or 6 reales to 18 to 20 reales per quintal.[2] The British invasions severely reduced the prices of textiles. Cottons of local manufacture sold at 2 to 2·75 reales per vara. British cottons were put on the market at 1·75. Locally manufactured ponchos sold for 7 pesos; a good-quality Yorkshire poncho sold for 3 pesos.[3] The revolution only accelerated the process of price competition. Although the British merchants were wrong in supposing that an alteration in the terms of trade favourable to Buenos Aires was a new phenomenon, they were correct when they reported to their Consul-General in July 1824 that, 'while the colonial System existed, all Manufactures and other European goods sold here at three times their present prices; while the produce of the Country was given in exchange, at a fourth part of what is now paid for it'.[4]

We have no means of measuring precisely how cheap British goods were when compared with other goods, but the fact of their cheapness was a matter of common observation. 'The consumption of British manufactures has of late greatly increased', observed a group of British merchants who waited on Castlereagh in July 1812, 'the abundance and consequent low prices of Goods has placed within the reach of the Inhabitants, articles which from their first cheapness they were induced to wear, and which, being now accustomed to, has created new wants.'[5] Reflecting upon his great experience of Anglo-Argentine intercourse forty years later, Sir Woodbine Parish had little to add to the observation of 1812.

The low prices of British goods, [he wrote in 1852] especially those suited to the consumption of the masses of the population of these countries, ensured a demand for them from the first opening of the trade. They are now become articles of the first necessity to the lower orders in South America . . . thus it is that every improvement in our machinery at home which lowers the price of these

---

[1] Puiggros, *Historia económica*, p. 39.   [2] Coni, *Historia del gaucho*, p. 48.

[3] Puiggros, *Historia económica*, p. 21.

[4] F.O. 6/4, enclosure in Parish to Canning, 30 July 1824, printed in Humphreys, *Consular Reports*, pp. 27–62.

[5] F.O. 72/157, British merchants to Castlereagh, 2 July 1812.

manufactures, tends to contribute (we hardly perhaps know how much) to the comforts of the poorer classes in these remote countries, and to perpetuate our hold over their markets.[1]

On the strength of this capacity to sell at prices attractive in a market made up largely of absolutely poor people, Great Britain soon came to occupy a position of predominance in some branches of the River Plate trade. In 1822, for example, a year for which a complete return from the Buenos Aires' customs house is available, imports of British origin amounted to $5,730,952 of a total importation of $11,267,622 or 50·9 per cent. Brazil, the second largest exporter to the River Plate, was responsible for 12·5 per cent. and the United States, a close third, for 12 per cent. The entire continent of Europe was the place of origin of only 19·8 per cent. of Argentine imports in 1822.

But it must not be supposed that Britain predominated in every line of trade. Indeed, the trade of the River Plate, when it was first opened widely to international commerce, was specialized along lines formed by technological advance or geographic circumstance. Britain was primarily a supplier of textiles —particularly cotton and woollens.[2] The accounts of the first year for which we have records specifically identifying in detail exports to Buenos Aires reveal that 85·5 per cent. of British goods by value were textiles. 'We have . . . successfully supplanted German and French fabrics', some British merchants told the Foreign Office in 1812.[3] They might have added that they were also supplanting local production wherever British goods were allowed to compete. But Germany still predominated, for example, in the hardware trade. Flour and lumber were handled almost exclusively by the Americans. Brazil supplied sugar, yerba mate, rum, rice, coffee, and some textiles, of which a proportion were re-exports from India.

But if the British were sellers, they were also buyers. Equipped with a large commercial capital, connected with and knowing the markets not only of Britain but the continent of Europe and the Far East, British merchants soon demonstrated their capacity to take up a substantial proportion of the main export

[1] Parish, *Buenos Ayres* (1852 ed.), p. 362.
[2] H. S. Ferns, 'Investment and Trade between Britain and Argentina in the Nineteenth Century', *Economic History Review*, 2nd series, vol. iii, no. 2, 1950, p. 203.
[3] F.O. 72/157; British merchants to Castlereagh, 2 July 1812.

staples of the country—hides, tallow, hair, bones, and—as long as the supply lasted—bullion. Of 5,652,768 hides imported into Britain during the years 1810–15, 3,089,694, or 54 per cent., came from the River Plate.[1] This percentage declined after Waterloo, but Britain remained for many years Argentina's best market for hides. Britain's capacity to buy hides was not the only factor, however; for British merchants were willing to take up everything offered, confident that they had the connexions in Europe and elsewhere to dispose of their purchases.

And they were willing and able to give credit. The Robertson brothers, who played an active part in British trade with Buenos Aires from its first establishment after the revolution in 1810, have left us a vivid and detailed account of their experiences and their modes of operation. 'The universal system of doing business in the interior parts of South America', they record, 'is by giving what are called *habilitaciones*, that is advancing to the grower or collector of produce a certain sum in money and goods, which he engages to repay in his produce in a given time, and at a stipulated price.'[2] From the Robertsons' description we get a picture of a British mercantile firm widely ramified through the countryside buying produce and selling manufactured goods, salt, mate, and tobacco, hiring carters, chartering transport vessels, and even recruiting and paying the agencies of law and order. During the first wave of British commercial penetration merchants like the Robertsons appear to have undertaken the superintendence and financing of all the operations of hide production. One contract described by the Robertsons reveals them contracting with an *estanciero* for 10,000 horses at threepence per head. They spent another threepence per head on slaughter; another threepence on cleaning and drying the hides; and threepence more on transport to Goya on the Río Paraná. A horse hide costing the Robertsons a shilling in Goya could be sold for three shillings, more or less, in Buenos Aires in the 1820's and for seven to eight shillings in Liverpool or London.[3]

A selling price of a hide at 2,800 to 3,200 per cent. of the first cost of a horse in Corrientes suggests large profits. Transport costs, however, were high. Fifty per cent. of the price of a hide in Buenos Aires was accounted for by transport according to

---

[1] *Parliamentary Papers*, 1830, xxv, pp. 264–5.
[2] Robertson, *Letters on South America*, i, p. 174.   [3] Ibid., ii, p. 263.

one estimate.[1] If land carriage was involved transport might be much higher. Parish's estimates of land transport costs in the pre-railway age suggest that it cost about one shilling and threepence to carry a hide fifty miles.[2] Marine freight charges and insurance absorbed an indeterminate proportion of cost, but never less than 25 per cent. of the final selling price. A British merchant, operating on the scale of the Robertsons with an ample capital to finance a large turnover and with good mercantile connexions in Liverpool and London (the Robertsons were connected with the Gladstones), was able to make a very substantial total profit on his capital and at the same time cut profit margins on both buying and selling in a way which smaller Creole merchants were unable to do.

The very scale and effectiveness of British mercantile operations were the cause of the eventual limitation put upon them and of the establishment of a division of business which left the commercial activity of the interior very largely in Creole hands and confined British mercantile activity to Buenos Aires and to international commerce. Almost everyone who was not a working gaucho aspired to be a trader. 'Throughout South America all men in authority are petty traders', one British traveller discovered.[3] *Estancieros* soon discovered that a *pulpería* —a combined shop and saloon—was a profitable addition to their establishments. Political and military leaders became traders—particularly on the pampas. Indeed, the social hierarchy on the pampas corresponded to the scale of commercial operations. 'Even the term huckster, or retail dealer, implies always in Corrientes, something respectable', the Robertsons inform us, 'that of *comerciante* something aristocratic; but that of *comerciante gueso* or *poderoso*, something magnificent.'[4] Candioti, the Prince of the Santa Fecino gauchos, was a great merchant reputedly possessed of half a million gold dollars in working capital. The great *caudillos* including the most famous of all, General Juan Manuel Rosas and General Urquiza, were great merchants as well as *estancieros*.

These Creole traders, both big and little, looked with the

[1] *Gaceta Mercantil*, no. 3235, assuming transport of 240 leagues.
[2] Parish, *Buenos Ayres* (1852, ed.), p. 276.
[3] J. Miers, *Travels in Chile and La Plata* (London, 1826), i, p. 102.
[4] Robertson, *Letters on South America*, i, p. 237.

eye of malevolence and envy upon the operations of British merchants in the interior. The Robertsons eventually confined their activities to Buenos Aires and finally became bankrupt. They found it a relief to live in Buenos Aires, for in Corrientes they believed themselves to be 'marked men'. They dreaded the gaucho's sabre (and behind the gaucho stood the *caudillo*-merchant such as Candioti or Urquiza or Ramírez) and the prisons of Dr. Francia, the Paraguayan dictator.

Another source of petty annoyance to us [the Robertsons reported] arose out of the jealousy and envy of small merchants, who fancied themselves aggrieved by our gigantic operations. They could not, with their mole-like blindness, see—perhaps they would not—that although a large and new field opened up for us, their old and narrow one was not involved. We were no monopolists. There was ample room for the free competition of all. But then again, the would-be little monopolists complained that, by paying high prices we ruined their trade; so that, if they resolved not, they cut short the problem thus:—'These great dealers, one way or the other, are in possession of all the trade; let us, by hook or by crook, get quit of them, and then the trade will be divided among us'.[1]

Looking back across nearly a century and a half we see in our mind's eye a little English-speaking community on the shores of the Río de la Plata, lively, expansive, dominated by men willing to try first one line of endeavour and then another in their search for fortune; travellers in a strange land whose possibilities excited their enthusiasm and whose realities often disappointed them in like measure. These early pioneers of British enterprise in Argentina were truly adventurers; for in those revolutionary times all their undertakings and sometimes even their lives were things about the fate of which no man could be sure. Although they were men of business, large and small, they knew no security of property in a society where revolutionary soldiers and politicians driven by the necessities of the hour might seize their funds, or, impelled by some ideal conception of improved human institutions, might challenge the very notion of property itself. They were welcomed as friends and reviled as enemies according to the shifting circumstances of politics on both sides of the Atlantic. They were sometimes compelled to make forced loans to the Government,[2]

[1] Ibid. i, p. 282.
[2] On one occasion the British community attempted to head off a forced loan

and sometimes they were threatened with the conscription of their persons into the revolutionary armies. On one occasion the whole British community was threatened with death as a reprisal for the seizure of an Argentine brig by a British naval commander.[1] On another occasion an Englishman was beaten to death in the streets of Buenos Aires for not falling on his knees quickly enough in the presence of the Host. If there were difficulties in living, there were likewise difficulties in dying, and the burial of the dead was one of the subjects provided for in the Treaty of Friendship, Commerce, and Navigation of 1825.[2]

The character and activity of the British community in the Río de la Plata were shaped by the course of revolution there. At first it looked as if the breakdown of Spanish monarchal authority, the opening of the country to foreign penetration, and the establishment of the free market as the central organizing mechanism of society would lead to a rapid expansion of British as well as native business activity. Indeed, the popular enthusiasm in Britain about Spanish America and the warmth of the expectations concerning it were greater than anything felt during the 1820's for the United States, Canada, or New South Wales. But in spite of these expansive hopes, the River Plate trade at this time accounted for only a very small part of British overseas commerce.

The nature and needs of the Argentine democratic movement set severe limits to what could be done in the Río de la Plata. There were, of course, certain natural factors of geography which postponed rapid economic development until the capital resources and technical knowledge were equal to the challenge of the pampas, but of equal importance, checking rapid development and extensive foreign penetration, was the nature of the new-born democracy of the Río de la Plata. The democratic movement in Argentina may never have produced consistently workable representative institutions for the government of society but, as a result of the British invasion and the revolution which followed, Argentina developed rapidly into a community in which the *montoneros* (the mass of common men

by making a voluntary contribution. When the forced loan was ordered in spite of this, the senior British naval officer issued a grave warning to the Government, and it desisted. Adm. 1/23, Bowles to the Admiralty, 2 Oct. 1818.

[1] Mulhall, *English in South America*, p. 326.   [2] Article XII.

in arms against authority) exercised a predominance. The gauchos of the plains and the lower orders of Buenos Aires may seldom have possessed a rational appreciation of their own material interests, they may frequently have been duped and more often exploited by leaders who gained wealth from their labour and social prestige from their willingness both to fight and to capitulate, but these people could never be left out of account after the revolution. Democracy meant appealing to them, and their response to the appeal. This had two important consequences for foreign new-comers and particularly for the British. First, it set a limit to their business activity and reserved to the natives small business, business in the interior provinces, and all but the most complicated crafts and commercial operations. Secondly, Argentine democracy was prejudicial to the ideas and scheme of values at the root of business enterprise. Many of the revolutionaries were children of the enlightenment: rationalists, utilitarians, atheists, and deists. The gauchos were otherwise. Facundo Quiroga, the Tiger of the Pampas, inscribed on the banners of his army the slogan 'Religion or death!' These savage men of the plains had some very imperfect ideas concerning the Christian religion, but they entertained none the less a strong feeling of hostility to men who worshipped strange gods unknown to them or who did not worship any gods at all. They had no feeling whatever for gods whose magic resided in dull and unmanly institutions such as schools and universities. They loved a Man who suffered and died bravely, Who was a part of God, Who rose again and Whose power and glory came to everyone in the Host, Whose presence they could seek when impelled to do so. That was the long and short of religion for the gauchos, and they cared nothing at all for the morality, discipline, gentleness, and subterfuge with which townsmen cluttered up the worship of God and impaired the liberty of men. Rivadavia, the liberal revolutionary, proposed to build schools, and he was driven out; Rosas, the gaucho revolutionary, built churches and he endured.

If democracy means rule susceptible to the influence of men as they are, and not as they exist in the mind of a revolutionary leader, then Argentina in 1820 was a democracy, and as such, a community to which the British business class and immigrant workers could not adjust without some effort. But they did find a place in the Argentine community, and this was partly their own doing and partly that of their Government.

As we have already observed there existed at the very commencement of the developments we are seeking to describe an appreciation in the guiding mind of the British nation of the essentials of the situation in which Britain and the South American nations found themselves during the Napoleonic Wars. Castlereagh saw clearly that Britain's principal interest was the development of commercial opportunities; that flags, bayonets, and artillery were not the keys to such opportunities; and that delicate navigation in the direction of the flowing tide of events might lead to safer harbours and richer rewards than marching armies could ever reach. But the perils were many and the British Cabinet had greater commitments elsewhere which might at any moment contradict their policies in South America. How, for example, could the necessity of supporting Spain in Europe be reconciled with the objective of creating new commercial opportunities, which royalist and liberal Spaniards alike abominated? How could the omelette be made without breaking eggs? British statesmen had set themselves up as men who hated the breaker of eggs, but they were as greedy as any European statesman—more so in fact—for omelettes of the most liberal size and constituency.

So long as Spain was an ally of Napoleon the interests of the revolutionary forces in South America, such as they were, ran parallel with those of the British Government. The risings in Spain, the formation of the Juntas, and the dissolution of the authority of the hereditary monarch ended the alliance of Spain with Napoleon. In July 1808 Great Britain concluded a peace with the *ad hoc* Spanish authorities, and in January 1809 entered into an alliance with Spain against Napoleon. Henceforward it was Britain's interest and duty to give the Spanish authorities the strongest possible support. On the highest level of diplomacy the British Government never departed from acknowledgement of the sovereignty of the Spanish authorities over its transatlantic empire. But, from the beginning of the alliance, the British Government differed from the Spanish authorities over the consequences of Spanish hegemony in the sphere of trade and finally of politics. It was soon discovered that the Spanish Cortes was even more determined than the Spanish Crown to preserve for Spanish enterprise the opportunities of Spanish America and that only the want of power at the moment prevented them from coming forcibly to the assistance of their partisans, such as Álzaga in Buenos Aires, for the purpose of maintaining the commercial monopoly of the mother country. Thus, so long as Britain and Spain were alike fighting Napoleon and their main resources were absorbed in this struggle, the British Government lacked the disposition formally to come to the assistance of its subjects trading and working in South America and likewise Spain lacked the capacity to check their activities or to discipline the local authorities, still nominally under their control, who welcomed the presence of the British.

The British in Buenos Aires were conscious, from their first coming there, of the necessity of some security for their persons and their property, and they sought this from two sources: from the local authorities and from the organs of power of the British Crown. As we have noticed, the Junta of May 1810 made them a general promise, but the British merchants also turned naturally to the British Government for assistance.

The nearest agent of the British Government was the British Minister at the Portuguese Court in Rio de Janeiro, Lord Strangford. From almost the first moment of his arrival in Brazil, Strangford was concerned actively with both the diplomatic and commercial aspects of events in the Río de la Plata. Within the limits of the necessities of the Anglo-Spanish alliance he worked skilfully to maintain a friendly relationship with all concerned: to restrain the Portuguese from attempting to seize the Spanish possessions; to retain the goodwill of the Spanish authorities; to encourage the revolutionaries to believe that Britain was their friend; to secure opportunities for British mercantile enterprise; and to teach British naval commanders their duty in these confusing circumstances.[1]

But Strangford was far away in Rio de Janeiro, and the British in Buenos Aires asked for someone immediately at hand to represent and protect them. In response to a direct request to the Foreign Office, the British Government appointed Robert

[1] J. Street, 'Lord Strangford and Río de la Plata, 1808–1815', *H.A.H.R.* xxxiii, 1953, pp. 477–510.

Staples, and, as they were bound to do by the custom and law of nations, they asked the Spanish authorities to accept Staples as an official spokesman and to endow him with the requisite rights and powers. The authorities at Cadiz refused to accept Staples. But the Foreign Office let Staples go to Buenos Aires, although a nameless official recorded his 'doubt of the possibility of giving him an official character'.[1] In Buenos Aires the 'Superior Government of the United Provinces of the River de la Plata' was as alive to the implications of Staples's appointment as the authorities in Cadiz. Rivadavia, the secretary of the Triumvirate, returned Staples's diploma 'hasta que lo no acompane Vd. con una nota oficial',[2] but he added that 'it has given the greatest satisfaction to the Superior Government of the United Provinces of the River de la Plata to have received from the British Government, for the first time, an indication of its desire to communicate . . .'.[3] Eighteen British merchants in Buenos Aires promptly wrote to the Foreign Office to express their regret that Staples had not been recognized.

And well they might, for the difficult situation in which the British Government found itself, wishing to support Spain and to trade with her insubordinate colonies, had its effect upon the fortunes of the British community in Buenos Aires. The royalist Governor, Elío, had established himself in Montevideo. The Spanish authorities found somehow the means to reinforce him, or at least, seemed to do so.

I found on my arrival here [Staples wrote from Buenos Aires] that the reinforcements arrived at Montevideo from Spain had given much alarm, and the opinion that something more than the connivance of the British Government was necessary to enable troops to come from that Country, was still, among many classes of people, received here. The effects of this have been an almost total cessation of Commerce for several months past, and the finances of the Government have been much reduced . . . .[4]

To relieve their financial distress the Triumvirate at Buenos Aires levied a forced contribution on the old Spaniards, and, if it were true that Britain was aiding the counter-revolutionary

[1] F.O. 72/157, added to letter from Staples to the Foreign Office, 13 Apr. 1813.
[2] F.O. 72/157, Rivadavia to Staples, 24 Mar. 1812.
[3] F.O. 6/1, from a Memorandum on Robert Ponsonby Staples, 26 June 1823.
[4] F.O. 72/157, Staples to the Foreign Office, 18 Nov. 1813.

forces, the British merchants could reasonably expect to be the next to suffer confiscations.

This was not the only difficulty stemming from the policy of the British Government. 'Suspicions of this nature [that Britain was aiding the Spanish authorities at Montevideo] are kept alive by the Americans, who use every means to insinuate themselves into the confidence of this Government', Staples informed the Secretary of State for Foreign Affairs.[1]

The suspicions of the authorities and the people in Buenos Aires were further reinforced by the actions of some of the senior British naval officers on the South American station. Captain Fabian of H.M.S. *Mutine* had broken out bunting and saluted the revolution with salvoes of cannon—quite understandably, for the revolution had solved the immediate problem he faced of saving British property from confiscation by the viceregal authorities. Within a few months, however, the facts of politics in Peninsular Spain, the strengthening of Spanish authority in Montevideo, and the momentary pause in the spread of revolution beyond the Province of Buenos Aires caused the British naval commander in the River Plate to restrain any enthusiasm he may have privately felt for the revolution. Captain Elliot, who succeeded Fabian as senior officer, was confronted with a request from Montevideo that he co-operate in blockading Buenos Aires where there were forces in revolt against the ally of Great Britain, the King of Spain. Elliot tried to prevent the blockade, but when the Spanish Governor insisted, Elliot felt obliged to co-operate and to order British vessels to cease entering Buenos Aires.[2]

Elliot appears to have interpreted the letter of the law rather better than he did the subtle mind of Lord Strangford. When Strangford heard of Elliot's action he dispatched Admiral de Courcy, the Commander-in-Chief on the South American station, to the River Plate. Upon his arrival off Montevideo, de Courcy learned that the revolution had spread to Chile and that revolutionary antagonisms were even gnawing at authority in Montevideo itself. He, therefore, took a very strong line, inviting the Spaniards to agree not to interfere with British ships at Buenos Aires. 'After a pause', de Courcy reported, '[the Spanish Governor] gave in, adding that he yielded to superior

[1] Ibid.   [2] Adm. 1/20, Elliot to de Courcy, 10 Sept. 1810.

force without being at all satisfied with the justice of my conduct. . . . It was agreed that the blockade should be relinquished on the day following.'[1]

de Courcy had some doubts about his conduct, and he asked for positive instructions over and above those given by Lord Strangford. In the meantime, the British merchant vessels counted up their guns, took on crews capable of firing them, and defied the Spanish cruisers.[2] Finally, in July 1812, instructions were devised ordering that 'in the event of . . . finding the Blockade of Buenos Ayres renewed and enforced by the Governor of Monte Video, he was not to allow any interruption whatever to be given to the legitimate commercial Intercourse of His Majesty's Subjects with all the Ports in the possession of the former'.[3] A zeal quite unlike the caution of Captain Elliot animated the officers who followed him, for one British commander forced the surrender of the Spanish frigate *Mercurio*, cruising off Buenos Aires.

Thus the British Government succeeded in keeping its left hand unentangled with its right. With the Spanish authorities, the Foreign Office was correct. When Staples returned to London from Buenos Aires early in 1813, he was paid £1,200 for his services and he was appointed a Treasury agent for the purchase of bullion in the River Plate, but Castlereagh refused to 'give him an official character'. From time to time Staples wrote to the Foreign Office about events in Buenos Aires, and the Foreign Office sent him consular circulars. But, like the agents in London of the various Juntas, Triumvirates, and supreme Governments of the Río de la Plata, Staples was not a recognized channel of communication and he had no public authority. Less than a week after the Congress at Tucumán proclaimed the independence of the United Provinces in July 1816 the British merchants in Buenos Aires called a public meeting at which they resolved to request Mr. Staples to acquaint the British Government that they had called upon him to represent them.[4] At a subsequent meeting they agreed to pay Staples by levying a 'Consulage of One Half per Cent on

---

[1] Adm. 1/20, de Courcy to the Admiralty, 5 Nov. 1810.
[2] Ibid., de Courcy to the Admiralty, 25 Jan. 1811, enclosures.
[3] F.O. 63/122, Castlereagh to Strangford, 13 July 1812.
[4] F.O. 6/1, Memorandum on Robert Ponsonby Staples, 26 June 1823.

the total Invoice Amount of all Goods imported in British
Vessels' and 'One Real per Ton for Consulage on the Register
Tonnage of all British Vessels arriving at Buenos Ayres'.[1]

This 'recognition' of Argentine independence by the British
merchants and their 'appointment' of a Consul ironically illus-
trates the contradiction between the facts of the situation and
the necessities, and, in some quarters, the prejudices, of British
high policy. What Staples was able to do on behalf of the
British mercantile community is not entirely clear. His main
function seems to have been that of an adviser, information
officer, and contact man with the public authorities. He was
regarded, however, with sufficient seriousness in Buenos Aires to
cause General San Martín to seek an interview with him early
in 1817, before he set out to liberate Chile. Indeed, San Martín
placed before Staples his views on future developments, and
expressed to him the hope that 'some British naval force should
be stationed in those seas [off the coast of Chile] which, acting
even on the principle of strict neutrality, would prevent many
acts of an arbitrary and oppressive nature to which all commerce on that coast is now exposed'.[2]

From 1816 onward the Government at Buenos Aires was, of
course, striving for recognition as an independent state. In the
conduct of this struggle it was proposed not only to use informal
channels of communication such as Staples and the local British
naval commanders provided, but also to break off communication as a form of pressure. In October 1818, for example, the
Government refused to discuss commercial questions with
British naval officers and stated that such matters would only
be discussed with a properly accredited Consul. On the British
side the complications of European policy, uncertainty about
the prospects of a Spanish counter-revolution, and anti-revolu-
tionary sentiment among British political leaders pushed them
to dissociate themselves further from Staples. Early in 1819 he
was told specifically by the British Government that he could
not be appointed a consul, and in June of the same year the
British merchants resolved to change his title to that of British
Commercial Agent. Following this Staples ceased writing to
the Foreign Office, although, such was the inertia of the Foreign
Office, it required some years before they stopped writing to him.

[1] Ibid.   [2] F.O. 72/202, Staples to Hamilton, 25 May 1817.

The best security of the British residents in the United Provinces during these years of uncertainty was their importance
to the Argentine community. Political cries might be raised
against them as foreigners, Protestants, and men of opulence;
they might be threatened with confiscation and conscription;
but no government could take any concerted action against
them because they provided one of the principal channels by
which the products of the main Argentine industry flowed into
the world market, and the trade carried on by the British constituted, through its effects on customs dues, the chief source of
revenue for the state authorities. British merchants, sometimes
reluctantly and sometimes willingly, became likewise one of
the chief sources of public borrowing. Indirectly through their
influence and interest in London, in the British press, in Parliament, and in the Cabinet, the River Plate interest was becoming the biggest single, positive factor in the struggle for the
recognition of the United Provinces of the Río de la Plata as an
independent state.[1] Thus, the British community in Buenos
Aires had as its best protector the interest of all but the most
xenophobic forces on the extreme wings of Argentine politics.

An historian of Anglo-Argentine relations can present no
rational narrative of events during these formative years if he
confines himself narrowly to a description of the fortunes and
character of the British community in Buenos Aires and its
relations with London. The United Provinces of the Río de la
Plata[2] enjoyed during the course of the revolution the enviable
distinction among the Spanish colonies of never experiencing a
counter-revolution by Spanish forces. Elsewhere in Spanish
America the revolution was never the 'sure thing' it appeared
to be in Buenos Aires. Viewed within the horizon of events in
the River Plate, the British Government's policies from 1810

---

[1] J. C. J. Metford, 'The Recognition by Great Britain of the United Provinces of
Río de la Plata', *Bulletin of Hispanic Studies*, vol. xxix, no. 116, 1952, pp. 201–44.
Metford has explored the ramifications of the 'River Plate interest' in British
politics during the period, and he has discovered evidence that speculation in
River Plate funds was suspected even among the confidants of George IV, p.
203 (n.).

[2] This name was used officially for many years. The term Republica Argentina
was first used in the abortive Constitution of 1826. In the Anglo-Argentine Treaty
of 1849, for example, the official designation was the Argentine Confederation, but
in the Treaty of 1825 the designation was the United Provinces of the Río de la
Plata.

until 1824 may have seemed full of unnecessary ambiguities, hesitations, and reactionary preferences, but, viewed in the context of events in Spanish America generally, there is some explanation for the shortcomings which often drove Argentine politicians towards an anti-British position.[1]

On the whole, British policy from the first outbreaks of colonial insubordination until the final recognition of the independence of the several successive states of Spanish America was designed to achieve the two objectives Castlereagh had defined in 1807: the development of the British commercial connexion and the diminution of the British political commitment in Latin America. In the first stage of the trouble Britain strove to mediate between the Spanish authorities and transatlantic colonies of Spain on the basis of admitting the colonies to a share in the government of the Spanish Kingdom, of 'securing to the Inhabitants of Spanish America their due Weight in the internal Administration of their respective Provinces, . . . and [of making] due provision . . . for the encouragement of commerce'.[2] Once Ferdinand VII was, as he imagined, firmly in the saddle after the expulsion of the Napoleonic forces from Spain, he began sending troops to America, and these were sufficient everywhere except in the River Plate to reduce greatly the power of the revolutionary forces. Assuming that it is possible to suppress a revolution by force of arms, there are good grounds for believing that during the years 1815–20 Ferdinand VII might have reasserted his authority everywhere in Spanish America, had he been able to obtain the material assistance which he required in the shape of ships and supplies to give full effect to the armies he had at his disposal. But Britain refused to give him such assistance, and refused to let other powers do so[3]—a refusal which British sea power could make effective. Likewise Britain refused to be bribed. The Spanish Crown was willing to grant to Great Britain 'a participation in the trade with Spanish America' on a principle of exclusion which would give British merchants privileges greater than other foreigners and less than

[1] e.g. Manuel Moreno and Rivadavia.

[2] F.O. 72/156, Instruction to the Commissioners of Mediation to Spanish America, 2 Apr. 1812; printed in C. K. Webster, *Britain and the Independence of Latin America, 1812–1820* (London, 1938), ii, p. 319.

[3] F.O. 72/177, Vaughan to Castlereagh, 16 Nov. 1815, printed in Webster, *Independence of Latin America*, ii, p. 341.

Spaniards. The price of these privileges was a 'special service
. . . under the stipulations of the Treaty of Utrecht', namely
armed support for the suppression of the revolution in America.
Britain's refusal to contemplate a return to mercantilist privileges and to old-fashioned instruments such as the Treaty of
Utrecht shows how deep-rooted the conception of a free market
had become as early as 1815 and how little of the 'new thinking'
of the post-American revolutionary period had, in fact, been
prejudiced by the experiences between 1791 and Waterloo.

The objective of mediation, as it was understood by the
British Government, was the achievement of a change in the
relationship between the Spanish Crown and the Spanish colonies of great economic as well as political significance. The
Spanish Crown was unwilling to accept such mediation, in
spite of the abundant evidence in South America, particularly
among the wealthier classes, of a disposition which might have
been moulded to an acceptance of a Spanish sovereignty permitting a wide area of local independence and initiative economically and politically.

As the Spanish Crown moved in a reactionary direction, re-
establishing the Inquisition, insisting upon absolute trade mono-
polies, destroying constitutional liberties, and manifesting all
the evidence of logical intransigence which people have come
to associate with the Spanish character, popular enthusiasm in
Britain for the revolution in South America began to mount.
Both the interest and the moral preferences of the British began
to run parallel. Large numbers of unemployed officers, soldiers,
and sailors began to seek service in the South American revolutionary armies. Speculators bought up discarded war materials
and dispatched them to the thriving markets of South America.
Trinidad became a cash-and-carry arsenal.[1] Influential newspapers such as *The Times* and the *Morning Chronicle*, as well as a
chorus of lesser journals, encouraged the public to believe that
unemployment and overstocking of warehouses would be relieved by a policy of opening up South America on liberal
principles. Merchants clubbed together to fit out privateers
for service in the revolutionary forces, and to dispatch arms,
ammunition, and uniforms to the partisans of liberty.

[1] A. Hasbrouck, *Foreign Legionaries in the Liberation of South America* (New York,
1928), p. 43.

For a variety of reasons, some relating to the complications of the European balance of power and others connected with the social and political preferences of the Court and the Cabinet, the British Government adhered to the policy of mediation. This policy, originally an obstacle to the reactionary policies of the Spanish Crown, was increasingly transformed by the movement of events into a prop of the Spanish Government. In the interests of neutrality the British Government responded to the complaints of the Spanish Ambassador by banning the export of arms and by passing a Foreign Enlistment Act in 1819. As the Government moved in one direction the people—or rather the financial and mercantile middle class—moved in the other. On one occasion an officer of the Coldstream Guards applied to the magistrates of the City of London for a warrant to search a ship in the Thames for deserters believed to be sailing for Venezuela. The Lord Mayor refused to grant the warrant, alleging that the ship was outside his jurisdiction.[1] Indeed, such was the pressure of the mercantile community that the Government was barely able to push the Foreign Enlistment Act through Parliament.

The years 1817–20 were critical for the fate of the revolution. In February 1817 San Martín, having marched his army across the Andes, encountered the Spanish army at Chacabuco and defeated it. He occupied Santiago and proclaimed the independence of Chile. More than a year later he encountered another Spanish army dispatched from its base of operations in Peru, and defeated it at Maipú in April 1818. Meanwhile, in the north, in Colombia and Venezuela, the Spanish commander, Pablo Morillo, had the situation well in hand, and Bolívar and the revolutionary forces were driven on to the defensive in a limited area at the mouth of the Orinoco River. In spite of Maipú no one could have confidently predicted the outcome of the struggle.

In 1818 the situation in the north began to mend from the point of view of the revolutionaries. Bolívar's proclamation freeing the slaves injected a popular element hitherto lacking in the Creole revolutionary activity in the north, and gradually the sympathy of the downtrodden began to swing from the royalist to the revolutionary side. Tomás Boves, the cowboy

[1] Ibid., p. 107.

leader, had paved the way for Morillo's victories for Ferdinand VII. Now José Paez, the *llanero*, began to rally the cowboys to the side of the revolution. The lower basin of the Orinoco was cleared of royalists. A congress was summoned to meet at Angostura. An army with a nucleus of formations organized, armed, and disciplined in the European manner (including the famous British Legion) was assembled. In August 1819 this army met and defeated the Spanish army at the Boyacá River and occupied Bogotá.

At this stage the revolutionary forces had firm bases in both the south and the north. The Spanish royalists, on the other hand, were still firmly based in Peru. The climax could not be far off. Then, in an unexpected quarter, came a dramatic break. In January 1820 troops destined for America revolted in Cadiz, under the leadership of Colonel Rafael Riego, and marched on Madrid. Ferdinand VII and the partisans of the absolutist reaction were obliged to pause both in Spain and America. But it was not a pause which refreshed the royalists. From the moment of Riego's revolt the Spanish Crown passed to the defensive. Disaster after disaster was visited upon its arms in America. Finally, in the high thin air on the field of Ayacucho, on the road between Lima and Cuzco, the last army of Ferdinand VII met its total defeat on 9 December 1824. There the last Spanish Viceroy in South America, La Serna, was taken into captivity; there the last Spanish commander, Canterac, laid down his arms.

By 1820 the policy of mediation was obviously out of date. A contest soon developed among the powers, including the United States of America, for the friendship of the new states either in being or about to be born. In Buenos Aires the possibility began to develop well before 1820 that Britain might lose this contest in spite of her pre-eminent economic position and the effective bar which the British Navy offered to any forcible penetration of influence by other great powers. This possibility developed partly out of the unwillingness of the British Government to push ahead precipitously with a policy of recognition, partly from the local jealousy of the very great place occupied by the British community in economic affairs, but chiefly from the political instability of the revolutionary period.

Nearly all the men who rose to positions of leadership in the revolutionary movement became afflicted eventually with a species of political schizophrenia. On the one hand the movement which had brought them to positions of authority required them in their own interest to oppose the Spanish Crown and to insist on independence. On the other hand the deep-seated conflicts in society threatened all authority, and experience taught that the careers of revolutionary leaders were often exciting but short. Desiring independence, these leaders wanted also to consolidate their positions and to still the dissensions of society so dangerous to themselves. Despairing of finding an internal source of stability they looked to an importation of foreign influence in some shape as an agency of salvation. Pueyrredón, Belgrano, Rivadavia, San Martín, Alvear, Sarratea, all entertained at some time or other a belief in the need to establish a monarchy in Buenos Aires, and to have that monarch drawn from among the royal families of Europe. In Europe there were candidates enough for the proposed throne, and Foreign Offices willing to test whether a blood connexion could establish an influence which the British were prepared to leave to merchants and naval commanders. The British Government discovered, for example, in the spring of 1820 that the French Foreign Office was actively discussing with an Argentine agent the candidature of the Prince of Lucca for the proposed throne in Buenos Aires.[1] Castlereagh, himself rather partial to the notion of monarchy in South America, was confronted by half a dozen projects all designed to import foreign influence into the new states by way of monarchical institutions. In fact, these projects were a more serious threat to the British position and prospects than the possibility that France, Russia, or Austria might somehow provide Ferdinand VII with the means of rebuilding his power in the dominions so rapidly slipping from his grasp.

Thus it was that the new situation created by the failing power of the Spanish Crown obliged the British Government to abandon the dead policy of mediation and find a new one. This was not difficult. Indeed, it was already implicit in the original ideas of Castlereagh expressed in 1807. Britain was herself unwilling to seek political power in South America, and equally she was unwilling to see other powers do so. At bottom

---

[1] F.O. 63/228, Thornton to Castlereagh, 18 Apr. 1820, printed in Webster, *Independence of Latin America*, i, p. 105.

this explains everything that Castlereagh and Canning said and did on the subject of South America during the years 1820–5. Once it was clear that Ferdinand VII could never reassert his power, recognition of the independence of the new states depended simply upon how soon they could show the viability necessary to participate in the international community. Every consideration of commerce and finance as well as international politics prompted action by Britain as soon as it could be demonstrated that there existed authorities in South America capable of undertaking the obligations implicit in recognition.

In the case of the United Provinces of the Río de la Plata the 'terrible year', 1820, seemed to offer no hope that the British Government, however willing, could find there anything to recognize. The Congress of Tucumán, first assembled in 1816, continued to give off constitutions like a fertile hen laying eggs. Its final production, the Constitution of 1819, aimed to create a unitary state, the executive authority of which would be an elected director and whose legislature would be a representative body of two chambers. This Constitution reduced the provinces to administrative units and ignored utterly the existence of organized and armed centres of local power. The men who sponsored this Constitution were not sincere republicans. Pueyrredón, the Supreme Director of the moment, was seriously compromised both by his intrigues with the French for the purpose of establishing the Prince of Lucca as a monarch in Buenos Aires and by his relations with the Court of Brazil directed to the overthrow of the Uruguayan *caudillo*, Artigas. Rondeau, his successor, was equally compromised. Finally, when the Congress was summoned in secret session to consider the establishment of a monarchy, the nadir of insincerity and lack of political principle was reached. The provincial gaucho leaders were opposed to a unitary state; they hated monarchy and all its social implications. Ramírez, the *caudillo* of Entre Rios, and López of Santa Fé revolted against the authority of the Congress. The Supreme Director, Rondeau, summoned to his assistance San Martín, at the head of the army in Chile, and Belgrano, the commander of the forces in Argentina proper. San Martín was preparing the invasion of Peru, and disobeyed the summons. Belgrano obeyed, but his army mutinied. Rondeau, with a remnant of the army, marched against Ramírez and López. But the strength of a disciplined army and the help, political and military, of gaucho guerillas was lacking. Rondeau was defeated at the battle of Cepeda. Ramírez dispersed the Directorate, the Congress, and all the organs of authority.

A Hobbesian state of nature seemed about to supervene, but even Ramírez required some form of authority. He summoned the *Cabildo* of Buenos Aires and ordered it to create a Government in that Province. This Government then signed the Treaty of Pilar on 20 February 1820, by the terms of which the Government in Buenos Aires recognized the existence of provincial jurisdictions and committed itself to sponsoring a federal state. The Treaty of Pilar is in some respects the social contract which created the form and character of Argentina; that primary polarization of elements upon which the community as a system depends. In spite of its positive importance as a fundamental social and political decision, the Treaty of Pilar was nevertheless a negative rather than a positive agreement: a pronouncement against a unitary state with one centre of power in Buenos Aires rather than a definition of the character and structure of the federal alternative. So negative, indeed, was the result of Ramírez's victory that for a space of time a state of anarchy was inaugurated. The passion for government was so intense and the capacity to consummate it so weak that at least twenty-four governments were born and died in the Province of Buenos Aires between February and November 1820. The peak of the fever was reached on 20 June when three governments rose and fell in one day.

The man who brought calm was Manuel Dorrego, a colonel of the army who had been exiled to the United States on account of his over-sympathetic views of gaucho activities. Dorrego was an educated townsman, a trained officer, and a man of civilized charm, native courage, and dignified bearing. Unlike many of his kind, however, he liked rather than despised the gauchos and the provincial politicans. He was prepared to accord them a place in the body politic. His sympathetic understanding of gaucho barbarism was the key to his realism as a politician. The only failure of this realism, shockingly proved by his cruel death, consisted in his inadequate appreciation of the savagery and lust for power which reposed beneath the surface in the men who called themselves the friends of civilization, enlightenment, and progress and among whom he moved on terms of social equality and friendship.

Under Dorrego's direction, elections were held in Buenos Aires Province. The Representative Chamber thus created chose Martín Rodríguez, one of the heroes of the British invasion, as Governor of the Province, and he brought into his service as Minister, Rivadavia, the man mainly responsible for the work of the Triumvirate of 1812–13. The Government of Rodríguez and Rivadavia at once set to work to devise, at least for the Province of Buenos Aires, a policy capable at once of promoting the internal development of the community and of securing the recognition and support of foreign powers—particularly Great Britain and the United States. The policy of Rivadavia (for he was the brain of the Government) may best be described by saying that its author aimed to become the Alexander Hamilton of the Argentine revolution. From a study of his particular acts of policy there emerges an impression of harmony and consistency both of ends and means. His end was to bring into being in Buenos Aires a state as liberal, democratic, secular, and civilian in its outer structure as that of the United States, and in terms of its concentration of authority and its regard for financial and mercantile activity as strong and positive as that of Great Britain. His means to this end was a financial policy which, like Hamilton's, sought to bring together and concentrate in support of the state the creditor interest, both domestic and foreign. This interest, he believed, would support his endeavours to secure the recognition of independence and at the same time would become the source of funds for promoting internal developments such as education, immigration, extension of the frontiers of settlement, harbour works, and municipal services.

In July 1821 a commission was appointed to report on the outstanding debts of the Province of Buenos Aires. Apart from the debts of the viceregal government these were discovered to amount to a sum between one and a half and two million pesos. A high percentage were in the form of treasury bills and other negotiable short-term instruments, which were presented regularly at the custom houses in payment of duties.[1] In the

---

[1] M. Burgin, *The Economic Aspects of Argentine Federalism, 1820–1852* (Cambridge, Mass., 1946), pp. 52 ff.

following October a law was passed by the Assembly authorizing the Government to issue bonds at 4 per cent. and 6 per cent., and a *Caja de Amortización* was set up.[1] Within a month creditors were invited to exchange their various instruments of debt for the new bonds: obligations contracted between 25 May 1810 and July 1821 being paid in 6 per cent. bonds and viceregal debts in 4 per cent. bonds. In order to back this debt a law of 3 November 1821 set aside all the movable and immovable property of the Province as security.[2]

The implementation of these aspects of Rivadavia's policy were immensely important to the British community. One-half of the public debt was supposed to be in British hands.[3] As the prospects of peace, independence, and financial policies beneficial to creditors began to grow rosier during 1822 and 1823, the enthusiasm for investment in River Plate funds, commencing in Buenos Aires, was communicated to London. For instance, the Robertson brothers in Buenos Aires began buying heavily[4] and also writing to their grandfather, John Parish of Bath, the head of their connexion, who was 'in the habit of occasionally communicating . . . political information to the Foreign Office, as well as to Lord Liverpool'.[5] William Parish Robertson told of how magnificently Rivadavia had acted in putting down a conspiracy—'two only shot for treason'. Shortly after this little disturbance he reported that developments were 'bearing out . . . what I prognosticated of the Funds in October last. . . . The dividends are paid with the same punctuality as those of the English consols'. The 6 per cents. were selling at 45 and 4 per cents. at 30. 'What makes me most anxious to commence [*sic*] purchases *now* to my friends is the absolute certainty which appears before me of the *general rate* of interest here declining, and consequently of the Funds advancing in proportion.'[6] Those who took Robertson's recommendations to heart and

---

[1] *Registro Oficial de la Provincia de Buenos Aires*, 69, i, pp. 118–24.

[2] E. Coni, *La Verdad sobre la Emfiteusis de Rivadavia* (Buenos Aires, 1937), p. 22.

[3] F.O. 6/3, Parish to Canning, 25 Apr. 1824; and E. J. Pratt, 'Anglo-American Commercial and Political Rivalry on the Plata, 1820–1830', *H.A.H.R.* xi, 1931, p. 306.

[4] Robertson told his grandfather in June 1823 that 'I now hold for myself and friends Eight shares of the Bank and about $200,000 of the public funds'. F.O. 6/1, Robertson to J. Parish, 11 June 1823.

[5] F.O. 6 1, J. Parish to the Foreign Office, 11 Aug. 1823.

[6] F.O. 6/1, W. P. Robertson to J. Parish, 11 June 1823.

bought River Plate funds—and sold them at the right moment
—profited handsomely, for by July 1824 the 6 per cents. stood
at 85.[1]

Meanwhile, another section of the creditor interest was experiencing the rich delights of Rivadavia's policy. The law of
22 June 1822[2] authorized the establishment of the *Banco de
Buenos Ayres*, a privately owned institution with a monopoly of
banking activity. This bank was endowed with the power to
discount bills up to ninety days, issue notes, deal in foreign
exchange, and act as a banking agency for the Government. Its
capital was 1,000,000 pesos divided into 1,000 shares, of which
200 pesos were payable on subscription, 200 upon the opening
of the Bank for business, and the remaining 600 at the demand
of the directors. Three of the nine founding directors were
British merchants: Joshua Thwaites, James Brittain, and James
Barton. Thomas Armstrong, one of the most influential men in
the British community in Buenos Aires for over half a century,
shortly became a director, and was believed to own 45 per
cent. of the shares. British merchants were supposed to own
58 per cent. of the shares.[3]

Within a year the shareholders of the Bank were reaping
their reward. 'The premium on Bank shares is still $17\frac{1}{2}\%$',
Robertson told his grandfather, who passed the letter on to the
Foreign Office, 'and it is calculated that about 10% will be
divided on the 31st August; and as the shares were paid up by 5
instalments, one every two months from 31st August 1822 to 31st
March 1823, . . . a Dividend of 10% will be equal to 15% p.a.'[4]

Neither the British community nor the Creoles were going
completely mad about the new prospects of making fortunes
through investment in the Bank and the funds. In spite of a
10 per cent. dividend, 400 of the Bank shares remained unsold
in mid-1823. This is perhaps explained by the fact that the rate
of interest in Buenos Aires was 12 per cent. at this time, and
there was a shortage of capital of all kinds. In Britain, on the

---

[1]　F. O. 6/4, Parish to Canning, 25 June 1824.

[2]　*Registro Oficial de la Provincia de Buenos Aires*, 735, i, p. 233.

[3]　R. Scalabrini Ortiz, *Política Británica en el Río de la Plata* (Buenos Aires, 1935),
p. 65. Ortiz's book is very anti-British and he cites no authorities for his statements.
However, there is no doubt about the role of the British community in founding
the *Banco de Buenos Ayres*, and Mulhall flatly asserts that it was a British enterprise.

[4]　F.O. 6/1, Robertson to J. Parish, 11 June 1823.

other hand, the rate of interest was falling, and the owners of investment funds were being attracted more and more to foreign securities offering higher rates.[1] In July 1822 a certain Mr. Bary (*sic*) appeared in Buenos Aires. Rivadavia wrote to him seeking a loan of two or more million pesos,[2] and undertook to provide adequate security. The law of 28 November 1822 authorized the Government to borrow up to 5,000,000 gold pesos and to negotiate with Baring Brothers on condition that the state received 70 per cent. of the face value and the rate of interest did not exceed 6 per cent.[3] The purpose of the law was to finance harbour works, frontier settlement, and municipal waterworks.

In the promotion of this loan the Robertsons acted as go-betweens. John Parish Robertson and Don Felix Castro jointly took up the entire issue of bonds at 70, retaining, however, a sum sufficient to pay the interest and amortization charges for two years. Thus, for a debt of £1,000,000 the Government of Buenos Aires Province received a credit of roughly £570,000.[4] The bonds were marketed in London by Barings at 85. The Robertsons and their associates and Baring Brothers made £150,000 on the transaction. The bonds themselves rose to 93⅞ in January 1825, the highest figure they reached before the bottom dropped out of River Plate stocks.

Another aspect of Rivadavia's policy was of direct concern to the British community: his revenue system. Rivadavia was a partisan of *laissez-faire* and free international commerce, and he had already had a part during the early days of his influence in 1812–13 in reducing obstacles to international trade. But he could not fail to notice that the customs houses yielded a heavy proportion of the state revenue. His objects were two: firstly, to clear away all restrictive and troublesome imposts in order that the maximum revenue could be derived from the maximum turnover in international trade; and secondly, to broaden the basis of the revenue system by levying taxes on other than the commercial interest.

To achieve his first object he abolished the *contribución de comercio* and the *alcabala de venta* together with a number of

---

[1] T. Tooke, *A History of Prices* (London, 1838), ii, pp. 148–9.

[2] *D.H.A.* xiv, p. 117.

[3] Burgin, *Argentine Federalism*, p. 55.

[4] R. W. Hidy, *The House of Baring in American Trade and Finance* (Cambridge, Mass., 1949), p. 66.

extraordinary levies on commerce established during the revolutionary wars. These reforms may be said to have established Buenos Aires as one of the freest international markets in the world at that time.

His second objective, of broadening the basis of taxation, involved many complications which, if we allow much to an economic interpretation of politics, were factors in his eventual failure. His *contribución directa* was a species of capital levy fixed at a rate of 0·08 per cent. on commercial establishments, 0·06 per cent. on manufacturing, 0·02 per cent. on grazing, and 0·01 per cent. on agriculture. These rates can hardly be described as discriminatory against the landed interest, but they had the supreme defect of being the first endeavour to bring rural interests within the scope of the revenue system. Landowners, ranchers, and peasants in every country at all times seem to regard taxation levied on themselves as a form of gross injustice, and the Argentine rural interest was no exception. So inadequate was the machinery of collection and so great was resistance to payment that the *contribución directa* never accounted for more than 3 per cent. of the state revenue before the administration of Rosas.[1]

In addition to his *contribución directa*, Rivadavia designed a system of land-holding which had implicit in it a method of distributing the national income in a manner advantageous to financial interests. Rivadavia's system of emphyteusis has been variously estimated. One writer has declared that 'at the behest of foreign masters he [Rivadavia] proclaimed the collectivization of the land and the nationalization of the soil'.[2] Others have seen in it a far-sighted effort to anticipate Henry George. Neither the Government which framed nor the Assembly which passed Rivadavia's Law of Emphyteusis on 27 April 1822 seems to have had in mind anything more than a device for raising revenue.[3] The system itself, briefly described, involved the national ownership of all land which was then rented to tenants at rates determined periodically by juries. If the system could have been made to work, it would undoubtedly have been the

---

[1] Burgin, *Argentine Federalism*, p. 48.

[2] A. L. Palacios quoted in Coni, *La Verdad*, p. 22.

[3] Statement of the Minister of Government to the Sala de Representantes, 10 May 1826, in *Asambleas Constituyentes Argentinas* (Buenos Aires, 1937), ii, p. 1199, when the system was being extended to the entire Republic.

means by which part at least of the rent of land would have passed directly to the public treasury and, thence, under the financial system then growing up, into the pockets of persons financing the public expenditure. As it turned out, tenants rented land, often in blocs of a 100,000 acres, but they did not pay the rent. One student of the subject has estimated that in eight years the Government collected only 5,008 pesos in rent.[1]

On the expenditure side Rivadavia sought to cut the principal item of public expenditure since the revolution, the cost of the armed forces. In 1822 the War Department absorbed 38·4 per cent. of all expenditure and in 1824 42·4 per cent.,[2] but when the army was being expanded to meet a serious danger it would absorb nearly 80 per cent. of the expenditure, as it did in 1829. We have no exact figures for the cost of San Martín's army, but it is reasonable to suppose that it cannot have cost a very much smaller proportion of the state revenue than the army which fought Brazil from 1826–8.[3] The object of the law of 28 February 1822 was to disband the army except for a small frontier force and to pay off the officers and soldiers with bonds. This conversion of the state to a peace footing was one of the most attractive features from the point of view of the British community. In his first report to the Foreign Office the Consul-General emphasized the central fact that 'the Army of Buenos Ayres which crossed the Andes under San Martín, and which established the Independence of the Western Provinces of South America, no longer exists',[4] and he considered it the act of government which made possible 'the formation of a more regular system of finance'.

Thus, the character of the Government in Buenos Aires, as well as the movement of events in the sphere of arms and diplomacy, were working during the years 1821 and 1822 towards the recognition of Argentine independence. In April 1821 King

[1] Coni, *La Verdad*, p. 36.   [2] Burgin, *Argentine Federalism*, p. 49.

[3] F. L. Hoffman, in 'The Financing of San Martín's Expeditions', *H.A.H.R.* xxxii, 1952, pp. 634–8, estimates the Argentine share of the cost of the expedition to Peru at 1,500,000 to 2,000,000 pesos at a time when the state revenue was in the neighbourhood of 2,000,000 pesos a year. But there is no clear evidence about how much of the cost was borne by the treasury of Buenos Aires.

[4] F. O. 6/4, General report on the rise and progress of the present government of Buenos Ayres, enclosure in Parish to Canning, 25 June 1824, printed in Humphreys, *Consular Reports*, p. 22.

John VI of Portugal recognized the independence of the United Provinces of the Río de la Plata. The United States followed in March 1822. Mercantile and banking firms in London and Liverpool began pressing the Government to do as the Americans had done. In June the British Parliament in the course of revising the Navigation Acts legislated to recognize the mercantile flags of the revolted states of Spanish America. In July 1822 Castlereagh told the House of Commons 'he had no hesitation in saying, that he did not think Spain entitled to detain British vessels, trading with those parts of South America which had declared themselves independent and had obtained a recognition of their independence from other nations'.[1]

At this time Castlereagh was preparing to meet the representatives of the Congress of Europe at Verona. He intended to press there for recognition of the Latin American states.[2] But he committed suicide before his departure, and Wellington, who took his place as a delegate, neither understood Castlereagh's policy nor sympathized with the notion of recognizing revolutionary colonies. Canning, who succeeded to the Foreign Office, could hardly be expected to achieve overnight what Castlereagh knew he could only attain by the subtlest of sympathy with monarchy and reaction.

And so the movement towards recognition which seemed so strong during 1822 received a check. During 1823 opposition to recognition hardened both in the British Cabinet and in the chancelleries of Europe. In the spring the French invaded Spain. In August the Spanish partisans of constitutionalism were defeated and Ferdinand VII was restored to absolute power. Could he carry reaction across the Atlantic? Canning was determined that he should not do so.

In these circumstances the pressure from below of the mercantile and financial interests began to grow. 'I should suppose', wrote Robertson from Buenos Aires, 'the General acknowledgement of the Independence of this Country would greatly increase its intercourse with Europe, and would naturally give solidity to her opening Commerce, Credit and resources. It would in a particular degree give confidence to the Holders of Public Stock and enhance its price certainly much beyond its

---

[1] *Parliamentary Debates*, 2nd series, vii, p. 1649.
[2] Webster, *Independence of Latin America*, i, p. 31.

present value.'[1] Canning and Liverpool worked hard to express this point of view in policy against Wellington and the King. In politics one is forced frequently to find bad or irrelevant reasons for doing good. Castlereagh had been prepared to dress up recognition in the trappings of monarchy. Canning now made it out to be an anti-French *coup*. He arranged it to appear that he was saving Latin America not from the reaction of Ferdinand but from the designs of Polignac and Charles X. As early as March 1823 Canning declared himself satisfied that France would do nothing 'to bring under her Dominion' the late colonies of Spain,[2] but throughout that year he thundered in Whitehall, Windsor, and Washington like a new-born Pitt come to save Britain and the world from French domination. He even invited the United States to join him in this enterprise, whose real object was to force the British recognition of Latin American independence upon his reluctant colleagues and sovereign. Having themselves already recognized the new states, Monroe and Adams declined the offer. They drew the correct conclusion that the safety of the revolution was now ensured by a split in both British and European sentiment at the highest levels, and seized the opportunity to make Latin American salvation an enterprise of their own by Monroe's celebrated declaration of December 1823.

The Foreign Office had begun to prepare instructions for consular agents in South America as early as July 1823. In October letters of appointment and instructions to consuls in 'Peru, Chile and Buenos Ayres' were placed in the records and individuals were selected to hold these posts. In the case of Mexico and Colombia commissioners were appointed to report on the state of affairs in those countries. In December the King was persuaded to permit the production of three snuff-boxes with His Majesty's portrait in medallion for presentation 'to the persons of the highest consideration and Influence in the Administration of the State of Buenos Ayres'.[3] If His Majesty could be brought to the point of snuff-boxes, perhaps, he could be brought to the recognition of revolutionary states. And so it

[1] F.O. 6/1, W. P. Robertson to J. Parish, 25 July 1823, enclosed with Parish to Planta, 18 Oct. 1823.

[2] F.O. 27/284, Canning to Stuart, 31 Mar. 1823, printed in Webster, *Independence of Latin America*, ii, pp. 111–12.

[3] F.O. 6/1, Planta to Consul-General in Buenos Aires, 15 Dec. 1823.

turned out. The decision of the Prime Minister and the Foreign Secretary to resign if the King further obstructed recognition was sufficient to clarify the mind of George IV and extinguish the resistance of the Duke of Wellington. On 15 December 1823 the recognition of Buenos Aires, Mexico, and Colombia was decided upon by the British Government.[1]

[1] H. Temperley, *The Foreign Policy of Canning, 1822–1827* (London, 1925), p. 147.

IV

THE ANGLO-ARGENTINE TREATY

We have been taught to see the reputation of the Rt. Hon. George Canning resting solidly upon the record of his brilliant diplomatic and political manœuvres in the face of obscurantist resistance at home and abroad to his policies of a free hand for Britain in the affairs of the world. How far he went beyond Castlereagh and how far he improved upon his predecessor's policies in the large sphere of international politics, it is difficult to see clearly. Less obscure, however, is his achievement in working out the principles upon which British intercourse with the Latin American states were to rest for more than a century.

Canning followed Castlereagh in assuming that Britain's interest in the United Provinces of the Río de la Plata, like her interest elsewhere in Latin America, was primarily economic and that good political relations would emerge from good economic relations. The originality of Canning and his advisers consisted in the meaning and form which they gave to the term 'good economic relations'. Devotion to the economic interests of Great Britain had prompted the British Government to negotiate a Treaty with Portugal in 1810 which gave to British commercial interests a special place in the economy of Brazil. This Treaty, for example, fixed the tariff on British imports permanently at a preferential rate of 15 per cent. and obliged the Portuguese Government to reduce this tariff if it made reductions on goods coming from other states. In short, this Treaty limited the sovereignty of the public authorities in Brazil in the matter of commercial policy. Likewise it placed British merchants under the authority of a Judge Conservator, which meant that they enjoyed extraterritorial privileges in Brazil and were not subject to Portuguese–Brazilian authority. Canning had himself given the instructions for the negotiation of this Treaty in 1809, but he had described it as 'odious and impolitic' and claimed that it had been forced upon him by the Board of Trade.[1]

Although Canning never completely jettisoned this policy of seeking economic and commercial privileges in Brazil, he seized the opportunity of applying consistently liberal principles in establishing the treaty basis for Anglo-Argentine intercourse. His letter of instructions to the first Consul-General in Buenos Aires made plain the intention of seeking to make the public authorities in Buenos Aires, not the British Government, the protectors of British trade and to teach British interests that their surest security in the United Provinces of the Río de la Plata was obedience to the laws of the United Provinces. 'The Consul General will', Canning wrote, 'bear in mind that his principal duty will be to protect, to support and to further the lawful Trade and trading Interests of the United Kingdom by every fair and proper means.'[2] The 'fair and proper means' which Canning advised consisted in knowing the laws of Buenos Aires, 'so that he [the Consul-General] may admonish all British Subjects against carrying on an illicit Commerce, and discourage by all proper means in his power such proceedings to the detriment of the Revenues, and in violation of the Laws and Regulations of . . . [the] country . . .'. And Canning made it clear that the Consul General must be very careful 'on no account [to] urge on behalf of His Majesty's Subjects claims to which they are not justly and fairly entitled'.

Canning's policy, as it eventually took shape in the Anglo-Argentine Treaty of 1825, was to establish a complete legal and political equality between the British and the Argentine states. Britain recognized unreservedly the sovereignty of the Argentine public authorities in the territory over which they claimed jurisdiction, and the full powers of those authorities to legislate concerning, to govern, and to judge all persons living within its territory. The Argentine public authorities recognized a similar power to reside in the British Crown within its territories. In his first instructions to H.M. Consul-General at Buenos Aires

---

[1] A. G. Stapleton, *George Canning and his Times* (London, 1859), p. 509; Webster, *Independence of Latin America*, i, 53–54, and generally, A. K. Manchester, *British Preëminence in Brazil, its Rise and Decline* (Chapel Hill, 1933). Canning had an opportunity in 1825 to sign a more liberal treaty negotiated by his agent in Rio de Janeiro, but he insisted on the renewal of the original Treaty of 1810.

[2] F.O. 6/1, Letter of Instructions, 10 Oct. 1823.

Canning made it plain beyond mistake that Britain sought no special political position in the River Plate and wished to deal with completely independent public authorities.

It may perhaps be unnecessary to state to you, [he wrote] but it is very material, that it should be understood by the persons with whom you communicate in Buenos Ayres; that so far is Great Britain from looking to any more intimate connection with any of the late Spanish Provinces, than that of friendly political and commercial Intercourse, that His Majesty could not be induced by any consideration to enter into any engagement which might be considered as bringing them under His Dominion. Neither, on the other hand, would His Majesty consent to see them (in the event of their final separation from Spain) brought under the Dominion of any other Power.[1]

Canning was as determined as any of his predecessors to protect British commercial interests. The novelty of his views consisted in his conception of the institutional framework for this protection. If he followed the example of the treaties made with Spain during the seventeenth and eighteenth centuries he would have been obliged to seek for special treaty rights governing the residence and activity of British subjects in the United Provinces of the Río de la Plata. Instead, he sought only the same treatment for British subjects as the Argentine state accorded all foreigners and as the British Government accorded Argentine nationals. Article II of the Treaty[2] provided that

the inhabitants of the two countries, respectively, shall have liberty freely and securely to come, with their ships and cargoes, to all such places, ports, rivers, . . . to which other foreigners are or may be permitted to come, to enter into the same, and to remain and reside in any port of the said territories respectively; also to hire and occupy houses and warehouses for the purpose of their commerce; and generally, the merchants and traders of each nation, respectively, shall enjoy the most complete protection of the laws and statutes of the two countries respectively.

The remainder of the Treaty was devoted to working out the particular details of these principles upon which was to be founded 'the perpetual unity between the dominions and

[1] Ibid.
[2] L. Hertslet, *A Complete Collection of the Treaties between Great Britain and Foreign Powers; so far as they relate to Commerce and Navigation,* &c. (London, 1820–), ii, pp. 27–65.

inhabitants' of the parties. Neither party, for example, sought to limit the liberty of the other to impose taxes, tariffs, and other economic and commercial controls, but they bound themselves not to discriminate against each other's subjects or citizens in so doing. Again, Articles VIII and IX guaranteed freedom of enterprise and business activity for British subjects in the United Provinces and for citizens of the United Provinces in Great Britain. Article VIII stated that

all merchants, commanders of ships and others, subjects of His Britannick Majesty, shall have the same liberty, in all the Territories of the said United Provinces, as the natives thereof, to manage their own affairs themselves or commit them to the management of whomsoever they please, as broker, factor, agent or interpreter; nor shall they be obliged to employ any other persons for those purposes, nor to pay them any salary or remuneration, unless they choose to employ them; and absolute freedom shall be allowed, in all cases; to the buyer and seller to bargain and fix the price of goods, wares, or merchandise imported into, or exported from the said United Provinces, as they shall see good.

Other articles ensured British subjects in the United Provinces and citizens of the United Provinces in Great Britain exemption from military service, from 'all forced loans, or military exactions and requisitions; neither shall they be compelled to pay any ordinary taxes, under any pretext whatsoever, greater than those paid by native subjects or citizens'. The only clauses of the Treaty which might be described as technically one-sided were not in fact so. These had to do with religious freedom. The Treaty bound the United Provinces to guarantee to British subjects 'perfect liberty of conscience', the right 'to celebrate divine service either within their own private houses or in their particular churches or chapels, which they shall be at liberty to build and maintain in convenient places, approved by the Government of the said United Provinces', and the right to bury their dead in their own burial grounds. In Britain practical religious toleration was a long-established fact, whereas in Argentina the Inquisition was only lately dead and the inclination to persecute Protestants and non-believers, though much abated, had not been entirely eradicated.

The final clause of the Treaty bound both parties to co-operate in the suppression of the slave trade. This joint undertaking symbolized in a sense the union of hearts of Britain and Argentina, for both communities at this stage in their histories regarded opposition to slavery as the test of enlightenment: an assurance to themselves and the world that they were in the vanguard of progress and that they entertained the highest moral and social ideals.

The policy of Canning expressed in the Anglo-Argentine Treaty of Friendship, Commerce, and Navigation was a simple, mature, and, in many ways, the earliest and best instance of the new liberalism in economics and politics. It represented an effort to create a free-market relationship between an industrial community and a raw-material-producing community. In this relationship the role of the state was reduced to that of guaranteeing the operation of an automatic market mechanism. The only traces of the old mercantilism in the Treaty were those provisions against its revival. In neither community were the *laissez-faire* assumptions of the Treaty entirely acceptable, but in both the classes of people who saw in the free market the best guarantee of their prospects and interests were in the ascendancy. This was rather more the case in Britain than in Argentina. In Britain the old mercantilism was being rapidly dismantled, and the Treaty must be viewed as an incident in a general process. In Argentina the ascendancy of the export interests—the ranchers who produced staples for the international market— was in 1825 sure only in the Province of Buenos Aires, but the balance of forces both domestic and international was favourable to the Treaty. Indeed, Argentina grew into the Treaty, and the Treaty remained the legal foundation of Anglo-Argentine intercourse until the return to mercantilism in the 1930's, which had its first beginnings in so far as Britain and Argentina are concerned in the Roca–Runciman agreement of 1933.

The man chosen by Canning to execute his policy in the United Provinces of the Río de la Plata was Woodbine Parish. In October 1823, when he was appointed 'His Britannic Majesty's Consul-General at Buenos Ayres', Woodbine Parish was twenty-seven years old. In his energy, the variety of his interests, his optimism, his abundant practical capacities, and his philoprogenitiveness, he, like Sir Home Popham, presented a splendid manifestation of the expansive imagination and dynamic power of the British people during their industrial revolution. He was the son of a Lincolnshire clergyman connected at several removes with Irish landlords and Hamburg merchants, one of whom, John Parish of Bath, has already figured in this account as a moving agent in the 'River Plate interest'. Parish was educated at Eton, whence he entered the diplomatic service as an assistant to Joseph Planta, the private secretary of Castlereagh. While still little more than a boy he was engaged in mighty affairs. He crossed the field of Waterloo, on which the dead lay still unburied, bearing dispatches from the Court of Naples. The treaty of peace with the French in 1815 is in his handwriting.

He found Buenos Aires a 'disagreeable and disheartening Place',[1] but he remained there for nine years without complaint studying the economy, the geology, and the flora and fauna of the country with enthusiasm and sympathy while all the time engaged in political and official duties amid international and civil wars. He had the qualities both of pride and deference: a pride which prompted him to insist upon £3,000 a year instead of £2,000 as a necessity of his station[2] and a deference which enabled him to accord graciously to Lord Ponsonby, the first Minister to the United Provinces, all the dignity of office while he did all the work which that nobleman was ill qualified to perform. In his intercourse with Argentine leaders he never lost his temper, never hesitated plainly to speak his mind, and always displayed a readiness to assist and support any man regardless of party who exhibited the least trace of what Parish conceived to be common sense and the spirit of conciliation. Parish possessed strong critical faculties, but his optimism always prompted him to give people the benefit of every doubt. When he was leaving Buenos Aires the Government conferred upon him the citizenship of the United Provinces, and by law he and his descendants were entitled to incorporate into their family arms the arms of the Argentine Republic.

Parish arrived in Buenos Aires late in March 1824. He found the attention of the town focused almost exclusively upon the election of a new Governor by the Provincial Assembly of Buenos Aires. He decided, therefore, to postpone for a few days

---

[1] F.O. 6/27, in a private letter to Lord Dunglass, 20 Aug. 1829.
[2] F.O. 6/5, Parish to Canning, 31 Dec. 1824.

the official notification of his arrival. On 3 April the election was declared over and the result announced. By a vote of twenty-six to thirty-six, General Rodríguez, the veteran revolutionary soldier and politician, was replaced by General Las Heras as Governor of the Province of Buenos Aires, and by virtue of that office the premier official of the Argentine community. In spite of his brief acquaintance with the politics of Buenos Aires, Parish's conclusions concerning the change were sound; namely, that Las Heras and Rodríguez were of the same political principles and that the change of Governors would mean no change in the policies or the key personnel of the Administration. Having so formed this opinion, Parish called officially upon the principal minister, Don Bernardino Rivadavia.

Parish had been taught by his kinsmen, the Robertsons and the Parishes, to regard Rivadavia as a man who had 'done as much *good*, as all the others before him [had] done *harm* to the Country, which is saying a good deal.'[1] None the less, Parish discovered within twenty-four hours that the policies which made him so estimable in the eyes of the commercial interests did not prevent him from being a slippery and difficult politician. Parish's first duty consisted in delivering to Rivadavia Canning's sealed letter to 'the Secretary of the Government of Buenos Ayres' in which Canning told that official how 'the King, My master having determined to take measures for the effectual protection of the Trade of His Majesty's Subjects in Buenos Ayres . . . and with a view to such measures as may eventually lead to the establishment of friendly relations with the Government of Buenos Ayres' had sent out a Consul-General in the person of the bearer. Rivadavia broke open the letter, read it, and exchanged compliments. 'I quitted Mr. Rivadavia with every reason to feel satisfied at my first Reception', Parish reported.[2]

The next day Parish was able to read the sealed letter in the newspapers. Rivadavia had given it to the press. 'I did not hesitate to express to Mr. Rivadavia my feelings upon this subject', Parish wrote. He pointed out 'how much inconvenience might be occasioned if all the Communications [they] were to

---

[1] F.O. 6/1, W. P. Robertson to J. Parish, 25 July 1823, enclosed with Parish to Planta, 18 Oct. 1823.

[2] F.O. 6/3, Parish to Canning, 6 Apr. 1824.

hold together in future were to be so abruptly laid open to general observation'. Parish begged Rivadavia 'at least [to] have the goodness to apprize me of any similar intentions'. Rivadavia, however, had a thick skin. He shrugged off the rebuke with the remark that the publication of letters was a custom of the country. He had succeeded in telling the world that the British Government was very close to recognition.

Round one being concluded, Parish met Rivadavia a few days later for an extended political discussion. Parish opened by suggesting that the Buenos Aires Government would make recognition easier for all concerned if they could get Spain to recognize their independence. Britain, Parish argued, would help in every way possible. Rivadavia replied that the Spanish liberals had been difficult on this matter and in fact wanted privileges and powers as great as those of colonial times, and that since reaction was now triumphant in Spain there was not the remotest hope of obtaining Spanish recognition of independence. Rivadavia continually emphasized the Spanish desire for commercial and economic privileges and the liberal and egalitarian character of his own Government. 'Both Natives and Foreigners [are] here upon the same footing', he declared, 'and Spain [can] hardly expect exclusive Privileges from the enjoyment of which the Natives themselves [are] debarred.'[1]

One of the most difficult tasks which can face a diplomatic agent is the discovery, for the information of his Government, of the extent to which the activities of men in office are supported, or at least not actively opposed, by the community and of the extent to which their activities are directed to the preservation of their own position in office. In the case of Rivadavia this task demanded great acuteness of perception for Rivadavia was at once an imaginative and creative maker of policy who understood the practical measures needed to achieve revolutionary ideals and a devious, vain, and intensely ambitious individual ever bent on perfecting a personal political machine. No sooner had he received Parish than he busied himself with the appointment of someone to represent his Government in London. He made the strange but not inexplicable choice of an Englishman who was a partner in the London mercantile and banking firm of Hullett Brothers and Company. This annoyed Canning.

[1] F.O. 6/3, Parish to Canning, 12 Apr. 1824.

I cannot consistently with my publick Duty [he wrote] or with any sense of propriety admit an English Gentleman of the mercantile profession into political communication as the Agent of a Foreign State. I have no reason to doubt Mr. Hullett's probity: but for his sake as well as for the credit of the Government generally, I must take care that in the fluctuations of the South American Funds which take place upon every arrival of intelligence from the River Plate, no suspicion shall be excited that one mercantile house has an advantage over the rest, through the political character of its partners.[1]

Canning insisted that a native of Buenos Aires be appointed. How right he was can be judged from the facts subsequently revealed that Hullett Brothers and Company were the promoters of several mining companies whose shares were offered to the public and that they were the rivals of Baring Brothers in a quarrel of vast proportions, but obscure character, of which there are several hints in the Foreign Office files.[2]

Rivadavia soon busied himself also in endeavours to draw the British Government into the rivalries of Argentine politics. The biggest figure in the revolutionary movement at that time was, of course, General José de San Martín. San Martín was out of office and out of a job. Rivadavia depicted himself to Parish as the intimate friend of San Martín to whom the Liberator's heart and mind had been revealed. His 'arrival in England', Rivadavia told Parish, 'and [his] supposed Intention to communicate if possible with His Majesty's Government might at this moment be thought [to] be productive of some Embarrassment'. Rivadavia then warned Parish that San Martín was a monarchist whose ambition was to plant a European dynasty in America. San Martín was not going to Europe simply to superintend his daughter's education, as he had publicly asserted, but to forward the cause of some European prince. Rivadavia, however, had saved the situation for Britain.

But added Mr. Rivadavia (and he dwelt particularly upon this) [San Martín had departed to Europe] under a solemn promise of

[1] F.O. 6/2, Canning to Parish, 19 Nov. 1824.
[2] e.g. F.O. 6/13, Lord Ponsonby writes, 20 October, 1826: 'He [Rivadavia] has supported the War by recurrence to a Paper Monetary System of the worst nature . . . having previously in London, by an act of folly, taken the Money business of this country out of the hands of Alexander Baring, and placed it in the hands of Messrs. Hullett and Co. from whom he can receive no help in his utmost need.'

taking no step whatever which might in any way tend to any alteration in the present Constitution of these Governments against the
opinion and feeling of the British Government, or indeed without
previously laying before them for their concurrence any Plan he
might wish to bring forward.[1]

Parish to his credit did not permit himself to be drawn into
Rivadavia's intrigues. His mission was to report and not to
negotiate, and this he did. His dispatches during April, May,
June, and July were devoted mainly to telling Canning about
the form and character of the state and economy which he
found in Buenos Aires. His sources of information were his own
observations, the Government of Buenos Aires, and a committee
of seven leading British merchants in Buenos Aires. His formal
'General report on the rise and progress of the present government of Buenos Ayres'[2] was dispatched to the Foreign Office
at the end of June; the report of the committee of merchants[3] at
the end of July.

Both the formal reports stressed the enormous economic and
commercial potential of the republic where 'Nature has done
her utmost in climate and situation'. They forbore to add that
only man in these parts was vile, but they did suggest that the
enthusiasm which their authors felt for the régime was qualified
by political considerations. If the Republic could achieve the
right kind of political institutions and maintain them in a condition of peace and stability, prospects of vast development would
be realized; if not, who could say? Parish's enthusiasm was less
qualified than that of the mercantile committee. He was able to
present evidence supplied to him by Rivadavia that the laws
of the Republic, or at least of the Province of Buenos Aires,
guaranteed the inviolability of private property both to natives
and foreigners; that religious freedom and freedom of the press
were protected by law; that taxes were equal for all; that trade
was free; that finances were becoming better ordered; that
inter-provincial animosities were yielding to a liberal policy of
federal freedom; that the army was being reduced. Parish went
so far as to say that Buenos Aires was 'at present in the enjoyment of the blessings of a good, well organized and stable

---

[1] F.O. 6/3, Parish to Canning, 25 Apr. 1824.
[2] F.O. 6/4, printed in Humphreys, *Consular Reports*, pp. 2–25.
[3] Ibid., pp. 28–62.

Government'. An acute observer would notice the words 'at present' and someone with a knowledge of the River Plate (a *rara avis* in Whitehall in 1824) would be put on guard by the restriction of the description to Buenos Aires: two important qualifications, which Parish might well have elaborated. Like many a diplomatic agent before and since, Parish knew what his superior at home wanted to hear, and without deliberate misrepresentation he was distributing an agreeable emphasis in the necessary places in his report. Nowhere in his formal and comprehensive report did he attempt to estimate how strong or how permanent was the Government which had legislated in the liberal manner he had described. In the light of subsequent events, the report of the mercantile committee was more accurate than Parish's, for the committee did not describe the Government of Buenos Aires as stable. They said plainly something quite different; that *'when once* Political order and Stability are restored, and the Country consolidated in a general Union, the trade of the River plate will be found susceptible of an immense extension, and must ultimately prove of very great importance to the Commercial Interests of Great Britain'.[1]

In making up their minds about recognition Canning and his colleagues in the Cabinet had before them not only the two formal reports from Buenos Aires but also Parish's dispatches. These present a rather different picture of political developments to that painted in the formal report. Indeed, the dispatches depict a society full of dynamic tension: the old in conflict with the new, fresh hopes, old hates, and new-born animosities. Certainty concerning the outcome of these conflicts flowed from Parish's heart rather than from anything he could see or measure; for he was full of that cool, lofty optimism of his age, his race, and his class which prompted him to accept as certain the creative use by men of the gifts bestowed by nature.

In one of his first dispatches he described the constitution of the Government of the Province as 'extremely simple, consisting of a Hall of Representatives (Sala de Representantes) elected by Universal Suffrage, one Half... annually renewed in Rotation'.[2] Every three years this Assembly elected the chief executive,

---

[1] Ibid., Author's italics.
[2] F.O. 6/3, Parish to Canning, 25 Apr. 1824.

who bore the name of Governor and Captain-General. The Governor in his turn appointed a Cabinet of three Secretaries of State: for Foreign Affairs, Finance, and War. The rules of the Sala were modelled on those of the Congress of the United States. Debate was free and public and fully reported in the newspapers.

So far so good; but it is hard to see how the Duke of Wellington would receive this intelligence. Two days after setting down this description of democratic simplicity in government Parish reported that all was not harmony in the Sala. It was, in fact, afflicted with differences about religion and the place of the army in public life quite comparable with the great conflicts which had often turned Europe into a battlefield of civil and international war. 'In carrying his Plans into effect', Parish wrote,[1] 'M. Rivadavia has necessarily created many personal enemies especially amongst the Military and the Clergy.' Soldiers and priests 'have since the election of the New Governor been actively employed to raise a feeling against M. Rivadavia and I am sorry to add apparently not without some success'. In fact Parish reported that the opposition had won the recent election, and Rivadavia had decided that, like San Martín, he would be wise to commence the superintendence of his children's education in Europe. He feared, he told Parish, that his retirement 'might produce a hesitation on the part of His Majesty's Government', but he assured him at the same time that his policies were accepted by 'every party in this Country'.

Parish accepted this view. The 'propriety and order' which Parish observed in the Sala de Representantes he believed to extend throughout the Province. He argued that the growth of private property and wealth had increased social tension, but that the administrative instruments to control this tension had also been improved.

The System of Police [he reported Rivadavia as saying] has been improved with greater Economy. The execution of the Law of the 20th of December last has placed in the hands of the Citizens that Duty purely civil, with which the Army was formerly improperly entrusted. The moveable Property in the Country which becomes more liable to be attacked in proportion to its increase is

[1] F.O. 6/3, Parish to Canning, 27 Apr. 1824.

better secured against robbery and the means adopted to regulate the Service in the Plains have produced the best Effects.'

Parish was impressed by the attention which the Government was paying to education, particularly secondary and university education. He was also attracted by its content. 'The study of Political Economy has been commenced this Year, a knowledge of which will tend to ensure us hereafter intelligent Officers.' Parish could detect already the beneficent effects of political economy in the financial policies of the Government, for he believed they had come to consider 'Sacred this Principle viz. "That the just Payment of our Debts is itself a Fund of Riches". . . . The system of Public Credit is becoming more intelligible even to the most prejudiced'.[2]

In spite of this rapid spread of bourgeois enlightenment Rivadavia still felt it wise to withdraw from the scene of his labours, *reculer pour mieux sauter*. Upon his resignation he was presented with a public address signed by '3 to 4000 of the principal respectable and independent Inhabitants of the Place'.[3] It is a pity that Parish, so acute in most things, did not pay more attention to the unrespectable and dependent inhabitants, for they, too, were a factor in the situation. But, perhaps, it is too much to expect the son of a clergyman, educated at Eton and apprenticed under Castlereagh in the age of Bentham and Ricardo, to have taken much account of the men who fetched and carried but who, on the pampas, also rode horses, carried knives, and worshipped a very old God. Instead, Parish concluded that 'the spontaneous Expression of so universal a Public Feeling with respect to M. Rivadavia's Administration, is the best proof which can be given of the general and great Anxiety felt here, for the Continuance and Preservation of that System which has been so beneficial to every real Interest in this Country'.[4]

If Parish was ill equipped to reckon the power of the lower classes, he was proportionately well equipped to react sensitively to the smallest eddies in the flow of international politics. Particularly he was concerned to warn the Foreign Secretary of the dangers to British commerce of any concessions to Spain

[1] F.O. 6/3, Rivadavia's address to House of Representatives, 3 May, enclosed with Parish to Canning, 12 May 1824.   [2] Ibid.
[3] F.O. 6/3, Parish to Canning, 17 May 1824.   [4] Ibid.

and, to the British political position, of the activity of the
United States. To impress upon London the first of these
dangers, he invited Canning to look at what was happening to
British trade in Callao where a Spanish commander had occupied the port. Tariffs on imports had been raised, and the
British warned that entry of foreign goods, unless specifically
permitted, was prohibited.[1] To impress upon Canning the
second danger, Parish reminded his superior that the United
States was not only the second trading power in the River Plate
but the object of much affection on account of the recognition
it had accorded the United Provinces. On the fourteenth anniversary of the deposition of the Spanish Viceroy, the United
States Minister had been selected for the honour of a special
dinner, and 'the whole Entertainment was managed with as
much Order,' Parish reported, 'and I may add Elegance, as
could have been expected even in any of the Capitals of
Europe'.[2]

Undismayed, Parish went about establishing his connexions
in Argentine society. He presented the royal snuff-boxes; one
to the Governor, one to Rivadavia, and one to the Minister of
War. The receipt of a snuff-box became such an honour that
Parish sent for three more, 'which should not be of less value
than the best of those I have already brought out'.[3] He particularly wanted to give one to Manuel García, the under-secretary
in the Ministry of Foreign Affairs. The choice of García is a
revelation of Parish's judgement, for García was, perhaps,
technically the ablest man in the Argentine Government service: practical, well versed in international law, diplomatic
practice, and finance, and gifted with a subtle intelligence
masked by a modest, self-effacing disposition.

For lesser figures, Parish ordered 'a few good Prints of His
Majesty handsomely framed . . . [for] some of those Persons who
are furnishing me with information, and are disposed to be
otherwise of Service'.[4] Some of these services were of an extraordinary character. Parish was able to send Canning copies of
General Alvear's correspondence with his Government during
the latter's visit to Great Britain. 'These Papers have been

---

[1] F.O. 6/3, Monet to the commander of His Britannic Majesty in the Pacific,
1 Mar. 1824, enclosed with Parish to Canning, 12 May 1824.
[2] F.O. 6/3, Parish to Canning, 4 June 1824.   [3] Ibid.   [4] Ibid.

communicated to me by an Employé of the Government in the strictest confidence', Parish told the Foreign Secretary.[1]

When Parish arrived in Buenos Aires it was decided by the political authorities there to send abroad an agent of the highest distinction. San Martín had disassociated himself from those possessing power in the Río de la Plata, but there remained General Carlos de Alvear who had come to Buenos Aires with San Martín in 1812. He was dispatched to the United States by way of Britain to see what could be done to advance recognition and to report to Buenos Aires on the condition of politics.

General Alvear arrived in Britain when Parish's first dispatches from Buenos Aires were beginning to arrive at the Foreign Office. He landed in Liverpool after eighty-four days at sea. He had hardly recovered his capacity to stand straight on dry land before a delegation of merchants waited on him to 'compliment him and hear news from South America'.[2] Alvear reached Birmingham on 10 June, and the next day he learned that 11 June had been appointed for a town meeting 'composed of the merchants and manufacturers, with the same view as that before mentioned at Liverpool'.[3]

Alvear's impressions of the political situation in Britain *vis-à-vis* the Latin American republics is worth recording.

The sentiments of the Ministers Mr. Canning and Lord Liverpool, in both houses of Parliament, evidently show that the intentions of the British Government, with respect to America, are of the most favourable kind; and to judge from circumstances this impression is in unison with the ideas of the public at large, which evidently desires most anxiously the independence of The New World. This opinion is entertained by all the Deputies of America residing here, and also by Mr. Rush, Minister Plenipotentiary of the United States. This frank and liberal conduct (of the British Government) has been greatly decried by the European Journalists in the pay of the Holy Alliance, who in their diatribes have shown the deadly venom which lurks in that famous body. Notwithstanding, in spite of the great influence of Mr. Canning who is at the head of the party who favour the recognition of the American states, of which the members are 1st Lord Liverpool, Prime Minister, Mr. Peel, Minister of the Interior, Mr. Robinson, Chancellor of the

[1] F.O. 6/5, Parish to Canning, 6 Nov. 1824.
[2] F.O. 6/5, Alvear to Rivadavia, 15 June 1824.   [3] Ibid.

Exchequer, and Mr. [*sic*] Bathurst, Minister of War, there is an opposite party headed by the Lord Chancellor, in which are ranked Lord Wellington and Lord Harrowby; and the influence of the second is great, on account of his intimacy with the King, although now he begins to give up his obstinacy, as well on account of the national interests as to support the Government, which in some measure is pledged to oppose the views of the Holy Alliance as regards America.[1]

Alvear's analysis of British political alignments on the subject of recognition were not far wrong. When Parish's dispatches and reports were laid before the Cabinet the weight of opinion in the community and particularly in London had shifted markedly in favour of recognition. The petitions for recognition from Liverpool and London bearing the names of some of the largest firms had been received in June. In July, Baring Brothers offered stock of the Buenos Aires Government at 85, and it had been taken up and was appreciating on the market. Mining companies, immigration companies, and fanciful projects for the transportation of milkmaids to the River Plate were being organized in an atmosphere recalling the South Sea mania of a century previous.

Neither Parish's reports from the River Plate nor the clamour and enthusiasm in London were sufficient to force the Cabinet to take immediate action.

Your Despatches [Canning informed Parish] contain generally speaking, a satisfactory report of the Situation of Buenos Ayres; of the moderate principles of the Government, of its tendency to a stable and tranquil Settlement; and of the disposition manifested . . . to cultivate with this country the closest relations of friendly intercourse.[2]

But the Cabinet wanted further proofs:

1st. That any such State has renounced finally and irrecoverably all political connection with Spain. 2ndly. That it has the power as well as the will to maintain the Independence which it has established, and 3rdly. That the frame of its Government is such as to afford a reasonable security for the continuance of its internal peace, and for the good faith with which it would be enabled to maintain whatever relations it might contract with other Powers.[3]

[1] F.O. 6/5, Alvear to Rivadavia, 29 June 1824.
[2] F.O. 6/2, Canning to Parish, 23 Aug. 1824, printed in Webster, *Independence of Latin America*, i, pp. 114–16. [3] Ibid.

Wellington seized upon the fact that the Government at Buenos Aires did not appear to control the whole of Argentina. He was thus able to delay matters by insisting that recognition be made to depend upon 'the power of the Government of Buenos Ayres to bind by its stipulations with a foreign State, all the members of the Confederacy constituting the United States of Río de la Plata'.[1] But even Wellington was not irreconcilable, and he seems to have felt that further delay might be the means of bargaining with Buenos Aires.[2] A draft Treaty was sent to Parish with the advice that he would be given a full power to negotiate once the terms stated above had been complied with.

Thus, as the spring was coming in Buenos Aires in September 1824, Parish was instructed to look for those evidences of power and policy which would enable Canning to satisfy his critics and Great Britain to recognize the new state.

Once Parish had got out of the way his general reports he was free to explore the possibilities of a treaty based upon the general principles outlined in his first instructions. By this time Rivadavia had departed from Buenos Aires for Europe and his place had been taken by García. Parish addressed to the new Minister for Foreign Affairs a note dated 9 August 1824 in which he wished to explore the possibilities of claiming 'for British subjects who may establish themselves in Buenos Ayres the enjoyment of certain Civil Privileges, as well as certain Immunities with respect to Religion, which are considered . . . to be necessary for the satisfactory Domiciliation of the Subjects of one friendly State in the Territories of another'.[3] Parish admitted that both law and public opinion had already confirmed a number of privileges for British subjects, but he suggested that some additional protection for the property, persons, and beliefs of his compatriots might be considered. He stated, however, that when he spoke of privileges he did not mean special treatment or immunities for British subjects. He wished

to assure them that it will be ever considered by H.M. Government to be the especial duty of British Subjects . . . to avoid any offensive or ostentatious display of their Religious Worship and Ceremonies,

---

[1] Webster, *Independence of Latin America*, i, p. 23 and p. 115.
[2] Metford, *Bulletin of Hispanic Studies*, xxix, 1952, p. 216.
[3] F.O. 6/4, Note to the Government of Buenos Ayres, 9 Aug. 1824.

to conduct themselves in all things not only in a peaceable and orderly manner, but with due deference and submission to the Government, under whose Protection they live, with strict obedience to the Laws, and with a most scrupulous Respect for the Customs, Usages, and Institutions Civil and Religious of the Inhabitants.[1]

García replied by providing Parish with a number of examples of laws which guaranteed the rights of both foreigners and citizens in a manner which must be agreeable to the British Government. On the subject of religion, however, he was willing to concede that there might be a difficulty. The Government was working towards religious toleration and great advances had been made, and they would move farther and faster except for 'the conviction that any Precipitation in such matters, and much more so with a people educated exclusively in the Roman Catholic Doctrines, might expose them to failure'.[2]

Apart from religion there was the critical obstacle behind which the Duke of Wellington had barricaded himself in resistance to recognition: the authority of the Government in Buenos Aires over the provinces and its capacity to bind them in international relations. In October Parish began to go over this matter with García. In a formal Note, García explained that each province 'has indeed its own separate Administration for its domestic Affairs, but with respect to any general question of National Interest, or of pecuniary Means, especially in furtherance of their Independence, they all look to the measures of the Government of Buenos Ayres which, with their common acquiescence, since the breaking up of the Congress in 1820 has taken upon itself the lead in all such matters'.[3] García then gave a number of particular instances of the working of this system by which Buenos Aires paid the bills and made the foreign policy of the nation. In each case of action, such as the negotiation with the Spanish Commissioners and the appointment of Ministers to Chile, Peru, and Colombia, the Province of Buenos Aires had selected the people and undertaken the work with the specific concurrence of the provinces. Parish, however, did not feel that the arrangement was 'sufficiently formal' to justify acting upon Canning's instructions.

[1] F.O. 6/4, Note to the Government of Buenos Ayres, 9 Aug. 1824.
[2] F.O. 6/4, García to Parish, 14 Aug. 1824.
[3] F.O. 6/5, Parish to Canning, 15 Oct. 1824.

He disclosed to García the rewards which would be Argentina's if an agreeable development in the form of government took place. He let García read Canning's instructions in strictest confidence. 'I can ill describe the satisfaction with which this Communication was received by the Buenos Ayrean Minister,' Parish told Canning, 'nor had I the smallest difficulty in convincing him of the obvious necessity of the Existence of a formal Authority on the part of the whole of the United Provinces, before the Negotiations could be in any way opened.'[1]

Parish talked not only to García but to 'some of the leading Deputies' of the Sala. Like García these deputies appear to have apprehended the wisdom of calling a general Congress of the provinces not with a view to rekindling the old quarrels about a weak federal state or a strong unitary one but for the purpose of doing 'little more than reconstitut[ing] their National Representation and appoint[ing] a President and such other Authorities as may be absolutely necessary for National Purposes'.[2] Parish was very pleased to observe very little disposition on the part of the politicians in Buenos Aires to interfere in the internal administration and political activity of the sister provinces.

Late in November something happened which should have shaken Parish's faith in the enthusiasm of the Buenos Aireans for free trade. By a majority of one the Sala voted to prohibit the importation of American flour. During the year 76,000 barrels of flour had been imported in American ships, and local milling and cereal farming interests were being affected. Parish, however, appears to have preferred to rely upon the fact that the Government opposed the prohibition. Incidents of this kind, portentous as they might be for the future, were soon forgotten in the excitement of the General Congress which began to assemble in the first week in December.

The first question considered concerned the oath to be taken by the deputies to the Congress. The resolution of this question satisfied one of the conditions made by Canning, although it tended to suggest that the religious difficulty might be even more intractable than García believed. The oath formally committed the Congress and each of its members 'especially to maintain the Integrity, Liberty and absolute Independence of the Nation under a Republican Representative Government'.

[1] F.O. 6/5, Parish to Canning, 24 Oct. 1824.   [2] Ibid., 6 Nov. 1824.

But it also was an oath 'before God and the Holy Evangelists ... 3rdly to protect the Catholic Religion'.

García and the Ministers of Buenos Aires appear to have had some second thoughts about a treaty with Great Britain. In the message of their Government to the Congress they emphasized the security of property, the equality before the law and the liberty of conscience which existed by law in Buenos Aires. To these essentials they urged that there be 'add[ed], Gentlemen, the free Competition of human Industry within the Territory of the United Provinces'. Free competition, they argued, 'will strengthen the vital Principle of the Union of the Provinces, will speedily destroy the seeds of any jealousies or local dissension . . . and finally will prevent the necessity of Treaties of Commerce, which, the offspring of Ignorance . . . have been the causes of sanguinary Wars, useless even to the Conquerors'.[1]

Some graceful compliments were broadcast to the Congress. The United States was described as the 'Republic which from its Origin presides over the civilization of the New World', while the United Kingdom was stated to be 'the most civilized, the most independent and certainly the most powerful in Europe'.

Parish still held back from negotiation about a treaty. The proceedings of the Congress revealed the strength of provincial independence. The delegates from the Province of Córdoba proposed the loosest kind of federation in which the finances of the Confederation would be provided by grants from the provinces, and that the army be raised by provincial levies, the officers of which, from colonel downward, would be appointed by the provincial authorities. Through January discussion centred around these and similar matters of domestic concern.

At nine o'clock in the evening of 22 January 1825 Parish received the news that more than a month previously La Serna, Canterac, and Valdes had laid down their arms after their defeat. This news quickened the proceedings of the Congress. They turned down a proposal to adopt a constitution on the model of the United States, and then promptly made that alternative provision so fundamental to Parish's negotiation. The Executive Power of the whole Confederation in so far as it related to foreign affairs was by a unanimous vote placed in the hands of

[1] F.O. 6/5, Parish to Canning, 22 Dec. 1824.

the Government of Buenos Aires on 23 January 1825. 'There no longer remains any impediment to my entering now upon [your] Instructions', Parish wrote, '. . . and I shall proceed in consequence at once to open the negotiation.'[1]

In these negotiations no serious difficulties were encountered. Parish exchanged full powers with García on 30 January, and the Treaty was signed within a fortnight. The Congress examined the Treaty in secret session almost immediately, and on 19 February 1825 Governor Las Heras delivered to Parish the ratification by his Government.

In the negotiations three general problems required resolution. Parish discovered that 'there . . . [is] a great deal of intrigue against our Treaty . . . principally set going by the Yankees'.[2] The American chargé d'affaires went to the length of addressing a Note to the Government. Parish obtained a copy privately and he discovered that the Americans were insisting upon a promise given them by Rivadavia that no commercial privileges would be granted to any nation. This presented no difficulty because Britain was seeking no commercial privileges, but only treaty guarantees of rights already declared to belong to Argentine citizens. The only serious 'privilege' which Parish sought was that of exemption for British subjects from compulsory service in the Argentine armed forces.

The second question centred on the matter of reciprocity of rights. From the Argentine point of view reciprocity was of political and emotional importance; in practice it meant very little, given the character of society, opinion, and law in Great Britain. When García raised the point Parish instantly agreed that all guarantees should be reciprocal.[3]

The third question concerned religion.

I had the most difficulty in bringing Mr. Garcia to agree . . . [to the 12th Article on religious toleration], not from any feeling against it in the Province of Buenos Ayres, where alone the case is really likely to arise, but from the still remaining Prejudices existing more or less in some of the interior Provinces where the hearing of such concession, he thought, would create alarm amongst the Priests and those still under their influence.[3]

---

[1] F.O. 6/8, Parish to Canning, 24 Jan. 1825.
[2] F.O. 6/8, Parish to Planta, 18 Feb. 1825.
[3] F.O. 6/8, Parish to Canning, 19 Feb. 1825.

García was right about this. In the Congress Article XII gave some difficulty, but the Minister was able to circumvent the opposition, and it was accepted.

The Treaty was ratified in Buenos Aires and London without delay. Negotiated and ratified in less than three weeks, it endured for more than a century: the solid foundation of Anglo-Argentine intercourse which supported much folly and vast change.

V

THE FAILURE OF THE LOAN OF 1824

WHEN the editor of the *Annual Register* sat down to write a preface to his account of the year 1825, he gave first place among political events to the 'increased strength and . . . more decided character' of Britain's relations with the states of South America. In the sphere of industry, commerce, and finance he saw on the other hand only the sharp change from optimism to pessimism which developed within nine months of the recognition of the independence of the revolted Spanish colonies. In 1824 such had been the state of optimism and prosperity that 'even country gentlemen—the most querulous of all classes, the least accustomed to suffer . . . could no longer complain'. Prices were rising; credit was easy; employment opportunities were good and 'all the gambling propensities of human nature were constantly [being] solicited into action'.[1] The atmosphere and circumstances of boom persisted into 1825. When the Anglo-Argentine Treaty was signed in February and ratified in London in May 1825, the enthusiasm for new enterprises had passed its peak, but it was not until after the rising of Parliament in August that the hurricane began to blow through the City scattering paper dreams in all directions.

Far removed as we are from the dayspring of English liberalism, only an exercise of the historical imagination addressed to facts and fancies of that age can picture for us the close union of political enthusiasm and economic hope which gave character and direction to the broad mass of Englishmen regardless of social status, income, form of work, party affiliation, or religious belief. Well before they began to concern themselves with parliamentary reform and the formal domestic aspects of the march towards democracy a lively core of the community understood the connexion between the dismantling of static political and economic structures and economic development. Likewise they

[1] *Annual Register*, 1824, pp. 1 and 3; 1825, preface.

saw in liberty, freedom, and economic development, no matter where, opportunities for themselves as investors and workers. Advocating the cause of freedom and independence in South America, Lord Lansdowne, for example, asked the House of Lords in 1824 to look at the United States.[1] There, he said, a population of three million had increased in fifty years of freedom to ten million. In South America their Lordships could reasonably expect fifty years of freedom would produce a population of sixty million 'of a consuming character', which would buy British goods and afford opportunities for the investment of British capital. Free political institutions meant free markets; and free markets spelt economic progress.

We know now that the assumptions of the liberals were too simple and their facts too few for an adequate understanding of all situations. Certainly this was so in the case of the Río de la Plata. Neither the general optimism of Lord Lansdowne nor the particular enthusiasm of Sir Woodbine Parish[2] was justified by anything which happened in the Argentine Republic for more than a quarter of a century. By any test, moral, political, or commercial, the assurances and hopes of the year 1825 concerning developing opportunities at Buenos Aires were without foundation. And yet there was great wisdom in the liberal judgement which lay at the foundation of the Treaty with Argentina. Thinkers like Adam Smith and Ricardo and politicians like Canning, Lansdowne, and Palmerston were great artists who saw into the human situation in a phase of time and found a mode of expressing its predominant necessities.

In 1824 British exports to the River Plate exceeded £1,000,000 in value. Twenty-seven per cent. of the ships and 23 per cent. of the tonnage entering the ports of the Argentine Republic were British.[3] Investors in London had taken up bonds of Buenos Aires valued at £1,000,000 on their face. British merchants in Buenos Aires had invested in an Argentine bank. Several mining and immigration and land companies were planned and money was spent to bring them into being. They did not include the chimerical joint-stock enterprises born in 1824 and 1825 to import milkmaids into Santa Fé and to market Paraguayan tea

---

[1] *Parliamentary Debates*, 1824, 2nd series, x, p. 989.
[2] Created Knight of the Guelphic Hanoverian Order in 1835.
[3] Based on Consular Shipping Returns in F.O. 6/19.

in Liverpool. A quarter of a century later, in 1850, the value of British exports to Argentina was less than £1,000,000 and had only surpassed the total of 1824 on one occasion, in 1849. The number of British ships which entered the ports of the Republic in 1850 was ninety-one compared with eighty-three in 1824 and the tonnage was only 19,507 compared with 16,666 twenty-five years earlier. The proportion of British ships and tonnage had declined to 20 per cent. of ships and a similar percentage of tonnage. In 1850 no British joint-stock enterprises existed in the Republic and the bonds marketed by Baring Brothers in 1824 were in default. And from the point of view of trade 1850 was a good year for British merchants. In bad years such as 1827 and 1845 British exports to Argentina were worth less than £200,000, and a year when exports to the Republic exceeded £700,000 could be counted above average.

During the period between the recognition of Argentine independence and the launching of the first long-distance railway in 1863 Argentina was a far less important market than Brazil, not such a good market as Chile, and in no way comparable with Australia.[1] British trade with Argentina expanded at a much slower rate than British trade with the world as a whole. Any quantitative economic test we care to make reveals that the expectations of 1824–5 concerning the Río de la Plata were in no way justified. Indeed, there is much evidence that the American, French, and German economic connexions with Argentina grew more rapidly during this period than the British.

Liberal expectations were as blighted in the sphere of morals and politics as they were in that of commerce and finance. Liberty in Argentina did not lead to liberalism. In a note addressed to the Argentine Minister in London Palmerston once described the ruling political club in Buenos Aires as 'a ferocious gang of Murderers', and he deplored the fact that 'no elevation of Rank afforded protection against these Ruffians, and no humbleness of condition gave security . . .' from them.[2] Anything resembling the English conceptions of peace, liberty, and progress were utterly wanting year after year on the shores of the River Plate. And yet meaning and movement can be

---

[1] W. Page (editor), *Commerce and Industry, Tables of Statistics for the British Empire from 1815* (London, 1919), pp. 110–11, 114–15.

[2] F.O. 6/81, Palmerston to Moreno, 9 Feb. 1841.

discerned in this scene of disillusionment, and it is necessary to see them, if we care to understand why, between 1860 and 1914, Argentina grew into one of the cornerstones of the British economy.

The failure of the attempt made between 1821 and 1825 to establish a British investment interest in Argentina requires our first attention. This interest had several branches of which some merit study and some do not. We can safely ignore the fraudulent enterprises undertaken by rogues or fools who employed the magic and popular words 'Río de la Plata' as a means of capitalizing on the ignorance and greed of people with surplus money. Serious investments were of three sorts: those made by British investors resident in Britain in joint-stock enterprises which it was proposed to establish in Argentina; investments by British residents in Argentina in financial or industrial enterprises developed there; and, finally, British investments in Argentine public securities.

The joint-stock enterprises organized in Great Britain and having the Río de la Plata as their proposed scene of operations were plausible enough. From the days of Drake an aura of silver and gold had shone around the Spanish Indies and the very names Mexico, Peru, and the Río de la Plata glistened with precious metal. The myth with which the South Sea Bubble had been blown up still persisted, and the fact is that the Spanish colonies *did* produce bullion in large quantities. A small group of English capitalists had reasoned that, if Spaniards employing the techniques of the sixteenth century, could produce bullion in Mexico and Peru, Englishmen employing steam and hydraulic apparatus in the nineteenth century could greatly improve upon their example. And so they did. The Real del Monte Association was a serious enterprise in Mexico which did produce silver bullion, not perhaps in sufficient quantity to justify the appreciation of its shares 1,200 per cent. in a matter of weeks, but enough to give substance to the growing belief that profits would come to those who backed such enterprises.

One of Rivadavia's favourite beliefs concerned the desirability of foreign investments in his country. He sought out the capitalists. They did not inflict themselves on Argentina. In November 1823 he wrote to his agents in London, Hullett &

Company, informing them that 'the United Provinces possess rich mineral deposits both gold and silver in a virgin state',[1] and he referred to *las celebradas minas de Famatina*, as if everyone was bound to know the riches *they* produced. Authority was granted for the formation of an English mining company.[2] In February 1824 Rivadavia descended to particularities. 'An immense mineral deposit', he wrote, 'is situated in the midst of fertile plains in a climate healthful and temperate, provided with all kinds of fuel, water and the means of obtaining cattle and all kinds of vegetables, and, it should be added, located only 20 easy miles from the city of Mendoza.'[3]

It only required the application of an imagination like Disraeli's[4] to an official statement of this description to produce a wonderful prospectus, and, as Mr. Hartlepod said to Mr. Wharton,[5] 'if that prospectus won't make a man confident I don't know what will'. Hullett & Company organized the Río de la Plata Mining Company with a nominal capital of £1,000,000, and commenced peddling the shares. At the same time a group of Argentine politicians and landowners acquired a concession from the Governor of the Province of La Rioja which they sold to a British company organized by the Robertson brothers and entitled the Famatina Mining Company. This company had a capital of £250,000, and it too began peddling shares. Unfortunately there were defects common to both enterprises. In the first place Rivadavia seems to have been a better politician than a geologist, for *las celebradas minas de Famatina* did not answer to the description he had sent to his agents. Even as a politician he did not emerge brilliantly from this episode; for in the second place, the properties which both companies proposed to work were identical. Rivadavia and the Government at Buenos Aires had granted the property to the Río de la Plata Company which the Governor and Junta of the Province of La Rioja had simultaneously granted to the Famatina Company. Neither company sought to conceal

---

[1] *D.H.A.* xiv, p. 371.

[2] *Registro Oficial de la Republica Argentina*, 1704, ii, pp. 46–47.

[3] *D.H.A.* xiv, pp. 461–2.

[4] Benjamin Disraeli, at this time a stockbroker's clerk, was employed to write prospectuses. There is no authority for supposing that he wrote the prospectuses of the mining companies operating in Argentina.

[5] In Trollope's novel *The Prime Minister*.

this confusion from the public for in one prospectus the authors dismissed the matter as a mere trifle saying that 'if any claims should arise, it is presumed that they will be satisfied at an easy rate'.[1]

The directors of the Río de la Plata Company soon discovered that their claims could not be so satisfied; indeed, that they could not gain possession of their property and finally that, even if successful, they could not work it. Sir Francis Bond Head was selected as the manager in Argentina. He assembled a party of Cornish miners and capital equipment, and with these he sailed to Buenos Aires. He soon discovered that there was a serious contradiction between the facts on the spot and the facts in the company's prospectus. In January 1825 a law had been adopted by the Government in Buenos Aires that it belonged to each province to regulate itself. Head found Rivadavia weak in the presence of difficulties. 'I easily perceived', he told the directors, 'that private interests were strongly opposing our progress; that Mr. Rivadavia's political opponents were striving to overturn all his plans; that he had evidently no inclination to assist us.'[2] But Head was not content to talk in Buenos Aires. He made what he later described as 'some rapid journeys across the Pampas and among the Andes' in order to see for himself what was possible and what was not. He reported to his directors without any ambiguity that 'the working of mines in the province of Río de la Plata by an English Association, is politically unsafe. And secondly that if there was no such risk, the expense would far exceed the returns.' Head's analysis[3] of the social and political situation, as well as his description of the resources of the sub-Andean provinces which it had been proposed to exploit, constitutes the best explanation of why capital investment by Europeans in industrial enterprises in Argentina at this time was impossible. The formidable obstacle of distance made impossible the transport and use of heavy steam-driven equipment in the interior areas. Where the ore bodies were workable, revolutionary upheavals had so

[1] H. English, *A General Guide to the Companies Formed for the Working of Foreign Mines* (London, 1825), pp. 27–30, 56–58.

[2] F. B. Head, *Reports relating to the Failure of the Río Plata Mining Association* (London, 1827), p. 6.

[3] F. B. Head, *Rough Notes taken during some rapid journeys across the Pampas and among the Andes* (London, 1826).

disorganized social relations that the labour force had been seriously diminished or dispersed, and that which remained in parts of Chile was so exploited that 'only a system of cruelty and tyranny' could maintain the mines in operation. Even his Cornish miners had been demoralized by the cheapness of wine and the atmosphere of freedom which the revolution had created.

Although the Río de la Plata Mining Company had a nominal capital of £1,000,000, the amount actually lost in the Argentine venture amounted only to £52,500. For this the directors had no thanks to offer Head. They blamed him for everything, and succeeded in losing additional sums in Chile. As for the Famatina Company, its prospects withered. In 1827 its shares on which £50 had been paid were selling for £2, and its misfortunes seem to have been one element in the bankruptcy of the Robertson brothers, whose firm had been one of the greatest and best connected in the River Plate trade.

The other form of enterprise into which Rivadavia sought to attract the investment of capital was immigration and agricultural developments. In this, as in so many other of his plans, Rivadavia's notions had a rational plausibility about them which sprang from evident necessities of the community which he endeavoured to govern and improve. Always short of food supplies, save meat, Buenos Aires had experienced since the opening of the market to world trade a growing scarcity of cereals, fruit, dairy produce, and vegetable oils—in fact every food which required for its production a large and orderly expenditure of labour. The Brazilians captured the sugar market; the Americans the flour trade; and the French and Spaniards intruded into the wine market. Even English merchants handled consignments of pickles, sweets, and confectionery among their bolts of cotton and woollen goods. In Buenos Aires in the 1820's a pound of butter cost more than a sheep, and an egg more than either. The fact is that prolonged war had unsettled and absorbed into the armies a substantial part of the small farming class, never at any time a thriving or powerful part of the community. The comparative advantages of ranching and the hide and meat trade, the most profitable business and the one requiring the least supplies of orderly and sustained labour, further undermined the agricultural interest. Argentina

experienced the same antithesis between the agricultural and
pastoral interests which had afflicted old Spain and gave
character to contemporary Texas.[1] It appeared to be a law of
nature that the producers of cash crops sold in the world market were destined to oust small-scale producers satisfying local
markets.

Rivadavia, however, considered it socially, politically, and
economically desirable that agricultural enterprise should be reinforced and the community given a more varied and balanced
composition. To this end he proposed to introduce immigrants,
particularly from the northern regions of Europe, whose people,
he believed, possessed the habits of industry, enterprise, and
willing submission to the discipline of production so conspicu-
ously lacking among the gauchos. Very soon after his appointment as a Minister, Rivadavia received a proposal concerning
colonization from an Englishman, Barber Beaumont. He referred Beaumont to his agents in London, Hullett & Company,
and he sought to impress upon Hullett's the importance of immigration by suggesting that they should frame legislation on the
subject designed to attract enterprise in this field.[2] Negotiations
proceeded during 1822 and 1823. Beaumont wanted an outright grant of land for colonization purposes; Rivadavia, on the
other hand, wished to preserve the principle of emphyteusis,
viz. that all land belonged to the state which rented it out to
tenants. He assured Beaumont that all tithes had been abolished.
He was prepared to exempt colonists from all land rents for
four years and he was prepared to pay married couples a subsidy of 200 pesos and single men 100 pesos upon arrival. In the
end Rivadavia agreed to grant Beaumont land within ten
leagues of the frontier in Buenos Aires Province in perpetuity
at an unspecified low rental and to pay passage money and a
subsidy to colonists upon arrival. The land grant was made to
depend upon the number of people brought to the country and
the capital invested.

Rivadavia ordered Hullett's to advertise widely in the European press the terms made with Beaumont.[3] Other enterprises
were undertaken in Scotland, Holland, and Sweden. The

---

[1] See A. M. Klein, *The Mesta* (Cambridge, Mass., 1922), and W. P. Webb, *The Great Plains* (Boston, 1931).

[2] *D.H.A.* xiv, p. 52.   [3] *D.H.A.* xiv, p. 166.

Scottish enterprise was undertaken by John Parish Robertson and his brother William. Being directed by men who knew the country and were capable of quick decisions on the spot, the Robertson colony enjoyed some success. The Robertsons entered into an agreement with the Government along the lines of the Beaumont agreement, but, finding that the occupation of land on the frontier was impracticable at the moment, they boldly purchased 16,000 acres near Buenos Aires from private owners. They recruited the colonists in the south-western Lowlands of Scotland: farmers, bricklayers, carpenters, blacksmiths, sawyers, coopers, gardeners, clerks, a doctor, an architect, land surveyors, and farm labourers. Altogether 220 persons, married and single, adults and children, and all Presbyterians, took ship at Leith in May 1825 and landed in Buenos Aires in August. The voyage was well managed. It began with songs and ended with rounds of whisky, *Auld Lang Syne*, and three times three rounds of cheers for the captain and the ship which had brought them to the River Plate.[1] No one died during the passage out. One colonist wrote a poem to celebrate the occasion in which he related that

> They wondered what people the Argentines were,
>   Savage or civilised—colour and figure,
> And lassies resolved they would droon themselves ere
>   They'd gang without claes or be kissed by a nigger.

The Robertsons soon had the colonists at work on their property at Monte Grande. They spent altogether £60,000 on the enterprise enabling the colonists to build thirty-one brick houses and forty-seven ranchos or mud cottages, a mill, barns and granaries, and a church. By 1828 they possessed 1,000 acres of orchards and plantations, 2,500 acres in cereals, and 12,500 acres of unfenced pasture. This was a considerable achievement, but in spite of it the colony failed. The Robertsons were seriously affected and finally bankrupted by the financial collapse and the war with Brazil. They could put no further capital into the enterprise. The farm labourers claimed that the farmers were not providing what they had promised, and the farmers claimed that the Robertsons were not providing what they had promised, and the Robertsons blamed the Government. Various

[1] James Dodds, *Records of the Scottish Settlers in the River Plate and their Churches* (Buenos Aires, 1897).

explanations were offered for the failure such as the disorganization of the currency in 1827 and afterwards. In fact the establishment of an elaborate agricultural enterprise based on wage labour and the renting of land was not an economic proposition in Argentina at that date. Total returns were insufficient to cover costs, and there was ever present the attraction of high wages in other employments in Buenos Aires.

When, finally, soldiers began plundering the colony during the civil war in 1829, the enterprise broke up, and only a few farmers remained. The rest went their own various ways, and many prospered. Most went to Buenos Aires and set themselves up as builders and craftsmen. The bailiff and three of the farmers established cartage enterprises in the city, introducing the English farm wagon as a means of carting merchandise superior to the high-wheeled wagons of colonial times. For sixty years the firm of James and William White was the most important cartage firm in Buenos Aires. Several of the farm labourers became rich men, having first become dairymen and then landed proprietors. One farm labourer, Thomas Young, died in possession of more acres than the Duke of Bedford. Several others founded landed dynasties in the Province of Buenos Aires, whose names were still well known as local dignitaries in Quilmes, San Vincente, and Chascomús when the nineteenth century came to an end.[1]

Writing ten years after the immigration projects were first discussed, the British Minister in Buenos Aires concluded that they were the work of 'vile and corrupt speculators and companymongers who . . . brought ruin upon so many industrious families and disgrace upon the British name in South America'.[2] Roguery there may have been (the Foreign Office refused to take up Beaumont's alleged claims against the Argentine Government),[3] but the fault of the individuals concerned seems to have consisted mainly in misjudgement[4] of social and political circumstances and of underestimating the difficulties of transferring people between communities so different in their

[2] Dodds, *Scottish Settlers*, p. 61.
[2] F.O. 6/34, Fox to Palmerston, 15 Oct. 1832.
[3] F.O. 6/14, de Walden to Beaumont, 27 Apr. 1826.
[4] Lord Ponsonby told Canning that the general opinion in Buenos Aires was that Beaumont had displayed a lack of foresight and that his agents had behaved criminally. F.O. 6/17, Ponsonby to Canning, 4 June 1827.

history and character as Britain and Argentina. The several hundred working people from the United Kingdom who were cast adrift on the shores of the Río de la Plata by the failure of the immigration schemes were the victims of the optimism concerning human affairs and the simple-minded theories of human nature which characterized the utilitarian enthusiasts so numerous among the enterprising classes of Great Britain then engaged in revolutionizing the world. While the schemes failed, the ruin of which the British Minister spoke does not appear to have been any more tragic in the case of Beaumont's colonists than the Robertsons'. In fact, there was a severe shortage of labour in Buenos Aires even in bad years, and skilled and unskilled alike could command wages as high as one pound a day.[1] The effect of the failure of Beaumont's scheme was not to leave stranded in Buenos Aires a group of hopelessly destitute people—for they seem to have been absorbed into the community without prolonged difficulty—but to destroy for many years the prospect of the organized migration of large groups for the purpose of agricultural development. Immigration did not cease, but it was henceforward and for many years a matter of individual decision based upon particular opportunities and dependent upon individual resources. This, in the circumstances of the time, seems to have been the only practical possibility.

The biggest capital investment of this period was, of course, that undertaken by the firm of Baring Brothers on behalf of the Government of the Province of Buenos Aires. A debt of £1,000,000 held by English investors and the clients of an English banking firm represented the biggest single foreign interest in the Republic, and a kind of investment which was then, and remained until recent times, quantitatively the most important source of British claims upon the Argentine community. Like the other investments which Rivadavia invited, the establishment of a sterling debt had about it a rational plausibility relating to the necessities of the community. Rivadavia intended that the income from the sale of the bonds should be used to foster economic and social developments capable of rendering the Republic more productive and, hence, able to carry the debt and to liquidate it through the means of a sinking

[1] F.O. 6/14, Beaumont to the Foreign Office, 19 Apr. 1826.

fund. The annual cost of the debt was approximately £65,000, or in the neighbourhood of 13 per cent. of the revenue of the Province of Buenos Aires in the year 1824. An increase of claims on revenue of such dimensions can be described as sharp for an economy of a primitive kind, but it was not unbearable provided the assumptions of Rivadavia and the promoters and agents of the operation were correct. These assumptions were: firstly, that the expenditure upon the war department would decline after the recognition of independence and the conclusion of the revolutionary contest with Spain; and secondly, that the expansion, or at least the maintenance, of existing levels of international trading from which the principal state revenues were derived would take place. Woodbine Parish in his reports to the Foreign Office produced evidence that these assumptions were sound. His kinsman, John Parish of Bath and John Parish's grandsons, the Robertson brothers, who helped promote the loan, certainly shared the Consul-General's belief in the correctness of the assumptions. Assuming that bankers do make rational judgements on behalf of their clients, the firm of Baring Brothers appears to have been convinced, and in turn to have convinced the public by the use of their name, that the situation in Argentina justified the advance of cash in return for bonds.

Since the revolution of 1688 a growing body of Englishmen possessed of wealth beyond their current needs had been discovering that it was possible to lend money to the state without losing it; that the state would and could pay interest upon loans to it; and that by lending to the state they strengthened the power of the state upon which economic opportunities abroad were supposed to depend. This was the English experience. After Waterloo several successful financial operations on the continent of Europe had encouraged the belief that Englishmen could safely lend money not only to their own Government, upon which the creditor class had some influence, but to foreign governments, upon which they had none. Reliance upon state authorities had thus by 1824 become a widely acceptable mode of making income-yielding investments on the part of the owners of wealth who had either no ability or no inclination to use their resources directly in productive activity. It is necessary to relate this general experience of the English investing class in order to understand why great numbers of presumably rational men living in comfortable houses in Bloomsbury[1] were suddenly induced to invest considerable sums in the bonds of a new-born government of a remote community about which they could have known next to nothing at first hand. It is likewise necessary in order to understand the significance of diplomatic recognition. Neither Woodbine Parish in his reports to the Foreign Office nor Canning in Parliament ever said specifically that investors could safely deal with the Government of the United Provinces of the Río de la Plata, but the conditions which Canning in his instructions to Parish laid down for recognition were also the conditions which satisfied an investor in public funds. In examining whether Canning's conditions were satisfied Woodbine Parish produced evidence concerning the state of the revenues, the character of expenditure, and the disposition and legislative activity of the Government which would have as fully justified an investment of capital in the bonds of the Government as they did recognition by the British Government.

An examination of the failure of the Loan of 1824 takes us to the heart of Argentine political and economic developments at this time and affords us at the same time a guide to Anglo-Argentine intercourse from the Treaty of 1825 to the re-establishment of the investment process after the overthrow of General Rosas in 1852. The first explanation is simple. The Government of the Province of Buenos Aires could not find the money to pay its sterling creditors. The two general explanations of this shortage are equally simple: war and a decline in international trade through the port of Buenos Aires. Once we pass beyond these simple and obvious explanations to an examination of political and economic alignments of the Platine community we enter a sphere of sometimes bewildering complexity in which one is tempted to attribute the chaos of those times to the barbaric propensities of the Spanish and Indian races. Various British diplomats, Argentine intellectuals, and foreign travellers yielded to this temptation. Even General Rosas in a despairing moment remarked that a vein of savagery

---

[1] The men who complained to the Foreign Office about the failure of their investments in Buenos Aires bonds seem mainly to have lived in the vicinity of Bedford Square.

so characterized his countrymen that they presented a unique problem in government. We, however, prefer to follow the example of Sir Woodbine Parish, who, for all his misjudgements of particular tendencies, saw in events in Argentina rational motives at work among the various contending forces and that certain rational hypotheses fit the facts and others do not. Least satisfactory of all is the hypothesis which assumes that the Argentine community at this period of its history had a uniquely barbaric character completely unlike that of the European or North American states.

It is one of the arguments of this book, offered as a first hypothesis concerning the course of politics in the Río de la Plata, that the revolution which overthrew Spanish power produced a quite exceptional community in Argentina. The exceptional element in the community was its domination by a class of poor rich, of men rich in land but poor in capital. With the progress of time this class became both richer and poorer: they acquired more and more land or their holdings became smaller in size but more and more productive, but at the same time they became more and more dependent on the import of capital. Unlike the communities of Europe the Argentine Republic did not possess an abundance of people whom its dominant class could easily put to useful labour, nor, in the primitive condition of its economy during most of the nineteenth century, did it possess an abundance of machines which are a substitute for labour. Hence the dominant class of the Argentine Republic were unusually dependent upon foreign communities for capital and labour, and hence they were a debtor class. In the Argentine community political power always belonged in the final reckoning to this debtor class—the landed interest. This was an exceptional situation—unlike that in the United States or Canada or Australia or any European country. Even in South America it had few close parallels.

Elsewhere in the civilized world the creditor classes possessed political power, not always absolute but in the majority of instances sufficient. In agrarian and pastoral communities at almost any period before World War I the dominance of bankers, merchants, and railway capitalists was a common theme of political agitation. In Argentina, however, the landed class determined the policies of the state and gave to its credit policies, its commercial policies, and its currency system a character atypical of the nineteenth and early twentieth centuries. For 78 out of the 104 years between independence and World War I the Argentine economy operated with a paper currency for domestic purposes. Argentina alternated between having no banks at all or operating them under extremely lax legislation or legislation which was systematically ignored even by the state authorities. The Republic was a free-trading state longer than Great Britain, and in few rapidly developing communities did the state make so few and such feeble attempts at industrialization. The debtor class which dominated Argentina wore no ragged overalls nor did they preach co-operation and a descent from the cross of gold on which mankind was allegedly crucified. They sent their sons to English public schools and they built palaces in the Avenue Kléber and on the Riviera, while they allowed their country to accumulate by 1914 the biggest *per capita* volume of foreign claims of any nation in the world. At the reckoning day their political power always told to their advantage. Things were invariably arranged so that either the Argentine workers and sharecroppers or the foreign capitalists or both carried the burden of economic development.

This hypothesis concerning debtor and creditor interests does not serve immediately to illuminate the crisis of 1825 in Buenos Aires. The respectable classes, about whom Parish wrote, were not at that moment imperilled by clamorous debtors. Their troubles were of a rather more familiar sort. Parish rejoiced to report to Canning in April 1828 that everywhere in Argentina progress was being made towards constitutional government. But candour and truth obliged him to notice a 'solitary but striking exception'. In the Province of Córdoba, General Bustos had been installed in the Governor's office by a mob, which had assembled in the streets of the provincial capital. This breach of constitutional procedure Parish attributed to the University of Córdoba, 'the Nursery of all those bigotted notions and principles which under the Spanish system held the People of these Countries in ignorance and subjection'. Parish explained to Canning that 'as the Priests and Monks have been rooted out of the other Provinces, they have taken refuge at Cordova, and have formed there a Party proportionably violent and inimical to the establishment of all liberal principles and

forms of Government'.[1] General Bustos enjoyed not only the
support of the priests but he also possessed an army, and it
was therefore unlikely that in Córdoba there would be an
earnest effort 'to regulate the interior administration . . . upon
a Footing of the strictest Economy', in the manner recommended by the National Congress. Furthermore, the Cordobans
were notorious for their zeal to preserve their own industries
and, if possible, to reserve the markets of the Republic for their
own wines, sugar, and cloth. When, a few weeks later, Bustos
put himself in accord with the customs of the age by holding an
election which he of course won, Parish was not able to derive
much satisfaction from the event.

Almost immediately after the distressing commotion in Córdoba, a band of sixty or seventy refugees[2] from the Banda
Oriental crossed the river from Buenos Aires with the object of
promoting the revolutionary overthrow of the Imperial Brazilian authorities established at Montevideo. Parish immediately
waited upon the Minister of Foreign Affairs to sound him on
this truly alarming development. 'Mr. Garcia affects to treat
[the matter] lightly', Parish reported to Canning, '. . . a mere
ebullition of feeling on the part of a few ruined and desperate
individuals . . . but . . . I have reason to believe that the
Government is seriously anxious and uneasy as to its Consequences.'[3]

And well it might be, for the entry of General Lavalleja into
the Banda Oriental inaugurated a struggle for power in Uruguay which lasted almost without a break for a quarter of a
century and involved before its conclusion not only Brazil and
Argentina but France and Britain. The wars in Uruguay wrote
finis to all the fine plans of Rivadavia not only by interfering
with trade and diverting an already pitifully weak and un-
disciplined labour force from the pursuits of peace but also by
creating an emotional and political atmosphere of xenophobia
greatly advantageous to the pastoral interests and inimical to
urban and foreign creditor groups.

In April and May 1825 these events in Córdoba and in the

---

[1] F.O. 6/8, Parish to Canning, 8 Apr. 1825.
[2] These are Parish's figures. The band are popularly remembered as the *Treinta
y Tres.*
[3] F.O. 6/8, Parish to Canning, 1 May 1825.

Banda Oriental were only little clouds upon the horizon. In the foreground and occupying the principal attention were ambitious plans for public improvement. The Governor's message to the Provincial Assembly of Buenos Aires, delivered on 19 May, told of 'the increasing Prosperity of our Commerce, the activity of our Industry, and the general welfare of the labouring Classes' which nourished the principles of liberal government. Hopefully the Governor believed that liberal principles would spread 'even among the lower orders of Society that just sense or rather instinct of liberty and order which destroys and baffles the machinations of the ambitious'. After telling the Assembly of the harbours and schools and churches the Government hoped to build, of the police forces they planned to strengthen in order to check the increase of cattle stealing, and of the land laws they intended to improve, the Governor closed on a note of warning that, perhaps, all was not what it seemed and that the power of the liberal improvers who borrowed money in Europe was not so absolute as one might suppose. 'The spirit of anarchy', declared the Governor, 'disguised in a thousand forms may corrupt our Institutions, and the Aristocracy which has sprung out of our revolution will try all possible means to discredit them.'[1]

While the Provincial Assembly of Buenos Aires was thus encouraged to fix its eyes on the future and to cock its ear to the present, the National Congress was at work endeavouring to set up a National Government and frame a constitution. Parish described to Canning the manœuvres by which the partisans of a strong, central Government hoped to circumvent their opponents and rally their supporters in the provinces. The National Assembly framed the question 'Do you wish a Central or a Federal Government?' which was sent to all the provincial assemblies. 'There seems to be little doubt', Parish explained to Canning, 'that the Assemblies will almost unanimously declare for the former, and the object in referring the question to them is, as far as I can learn, to obtain a fair declaration of this feeling, and to take it out of the hands of the Governors of the Provinces.'[2] Each of the governors controlled a militia force

---

[1] Quoted in F.O. 6/8, Governor to the Assembly, 19 May 1825. Also in H. Mabragaña, ed., *Los Mensajes* (Buenos Aires, 1910), i, p. 220.
[2] F.O. 6/8, Parish to Canning, 10 June 1825.

and these forces were the controlling political machines of each province. An appeal to the provincial assemblies was thus an invitation to any rivals of the governors to rally round the National Congress and the National Executive which it hoped to bring into being. As events were to demonstrate, provincial governors either were or soon became the central figures of the rural cattle-breeding interests, and, as such, advocates of a wide provincial independence; whereas the advocates of strong central government tended to express the aspirations and needs of the dominant classes in the city of Buenos Aires.

Constitutional questions were at this moment becoming inaudible amid the clatter of arms and the shouts of patriotic crowds. The 'ruined and desperate individuals' who had crossed the river Uruguay in May were winning successes against the Brazilian authorities. Parish's agents informed him that General Lavalleja had assembled six divisions 'in the most wretched condition and without discipline [but] . . . accustomed to the use of firearms . . . [and] excellent horsemen, acquainted with the intricacies of the Country'.[1] The officers were mainly landed proprietors. Lavalleja's successes completely unsettled the Imperial power at Montevideo. The senior Uruguayan commander in the Brazilian service, General Fructuoso Rivera, abandoned his oath to the Emperor of Brazil and joined the rebels with the troops under his command. This bird of ill omen had already abundantly displayed his genius for desertion, and now he demonstrated, as he did repeatedly during his long and troublesome life, that an act of treachery on his part was the inaugural sign of a terrible public calamity.

In Buenos Aires the news of Lavalleja's success and Rivera's treachery was variously received. The public was excited and enthusiastic and the members of the National Congress and the Provincial Assembly of Buenos Aires were joyfully awaiting the return of the Banda Oriental to the Argentine family. The Government, however, was worried. García, the Foreign Minister, shared with his countrymen an antipathy to the presence of Brazilian power in Montevideo, but he was also aware in a lively fashion of the fatal dangers for constitutional and economic progress of a war with Brazil. Brazil possessed a substantial navy largely officered and manned by veteran

[1] F.O. 6/9, enclosed with Parish to Canning, 20 July 1825.

British sailors, and with this it could cut Buenos Aires's connexion with the world market. By comparison with Argentina, Brazil was a rich and populous country which had avoided the exhausting experience of revolutionary war. Although it was a slave-owning monarchy vulnerable to revolutionary agitation, the Brazilian state had demonstrated in the Banda Oriental that by the use of organized force it could establish itself even in the presence of an alien and revolutionary population.

Parish found that the news of revolutionary successes in the Banda Oriental made the Government more rather than less uneasy. García assured Parish once again that he wished to avoid a conflict. In order to demonstrate their neutrality the Government issued a proclamation early in June prohibiting the fitting out of rebel privateers in the ports of the Confederation. But it was evident that García and his colleagues were not going to purchase peace at any price. General Alvear was dispatched to congratulate General Bolívar on the defeat of the Spanish forces, and it was assumed that he would discuss not only the status of Alto Peru but the formation of a grand republican alliance of free men against the slave monarchy of Brazil.[1] The Argentine forces on the Uruguay were strengthened and Chile was invited to lend the assistance of her navy as recompense for Argentina's contribution to Chilean independence.

Early in July a Brazilian squadron comprising four 74-gun frigates and two gunboats appeared in the Río de la Plata under the command of Admiral Lobos. The Brazilians seemed determined to appeal to a variety of affections in the community, for one of their 74's was named the *Maria de Gloria* and another the *Liberal*. The Admiral himself, however, was bent on threatening the Argentine Government. In a note to the Government Lobos accused them on behalf of His Majesty the Emperor and Perpetual Defender of Brazil of permitting subjects of the Government of Buenos Aires to 'seduce the unguarded people and to unite with the perfidious rebel Fructuoso Rivera'. García returned a soft but insolent answer saying that he was ready to discuss the subjects alluded to by the Brazilian commander 'as soon as it shall appear that the Vice-Admiral is

[1] F.O. 6/8, Parish to Canning, 22 June 1825, and F.O. 6/9, Parish to Canning, 20 July 1825.

properly and sufficiently provided with Credentials conformably with established custom'. At the same time he prepared to dispatch an official envoy to Rio de Janeiro.

The appearance of the Brazilian ships off Buenos Aires put the people and the politicians in a froth. One outspoken Buenos Airean delegate in the National Congress, Agüero, who was generally esteemed a supporter of the Government, demanded a full explanation of the situation. The Government of Buenos Aires, which was still acting as the executive authority of the Confederation in accordance with the request of the National Congress, wished for a secret committee to hear the report on the course of events. Agüero would have none of this. He insisted on publicity, asserting that he was 'best consulting the interest of the Country by forcing a Public disclosure of the real state of affairs upon this question'. He argued that the people should know the strength of the Government, and, if it was weak and unprepared, 'it were better to open the Eyes of the Nation to that weakness in order to prove to all classes the necessity of proportional exertions'.[1]

In the face of this upsurge the Government exhibited the weakness which became only too familiar a feature of authority in Buenos Aires. The Minister of War, General Cruz, resigned. García, for his part, agreed to report to the Congress publicly. On the evening of 9 July he faced a crowded assembly of the National Congress. The galleries were packed. He told the Congress that the Governments of both Buenos Aires and Entre Rios were making every effort to prepare for any eventuality; that the Provincial Assembly of Buenos Aires had placed $500,000 at the disposal of the Government (more than a year's debt service on the London loan), and that Entre Rios and Santa Fé had exceeded the quota of their contributions of men to the Army. He then complained about the jealousy of Buenos Aires exhibited by some of the delegates from other provinces, and assured the Congress that the Government of Buenos Aires was fulfilling the obligations of national leadership undertaken on behalf of the National Congress. Agüero then asked García what the Government knew about the intentions of Brazil. García commenced his answer by saying that he only knew

[1] F.O. 6/8, Parish to Canning, 22 June 1825, and F.O. 6/9, Parish to Canning, 20 July 1825.

what he read in the newspapers, but he concluded with a revelation which was either a manœuvre to capture leadership of the popular war party or else a manifestation of a serious resolve to fight Brazil. He simply stated that he had reason to believe that the Emperor of Brazil intended to seize the Province of Entre Rios and to blockade the port of Buenos Aires if he thought such action was necessary to defeat General Lavalleja and maintain Brazilian power in Montevideo.

After the meeting García told Parish that Agüero and his friends had won a victory over the Government, thus seeming to suggest to the British chargé d'affaires that war with Brazil was not really the Government's intention. There might be a legitimate doubt about this, but there could be none about the determination of the Government to maintain its authority and strengthen its popularity. The next day García and his colleagues in the Government of Buenos Aires placed before the National Congress a request to be relieved of their responsibilities as a National Government acting for the provinces. This request silenced the critics. After examination by a committee from which the representatives of Buenos Aires absented themselves, the National Congress voted unanimously to ask the Government of the Province of Buenos Aires to continue to act for the United Provinces in matters of foreign affairs, finance, and defence. Parish was much impressed by the entire performance. 'It has given [the Government]', he reported to Canning, 'an impulse, and an additional moral Force which will be of the greatest consequence to them, not only here but throughout the Union.'[1]

A pause in the movement of events now intruded itself during the rest of July and through August and September. Sailors and officers from the Brazilian ships came ashore and were seen about the streets of Buenos Aires. The windows of the Brazilian Consulate remained intact. The National Congress directed its attention once more to the work of making a constitution. The Provincial Assembly of Buenos Aires resumed the discussion of the conditions under which citizens might worship God, and it resolved that 'the right of every Man to worship the Almighty according to his Conscience is inviolable in this Province'. But the committee studying the subject felt some uneasiness 'that

[1] F.O. 6/9, Parish to Canning, 20 July 1825.

the principal work of our glorious regeneration remained incomplete in various of its branches, because Philosophy was unable at once to decompose and generally extirpate maxims which time had fixed in the hearts of the multitude.'[1] This was only too true, for in San Juan Province '[some fanatical] Priests succeeded in collecting a considerable party against the Government'.[2] Dr. Gillies, a Scottish naval surgeon on the retired list, who lived in Mendoza, reported to Parish that in his place of residence the priests had raised a new flag and proclaimed a fight for the Catholic religion. Parish was relieved to inform Canning, however, that, after a round of executions and expulsions to Chile, the interior provinces had been restored to the ways of liberalism, and he 'hoped that this is the last struggle of the Priesthood for their old influence in this Country'.[3]

In Buenos Aires itself Parish rejoiced to see that freedom of religious belief was beginning to march parallel with freedom of enterprise. The British community purchased a disused chapel of the Jesuits, and the Bible Society provided a minister in the person of the Rev. John Armstrong. On 25 September the first Protestant church in South America was opened for worship. Parish took for granted the theological and moral excellence of the Protestant faith, and this being so, he called attention to the solidity of the rock on which his church was founded: the XIIth Article of the Treaty, a numerous congregation of His Majesty's subjects, and the respectable demeanour of all concerned. Respectability Parish regarded as a species of witness. 'The opening of a Protestant Church for the first time in South America naturally excites much attention and observation on the part of the Natives of the Country', he told Canning, 'and it is of proportionate importance that our Service should be respectably performed.'[3] Mr. Armstrong in consultation with Parish devised a prayer for the state 'under whose protection we live'. 'Give heavenly wisdom to the principal Governors and Ministers of these United Provinces, and let Thine arm strengthen and support them', concluded their appeal to God. The Foreign Office, at least, appears to have

[1] F.O. 6/9, *Dictamen de la comisión de negocios constitucionales de la honorable junta de representantes de la provincia en el proyecto de ley pasado por el gobierno sobre la libertad de cultos*, enclosed with Parish to Canning, 10 Oct. 1825.

[2] F.O. 6/9, Parish to Canning, 10 Sept. 1825.   [3] Ibid., 10 Oct. 1825.

been satisfied, for Canning had no comment to make. Nor should he, for the prayer had the merit of brevity, political accuracy, and honesty. Parish and Canning did not seek to mislead the Almighty about the unity of the Argentine state in the way they had the Duke of Wellington.

With the coming of spring the pace of events began to quicken. As the pastures freshened armies could move more easily. The day before the Protestant church was opened in Buenos Aires General Rivera defeated a small Brazilian force at the Rincón de las Gallinas beyond the Uruguay. The main Brazilian force began to concentrate south of the Río Negro under the imperial commander General Veritus Manoel. In the first week of October the main force of General Lavalleja began to make contact with this force, and on 12 October at Sarandí on the Río Negro in the heart of the Uruguayan pampas the forces of Lavalleja were completely victorious.

When the news of the victory at Sarandí was received in Buenos Aires a wave of patriotic and revolutionary passion overwhelmed the Government and deprived it of control of its course. Lavalleja's Orders of the Day were laid before the National Congress. The Congress debated them from 21 to 25 October, when it was resolved to reincorporate the Banda Oriental in the United Provinces and to seat the delegates of the Uruguayan Province. The Government fought this resolution. The Congress insisted on seeing García's communications with the Brazilian Government, and strong disapproval of his temporizing policies was expressed. García gave way and accepted the policy of incorporating the Banda in the Republic. In a formal Note he asked Britain to mediate with Brazil on the assumption that the Government in Buenos Aires would pay Brazil a substantial sum of money for the right to re-embrace the Uruguayan Province in the Argentine family.[1]

Tempers began to rise. During this excitement a British subject was pulled from his horse and killed by a mob for failing to sink to his knees during a procession of the Host. Brazilian sailors could no longer safely appear in the streets. Rivadavia returned from Europe ambitious to preside over the scene of tumult. General Rodríguez was appointed Commander-in-Chief of the Argentine forces and he was ordered to cross the

[1] F.O. 6/9, García to Parish, 18 Dec. 1825.

River Uruguay 'to maintain possession of the country which Lavalleja had liberated'.[1] As the year which had begun with the optimistic negotiations of the Anglo-Argentine Treaty drew to a close, Parish sent to the Admiral on the South American station at Rio de Janeiro for H.M. ships of war 'for the protection of our trade from more than necessary inconvenience'.[2] In less than twelve months, the hope of industrial development, immigration, and foreign investment in public securities had been blasted, and now trade itself was facing the prospect of disaster.

[1] F.O. 6/9, Parish to Canning, 18 Dec. 1825.
[2] Ibid. 31 Dec. 1825.

VI

BRITAIN AND THE WAR BETWEEN ARGENTINA AND BRAZIL

FROM the Treaty of Utrecht until the extinction of the Spanish authority in South America the British Government had concerned itself with the balance of power in the Río de la Plata and the political questions relating to the control of the military and commercial centres at the mouth of the Plata–Paraná river system. So long as the Spanish Crown maintained an exclusive commercial policy, Britain had supported the Portuguese claims to control the Banda Oriental—the eastern bank of the River Uruguay. When, however, Colonia do Sacramento was lost irrecoverably to Spain in 1777, Britain ceased seriously to dispute the settlement of the Río de la Plata question in favour of the power in occupation.

When the Portuguese Court withdrew from Lisbon to Rio de Janeiro and a revolutionary movement developed in Buenos Aires, the problem of the Río de la Plata was reopened, and in a much more complicated form than had been the case when Spain and Portugal were engaged in a simple rivalry for control. Britain was the ally of Portugal and, after the Treaties of 1810, was granted special commercial privileges in Brazil. Logically one might expect that British interest would have aligned Britain completely with Portugal and Brazil. The progressive opening of the Buenos Aires market to world trade after 1810, however, eliminated one ground for British opposition to Spanish hegemony in the Río de la Plata, while consideration for the new-found ally, Spain, prompted Castlereagh and his agent in Rio de Janeiro, Lord Strangford, to seek to restrain Portuguese and Brazilian endeavours to take advantage of Spanish weakness. The situation was additionally complicated by the growing disposition, first of the Spanish authorities like Governor Elío at Montevideo and then of the conservative wing of the revolutionary movement on both sides of the Río de la Plata to seek assistance from Rio de Janeiro in the struggle for the power to determine the character of their society. Finally, among the revolutionary forces in the Banda Oriental itself, there emerged under the leadership of General Artigas a movement for the independence of the Banda from all control by external agencies, whether Spanish, Argentine, or Brazilian.

In response to the complications of events between 1810–16 the British Government evolved a policy the object of which was to restrain Portuguese attempts to conquer the area and to subject Buenos Aires itself, perhaps, to Portuguese control. In the armistice arranged by Lieutenant-Colonel J. Rademaker in May 1812 between the forces of Portugal and Buenos Aires we can discern the first manifestation of the British policy of maintaining, if possible, a balance of power in the Río de la Plata. The restraints imposed on the Portuguese by Britain helped to establish the circumstances in which the revolutionary forces first eliminated all Spanish power in the Banda Oriental and finally the authority of Buenos Aires. By 1815 the embryo of a buffer state had come into being, separating Argentina from Brazil and ensuring more completely a balance of power in the Río de la Plata.

In 1816 the Portuguese marched into the Banda Oriental on the pretext of assisting in the restoration of the authority of Ferdinand VII. Britain never supported or endorsed this move, but, inasmuch as Britain was herself supposed to be mediating at this time between Ferdinand and his rebellious subjects, Castlereagh felt obliged to take upon himself the ironic burden of restraining Portugal from seizing the territory of a monarch who had already lost it to a third party of native revolutionaries.

When the British policy of mediation between Spain and her rebellious colonies came to an end and recognition of the new states was undertaken, the position of the Banda Oriental was passed over in silence. When Brazil became an independent state in 1821, the Banda Oriental was incorporated in the Empire as the Cisplatine Province. Britain neither accepted nor challenged this action. The Government at Buenos Aires, however, did. They refused to receive a Brazilian envoy unless he renounced the Brazilian claims. In 1823 an agent was dispatched to Rio de Janeiro from Buenos Aires to see what might be achieved by negotiation. The result was nothing. In his first report to the Foreign Office, Parish explained the state of this affair, but at the same time he left the impression that the policy of the Government in Buenos Aires was one of peace and that the army was being reduced. This may, indeed, have been so, for the Government seems to have been relying upon twin hopes for a solution: firstly, action in the field against Brazil by the revolutionary leaders Bolívar and Sucre, of whom the latter was still seeking for people to liberate and republics to proclaim; and, secondly, popular revolution against Brazil in the Banda Oriental itself. García always conveyed the impression to Parish that he was a man of peace and much devoted to the belief that orderly finances and public economy are more important agencies of salvation than military glory and territorial conquest. In 1824 there had been a slight increase in the proportion of public expenditure devoted to the war department compared with the year 1822, but this hardly pointed to a plan for war. Indeed, the Government had very few troops and no warships of any consequence at its disposal when the Brazilian fleet first appeared off Buenos Aires. The balance of evidence seems to indicate that the Government and the public in Buenos Aires were both much alive to the problem of the Banda Oriental, but that the Government was not planning a solution by force of arms at any time prior to the outbreak of revolution in the Banda Oriental, and then only when they apprehended an attack from Brazil.[1]

What object the Emperor of Brazil had in mind in attacking Argentina is difficult to discover. Faced with a revolutionary movement he and his ministers adopted an idea congenial to well-entrenched governments of socially static communities, namely, that revolution at home can best be wiped out by attacking its sympathizers abroad, thus combining the business of counter-revolution with the delights of conquest. This idea was encouraged by the knowledge that Brazil possessed a formidable navy and a respectable army which, if no account is taken of geography and politics, was far larger and stronger than the forces at the command of Buenos Aires. Judged by his

---

[1] There does not appear to be sufficient evidence for the assertions made by several authorities that Buenos Aires was preparing for or contemplating war, e.g. Humphreys, *Consular Reports*, p. 19, note 3, and Webster, *Independence of Latin America*, i, p. 69.

actions the Emperor of Brazil seems to have believed that by assaulting Argentina and destroying its commerce he could teach the Government in Buenos Aires that peace and friendship with Brazil depended upon assisting him in suppressing revolution in the Banda Oriental.

Given the freedom of trade which the revolution had brought to the Río de la Plata and which had been secured by treaties both with Argentina and Brazil, Britain in 1825 had only one object: peace. An absurd situation was developing in which the Brazilian navy, manned largely by British subjects, would be fighting an Argentine Navy manned largely by British subjects in the process of which a commerce conducted largely by British subjects would be destroyed. All the parties were seeking their own self-interest according to the approved canons of utilitarian orthodoxy, and yet somewhere a devil was at work guiding them all to destruction in the estuary of the Río de la Plata. The Foreign Office, however, did not go chasing after this devil hoping to find peace by exorcism. Canning sought, instead, to save and build, working with the corrupt material of the state of nature in South America. Could not a deal be arranged?—something involving the commodity everyone understood and loved, money? During the course of his mediation Castlereagh had proposed that the King of Spain pay the King of Portugal a comfortable sum to get out of the Banda Oriental, representing the payment as compensation to His Most Faithful Majesty for putting down rebellion in a province of His Most Catholic Majesty. This suggestion was now revived and advanced.[1]

At the same time Canning sought to explore the possibility of having the question examined and, perhaps, settled by the proposed Congress of American States. Canning never developed any clear or precise idea about this possibility. Writing to Parish in October 1825 he envisaged the Congress in the role of a mediator,[2] but later, in March the next year, he was disposed to use the meeting of the Congress as a threat to Brazil by ordering Ponsonby to warn the Emperor of Brazil against the likelihood that, failing a quick settlement, the Government of

---

[1] F.O. 13/2, Canning to Stuart, 16 June 1825, and F.O. 6/7, Canning to Parish, 20 June 1825.

[2] F.O. 6/7, Canning to Parish, 19 Oct. 1825.

Buenos Aires would appeal to the Congress and find a sympathetic hearing for its case.[1]

At the time of the war's approach Rivadavia was in London in the capacity of chargé d'affaires. There he was seeking an advocate, not a mediator. He thrust himself upon Canning alleging that at the time of the armistice in Uruguay, arranged in 1812, Lord Strangford, the British Minister in Rio de Janeiro, had given a British guarantee concerning the independence of the Banda Oriental from Portuguese control. Canning was extremely annoyed by Rivadavia's allegation. He complained about Rivadavia's commercial connexions as unbecoming to a diplomat. He denied that so solemn a diplomatic act as a guarantee could ever be a matter of mere words spoken between agents. But Canning seems to have been worried, for he questioned Lord Strangford about his proceedings in 1812. Fortunately Rivadavia decided to return to Buenos Aires, and Canning allowed his relief to creep even into his official dispatches; and naturally so. Canning was determined to work for peace from a position of neutrality, and to avoid commitment to either Brazil or Buenos Aires.

In an important sense Britain was not, however, completely neutral. The British Government had never formally acknowledged the incorporation of the Banda Oriental into the Brazilian Empire. The impression certainly emerges, although it cannot be illustrated by any specific statement, that Canning and his colleagues hoped to see created a buffer state independent of both Argentina and Brazil. When Parish announced the British intention not to interfere in the affair, García observed that he did not believe this decision was a final one and concluded pointedly that 'he felt . . . considerably relieved by the assurance that His Majesty's Government disclaimed any intention on their part of recognizing . . . the pretensions of Don Pedro to the *permanent* right of possession over that province'.[2]

While diplomatic manœuvring of this description was in progress the consequences of conflict began to manifest themselves to the British community. When Admiral Lobos announced the blockade of Buenos Aires, Parish was besought by the mercantile community to negotiate an extension of the

[1] F.O. 6/12, Canning to Ponsonby, 18 Mar. 1826.
[2] F.O. 6/9, Parish to Canning, 10 Sept. 1825.

period of fourteen days which the Brazilians allowed to neutrals
for the purpose of moving their ships and goods from Buenos
Aires. Parish saw his fine scheme of appointing consuls in the
interior provinces dissipated, since the commercial future looked
black and provided no justification for appointing men to promote mercantile penetration.[1] Anarchic passions concerning
land, cattle, victory, and death were once more abroad among
a race of landlords and cowboys who could live for years, if
necessary, without money or peace or trade or the amenities
of city life. 'I fear [this] will give rise to much Mercantile
Distress', Parish reported, 'which will fall upon none more
heavily than the British Establishments in this Country.'[2]

Parish had every reason for such apprehension. The Brazilian
force in the river consisted of forty-two vessels several of them
heavy, well-armed frigates. The Buenos Aires Government, on
the other hand, possessed only twelve gunboats and three brigs
of war. Two frigates and four smaller vessels were purchased
and added to this force, and it was hoped to obtain several ships
from the Chilean Navy. As if to compensate for a deficiency of
ships with a sufficiency of men, the Government recalled to the
service an Irish sailor, William Brown. Almirante Guillermo
Brown was the creator of the Argentine Navy. Possessed of a
wide range of capacities, enormous energy, great courage, and
an implacable will-to-victory, Brown made one ship count for
two and a few guns for many. He considered it his main business
to fight the enemy wherever he found him. From the first
moment of the Brazilian blockade he sprang to the attack,
sailing with an inferior force into the main body of the Brazilian
fleet firing all guns. This unexpected cannonade caused the
Brazilians to retreat down river, but before they could escape
Brown's ships cut out a large Brazilian gunboat, and brought it
with stricken colours to anchor off the Fort at Buenos Aires.
The enthusiasm of the people boiled up, and within a fortnight
Brown gave them another show. Faced with the main Brazilian
force off Buenos Aires he brought his flagship to close action
with the largest enemy vessel although the rest of his fleet
veered away in the face of enemy superiority. He continued
firing until his powder magazines were exhausted, and only
then retreated behind the protection of the shore batteries. He

[1] F.O. 6/11, Parish to Canning, 18 Jan. 1826.   [2] Ibid., 23 Jan. 1826.

immediately came ashore, and ordered the court martial of his captains who had not followed him into the fight. Thus was popular sentiment aroused and engaged. Being witnesses to scenes of victory and defeat, the populace of Buenos Aires became a force in the political struggle which made difficult any policy of the Government not committed to complete victory even when foresight and wisdom suggested the necessity of less.

The pattern of the war, which determined its outcome, soon established itself. After the victory at Sarandí in October 1825 the Brazilian forces in the Banda Oriental lost control of the open country, and were confined henceforth to the fortified towns of Montevideo and Colonia, which were supplied by sea. During the summer of 1826-7 they ventured into the open country with the object of defeating the combined forces of Buenos Aires and the Oriental revolutionaries, but at Ituzaingo in February 1827 the Brazilian forces under the Marquis vf Barbacena suffered a heavy defeat from which they never recovered. On the other hand the army of Buenos Aires under Alvear and the Oriental revolutionary forces were never able to gather a sufficiency of fire power or a large enough body of skilled and trained men to carry the strong place of Montevideo by assault. Indeed, they did not try.

At sea a similar stalemate developed. The superior Brazilian forces were able to maintain a blockade, a task made easier for them by the fact that Britain maintained a doctrine of strict blockade, and British merchants and shipowners could not insure cargoes and ships destined for a port the blockade of which was recognized by the British Government.[1] Thus the British doctrine of blockade made the blockade of Buenos Aires more complete than the Brazilian Navy had any capacity to do. Although the Brazilians, assisted in this way, succeeded in reducing the trade of Buenos Aires, they failed equally to control the Río de la Plata militarily, and never had the slightest success in cutting off the Argentine Army from its home bases in Buenos Aires, Entre Rios, and Santa Fé. On the other hand, Admiral Brown never succeeded in doing more than inflict partial defeats upon the Brazilians. He never broke their main

---

[1] F.O. 6/19, Ponsonby to Dudley and Ward (John William Ward, Viscount Dudley and Ward of Dudley, created Earl Dudley of Dudley Castle, Oct. 1827), 4 Dec. 1827.

force, and his principal success consisted in breaking out of the Río de la Plata, where, cruising off the coast of Brazil, he harassed their shipping. His action also enabled the Buenos Aires Government to commission numerous privateers whose piratical assaults upon all shipping had the dubious advantage finally of provoking the British Government to speak out with sharp threats against all forms of interference with shipping on the high seas.

On the political front the Emperor of Brazil was soon put on the defensive. From the beginning he had the disadvantage of no clear objective except the suppression of revolution in the Banda Oriental. Inflated talk about the 'tenebrous machinations . . . revolutionary licentiousness and . . . ugly vice'[1] of Buenos Aires might evoke some response in the Courts of Vienna, St. Petersburg, and Paris, but unfortunately for Don Pedro the only powers capable of affecting the situation and coming to his assistance were Great Britain and the United States, both of which entertained a different view of Buenos Aires derived from the solid commercial opportunities which revolution had opened up for them. By taking a high line based on monarchical principle the Emperor left all the advantages of appearing reasonable to the Buenos Aires Government. They had already indicated a willingness to negotiate both directly and through the mediation of Great Britain.[2] In January 1826 the Argentine Minister in London, Sarratea, announced to Canning that the Banda Oriental had been admitted to the National Congress of the Argentine Provinces,[3] but he also indicated a willingness still to negotiate by promising a money payment to Brazil. Thus, the Government in Buenos Aires succeeded in creating circumstances very congenial to Great Britain, wherein Britain could arrange for Argentina to win the war by getting the Brazilians out of the Banda Oriental and for Brazil to win by getting the Argentines out of the same place.

On the level of warfare, the Emperor of Brazil was likewise put on the defensive. Monarchy at that time was a symbol of order. But society in South America was broken and restless,

---

[1] F.O. 6/12, Inhambupé to Ponsonby, 10 June 1826, enclosed with Ponsonby to Canning, 13 June 1826.

[2] F.O. 6/11, Sarratea to Canning, 11 Mar. 1826.

[3] F.O. 6/14, Sarratea to Canning, 28 Jan. 1826.

and no one seemed to care about this. Unable completely to defeat the Emperor, the Government of Buenos Aires and the revolutionary forces took up the weapon of revolution. They proposed to do this in two ways: firstly, to stimulate revolutionary leaders like Sucre to carry the republican assault on a gigantic scale into monarchical Brazil, and secondly, to carry their own species of revolution into the Brazilian Province of Río Grande do Sul with the object of detaching it from the Empire. Competing in this field of warfare, the Brazilian Emperor had little to offer communities which a long course of revolution had taught to live without settled authority.

But the Emperor was not without some advantage in the political field. The Buenos Aires Government were nearly as frightened of Bolívar and Sucre as they were of the Emperor of Brazil. When, at the beginning of the war, Parish told García about the high regard which the British Government entertained for the Brazilian monarchy, García assured him that, although he was not willing to exclude the possibility of the republics of South America making common cause against the Emperor, the Government of Buenos Aires did not seek to make a 'war of principles'. Subsequently the Government of Buenos Aires displayed the greatest reluctance to enter into too intimate a contact with Bolívar,[1] and within a matter of months were embroiled with Sucre's new republic of Bolivia. Before the war with Brazil ended, Colombia emerged as a mediator, but not as an ally of Buenos Aires.

The second weapon upon which Buenos Aires relied—the provocation of revolution in peripheral provinces of the Empire —was double-edged and, as it turned out, self-acting. The Emperor disdained to provoke revolution, but revolution began to act in the end to terminate hostilities between himself and the Government at Buenos Aires; for the revolutionary movement in the Banda Oriental, allegedly instigated by Buenos Aires, finally turned against its Argentine allies. Once the Emperor abandoned his efforts to control the Banda Oriental and left the revolutionary forces free to create their own government, this government soon began to exercise an attractive power to the federalist leaders in the Argentine Provinces of Santa Fé and Entre Rios. Independent Montevideo became

[1] F.O. 6/11, Parish to Canning, 21 Apr. 1826.

more of a thorn in the side of Buenos Aires than in that of the Emperor.

Thus were the total forces, political and military, of Buenos Aires and the Emperor of Brazil locked in a balance during the course of the war.

It is the argument at this stage of our history that the war with Brazil brought to an end the experiment in British financial participation in the development of the Argentine community, and compelled the return to the commercial connexion characteristic of the decade following the overthrow of Spanish power. In fact the war all but terminated the commercial connexion as well. Had not hostilities been brought to a speedy conclusion in 1828, the British mercantile community might well have been obliged either to abandon Buenos Aires entirely or commence operations anew after complete bankruptcy.

In order to understand this development, it is necessary to record briefly the economic history of these years. Britain's interest in the Río de la Plata was unashamedly economic. Neither Parish nor Ponsonby, the British Minister, ever considered their diplomacy to have any objective but the use of British influence to establish a practical political arrangement which would make commercial activity possible. There is a direct correlation between the changes in condition of the British interest in Buenos Aires and the course of British diplomacy: a relaxed neutrality and good offices at one stage; an urgent, pertinacious, and almost threatening mediation at the stage when the final commercial crisis was in sight in 1827.

When the war broke out, the British equity in Argentina was estimated at £1,536,411, consisting mainly of goods for export and specie. In addition, British holdings of government and bank stock in Buenos Aires amounted roughly to £750,000.[1] This did not include the Baring Loan, a claim amounting by 1827 to approximately £970,000. As soon as the threat of blockade developed, the British merchants in Buenos Aires began shipping as much produce as possible. The effect of the blockade was catastrophic as far as the shipment of produce was concerned. In 1825 ninety-five British vessels had entered the ports of the Republic and eighty-five had cleared thence. In 1826 the number entering fell to seven and in 1827 to one.

---

[1] F.O. 6/20, Parish to Bidwell, 31 Dec. 1827.

In 1826 twenty-three British vessels departed, all of them during the period allowed by the Brazilian Admiral to neutrals, and in 1827 only one British vessel left Buenos Aires.[1] Once the possibility of liquidating assets by the shipment of produce abroad was terminated, British merchants commenced purchasing specie, which could still be shipped abroad in the British packet allowed through the blockade carrying dispatches and mail for H.M. Government. In August 1826 the Brazilian Admiral objected to this practice because it served 'to uphold . . . the expiring credit' of the enemy. 'It would be of vital importance . . . to many British Establishments connected with this Country', Parish warned, 'if they were to be deprived at this moment of the only means, which remains to them of receiving their Remittances from hence [sic].'[2] The Brazilians did not succeed in stopping the flow of specie abroad. In the first half of 1827 587,874 hard dollars were shipped out of Buenos Aires. In July 1827 the Buenos Aires Government attempted what the Brazilian Navy had failed to do. They prohibited exports of gold and silver in spite of the British Minister's protest, in response to the demand of Señor Anchorena, a great ranch owner who was Minister of Finance. This prohibition came a little late, for the country was already denuded of bullion, and had reached the limits of trading by the export of specie.

The export of bullion, together with the heavy Government borrowing from the National Bank and the printing of paper currency and treasury bills, had a profound but not always uniform effect on prices. While the British merchants were attempting to liquidate their assets by shipping bullion abroad, they sought to overcome the limitations of this method and to continue their connexion in Buenos Aires by hedging against price changes through investment in land and livestock and by purchasing hides, which could be stored for a period up to two years without serious loss by deterioration. By the end of 1827 British assets in Buenos Aires had declined to £492,000 according to Parish's estimate, of which £220,000 were represented by holdings of hides and £75,000 in land.[3]

[1] F.O. 6/19, Consular Shipping Returns, 1822–7.
[2] F.O. 6/11, Parish to Hood, 2 Aug. 1826.
[3] F.O. 6/20, Parish to Bidwell, 31 Dec. 1827.

The effect of the blockade on the Argentine economy itself was not altogether disastrous. Indeed, to some parts of the economy it came as a restorative blessing.

It is curious to remark [Parish reported to the Foreign Office] that while the operation of these two great effects of the war—the suspension of the foreign trading and the depreciation in the paper currency has been ruinous to individuals and chiefly to neutral parties, it . . . has suspended no internal branch of trade, nor checked, any of the resources of national industry—it has drawn a large amount of native and foreign capital—partly on account of there being no other means of employing it, but chiefly to avoid the dangers of the paper currency—into the improvement and extension of Cattle Establishments—the great Source of the wealth of Buenos Ayres, and in that respect the province was never in so flourishing a state as now.[1]

The blockade operated as a measure of protection for native industry better than any which had existed since the overthrow of the Spanish Viceroy. Within three months of the imposition of the blockade Parish reported the distress felt by the British merchants and added that 'in some of the interior Provinces, however, large sales of native Produce have been effected at very high prices for Buenos Ayres, which makes the war popular in those Districts'.[2] There is some evidence that the war enabled the economies of provinces like Córdoba, enfeebled and harassed by foreign competition in the Buenos Aires market, to stagger once more to their feet. It is, perhaps permissible to see some connexion between this resurgence of the provincial economy and the counter-offensive of the federalist forces, which brought down Rivadavia and his system and prepared the way for General Rosas. General Bustos, who led the offensive against the unitary constitution designed by the National Congress of 1826, in which Rivadavia had such great influence, was the Governor of Córdoba, the most strongly protectionist of the Argentine provinces and the one most injured by international competition.

Another peril to the British interest began to emerge as the war drew to a close and the physical capacity of the Brazilian navy to enforce the blockade diminished. This took the shape of

---

[1] F.O. 6/20, Report of British Merchants in Buenos Aires, enclosed with Parish to Bidwell, 31 Dec. 1827.   [2] F.O. 6/11, Parish to Canning, 30 May 1826.

the United States. The Americans had had a very large place in the carrying trade into and out of the River Plate since the opening of Buenos Aires to international commerce. In 1824 the number of American vessels entering the Río de la Plata exceeded the number of British vessels by 45 per cent. When the war came the American ships disappeared from the trade, but in 1827 they began to reappear. Thirty-five American vessels entered the ports of the Republic in that year compared with one British. The Americans were uninhibited by the doctrine of strict blockade, and in Boston, New York, Baltimore, and Philadelphia shipowners could insure against the risks of trade without the fear that American courts would invalidate the contracts of insurance. In the end, the British Minister declared to the Foreign Secretary that, if the United States Government followed the example of American ship-masters and ignored the Brazilian declaration of blockade, Britain would be obliged to demand equal rights at once.[1]

There is no means of directly calculating British losses due to the war. Parish and Ponsonby spoke freely of ruin, but it is surprising to discover that a substantial proportion of the British merchants who subscribed to the support of the British chapel in 1825 were still subscribing after the war was over. They had not disappeared without trace and without money. The people who suffered most were those who had invested too heavy a proportion of their wealth in public funds or were too inexperienced or insufficiently agile in shifting their capital from one form of investment to another. In so far as the holders of sterling bonds received nothing after 1827 and the holders of Argentine dollar securities were paid in depreciated paper, they suffered a direct loss. Manufacturers and shipowners suffered losses from prolonged exclusion from the Buenos Aires market, but they had alternative opportunities, some of which were far more valuable than those in Buenos Aires. Indeed, the marginal character of the Buenos Aires market in the entire international market of Great Britain helps to explain the hesitancies of British policy obliged to consider other and more important spheres of interest such as Brazil.

The British merchants in Buenos Aires suffered probably least for they were able to diversify their activities and investments

[1] F.O. 6/22, Ponsonby to Dudley and Ward, 28 Jan. 1828.

and, as it turned out, the blockade was lifted in time to bring them relief. In the long run the necessities of their situation gave them valuable experience which became one of the secrets of British success when, forty years on, they and their sons began to undertake large-scale investments in railways, public utilities, and banks. They were learning the nuances of the Argentine environment. They were learning, likewise, how to conduct business enterprises in a community with an unfamiliar book of rules or no rules at all; where there was no gold standard, no predictable credit policies, a capricious political order, and a jealous and xenophobic public temper.

Just as the game was getting well under way, the principal players were suddenly changed. Shortly before the Brazilian blockade was proclaimed, Rivadavia appeared once more in Buenos Aires, and in February 1826 the National Congress decided to establish a National Executive in the place of the Government of Buenos Aires, which had hitherto conducted the affairs of the Republic. On 7 February Rivadavia was elected President of the United Provinces by the vote of thirty-five of the thirty-nine members of the Congress. He proceeded at once to construct a new Government which was to serve at the same time as a party machine for the implementation of his favourite political theories concerning centralized government and administration. García dropped out. 'I hardly know how the Government can long go on without him', Parish told Canning.[1] In fact, it could, but not in the right direction. Rivadavia had chosen as his Minister of Government, Agüero, the wildest of the war party, and García refused under any circumstances to serve in a Cabinet in which Agüero was a member. At the same time Rivadavia had installed in office as Minister of Finance Dr. José Carril, the principal advocate of centralized government from the interior provinces. It was thus made apparent that Rivadavia intended two objectives, the wisdom of which García seriously doubted: war *à outrance* against Brazil and the establishment of a unitary constitution.

While these changes were in progress, Canning decided to appoint a Minister in Buenos Aires to take over the work Parish had been doing. Shortly after this, Rivadavia decided to remove

---

[1] F.O. 6/11, Parish to Canning, 12 Feb. 1826.

the Argentine Minister in London, Sarratea, because he had discovered by accident some of Sarratea's criticisms of himself.[1] At the same time, the new Minister of War, Alvear, decided to take the field as Commander-in-Chief in the Banda Oriental. Thus, towards the end of the first act, we are presented with new dramatis personae to whose presence we are now obliged to adjust ourselves. Only the far-away Emperor of Brazil, Don Pedro, retained an aspect of permanence, and even he changed his generals and admirals with the ease of a boy playing with plastic soldiers.

Canning's choice as the first British Minister to the United Provinces of the Río de la Plata was John Ponsonby, Viscount Ponsonby in the peerage of Ireland. Ponsonby was accounted the handsomest man in the three kingdoms, and he had attracted the attention of Lady Conyngham, the favourite of George IV. Having encountered vast difficulties with His Majesty over the recognition of Argentina, Canning decided to show that Buenos Aires had a use which his Royal Master could appreciate.[2] He appointed Ponsonby to Buenos Aires. Ponsonby hated the scene of his exile. 'It is the vilest place I ever saw', he told the Under Secretary at the Foreign Office, 'and I certainly should hang myself if I could find a tree tall enough to swing on. . . . It is a beastly place.'[3] He complained about the 'republican conceit', which he thought was about as bad in Buenos Aires as in Washington. Rivadavia he considered to be 'a man of whom I can say nothing good',[4] and, although he admitted that he had a few acceptable ideas about policy and economics, Rivadavia deserved nothing 'beyond the praise that might be due to the bustling Mayor of a small town'. Rivadavia's successor, Dorrego, Ponsonby invariably described, on no evidence at all, as corrupt and unpatriotic.

If Ponsonby hated Buenos Aires and its leading political figures, he loved politics. There is little evidence that he pined

---

[1] F.O. 6/11, Parish to Canning, 20 July 1826.

[2] In the Hatfield House manuscripts there is a record made by Lady Salisbury in April 1838 of the Duke of Wellington's belief that George IV's jealousy of Ponsonby prompted His Majesty to approach Canning to find a foreign employment for his rival, and that this influenced the recognition of the succession states of the Spanish Empire.

[3] F.O. 6/13, Ponsonby to Howard de Walden, 4 Dec. 1826.

[4] F.O. 6/18, Ponsonby to Canning, 20 July 1827.

for Lady Conyngham or anyone else. His voluminous and badly organized dispatches breathe through their tumbled and official prose the spirit of a man who found a robust pleasure in politics; who was completely confident of his own powers in the presence of the most difficult and slippery characters with whom foreign sovereigns might care to confront him. He complained that he was seldom given instructions, but in a tone which suggested that he would not have noticed them much if he had received them. Ponsonby had a clear vision of British policy, and he was attentive to immediate necessities. He never thought of using force to solve difficulties, but he was prepared to do anything else. Endowed with a strong imagination, he invented characters and situations to suit the purposes of the moment. At one stage, when he considered it desirable to frighten the Emperor of Brazil out of his wits and into a course of action Ponsonby thought good, he invented a revolutionary plot, which, according to the British Minister in Rio de Janeiro, was 'without one single proof of . . . veracity'.[1] This troubled Ponsonby not at all. He told his colleague in Rio that the cause of peace and British interests would be well served if he terrified the Perpetual Defender of Brazil as he deserved to be.[2]

So long as the British diplomatic agent in Buenos Aires had to deal with García, he was working with a man who genuinely considered the war with Brazil a disaster. Once Rivadavia became President and had installed his factotum, General Cruz, at the Foreign Office, Parish and then Ponsonby were dealing with a man who considered the war an opportunity not only to win glory and reputation at the expense of Brazil but also as means of baffling and defeating the internal opponents to his scheme of centralized government. Rivadavia appears to have believed that by giving the war party their head he could create the public enthusiasm and, at the same time, the military instrument with which he would be able to deal with the partisans of a federal constitution such as General Bustos of Córdoba. In this Rivadavia made the final mistake of his life. The enthusiasts for the war were chiefly the landowning

---

[1] F.O. 13/47, Gordon to the Foreign Office, separate and confidential, 17 Mar. 1828.

[2] Suggested in F.O. 6/18, Ponsonby to Canning, 20 July 1827, and F.O. 6/22, Ponsonby to Dudley and Ward, 13 May 1828.

class and their gaucho dependants. They suffered least and benefited most by the war. So did the small producers of the interior provinces, who found in the Brazilian blockade the protection from competition which the revolution had destroyed. The groups which suffered most from the war were precisely those 'respectable classes', as Parish described them, who were the best support for a unified liberal state.

Rivadavia had liberal objectives and he had designed beneficial legislation about which Parish, Canning, and Ponsonby could enthuse, but he resembled closely those politicians and philosophers whose love of humanity in general absolves them from all care or consideration for men in particular. Rivadavia was incapable of loyalty, honesty, or even good manners in his relations with the men immediately about him and with whom he was obliged to conduct the business of the community. He envied and hated men more conspicuous or successful than himself. There was nothing too malign for him to say about San Martín or Bolívar. Insensitive to the point of stupidity, he seems to have been incapable of grasping not only the inhumanity but the folly of attempting to drive from public life men as able and disinterested as García or as well loved as Dorrego. There is no evidence that anybody liked Rivadavia or trusted him, and that, perhaps, sums up his tragedy and explains the failure of his ideals.

When Parish first encountered him in his presidential office, he found Rivadavia disposed to 'extreme formality . . . so strikingly different from the frank, and cordial manner, which had given me so much satisfaction on all former public occasions in this Country'.[1] From his icy eminence Rivadavia assured Parish of his 'attachment to all that was English'. It soon became evident, however, that Rivadavia had not utterly banished from his mind the hope that Britain could be converted into an ally against Brazil. In April 1826 Parish had an interview with Rivadavia (General Cruz, the Foreign Minister, seems to have had only a limited capacity for attending to serious business) for the purpose of discussing with him Canning's note to Baron de Etabayana informing the Brazilian Government of the desire of Buenos Aires to negotiate a settlement. Rivadavia at once seized the opportunity to suggest that

[1] F.O. 6/11, Parish to Canning, 12 Feb. 1826.

Britain could best avoid the fresh calamity of a renewed revolutionary war carried into the heart of Brazil by putting pressure on the Emperor of Brazil to settle at once and in favour of Buenos Aires. He did not scruple to depict Bolívar as a supreme villain and at the same time as the author of the action which would finally bring down the enemy of Argentina. He insinuated that Britain was the real ruler of Brazil and that the British Minister in Rio de Janeiro had 'a particular influence over the Councils of His Imperial Majesty which no other Government could urge with the same justice and force'.[1] When Parish informed Rivadavia that the British Government had received the most positive assurances from Bolívar that Colombia would not attack Brazil, he did not accept this statement as a fundamental defect in his prognostication of a calamity for Brazil but as an excuse to give expression to his hatred and jealousy of Bolívar.

During the winter of 1826 diplomatic activity concerning the war all but ceased in Buenos Aires. Ponsonby had been appointed early in the year, and once Parish had notified the Government that Ponsonby was about to take over, his status became that of an observer. Ponsonby himself was ordered to stop in Rio de Janeiro on his way out to Buenos Aires in order to see what he might achieve by direct contact with the Imperial Government. His instructions made no mistake about the anxiety Britain felt for a quick termination of hostilities. Canning wanted Ponsonby to make it abundantly plain to the Emperor that continued disorder among the new states of America was an invitation to foreign intervention and that war might very well lead to revolution in Brazil. Canning mentioned no names when he spoke of intervention, but the comments and asides of the Foreign Office at this time suggest that France and the United States were never far from their minds. In his discussions with the Court of Brazil Ponsonby refused to discuss the rights or wrongs of the Brazilian position in the Banda Oriental. He urged the Brazilian Foreign Minister, the Visconde de Inhambupé, and Don Pedro himself to concentrate upon what was expedient and most likely to bring peace and stability. Inhambupé was inclined to sympathy with the

---

[1] F.O. 6/11, Parish to Canning, 21 Apr. 1826. This dispatch, illustrative of Rivadavia's technique, is printed in Webster, *Independence of Latin America*, i, pp. 144–7.

expedient, and though he naturally never repudiated the objectives of his royal master as expressed in Admiral Lobos's note to the Argentine Government, Inhambupé suggested that the serious objective of Brazil was to prevent the Argentine Government from exercising exclusive control of the Plata–Paraná river system. According to Ponsonby's information, the entire Imperial Council was favourable to negotiation on the basis of compromise, but that 'the Emperor alone rejected [negotiation] declaring with great violence, that he was resolved never to yield anything'.[1]

The proposals made by the Brazilian Government amounted to nothing more than an acknowledgement by Buenos Aires of the Imperial possession of the Banda Oriental, in return for which Montevideo would be declared a free port open to the ships of all nations, including Argentina, and a port of shelter available to Argentine ships without payment of duties. Ponsonby declared the Brazilian proposals to be futile, and he candidly told Inhambupé that the Emperor 'demands everything and offers nothing in return',[2] and that the proposals were an insult to the Government of Buenos Aires and to the King of Great Britain, whose mediation had been sought. Don Pedro, however, declared that he had nothing new to propose. If the Emperor could be obstinate in his ivory tower of monarchical rectitude, Ponsonby could also speak with the candour of an English aristocrat accustomed to look kings squarely in the face. He urged the Brazilian Foreign Minister to 'consider that credit was gone. No more loans—that he knew the state of his bank and the *disposition* of the Chamber of Deputies.'[3] Finally he told the Brazilian Government that 'I am further commanded not to disguise that the wishes of the British Government, while scrupulously neutral in conduct, cannot fail to be in favour of that Belligerent who shall have shewn the readiest disposition to bring the dispute to a friendly termination.'[4] He closed his last letter to the Visconde de Inhambupé

[1] F.O. 6/12, Ponsonby to Canning, 13 June 1826.
[2] F.O. 6/12, Ponsonby to Inhambupé, 11 Aug. 1826.
[3] F.O. 6/12, Ponsonby to Canning, 11 Aug. 1826. Webster has neglected to print this part of Ponsonby's dispatch, just as he has omitted Ponsonby's threat to exercise the rights of neutrality in a way favourable to Buenos Aires. See Webster, *Independence of Latin America*, i, pp. 312–14.
[4] F.O. 6/12, Ponsonby to Inhambupé, 11 Aug. 1826.

with these words: 'It is with infinite regret that I finally abandon all hope of a successful termination of the business committed to my care by His Majesty the King.'

Dark and threatening as the atmosphere in Rio de Janeiro seemed when Ponsonby departed for Buenos Aires, there were, none the less, a few patches of light to be discerned. At the ministerial, as distinct from the imperial, level of politics there existed a determination which was in accordance with one point in Canning's instructions to Ponsonby, namely, to secure for Brazil the free navigation of the Plata–Paraná river system. Canning was prepared to go so far as to offer a British guarantee of free navigation of these rivers. 'Every precaution', Canning wrote, 'should be taken by precise stipulations in the Treaty of an arrangement to secure to Brazil uninterrupted enjoyment of the navigation of the River Plate. His Majesty would, if required, not refuse to lend his guarantee for the observance of such stipulation.'[1] On the other hand, it should be added, this was as far as Canning was prepared to go in involving Britain in the affairs of the River Plate. Ponsonby was firmly warned not to give any British guarantee concerning territorial arrangements.

While Ponsonby was laying about him in Rio, Parish was endeavouring to prepare the way for the new Minister in Buenos Aires. This was rocky enough. General Cruz summoned him to inquire what was going on. Parish said he had no news himself. He warned Cruz to expect little softening in the Emperor's attitude, and he hinted that Rivadavia and his Minister ought to consider the independence of the Banda Oriental as a practical compromise. Cruz burst out 'that his Government will never listen to any arrangement which should tend to separate the Banda Oriental from the rest of the Provinces in any manner whatever'.[2]

While this mid-winter stillness prevailed in the sphere of diplomacy and while the armies across the Uruguay did nothing, there was only too much domestic political activity in Buenos Aires, and all of it bad. Once he was installed in power, Rivadavia set about the business of destroying the centres of provincial power which were obstacles to his plans for a centralized

---

[1] F.O. 6/12, Canning to Ponsonby, 18 Mar. 1826.
[2] F.O. 6/11, Parish to Canning, 3 Aug. 1826.

Government. The National Congress, whose express purpose in meeting was to devise a constitution and which had already passed beyond its terms of reference in setting up a National Executive, now prepared a law suppressing the Provincial Government and Assembly of Buenos Aires, separating Buenos Aires city from the surrounding countryside and declaring the city and its administration a national entity. Thus, by one startling and sudden breach of faith, Rivadavia sought to destroy the strongest of all the provincial governments and to turn out of office men who had successfully conducted the affairs of the whole nation for several years. 'General Las Heras (the Governor)', Parish reported, 'has been treated by Mr. Rivadavia with the most marked disrespect, deprived of the Command of his Troops, turned out of his Residence, and personally annoyed by every possible petty vexation.'[1] With great forbearance General Las Heras refused to speak out. He retired to Chile and thence to Europe. But his supporters—and they constituted the strongest interest in the country outside the city of Buenos Aires—remained. If they were obliged for the moment to be silent, this was not the case with the partisans of federalism in the interior. General Bustos called his Junta together and this body declared that Córdoba refused to recognize the law of the National Congress which had established the National Executive and had permitted the election of Rivadavia to the presidency. Parish's sympathies were entirely opposed to Bustos, whom he regarded, and rightly so, as an enemy of liberal policies, but he was candid enough to report to Canning that

unluckily for this question M. de Rivadavia's personal Conduct since he has been appointed President, has had a tendency to bring odium, and I may almost add Ridicule upon anything like a Supreme Authority . . . his abrupt dissolution of the late Government of Buenos Ayres . . . has prematurely alarmed the other Provinces for their own fate, and brought the question of Federalism or No-Federalism, under their consideration at a moment, and in a manner which may make it very difficult for the Government to carry their Plans into effect.[2]

Imprisoned within the wall [of his own ego and animated by his vision of a new state organized on rational principles,

[1] Ibid., 14 Mar. 1826.   [2] Ibid., 20 June 1826.

Rivadavia pressed on, regardless of the gathering storm. In July the Committee on the Constitution reported to the National Congress, rejecting completely the principles of federalism. The Committee demonstrated with an abundance of detail how the poverty and sparse population of most provinces made them incapable of supporting a government and exposed the people to the arbitrary authority of the strongest landowner or soldier or bandit in the area. 'The ultimate end of every political Society is happiness', the report concluded. 'Men cannot be happy without being virtuous, and they cannot be virtuous without possessing the liberty of exercising all those rights which enable them to fulfil their duties.'[1] The presupposition was that Rivadavia's centralized Government would make the gauchos free, and freedom would make the Argentine people virtuous; a provincial government run by General Bustos or Facundo Quiroga would do the contrary. The Congress accepted the Report by a vote of fifty-four to forty-four.

The Constitution which was devised in response to this report did not make so many concessions to freedom as the generalities of Rivadavia might have prompted one to expect. Article 6 gave the vote to everyone except women, unmarried men under twenty, illiterates (but the literacy qualification was suspended for fifteen years), bankrupts, insane persons, private soldiers, day labourers, servants working for wages, notorious vagabonds, and persons accused of crime. In the light of this clause a gaucho could be excused for preferring to rely for his position in society upon a knife which he knew how to use than upon a vote which he could not cast. Deputies were obliged to possess a capital of $4,000 and Senators of $10,000. Both the Senators and the President were to be indirectly elected for periods of nine years. In fact, these provisions were hardly matters of practical controversy. The really serious objection to the Constitution of 1826 which affected the men who actually had some authority in the provinces and country districts was Chapter 3, articles 140–59, concerning provincial administration. Rivadavia's solution of the federal question, set forth in these articles, consisted of a plan by which the central authority

---

[1] *Informe de la comisión de negocios constitucionales sobre la forma de gobierno que ha de servir de base a la constitución*, enclosed with Parish to Canning, 20 July 1826, in F.O. 6/11.

would have the continuous right of interfering in provincial affairs and of influencing the creation and staffing of the provincial agencies of government. It does not require much imagination to know how dismally the authors of the American Constitution would have failed had they proposed to endow the President and Congress of the United States with the power to select the State Governors and to transform the State Legislatures into appointed bodies. This is, however, what Rivadavia's partisans attempted to do in 1826 in the Argentine Republic.

Rivadavia may have proposed but society in more places than the Province of Córdoba was indisposed to accept his policies. In the Banda Oriental dissension began to develop in the winter of 1826 between the Argentine commander-in-chief and Lavalleja, the revolutionary leader who had lately assumed the office of Governor of the Banda Oriental. Lavalleja desired to keep his troops separate from the Argentine Army and under his sole command. In July an envoy was dispatched from Buenos Aires to attempt a reconciliation, and this was temporarily brought about, largely, according to Parish's intelligence, because Lavalleja's men were short of supplies and were deserting his forces for the better supplied army of Rodríguez.[1]

The same determination to maintain local independence and the power of local military chieftains and landowners (who were frequently interchangeable characters, the officers of the armies being *estancieros* and the *estancieros* officers) was as much at work beyond the Uruguay as it was at the foot of the Andes. One of the purposes of replacing Rodríquez by Alvear was the strengthening of the Buenos Airean hold over the Oriental forces by transforming them into a body disciplined and equipped along European lines. One of Ponsonby's agents in the Banda Oriental, a British merchant who lived with the army encamped at the Arroyo Grande, described how deeply the antagonism between Alvear and Lavalleja had penetrated all ranks.

> Great Repugnance on the part of the Orientales to the Numbering and other Measures of Organization and discipline adopted by Alviar [prevails]; there has been some disgust occasioned by the superseding of Orientales officers of old standing to put Porteño Officers in their Stead. Desertions have taken place . . . and some

[1] F.O. 6/11, Parish to Canning, 20 July 1826.

have been punished with Death. The exterior Appearance of the
Army is favorable. . . . It is the Opinion, however, that they would
fight better, were they under the Command of a Chief accustomed
to their Habits, and without the Inconvenience of much military
Parade. There has also been a Change in the Manner of supplying
them with Necessaries since Alviar has taken the Command. Formerly their half Indian Girls were allowed them, a small Quantity
of Soap, Tobacco, Yerva [Paraguayan tea], and a few Rials given
them at the Close of the Month to gamble with; this is all they need
besides their Ration of Beef. Their dress equally simple and un-
expensive, a full large Cloth Poncho their Clothing by day and their
Covering by Night; the Recado, their Saddle and Bed, and this
with a spare Shirt and Cotton Trousers or drawers of the Fashion of
the Country all the Luggage they had need to cumber their Horses
with. Portmanteaus have been introduced and more trappings, the
Comforts described above have been curtailed, and a larger Allowance of Pay substituted, but this in Paper, and often diminished by
Sets Off and deductions which the men cannot understand.[1]

It may be said on Alvear's behalf that he realized the necessity of a well-equipped and well-disciplined army if ever the
forces in the Banda Oriental were to take the strong places of
Montevideo and Colonia. Auchmuty had demonstrated that
Montevideo could be taken, but those acquainted with this feat
know that it was performed by British regiments of the line so
finely trained that they could advance steadily under heavy
fire from cover, scale walls under fire, and penetrate breaches
opened by heavy artillery. Alvear was aiming not only at a
control of the Oriental forces by Buenos Aires but at the construction of an army like the British Army which could take
Montevideo. But he encountered a state of society and of
human character formed in that society which set limits to
what he or any governor could do. Montevideo changed hands
but it was never taken in this war or in any of the many contests
which followed. Like Troy, Montevideo was long besieged, and
like Troy it fell through an operation upon the spirits and souls
of its defenders by attackers incapable of the social organization
and discipline required for a main assault.

Lord Ponsonby arrived in Buenos Aires on 16 September.
Rivadavia was quick to see the political capital which could be
made out of the appointment of so distinguished a personage as

[1] F.O. 6/13, enclosure with a private letter of Ponsonby to Canning, 27 Nov. 1826.

a British peer drawn from Court circles as the first British Minister to the Republic. He sent Ponsonby a message appointing the 19th as the day for his official reception, and he expressed the desire that this should be public and that Ponsonby should 'say a few words' when he delivered his letter of credence. Ponsonby agreed to this.

On the day appointed the President's coach drawn by six horses and attended by other carriages was sent to Ponsonby's residence. Accompanied by the General commanding the artillery, the Under Secretary of State, and Woodbine Parish, he was conducted to the Fort where he was received by a guard of honour and a salute by the artillery. Ponsonby was satisfied with the propriety of these proceedings, but he was not deceived into committing himself to anything. His speech was short and cautious, and he limited himself to the promise that he would strive 'to maintain and promote the amicable relations which so happily exist between the King my Master and this Republick'. In his reply, Rivadavia hinted at the tactic which he was pursuing, for he chose to call special attention to the recognition accorded to Argentina by Great Britain when the other European powers had 'maintained a close Reserve upon that Point', and expatiated upon the particular place which the people of the Republic held in their hearts for His Majesty, King George IV.

The next day Ponsonby came to grips with Rivadavia. Like Canning and Parish, he soon discovered Rivadavia to be as full of tricks as a bazaar dealer, determined to draw Britain into supporting the claims of Buenos Aires and convinced that by some slip on Ponsonby's part this might be achieved. In the opening interview Ponsonby presented Rivadavia with the Brazilian proposals. Rivadavia read them through attentively, and declared that they were not worth discussing. Ponsonby made no comment and asked to be excused.

It was characteristic of Ponsonby to have his own vision of a solution, to ignore everyone who might stand in his way, and to cultivate all those who could contribute to his endeavours. As soon as he had left Rivadavia he called into consultation Parish and García. He excused himself for this course on the grounds that García had been lately nominated Argentine Minister in London in the place of Sarratea, and that, therefore, he was a right and proper person to consult. García had the added advantage of being a man who agreed with Ponsonby that peace was an immediate necessity and could most likely be established by consulting the realities in the Banda Oriental and not the aspirations in the heart of Señor Agüero or the Emperor of Brazil. García encouraged Ponsonby to believe that Rivadavia's views were changing, and that a compromise based on the independence of the Banda Oriental had some chance of acceptance. Ponsonby promptly declared that he would put this to Rivadavia.

At the next interview Ponsonby unveiled his proposals. To them he appended 'a hint that it might not be impossible to obtain from His Majesty's Government . . . his Guarantee of the Free Navigation of the River Plate . . .'.[1] To hint at more than one was immediately prepared to do to a man as sharp as Rivadavia was always a mistake. He at once seized on Ponsonby's suggestion and began to extend it in accordance with his favourite notion that Britain should underwrite every enterprise of the Argentine Government. 'It is absolutely necessary', he argued, 'to have whatever treaty might be founded upon the Basis mentioned . . . [and] guaranteed in all its provisions by Great Britain.' Ponsonby promptly jumped on the lid of Pandora's box. 'I told him', he reported to Canning, 'that Great Britain would never consent to any such Guarantee, and that in telling him this, I spoke with a perfect knowledge of the fact, and that I could not consent to propose it to my Government.'

Rivadavia became stubborn. He told Ponsonby flatly that he would do nothing unless Britain guaranteed the territorial independence of the entire Banda Oriental from Brazil. Ponsonby was as little disposed to mince words with a president of a republic as with the emperor of a vast domain. He stood up with the draft of his proposed settlement in his hand. 'It is useless, he said, 'to talk any more . . . it only remains for me to throw [this] Paper into the Fire and repeat to my Government the failure of my efforts to produce any advancement towards peace.'

Rivadavia now began to retreat. He begged Ponsonby not to terminate the discussion, and he asked him to send him a copy of his proposals through the Minister of Foreign Affairs.

[1] F.O. 6/13, Ponsonby to Canning, 2 Oct. 1826.

Ponsonby agreed to do this, but, he told Canning, he thought the purpose of this might 'be to entrap me into giving an official and public Character to a communication which was entirely confidential'. In spite of his fears, he sent Rivadavia the proposals, making plain, however, that they were private, and that 'it was for His Government to originate their own measures officially'.

It is easy to see why men obliged to do business with Rivadavia, no matter what their race or nationality, came to hate him heartily. He invariably seized on any gesture of amiability or compliance in order to baffle or entrap a man for his own purposes. In this case he privately told Ponsonby that he would not act on Ponsonby's proposals unless he could lay them before the Congress and, thus, gain support. Quite rightly, Ponsonby could think of no course of action more likely to encourage the war party and to enrage the Emperor of Brazil. Simultaneously with his request to lay a private communication before the Congress, Rivadavia invited Ponsonby to dine publicly with him; and this at a moment when news of Ponsonby's initiative was leaking out to all the leading political figures.

It began to look as if Rivadavia was going to succeed in making a fool of Ponsonby within a fortnight. Ponsonby, however, turned on him. He refused to dine with Rivadavia publicly or privately, and he addressed a note to the Foreign Minister making plain the fact that Britain was not going to the support of anyone, any party, or any nation in South America.

England [Ponsonby declared in his Note] is not likely to take upon herself such a charge, and respects too highly the Independency of the Republick to give a pretext for the accusation of attempting to establish any other influence in her councils, but that which Great Britain may deserve from a disinterested friendship. It is an error of the first magnitude to suppose that England has some predominant Interest in the settlement of the Affairs of this Country, which could induce the British Government to depart from its known policy so far as to give ground for a supposition that it could consent to guarantee any territorial arrangement in South America. . . . England is the friend of the Republic of Río de la Plata, and of the Empire of Brazil, and desires the restoration of Peace between them for their own joint Advantage. England places her interest (and justly) in their common prosperity.[1]

[1] F.O. 6/13, Ponsonby to Cruz, 9 Oct. 1826.

Rivadavia now seems to have begun to realize that the policies of a great state cannot be influenced by petty tricks. He sent García to apologize to Ponsonby, asking that 'the whole affair might be considered as not having occurred'.[1] Ponsonby then accepted the President's invitation to dinner on the understanding that he would not be obliged in any circumstance to make a speech. Rivadavia accepted these conditions, and Ponsonby found himself once more in a position to mediate from a position of neutrality.

Once these preliminary excitements were over, Ponsonby surveyed the situation for Canning. His observation revealed nothing essentially new. He repeated the familiar view that Rivadavia had 'contributed much to give a useful direction to [the] new energies' of Buenos Aires, and that he was 'the author of many sound and beneficial internal laws and regulations' but that his immediate policies were thoroughly bad. Ponsonby believed that financial weakness—which he attributed in part to Rivadavia's preference for Hullett and Company instead of Baring Brothers—and a wrong emphasis upon land operations made it impossible for Buenos Aires to break the stalemate. According to Ponsonby, the Government was relying entirely upon one tactic: 'to march the Army into the Province of Rio Grande, to raise the people against the Emperor and to set the Blacks free.' When, later, Ponsonby discussed the state of affairs with the leader of the war party, Agüero, he found this enthusiast relying almost entirely upon the larger hope that all the Spanish states would combine to attack Brazil in a renewed outburst of revolution.

Like Parish, Ponsonby felt the greatest enthusiasm about the commercial possibilities of Argentina, and he used this argument to strengthen his advocacy of his policy of a British guarantee of free navigation. 'The Settler', he enthused, 'finds here an abundance of Horses and Cattle, a rich soil, and a constant and easy communication with England: Religion not only tolerated but respected; and persons and property as well protected as the persons and property of the native inhabitants, and a prospect, almost a certainty, that by industry and skill a considerable fortune may be rapidly accumulated.'[2] Ponsonby went on from this to envisage the Río de la Plata swarming with

[1] F.O. 6/13, Ponsonby to Canning, 20 Oct. 1826.   [2] Ibid.

busy Britishers making their fortunes and in the process developing a demand 'which can only be supplied and gratified by English productions'. 'But', Ponsonby concluded, 'every advantage existing now, or to be hoped for in the future, depends upon the security of the freedom of navigation of the Plate.'

At the end of October Rivadavia agreed to invite the British Government to attempt a peace settlement and he also agreed, reluctantly, not to seek more than a British guarantee of free navigation. Privately García hinted that Rivadavia was not in earnest, but, in spite of Ponsonby's belief that opinion was veering towards peace, Rivadavia refused to put anything concerning the independence of the Banda Oriental in writing. In fact, Rivadavia and his Ministers were still hoping for the complete defeat of Brazil. Alvear was full of enthusiasm about the land operations and, in spite of financial difficulties and inflation in Buenos Aires, the Government was able to find £200,000 in London for expenditure on the Navy.[1] In Downing Street the Cabinet was contributing to the hopes in the Fort at Buenos Aires, for in November they agreed to permit Captain Ramsey, a half-pay officer, to take service in the Argentine Navy as an organizer and purchaser of equipment.[2]

In January and February the Argentine and Oriental forces won the series of victories on land and at sea which culminated in the defeat of the Imperial forces at Ituzaingo. The consequence of this was a growth of internal political tension in Buenos Aires between the Government and its opponents, for it was becoming apparent to all that the unresolved conflict over the constitution could not be far off. Ponsonby dispatched an urgent message to Admiral Sir Robert Otway 'in order that he may use his discretion respecting the protection it may be adviseable to give the British Interests here, and perhaps to the persons of His Majesty's Subjects'.[3]

Simultaneously, he pressed the Government to consider seeking peace, and urged Gordon in Rio de Janeiro to do all he could to have the Emperor accept the principle of independence

[1] Ibid., 4 Dec. 1826.
[2] F.O. 6/13, Captain Ramsey to Ponsonby, 22 Nov. 1826.
[3] F.O. 6/17, Ponsonby to Canning, 9 Mar. 1827.

for the Banda Oriental. On the 10th, 12th, and 14th of April Ponsonby had a series of interviews with General Cruz, the Foreign Minister, at which he showed him some of Canning's dispatches wherein Canning had predicted that Brazil would ultimately accept the independence of the Banda. He likewise assured Cruz that the British Minister in Rio could guarantee an honourable reception for the Argentine envoy. Cruz then put to Ponsonby a declaration of three points of which the last was critical: namely,

> That . . . the Government of the Republic animated always by the same Policy would not object [*distaria*] to send a Minister to the Court of Rio de Janeiro to treat of Peace upon the Basis of Independency of the Banda Oriental, provided they could hear from Lord Ponsonby enough to assure them, that such a Minister would be properly received by His Imperial Majesty The Emperor of Brazil, to treat upon the Basis above referred to.[1]

In the final interview, Ponsonby gave the assurance required. A British man-of-war was summoned to carry García to Rio to negotiate.

Something went wrong. Ponsonby preferred to think that Gordon at Rio had not done enough to impress upon the Emperor the necessity of climbing off his high horse.[2] It is possible to believe, however, that Ponsonby had given Cruz an assurance about the willingness of the Emperor to negotiate on the basis of the independence of the Banda Oriental which sprang more from his own hopes than from anything the Emperor had said. When García arrived in Rio de Janeiro, he discovered that the Emperor was willing to make peace and to raise the blockade, but that he was not willing to grant independence to the Banda Oriental. García seems to have had an appreciation of every political reality except passion. Peace, he believed, was the greatest necessity of Buenos Aires. Let the Emperor of Brazil accept the responsibility of settling with the revolutionary forces beyond the Uruguay, he reasoned, while Buenos Aires grows strong through trade, development, and peace.[3] Arguing with himself in this way, García concluded a draft peace Treaty which acknowledged the Emperor's sove-

---

[1] F.O. 6/17, Memorandum enclosed with Ponsonby to Canning, 21 Apr. 1827.
[2] F.O. 6/18, Ponsonby to Canning, 20 July 1827.
[3] Ibid., from García's published defence of his conduct.

reignty in the Banda Oriental and which committed both parties to seek a British guarantee of free navigation. He signed
this on 24 May 1827 and returned to Buenos Aires.

While the ship bearing García home was still at sea, there
arrived in Buenos Aires news which meant either civil war or
the end of Rivadavia's rule. By a decree of 5 April 1827 the
Junta of San Juan repudiated the presidential authority, and
one by one nine other provincial juntas issued similar decrees.
When García came ashore on 20 June 1827 Rivadavia was at
his last gasp politically, but he was not dead. He saw in García's
Treaty one last hope of saving himself by appealing to patriotic
passion and by presenting himself as a saviour.

Privately, Ponsonby was dismayed by García's handiwork,
for it left him standing in a very unlovely posture exposed to the
justifiable charge that he had misrepresented the mind of the
Emperor of Brazil. Before Rivadavia, however, he was prepared
to fight for the Treaty's acceptance. He at once waited on the
Foreign Minister and put to him a straight question, which was
the only question: 'Do [you] to the best of [your] knowledge,
believe that the Republick ha[s] the means of continuing the
War, without risking to the greatest Degree, bringing upon
itself the most serious Evils, if not ruin?'[1] General Cruz refused
an answer. Instead, he asked Ponsonby for his opinion about
what to do. Ponsonby asked for time—even a few hours—to
think this over.

In fact Rivadavia had already decided upon his course of
action. Cruz blurted out that there was no point in waiting for
an opinion from Ponsonby because the President had already
decided to send a message to the Congress denouncing the
draft Treaty. Two hours later Ponsonby received an official
Note stating that Rivadavia intended to do this, and asking
him to attend upon the President for an interview the next day.
This discourtesy enraged Ponsonby. He sat down immediately
and wrote to Rivadavia saying that 'I thought it might be
better to save His Excellency the trouble of an Interview and
confine myself to simply informing him in writing that the
Rejection of the Preliminary Convention would put an end to
the British Mediation unless some reasonable or very plausible
ground could be found for its Continuation'.

[1] F.O. 6/18, Ponsonby to Canning, 15 July 1827.

Rivadavia was now beyond argument. The welfare of Señor Rivadavia and not Argentina was his main concern. On 25 June he sent the rejection of the Treaty to Congress. His chief spokesman in the Congress, Gomez, made a violent personal attack on García, who went in peril of his life. There were scenes of abandoned enthusiasm, and even in the secret session of the Committee set up to examine the President's message, the war hysteria (according to Ponsonby's intelligence) was so strong that any rational discussion of whether Argentina had the means to make further war was impossible. Placards printed in the Government Printing Office began to appear on the walls denouncing García and the English. One read: 'Buenos Ayres, and Banda Oriental! García has betrayed you! The English want to have a share in the spoil! If we do not open our Eyes, we shall have the times of Beresford back again!'[1]

Ponsonby began to fear an assault upon the British Legation. He sent for H.M.S. *Forte*, which was cruising in the estuary, and her captain 'with his characteristic Zeal and Energy moved the Frigate up the River'.

As the excitement mounted—a combination of newly born national pride and ancient Spanish xenophobia—Rivadavia made his last and fatal mistake. Thinking no doubt that he was now an indispensable hero, he sent a message to the Congress resigning his office as President. His friends began to press for the rejection of this resignation. Excitement or no excitement, the enemies of Rivadavia were not willing to forgo this opportunity. In a house of fifty members forty-eight voted to accept the resignation of Bernardino Rivadavia.

The rest of the winter until the last week of August 1827 was occupied in winding up the National Congress and ending the system of Rivadavia. Dr. López, an amiable and honest member of the Congress from the Province of Buenos Aires, was appointed provisional President by the Congress. He was charged with only two responsibilities: to direct for the time being the foreign and financial affairs of the Republic and to superintend the election of an Assembly for the Province of Buenos Aires. In that Province he made an appointment which presaged the new order about to be born. He raised General Juan Manuel Rosas, 'a man of very great activity and extreme

[1] F.O. 6/18, Ponsonby to Canning, 15 July 1827.

popularity amongst the class of gauchos',[1] to the command
of the provincial militia of Buenos Aires. Then he ordered the
elections.

In this contest the partisans of Rivadavia failed completely
—failed, Ponsonby believed, 'so as to destroy all hopes they
might have of future success'. When the Assembly met and
appointed a Junta, Colonel Manuel Dorrego was in turn appointed Governor and Captain-General of the Province of
Buenos Aires. Dr. López then resigned as the provisional
President of the Republic, and the National Congress by its
own resolution dissolved. Legally the United Provinces of the
Río de la Plata had ceased to exist, and Ponsonby was now the
Minister accredited to nothing.

The fall of Rivadavia had some immediate consequences for
British interests. The date for payment of charges on the Baring
Loan—the first to be paid out of the revenues of the Government—came and went without the annual payment of interest
being transmitted. A decree prohibiting the export of gold and
silver was issued, and a fresh complication was thus introduced
into the affairs of the British mercantile community. There
seemed no immediate prospect of peace and of the opening of
the river to trade. Ponsonby, however, was not idle. He put
himself in communication with López immediately upon his
installation in office, and protested in frank terms about the
anti-British sentiment which had been stimulated by the late
Government. Having regard for the opinion Ponsonby entertained concerning the economic importance of the Río de la
Plata, he pursued a very curious line of argument with the
provisional President. He listed the British interests in Buenos
Aires, and then 'I asked him, if he could believe the Government of the richest Country in the Universe could be influenced
in their counsels by such trifling pecuniary concerns, not so
great as many of the private merchants of England were in the
daily habit of transacting with disinterestedness and almost indifference'.[1]

The dissolution of the National Government left Ponsonby
in a difficult position. The Government to which he was accredited had ceased to exist and none had yet been authorized to
take its place. Ponsonby assumed that it was 'not the intention

[1] Ibid., 20 July 1827.

of His Majesty's Government that my Mission should be considered terminated.'[1] He waited on Dorrego in his private capacity, and Dorrego assured him that he intended to seek from the provincial authorities the power to act for them in foreign affairs. He warned Ponsonby that this might take time because it was his policy to do nothing without the full and willing support of the provincial governors. In fact he did not receive the required authority from a majority of the provinces until the end of the year, but Ponsonby took a practical view of matters and carried on without regard for protocol or legal niceties.

When Dorrego took office Ponsonby reported to the Foreign Office that the new Governor was a brave soldier who was said to be an honest man. Ponsonby considered that he was not very well informed about the larger world outside the Río de la Plata. On the other hand, Ponsonby had a high opinion of the honesty, knowledge, and intentions of Dr. Manuel Moreno, whom Dorrego had chosen as his Minister of Government and Foreign Affairs. Moreno was one of the few members of the Congress who had dissociated himself from the war hysteria set alight during Rivadavia's last hours. In his grasp of the realities of politics Moreno much resembled García, and his final objectives were not unlike his.

The advent of Dorrego led to a diminution of British influence on the course of events at a time when the difficulties of British interests were increasing in the manner we have already described. Ponsonby soon turned against Dorrego, convinced that the Governor intended to continue the war indefinitely. He abandoned his good opinion of Dorrego's honesty, and described him in his reports to the Foreign Office as corrupt and animated by speculative, personal interest in prolonging the war. When Moreno told Ponsonby that there were moves on foot at one stage to overthrow Dorrego and replace him by General Rosas, Ponsonby went to the length of saying that 'I am not authorized to put Dorrego on his guard. I shall see his fall, if it takes place, with pleasure.'[2] Ponsonby finally depicted Dorrego as the central figure in his fanciful plot to overthrow the Emperor of Brazil.

---

[1] F.O. 6/18, Ponsonby to Dudley and Ward, 27 Aug. 1827.
[2] F.O. 6/19, Ponsonby to Dudley and Ward, 27 Dec. 1827.

There is no simple explanation of Ponsonby's animus towards Dorrego. At the time of the Governor's death in 1829 Parish categorically contradicted the allegations of his corruption. Dorrego's Government finally moved in the direction which Ponsonby had always advocated. They made peace with Brazil. They recognized the independence of the Banda Oriental. They adopted a domestic policy which promised at least some prospect of internal peace. They even tried to stabilize the currency.

An inference from the narrative of events is that Ponsonby came to hate Dorrego because Dorrego and his Government ceased to rely seriously on British mediation and turned to Colombia as a means of finding the way to peace with Brazil. In September Ponsonby discussed a plan of mediation with the Government which much resembled García's abortive Treaty. Moreno did not like such a proposal and urged Ponsonby to accept the independence of the Banda Oriental as indispensable to any discussions. Ponsonby half-heartedly agreed to advance this proposal, in which he himself had always believed, but which he now considered that the Emperor of Brazil would never accept. Through October he was extremely discouraged and asserted that he was 'almost certain that if left to themselves, His Imperial Majesty and the Republick or rather Buenos Aires will never come to any understanding'.[1] At the same time the British merchants were becoming very anxious about the produce they had been accumulating for export. Ponsonby tacitly admitted his failure to influence events by consenting that they should petition the Emperor of Brazil to permit them to take cargoes through the blockade.

Through a secret source Parish discovered in December that Dorrego's Government had approached the Colombian Government to undertake the task of mediating between themselves and Brazil. Ponsonby sought to belittle the results of the Colombian mediation when he learned officially of its existence. The Emperor of Brazil was conceding nothing new. To Moreno Ponsonby addressed some searching inquiries. 'I have no reason to believe', he reported, 'that Dr. Moreno had the smallest intention of getting rid of the British interference in the affair of the Peace when he wrote to Señor Palacios'. But he was not

[1] Ibid., 15 Oct. 1827.

sure. 'I could clear up this point by desiring to see Dr. Moreno's letter to Señor Palacios, but I think it better to show no suspicion of a man who [sic] I intend to trust.'[1] Moreno was very tactful. He said that he had only wished to draw the Colombian Government into the negotiations in order to strengthen the peace forces. This was a good argument which Ponsonby did not seem properly to appreciate. The Colombian mediation was in fact a stroke of genius, for it deprived the war party in Buenos Aires of one of their main delusions—that Colombia would attack Brazil. It likewise served to allay one of the Emperor of Brazil's chief fears. Ponsonby, indeed, seems to have failed to understand that both he and the British Government had greatly weakened their position by the part they had played in the García mission and that, for the time being at least, they could serve the cause of peace best by not pushing too sharply forward.

From the moment of learning of the Colombian mediation Ponsonby began describing Dorrego as 'false to all his engagements, and principles, and intent only upon amassing a private fortune, at the expense of the country and its true policy'.[2] He hoped for Dorrego's fall. Dorrego did not fall, but Moreno did. There is some suspicion that he may have compromised himself by too close an attachment to Ponsonby and by too free a disclosure of the policies of the Government towards the Banda Oriental; for Ponsonby felt obliged to say that 'Moreno communicated . . . [with me] as a private individual, and as such I listened. I have not meddled with party matters and domestick politics'.[3]

In spite of Ponsonby's hostility to Dorrego and his preference for Moreno, Moreno's resignation opened the way for a renewal of positive activity as a mediator on the part of the British Minister. Early in January 1828 Balcarce, the new Foreign Minister, asked Ponsonby to undertake the negotiation of an armistice. The request showed how wrong Ponsonby was in his judgement of Dorrego, for at this moment there was much jubilation about the fresh victories over the Brazilians in the Banda Oriental and news that even the German mercenaries in the Brazilian army were deserting in substantial numbers. If Dorrego was bent on war there was never a better opportunity

---

[1] F.O. 6/19, Ponsonby to Dudley and Ward, 27 Dec. 1827.   [2] Ibid.   [3] Ibid.

for pursuing it. In fact, Dorrego proved himself very open to argument and eager for peace, if only he could find some means of making it palatable to public opinion and of disarming those in Rivadavia's party who were waiting to cry 'Traitor!' at anyone seeming to win less than a total victory. Dorrego appears to have believed that when Ponsonby spoke of an independent Banda Oriental he meant to leave Brazil in possession of Montevideo and Colonia. When Ponsonby explained that he meant a truly independent state, Dorrego came rapidly around and, indeed, took the initiative in suggesting a formula which would secure independence and at the same time save his own face. Ponsonby asked him the straight question: will you make peace on the basis of the belligerents' withdrawing and leaving the Banda Oriental free to choose its own course, either independence or union with either of the belligerents? Dorrego replied without equivocation, 'Yes'.[1]

Now that he was once more in the game and in a winning position, Ponsonby let himself go. This was the occasion when he invented his great plot against the Emperor of Brazil. Undoubtedly there had been, and probably still were, plots afoot to promote revolution in Brazil. Lavalleja was in communication with the Brazilian commander, General Lecor, concerning a proposal to join forces to form a new state consisting of the Banda Oriental and Rio Grande do Sul.[2] And there were other plots reported. Ponsonby's plot exceeded all these in the power of its central figures, and the scope of its objectives. Colonel Dorrego was one of the authors and architects. The mysterious and powerful Andrada brothers were at sea in privateers. An English house was drawing bills. Agents were purchasing arms in New York. German mercenaries were being seduced. A French captain of privateers was cruising off São Paolo. The Imperial family were to be overthrown. No less than five republics were to be proclaimed. Ponsonby put all this in code, and sent it to the Foreign Office and the British Minister in Rio de Janeiro.[3] The dispatch was hardly coded when Ponsonby found a new detail. The Marquis of Quebuz, a former Imperial Minister, was one of the conspirators. Finally, to give the whole

---

[1] F.O. 6/22, Ponsonby to Dudley and Ward, 28 Jan. 1828.
[2] F.O. 6/19, Ponsonby to Dudley and Ward, 15 Oct. 1827.
[3] F.O. 6/22, Ponsonby to Dudley and Ward, 12 Feb. 1828.

potion the right flavour, Ponsonby dispatched Admiral Sir Robert Otway to Rio to 'save the Emperor's life'.[1]

The value of this whole manœuvre depended upon its frightening the Emperor. Unfortunately, the plot had a damp fuse in the shape of the British Minister in Rio. Gordon did not believe a word Ponsonby had to say, and he intimated to the Emperor that he should not believe a word either. Happily for the cause of peace the Emperor was already sufficiently frightened, or at least rendered sufficiently anxious, by the state of his army in the Banda Oriental to make new proposals more likely to produce a serious negotiation. On 24 February 1828 Gordon transmitted to Ponsonby a brief summary of the Emperor's proposals which involved an independent Banda Oriental, the strong points of which should be delivered into the hands of the Oriental forces but not of the Argentine forces.

Ponsonby then played a trick on Dorrego, which fortunately worked. He took the summary of the proposals to Dorrego, but he kept from the Governor the detailed proposals. There was a serious difference between the summary and the proposals themselves; for the summary omitted or failed to amplify the second article, in which the Emperor 'promette do modo mais solemne crear, erigir, e constituir completamente a Provincia Cisplatina, ere huim Estado livre, separado e independente'. This article meant that the independence of the Banda Oriental would be granted by the Emperor and would not derive from the agreement of the powers—a very substantial difference, which left to the Emperor the power of decision and of negotiating with the revolutionary forces.

Ponsonby was quite candid about his reason for presenting Dorrego with the summary only. The Governor 'might have found ground for cavilling or delay'. As it was, Dorrego accepted the basis of negotiation represented to him.

At this stage Ponsonby received notice of his transfer from Buenos Aires to Rio de Janeiro. He had emerged as the most ardent and determined, if not always the wisest, advocate of peace, and peace was very much what the British Government wanted. The pressure of manufacturing and commercial interests in Great Britain for a quick settlement intensified sharply during the later part of 1827 and through the late winter and

[1] F.O. 6/22, Ponsonby to Dudley and Ward, 13 Feb. 1828.

spring of 1828. In January 1828 the Chamber of Commerce and Manufacturers of Glasgow presented a strongly worded memorial, and several London commercial houses wrote complainingly to the Foreign Secretary about the blockade.[1] In the presence of this growing impatience the Foreign Office began to move towards making good the threats which Ponsonby had uttered in Rio de Janeiro in August 1826. Gordon suggested a new basis for negotiation to the Emperor in January.[2] The Foreign Office instructed him to assist the merchants of Glasgow in their application to pass the Brazilian blockade with ships in ballast and to repass loaded with Argentine produce belonging to British merchants. At the same time the legality of the Brazilian blockade was referred to the King's Advocate. When he reported late in March 1828 Gordon was instructed to implement Ponsonby's threat. 'You will . . . acquaint them [the Brazilian Government]', he was ordered, 'with the firm determination of His Majesty no longer to endure that his own subjects should suffer by a restraint which is not equally imposed upon the commercial navigation of other countries . . . his Admiral will receive orders to protect the English trade.'[3] Finally, as if to underline the threat and to give it a lively voice, the Foreign Office replaced the soft and reverential Gordon by the man who had no hesitation in kicking a king or seducing his mistress.

While Ponsonby's servants were packing his valises and trunks in preparation for his departure to Rio, the Brazilian control of the situation was weakening visibly. The Brazilian Navy could not stop or catch the Argentine privateers. American ships were repeatedly passing the blockade. The British Navy was becoming increasingly active to stop the drift towards chaos in the Río de la Plata and along the coast of Brazil. H.M.S. *Forte* went to the aid of the brig *Anne* out of Liverpool when she was assailed by an Argentine privateer under the notorious Catalan commander, Pepe Onza. The *Forte* recovered the vessel and put the privateer's crew in irons. One of Ponsonby's last acts in Buenos Aires was to demand satisfaction for the 'misconduct of certain officers of the Republican marine', with the consequence that two commanders of privateers,

[1] F.O. 6/25.   [2] F.O. 13/47, Gordon to Dudley and Ward, 17 Jan. 1828.
[3] F.O. 13/46, Dudley and Ward to Gordon, 5 Apr. 1828.

Fournier and Costa, were dismissed from the service and Dorrego's Government promised to restrict the granting of letters of marque.

In May 1828 Dorrego greatly strengthened his hand by holding an election in the Province of Buenos Aires which he won handsomely. Any man in office could win an election; the encouraging and fortifying factor was the kind of support he received from men like García. Once the election was over, Dorrego agreed to send a mission to Rio de Janeiro. In his final interview with Ponsonby, the Governor agreed to an armistice and to negotiate a peace settlement on the basis of an independent Banda Oriental from which the forces of both belligerents would retire. On 8 August Ponsonby went aboard H.M.S. *Thetis* to depart, but before the ship cleared from the roadstead he sat down and wrote to Dorrego warning him that he wanted no tricks.

> Your Excellency no doubt knows [he wrote] that I have for a long time been acquainted with some of the more secret operations and designs of persons belonging to the Republick and to Brazil, and it will be enough that I mention to your Excellency the name of Bonifacio Credenda and that I know where he has been living more than a year past and where he now is.

This dark hint that Ponsonby knew all and would forgive nothing was introductory to the solemn and sensible argument which he had used two years earlier with the Emperor of Brazil. Continued revolution, disorder, and war would greatly increase the will and the opportunity for European powers to intervene in South America and, perhaps, re-establish a colonial control.

> Your Excellency cannot have any respect for the doctrine set up by some crude theorists 'that America ought to have a political existence separate from the political existence of Europe': Commerce and the common Interest of Individuals have formed ties between Europe and America which no Governments nor perhaps any power possessed by Man can now unloose, and whilst they exist Europe will have the right and certainly will not want the means, nor the will to interfere with the policy of America, at least so far as shall be necessary for the security of European Interests.[1]

Then, having sent this message ashore, he departed.

[1] F.O. 13/50, Ponsonby to Dorrego, 8 Aug. 1828.

VII

CIVIL WAR AND DICTATORSHIP

WITH the spring came peace between Argentina and Brazil, and to the Banda Oriental of Uruguay came independence. Peace, it had long been supposed by British diplomatists and merchants, would inaugurate an era of flourishing commerce, investment, and immigration. But this was not to be. Instead, there commenced a quarter of a century of commercial stagnation, debt repudiation, political tension, and blighted hopes. International peace in the River Plate brought civil war in Argentina.

In November 1828 the regular formations of the Argentine Army began to withdraw from the territory of the Oriental Republic of Uruguay in accordance with the preliminaries of the peace treaty being negotiated in Rio de Janeiro. Late in the month the principal regiments under the command of General Juan Lavalle had established themselves in and around the capital city. On 2 December Parish wrote in haste to the Earl of Aberdeen: 'I avail myself of a Merchant Vessel which sails this Evening, and which may reach England before the Packet, to acquaint your Lordship briefly with the Circumstances of a Revolutionary Movement which took place Yesterday in this City, and which has put an end to the Government of General Dorrego.'[1]

The overthrow of Dorrego was the bloodless work of a few hours. There followed upon it, within a matter of days, years of blood and bitterness, the traces of which still are visible in the life of the Argentine nation. The overthrow was planned by Rivadavia and his associates and carried into execution by General Lavalle, General La Madrid, General Paz, and Admiral Brown. A few days before the fatal event Dorrego told Parish that he was aware of the proposed attack upon his authority, but he and his ministers believed that a military rising was so out of keeping with the liberal principles professed

[1] F.O. 6/23, Parish to Aberdeen, 2 Dec. 1828.

by the 'friends of good order' that he and his colleagues refused to take seriously the threatened action against a Government constituted by a vote of a constituent assembly, subsequently supported by an election in the Province of Buenos Aires, and acknowledged by a majority of the provinces of the Republic.[1] A few hours before the rising Dorrego received information which cast doubt upon his trust in the principles of his political opponents. In his capacity as Captain-General of Buenos Aires he immediately sent a message to General Lavalle to wait upon him. Lavalle replied that he would obey this order at the head of his troops. Dorrego then ordered that the Fort, which was his official residence, be put in an attitude of defence. He found he had only 600 men at his disposal and very little food or ammunition. When morning broke on 1 December 1828, 2,500 regular troops were discovered in occupation of all the streets and squares leading to the seat of government. Governor Dorrego was unwilling to yield unreservedly, but, recognizing the impossibility of any resistance at the moment, he fled alone to the open country to a refuge among the rural militia, which was the only force he could still command. His ministers, General Balcarce and General Guido, surrendered to General Lavalle, and offered to transfer their authority to any body selected by the Provincial Assembly of Buenos Aires.

General Lavalle refused to recognize or deal with the Provincial Assembly. A proclamation was issued after breakfast, inviting 'the respectable inhabitants of the City to name a *provisional Government*'.[2] At one o'clock a group of citizens met in one of the churches under the supervision of Rivadavia's partisans and elected General Lavalle provisional Governor until a new Provincial Assembly was chosen to establish a 'regular' Government.

In charge again since Ponsonby's transfer to Rio de Janeiro. Parish's first reaction to these events was cautious but slightly favourable. 'We *may* perhaps have a more respectable Government and one which will enjoy more generally the Confidence of the better Classes of the People here than that of General Dorrego', he told Aberdeen, 'but', he added, 'the manner in which the change has been effected is lamented exceedingly by all well disposed and considerate persons.'[3] Parish appears

---

[1] F.O. 6/23, Parish to Aberdeen, 2 Dec. 1828.   [2] Ibid.   [3] Ibid.

to have shared Ponsonby's general suspicion of Dorrego, but neither he nor Ponsonby ever clearly formulated any grounds for disliking the Governor except that he was disliked by the majority of the respectable class. When Lavalle's newspapers began to expose the crimes of Dorrego they had nothing of consequence to say beyond what can be said of any politician at any time: that he loved power, was guilty of petty graft and tyranny, and had placed obstacles in the way of opposition propaganda. It was suggested that he was seeking to ruin the *Banco Nacional*, but nothing precise ever emerged on this subject. Neither Parish nor Dorrego's critics mentioned one of Dorrego's most popular measures: the fixing of the price of meat, the staple of Argentine diet among all classes.

Parish had scarcely finished setting forth his preliminary view of the situation to the Foreign Secretary when he received a letter from General Lavalle, which, if he acknowledged it, would imply a recognition of the General's authority. Parish decided to let it go unanswered, 'especially as I understand this Morning that a considerable Re-action in favor of General Dorrego is taking place particularly amongst the lower orders, and that many of that Class are arming, and leaving the City to join him, and further, that the Soldiery who are connected with them, have also shown a great disposition to desertion'.[1]

Dorrego had made good his escape, and General Rosas, the commander of the rural militia, was reported to be on the move. Whether Rosas would support the Governor or effect a compromise with General Lavalle was uncertain. On this alternative depended civil peace or war. During this first critical week Dorrego did not join forces with Rosas, but acted independently. It was not, however, clear whether this was due to the circumstance of time and locality, or to political calculation on the part of either Rosas or Dorrego, or both. In Buenos Aires the representatives of the foreign powers—Parish, the French Consul-General, M. de Mendeville, and the American chargé d'affaires, Colonel Forbes—consulted on a course of action in response to Lavalle's invitation to recognize the new régime. In the light of subsequent events the decisions made at this moment were immensely important, for upon them depended the involvement or non-involvement of foreign states

[1] F.O. 6/23, Parish to Aberdeen, 3 Dec. 1828.

in Argentine politics. Parish was resolutely opposed to quick
recognition of General Lavalle. At first his French and American colleagues agreed, but after adhering to this course for two
or three days the American chargé d'affaires changed his policy
and wrote to General Lavalle 'rather a long Note . . . about the
Rights of the People, and the deference of his Government at
all times to an expression of "the Public Will"; which he flattered
himself was necessary as a Mark of Civility towards the existing
Authorities, whilst he was of the opinion that its meaning was
sufficiently indefinite to save him from any inconvenient Construction being put upon it'.[1] The French Consul-General,
however, adhered to Parish's line. Parish told Aberdeen that
his silence was much remarked upon by Lavalle's supporters
and was attributed to Parish's hostility to the party of Rivadavia.

Preoccupations of this description were pushed into the
background by the dramatic events of the succeeding week.
Dorrego gathered around him a force of 2,000 militia, with
which he moved northward away from Buenos Aires. He was
suddenly attacked by a force under General Lavalle at Navarro,
a point some forty miles from the capital. Lavalle won a quick
but bloody victory. Parish estimated casualties on both sides at
20 per cent. including several of the senior officers. This action
took place on 9 December. On the 10th Dorrego appeared at a
post of frontier guards, but when they learned of his defeat, he
was arrested on the orders of one of the officers of the post, and
delivered to General Lavalle. It now seemed that the *coup d'état*
was over, and that Lavalle and his backers possessed the power
of government. 'It is generally supposed', wrote Parish, 'that
Rosas will now no longer oppose the existing Authorities and
that he will easily be induced to send his Gauchos to their
homes.'[2]

Parish had scarcely concluded writing these words and sealing the dispatch, when he was asked to receive a deputation of
Dorrego's friends. He met them at once. They told Parish that
they had a serious fear that Colonel Dorrego was about to be
executed, and they begged Parish to intervene in an effort to
spare the former Governor's life. Parish could scarcely credit

---

[1] F.O. 6/23, Parish to Aberdeen, 10 Dec. 1828.
[2] Ibid., 13 Dec. 1828.

this development, although he acknowledged that he had heard the matter 'coolly discussed . . . amongst respectable people'.[1]

Parish immediately went to see Diaz-Vélez, the man whom Lavalle had appointed Minister General to act while he was conducting military operations. Diaz-Vélez assured Parish categorically that there was no intention of executing Dorrego. Parish accepted this assurance, and dismissed the matter as outside the realm of possibility. He stayed on talking with Diaz-Vélez, warning him of the unwisdom of recalling Moreno from his post in London and, thus, increasing the already unfortunate impression at the Court of St. James of political instability in Buenos Aires. While Parish and Diaz-Vélez talked in Buenos Aires, forty miles away in a field outside the village of Navarro Colonel Dorrego was being led out to die.

The next morning a bulletin appeared in Buenos Aires.

Señor Ministro:

I wish to inform the provincial government that Colonel Don Manuel Dorrego has just been shot by my order at the head of the Regiments which compose this division.

History, Señor Ministro, will judge impartially whether Colonel Dorrego ought to have died or not and whether in sacrificing him to the public tranquility which he disturbed, I was possessed of any sentiment but that of the public good. . . .

Greetings to the Señor Ministro

Juan Lavalle.

His Excellency, Señor Ministro de Gobierno,
Dr. D. José Miguel Diaz-Vélez.

Thus was the blood feud born which raged in the vitals of Argentine society for thirty years, sometimes slumbering and quiescent, at others burning at fever heat.

Dorrego died with the composed simplicity of a Roman hero and the forgiving sweetness of a Christian saint. A wave of revulsion against Lavalle and his supporters swept 'from one end to the other of the Republic among all classes'.[2] Rosas no longer hesitated but moved more resolutely against the usurpers, swearing to avenge the death of the federalist leader. In Santa Fé, General López, and in Córdoba, General Bustos began to prepare for an armed settlement. Within a matter of days

---

[1] Ibid., 14 Dec. 1828.
[2] F.O. 6/26, Parish to Aberdeen, 10 Jan. 1829.

copies of Dorrego's last letters to his wife, his daughters, and his friend, Don Miguel de Ascuenga, began to circulate from hand to hand like blessed relics. They were moving in their simple brevity and loaded with menace for the liberals and atheists who had done the deed. The letter to Ascuenga read:

My friend and thru' you to all my friends: In an hour I am about to die. I know not why, but Providence has willed it so:—Adieu, my friends,—remember your friend,

Manuel Dorrego

At this moment the Catholic Religion is my only Consolation.[1]

Out on the camp the gaucho militia began to gather. In Buenos Aires itself popular feeling turned rapidly against the provisional Government.

The lower Classes [Parish reported]. . . were loud in their execrations against [the] Murderers, and employed themselves actively and with success in seducing the Soldiery . . . Señor Rivadavia and others were threatened with personal violence, and that individual became so alarmed for his own safety as to take out his Passport to be in readiness to fly to France. A great many persons in the Higher Classes who were opposed to the late Government, and to General Dorrego have been amongst the foremost to deprecate the action of General Lavalle.[2]

Early in January 1829 Rosas and his forces began to move on Buenos Aires, but they declined a pitched battle with Lavalle. Lavalle's men began to desert through want of pay, while in Buenos Aires Admiral Brown's sailors, who were acting as a garrison, broke out in disorder, claiming to collect direct from the citizens the arrears owing to them. As the situation grew worse for the provisional Government they resorted to increasingly discreditable devices, such as releasing murderers from prison on the understanding that they directed their talents at General Rosas.[3] Attempts were being made to saddle Lavalle with the sole responsibility for Dorrego's death, and Lavalle was reported to have placed the papers revealing his orders to do the deed in the safekeeping of his family.

Early in February Lavalle won a small victory over a detachment of Rosas's militia. Again Lavalle resorted to terror. Major

---

[1] F.O. 6/26, Parish to Aberdeen, 10 Jan. 1829.
[2] Ibid., 12 Jan. 1829.   [3] Ibid.

Mesa, a prisoner taken in the action, was tried by court martial and shot in a public square in Buenos Aires. Like Dorrego, whose orders he said he was obeying, he died with composure, and so recharged the public indignation.

At this stage Parish was inclined to think a long and bloody civil war inevitable. Rivadavia and his friends believed that the regular army could establish and maintain their power, although General Lavalle was reported already to doubt his capacity to do more than control the Province of Buenos Aires. The federalists were arguing that even if Lavalle and Rivadavia could put a garrison in every province they could not pay their troops, and revolt would inevitably follow. Parish reported gloomily that there seemed little prospect of settling outstanding British claims; that the exchange on Britain had fallen to the worst levels of the Brazilian war; that the harvest was rotting in the fields because all the gauchos had joined Rosas, and finally and ominously, that the possibility now existed that France would begin fishing in the troubled waters.[1]

Indeed, this last proved to be a major complicating factor for British policy in the Río de la Plata during the next twenty years. At this time France occupied a place of little consequence in Buenos Aires. Bourbon opposition to the revolution in Latin America and the French monarch's endeavours to gain influence through supporting Ferdinand VII had doomed France seemingly to exclusion from Argentina. During the war between Argentina and Brazil, however, French policy began to change as it became evident that Britain was not only establishing a firm position in South America but was also encountering difficulties arising out of the conflicts and antagonisms both between and inside the new states. The Bourbon monarchy had not gone to the length of recognizing completely the Argentine Republic by an exchange of ministers and by the negotiation of a treaty, but towards the end of the Brazilian war a French Consul-General had come to Buenos Aires and French immigrants had begun to establish themselves in the Province mainly as shopkeepers, craftsmen, labourers, and merchants. Simultaneously Rivadavia, both before and after his fall from power, made overtures to France and several of his most successful captains of privateers were Frenchmen. In

[1] Ibid., 20 Feb. 1829.

spite of these developments, however, the position of Frenchmen in Argentina was uncertain. Formal recognition was tentative and incomplete. French nationals were completely subject
to the domestic laws of the Republic, which, for example, put
them under the obligation to serve in the militia, and their
Government had no treaty right to protect them.

After the overthrow of Dorrego, the French Consul-General
sought to preserve his neutrality in the domestic dispute in
progress before his eyes, and Parish reported that M. de Mendeville had not cultivated Rivadavia or members of his party.
In this he did not show the inclination of at least some elements in France to take advantage of the situation, for in
January 1829 there appeared in Buenos Aires the Comte de la
Rochefoucauld, the secretary of the French mission in Brazil.
Parish considered that the Count remained an unnecessarily
long time in Buenos Aires and he reported that Rochefoucauld
was much given to consorting with the members of Rivadavia's party. Rivadavia's chief press propaganda officer was a
Frenchman, who spent much effort discrediting the British
Government by skilfully quoting from opposition newspapers
in Britain.[1]

Had the French limited themselves to these relatively innocent activities it is unlikely that they would have created any
difficulty either for themselves or others. Unfortunately M. de
Mendeville was either persuaded or ordered to abandon his
neutrality and to adopt a course of action favourable to the
party of Lavalle and Rivadavia. This in turn precipitated a
crisis for the entire foreign community in Buenos Aires and not
least for the British community and the British Government's
representative.

This situation came about as a result of the final collision
between Lavalle and Rivadavia on the one hand, and Rosas,
López, and Bustos on the other. Late in February General San
Martín had reappeared in the Río de la Plata, thinking to compose the tension of his country and to rally all elements under
him in a united national state. It became apparent to him
before he landed that the jealousy felt for himself by Rivadavia
and the antagonisms of the rival parties were insuperable obstacles to reconciliation and social peace. And so San Martín

[1] F.O. 6/26, Parish to Aberdeen, 20 Feb. 1829.

sailed away to Europe once more, and in Buenos Aires Lavalle's officers began arresting the federalist leaders: General Balcarce, General Martínez, Colonel Iriarte, Señor Aguirre, the brother-in-law of García, and the Anchorena brothers, whom Parish described as 'by far the most wealthy and powerful Citizens in this Republick'. Curiously General Guido, Dorrego's Minister and emissary to Brazil, whom Ponsonby so admired, remained, like García, at large. Guido, indeed, seemed to enjoy everyone's confidence, for he went back and forth among the bitter factions as if his life were charmed.

Lavalle had learned something of moderation for he did not shoot Balcarce and the others in his power. Instead, he sent them into exile, and Parish provided them with letters asking British subjects to succour the unfortunates wherever they might find themselves. In the case of the Anchorenas he seems to have done even more. They were taken aboard one of H.M. ships, and they appear to have been so lavishly entertained that the naval officers concerned thought the Admiralty ought to foot the bills and not themselves.[1] The Admiralty in turn thought the bills were the affair of the Foreign Office.

These arrests were a sign of weakness rather than strength. The disorganization of society by the politicians and generals was becoming intolerable. The denuding of the frontier guard posts and the concern of the militia and regular army with civil war rather than national defence opened the way for Indian raiding parties which penetrated almost to Buenos Aires. The only reply of the Government to the aggrieved ranchers was advice to look after themselves. But even the Indian peril did not weaken the resolution of Lavalle and his friends to keep what little power they had or the determination of Rosas and his allies to drive out these murderers of Dorrego.

In April Lavalle set out to reduce the Province of Santa Fé to his authority. He left a small force of troops under Colonel Estomba to hold Rosas in check in the southern part of the Province of Buenos Aires. This dispersal of the main force of the regular army was just the opportunity which Rosas's militia required. They fell on Estomba's force, and harried it until Estomba himself went insane, and the authority of the Govern-

[1] F.O. 6/28, Captain Bingham, the commander of *Thetis*, to the Admiralty, 26 Aug. 1829.

ment ceased to exist beyond the city of Buenos Aires. Lavalle detached another force under a German officer, Colonel Rauch, to restore the position, but this force was likewise harried and destroyed so that in the end Rauch shot himself.

In Buenos Aires anxiety concerning an attack upon the city by Rosas's forces began to mount, and the hysteria was not diminished by Rivadavia's press, which assured the people that the gauchos and their Indian allies would kill and loot indiscriminately. A military council was formed in which General Guido played an active part, and this Council decided to summon Lavalle back to defend the city. Lavalle obeyed, first detaching a force under his ablest commander, General Paz, who continued to move northward towards the remote interior Provinces of Tucumán and La Rioja, where opposition to the federalist *caudillos* still flourished.

In the situation of near panic which obtained in Buenos Aires the French, Spanish, and Italian communities decided to form a Foreign Battalion under French officers. M. de Mendeville gave the enterprise his blessing. Parish warned British subjects to have nothing to do with the Battalion, and the Americans similarly dissociated themselves. As Rosas advanced, the French seem to have had some second thoughts about what they were doing, for M. de Mendeville tried to draw the British and Americans in by depicting the Battalion as simply a guard for foreign lives and property and not an auxiliary force of the provisional Government. The provisional Government, meanwhile, was not adverse to drawing the foreign communities and foreign Governments into their quarrel. Early in April they were preparing to decree the enlistment of all foreign nationals in the defence forces.

On the evening of 9 April Parish learned that the decree was about to be issued. The next morning he summoned to him the officer commanding H.M.S. *Cadmus* anchored in the outer roads. He ordered this officer to wait upon the military Governor of the city, Admiral Brown, 'to ask him if there was any foundation for the Report', and to warn him that such a decree would be 'a gross Violation of our Treaty', and that Great Britain would 'be obliged to act accordingly'.[1] Brown assured the captain of the *Cadmus* that there was no truth in the report.

[1] F.O. 6/26, Parish to Aberdeen, 25 Apr. 1829.

Parish's connexion with the Government Printing Office seems still to have been in good order, for he obtained a copy of the proposed decree. He went immediately to Admiral Brown and the ministers of the provisional Government and confronted them with the decree. He spoke very plainly. He told them that British subjects had 'many valuable Establishments in the Country as well as in the Town, which would at once become endangered, and subject to vengeance of the Party outside, if the Proprietors were known to be giving any support whatever to their opponents in the City'.[1] He stated that he had ordered British subjects to preserve the strictest neutrality in the civil war in progress in the closest conformity with the terms of the Treaty, and that he expected the authorities on their part to adhere to the Treaty. As soon as he had seen Admiral Brown and his colleagues he sent for the frigate H.M.S. *Thetis* to reinforce the *Cadmus*.

At this moment the provisional Government had more to think about than the expediency of conscripting British subjects. General Lavalle's force, falling back to defend Buenos Aires, was overtaken by the federalist militia at the Rio Conchas fifteen miles from Buenos Aires. There it was forced to make a stand, weary from a long retreat, weakened by desertions, and cut off by Rosas from its supplies of horses. In the battle Lavalle's once well-disciplined force of regulars was cut to pieces. The gauchos had conquered. When Lavalle entered the city there was no alternative open but negotiation with Rosas.

It may be said of General Lavalle that he was a brave man and a competent officer even though he was a traitor and the dupe of unscrupulous politicians. He remained in the city ready to the end to fight or to negotiate as circumstances would permit. Rivadavia was prepared to do neither. He fled accompanied by the leading members of his party. On 1 May 1829 Parish reported that they had taken ship bound for France.

Throughout May Rosas waited, shrewdly aware of the limitations of his gaucho troops and the disaster which might befall them if they attempted to take Buenos Aires by military force. Politics was Rosas's best *métier*, and it was upon political manœuvre that he now relied. He declared that he did not wish to deliver an assault upon Buenos Aires. He even persuaded his

[1] Ibid.

ally, López, to retire to Santa Fé and thus presented himself to the capital as a true son of Buenos Aires, seeking only to restore the laws and institutions of his native Province. This moderation won over many waverers in spite of the rumours put about concerning gaucho and Indian atrocities. Rosas himself seems to have tried hard to keep order among his forces. He mercilessly punished murderers and looters among his own following, and he either paid money or gave receipts signed by his commissaries for all supplies taken by his troops. But there were disorders enough. The seizure of property and the frightening presence of the gaucho cavalry, who quartered themselves in the Presbyterian chapel, were the last blows which finally destroyed the Scottish settlement at Monte Grande. Parish was confident that Rosas was as capable of keeping order as any other Argentine general, but even he ordered his ciphers and archives aboard a ship of war and garrisoned his legation with Royal Marines when the gauchos finally began to enter the city early in June.

Meanwhile a mistake on the part of the French authorities helped further to unite the rival parties manœuvring cautiously for a compromise. The decree enlisting foreigners was not applied to British subjects, but it was to the French. When M. de Mendeville discovered that French subjects were being forced into the Argentine formations preparing to defend the city, he began to regret his countrymen's ill-advised Foreign Battalion. He protested to the authorities, but they found the opportunity to abuse foreigners a political blessing calculated to obscure their own shortcomings. At the beginning of May, de Mendeville was left no other course but to demand his passports as a protest against 'des persécutions qu'il a exercées contre la Population Française de cette ville'. On 18 May the French frigate *Magicienne* under the command of the Vicomte de Venancourt appeared off Buenos Aires, and on the 21st without warning boarded eight Argentine vessels of war while they were at anchor and burned them to the water. Having performed this act, de Venancourt addressed a Note to the authorities offering to make a peaceful settlement. The Argentine reply was a blast of newspaper abuse against France in which the opposed parties vied with each other in their vows of vengeance. The French for their part had no regrets. In July the French admiral in Rio de Janeiro expressed satisfaction with the behaviour of the captain of the *Magicienne*.

Early in June the peace negotiations between Rosas and Lavalle began to make progress. Parish's intimate connexion with General Guido and Señor García enabled him to follow events closely and, perhaps, to influence their course. There is no evidence, however, that Parish officially gave any advice, and certainly he never employed the power of the British Government on behalf of any faction or even to compel compromise between them.

The first stage in these negotiations was a reshuffle of Lavalle's ministers which involved the replacement of Admiral Brown as the Governor of the city and the entry of General Alvear into the office of War Minister. Politicians and generals (the distinction is a very fine one) moved about in subtle variations. While they danced in the foreground, General Lavalle secretly beckoned to General Guido, who came to him. Unbeknown to the slowly twisting lesser artists, they talked in whispers which Parish was privileged to hear. A deal was made. Lavalle would resign the Government to Guido if Guido would guarantee Lavalle his life and the lives of his officers. Guido then wrote to Rosas, and Rosas sent for Señor García.

The outcome was a further compromise. Lavalle retained the office of provisional Governor and Guido and García became his principal ministers. It was agreed to hold a provincial election and to reconstitute the provincial institutions violently overthrown by Lavalle. In a secret article it was agreed between Rosas and Lavalle that the party of compromise would win the election.[1] When all was settled Rosas's forces began to move into the city.

Unfortunately matters were not yet entirely settled. Although Rosas had clearly the advantage in Buenos Aires Province, General Paz had defeated General Bustos and had gained control of the Province of Córdoba. All, therefore, was not yet lost to the unitarian[2] forces and they were still driven by ambition and folly to hope for better than a compromise. Contrary

---

[1] F.O. 6/27, Parish to Aberdeen, 30 July 1829.

[2] The party opposed to Rosas became known as the unitarians, i.e. those advocating a strong centralized government of the 'united' provinces. Rosas's supporters were known as the federalists, i.e. the supporters of the principle of provincial independence.

to the secret undertaking given to Rosas, the supporters of
Lavalle broke from his control and proceeded to win the elections by the simple device of sending regular soldiers to drive
federalist voters away from the polling points in the city. The
federalists fled to Rosas's camp. García and Guido urged the
unwisdom of Lavalle's supporters' winning the election, and
finally it was agreed that Rosas and Lavalle would jointly
nominate a provisional Governor for six months, whose main
business would be to hold an election in the spirit of the agreement between the parties. General Viamonte, a man of much
the same views as General Guido, became the Governor, with
Guido and García as his principal ministers.

The civil war was over in the Province of Buenos Aires, but
political tension was not at an end. A compromise at the top
of society had not stabilized and solidified the base. Struggles
like those which afflicted France in the fourteenth century and
England during the Wars of the Roses persisted in the interior
with no meaning, it seemed, but death for the victims and ruin
for the community. Conditions beyond the limits of the Province of Buenos Aires were in Parish's opinion 'a disgrace to
any Christian Country'.[1] Within the Province the compromise
between Lavalle and Rosas was proving itself but a stage in
the total overthrow of the unitarian party. Lavalle had been
appointed to the command of the regular cavalry and several
leading personalities among his followers, who had proved
their *bona fides* by not accompanying Rivadavia into exile, had
been given places in the provisional council which was acting
as an interim legislative body until the provincial elections were
complete. But in October Lavalle decided to retire to the safety
of Montevideo, where he was shortly reported to have gone
mad. Admiral Brown followed Lavalle to Uruguay. The regiments of the regular Army were broken up and their officers
either dismissed or reassigned to new formations. The Navy
was reduced to a peace footing.

Dorrego's friends were still crying aloud for vengeance, and
he was not allowed to rest in his grave at Navarro where he
had died. His body was brought back for burial in Buenos
Aires and a solemn service was held in the cathedral to sanctify
his reinterment. This became a great popular demonstration,

[1] F.O. 6/27, Parish to Aberdeen, 12 Sept. 1829.

a prelude to the reconvocation of the old Provincial Assembly which Lavalle had dispersed. Rosas advised that the Assembly should meet before the election was held. In December it came together, and its first act was to elect with no dissenting voices Juan Manuel Rosas Governor and Captain-General of the Province of Buenos Aires. On 5 December 1829 he was proclaimed amid great popular excitement. His supporters swarmed in the streets shouting 'Viva el General Rosas! Viva el Liberador de la Patria! Viva el nuevo Gobernador!'[1]

Parish was becoming discouraged by the course of events. Privately he described Argentina as a 'disagreeable and disheartening . . . place'.[2] Officially, however, the victory of Rosas revived his spirits. 'I have had great satisfaction in seeing much of him', Parish reported. 'His Power in the country is as extraordinary as his modesty and moderation.' Rosas's ministerial appointments won his hearty approval, for the new Governor retained García and Guido. Indeed, Parish declared the Rosas cabinet 'are all honest and well disposed men'.[3]

The Rosas régime thus installed endured for more than twenty-one years. The modesty and moderation which attracted Parish's attention did not, however, become the leading characteristics of that régime. Rosas's political techniques and the institutions he developed were more typical of the twentieth than the nineteenth century. He preserved the institutions of government which had been designed by the liberals of the revolutionary period. Indeed, he was described as the restorer of the laws in order to distinguish him from what his party described as the anarchists, who had tried to destroy the constitutional foundations of society. But with Rosas neither the legislature nor even his cabinet were the repositories of final authority nor were they the architects of policy. At the beginning of his career Rosas had hung back from a public assumption of final authority and he had let others negotiate on his behalf and accept responsibility. At the end of his career he still employed the tactics of reluctance and remoteness. In January 1851, a year before his overthrow, the British Minister reported that Rosas had not seen his Foreign Minister for more

---

[1] F.O. 6/27, Parish to Lord Dunglass, 20 Aug. 1829.
[2] F.O. 6/27, Parish to Aberdeen, 12 Dec. 1829.
[3] Ibid.

than two years.[1] At the height of the political terror of 1841–2
he told the British Minister that he did not know what was
happening nightly in Buenos Aires and in the military prison
at Santos Lugares. When, in response to the British Minister's
protests, he visited Buenos Aires, he professed to be shocked by
what he learned about the wholesale killing of the opposition
then in progress.[2] It is, perhaps, a sufficient comment to say
that the political murders ceased once he had personally received the British protest.

Like a skilful monarch Rosas left much formal authority and
nearly all the details of government to subordinates, whom he
could change according to whim or circumstance. Power he
retained in his own hands so that the Provincial Assembly of
Buenos Aires, the cabinet, the staff of the Army, the Navy, and
the militia, the Police, and his secret political society, the Mazorca, were all instruments for his use, and none of them, save
perhaps the Mazorca, was a source of policy or of decision.
There can be little doubt that Rosas willed it so. Repeatedly
during his career he appeared before the people as a reluctant
leader. His favourite device in any difficulty was a threat to
retire, and in fact he did retire at the end of his first term of
office. But he always managed to acquire greater power after
each threat of retirement, whether he carried it out or not.
He was convinced that the Argentine Republic 'could not be
governed by European methods',[3] by which he meant that no
power of policy-making could be left to the legislature and that
it should have no influence upon the personnel or path of the
Government. Its business was to register popular assent and to
strengthen the hand of authority. Elections served the same
purpose. They were not conceived of as a social device for
establishing a government for a limited period of time and for
limited purposes. Rosas asked for the widest powers to serve the
most general purposes. When the Provincial Assembly voted
him dictatorial powers for five years in March 1835, they did so
for two purposes: firstly, to save and defend the Roman Aposto-
lic and Catholic religion and, secondly, to defend the Argentine

[1] F.O. 6/157, Southern to Palmerston, 11 Jan. 1851.
[2] F.O. 6/83, Mandeville to Aberdeen, 23 Apr. 1842, and Mandeville to Viscount
Canning (private), 24 Apr. 1842.
[3] F.O. 6/158, Southern to Palmerston, 25 June 1851.

Confederation. Not content with receiving dictatorial powers from the Assembly by a vote of thirty-one out of thirty-three (the two voting against him were his brother and his business partner, who out of an excess of delicacy voted for Rosas's cousin Nicolás Anchorena), he held a plebiscite, which ratified the action of the Assembly by 9,320 votes to 4.

The original source of Rosas's power was the gaucho militia which he had commanded for many years prior to his emergence on the political stage. We have already observed how this militia was employed to defeat the party of Rivadavia which depended upon the regular army. Rosas employed the militia again to displace his successor General Balcarce when that unfortunate man permitted liberal elements to gain too much authority in his Government during the years 1832–3. But Rosas did not rely exclusively upon the gaucho militia. Indeed, in the end the militia and the regular army which he built up after the dissolution of Lavalle's forces came to occupy a subordinate place in his apparatus of power. Rosas had always inclined strongly towards the Church as a bulwark against liberal courses, so much so that British Ministers in Buenos Aires frequently referred to Rosas's supporters as the Apostolical Party. Parish reported in 1831 that Rosas's Government was pursuing an active policy of paying priests, erecting new parishes, building churches, and rebuilding old ones.[1] One British Minister, at least, did not regard the clerical side of Rosas's policy with so much indulgence as Parish. Hamilton, who served in Buenos Aires while Rosas was establishing his dictatorship, spoke of the Governor's supporters as 'the bigoted and besotted remnant of the old Spanish dominion',[2] and he described 'some of his alterations . . . [as] far from being improvements [and] calculated rather to restore and perpetuate . . . uncivilized manners and mental prostration . . . namely the revival of the bull fight, and the reopening of the convent of the Dominicans. '[3] There was as much of design as of piety in Rosas's policy, for he was firmly Erastian. One of his last and, perhaps, fatal political encounters was with the Holy See. In 1851 he emerged the victor in a trial of strength with Count

[1] F.O. 6/32, enclosed with Parish to Palmerston, 25 May 1831.
[2] F.O. 6/47, Hamilton to Wellington, 14 Apr. 1835.
[3] F.O. 6/48, Hamilton to Wellington, 14 Nov. 1835.

Bessi, Archbishop of Canopo, a delegate sent from Rome to assert the Church's authority in the selection of a new bishop and the disciplining of an old one.[1]

In order to buttress his power originally acquired through the agency of the gaucho militia, Rosas developed a political party operating directly among and upon the populace both as a means of expressing enthusiasm and suppressing the lack of it. All the British representatives in Buenos Aires agreed in their observation that Rosas was supported by a 'majority of the middle and lower classes of the inhabitants, both of the Capital, and of the Province of Buenos Aires'.[2] One representative described the Province as one of the 'Democracies of the purest, but of the lowest description',[3] and another declared that the régime excited little enthusiasm among those 'of any rank and consideration in society'.[4] In order to bring this support of the lower strata to bear there was brought into being the secret political society, the Mazorca. This organization acted to stimulate mass enthusiasm by such devices as making obligatory under pain, not of official but of popular reprisal, the wearing of the crimson colour of the Rosas party. The Mazorca selected and killed the enemies or supposed enemies of the régime in moments of crisis such as that which existed during the French and again during the Anglo-French intervention. The Argentine Foreign Minister once admitted that 'in these cases the Police are as much afraid as any other person, or as I am'.[5] The Mazorca even imposed itself upon the armed forces to the extent that on one occasion the guards at the Fort stopped the British Minister and denied him entry because he did not wear a crimson emblem. On that occasion Hamilton seized the opportunity to insist that British subjects were entitled and indeed bound by Treaty to maintain political neutrality, and he secured an apology from the Government which subsequently was interpreted not merely as the immunity of a diplomat but as a guarantee to British subjects of liberty to abstain from political demonstrations.[6]

Rosas, of course, controlled the press and the organs of public

[1] F.O. 6/157, Southern to Palmerston, 27 Apr. 1851.
[2] F.O. 6/34, Gore to Palmerston, 28 Nov. 1832.
[3] F.O. 6/40, Gore to Palmerston, 27 Feb. 1834.
[4] F.O. 6/47, Hamilton to Wellington, 14 Apr. 1835.
[5] F.O. 6/83, Mandeville to Aberdeen, 18 Apr. 1842.
[6] F.O. 6/47, Hamilton to Wellington, 11 May 1835.

information. He was aware of the advantages of employing competent journalists and propagandists to place the case for the régime before not only the Argentine people but those foreigners both at home and abroad who were interested in the politics of the River Plate. An Italian immigrant scholar, Pedro de Angelis, emerged as the most persuasive and learned apologist for the régime. de Angelis sought to explain Rosas simply by presenting to the world the history of Argentina. His *Archivo Americano* is a permanent contribution to any serious consideration of Argentine development. But de Angelis leaves the impression of being a sophisticated European whose racial and national memories had rendered him impervious alike to enthusiasm or indignation and who could see nothing novel or horrible in the history of Buenos Aires or anything attractive or enlightened in the activities and objectives of Rosas's liberal critics. That Rosas should have abandoned not only the plans but the hopes of universal education and that he should have impoverished and controlled the University of Buenos Aires in the interests of economy and the Roman Catholic Church did not seem crimes to a man who set his sights as low as de Angelis.

Rosas's propaganda was prepared for two classes of consumers. de Angelis presented the serious case, which was based upon an experience of man and particularly man on the pampas in the first half of the nineteenth century. In essence de Angelis, like Rosas, argued that the policies of the régime were necessities springing from the ungovernable wickedness of man and society. The popular case was stated otherwise in glaring black and white. Rosas and his allies in the Argentine Confederation manned the armed fortress of righteousness. This armed camp was beset by criminals who appeared in various guises sometimes as Frenchmen, atheists, North Americans, liberals, monarchists, old Spaniards, and foreigners. These criminals, though numerous and dangerous, were but the allies, however, of a comprehensive class of the most debased, treacherous, and insinuating murderers who ever threatened an ordered Christian community, namely, the vile unitarians, a misbegotten band of lying, libellous, cut-throats who wished to seize the Government for the purpose of oppressing the humble folk who worked in Buenos Aires and the free and noble plainsmen of Buenos Aires Province. Not only this. Having seized Buenos

Aires they would impose upon the other provinces a rule even more oppressive than that with which they would afflict Buenos Aires itself. Like any effective propaganda the arguments of the Rosista journalists and pamphleteers contained a kernel of truth. There *was* a contradiction between the professions of Rosas's critics and their actions. Parish once described the unitarian party as 'in general a brawling, worthless set of unemployed Officers and broken Speculators'.[1] But the passage of time rendered the stereotypes of Rosas's propaganda flat and ineffective. By the time of his overthrow, the memories of Dorrego's martyrdom and Lavalle's revolt were dim. Even the memory of the French intervention was not green enough to dazzle the popular vision.

Rosas belonged to that class of politician which specializes in bold simple alternatives in order both to get power and to keep a free hand for its exercise. He always tended to suggest that the alternative to Rosas was chaos. And he was widely believed. As late as 1851 the British Minister, Henry Southern, as cool an observer as one could encounter, reported to Palmerston:

> It is not wise to judge lightly the motives of a man who has discovered the means of governing one of the most turbulent and restless People in the World, and with such success that, though there is much cause for complaint, and not a little discontent, still the death or fall of General Rosas would be considered by every man in the Country as the direst misfortune. It certainly would be the signal of disorder and of intestine quarrels which could reduce the Country to misery.[2]

By the time Southern wrote these words, Rosas was no longer the indispensable alternative to chaos. He had created the conditions for his own suppression. When he swore to defend the Argentine Federation he had undertaken to respect the independence of the Argentine provinces, and by that fact to acknowledge a severality of authorities within the Republic. Rosas assumed that each provincial Governor would share his vision of a federal state, would not strive to assert an authority outside the boundaries of his own province, and would give to the Governor of Buenos Aires a free hand in foreign affairs. Eventually Rosas's conditions for successful federal government were realized. The unitarian politicans and armies were rooted

[1] F.O. 6/32, Parish to Palmerston, 25 May 1831.
[2] F.O. 6/157, Southern to Palmerston, 10 Jan. 1851.

out of the provinces. The economic complaints of provinces like Mendoza were given a hearing, and protection from foreign competition was accorded to some of their industries.

As the provincial régimes grew stronger and more stable their dependence upon Rosas diminished. This stability had a social foundation. Rosas had never sought to turn the gauchos and Indians into literate, liberal voters, as Rivadavia wished to do. He aimed lower and got at least on the target. He turned the gauchos into soldiers, sorted them out in the army, and through his distribution of land converted them into land owners and ranch hands. *Caudillismo* in every province tended towards this transformation. There was nothing novel in what Rosas did. The process can be discerned in pre-revolutionary times. Rosas's contribution consisted in maintaining the process and in rejecting premature endeavours to make the market the organizing agency of society. Judged by democratic and egalitarian criteria, there was much wrong with the land distribution effected by Rosas, and it undoubtedly left a legacy of poverty and parasitism which are still unresolved problems of Argentine society, but it did create viable units of production and social living which enabled Argentina to maintain and develop her connexions with the rest of the world. This is simply a roundabout way of saying what a Liverpool merchant was not alone in remarking: 'Altho' much can undoubtedly be said against him, it cannot be denied, that his policy has the great recommendation . . . of having produced almost perfect tranquillity throughout the Argentine provinces, of having raised the Exchange . . . [and of having] improved the credit of the Government securities both at home and abroad.'[1]

The creation of 'perfect tranquillity' may have been Rosas's objective, but it was one he achieved for only short periods during his ascendancy. When he did achieve it, as he did for a period in 1840–3 following the French intervention and again in 1848–51 following the Anglo-French interference, Rosas's Argentina experienced a rapid expansion of economic activity. In the last period the volume of immigration grew rapidly, supplying the country with that element which it needed most: a body of men willing and able to do disciplined work, without which the importation of capital is meaningless and its creation impossible.

[1] F.O. 6/110, George Nicholson to Aberdeen, 10 Feb. 1845.

To the outsider, Argentina during the 1830's, 1840's, and 1850's may have seemed a disappointing community, wanting in a liberal and progressive character and slow in its economic development. To those more closely acquainted with the country as a community, it presented a rather different aspect. Under the dictatorship of General Rosas a kind of progress was made upon which later generations were able to build. Peace was preserved for a long period of time within the extensive Province of Buenos Aires. The frontier was pushed southward and westward. Social disturbances were eliminated. The national independence was preserved. Property was made secure for all who obeyed the public authorities. The treaty rights of foreigners were carefully preserved. The development of commercial sheep-raising added variety and strength to the economy. There is some evidence of wealth accumulating in private hands both native and foreign.

To men in other communities and other ages accustomed to assume peace and opportunities to work as a natural state, the achievements of General Rosas seem small enough. His abandonment of plans for universal and higher education, his tolerance of religious obscurantism, his belief that from time to time the murder of political opponents is justifiable and necessary, his prolonged quarrels with his neighbours—all these aspects of his policy counted against him in the minds of his contemporaries, but to those experienced in the social instability and political anarchy always so close at hand, the régime of General Rosas presented itself as a working alternative not to good government but to no government. It is possible to imagine the virtues of 'no government' acceptable to Indians and hunters, but by the 1830's there existed too many men both in the towns and on the camp, and too many connexions with North America, Europe, and Brazil had been established for a primitive anarchy to prevail. The régime of General Rosas represented a practical compromise: less agreeable than the most civilized men might desire but a good deal more bearable than the best Indian *cacique* or the worst gaucho *caudillo* would permit.

The régime of General Rosas did not suddenly present itself to the world to be admired or reviled according to taste or interest, nor did his régime assume a sudden definite character distinguishing it from its predecessors and successors. It emerged slowly and its character was formed as much in response to events as by the design of the man who gave it a name. Because General Rosas was for many years the central figure of political controversy so that in the end he became almost a symbolic figure, he seemed to assume a unique moral character, but to the student of the ordinary activities of his Government carried on from month to month and year to year his policies do not outline themselves in black and white. When we have said that General Rosas stood firmly for the independence of the Argentine Republic in resistance to foreign interference and as firmly for the freedom of the Province of Buenos Aires within the Confederation of Argentine Provinces we have said all there is to say about his principles. All else was a matter of expediency and arrangement, of growth and of pressure exerted first in one quarter and then in another. That, perhaps, explains the repeated failures of his enemies, for they always tended to judge him by his most extreme statements and his worst acts, thus blinding themselves to his gift for shrewd and guileful compromise.

This talent for compromise—this core of moderation within a rind of ferocity—must be kept in mind when we examine the relations between Britain and Argentina in this period when liberal ideas and tendencies were all but extinguished in Buenos Aires and its associated provinces. For Britain the principal problem was to devise a policy and establish a mode of behaviour suitable to the circumstances of reaction in which some of the main hopes of the revolution were being disappointed. The temptation to think that some alternative to General Rosas could be found or to believe that he could be coerced into more liberal courses was often very great. Curiously it was the Conservative, Aberdeen, who went the farthest in yielding to such temptations and the Whig, Palmerston, who most resisted them. But then, there was something of the Whig in General Rosas, and like spoke to like across the equator. Indeed, when Sir Woodbine Parish visited Rosas on his farm in Hampshire, where he spent his years of exile, the former Consul-General found the former Captain-General 'very like an English country gentleman, with a benevolent countenance and very polite manners'.[1]

---

[1] From Sir Woodbine Parish's diary, 13 Dec. 1853, in Shuttleworth, *Sir Woodbine Parish*, p. 414.

VIII

SOME ANGLO-ARGENTINE
PROBLEMS

I. CLAIMS AND LOANS
II. THE FALKLAND ISLANDS
III. RELIGION

WHEN Rosas came to power in 1829 there were three questions outstanding, none of which singly could have wrecked Anglo-Argentine relations, but which cumulatively might well have led to serious trouble. These questions were: the British claims on account of losses sustained to British shipowners, merchants, and others during the war with Brazil; the default on the London Loan of 1824; and the status of the Falkland Islands. As Rosas moved away from liberalism additional problems arose concerning the status and rights of non-Roman Catholic British subjects, the civil liberties and security of property of British residents in Argentina, the level of customs dues, and the navigation of the River Plate and its tributaries. It must not be supposed that these questions concerned only the liberty and opportunities of British subjects. The Treaty had been designed to protect Argentine rights and liberties as well as British, and the working of the Treaty required something from Britain as well as something from the Government in Buenos Aires. In the matter of customs dues the Argentine Government formally and successfully protested against breaches of the Treaty by the customs officers in Liverpool,[1] whereas Britain never had grounds for complaint about customs duties levied in Buenos Aires. In matters of religion, too, the Treaty served to limit the zeal and enthusiasm of British subjects as often as it put restraints upon Argentine religious preferences.

The question of claims, whether of compensation for damages

---

[1] F.O. 6/25, Foreign Office to Torres, 19 Dec. 1828. This was before Rosas came to power.

and confiscations or for defaulted interest on loans, was never a moral or political one. The Government in Buenos Aires readily and repeatedly acknowledged that they owed money to British subjects for a variety of reasons. The questions were, could they pay? and, if they could, how far should the British Government go in insisting upon payment? Parish and his successors freely recognized the economic difficulties. With the separation of the mining regions from Buenos Aires and the partial destruction of the mining industry during the revolution, the Argentine Confederation lost one of its sources of precious metals and the principal means in colonial times of satisfying its European creditors. When Rosas came to power the only means of paying claims or interest charges was a surplus on export account after paying for imports and, secondarily, a surplus in the public revenues after paying the soldiers and officers of the state and the bills for the goods and services they required. Export surpluses as a first means to pay foreign debts were not easy to come by at any time in the 1830's and 1840's. A severe drought prostrated the country in 1830-1, and again in 1833-4. Civil disturbances and foreign intervention afflicted trade and production on two other occasions. Not only were there physical interruptions of trade but the prices of hides, horns, bones, wool, and tallow tended generally downwards during the period.[1] This downward course of prices was masked somewhat in Argentina by the rise in prices expressed in paper currency, but the power of pastoral products to secure the gold needed to pay foreign debts declined. Knowledge of export prices is more reliable than that of import prices, but there are good reasons for supposing that the decline in export prices was offset, and perhaps more than offset, by declines in the prices of imported textiles, iron ware, and flour. It is also necessary to remark that the ranching area considerably increased as the frontier was pushed back and the range of pastoral products extended to include wool and tallow.

During the period of Rosas's ascendancy Argentina's international economic position was thus difficult but not impossible. There may even have been some advantage to Argentina in the terms of trade. It is possible to suppose that theoretically Rosas's

[1] J. Broide, *La Evolución de los precios pecuarios argentinos en el periodo 1830-1850* (Buenos Aires, 1951), table 15.

Government could have paid its foreign creditors except during the years of drought and blockade. But what may have been theoretically possible was impractical having regard for the character of the Rosas party. Understandably Rosas preferred paying his soldiers, civil servants, and domestic creditors to paying foreign bondholders and claimants for redress. Sometimes even the claimants close at hand were forced to go short, and the depreciation of the currency left many employees of the Government in desperate straits. Although Rosas was a dictator and supposedly all powerful, he was, during all but the last years of his rule, short of money. On the one hand his policies required the maintenance of armed forces large in relation to the size of the country; on the other hand his was a 'popular' government unwilling to tax the wealthiest class, the landowners, and afraid, and perhaps unwilling, to force up the cost of living of the mass of the people by either direct or indirect taxation. Levies on foreign imports and exports to foreign countries provided the bulk of the state revenues. The sale of public land, which in the contemporary United States yielded an ample revenue, yielded next to nothing in Argentina. The taxes on landowners amounted to nothing, and the system of renting public land under contract of emphyteusis was deliberately allowed to fall to pieces so that it rendered no assistance to the public revenues. Neither Parish nor any of his successors even conceived of the possibility of Rosas's broadening the bases of his revenue system; they always looked hopefully and exclusively to economies and economic expansion as means of satisfying English bondholders and other claimants. The news that Rosas had retired a body of officers or discharged a few state servants usually evoked expressions of hope from them; whereas the raising of fresh troops filled them with gloom.

That Rosas never altered his financial policies in order to meet the claims of foreign creditors is due in part to the unwillingness of the British Government to apply any pressure on behalf of the bondholders. In the case of claims arising out of seizures during the Brazilian War the Foreign Office took a stricter view of Argentine obligations, but in this case the sums were small and they did not represent a continuous annual strain upon the resources of the Government in Buenos Aires. Even in the case of these claims the British Government was as much concerned to keep the claims within the bounds of justice as they were to collect them. Parish had grave doubts about the validity of some,[1] and in the end recommended that their investigation be undertaken in London where reliable evidence from insurance firms could be collected. The Mixed Commission in Buenos Aires made up of representatives of the Argentine Government and the British commercial community were sometimes unanimous in thinking reductions of claims to be justified. In one long-drawn-out case, that of the schooner *Huskisson*, Parish intervened. He studied the claim and decided £6,000 could be justified. He then went to the owner and asked what he would accept. The owner said he would be more than happy to receive £5,000. Parish then went to General Guido and proposed that he settle at once for £5,000, which he did. In July 1830 the business of settlement was transferred to London, where the new Mixed Commission was established consisting of Manuel Moreno, the Argentine Minister at the Court of St. James, and Michael Bruce, a British barrister. Palmerston's instructions to the British Commissioner were to act 'judicially and uniformly, [to] endeavour to combine a fair and conscientious zeal for the private Interests of H.M. subjects with the maintenance of the strictest justice towards the Government of Buenos Aires and with the promotion of a Spirit of Conciliation and Harmony between the two Countries'.[2] The Commissioners appointed an arbitrator, and soon settled the claims. The Argentine Government sold two frigates, remnants of the war with Brazil, to provide some of the funds to meet the claims. From time to time there were complaints that payments were not being made on the due dates, but in the end the claims were settled amicably. The settlement provided a contrast to the difficulties encountered by the Brazilians, who threatened a renewed war over claims, and by the Americans, who sent several warships into Buenos Aires harbour, only to be told that amicable negotiations were impossible while a sword hung overhead.[3]

The total British claims amounted to a sum between £20,000 and £25,000. The annual charges arising out of the Loan of

[1] F.O. 6/30, Parish to Aberdeen, 13 Mar. 1830.
[2] F.O. 6/36, Palmerston to Bruce, 18 Oct. 1831.
[3] F.O. 6/41, Hamilton to Palmerston, 11 Dec. 1834.

1824 were nearly three times this sum, amounting roughly to £65,000 per annum. In a comparatively good year from the economic and commercial point of view, say 1832 for example, this sum of £65,000 amounted to 2,250,000 pesos in paper currency. That year the total revenues of the Province of Buenos Aires, which was responsible for the Loan of 1824, amounted only to 10,657,322 pesos. The expenditure that year was 12,200,397 pesos. In bad years of blockade or drought when the pesos declined to 2*d*. the Loan of 1824 would require for its service as much as 6,500,000 pesos. It is easy to see that the payment of full interest plus amortization charges plus arrears would have required a complete revision of the revenue system on new principles designed to tax severely new sources of wealth, or a cut in expenditure so drastic that the character and activities of the Government would have been completely changed, or a rate of economic growth such as conditions in the country made impossible at that time. There is no evidence that Lord Palmerston, when petitioned by the bondholders, or any of his agents in Buenos Aires, turned to the science of economics for guidance. But they got just as realistic instruction from morality and law.

When Rosas first came to power, Parish was full of hope concerning the Loan of 1824. 'I am persuaded . . .', he reported early in 1830, 'that the resources of this Country are ample, if well managed, to satisfy all the public Creditors as well abroad as at home.'[1] Rosas himself encouraged the hope. In the first Message of the Executive Power to the Assembly after he took office it was stated to be 'necessary to recover our credit jeopardized abroad, and promptly to ameliorate our circulating medium, whose depreciation paralyses industry, disturbs security, and prepares the road to misery'.[2] The drought which came upon the country at this time and the continued political disturbances in the interior provinces soon put an end to expectations of payment. The year 1830 saw no action to satisfy the creditors in London nor did 1831. Late that year a committee of the bondholders wrote to the Foreign Secretary. Palmerston directed the Under Secretary 'to inform [them] that the grievance of which [they] complain arising as it does out of

---

[1] F.O. 6/30, Parish to Aberdeen, 24 May 1830.
[2] Mabragaña, *Los Mensajes*, i, p. 248.

a speculation of a purely private nature, His Majesty's Government cannot properly make any official application to the Government of Buenos Ayres'.[1] Palmerston promised, however, to instruct H.M. Minister to employ his good offices in bringing the question of the Loan to the attention of the Argentine authorities. The instructions to the British Minister were along these lines, and they were repeated from time to time in response to further representations from the creditors. In 1833, during the period of Rosas's nominal retirement when Balcarce was Governor, there was an effort made to introduce more liberal elements into the Buenos Aires Government, and at that time, Gore, the British chargé d'affaires, thought it proper to press the Government more strongly for payment. 'I am inclined to believe', he wrote, 'that the Buenos Ayres Government consider their obligations as sufficiently discharged by an annual acknowledgement of the Debt to their British creditors in the opening Message of the Government to the House of Representatives.'[2] Accordingly he presented an official note to the Government. Palmerston reproved him. Palmerston declared that he did not disapprove of the Note, but Gore had exceeded his instructions, and he was ordered to confine himself henceforth to unofficial representation on behalf of the bondholders.[3] This remained Palmerston's policy throughout, culminating in his famous Circular of 1849 stating the general principles of the British Government in relation to defaulted foreign loans.

While Aberdeen was at the Foreign Office from 1841 until 1846 there was no alteration in policy on this subject. The demand of the bondholders was no part of the case against General Rosas which led to the Anglo-French intervention. Indeed, the Committee of Spanish American Bondholders generally chose to rely on their own powers of negotiation rather than upon Government intervention. They took the view that political disturbances reduced economic activity and hence prejudiced the capacity of the debtor government to pay. At the time of the French intervention in 1838–9 the Committee's Report stated 'the blockade of the River Plate by the French must necessarily have greatly injured the commerce of

---

[1] F.O. 6/35, Jan. 1832.
[2] F.O. 6/37, Gore to Palmerston, 19 Sept. 1833.
[3] F.O. 6/40, Palmerston to Gore, 5 Feb. 1834.

the Country, and crippled the means of the Government in such a manner as to preclude any chance of an arrangement favourable to the Bondholders during its continuation'.[1] The Committee continued to adhere to this analysis. From time to time agents of the Committee connected with Baring Brothers visited Buenos Aires, and in 1844 Rosas began to pay the small sum of 5,000 silver pesos a month, which amounted to roughly 1 per cent. per annum. Although the bondholders had begun in 1830 by asking for Government support in their endeavours to collect their money, they appear to have welcomed, as heartily as any interested group connected with Argentina, Palmerston's decision, when he returned to office in 1846, to wind up the ill-conceived and disastrous policy of armed intervention undertaken by Aberdeen.

The dispute between Britain and Argentina concerning what one nation calls the Falkland Islands and the other Las Islas Malvinas is now more than a century and a quarter old.[2] The antiquity of the dispute is one of its illuminating peculiarities. It is neither important enough to solve nor unimportant enough to forget.

For the purposes of argument much has been said on both sides about the first discoverers of the Falkland Islands in the sixteenth century. It would be profitless to attempt to establish which Europeans first saw the two great windswept islands, each between 2,000 and 2,500 square miles in area, and the numerous small islands which comprise the group. When the Spanish, the French, the Portuguese, and the English have each advanced their claims to first discovery it will doubtless be found that some Viking or perhaps even Fijian or Chinese sailors have precedence. Practical interest in the Falkland Islands dates from the eighteenth century. The British interest in the islands fits into the pattern of policy pursued after the Seven Years' War of establishing off-shore commercial and military bases around the edge of the Spanish Empire. In 1771 Britain was prepared to go to war rather than yield to Spanish claims. The Spaniards acknowledged British claims when they discovered

[1] *Report of the Committee of Spanish American Bondholders*, 8 May 1839, p. 44.

[2] F. A. Kirkpatrick, *A History of the Argentine Republic* (Cambridge, 1931), appendix iv, and pp. 36–37, and J. Goebel, *The Struggle for the Falkland Islands* (New Haven, 1927).

that their ally France was unwilling at this time and for so slight a reason to support them in taking up the British challenge. The British Government had no sooner received the acknowledgement of their claims than they abandoned the islands. In 1774 the British settlement was removed, and only a British flag and some leaden markers remained to proclaim British possession. Almost at once the Spaniards moved in. Taking advantage of an opportunity to examine the archives in Buenos Aires concerning the islands, Woodbine Parish discovered that the Spanish Government paid 618,108 French livres to M. de Bougainville for his work in establishing a settlement at Soledad, the Spanish name for one of the islands.[1] In spite of a capital expenditure of these dimensions the Spaniards cannot be said to have established evidence of continuous and settled occupation. The islands became a place where the seal and whale fishermen of many nations, particularly of the United States and the British Empire, congregated, hunting, sheltering, watering, and refreshing themselves. Spanish naval vessels on several occasions made attempts to assert Spanish control over these activities, but with no success, for the good reason that Spanish resources to do so dwindled continuously as their troubles in Europe and in their colonies increased. During the period of the Napoleonic Wars the Falkland Islands belonged to no power in any practical sense. The claims of Britain and Spain can only be described at this stage as legal and theoretical.

In 1820 an Argentine naval officer, Daniel Jewitt, appeared in the islands in a ship commissioned by the Government at Buenos Aires. He proclaimed the possession of the islands for the Argentine Republic, raised the blue and white flag, warned the ships present of Argentine sovereignty, saluted, and sailed away. No one challenged this act, and there does not appear to have been much to challenge. Three years later, however, the Government at Buenos Aires appointed a Governor of the islands and granted two concessions of land, grazing, and fishing rights. One of these concessionaires was Louis Vernet, about whose allegiance or citizenship there is considerable uncertainty. He was believed to be a Frenchman by birth. He had lived for some time in the free city of Hamburg, and in the year 1820 he found himself in Buenos Aires. Parish met him in 1829. He

---

[1] F.O. 6/499, Parish to Aberdeen, 20 Nov. 1830.

described him as 'a very intelligent Person',[1] and certainly, from the account he gave of the Falkland islands to the British Consul-General, it is clear that he had a shrewd and comprehensive understanding of the commercial and productive possibilities of the group.

At the time of his interview with Parish, Vernet had already spent three winters in the Falklands. He believed that the pastures on the islands would sustain large flocks of sheep and herds of cattle. He estimated the herds of wild cattle, descendants of those brought in by Spanish settlers, at 15,000–20,000 head. Peat supplies were good, and fuel thus assured. There was an abundance of fresh water. Timber for building purposes was available on Staten Island. Vernet found that potatoes and vegetables flourished, and, although he had not yet done so in 1829, he was confident that cereals could be grown with success. Vernet believed that, if some order and control could be established in the islands which would prevent sealing crews from shooting cattle for provisions and fishing indiscriminately for seals among the islands, the sealing fleets would be obliged to call at the ports he proposed to establish there to buy supplies and to re-equip themselves. He believed, too, that if he could establish, with the assistance of some state, the power to control the coastal fisheries, he could, as a concessionaire, make a substantial profit from seals, either directly by fishing himself, or by licensing other fishermen.

In 1829 Vernet was appointed Governor of the Islands by the Government in Buenos Aires, thus joining political with economic authority. He undertook to colonize the islands. When Parish met him he had assembled a body of colonists and was about to set out. The party of colonists consisted of 10 white citizens of Buenos Aires, 10 seafaring men who were English or American, a brother and brother-in-law of Vernet, 18 negroes under ten-year indentures, 12 negro girls, and 7 single Germans. There were additionally 8 families of unspecified nationality, but presumably citizens of Argentina, and 4 families and 6 single men who were English.[2] Like Vernet himself his colonists were not specifically and completely citizens of any particular

---

[1] F.O. 6/499, Parish to Aberdeen, 25 Apr. 1829.
[2] F.O. 6/499, Memo. dated 20 Apr. 1829, attached to Parish to Aberdeen, 25 Apr. 1829.

nation. Legally, however, they were acting under the protection of the state, Argentina, which had done the most (and this was very little) to assert authority in the islands.

Vernet himself does not appear to have had any marked attachment to Buenos Aires. According to Parish, Vernet 'would I believe be very happy if His Majesty's Government would take his Settlement under their protection'.[1] In 1831 Vernet made an extensive grant of land to an Englishman, Lieutenant William Langdon of the Royal Navy. Langdon also stated that 'from a conversation I had with M. Vernet upon the subject, I am authorized in saying, no objection would be made to occupation of it by the British Government'.[2] Subsequently Vernet himself applied for reinstatement in his economic and commercial rights after the British occupation had been established.

At the time of Parish's interview with Vernet in 1829 other Englishmen appear to have become interested in the Falkland Islands. In July of that year a man named Beckington wrote a long and intelligent letter to the Foreign Secretary urging that a British colony be established in the islands. He believed the Falklands to be of very great importance in strengthening British sea power, and in providing a base for the suppression of privateering and piracy and for whale fishing. When Langdon wrote to the Foreign Office eighteen months later he supported Beckington's arguments, and added one of his own: the advantage of the Falkland Islands to the increased shipping in the Australian trade.

Shortly after receiving Beckington's letter, Aberdeen wrote to Parish instructing him to protest to the Government in Buenos Aires against the actions 'done without reference to the validity of the claims which His Majesty had constantly asserted to the sovereignty of the Islands.'[3] In November Parish delivered an official Note of protest to General Guido, the Minister of Foreign Affairs. At this moment Argentina was still rumbling with civil war, and General Rosas was just settling into authority in Buenos Aires Province. Guido merely acknowledged the Note, promising that 'The Government will give their particular

---

[1] F.O. 6/499, Parish to Aberdeen, 25 Apr. 1829.
[2] F.O. 6/499, Langdon to Hay, 20 Jan. 1832.
[3] F.O. 6/499, Aberdeen to Parish, 8 Aug. 1829.

consideration to the said Note . . . and will have the satisfaction of communicating . . . their resolution upon it, as soon as [the undersigned] receives orders to do so.'[1]

General Rosas's Government never managed to come to any resolution on the subject. There were a good many other things to think about during the year 1830 in Buenos Aires. In November of that year Vernet's principal lieutenant, Captain Brisbane, a British subject, appeared in Buenos Aires, where he published for ships' captains to read an order of Governor Vernet prohibiting the shooting of cattle in the islands and unauthorized fishing for seals on their coasts. Parish waited upon Captain Brisbane to warn him that the British Government claimed the islands and that Vernet should be careful not to interfere with any of His Majesty's subjects. 'Mr. Brisbane promised me', Parish reported, 'he would take care that my caution should be attended to; that the truth was, the Notice was more intended to draw Vessels to Soledad for Supplies, than to hinder their coming there, which in fact they had no means whatever at their disposal to prevent.'[2] In fact no British vessel or crew was ever obstructed in any activity of any kind in the Falkland Islands.

Sometime in 1831 Louis Vernet decided to commence enforcing his orders against the shooting of cattle and unauthorized fishing, at least against the Americans. In July and August he arrested three American vessels. One escaped from his custody. The captain of the second made a deal with Vernet by the terms of which he agreed to fish for seals in the Pacific and split the profits with Vernet. The third ship and its crew were sent to Buenos Aires for trial by an Argentine court.

At this moment the United States Consul at Buenos Aires was an inexperienced patriot named George Washington Slacum. Mr. Slacum believed that the essential element in diplomacy was to assert, in the most intemperate language at his command, the self-evident and natural rights of the people of the United States to shoot and fish where they pleased. Unfortunately the Foreign Minister in Buenos Aires at this time was Nicolás Anchorena, who was a patriot of Mr. Slacum's own kidney. He replied to Slacum by denying him diplomatic status.

---

[1] F.O. 6/499, Guido to Parish, 25 Nov. 1829.
[2] F.O. 6/499, Parish to Aberdeen, 20 Nov. 1830.

At this stage the U.S.S. *Lexington* appeared off Buenos Aires. Its captain presented himself to Señor Anchorena and described Governor Vernet as a pirate and robber. He ordered Anchorena to arrest Vernet and send him for trial. Naturally Anchorena refused to listen to Captain Duncan. Duncan thereupon went back aboard his ship and, in the company of the U.S.S. *Warren* from Rio, sailed for the Falklands. A party was landed at Port Louis. They spiked the Argentine guns, blew up the powder magazine, sacked the dwelling houses, seized a store of seal skins, arrested the inhabitants, put the leading ones in irons, and carried them away to be tried as pirates.

In Buenos Aires and Montevideo the feeling against the United States was intense. Buenos Aires, however, was experiencing a liberal interlude between the first and second Governorships of General Rosas. Señor de Maza, the Foreign Minister, consented to see the newly appointed chargé of the United States, but Mr. Francis Baylies only succeeded in compounding the error of Mr. Slacum by attempting to get Señor Maza to agree that Governor Vernet was a pirate. Maza saw Baylies twice, and then gave him his passports. Diplomatic intercourse between Argentina and the United States ceased for eleven years, and as late as 1885 the two Governments were still discussing the actions of the U.S.S. *Lexington*.

In the interval between the seizure of the American sealers and the arrival of the *Lexington* Governor Vernet made another flirtatious overture to the British. He sent Parish a list of all the ships which had called at Port Louis during his presence in the islands between 1826 and 1831. He also wrote, for Parish's benefit, an extensive description of the islands in which he argued that, as a port of call on the way round the Horn, East Falkland had many advantages in health over the River Plate or Brazil ports. Vernet emphasized the abundance of fresh supplies and antiscorbutic vegetables which a colony could make available, and he called attention to the way in which crews could recover from long months at sea by hunting the abundant game on the healthy moors of the islands.[1]

By the time this description reached London, Vernet's colony was a shambles. H.M.S. *Rattlesnake* visited the islands, and its captain reported to Parish, who was on his way home to Britain,

[1] F.O. 6/499, enclosed with Parish to Palmerston, 14 Dec. 1831.

that the Americans were taking the entire settlement away for trial as pirates. Whether the Americans deported everyone or only some is a point of detail. The plain fact is that their action destroyed the colony as a growing community, and the Falkland Islands momentarily relapsed into a state of nature, free to all comers.

This condition did not last long. The Hon. Henry Fox, the new British Minister to Buenos Aires, arrived there in December 1831. He appears at first to have succumbed to American influences, for he joined the Americans in describing Vernet's colony as a gathering of vagabonds and pirates.[1] Palmerston replied to Fox's first communication with instructions to demand at once from the Government in Buenos Aires a revocation of the authority granted Vernet.[2] By the time Fox received Palmerston's instructions he had had time to think things over and to get a better view of what was happening. He put Palmerston's instructions aside, arguing that it would be just as well to let the Americans do their own quarrelling in Buenos Aires, and that in any case an assertion of British sovereignty might very well involve Britain in disputes with the Americans about fishing rights. The American chargé told Fox that his Government was quite willing to acknowledge British sovereignty, but that the U.S. Government as a successor state of Great Britain in the Americas claimed the same fishing rights as those of Great Britain.[3]

At this stage the United States and Argentina broke off diplomatic relations. In London, Fox's arguments about possible involvement with the United States over fishing rights appears to have had little effect. In August 1832 the Admiralty sent to the Foreign Office a draft order which they proposed to issue to the Admiral on the South American station 'to take measures for periodically exercising the right of sovereignty on behalf of His Majesty in the Falkland Islands'. Palmerston agreed to the order.

Meanwhile the Government in Buenos Aires appointed a new Governor with the object of establishing a penal colony. Under the escort of the Argentine vessel of war *Sarandí* a small fleet

[1] F.O. 6/499, Fox to Palmerston, no date, Dec. 1831.
[2] F.O. 6/499, Palmerston to Fox, 22 Mar. 1832.
[3] F.O. 6/500, Fox to Palmerston, 15 Oct. 1832.

was dispatched to the islands. Once there, the convicts mutinied and murdered the Governor. The officers and crew of the *Sarandi* had just succeeded in re-establishing authority when H.M.S. *Clio* appeared off Port Louis (Port Egremont, to the British). The captain of the *Clio* came ashore. He stated to the captain of the *Sarandi* that he was obliged to order him to strike the Argentine flag and that he was present for the purpose of asserting the sovereignty of His Majesty King William IV in the Falkland Islands. The captain of the *Sarandi* naturally refused to obey. A party of Royal Marines was landed. They struck the Argentine flag and broke out the Union Jack. Having delivered a protest at this action, the captain of the *Sarandi* embarked and sailed away. Shortly after, a small permanent British naval base was established.

When news of this action reached Buenos Aires, the British chargé, Philip Gore, was unaware of what had taken place. He was summoned to the Foreign Office at once. Señor de Maza declared that 'the Government of Buenos Ayres could not but see a *gratuitous* exercise of the "Right of the Strongest" . . . to humiliate and depress a powerless and an infant people';[1] Gore replied that the British Government had repeatedly raised the question of the possession of the islands, but had had no reply. Fox had protested against the appointment of the late Governor, but had received only a promise to discuss the matter in the future.

In Buenos Aires the indignation against Great Britain was very great. But amid the indignation there was a note of caution. The newspaper *Lucero* expressed this very well.

If one should be asked [wrote the editor] 'what ought to be the conduct of the Government, in the difficult position in which it has been placed, through the usurpation of a part of its territory by a friendly nation?' we should say without hesitation, that nothing would appear to us more inopportune than to retort upon that Nation by the abrogation of existing Treaties, without having acquired the proof, of absence of all disposition on the part of England to repair the offence committed against the Flag and our Rights.[2]

Señor Moreno, the Argentine Minister in London, presented a Note of protest asserting the Argentine claim to sovereignty.

[1] F.O. 6/500, Gore to Palmerston, 14 Feb. 1833.
[2] *Lucero*, 28 Jan. 1833, enclosed in F.O. 6/500, Gore to Palmerston, 14 Feb. 1833.

In June 1833 he had this Note and its supporting documents published in French and English and circulated in the capitals of Europe. The British chargé in Buenos Aires thought Palmerston ought to circulate publicly a Spanish translation of the British documents on the subject.

Thus the matter stood at the end of 1833, and so it has continued to stand since then. The British continued to occupy the islands and the Argentine Government continued to complain. At first the complaints were loud and menacing. The mercantile community was thoroughly uneasy immediately after the crisis. In the winter of 1833 a rumour that the Argentine Government planned to recall their Minister in London greatly upset British merchants. The British chargé waited on the Foreign Minister with a copy of *El Monitor* in his hand in which the rumour was stated as fact with great explicitness. 'His Excellency, in reply, assured me', Gore reported, 'that the language to which I adverted had been wholly unauthorized; . . . that whatever might have been the intentions of the Buenos Ayres Cabinet, at one period, with respect to such a course, they no longer existed'.[1] This determination not to make a fundamental issue of the Falkland Islands remained the policy of the Government. Gradually the dispute became an accepted part of Anglo-Argentine intercourse like the fixed faults of a husband or wife about which one complains and the other does nothing. A reference to the Falkland Islands became as much a part of the Governor's annual message as the petition for Divine guidance. General Rosas attached as little importance to one as to the other. In 1841 each disputant restated his case in an elaborate exchange of Notes. Following upon this Rosas proposed a simple deal: if the British would forget the Loan of 1824, he would forget the Falkland Islands.[2] This was an altogether too unequal transaction from the British point of view. For Rosas the Falkland Islands were bargaining counters. The whole energy of his régime and of the régimes which came after him was directed towards the land frontiers. Cows and sheep not whales and seals were the preoccupation of his principal supporters, and the main objects of their affections and

---

[1] F.O. 6/501, Gore to Palmerston, 29 Aug. 1834.
[2] This story is reported in H. E. Peters, *Foreign Debt of the Argentine Republic* (Baltimore, 1934), p. 20, but there is no evidence for it in the F.O. papers.

capital investments. A greater influence of the mercantile elements in the affairs of Buenos Aires might conceivably have
altered the temperature of the Falkland Islands question, but
the ascendancy of the landed interest was the best guarantee
that it would be left in cold storage, a frozen asset in the game
of diplomacy, but nothing more.

The real sufferers in this dispute were the men who knew
something about the Falklands and had some enthusiasm for
their potentialities as an habitation for human beings. In 1835
Vernet applied to the British Government for reinstatement in
his property rights. He was permitted to take away what remained of his movable property, but the British Government
refused to recognize any of his claims lest by doing so they
tacitly admitted the right of the Government in Buenos Aires
to make the grants which had been originally made to Vernet.
Lieutenant Langdon, as a sub-grantee of Vernet, suffered the
same fate. As for the original colonists, they were scattered
across the world. When H.M.S. *Clio* visited Port Louis for the
purpose of asserting the sovereignty of Great Britain, they found
only twelve gauchos, two Britons, two Germans, one Frenchman, and a negro from Jamaica, the remnants of the Argentine
convict settlement left behind when the *Sarandi* sailed away.
For many years the islands were bare of permanent inhabitants,
save for the small detachment of the Royal Navy amounting to
little more than a boat's crew. From time to time men wrote to
the Foreign or Colonial Offices pointing out the many advantages of the Falkland Islands to a maritime nation, but nothing
has ever happened to transform in any dramatic way these
windswept dots of land at the end of the world.

The experiences of the Roman Catholic Church in Argentina
during the revolutions which overthrew Spanish authority bear
some resemblance to those of the Church of France during the
French Revolution. The revolutionaries had been in varying
degrees under the influence of the enlightened rationalists of
eighteenth-century France and the utilitarians of the Bentham-
ite school. The Church had suffered a considerable diminution
of its authority and a reduction of its wealth. The sufferings
of the Church during the revolution were not, however, a
martyrdom but merely a stimulus sufficiently sharp to awaken

it from its slumbering apathy. As the revolutionary movement grew in strength and drew unto itself wider and wider strata of the population the influence of the liberal intelligentsia of the towns correspondingly diminished and the strength of the Church was correspondingly renewed. The provincial *caudillos* discovered in religion their political slogans. Rosas proclaimed the defence of the Catholic Church as the first purpose of politics. In all the constitutions, even the most liberal, the Roman Catholic Church had been accorded a special, official status, but Rosas went beyond mere official recognition. He diverted such funds as there were from secular schemes of education projected by the liberals into the hands of the Church, and he allowed secular education to die.

The resurgence of the Church, linked as it was with xenophobic tendencies in politics and protectionist tendencies in commercial policy, presented a potential difficulty to a community like the British gathered in Buenos Aires. The religious freedom of British subjects was guaranteed by Treaty, but religious freedom has many particular aspects of which the right to worship is only one, and for many not the most important. The laws governing marriage, burial, educational activities, the custody of children, and the taking of oaths are matters of some concern to persons spending their lives under the authority of a government not their own and in a community in which they are a small minority. A minority can be harassed out of existence or at least driven to departure by laws governing such matters, if they are designed and applied in a hostile manner.

On the British side, there were not wanting elements of difficulty. Zeal for the true reformed religion was at this time still lively in the hearts of many of His Majesty's subjects, and not least in the hearts of those who had sought improvement of their lot in foreign parts. Many knew and many learned that neutrality, if not indifference, in matters of faith is often a necessity of commerce, but there still remained some, particularly of the humbler orders, who, given a lead, were ready enough to proclaim the truth among the Papists and heathens. In addition to zeal, and perhaps as an aspect of it, there were differences among British subjects about which manifestation of Divine Knowledge ought to receive the protection of the Treaty of 1825 and the financial assistance of His Majesty's Government under the authority of 6 George IV, cap. 87.

Parish had taken the view that Protestant British subjects could find the satisfaction of their religious needs in a chapel supported by subscription, assisted by a grant from the British Government and opened with the permission of the Government of Buenos Aires. The first man placed in charge of this chapel, the Rev. John Armstrong, was a man of broad and comprehensive views, but he was none the less a member of the priesthood of the Church of England owning the authority of the Bishop of London. At first this fact presented no difficulty, but in 1829 there appeared in Buenos Aires the Rev. John Brown, the minister of the Kirk established under the patronage of the Robertson brothers in their settlement at Monte Grande. Brown and the members of his congregation had fled from the settlement during the disorders of that year, and were now in Buenos Aires re-establishing themselves. Brown argued that he and his congregation, being part of the established church in Scotland, could properly claim the protection of the Treaty and the financial support of the British Government. When the erection of a new chapel was under discussion, the Rev. Mr. Brown and some of his followers, led by his principal lieutenant, a schoolmaster named Gilbert Ramsay, appeared at one of the meetings and began to state their case not, as Parish reported, 'in the most decorous manner'. Parish was the chairman of the meeting. He was satisfied that 'every Merchant of Respectability who attends Church at all, support[ed] that established with the sanction of His Majesty's Government', whereas Brown's congregation consisted of 'the lower orders of his countrymen . . . chiefly mechanics and Agricultural Emigrants . . . to whom may be added . . . a very few of the Clerks belonging to some of the Mercantile Houses'.[1] This being so, Parish thought it proper to rule the Rev. Mr. Brown and Mr. Ramsay out of order and ineligible to vote 'unless they chose to subscribe to the real objects of the meeting'.

Brown was an able and determined man. When summoned to see Parish, he told the Consul-General that he intended to bring his case before the General Assembly of the Church of Scotland and before Parliament. Parish warned him of the

[1] F.O. 6/30, Parish to Aberdeen, 13 Mar. 1830.

scandal a religious controversy would cause and the dangers it might bring to Protestants generally. Brown promised not to publicize the controversy, but in a long and closely argued letter ranging over the subject of Church Government from Genesis to George IV he threatened to place an advertisement of his case in one of the Buenos Aires newspapers. Parish's answer to this threat was a visit to General Guido to whom he exposed the many embarrassments likely to follow from the dispute. General Guido took the hint, summoned Brown before him, and 'told him plainly that he ran a risk of having his Chapel closed altogether if he chose to persist in a course which he was once sufficiently warned might be highly inconvenient to the Government'.[1]

This silenced the Rev. Mr. Brown, but only in Buenos Aires. The Earl of Aberdeen heard his plea, and to some effect. Parish's successor, Fox, was instructed to seek from Rosas permission for the Presbyterians to build a chapel of their own which was to share in the subsidy provided by Parliament. He encountered no opposition from Rosas or his ministers. But Fox was a cool sceptic, who lamented the zealous absurdities of his countrymen.

When the British Church was first established [he told Palmerston] there would have been less difficulty in reconciling the interests of the two Sects, but, unfortunately, more importance seems to have been attached, even in this distant quarter of the globe, to securing for the followers of the Church of England a triumph over their Presbyterian fellow Countrymen, than to extending the benefit of His Majesty's bounty over the greatest number of His Majesty's subjects.[2]

The zeal of the Rev. Mr. Armstrong created embarrassment in another direction. He wrote to his Bishop calling attention to the dangers of a falling away 'from the true religion' owing to the scarcity of chaplains and to the lamentable failure of the true Church to bring the light of their witness into the many dark places of South America. The Bishop of London at once wrote to the Foreign Secretary urging him to make more and better use of 6 George IV, cap. 87 to the end that boundaries of light might be extended. Aberdeen did not consider the Treaty of 1825 a licence to convert men from error, but only a defence

[1] F.O. 6/30, Parish to Aberdeen, 13 Mar. 1830.
[2] F.O. 6/34, Fox to Palmerston, 15 Oct. 1832.

of a British subject's right to keep his own truth. 'I cannot but express to your Lordship', he wrote, 'the strong doubts which I entertain of the practicability or expediency of the plan proposed by the Rev. Mr. Armstrong of appointing Itinerant Clergymen in the new States of America for the purpose of propagating . . . among the Roman Catholic Inhabitants of those States the reformed doctrines of the Church of England.'[1] After this exchange there were no further efforts made to obtain official sponsorship and help for missionary enterprise.

The zeal and professional interest of the Anglican and Presbyterian clergymen created only a potential difficulty in the practical interpretation of the religious clauses in the Treaty. A real difficulty loaded with political overtones arose over the marriage practices of the Argentine community. This difficulty was brought into public view in the Lafone marriage case, the dramatic qualities and moral ambiguities of which defied improvement for the purpose of inflaming indignation and prejudice among both Catholics and Protestants.

The *dramatis personae* of this episode were Mr. Samuel Lafone, a wealthy dealer in hides connected with a large firm of tanners in Liverpool, his brother Alexander Lafone, an Argentine lady, Doña Maria Fliga de Quevedo y Alcina, her mother, her father, a young American named Horne, and an unnamed Frenchman. In paying court to Doña Maria Fliga, Samuel Lafone encountered the opposition of the father but the encouragement of the mother of his beloved. Quevedo proving stubborn, Lafone planned to marry the lady in spite of everything. He applied to the Rev. Mr. Armstrong to perform the ceremony, but Armstrong refused. The Rev. Mr. Brown, however, had no scruples or was unacquainted with the laws of the Argentine Republic, for he agreed. The ceremony was performed in the house of the lady's mother in the presence of the mother, Lafone's brother, and the American and French friends of the couple. Enraged by these proceedings Quevedo lodged a complaint with the Government of Buenos Aires. Lafone and his bride, the bride's mother, and the witnesses were arrested and hailed before both the civil and the ecclesiastical courts. The civil court sentenced the bridegroom, his brother, and the witnesses to banishment from the Province. The ecclesiastical

[1] F.O. 6/28, Aberdeen to the Bishop of London, 10 Mar. 1829.

court annulled the marriage, fined Lafone 1,000 pesos (about £29), and sentenced the ladies to correction in a convent. Protestant susceptibilities were further rubbed raw by the offer of the ecclesiastical court to validate the marriage if Lafone turned Catholic.

At once there was a loud public outcry of liberal indignation from the British residents and of outraged patriarchal virtue from the Argentinos. The case was pushed before the British Minister, the sceptic Fox. After studying it he refused to do anything more than apply privately to the Governor of Buenos Aires to deal mercifully with Lafone. Fox declared that it was the duty of British subjects to obey the laws of the Argentine Republic and to respect the jurisdiction of the Argentine courts. He repudiated the suggestion in the memorial drawn up by the British residents that they 'are to be considered a separate community exempt as British subjects from the operation of the law of the land and enjoying rights distinct from those of the Citizens of the Republick'.[1] The British residents then called a general meeting to consider the conduct of the British Minister. Fox told them that he did not propose to accept his instruction from a meeting of British residents and that he was responsible only to His Majesty's Government. 'It is due to the Buenos Ayrean Government', he told Palmerston, 'to observe that ever since the signature of the Treaty with Great Britain, they have been not only scrupulously exact in fulfilling their obligations under the article of religious toleration, but upon several occasions, liberal beyond the letter of those engagements. And the more credit belongs to them, therefore, as there have been, I believe, great difficulties to overcome.'[2] Fox concluded by saying that behaviour such as Lafone's was encouraging ill will and jealousy towards foreigners.

The essential difficulty in the Lafone case was the illegality of marriages between Catholics and Protestants. Such a marriage could only take place if the Catholic party received a dispensation from the Papal Nuncio. For some years the Argentine authorities had simply issued a licence in lieu of a dispensation, but when formal ties were re-established with the See of Rome the dispensing power was resumed by the Pope's representative.

---

[1] F.O. 6/34, Fox to Palmerston, 24 Sept. 1832.
[2] Ibid.

Inasmuch as he ordinarily resided in Rio de Janeiro, the difficulties of a mixed marriage were formidable. Unquestionably Lafone had been guilty of gross breaches of law. This was the opinion of the law officers of the Crown.[1] In spite of his offence, his sentence of banishment was revoked, and in May 1833 the Provincial Assembly passed a law removing civil obstacles to mixed marriages and giving to the Governor the power to dispense, although leaving intact the ecclesiastical power to impose spiritual penalties upon Catholics contracting marriages without the Church's sanction.

The Lafone case served to demonstrate the good faith of the British Government in the observation of the religious clauses. Although Rosas's régime became steadily more severe, nothing happened to impair the religious liberty of British subjects. They extended the area of their burial grounds. In the course of the next half-century they built churches both in the cities and in the rural areas and opened schools. The Roman Catholic Church, of course, never slumbered in its attention to questions like birth, death, and marriage, and as late as the 1890's British residents were complaining about the high cost and difficulty of marrying in the Argentine Republic even among Protestants. But, in fact, the question was solved as a political difficulty by 1833. The British Government for its part was prepared neither to countenance law-breaking by British subjects nor to support them if they did, nor was it willing to encourage missionary activities by Protestants; the Argentine Government in return was prepared to accord religious liberty both in theory and in practical detail.

[1] F.O. 6/40, Palmerston to Gore, 7 Jan. 1834.

IX

BRITAIN, FRANCE, AND
GENERAL ROSAS

IN the immediately previous pages we have considered what may be described as the private problems of Britain and Argentina during the ascendancy of General Rosas. These were differences which primarily concerned Britain and Argentina without reference to other powers. Now we must tell about the relations of the two states as they were affected during these years by the activities and policies of other nations in the River Plate. In the main this means a consideration of the place of France and of the new-born state of Uruguay created out of the Banda Oriental by the peace treaty with Brazil in 1828.

By the time General Rosas came to power the crudity and confusion of Bourbon diplomacy had all but extinguished the Franco-Argentine connexion at the moment of its institution. When Louis Philippe came to the throne of France a softer approach was tried. Almost at once the Orleanist Government unconditionally recognized the independence of the Argentine Confederation without bargaining, as the British had done, about a treaty setting forth general but explicit rules governing the intercourse of the two communities. Unfortunately, the impulsive generosity of the Orleanists was as unproductive of understanding as Bourbon arrogance and violence. General Rosas and his followers were little disposed to extend the number of their contacts with the outer world, and particularly with the French whose naval commanders had burnt Argentine warships at anchor within sight of Buenos Aires and whose wines and craft products competed with old-established enterprises of the interior provinces. The federalist party in Buenos Aires were not opposed to the growing immigration of Frenchmen to the River Plate, but the notion implicit in any treaty with the French that Frenchmen resident in Argentina enjoyed the special protection of the French Government was an anathema to them. General Rosas's suspicions of the Orleanist liberality were only too well founded. Events in Algeria, in the Pacific, and in South America itself soon revealed that the soft persuasive words of the July Monarchy were but a stage in the establishment of French authority over other peoples and that French immigrants, whether they liked it or not, were an advance band of the French mission to civilize and rule.

During the brief liberal interlude while General Balcarce was Governor the French representative in Buenos Aires made some progress in the negotiation of an agreement along the lines of the Anglo-Argentine Treaty. In September 1833 the Rosista reaction commenced. A turbulent flood of anti-foreign feeling accompanied the establishment of the dictatorship. When the draft of the agreement was placed before a secret session of the Assembly in June 1834 the British chargé predicted that it would never survive.[1] He was right. The xenophobic enthusiasts in the Chamber refused to see what Rosas himself was able to grasp, namely, that a treaty, if it embraces the notion of equality as the Anglo-Argentine Treaty did, is a means of shackling foreign states and restraining impulses to imperialism whenever they infect the lifestream of a great power.

From the winter of 1834 onwards Franco-Argentine relations deteriorated. Rebuffed by the régime in Buenos Aires the French Government ceased to strive for a treaty binding themselves and the established Government in Buenos Aires. They turned instead to a policy of allying themselves with the enemies of General Rosas and, in concert with the opposition, to the use of force. The precise objects of the French Government are not clear. The successful employment of such a policy in Tahiti led to a protectorate; in Algeria to annexation. In the case of the River Plate intentions were probably more modest, but the French, like the British thirty years before, had not yet clearly defined their objectives nor discovered a settled policy for their achievement. In addition the Orleanist Monarchy suffered more than any British Government from the pushing and hauling of incompatible interests, the commercial classes wanting one thing, the military caste another, with the Government irresolutely in the centre of these contentions.[2]

[1] F.O. 6/40, Gore to Palmerston, 16 June 1834.
[2] J. F. Cady, *Foreign Intervention in the Río de la Plata* (Philadelphia, 1929), pp. 42, 82.

In Algeria French action had begun over a fly-swatter; in
Argentina it was a matter of maps. In May 1837, when he was
preparing for war against Bolivia, General Rosas placed an
order for maps and plans with a French lithographer in Buenos
Aires, César Hipolyte Bâcle. Bâcle appears to have been selective
in the business he undertook, for he declined the order on the
excuse of ill health. In order to recruit his strength he moved
to the interior where he believed the climate was better and
where, Rosas believed, he was nearer the Bolivian frontier and
the centres of unitarian resistance to the dictator's régime.
Bâcle was seized, and it was alleged that he was found with
plans and papers in his possession of value to the enemies of
General Rosas. He was ordered to reside in Santa Fé under the
eye of Rosas's best political ally, General López. There Bâcle
died. The French Vice-Consul Roger presented a claim upon
the Government of Buenos Aires for the losses suffered by Bâcle.
Unfortunately, the language in which the claim was made was
provocative and threatening, and Rosas handed Roger his passports and told him to leave the country.

L'affaire Bâcle was only one of several difficulties. Roger had
repeatedly complained that the Argentine Government was
compelling French subjects to serve in the Argentine Army.
The Argentine Government replied that the service of foreign
nationals in the Argentine forces was the law of the country
applied equally to all foreigners except those exempted by
treaty; that in fact the number of Frenchmen serving amounted
only to half a dozen of whom five were volunteers and the sixth
was a convicted criminal serving his sentence in the army.[1] The
French grievance was small in fact, but large in principle, for
service in the Army could be used as a means of political
pressure. The Argentine argument was likewise worthy of
consideration, for the French had once already swung their
influence at a critical moment against the partisans of Rosas,
and it was well known that enemies of the régime had found
a friendly place of asylum in France.

The expulsion of Roger provoked in the French a determination to bring Rosas down or at least to compel him to admit
French influence in Buenos Aires on something approximating
to French terms. Early in 1838 a French fleet appeared off

[1] Levene, *A History of Argentina*, p. 424.

Buenos Aires, and Admiral Leblanc came ashore to negotiate. Meanwhile in Montevideo French diplomatic agents were busy helping to install the adventurer, Fructuoso Rivera, as President of the Oriental Republic and to line up for action all the liberal enemies of Rosas under the leadership of General Lavalle.

In this situation Rosas displayed his political genius at its best. With his followers he had no difficulties. A popular movement in Buenos Aires threatened with death the four deputies in the Assembly who had spoken haltingly about negotiating with France.[1] Rosas for his part obeyed the voice of the people. He told Admiral Leblanc to go back where he came from. Admiral Leblanc, however, merely went back aboard his frigate and proclaimed the blockade of Buenos Aires. Rosas's answer to this was a promise to Britain to reduce all duties on foreign merchandise by one-third from the level before the blockade was proclaimed.[2]

The popular British response to the French action was very hostile both in Buenos Aires and in Britain. In June 1838, and again in August, *The Times* denounced the French for their actions, and mercantile firms and associations wrote protesting to the Foreign Office. After the blockade had run on for more than a year Lord Ashburton of Baring Brothers declared that a continuation of French interference in the Río de la Plata would justify Britain in going to war with Louis Philippe.

Palmerston's policy was directed towards mediation. He protested to France,[3] while Mandeville, the British Minister in Buenos Aires, urged Rosas to negotiate.[4] This was on the level of diplomacy. On the level of action the British cruisers did nothing to assist the French blockade, and the principle of strict blockade, which had operated so favourably for the Brazilians during the first stages of the Brazilian war against Argentina, was now forgotten. So little effect did the blockade have on British trade that in both 1838 and 1839 the level of British exports to Buenos Aires was above the average of the previous five years, and in 1840 it was only 11 per cent. below that average.

---

[1] Cady, *Foreign Intervention*, p. 27.
[2] F.O. 6/64, Mandeville to Palmerston, 14 June 1838.
[3] F.O. 27/556, Palmerston to Granville, 12 June 1838.
[4] F.O. 6/64, Mandeville to Palmerston, 14 June 1838.

At first the French had a number of successes against Rosas on the periphery of his power. Rivera managed to overthrow Oribe, the President of Uruguay, and to install himself in a position to win the elections required by the constitution of that unhappy country. Rivera accepted French assistance and actively helped to organize the Argentine opposition forces seeking to overthrow Rosas. In Corrientes the Governor, Berón de Astrada, denounced Rosas and called upon his fellow provincial governors to strip Rosas of his power to negotiate with foreign nations in the name of the Argentine Confederation. In Buenos Aires itself the son of one of Rosas's former ministers, Colonel Ramon Maza, organized a conspiracy against the Governor.

But, with a French fleet in the river, Rosas was at his best. The Governor of Entre Rios refused to respond to the appeal of his neighbour, the Governor of Corrientes. Instead, he marched into Corrientes and, in the name of the Argentine Confederation and the federalist cause, defeated Berón de Astrada and his Uruguayan allies at Pago Largo on 31 March 1839. In Buenos Aires Rosas's police discovered the conspiracy of Colonel Maza. His father was murdered in his office in the hall of the Provincial Assembly and Colonel Maza himself was shot the next day.

When the winter rains began to lift, a force of Argentine enemies of Rosas under Lavalle was assembled in Uruguay. This was equipped by the French and strengthened with a force of French marines and artillery. The joint army was launched at the island of Martín García, which fell after a bitter defence by Rosas. The fall of Martín García was the signal for a rising in the southern part of Buenos Aires Province. Lavalle, however, misdirected his force towards Entre Rios, while Rosas's brother Prudencio moved rapidly against the rebels in the southern pampas, defeating them band by band before they could concentrate their forces. The square in Chascomús was decorated with the severed heads of the defeated.

Away to the north Lavalle gained a series of tactical victories over the Governors of Entre Rios and Santa Fé. Far in the north-west another revolutionary movement under Marceo de Avellaneda broke out in April 1840 in Tucumán. As the winter approached it looked as if the enemies of Rosas were assembling for an assault on the central bastion of the dictator's authority.

The French were reported in London to be preparing a fresh naval reinforcement for the support of their protégés in the Río de la Plata.

At this stage Palmerston intervened. This was the climactic moment of his struggle to frustrate French policy in the Middle East where another of their protégés, Mehemet Ali, was seeking to destroy the Sultan of Turkey. Palmerston had put together all the information he could find about French intrigues with the enemies of the established authorities in Argentina. It made up a document of 134 pages. Palmerston sent this to the British Ambassador in Paris with instructions that it be delivered to the French Foreign Minister.[1] Nothing was said. No threats were made. But there was the ammunition for the destruction of French influence in South America. Almost simultaneously the announcement was made that Britain, Russia, Prussia, and Austria were prepared to support the Sultan against Mehemet Ali. Louis Philippe and his Ministers decided that the time had come to shorten their lines of defence. An officer of the French Admiralty was sent to request British assistance in coming to terms with General Rosas.

News of the French decision appears to have leaked out to Lavalle. He lost heart. His force, poised to strike at Buenos Aires, turned aside from its objective, and then drew back. Rosas passed to the offensive and so did his allies in Santa Fé and Entre Rios. His enemies scattered before his wrath. Far away on the borders of Bolivia Lavalle, who had asked history to judge him for the death of Dorrego, himself reached the end of his long and blood-stained journey. In the Province of Salta a party of Rosistas surrounded a house where he was being entertained. They fired into the house, and Lavalle fell. His body was borne away across the border by his friends, and he was buried in the cathedral in Potosí.

Admiral de Mackau, the man sent by the French Government to reach a settlement, arrived off Buenos Aires on 12 October 1840, hoping still to achieve by talk what France had failed to gain by force. His draft proposals, which he disclosed to Mandeville before meeting the Argentine Foreign Minister, aimed at obtaining for France indemnities, an Argentine undertaking to accord French citizens the same rights and privileges

---

[1] F.O. 27/599, Palmerston to Granville, 16 June 1840, and F.O. 146/222.

enjoyed by British subjects resident in Argentina, a readmission to Argentina of the Argentine political exiles, and an Argentine undertaking to guarantee the independence of Uruguay. In return France offered to lift the blockade and evacuate Martín García. In fact de Mackau was proposing to establish France as the guarantor of Uruguayan independence and the protector of an Argentine political faction. de Mackau asked Mandeville to use his great influence with General Rosas to prevail upon the dictator to accept these proposals. Mandeville replied dryly that, if he had the influence with the Governor necessary to obtain agreement to the French terms, he would long since have used that power to stop the war in the River Plate. Mandeville was determined, however, to do what he could to effect a settlement. He believed that Rosas ought to grant French citizens the same rights as British subjects. If this were granted everything else demanded by the French could be overlooked.

When negotiations commenced, Arana, Rosas's Foreign Minister, rejected every French proposal but with a politeness which left it for the French to try again. de Mackau collapsed completely and quickly. To the surprise of everyone concerned he proposed to abandon all the French proposals of substance if Rosas would agree to a face-saving agreement to indemnify France for losses suffered by individuals. Mandeville asked why Arana hesitated over a settlement of this kind. Arana said he did not know whether Rosas would consent. Mandeville immediately sought out the Governor, who had just returned from a journey into the countryside. Rosas got out of bed to see Mandeville.

'I know what you have come for,' he said. 'Sit down. Sit down.'[1]

Without hesitation Rosas agreed to an indemnity to be determined by arbitration, to grant French citizens the same rights as those of the most favoured nation provided they claimed no rights in excess of those enjoyed by citizens of other South American states resident in Argentina. France's late political allies were completely abandoned. By the terms of the settlement Rosas was left as sole judge of how he should deal with Argentine political exiles. He undertook to respect the absolute independence of Uruguay 'without prejudice to his natural rights wherever justice, honour and Argentine security require'

[1] F.O. 6/75, Mandeville to Palmerston, 28 Oct. 1840.

[their assertion].[1] Article IV was thus loaded with trouble. In conjunction with Article III concerning political exiles this Article laid the basis in international law of Rosas's determination to destroy rather than compromise with his enemies. Neither Mandeville nor Palmerston appears to have detected such a possibility in what seemed a settlement both happily and quickly realized.

We have already observed with what determination the Foreign Office strove for the creation of an independent buffer state between Argentina and Brazil on the Banda Oriental of Uruguay and how cautiously they avoided assuming any responsibility for the government of the new Republic. In dealing with Uruguay Aberdeen, during his first tenure of the Foreign Office, and Palmerston applied strictly the principle of non-interference and neutrality *vis-à-vis* the internal politics of that Republic, and they sought no special position for British subjects beyond what might be conferred upon them by a treaty like that existing with Argentina. Even this modest objective they failed to achieve. In 1834 the British Minister in Buenos Aires visited Montevideo for the purpose of negotiating a treaty. The Uruguayan Foreign Minister was sympathetic, but the public hostility to foreign states was very great. The press in Montevideo cried out that treaties with great powers, even when they were based on principles of reciprocity, were useless. The British had seized the Falkland Islands in spite of a treaty. In Chile and Colombia the French were behaving in a high-handed fashion. The Uruguayan Chamber refused to consider any agreement with Britain, and the British Minister returned to Buenos Aires determined to let the Uruguayans cool off.[2]

Treaty or no treaty, the fact of Uruguay's existence began to produce complications for the Foreign Office. So long as the Banda Oriental was the scene of social and international war where armies ranged across the Uruguayan pampas killing and stealing the herds of cattle and destroying all settled institutions productive of exportable products, Montevideo, in spite of its excellent harbour, was a place of no commercial importance. Once a semblance of peace came to the pampas and the cattle

[1] Cady, *Foreign Intervention*, p. 87.
[2] F.O. 6/41, Hamilton to Palmerston, 30 Dec. 1834.

began to renew their numb ers on the rich grass, merchants and ranchers commenced again to congregate in Montevideo and prosperity returned. No longer was the British commercial interest i n the River Plate focused on one metropolis, Buenos Aires, but upon two. Indeed, as early as 1834 the British Minister hazarded the prediction that with the coming of steam navigation Montevideo would become a place of much greater consequence than Buenos Aires.[1] Quite naturally the British mercantile interest in Montevideo became involved with the Uruguayan régime, and quite as naturally looked to the British Government to see things from their point of view rather than from that of the interests in Buenos Aires.

The mercantile interests in both Buenos Aires and Montevideo were agreed about certain obvious propositions such as the dependence of their prosperity upon peace and order. About the way in which peace and order could be maintained and, when broken, restored, there were, however, differences, and these differences in the end became too great even for the Foreign Office to transcend. We have referred to the semblance of peace which created the prosperity of Montevideo and the British merchants dwelling there. The operative word is semblance; for independent Uruguay was a very unsettled community. The nature of its malaise is not susceptible to brief description, but it can be shortly stated for the purposes of this narrative that the commotion in the 1830's in Uruguay was due to the rivalry of the two revolutionaries who had led the struggle against the Emperor of Brazil. One leader, General Juan Lavalleja, had launched himself upon his revolutionary course from an Argentine base; the other, General Fructuoso Rivera, had been an officer in the Brazilian service. The rivalry of Argentina and Brazil continued, as it were, as a domestic contention in Uruguay after the war between Argentina and Brazil had ceased.

Rivera was the first President of Uruguay. In 1835 a supporter of General Lavalleja, General Manuel Oribe, was elected to the Presidency. Rivera stepped down peacefully, but when Oribe permitted the return to Uruguay of certain supporters of General Lavalleja who had attempted forcibly to overthrow General Rivera during his Presidency, Rivera commenced to

[1] F.O. 6/41, Hamilton to Palmerston, 11 Dec. 1834.

seek the means of turning General Oribe out of office. Fair is fair, and nothing beyond a few scuffles and assassinations would probably have occurred had it not been for Rivera's decision to ally himself with the anti-Rosista exiles from Buenos Aires and with the French agents who were certainly bent upon applying pressure to Rosas and, perhaps, even upon preparing for the establishment of French authority in the River Plate.

In 1838, while the French Admiral Leblanc was threatening Rosas at Buenos Aires, Rivera succeeded in overthrowing President Oribe, who fled to Argentina and the protection of General Rosas. Once again in office, Rivera commenced consolidating his position by close co-operation with the foreign residents of Montevideo. From the French he received arms, ammunition, and the assistance of French soldiers. Italians he enlisted in a legion devoted to the defence of the Uruguayan capital. The British community for the most part steered clear of commitments of this description, and the British Consul on several occasions reminded British residents of their duty to remain neutral in the domestic affairs of the places where they resided. Unfortunately, the conception of neutrality did not exclude the possibility of making money. Rivera was a prodigious borrower, and his financial difficulties increased the closer his enemies drew a ring around Montevideo. In the end he mortgaged the Montevidean customs revenues to foreign business interests which were in the main British.[1] Thus it came about that substantial British interests became so entangled with Rivera's régime that they were obliged to support the Government in Montevideo and to exert what pressure they could to secure an abandonment of the long-standing British policy of non-interference.

In most politicians who risk their lives and estates in the quest for public power there can be discovered some central affection or principle upon which they will not loosen their hold. With Fructuoso Rivera it was otherwise. He was an adventurer. He had deserted Artigas for the Brazilian service. He had deserted the Brazilians to serve with Lavalleja. Lavalleja he had outwitted and exiled. Oribe he had overthrown. He had used the French and they had betrayed him when they found themselves over-burdened with too many ambitions. Now Rivera turned

[1] F.O. 51/32, Hood to Aberdeen, 7 Mar. 1844.

to the British. Late in 1841 Mandeville travelled from Buenos Aires across the river to Montevideo with the modest purpose of negotiating a treaty concerning the slave trade. Suddenly he was confronted with a request by Vidal, the Uruguayan Foreign Minister, to establish a British protectorate over the Oriental Republic. No, Mandeville replied, the responsibilities of a protectorate were too great and the special privileges which it would give to British subjects were bound to produce endless friction with other powers.[1]

So far the British Government had managed to avoid involvement and at the same time to preserve freedom of commercial intercourse. At this point, however, the aspect of affairs began to change. In the River Plate General Rosas was preparing to assist on a massive scale the effort of General Oribe and his party, the Blancos, to upset General Rivera and his party, the Colorados. In London Aberdeen replaced Palmerston at the Foreign Office. These events occurring together were heavy with trouble.

The difficulties in which the Earl of Aberdeen became involved in the River Plate during the Prime Ministership of Sir Robert Peel are not easy to explain. It is tempting to believe that Aberdeen simply abandoned the policy of Castlereagh and Canning in favour of a disastrous experiment in the use of force. That is how the 'intervention' is remembered and characterized still in Argentina. Aberdeen himself did not in the end differ much from this judgement of the events for which he was responsible. Writing in 1846 a few months before he quit the Foreign Office he concluded that 'after shedding much blood, [we have given] him [General Rosas] just grounds for complaint against us'.[2] The Government of the United States supported this view. 'We cordially wish the Argentine Republic success in its struggle against foreign interference', Secretary of State Buchanan wrote[3] within a few days of Aberdeen's own indictment of himself and his agents.

And yet the use of force, the spilling of blood, and hostility to Argentina were not the policy of the British Government

---

[1] F.O. 6/79, Mandeville to Palmerston, 6 Dec. 1841.

[2] British Museum, Add. MSS. 43127, *Aberdeen Papers*, vol. lxxxix, Aberdeen to Ouseley, 4 Mar. 1846. (Hereafter cited as *A.P.*)

[3] *Diplomatic Correspondence of the United States, Inter-American Affairs, 1831–1860*, vol. i, *Argentine*, Buchanan to Harris, 30 Mar. 1846.

during the years 1841–6. There is no document in the archives of the Foreign Office, the Admiralty, the War Office, or the Board of Trade which plainly indicates a conscious departure from the established policy of neutrality in the political affairs of the River Plate. On the contrary, all the documents—particularly the instructions to ministers and naval commanders—place their emphasis on neutrality and the preservation of peace and friendship with Argentina and Uruguay. A similar emphasis is placed upon the preservation of British lives and property, but nowhere in the official papers nor in the private papers of the Earl of Aberdeen is there any suggestion that Britain either alone or in concert with France intended or planned to use force against Argentina. The contradiction between what was officially intended and what actually happened requires explaining—but not explaining away.

It must first be remembered that the Government of Sir Robert Peel was much concerned with winning the affections of the commercial and industrial classes[1] and that these classes like the wage workers were still much disturbed by the depression of 1836–7 which had operated with such a devastating effect not only upon the levels of employment and investment but upon the received ideas of what constituted correct commercial and monetary policies. Even in so unimportant a sphere of British commercial interest as Argentina a contrast can be observed between the attitude of the British Government in the days of high prosperity of the early and mid-1830's and the attitude on commercial questions displayed after depression had set in. When Rosas embarked upon a protectionist policy in 1835 with the object of conciliating the small business interests of the interior provinces, the British Government did not object. In reporting the new tariff schedules of 1835 the British Consul, Griffiths, could, indeed, see some good in them as a means of stimulating local industrial and agricultural enterprise.[2] News of a further round of tariff increases in Buenos Aires in 1837 was not received so calmly in the Foreign Office. Palmerston told the British Minister that he did not 'claim the Right to

---

[1] Add. MSS. 43063, *A.P.*, vol. lxxxviii. In a letter dated 26 Nov. 1843, Peel reminded Aberdeen that the 'commercial interest connected with Montevideo' were complaining about the Government's 'apathy' in the River Plate.

[2] F.O. 6/49, Griffiths to Palmerston, 28 Dec. 1835.

remonstrate formally', but he wished him to lecture the Buenos Aires Government on the virtues of free trade and the folly of high tariffs and to point out 'the pernicious effects upon the trade of their Country which are so sure to result'.[1]

As the movement of the British economy was bearing British leaders ever towards the ideal of *laissez-faire*, their attention began to turn towards 'opening up' the channels of trade. The phenomenal growth of commerce by way of the Mississippi and the port of New Orleans suggested that other great rivers flowing out of vast continents might be the means of comparable developments. In 1841 Palmerston cast his eye over the expanse of South America and wrote to the Board of Trade: 'At present the Plata, and the Amazon and Orinoco and the Rivers which fall into them have not been rendered available for Commercial Intercourse with the Interior of the Country, but it seems likely that in process of Time the use of them may render those great water communications . . . available for the Purposes of Commerce.'[2] Later in the year a *Memorandum on British Trade* was drawn up in the Foreign Office which stressed two points; the need for more markets and the ill effects of political disorders in South America.[3] Neither Palmerston nor the author of the *Memorandum* proposed any departure from the traditional policy of non-interference, but the *Memorandum* and some of the comments it invited pointed to a more positive policy of diplomatic support for régimes capable of maintaining peace. In thinking along these lines the Foreign Office was only keeping pace with a renewed interest in South America in commercial and governing circles which manifested itself in the publication at this time of several books such as the Robertson brothers' *Letters on Paraguay*. This particular work was an able and vivid stimulant to public interest which appeared with the assistance of eminent subscribers headed by the King of the Belgians and followed by a duchess, three dukes, a marquis, an earl, a viscount, a brace of barons, and sixty-eight leading commercial men from Liverpool and another seventy-nine from London.

This quickening of interest and enthusiasm in Britain for

---

[1] F.O. 6/62, Palmerston to Mandeville, 3 Jan. 1838.

[2] F.O. 96/20, Palmerston to the Board of Trade, 15 Feb. 1841.

[3] F.O. 97/284, Memorandum dated 31 Dec. 1841. The memorandum and its ramifications are discussed by V. G. Kiernan in 'Britain's First Contacts with Paraguay', *Atlante*, vol. iii, no. 4, Oct. 1955.

commercial expansion along river routes was not matched by increasing liberality on the banks of the Plata–Paraná system. Rosas's Government in Buenos Aires by agreement with the other Argentine provinces collected the customs dues and paid the bills of the Confederation, but in practice these were collected mainly from the foreign trade at Buenos Aires. The river ports in Santa Fé, Corrientes, and Entre Rios were in effect closed to foreign trade. It is doubtful whether in the period before railway building there were any economic advantages in direct foreign contact with, say, Rosario. Some years after free navigation was established by treaty in 1853, the British Vice-Consul at Rosario spoke of the voyage hence as 'a difficult, tedious and expensive navigation', and attributed the slow development of the port to the superior advantages of Buenos Aires as a market.[1] But, in the 1840's an increasing number of interested persons were coming to *believe* that free navigation of the Plata–Paraná system was desirable, and at the same time Rosas was manifesting an increasing determination to maintain control in Buenos Aires partly for the purpose of winning the support of the mercantile interests in the capital, partly for the purpose of baffling his political enemies in the litoral provinces, in Uruguay, and in Brazil, and partly in the hope of using control as a means of attracting, or forcing, Paraguay to join the Argentine family. There is no convincing evidence that free navigation beyond Buenos Aires had any appreciable effect upon the commercial opportunities of Great Britain or that it seriously benefited or injured any interest in Argentina, Uruguay, or Brazil, but none the less the matter became an issue which increasingly focused a number of other conflicting elements in the situation. Just as all social and personal difficulties tend in some ages to be interpreted in the grammar of religion and in others in the grammar of sex or class antagonisms or technology, so in the 1840's they tended to be interpreted in terms of *laissez-faire* economics. Such seems to be the only rational explanation of the concern for free navigation.

When Aberdeen returned to the Foreign Office in 1841 there was thus a current of opinion running in commercial and political circles on the subject of the River Plate. This opinion suggested, as objectives of British policy, the establishment of

---

[1] *Parliamentary Papers*, 1859, xxx, p. 4.

peace and order in the area and the opening up of the great
rivers to commerce. But opinion about ends gave little instruction about means. Traditionally, two means of preserving peace
and expanding commercial opportunities had been employed:
mediation between political rivals, which established peace
on the basis of a balance of power; and negotiation, which
depended upon the existence locally of interests strong enough
and so constituted as to welcome and maintain international
commercial connexions. There is no evidence that the Earl of
Aberdeen and his advisers ever decided consciously or uncon-
sciously to abandon either of these means and adopt new ones.
Unfortunately neither of the means was appropriate to the
circumstances which existed at that time in the River Plate, and
the perils which arose through attempting to employ them thus
arose not from a decision to use force but from mistakes and
incomprehension of what in fact the British Government was
seeking to do and how it was trying to do it.

The *Memorandum on British Trade*[1] prepared in December
1841 contained the germs of all the mistakes of the succeeding
years. It called attention to the very great expansion of British
opportunities which had taken place at Montevideo. The author
then proceeded to suggest that 'secret instructions might be
given to offer succour . . . [to the Government at Montevideo]
to enable [the British Consul-General] to procure from Montevideo a Treaty securing to British Commerce those Privileges
and that protection which Great Britain seeks under the usual
Treaties of Commerce'. The meaning of 'succour' was clearly
understood. It involved 'a small amount of force . . . sufficient
to defend Mt. Video against External aggression'. Montevideo,
it was argued, had 'peculiar claims to British protection'. This
was a proposal for a revision of policy and a redefinition of
means which never got into the instructions. It was, however,
a thought behind all the other thoughts which went into the
orders given to the British agents and naval commanders in
the River Plate. And it was loaded with disaster, because it
meant not neutrality but taking sides; not good offices but the
use of force, and, above all, it was profoundly wrong in supposing that a small force was all the case required. The fact is that

[1] F.O. 97/284. The whole volume is devoted to this Memorandum and the
comments thereon.

under the Earl of Aberdeen a split developed in British policy in the River Plate: one part of the official mind caused instructions to be drawn up about which General Rosas could scarcely have complained; the other part stimulated actions which Aberdeen admitted were wrong and injurious to Argentina.

There is no convincing evidence that the Earl of Aberdeen consciously based his policy upon the *Memorandum* of 1841, but the attitude he assumed indicated that he reacted sympathetically to the currents of opinion in Britain and in the British community in the River Plate of which the *Memorandum* was symptomatic. In the presence of an international-cum-civil war involving Argentina and Uruguay Aberdeen appears to have believed that he could act as a mediator bringing peace to the contending parties *and* as a supporter of one of the parties. The incompatibility of these two roles seems never to have occurred to him. This contradiction serves to explain in some measure why it always happened that Aberdeen's determination to bring peace ended up in the use of force against General Rosas.

Before he left office, Palmerston had instructed Mandeville to propose a peaceful settlement of the dispute between Rosas and Rivera. This was in July 1841. Both sides turned down the mediation. Rosas and his supporters had sworn never to deal with Rivera or with the vile unitarians who were Rivera's Argentine allies. 'Death to the Unitarians!' was inscribed on every public document of the Argentine Confederation to remind both those who wrote and those who read that the unconditional surrender of the enemy was the only condition they could accept. Rosas maintained from first to last that his party would turn the River Plate into a charnel house, a desert, and a chaos (he employed all these figures of speech unreservedly) rather than deal with Rivera, and that he would perish at the hands of his followers if he tried to compromise. It must not be supposed that General Rosas exaggerated. Some twenty years later Marshal López, the dictator of Paraguay, fought his enemies without compromise until scarcely a male Paraguayan over the age of eleven remained alive and unwounded. There was nothing in the character of General Rosas and the Argentine gauchos which suggests that the resolution to die rather than compromise was any weaker near the mouth of the Río Paraguay than near its source. This the Earl of Aberdeen did not understand, nor did the Englishmen and Scotsmen gathered in Buenos Aires and Montevideo.

When the mediation between Rosas and Rivera was first proposed, General Rivera and his allies controlled the Uruguayan pampas and the Argentine Province of Corrientes and they had a partial grip on the Argentine Province of Entre Rios. This was the condition of affairs when Vidal, the Uruguayan Foreign Minister, proposed that Uruguay be taken into British protection. British trade with Montevideo was growing more rapidly than that with Buenos Aires, and even the British community in Buenos Aires was beginning to turn away from Rosas to Rivera, believing him to be the best protector and promoter of foreign commerce. Furthermore, he looked as if he would win.

These were the circumstances in which Aberdeen began to develop a pro-Uruguayan bias in his policy. He reproved Mandeville sharply for not having seized the opportunity presented during his visit to Montevideo in December 1841 to sign a Treaty of Friendship and Navigation with the Uruguayan authorities. Ellauri, the Uruguayan Minister accredited to the British and French Courts, began to correspond with Aberdeen encouraging the notion that the Government in Montevideo wanted a close relationship with Britain and would do anything Britain required to seal the bond of friendship. Aberdeen responded, and his response culminated in the broad hint that Britain and France *might* resort to force in dealing with Rosas.[1]

In achieving the peace in the River Plate which he was being pressed to create by the agitation of commercial interests Aberdeen turned not only to Uruguay but to France. In February 1842 Lord Cowley, the British Ambassador in Paris, had a conversation with Guizot in which he disclosed Britain's refusal to assume the protection of Uruguay and at the same time invited France to join with Britain in a joint mediation designed to bring peace and to open the rivers to commerce. Guizot was anxious to co-operate with Britain, but he had no desire to embark France upon fresh adventures in the River Plate.[2] He assented to Cowley's proposals without seriously deciding any

[1] F.O. 51/21, Aberdeen to Ellauri, 16 Dec. 1842.
[2] D. Johnson, 'The Foreign Policy of Guizot, 1840–1848', *University of Birmingham Historical Journal*, vol. vi, no. 1, 1958, pp. 75–76.

more than Aberdeen had decided what to do if Rosas rejected an Anglo-French mediation.

With the necessary decisions thus half-baked and wanting certain essential ingredients, Aberdeen then composed a new set of instructions for Mandeville. On 12 March 1842 he ordered the British Minister in Buenos Aires to renew his proposals for termination of the hostilities between Rosas and Rivera. He concluded his dispatch with a sentence at once threatening, vague, and hostile to Rosas.

If notwithstanding all your efforts, the Buenos Ayres Government should continue to refuse mediation, and to persist in a War not justified by any National object, and carried on solely from personal animosity, you will inform the Argentine Minister that a just regard for the Commercial interests of Her Majesty's Government in the River Plate, may impose upon Her Majesty's Government the duty of resorting to other measures for the purpose of removing the obstacles which at present interrupt the peaceful navigation of these waters.[1]

From this sentence all the subsequent misfortunes flowed. They flowed, indeed, from the one word 'may', for this word revealed that Aberdeen did not understand what he was proposing or, alternatively, that he was trying to bluff General Rosas. This was most unfortunate, for the man whom Aberdeen misled was not General Rosas but the British Minister in Buenos Aires. He was led to believe that the British Government really intended not only to check General Rosas but to send the force necessary to do so. Mandeville did not believe necessarily that Aberdeen's policy was the right one, but he did believe it was a new policy and that it was his duty to warn Rosas of this fact.

While Aberdeen's instructions were on their way to Buenos Aires, Rosas struck a blow which made compromise and peace exceedingly difficult. His secret political society, the Mazorca, began killing the opposition as they had done in 1839 during the French intervention. A number of political prisoners and prisoners of war were shot, and murders became nightly, even hourly, events in Buenos Aires during the first fortnight in April. Mandeville went to see Rosas personally, and once again the murders stopped when the dictator called upon his followers

[1] F.O. 6/82, Aberdeen to Mandeville, 12 Mar. 1842.

to restore the public peace. Mandeville was severely reproved
by Aberdeen on two counts: for not having protested sooner
and for not having recommended H.M.S. *Pearl* to protect the
lives of British subjects.[1] Mandeville refused to accept the reproof. He pointed out to Aberdeen that he alone of all the
diplomats in Buenos Aires had protested; that as a result of his
protest the killing ceased, and that the presence of H.M.S.
Pearl would have increased, not diminished, the number of
deaths.[2]

It is fair to say that politics of this kind played by General
Rosas were outside the range of Aberdeen's comprehension.
He seems to have regarded Rosas's action as undifferentiated
savagery and not as a warning that the dictator of Buenos Aires
would not yield to pressure and that there existed no means of
making him come to terms with his enemies. Instead, Aberdeen
pressed righteously on. Mandeville was preparing once again to
go to Montevideo to negotiate a treaty with Rivera's Government. He seized the opportunity presented by his departure for
the Uruguayan capital to talk personally with Rosas. There can
be no mistake about the candour with which the two men
talked. Rosas declared at once that the British Government's
determination to negotiate a treaty with Rivera was an act of
assistance to his enemies. Mandeville replied that not only was
he going to negotiate a treaty with Rivera's Government but
that, upon the arrival of the French Minister, the British and
French Governments were going to propose a joint mediation
for the purpose of bringing the war between Rosas and Rivera
to a close. 'I now spoke to him', Mandeville reported himself as
saying,[3] 'in my public and private character as British Minister
and his friend . . . [Ending the war] is a subject which requires
his mature deliberation. Should he hesitate upon accepting [the
joint mediation] . . . that hesitation might be fatal in its consequences to himself and his Government.' This was Mandeville's interpretation of the warning and threat contained in
Aberdeen's instructions.

The two men were seated. General Rosas told Mandeville

[1] F.O. 6/82, Aberdeen to Mandeville, 3 Aug. 1842.
[2] F.O. 6/84, Mandeville to Aberdeen, 15 Oct. 1842.
[3] F.O. 6/84, Mandeville to Aberdeen, 7 July 1842. This dispatch is the basis of
this description of the interview.

plainly that he, the British Minister, knew Argentina and he knew the solemn undertakings which had been given to General Oribe and to the federalist party of Argentina by himself in his capacity as Governor of Buenos Aires and leader of the federalist cause. Then rising to his feet, General Rosas said 'in the most solemn manner', 'Should anything happen to me, I will not answer for the life of any foreigner in the country.'

Did the British Government want chaos? Rosas invited Mandeville and Aberdeen to face the facts. 'I know full well', he said, 'that Great Britain alone, much more Great Britain and France combined can take Buenos Ayres with their ships and men. What [will] happen then? Guerilla parties [will] surround the town, and it [will] soon be obliged to surrender to us through famine.'

Rosas invited Mandeville and Aberdeen to believe that he alone stood between the British community in Buenos Aires and chaos; that he was the protector of British interests because he had control of his followers. But that control would be lost if he made peace with Rivera.

My Party [he declared] consists of all men capable of bearing arms, a warlike and powerful Race, and I am no more at liberty to make peace with Rivera than Louis Philippe to ratify the Treaty for the extinction of slavery. . . . There is no aristocracy here to support a Government. Public Opinion and the Masses govern, and as I said, if I do not in some things, for instance war with Rivera, give way, I am lost, and then I repeat for the third time, not one Foreigner is safe in this Province. I carry on war with Rivera as your Country did with Buonaparte.

Before Mandeville departed General Rosas softened a little, not in his intention to continue to fight Rivera, but in his expression of friendship for the British Government. 'I am grieved', he said, 'that circumstances forbid me in this instance to yield to the desires of Her Majesty's Government.'

Mandeville went to Montevideo and negotiated a treaty with Rivera's Government. Upon his return he again visited General Rosas[1]—on the evening of 12 August, the anniversary of General Whitelocke's surrender. The two men had been chatting for, perhaps, half an hour when suddenly a 'band of

---

[1] F.O. 6/84, Mandeville to Aberdeen, 15 Aug. 1842, which is the basis of this description.

military music' was heard. Rosas said: 'What is it? I have not ordered it.' They listened. Then Mandeville said: 'Why is the town decorated with Flags this day? No demonstration of this kind has ever taken place on the anniversary of this day since I arrived in Buenos Ayres.' 'I have not ordered it', Rosas replied. 'It is a spontaneous act of the people, and I have not commanded it.' Then Rosas turned and, looking at Mandeville, said: 'There is a great agitation among the people at present, particularly among those of the country. Should anything happen to me, all foreigners, English as well as others, will be in the most imminent danger, particularly those living in the Country. It arises from your going to Montevideo, and being in communication with Rivera and having made a Treaty which is worth more to him than victories. In the minds of the common people Great Britain is an ally of our deadly foe, as Rivera is regarded by them and by me.'

Mandeville said people were drinking a toast 'Death to the English!' Rosas said he had not heard of this, and he reminded Mandeville that during the crisis over Mehemet Ali he had allowed a small force of British warships to shelter under the batteries of Buenos Aires while a superior French force cruised in the River Plate awaiting news of a declaration of war.

A few days after this interview Mandeville met the newly arrived French Minister, the Count de Lurde. Late in August they made their formal joint proposal of mediation between the warring parties. Rivera had already agreed to a settlement on the basis of recognizing the territorial integrity of the two Republics and of non-interference in each others' affairs. Unfortunately, this could not be taken at its face value because subsequently he sought to have the Argentine Province of Corrientes included in the settlement. Mandeville and de Lurde agreed to propose, in the event of an acceptance of the mediation by Rosas, that an armistice be arranged until 15 March 1843, when Rivera's term as President of Uruguay expired, and that a general amnesty be declared.

September passed. During the month Admiral Brown, Rosas's naval commander, fell upon the Montevidean fleet under the command of Garibaldi and destroyed it. There was no news of Rosas's reaction to the proposed joint mediation. An agent of Baring Brothers turned up seeking repayment of the

Loan of 1824. Rosas was friendly, but he told Falconnet that he would have to wait until peace came to collect on behalf of the bondholders. As spring came, the energies of the soldiers revived as the pastures freshened and their horses could eat abundantly as they moved. On 24 October Mandeville reported that General Oribe was moving across the Paraná through the desolation of Entre Rios, wasted by the armies of Rivera and his Corrientine ally, Ferré.

Mandeville and de Lurde were impatient to know the fate of their suggestions. Arana, the Foreign Minister, told them that General Rosas intended to place their proposals before the Chamber. More time passed. On 26 November the Commission of the Chamber appointed to examine the proposals reported. Out in the streets crowds paraded under the leadership of the Chief of Police crying 'Death to Rivera! Death to his friends!' Mandeville and de Lurde went to Arana complaining of the threats which had been made to them. Arana told them that 'complaints of so delicate a nature' should be made in writing. The proposed mediation was rejected.

Within a fortnight the whole situation was transformed. On 6 December General Oribe and his Argentine allies fell upon General Rivera and *his* Argentine allies at Arroyo Grande in the Province of Entre Rios. In a bloody battle Rivera's army was destroyed. Rivera himself only escaped by swimming his horse across the River Uruguay. All his baggage and his archives were captured. A few days later 1,100 of his infantry enlisted for service under General Oribe. The Governor of Corrientes was overthrown and a man loyal to General Rosas was installed in his place. Within six weeks Rivera was merely a leader of a band of guerrillas lost in the Uruguayan pampas, while General Oribe's forces were encamped before Montevideo. Inside the city José Paz, the Argentine unitarian general, was in command. He was technically the ablest soldier of this troubled epoch.

When news of Oribe's victory at Arroyo Grande reached Buenos Aires, Mandeville and de Lurde were much perplexed. It looked as if only one more blow was required to end the war and bring that peace which Aberdeen and Guizot believed was their object. That final blow was being prepared. Admiral Brown was loading his fleet with 'shells, hollow shot and

Congreve rockets' for the purpose of battering Montevideo into submission from the seaward side.[1] In the presence of these preparations Mandeville and de Lurde decided to do something. Unfortunately, doing nothing was all the case required. To Rosas they addressed a *note identique* requesting him to sign an armistice and to retain his forces within the territory of the Argentine Confederation .This was 'saving Rivera' with a vengeance. Mandeville had the common sense to observe that he had 'little hope that this would produce an immediate effect upon the mind of General Rosas'.

Simultaneously, Mandeville and de Lurde wrote to the British and French naval commanders urging them to prepare to protect the foreign population in Montevideo. Mandeville told the British commander 'to take whatever measures may appear necessary to you to the end that the British population established at that town may have nothing to fear'.[2] Then Mandeville made what he later admitted was a serious blunder, and one that could not be attributed entirely to the ambiguities and vagaries of Aberdeen and Guizot. In a response to a letter from the Under Secretary of the Uruguayan Foreign Ministry, Mandeville wrote to say that he and de Lurde could not understand why the Anglo-French naval forces, which it was rumoured were to leave Europe in the beginning or towards the end of October, had not arrived and that 'until they come we have neither authority to land troops nor to furnish assistance'.[3] Thus he clearly seemed to be promising help to Rivera's Government in the moment of its extremity.

This promise, together with the actions taken by Commodore J. B. Purvis, the British naval commander, and Admiral de Clerval, his French colleague, was enough to restore the spirits of the forces resisting Oribe in Montevideo. Between 80 and 90 per cent. of the city's inhabitants were foreigners. General Paz began enlisting a foreign legion to defend the city. Italians, French, and to a lesser extent the British filled the ranks, so that the army within the defence perimeter of the city could not be described as Uruguayan. Only the Government answered to that description, and even that began to change. Vidal, who

[1] F.O. 6/84, Mandeville to Aberdeen, 18 Dec. 1842.
[2] F.O. 6/84, Mandeville to Captain Haynes, 17 Dec. 1842.
[3] F.O. 6/88, Mandeville to Gelly, 7 Jan. 1843.

had negotiated the Anglo-Uruguayan Treaty yet to be ratified, quitted office, and it was suggested as part of a prospective deal that he should become Oribe's Foreign Minister.

Italians, French, and British, with a sprinkling of Uruguayans, defended the city on the landward side under the leadership of an Argentine general. On the seaward side the British and French naval forces were acting as a protective screen. Their first action was to negotiate with Admiral Brown, the Argentine commander, and to compel him (for they negotiated from strength) to abandon his plan of shelling the city from the sea. Brown agreed to blockade, not to bombard, the city into surrender. Purvis and de Clerval made this demand of Brown in the name of defending their own people in Montevideo.

At this stage General Oribe began to exhibit his incapacity for consummation. With the prize before him, he began to dilly-dally, and the siege of Montevideo began its nine years' course. Some time later Rosas impatiently declared to Mandeville that Oribe was taking months to do what his second in command, Pacheco, could have done in a week.[1] Although he had no heavy artillery, there does not seem to be any reason why Oribe did not deliver an assault, for the heavy fortifications which had confronted Popham and Auchmuty in the days of the Viceroyalty were no longer a means of defence. Oribe, however, chose to sit down before the city and play politics in the way Rosas had done before Buenos Aires in 1829. Unfortunately, the main force in Montevideo had come to believe, thanks to Mandeville and Purvis, and de Lurde and de Clerval, that they were underwritten by the two greatest powers on the Atlantic Ocean. At the same time Rivera, the main enemy, was safe in the wilderness on the borders of Rio Grande do Sul, where he was preparing fresh betrayals with Benito Gonzalez, the Brazilian revolutionary.

The vagueness of Aberdeen's instructions, and Mandeville's interpretation of the conditional mood, thus contributed not to peace but to prolonged war. Mandeville began to back track rapidly in the direction of neutrality. On the other hand, Purvis in the cabin of H.M.S. *Alfred*, off Montevideo, began to move towards war with Argentina and with General Oribe. In April, Oribe, thinking to win by threats what he had failed to gain by

[1] F.O. 6/90, Mandeville to Aberdeen, 12 Aug. 1843.

arms, issued a circular to the foreign consuls in Montevideo declaring his intention to execute every foreigner found in the ranks of the Montevidean army. Purvis sent an officer to Oribe to inform him that 'if [he] do[es] not recall his ill-advised and offensive circular note, he will justify any measure [I] may deem necessary for the protection of the lives and properties of British subjects in Montevideo'.[1] Mandeville supported Purvis by complaining to Arana, but when Purvis began to devise his own conception of neutrality and of the rules of blockade, Mandeville warned him that he might be misinterpreting the mind of Her Majesty's Government. In the end Purvis drew up an elaborate document in which he denied to the states of South America the right to proclaim blockades, because civil war was endemic in South America and because it interfered with British trade.[2] When Mandeville said he would show the document *privately* to the Government in Buenos Aires, the Commodore exploded with rage at the slur upon his capacities as an international legislator.

In Buenos Aires itself the dangers to the British community began to mount. Argentinos commenced pleading with English friends to leave the city before it was too late. General Rosas, however, was not yet prepared for a slaughter of foreigners. The supposedly hot-blooded gaucho was a much cooler and more calculating man than the supposedly cold Englishman who commanded Her Majesty's ships in the River Plate. When Mandeville called upon him early in March before going to Montevideo to ratify, in the besieged town, the Anglo-Uruguayan Treaty, Rosas asked him more in sorrow than in anger why he was making a gesture to Rivera which would only prolong the war and increase the danger to British lives. Buenos Aires may become a charnel house for foreigners, he said. But in order to ensure that murder might not yet be loosed, General Rosas rode with Mandeville into the city, 'whether for safety or from courtesy, I cannot say'.[3]

When Commodore Purvis began to act against General Oribe in April, the danger to the British community grew. On the 15th Mandeville and de Lurde were summoned to the

---

[1] F.O. 6/88, Mandeville to Aberdeen, 13 Apr. 1843.
[2] F.O. 6/88, Purvis to Mandeville, 31 Mar. 1843.
[3] F.O. 6/88, Mandeville to Aberdeen, 12 Mar. 1843.

Foreign Office, where they found Arana 'in a violent state of excitement and irritation'. Word had been brought by special messenger to General Rosas that Commodore Purvis had stopped an Austrian ship laden with troops and that he had ordered Admiral Brown not to move a single Argentine ship, save a dispatch vessel, from the anchorage. Arana told Mandeville that if Purvis was not repudiated at once the British residents in Buenos Aires would be held responsible for the action of the Royal Navy. Mandeville and de Lurde asked for time to think this demand over. The next day they returned, and Mandeville agreed to write to Purvis warning him that 'if the acts complained of by the Buenos Ayres Government were such as had been represented to us, they were acts of hostility against a Power with which Great Britain and France were at peace, and that he must be aware what the consequences would be if they were persevered in especially with regard to the interests and welfare of British Residents in this Republic'.[1]

Purvis denied that he had stopped an Austrian vessel or ordered Admiral Brown to remain at his anchorage, but he did pause in his course. Mandeville for his part fought back at Arana, declaring it an indefensible doctrine to make innocent people such as the British community in Buenos Aires responsible for the acts of their Government. If British residents had broken the laws of Argentina, let them be accused and tried in open court, but it was a piece of monstrous inhumanity and a gross breach of the eleventh article of the Treaty of 1825 for which the British Government would hold the Argentine Government responsible. Then softly Mandeville told Arana that he personally had no power to order Purvis to do anything; that Purvis owed his obedience to Her Majesty's Government and that General Rosas could rely upon Her Majesty's Government to do justice at all times.[2] In spite of this protest, Mandeville told Aberdeen that the British community had not behaved with scrupulous neutrality; that they had cheered and some had abetted the enemies of General Rosas.[3]

As it became evident that the British Government was not going to assist the Government in Montevideo beyond the

[1] F.O. 6/88, Mandeville to Aberdeen, 20 Apr. 1843.
[2] F.O. 6/88, Mandeville to Aberdeen, 16 May 1843.
[3] F.O. 6/88, Mandeville to Aberdeen, 2 June 1843.

lengths to which Mandeville and Purvis had already gone, and that, in fact, Britain was drawing back from the brink of war with Rosas, the political head of the Government in Monte-video, Vasquez, accused Mandeville of betrayal. Vasquez claimed that Uruguay had only signed the Treaty with Britain because Britain had promised protection. Mandeville did not flinch at the prospect of Vasquez publishing his letters. He told the Uruguayan Vice-President that he could do as he pleased because Britain was, and intended to remain, neutral.

As the dispatches bearing news of more and more trouble began to arrive at the Foreign Office in London, Aberdeen began to discover that his vague threats were not threats and that his conditional mood was indeed very conditional. Mande-ville was severely reproved for telling the Uruguayans that a fleet was on the way. 'I have no knowledge of the authority upon which you entertained any such expectation . . .', he wrote.[1] There was certainly no authority if one read Aberdeen's instructions very carefully, and if one read Lord Cowley's accounts of the talks with Guizot in the full knowledge that these gentlemen had only been engaged in conditional specula-tions about the 'imposing Force [which] might be necessary in the River Plate'.[2]

As the facts about the muddle began to come out, Aberdeen issued more positive instructions. On 1 August 1843 he told Mandeville that 'the Government of Buenos Ayres, being at war with the Government of Montevideo, had a right to issue the orders . . . prohibiting all Vessels from introducing Provi-sions and Munitions of War into the Port of Montevideo'.[3] Britain must conform to the rules of blockade. So much for Commodore Purvis's theories of international law! In Novem-ber 1843 Aberdeen felt obliged to have a note sent to the Admiralty about Purvis saying that 'it is indispensable that all Her Majesty's Publick Agents observe . . . neutrality in the strictest manner . . . and that it is farther the duty of that officer to abstain entirely from all interference whatever in the hostilities between the two . . . Republicks'.[4] Purvis was ordered

[1] F.O. 6/87, Aberdeen to Mandeville, 3 May 1843.
[2] F.O. 27/652, Cowley to Aberdeen, 12 Sept. 1842.
[3] F.O. 6/87, Aberdeen to Mandeville, 1 Aug. 1843.
[4] Adm. 1/5535, Addington to Herbert, 15 Nov. 1843.

to Rio de Janeiro out of harm's way. Thus ended the first phase of the so-called intervention.

Aberdeen had more or less followed Mandeville in his retreat to a position of neutrality. But he was still under pressure from the commercial interest 'to do something'. Writing privately to Mandeville in January 1844, Aberdeen said that 'the injury inflicted upon . . . British commerce is very serious', and that the 'war so senseless in its origin and so barbarously conducted has excited a feeling of impatience and indignation throughout this country which it is difficult to control'.[1] Aberdeen could still think of nothing but a joint mediation as a means of bringing peace. During 1844 he took steps which he believed would make the mediation more effective. He recalled Mandeville just as he had secured the transfer of Purvis, and he sent in a new team. He renewed his efforts to strengthen co-operation with France, and he induced Guizot, too, to send out new agents to the River Plate. Brazil he endeavoured to draw into the scheme for restoring peace, but with the Brazilians he tried too much: to draw them into the affairs of the River Plate on the Anglo-French side, to force them to co-operate in suppressing the slave trade, and to oblige them to renew the Anglo-Brazilian Treaty, giving commercial privileges to Britain contradictory to the principles of free trade which he was preaching to the Argentinos.

As for the war, it dragged on. Rivera was still at large on the pampas, but he ceased to occupy the Presidential Office. A new President of Uruguay was 'elected' to rule in Montevideo, while Oribe continued to 'rule' in the Uruguayan countryside. General Paz and his foreign legions held him in the trenches about the city. Oribe still possessed no heavy artillery and still wanted the courage to launch an assault on the city. His lack of energy revived the spirits of his enemies in the rear, and the longer he lingered before Montevideo the more forces he required to ensure that he was not brought to battle on the pampas and there defeated by Rivera. His plan to starve Montevideo was not working, for the blockade was ineffective. In Buenos Aires General Rosas was seriously ill, and Aberdeen looked hopefully to the death of the dictator as a solution better than mediation and armed intervention.[1]

[1] *A.P.*, vol. lxxxviii, Aberdeen to Mandeville, 3 Jan. 1844.

Rosas, however, had a leathery constitution and a good British doctor. He still had the measure of his enemies, and likewise of his friends and the would-be mediators in his affairs. His flirtation with the United States, begun in 1843, was ripening. The American envoy had discovered General Rosas to be 'a real General Jackson of a fellow, a great man of the people, one of nature's noblemen'.[1] Secretary of State Calhoun sent an apology to Rosas for the action of the U.S.S. *Congress* in interfering with the blockade of Montevideo,[2] and his successor, Buchanan, saw in Argentina an American nation struggling to be free from European oppression and entitled to the moral support of the United States.

Rosas was never a man to reject moral support nor one to rely upon it unduly. He busied himself with plans to divide the British against themselves and to separate the French from the British. In the second phase of the affair he turned from threats of murder to bribery in dealing with the British commercial interest. In his message to the Chamber in 1844 he held out a more substantial hope than at any time in the past of a resumption of payments on the Loan of 1824. He commenced at once paying French claims, and in March 1844 the Minister of Finance concluded with Baring Brothers' agent an agreement to pay 5,000 silver dollars a month (or more than 1 per cent. per annum) on the Loan. The agitation of the commercial and financial interests connected with Montevideo was still strong, but the war, the blockade, and the general uncertainty of affairs in Uruguay were severely diminishing the importance of commercial operations there. Furthermore, the cattle on the Uruguayan pampas were being driven into Rio Grande do Sul as a result of the war, and there slaughtered for the benefit of the merchants in Porto Alegre and Rio Grande. Indeed, at a later stage it was charged that commercial interests responsible for the pressure on the British Government to blockade Buenos Aires and Montevideo were connected with the trade through Rio Grande and that they wished to see the River Plate closed for their own advantage.[3]

The strength of the 'Montevidean interest' thus diminished

---

[1] Cady, *Foreign Intervention*, p. 161.
[2] *Diplomatic Correspondence of the United States*, i, Calhoun to Brent, 28 Dec. 1844.
[3] F.O. 6/128, Louis Lucas to the Foreign Office, 6 Jan. 1846.

as its commercial importance declined. Meanwhile, Buenos
Aires remained a free port. The year 1844 was one of the best
from the point of view of British exports to that market: some
£785,000 in amount. Thus a new element in the second phase
of the Earl of Aberdeen's River Plate policy was apparent,
namely the realignment of the British commercial interests
more on the side of General Rosas. When the crisis came, Rosas
found it unnecessary to threaten the British community with
annihilation, for this time a substantial British interest was at
work on his behalf petitioning the Foreign Office, writing books
explaining his virtues, and finally fighting in the Argentine
batteries against the ships of the Royal Navy.

Another new element in the second phase of the affair was
the lukewarm attitude of the French. Guizot and particularly
the Minister of Marine, Admiral de Mackau, had never been
enthusiastic about Aberdeen's mediation. de Mackau knew
Rosas personally, having negotiated with him in 1840, and he
quite liked the Argentine dictator. Early in 1843 at the height
of the first crisis de Mackau had written personally to Rosas
telling him that the French Government wished only the most
amicable relations between the two Governments, and Manuelita, Rosas's daughter, acknowledged the overture by sending an ostrich-feather carpet to the Queen of the French.
Mandeville had informed Aberdeen of these transactions, and
thus Aberdeen had no excuse for putting too much faith in
French enthusiasm. During the second phase de Mackau sent
a special envoy, Captain Pages, to reassure Rosas. So little did
the French Government enter into the spirit of the enterprise
that at its moment of crisis King Louis Philippe sent for
Mandeville, then in Paris, and asked him how the whole
unpleasant business was initiated and how it might be brought
to a close. 'Anything', His Majesty the King of the French
declared, 'Anything, Mr. Mandeville, is preferable to war!'[1]

The only actors in the second part of the drama who were
more, not less, enthusiastic were Aberdeen, Sir William Gore
Ouseley, selected to supersede Mandeville, and the new commander of the British forces on the River Plate station, Admiral
Sir Charles Hotham. Reading Aberdeen's letters after the event,

---

[1] *A.P.*, vol. lxxxviii, Mandeville to Aberdeen, 24 Nov. 1845. Also Ouseley's own
memorandum of 5 July 1845, F.O. 6/104.

one might even doubt his enthusiasm. About his enthusiasm while under pressure from the 'Montevidean interest' in Liverpool in 1844 there can be little question, however. His instructions to Ouseley were firmer than anything ever sent to Mandeville, although they still possessed the same quality of vagueness on the material point of what force was going to be sent for the realization of the policy. 'You will invite your [French] Colleague', Aberdeen wrote, 'to join with you in declaring, that, if by a certain day the support of the Argentine troops is not withdrawn from the besieging Army, and the Blockade of the City [of Montevideo] raised, the Commander of the English and French Squadrons will be directed to effect these objects by force. It is needless to say that this Declaration, when once made, must be adhered to.'[1]

Ouseley was a most unfortunate choice as an envoy. He was a kinsman of General Whitelocke and it appeared that the hereditary curse of this family was their destiny to preside over British disasters in the River Plate. But apart from his connexions, he was a silly and hysterical man, who, in spite of his experience in the United States and marriage to an American lady, appears to have derived his leading ideas about the revolutionary Americas from the pages of *Martin Chuzzlewit*. He was certainly no de Tocqueville; not even a Mandeville. He was a social climber and a man in whom personal spite and vanity ever had the upper hand. He had had a little experience at Rio de Janeiro but he had no first-hand knowledge of the River Plate. He belonged to that numerous school of 'experts' who talked freely about 'South American politicians' as if in South America there existed an undifferentiated class of savages without individuality, morality, or rational objectives of action. A man with such a conception was the least suited to deal with a man of General Rosas's calibre and subtlety.

Mandeville had had the advantage of long acquaintance with General Rosas and a sympathetic understanding of his character. Moreover, he possessed a relaxed, impersonal quality in his relations with his colleagues as well as the Argentine and Uruguayan politicians. Ouseley, on the other hand, was intensely personal as well as ignorant. Before ever reaching Buenos Aires he was in a rage about the intrusion of the United States

[1] F.O. 6/102, Aberdeen to Ouseley, 20 Feb. 1845.

Government in the affairs of the River Plate. He got the
American envoy's name wrong, but that did not matter. The
American agent was an imbecile, and senile into the bargain.[1]
While in Rio Ouseley made his first mistake—a thoroughly
immoral one—of which Rosas took full advantage. He told the
Argentine agent in Rio, the wily old General Guido, that the
French had territorial ambitions and really wished for armed
intervention.[2] Rosas chose to believe this monstrous lie, and
with the object of winning the British community in Buenos
Aires to his side circulated the view in the pages of the English
language press in Buenos Aires that he was bent on restraining
French ambition.

The situation which Ouseley encountered when he arrived
in the River Plate was absurdly similar to that which had existed
in December 1842. General Urquiza, a supporter of General
Rosas, had just crushingly defeated General Rivera at the battle
of India Muerta. This time Rivera finally disappeared from
Uruguay and history. General Oribe was once more poised
before Montevideo with his rear free from the danger of being
kicked. This time the French and British naval commanders
drew their forces back in order to let the Argentine fleet go in
for the kill. Then Ouseley arrived. Without waiting for the
arrival of his French colleague, he declared: 'Montevideo must
not be taken.' The Montevidean politicians broke off the negotiations with Oribe which were being superintended by the
American envoy on the basis of an orderly surrender of the city.

Rosas was naturally enough angry at this turn of events, but
he kept his temper and curbed the boiling passions of his supporters. On Queen Victoria's birthday he came forward with
a crafty set of proposals to the effect that he would observe in
his intercourse with Uruguay the same principles that foreign
powers observed in their intercourse with Argentina; and that
he would withdraw all Argentine troops from Uruguay as soon
as General Oribe wished. But he would not negotiate until
the powers recognized the blockade of Montevideo. As for the
Anglo-French mediation, he was sorry, but the United States
had been accepted already as a mediating power.

Ouseley rejected Rosas's proposals. The Baron de Deffaudis,

[1] *A.P.*, vol. lxxxix, Ouseley to Aberdeen, 20 Apr. 1845, from Rio de Janeiro.
[2] F.O. 6/103, Memorandum by Ouseley, 19 Apr. 1845.

the French envoy, had by now arrived. Partly out of personal pique at Ouseley's unilateral declarations and partly as the expression of the mind of his own Government, he was reluctant to take any positive action. He hung back, preferring to wait on events, but in the end he consented to join with Ouseley in ordering the British and French naval commanders to forestall the final attack on Montevideo and with this purpose to land British and French marines.

Like Whitelocke before him, Ouseley had a talent for doubting privately the wisdom of what he had been instructed by his superiors to do. On 5 July he wrote to Aberdeen questioning his instructions, arguing that the commerce of Montevideo would never balance the loss of that of Buenos Aires.[1] Three days later, however, he joined with Deffaudis in a statement that neither Britain nor France could recognize the legality of a Government under the direction of General Oribe if that Government was installed in the presence of Argentine forces. At the same time both Ouseley and Deffaudis were preparing to send assistance to General Paz, who was endeavouring in Entre Rios to overthrow the supporters of General Rosas.

While these threats and plans were being considered, softer approaches were also being tried. Deffaudis promised to disarm all Frenchmen in Uruguay if Rosas would withdraw Argentine troops and artillery from the Oriental Republic. Ouseley began to call on Manuelita Rosas. Her father, however, did nothing. He was not impressed by the threats nor tempted by the bribes.

In Britain the public enthusiasm for Ouseley's proceedings began to mount. A Hong Kong spirit seems to have got a grip upon the mercantile classes. On 27 June the Duke of Richmond presented a petition from the 'Bankers, Merchants and Traders of Liverpool' praying for the adoption of measures to enforce the free navigation of the River Plate. Lord Brougham presented a similar prayer from Manchester. Aberdeen was not prepared to go the whole way with these enthusiasts. He informed Parliament that the Government's intention was to secure peace in Uruguay, not to seize territory nor to force upon Argentina free navigation. 'We are bound', he said, 'to respect the rights of independent nations.'[2]

---

[1] F.O. 6/104, Ouseley to Aberdeen, 5 July 1845.
[2] *Parliamentary Debates*, 3rd series, lxxxi, 1845, p. 1306.

The enthusiasm on the banks of the Mersey was counter-balanced by the despair of the British and French mercantile community on the banks of the River Plate. In July 1845 a great petition reputed to bear 15,000 signatures was drawn up by the British and French residents of Buenos Aires, protesting against the course of Anglo-French policy. Rosas's press published statements from the diplomatic representatives of the United States, Portugal, and Bolivia testifying to his scrupulous protection of foreign lives and property. He even received one from the French chargé!

In spite of his private doubts and the public despair Ouseley pressed on with plans to force Rosas to cease assisting Oribe and to help in negotiating a settlement in Uruguay. Late in July he and Deffaudis asked for their passports and on the 30th left Buenos Aires. This was not a severance of relations, however. British and French chargés remained behind, on the assumption that the failure of Anglo-French mediation did not mean war. Ouseley himself began to experience at this stage a revival of his first belligerency. He asserted that Mandeville had persistently misled the British Government, that he had been bribed by Rosas, and that Rosas had provided Mandeville's mistress with a house.[1] Ouseley now wanted Aberdeen to declare war on Argentina, and, indeed, he began to plan something like war. Meanwhile Ouseley's doubts of early July had reached London, penetrated Aberdeen's head, and resounded across the Atlantic in the shape of instructions to preserve a strict neutrality between the parties in Uruguay.[2] But such instructions came too late. On 26 September the Anglo-French fleet declared a blockade of Buenos Aires. A combined force seized Martín García. At Ouseley's request the British Minister at Rio de Janeiro redirected the 45th regiment of foot, bound for South Africa, to Montevideo.[3] Through October a fleet was being made ready to force a passage up the River Paraná with the object of conducting a fleet of over 100 merchant ships to the ports in Entre Rios, Corrientes, and, perhaps, in Paraguay.

Rosas's naval forces may have been swept from the estuary

[1] *A.P.*, vol. lxxxix, Ouseley to Aberdeen, 23 July 1845.
[2] F.O. 6/102, Aberdeen to Ouseley, 5 Nov. 1845.
[3] Aberdeen told Ouseley, 'I have never known the Duke of Wellington so angry as at the detention of these Regiments which he considered a very gross offence'. *A.P.*, vol. lxxxix, Aberdeen to Ouseley, 5 May 1846.

and Montevideo may have been reinforced, but Rosas was not dismayed. He commenced fortifying the river pass of Tonelero at the Vuelta de Obligado. A great chain was fixed across the river, and batteries of artillery were established on the banks. On the 17 November the combined fleet, under the command of Admiral Hotham, set out to force the passage, and the next day it came to the barrier across the river.

The action which ensued brought great credit to the Englishmen fighting on both sides. English volunteers manned the Argentine batteries in company with Rosas's soldiers. Englishmen, of course, manned the main ships of war in the river. The fire of the shore batteries was intense and accurate. One hundred and seven balls penetrated H.M.S. *Dolphin* and according to a British naval captain the *San Martín* (a captured Argentine warship converted to the service of the Anglo-French force) was 'like a colander'.[1] But in spite of heavy casualties the Anglo-French fleet remained steady. Boat parties cut the chain under heavy fire. The ships moved inshore and used their guns to great effect. After several hours of cannonading the shore batteries were reduced to sporadic firing, and the passage was forced.

Unfortunately, the political and economic results of the action were negligible. In Entre Rios Governor Urquiza was in the process of crushing Rosas's enemy General Paz, and quite naturally refused to co-operate with a force one of whose purposes was to assist that unhappy warrior. In Corrientes the Governor was friendly but the people were not. In Paraguay Hotham found the First Consul López unfriendly, or at least willing to be friendly only if Britain undertook to guarantee Paraguayan independence. Commercially the venture was a fiasco. Sales were poor and some vessels returned as heavily laden as when they set out, their supercargoes having disposed of nothing.

By the time the tales of gallantry and of treason at the Vuelta de Obligado began to reach England the tide of mercantile opinion was turning against Aberdeen's forcible mediation. British exports to Buenos Aires during 1845 fell to £592,279. In 1846 they collapsed to £187,481. As orders began to dry up

[1] F.O. 6/128, Account by Captain Thornton Champneys to Purvis, 10 Dec. 1845.

and consignments could not be made to Buenos Aires, a new kind of complaint began to reach the Foreign Office. In January Louis Lucas delivered on behalf of a delegation of merchants a telling rebuttal of all previous complaints. The people who urged intervention, he argued, were not connected with the River Plate trade. A certain Mr. Holland, who had taken a large part in seeking to have Buenos Aires and Montevideo blockaded in the interests of peace, was, according to Lucas, a merchant in Rio Grande do Sul, and it was much to his personal advantage therefore to see the River Plate closed. It was ridiculous, Lucas continued, to believe that Rivera was a liberal. He had raised tariffs repeatedly whereas Rosas had maintained stability of customs duties. 'But it is very hard', Lucas concluded, 'upon those who have been led and mainly *so from the Declarations in parliament of those whom they have been accustomed to look up to as the safest guides*—to trust their property in Buenos Ayres, that they should be placed as it were between two fires —between the demands of H.M. Government and the resistance of Buenos Ayres and to be sacrificed in the contest.'[1]

Thomas Duguid, a leading merchant in Buenos Aires with thirty years' experience in the River Plate trade, appeared in London. He told Aberdeen plainly that 'a blockade of the province of Buenos Ayres will have no effect on General Rosas' power for years'.[2] Aberdeen invited Duguid to visit him. A few days later he received a letter from an enterprising correspondent named Dickson, who had sought General San Martín's opinion. From Naples the old revolutionary hero wrote: 'I must at once state my firm conviction that they [i.e. Britain and France] will not succeed—on the contrary their course of proceeding . . . will only have the effect of prolonging for an infinite time the evil which they propose to terminate.'[3] San Martín then explained why the vast extent of the country and the political character of Rosas's régime made even a large-scale invasion a hopeless undertaking.

Confidential complaints and advice of this description were reinforced by public agitation. Late in 1845 a handsomely printed book, *Rosas and his Calumniators*, was published in London

---

[1] F.O. 6/128, Louis Lucas to the Foreign Office, 6 Jan. 1846.
[2] F.O. 6/128, Duguid to the Foreign Office, 6 Jan. 1846.
[3] F.O. 6/128, San Martín to Dickson, 28 Dec. 1845.

over the pseudonym, Alfred Mallalieu. Mandeville, whom Aberdeen had recalled, endorsed it warmly in a letter to Rosas's daughter.[1] A pamphlet was circulated alleging that the legitimate interests of the River Plate merchants were being scandalously sacrificed to satisfy the greed of a few speculators who had purchased the right to collect the customs receipts of Montevideo.[2]

In the presence of pressure and agitation of this kind Aberdeen began to alter course. In December 1845 Moreno, the Argentine Minister in London, demanded the recall of Ouseley. Aberdeen refused at that time, but, when the demand was repeated in April after several public attacks on the policy being pursued,[3] the Foreign Secretary invited Moreno to call. He induced Moreno to withdraw his demand by promising to send out a special envoy in the person of Thomas Hood, sometime British Consul in Montevideo, long a practical opponent of French influence in the River Plate and a friend of Rosas and Oribe. Aberdeen was getting ready to throw in his towel. It only remained for him to blame Ouseley for everything. Early in May he duly informed Ouseley that he had exceeded his instructions.[4]

Persons accustomed to the comparatively simple and straightforward politics of Europe are sometimes baffled by the unexpectedness which gives to the public life of South America its fascinating character. An example of this capacity for surprise now manifested itself in Montevideo. General Oribe's forces once more began to weaken just as victory came into view. The Colorado forces in Montevideo began to rally as defeat seemed close at hand. But they did not rally to attack their domestic opponents. They turned, instead, upon their foreign allies. The British and French forces in Montevideo, landed there to save the Colorados from annihilation, now found themselves obliged to assume the defensive against the very people they were intended to protect.

It would be a bold man who ventures to speak with certainty

---

[1] *Papeles de Rozas*, ii, pp. 75–77, quoted in Cady, *Foreign Intervention*, pp. 196–7.

[2] *An Appeal on behalf of the British subjects residing in and connected with the River Plate* (London, 1846).

[3] e.g. Lord Beaumont's speech in the House of Lords, 19 Feb. 1846, in *Parliamentary Debates*, 3rd series, lxxxiii, pp. 1152–62.

[4] F.O. 6/114, Aberdeen to Ouseley, 5 May 1846.

about the motives and calculations of the Colorado leaders. They may have been moved to their attack upon the foreigners in Montevideo by a desire for revenge on account of the arrival of Hood, whose purpose was to settle with Rosas. They may equally well have calculated that an attack on foreigners at this time might be the means of arranging a deal with Rosas and possibly of taking over from Oribe. They may simply have become bored with fighting the Blancos, and the novelty of fighting the British and French may have appealed to them. Another explanation, not lightly to be considered, was the simple delight to be obtained from betraying allies. Fructuoso Rivera, their first leader, had always found such betrayals among the most satisfying of experiences.

At this stage Ouseley was attempting to persuade Aberdeen that Rosas was in full retreat.[1] Hood, on the other hand, was arranging for Rosas's total victory,[2] and not unexpectedly Rosas and Oribe agreed to accept all that Hood proposed. Unfortunately Hood found himself opposed not by any of the participants in the civil war but by Ouseley and Deffaudis. When Palmerston returned to the Foreign Office in July, it was beginning to look as if his first task would be to mediate between the various mediators.

There had been a sufficiency of public discussion about events in the River Plate to cause Lord Palmerston to give the situation there his personal attention immediately upon his resumption of the Foreign Secretaryship. He had a memorandum prepared setting out the course of policy from its first misconception to its final absurdity.[3] Palmerston acted quickly. He frankly told Guizot that he was determined to wind up the affair. The Governments in London and Paris agreed to recall Ouseley and Deffaudis. The British Admiral on the River Plate station was replaced and fresh instructions were prepared which concluded that 'it is not the wish or intention of Her Majesty's Government to take any further Part in any Hostilities which may continue to be carried on between Buenos Ayres and Montevideo'.[4]

---

[1] F.O. 6/119, Ouseley to Aberdeen, 28 June 1846.
[2] Hood proposed to recognize the belligerency of Argentina, evacuate Martín García, restore all captured Argentine vessels, and to disarm all foreigners in Montevideo.
[3] F.O. 6/130, Palmerston's memorandum on River Plate policy.
[4] F.O. 6/130, Palmerston to the Admiralty, 31 July 1846.

Repairing the damage done by Aberdeen was not so simple as it seemed. Palmerston had no hesitation in abandoning a policy which meant in its application an active alliance with one of the factions of River Plate politics. But he wished to save the Treaty of 1825 and to ensure, if possible, free navigation beyond Buenos Aires. Although he was anxious to return to the policy of Castlereagh and Canning, Palmerston did not seem at first to grasp the necessity of abandoning every feature of Aberdeen's policy. He quickly got British troops out of Montevideo, but on the other hand he did not order immediately the abandonment of the blockade. Instead, he instructed his envoy, Lord Howden, to co-operate with the new French envoy, Count Walewski, in negotiating a settlement with Rosas which would secure the independence of Uruguay.[1]

In this decision to continue in association with the French there was more of prudence than of failure to see all the implications of his determination to return to traditional British policy. Palmerston suspected French intention as much in the River Plate as anywhere else. He feared that they would seize this opportunity to establish a French colony or base in the area; so much so that he approved Howden's instructions authorizing the British commander on the River Plate station to seize Colonia if the French occupied Montevideo.[2] The evidence suggests that in continuing the blockade Palmerston considered it an assistance in the negotiation of a settlement in accordance with British ideas on free navigation and also—and perhaps primarily—as a means of controlling the French and bringing them into the settlement on the basis of something like or better than the *status quo ante*.

Lord Howden soon ran into difficulties in negotiating with Rosas which even a proposal to marry Manuelita could not overcome. Indeed, his regard for that lady seems to have undermined him rather than her father. On the subject of guaranteeing the independence of Uruguay Rosas argued that to give such a guarantee to European powers would be to contradict one of his dearest principles: that of American independence and freedom from European control. The Río Paraná, he declared, was solely in Argentine territory, and he could not

---

[1] F.O. 6/132, Palmerston to Howden, 22 Mar. 1847.
[2] F.O. 6/132, Palmerston to Howden, 22 Sept. 1847.

abandon Argentine control of its navigation. As for the Uruguay, its navigation was a matter of joint concern to the Argentine Confederation and the Oriental Republic, but not to European nations.

Howden did not accept Rosas's arguments, but he might just as well have done, for he decided, in spite of his instructions, to abandon the blockade. In June 1847 the British forces ceased stopping vessels bound for Buenos Aires. Howden explained his action on practical rather than diplomatic grounds. The blockade, he argued, was interfering with trade. He added that there was nothing worth defending in Montevideo.[1]

Palmerston approved of Howden's action. Indeed, Howden caused the affair to enter a new phase in which settlement at last seemed possible. Palmerston instructed the British Ambassador in Paris to tell the French Government that the blockade was useless and illegitimate. With the French Ambassador in London he was even more brusque. 'I have had a long conversation with Broglie', he wrote, 'about River Plate affairs, and have granted him as a favour that which I must have claimed as a right, namely, that England and France should finish in concert the bad business which they began together. . . . The blockade is piracy . . . I am very glad we are out of such a system.'[2]

Palmerston's effort to settle outstanding questions in collaboration with the French was never very persistent. The French for their part remained for some inexplicable reason under the spell of Montevideo's attractions. They kept a small force there, and continued to assist the Colorado politicians. Once trade began to revive, as it did during the latter half of 1847, the previous years of quarrelling became for the British a nightmare memory and the guaranteeing of Uruguayan independence and free navigation matters of only theoretical interest. Howden made no progress with Rosas, nor, it should be added, with his daughter, and he was recalled in June 1848.

His successor was a diplomat of literary interests, Henry Southern. He came to Buenos Aires prepared to admit anything in order to establish positive cordiality with Rosas. Palmerston's

[1] F.O. 6/134, Howden to Palmerston, 15 July 1847.
[2] H. L. Bulwer-Lytton, *The Life of Henry John Temple, Viscount Palmerston* (London, 1870-4), iii, pp. 324-6.

resolution to do this was founded upon a consideration of two possibilities: firstly, that the French might succeed in establishing a strong position in Uruguay and, secondly, that a combination of Brazil, Paraguay, and out-of-office Uruguayan politicians and soldiers might commence a fresh round of war. Palmerston seems to have come to the view entertained by Southern that, although Rosas was like many other South American politicians, illiberal and unenlightened, he had the merit of keeping order inside his own province and, in spite of provocation to the contrary, was inclined to preserve the liberty of foreigners better than politicians professing larger views than he. Palmerston's new envoy moved quickly to create the new cordiality Palmerston sought. He acknowledged that British policy under Aberdeen had been wrong. According to the treaty which he negotiated, relations were to be 'restored to [their] former state of good understanding and cordiality'.[1] Britain agreed to evacuate Martín García, to return all Argentine vessels of war as nearly as possible in the state in which they were when seized, and to salute the Argentine flag in acknowledgement of Argentine sovereignty in the river. Privately, Rosas agreed to withdraw his forces across the Uruguay when the French disarmed all foreigners serving in the forces of the Colorados.

While this treaty was being negotiated, the commercial optimism warming the world began to make itself felt in Buenos Aires. The year 1849 witnessed the largest export of British goods to Argentina in all the years of the Anglo-Argentine connexion. Immigrants began to flow to the River Plate for the first time in twenty-five years. Rosas began to talk about economic progress. But, like Liniers before him, he had stood firm and maintained the independence of his country, and his job was done. The forces were gathering to usher in a new age.

[1] Article VII.

X

BRITAIN AND THE NEW ARGENTINA, 1852-62

ONCE the victory of Rosas over foreign intervention was clearly established and the independence of the Argentine nation secured, the limitations of his régime in relation to the changing character of the community became increasingly apparent. Outwardly his system appeared as strong as ever, and the main trunk and all its branches seemed to flourish luxuriantly—commercially more prosperous than at any time in the past and politically safe. But somewhere, something was wrong, and Rosas himself began vaguely to sense the disorder. Nations seldom seek independence of foreigners as an end in itself. The power of free political decision is sought because there is something to decide, and the Argentinos in this respect differed little from other peoples who have struggled to be free. The King of Spain had gone; so had the danger from the Emperor of Brazil. The King of the French and the Queen of England had discovered the unwisdom of attempting to order the affairs of the River Plate. There now remained Rosas.

Originally Rosas was the heir of the system of federalism established by Dorrego, a system which recognized the independence and power of the provincial chieftains and their retainers and ensured the predominance of the large landed interest in the affairs of the Province of Buenos Aires. It ensured, too, the predominance of the old Church and the old rural way of life, the rusticity and roughness of which the sophisticated and liberal enemies of the dictator described as barbaric. In the consolidation of this system Rosas had been obliged to interfere in the internal politics of the various provinces to the point where the system of federalism became but a cloak for dictation by the Governor of the Province of Buenos Aires, whose Government controlled the customs houses and collected the principal revenues of the Confederation. Federalism was assumed to mean equality among the provinces. By 1850 the Governor of Entre Rios, a rich and dictatorial *estanciero* like Rosas himself, began to ask whether equality really meant the right of the Governor of Buenos Aires to inhibit and control the connexion of foreign traders with the ports of Entre Rios and the right of Buenos Aires to insist on the passage of goods through their customs house. He began to ask, and other provincials did likewise, why, in all the great affairs affecting the Argentine nation—its foreign relations and its commercial policies—the Government of Buenos Aires alone made the decisions. Certainly, the provinces had transferred their power in these matters to Buenos Aires on the assumption that Buenos Aires would guard and protect the nation and its provinces, but by 1850 it was becoming an open question whether guardianship by General Rosas was not costing too much.

Rosas had claimed his ample dictatorial powers on the plea of order, social peace, and national independence. Order and national independence he had achieved, but not peace. He had established sufficient order in the community, so that the people —and particularly the leading people—began to develop a taste for peace, an enthusiasm for economic development, and a desire to enjoy the fruits of the lands which they acquired in the course of the prolonged revolution in society. But still Rosas persisted in the course of war. Paraguay must be subdued. Oribe must be restored in Montevideo. Death must still be visited on the savage unitarians. Intelligent men, who had agreed that France and Britain must be resisted, who had stood aside or had actively helped while the Mazorca rooted out the opposition, now began to doubt that an unstable currency, a depletion of the scarce supplies of labour, and an atmosphere of insecurity unfavourable to trade and investment were justified in the interest of incorporating Paraguay in the Argentine Confederation and of installing a president in Montevideo agreeable to Rosas. Even the direct beneficiaries of Rosas's policies in the end deserted him. Oribe himself accepted a compromise with his enemies behind Rosas's back. When the crisis came in 1852 many of the men closest to Rosas were discovered to have made private arrangements with his enemies. Bernardo de Irigoyen, Rosas's private secretary and confidential adviser until the moment of his defeat, was only the most conspicuous example[1] of a general willingness to abandon the uncompromising ways of the dictator.

The collapse of Rosas cannot be explained in terms simply of the ambitions of individuals, the duplicity of the courtiers at Palermo, and failures of the police and administrative apparatus. Studying the behaviour and the utterances of a variety of Argentinos and foreigners in the late 1840's and the 1850's, one cannot escape the impression that a change of temper and of objectives was coming over Argentine society during these years, and that this change was having an effect upon the politics of the nation as profound as that which it had experienced during the heroic days of the British invasion and the revolution against Spain. Several words might be selected to describe the change. Perhaps the best one can do is to say that Argentina was becoming bourgeois. Sarmiento would have said it was becoming civilized. A modern sociologist may have a better word. But there can be no mistake about what was happening. In 1852 the firm of Baring Brothers sent out an agent to Buenos Aires in an endeavour to collect the money owing on the defaulted Loan of 1824. They provided the agent with a handsome rifle and a brace of pistols for presentation to the conqueror of Rosas. After a brief experience of Buenos Aires the agent decided to sell the presents to an officer of the Royal Navy, for, he wrote in his diary, 'things have changed exceedingly in this Country . . . all the . . . dignitaries and officials I have had to deal with are learned Doctors of Law and peaceful Civilians. The era of the caudillos has passed away: thank God.'[2]

The era had not quite passed away. Both the traditions of the gauchos and the naked realism of the Spanish manner in politics forbade the complete abandonment of the habit of carrying political differences to the field of battle. Between the overthrow of Rosas in February 1852 and the presidency of Bartolomé Mitre, which commenced in August 1862, Buenos Aires was twice at war with the other provinces. From 1865 to 1870 Argentina was one of an alliance waging a war of extermination against Paraguay. As late as 1880 an army recruited in Buenos Aires sought to overthrow the constitutional president of the

[1] F.O. 6/167, Gore to Granville, 29 Feb. 1852.
[2] Public Archives of Canada, *Baring Papers* (hereafter cited as *B.P.*), *Diary of Major Ferdinand White*, p. 182.

Republic, and in 1890 an outbreak of violence caused the resignation of President Juárez Celman. Interspersed among these major episodes of violence were many minor scuffles involving the overthrow or restoration of various provincial governments. Until 1886 Indian wars were of frequent occurrence. Indeed, a rifle and a brace of pistols would have been an entirely suitable gift for any of the successors of General Rosas. The new Argentina born of Rosas's overthrow was in many respects as violent as the old. And yet there was a difference.

The practice of killing the opposition, begun during the revolution and brought to the peak of perfection under Rosas, ceased after General Urquiza's victorious troops had executed 200 Rosistas the day following the dictator's defeat. Argentine politicians may have appealed to arms from time to time thereafter but more often they worked for compromise in the interest of domestic peace. Argentina never grew into a model democracy, but it became a liberal community bearing some resemblance, at least in the sphere of politics and social values, to the England which emerged after the Glorious Revolution of 1688. Rosas had risen to the top when Argentina was in the state of nature, and he had become a sovereign such as Hobbes had imagined. He prepared his country for the age of Locke: for a constitution which was a contract; for an economy which permitted the accumulation of the products of labour in private hands; for a state machine whose financial operations enriched the men who held its levers.

The commercial prosperity which followed the termination of the Anglo-French intervention and the influx of immigrants which accompanied the boom in trade contributed to the new temper now beginning to pervade Argentine society. Rosas himself talked of a more liberal régime and the encouragement of economic development.[1] He claimed to excuse his record on the grounds that he was educating his people for self-government.[2] Perhaps he was beginning to realize that the criticisms of his régime uttered by Argentine exiles had some truth: that, as Sarmiento argued, Argentina was falling behind nations like the United States because the community lacked adequate education, freedom of thought, and willingness to experiment

---

[1] F.O. 6/167, Gore to Palmerston, 2 Feb. 1852.
[2] F.O. 6/158, Southern to Palmerston, 27 May 1851.

and change. By the time Rosas approached his final crisis his ambassador in the United States was beginning to tell him that steam power and railroads were better foundations of national unity and power than arms and federal pacts.[1]

Whatever Rosas may have seen in his circumstances during the closing years of his power, he displayed no capacity dramatically or effectively to adjust his course and to overcome the inertia of his system. Brazil was determined that neither Uruguay nor Paraguay should become a dependency of Argentina. Rosas was determined that they should. A familiar social tragedy seemed about to be re-enacted. Brazilian ships of war appeared in the Río de la Plata in April 1851. Rosas had already begun strengthening his army and executing what the British Minister described as a 'large arrear of irredeemable ruffians'.[2] The European powers sought to mediate. The foreign communities in Buenos Aires were sunk in despair. Was the year 1827 come again?

This time no wave of spontaneous patriotism supported the Government and carried it forward. When Rosas offered his resignation, a procedure which had become a ritual introduction to the grant of full dictatorial powers, the Governor of Entre Rios, General Urquiza, wrote in 'the form of a bitter satire on the Governor of Buenos Ayres',[3] accepting the resignation and withdrawing the authority given the Government of Buenos Aires to conduct the foreign affairs of the Confederation. Quietly the supporters of Rosas began to make arrangements with his opponent. Colonel Garzon, in command of the forces on the border of Entre Rios, deserted with his troops in May. As Urquiza's forces began to cross the Uruguay into the Banda Oriental, Rosas's commander, General Mansilla, sat still, and made no move to take Urquiza in the rear. As Urquiza's army approached Oribe's forces, Oribe did not stand and fight. Instead, he revealed that an arrangement had been made with his enemies, and he asked the British Consul and the French Admiral, Le Prédour, to assist in evacuating the Argentine auxiliaries from Uruguay. Such was the element of magnanimity in Oribe's treachery.

---

[1] T. B. Davis, *Carlos de Alvear, Man of Revolution* (Durham, 1955), p. 190.
[2] F.O. 6/157, Southern to Palmerston, 10 Jan. 1851.
[3] F.O. 6/158, Southern to Palmerston, 26 May 1851.

By the end of October 1851 Rosas's authority was so undermined that the Brazilians, resolving not to assist him by opposing him, lifted the blockade of Buenos Aires. The deterioration continued. General Mansilla was Rosas's brother-in-law, but family feeling did not stiffen his courage. He retreated steadily as Urquiza crossed the Paraná. In December he resigned his command on the grounds of ill health. There 'appears a great want of enthusiasm', the British chargé d'affaires wrote in a private letter to Palmerston, '. . . the mass of the people desire Peace, which they believe they will obtain more easily if Urquiza is quietly permitted to destroy or drive away Rosas from Power; there is no sympathy for Urquiza in Buenos Aires, but there is a very general desire for Peace, to permit individuals to attend to their private affairs'.[1]

Through January the forces of Rosas and those of his opponent slowly gathered before Buenos Aires for the final conflict. The third of February found them confronting each other at Monte Caseros. Only the Division of Palermo, the personal troops of the dictator, stood their ground and fought. The rest fled. Rosas himself was slightly wounded. He wrote out his resignation in pencil in his florid ceremonial style, and sent it to the Assembly of Buenos Aires which had so often invested him with his dreadful authority. Then he rode into Buenos Aires disguised as a common soldier, knocked at the door of the house of the British chargé d'affaires, and was admitted. Upon his return from the urgent business of a panic day in the city, Captain Gore discovered his uninvited guest lying on his bed exhausted with fatigue.[2] By 4.30 the next morning General Rosas and his daughter were on board a British steamship bound for England. For twenty-five years more he lived on a farm near Southampton, visited from time to time by friends from the old days, who found him a kind, considerate, and entertaining host.

The collapse of General Rosas left the British Government in an isolated position. Until the very last moment the British diplomatic agents in Buenos Aires had looked upon Rosas as the one alternative to chaos, and they were unprepared for his overthrow. Henry Southern, the Minister, was so convinced of

[1] F.O. 6/167, Gore to Palmerston, 4 Jan. 1852.
[2] F.O. 6/167, Gore to Palmerston, 9 Feb. 1852.

the necessity of Rosas and his régime that he was openly partisan to a degree which prompted a rumour of his corruption by the dictator.[1] For Southern, Rosas was a genius who alone possessed the secret of governing a wild and restless people. Urquiza, on the other hand, had a record, in Southern's estimation, 'sanguinary and capricious beyond anything heard of in the Government of a white race'.[2] In the presence of this dramatic contrast between white and black there was only one course open to Southern: to support Rosas. He did this in spite of the fact that Rosas in 1851 was opposed by the Brazilians, the Paraguayans, the French, the Uruguayans, at least two Argentine provincial governors, and a growing body of his own followers.

Southern's support had consisted of attempting to enforce a British mediation between Argentina and Brazil and to refuse British recognition of the Brazilian blockade. When Oribe quit Rosas, Southern was prepared to let the Royal Navy evacuate the Argentine auxiliaries from Uruguay, and he came into conflict with Rear-Admiral Barrington Reynolds over this particular interpretation of political neutrality. The Brazilian blockade was so short-lived and was employed with such finesse that Palmerston was never obliged to instruct Southern positively about mediation. Because the withdrawal of the Argentine auxiliaries seemed to contribute to pacification, Palmerston backed Southern against the naval commander.[3]

At this critical moment of Argentine history the British Government acted unwittingly to its own advantage and to the injury of Rosas. In the year 1851 the popularity of cheeseparing in the public service was at its height. Lord Palmerston was no indifferent enemy of economy. Looking around for opportunities to save money, his eye lit upon the British representation in Buenos Aires. In November 1851 Rosas was told that Britain would henceforward do with a chargé d'affaires in Buenos Aires, and that Southern would be transferred to Rio de Janeiro. This decision 'produced some painful impression'[4] on the dictator. Southern laboured to persuade him that Britain's policy of

[1] B.P., *White's Diary*, p. 147.
[2] F.O. 6/157, Southern to Palmerston, 25 Feb. 1851.
[3] F.O. 6/156, Palmerston to Southern, 24 Nov. 1851.
[4] F.O. 6/160, Southern to Palmerston, 2 Nov. 1851.

friendliness had not changed. This seems genuinely to have been the case, but the public did not so interpret the coming of Captain Gore from the British Consulate in Montevideo. Rosas felt obliged to print a special edition of the *Gaceta Mercantil* bearing the full text of Queen Victoria's letter recalling her Minister. Thus the people might learn from Her Majesty's polite and ceremonial sentences that the Queen of the United Kingdom was still the friend of the Governor and Captain General of Buenos Aires. And not only the Queen. Gore had scarcely set foot on shore at Buenos Aires before he received a private invitation to visit Manuelita Rosas, who assured him that her father regarded Palmerston as his personal friend.

Gore shared Southern's view that Rosas was the alternative to chaos; that he was strong and that he was the best friend foreigners could have in the River Plate. 'I dislike and condemn the System of Rosas, as all liberal Men must do', Gore told Palmerston, 'but I conceive it would be a great Evil should He be vanquished, as this system gives protection to life and property, more particularly that of Foreigners, and it is based on Order.'[1] Within a month of writing these words Rosas was a refugee in Gore's house. Gore never hesitated in his loyalty to Rosas. The thought of surrendering Rosas to his enemies never crossed his mind, nor does it seem to have occurred to him that advantages might be gained for his Government by abandoning the fallen idol of the people. 'I was doing nothing but my duty as a British agent and an English gentleman, nothing but what was dictated by humanity and honorable principles.' At some risk to himself he conducted Rosas and his daughter past the guards of the revolutionary forces, and personally saw them embarked on a British vessel. When he met Urquiza for the first time on the day following Rosas's departure from the River Plate, he found the victorious General most stiff and formal. Gore was chilled by Urquiza's reference in his greeting to 'ungrateful strangers',[2] but he swallowed the insult on the grounds that Urquiza's words were general and that he would have lost his dignity in demanding an explanation.

If Gore was unprepared to sacrifice Rosas to the expediency

---

[1] F.O. 6/167, Gore to Palmerston, 4 Jan. 1852.
[2] F.O. 6/167, Gore to Palmerston, 11 Feb. 1852.

of the moment, some of his fellow countrymen had less scruple. They were so incensed by Gore's failure to ingratiate himself with the victorious party that one man threatened to waylay him and another broke into his house at midnight and threatened to shoot him. Gore, however, refused to keep out of sight, but he did commence carrying a cane.

The signs that the new régime might move in an anti-British direction soon began to fade. Even in the moment of victory Urquiza's position was uncertain, and he needed friends. Furthermore, the main sentiment which had borne him to the leadership of the Confederation was liberal, pacific, and favourable to international goodwill and co-operation. Gore was privately informed that Urquiza regretted his unfriendly words almost as soon as they were uttered, and within a few days he had begun to thaw. Gore and the British Admiral, who had connived at Rosas's escape, visited the General. After a few polite exchanges, Urquiza took Gore aside and 'entered into a summary statement of some of his future plans for the development of the resources of this magnificent rich Country; the opening of the Rivers to all Nations, Vessels freely to pass up Rivers and discharge and load Cargoes without previously touching at Buenos Aires'.[1]

Urquiza's statement of policy to Gore can be described as simply a hackneyed repetition of promises and hopes uttered on a most ample scale by Rivadavia a quarter of a century previously. But such a description would be incorrect. Rivadavia had voiced the plans and the hopes of the urban mercantile and professional classes of Buenos Aires, which, experience had demonstrated, were not the strongest elements in the Argentine community. Now the desire for economic development was being expressed by one of the greatest *estancieros* and *caudillos* of Argentina and the most powerful member of the strongest element in the Argentine nation. The fact that no significant interest in the community now opposed free trade, the investment of capital, and the importation of labour supplies was the new and historically important consequence of Rosas's overthrow.

The new 'business man's Argentina' did not spring instantly to life at Urquiza's command. Another ten years were to elapse before the particular legal and political foundations were truly

[1] F.O. 6/167, Gore to Palmerston, 15 Feb. 1852.

laid, but henceforward the Argentine politicians were in the position of men in a road race without rules. All were running along the same road in the same direction even though some were tripping others; some were shoving competitors in the ditches and still others were attempting to reach the goal by running across the fields parallel to the road. Those who thought that the game of life in Argentina was not road racing but wrestling, fencing, or brawling no longer controlled the situation.

In the presence of these new tendencies the British Government displayed a high order of tact and skill in diplomacy. In general the situation was favourable to British policy, but in its particular development there were constant demands on the powers of judgement of the British political agents and the Foreign Office, a failure of which could have been disastrous. Simultaneously, there developed a pushing and hauling of interests in the British community. Had these been allowed seriously to influence policy, they might very well have inflamed a civil war which it was the overall interest of Great Britain to prevent. But British policy emerged triumphant during the ten years of uncertainty from 1852 to 1862.

During this period the work of building the political foundations of a free commercial and financial connexion between Argentina and Great Britain, begun in 1824, was completed. British diplomacy was a diplomacy to end diplomacy. Thereafter a long succession of undistinguished and indistinguishable British Ministers and chargés managed the relations of Argentina and the United Kingdom, but the significant agreements and arrangements after 1862, until the rebirth of mercantilism in the 1930's, were the work of business men dealing directly with the Argentine public authorities and private Argentine business interests. There were several occasions after 1862 when political diplomacy threatened to supersede business diplomacy, but in fact this never happened during the epoch of decentralized decision-making to which we give the name *laissez-faire*.

The transition from political to business diplomacy was effected during the years between Urquiza's victory in February 1852 and his retirement from politics in 1862[1] after the

---

[1] Informally intimated to the British Minister in Jan. 1862. F.O. 6/239, Thornton to Russell, 22 Jan. 1862.

battle of Pavón, which took place in September 1861. These years witnessed three decisive events: the signature of the Treaty of Free Navigation, the prevention of a full-scale civil war between Buenos Aires and the other states of the Republic, and the agreement for the complete repayment of the Loan of 1824 with its defaulted interest. Each of these events was the result of positive diplomatic action carefully calculated, and, judging from the results, correctly applied. Together they were of the highest significance in establishing the character of both the Argentine state and the community, and of its relations with the great commercial and financial centres across the Atlantic.

The signature of the Treaty of Free Navigation in July 1853 was, perhaps, the least important of these events, but at the time it was believed to be a matter of the highest consequence. Both the Foreign Secretary who ordered its negotiation and the men who brought it to birth regarded it as the means of ensuring the free exchange of the abundant agricultural produce of a numerous peasantry for the manufactures of Europe.[1] In fact the Treaty was an echo of an age which was passing. None of the river ports beyond Buenos Aires in 1852 was capable of attracting any significant volume of maritime commerce. Even Rosario was an inconsiderable place until the building of the Central Argentine Railway transformed it by making possible the colonization of the northern pampas. The real significance of the Treaty was not the extent to which it opened up commerce, but the international guarantee which it gave to the economic and commercial equality of the Argentine provinces and of their emancipation from dominance by Buenos Aires. It is possible to argue, indeed, that General Urquiza signed the Treaty for this reason and not because the Treaty added anything to already existing arrangements governing a commerce of an extremely limited kind.

The abortion of civil war in Argentina was a matter of considerably greater significance. Sir Charles Hotham, remembered principally as the man who forced the Obligado in 1846 and as the negotiator of the Treaty of Free Navigation in 1853, should instead be remembered as the man whose skilful diplomacy contributed to the stalemate in Argentine politics, which in

[1] F.O. 59/2, Hotham to Malmesbury, 20 Feb. 1852.

turn produced and finally made possible the implementation of the Constitution of 1853. Those who do not see history as a series of inevitable developments and are attracted by speculation about the consequences of alternative courses of action are bound to ask whether, after the fall of Rosas, the hour of the urban mercantile class had not come and whether, in the absence of foreign pressure, this class might not have constructed on the banks of the River Plate a community like that of the United States after the Civil War: an expansive, financial, and industrial power unhampered by the obstruction of a powerful landed interest. But such speculation is not required to underline the significance of British and French action in helping to moderate the conflicts in Argentine society. Such action had immediate significance in guiding the contending powers away from the battlefield to the market place and the office of the railway concessionaire.

Most significant of the three events was the agreement to repay the Loan of 1824 and all its defaulted interest. It is possible to regard the collection of the principal and interest of this bond issue as simply the repayment of so much money lent through the agency of British bankers and stockbrokers to the Government of Buenos Aires. This is one view, and a very common one particularly among those who were involved in the transaction. It is also possible to see in the collection of this debt a larger question touching the character and purposes of society, the course of its development, and the distribution of the income from the work of the community. The undertaking to repay the Loan of 1824 and its execution signalized the establishment on an ample scale of the accumulative process in Argentina. Before this agreement individuals and families saved money, of course; and some of them invested in the public funds of the Argentine state authorities; but the service in sterling of a debt in excess of £2,500,000 by a community as limited in its resources of labour as Buenos Aires was in the 1850's marked a new condition of affairs. Not only did it mean that Argentina became linked to the great pools of investable funds which existed in western Europe and was nourished by the expanding industries of that part of the world, but it also meant that the Argentine community had become so organized that the systematic and repetitive distribution of the community's income between capital and labour was now taking place and that one of the prime social conditions of rapid economic development had come into being.

In describing the British diplomacy in the River Plate between the years 1852–62 as successful one must be careful not to ascribe too much meaning to the word. British diplomacy can be counted successful in that it contributed to the achievement of business opportunities which influential British interests sought, but it must not be inferred that British diplomacy achieved an exclusive power of decision for Britain in the area, or that it was based upon preponderant and unmistakable force. Quite the contrary. British diplomacy consisted in a skilful participation in the politics of the Argentine community, giving a little support to this interest and removing a little from that, careful always not to commit what little strength Britain possessed in the area unreservedly to any particular faction and determined always to preserve the appearance of non-interference. If the art of diplomacy consists in inducing others to take decisions one wishes to see them take, then the British agents in Argentina at this time practised that art to great effect.

A general view of Argentine politics during the period of Urquiza's influence is necessary in order to understand what British diplomacy was about. Under the leadership of General Urquiza three important changes were made in the structure and policy of Argentina. His first achievement was a redefinition of Argentine federalism. This consisted of depriving the Province of Buenos Aires of its delegated power to manage the foreign affairs and general finances of the Confederation and the establishment of a National Government based upon a written constitution, which provided for an executive and a legislature created by and representative of the entire Argentine community. General Urquiza's second achievement was a redefinition of Argentina's relations with her neighbours. Under Rosas the distinction between fighting wars of national independence and wars of aggrandizement had become blurred and uncertain. Urquiza recognized the independence of Paraguay, ceased interfering in the internal affairs of Uruguay, and made it plain to Brazil that he refused to make Uruguay a dependency of Argentina, and that he expected Brazil similarly to deny herself. The General's third achievement was to make equal the economic and commercial rights of all the Argentine provinces. This was effected through the opening of the rivers to the free navigation of foreign ships and the establishment of national customs houses elsewhere than in Buenos Aires.

The changes made by General Urquiza encountered the most strenuous opposition from the Province of Buenos Aires. With the overthrow of Rosas the unitarian exiles began to return, and some of them were taken into the Government of Buenos Aires Province. Valentín Alsina, who had edited an anti-Rosista newspaper in Montevideo, became the Minister of Government of the Province, and Peña, an ex-priest and teacher of mathematics and philosophy, became the Foreign Minister of the Confederation. At first Urquiza believed that he could co-operate with the unitarians, but he soon discovered that these men of the city, liberal protagonists of civilization and urban dominance, were as much, or even more, the enemies of his brand of federalism as that of Rosas. The great proprietors of Buenos Aires Province, both native and foreign, were displeased by Urquiza's willingness to compromise with the liberal and urban party. The liberal men of the city in their turn were not satisfied with Urquiza. When Urquiza insisted upon the display of the federalist colours a great coolness developed between him and Alsina, the leader of the unitarians. In a fit of frustration Urquiza was heard to declare 'there is only one man to govern the Argentine Nation; that is Don Juan Manuel; and I am ready to send to beg him to return here'.[1]

When the provincial governors met at San Nicolás de los Arroyos in May and agreed to call a constituent assembly for the purpose of establishing a constitution, the Provincial Assembly of Buenos Aires became a forum of embittered attack upon Urquiza and the federalists. The Provincial Government resigned. Urquiza dissolved the assembly and expelled the principal unitarian leaders from the country. When he could not find a Governor for Buenos Aires, Urquiza appointed himself Governor and placed authority in the hands of a Council of State which included Rosas's kinsman, Nicolás Anchorena, who was the wealthiest landowner in the country, Arana,

[1] F.O. 6/168, Gore to Malmesbury, 1 June 1852.

Rosas's Foreign Minister, and Guido, the man who had served Dorrego and Rosas.

These upheavals took place in June 1852. As soon as Urquiza departed for the Constituent Congress meeting in Santa Fé, the Provincial Assembly of Buenos Aires met and elected a provisional Governor, who appointed the exiled Alsina as Minister of Government. Urquiza's commander in Buenos Aires, General Flores, deserted to the new provincial authority with his troops, who were assured a year's pay. A provincial guard commanded by General Mitre was organized in which the commercial classes trained themselves in the use of arms.[1] A renewed civil war seemed in the making.

Urquiza, however, accepted the situation for the time being, and pressed ahead with the construction of a new federal constitution in which Buenos Aires would have a place, but not a dominant one. He established the national capital for the Argentine Confederation provisionally at Paraná in Entre Rios Province. He decreed the recognition of Paraguayan independence, and he opened the rivers to free navigation. The liberals of Buenos Aires were being beaten at their own game. They, too, decreed free navigation. They, too, recognized Paraguayan independence. They set up a Foreign Office of their own, and invited recognition by the foreign powers, as a separate entity independent of the Confederation.

The Constituent Congress produced a Constitution about which unitarians could have few complaints and liberals none. The 67th article proclaimed objectives upon which Rivadavia could not have improved.

Congress shall have the power to provide for all that conduces to the prosperity of the country, to the advancement and welfare of all the provinces, and to the advancement of the people by prescribing plans for general and university instruction and by promoting industrial enterprise, immigration, the construction of railways and navigable canals, the colonization of public lands, the introduction and establishment of new industries, and the importation of foreign capital.

Nor could the enlightened men of Buenos Aires accuse the Congress of sharing the xenophobic sentiments of Rosas's times. The 27th article of the Constitution stated that 'the Federal

[1] *B.P., White's Diary*, p. 159.

Government shall be bound to strengthen commercial and peaceful relations of the Argentine nation with foreign countries'.

Under Rosas the urban mercantile and professional classes were able to present themselves to the world as the protagonists of liberal enlightenment opposed to the obscurantist, clerical reaction and rustic barbarism of the dictator. Now that a great provincial *caudillo* had thus seized the mantle of liberalism it was no longer possible to quarrel about principles. There remained now only a naked struggle for power over the community between the urban groups and the landed interests: Buenos Aires versus the rest.

As the year 1852 drew to a close the ingredients for a new civil war were assembled. Buenos Aires sent an emissary to the provinces in the person of General Paz, armed with a credit of £200,000 and under instructions to seduce the provincial authorities from their allegiance to the Confederation. Another soldier, General Hornos, was sent with an army into Entre Rios to overthrow General Urquiza. Paz's mission failed and Hornos was crushingly defeated. Urquiza spoke words of reasonableness. He declared to the Constituent Congress that, though he regarded the unitarian system of centralized government as unsuited to Argentina, he did not regard unitarians as criminals, and he urged that a veil of oblivion be drawn over the past. None the less he prepared a fleet to lay down a blockade around Buenos Aires and choke it into submission with economic and naval pressure. Buenos Aires replied to this assault with an astute piece of bribery. They purchased the blockading navy from its officers. In the country districts of the Province, however, the rural militia made trouble for the city politicians. The leading soldier of the unitarians, General Flores, improving upon the example of his masters, bribed himself with the pay of the troops and departed to Montevideo.

The decline in military virtue and the rising esteem for money brought a period of peace. For the six years 1852–8 Buenos Aires remained independent of the Confederation, each manœuvring against the other; each preparing for a final decision.

Always at the centre and sometimes at the edge of this confusing and changing scene, we find a succession of British diplomatic agents urging moderation upon the actors in their most ferocious moods, tripping up some as they advanced and giving others a shove in the direction they conceived to be right. There was nothing haphazard or random in their tripping and pushing, however, for they obeyed that grand design of policy planned by Castlereagh and now adapted to the needs of the moment by Malmesbury and Clarendon. They worked for the emergence of a united, peaceful, liberal Argentina, and they assigned exactly that order to their objectives. There was nothing novel in this. Every Argentine politician of any consequence had similar goals, but they differed among themselves about the method of achievement. The British diplomatic agents did not.

Among these agents the man of greatest influence was Admiral Sir Charles Hotham. As soon as the news of Rosas's overthrow reached London, Hotham wrote to the Earl of Malmesbury at the Foreign Office advocating the negotiation, if possible, of a treaty with the new authorities which would open the Plata–Paraná system to the free navigation of the maritime nations.[1] His letter to Malmesbury can be interpreted as an endeavour to justify his naval triumph at the Obligado, for he sought to deny in the letter that his military victory had been a commercial and political failure and he implied that the opportunity now perhaps existed to accomplish what should have been accomplished in 1846. Although Hotham persisted in attaching a commercial importance to the free navigation of the rivers Paraguay and Uruguay which subsequent events failed to confirm, he none the less emerges from the record of these years as the greatest creative figure on the British side working in the field of Argentine developments. Hotham established the main lines of British policy in response to the events of 1852–3 and he employed his influence, and by persuasion reinforced it with that of his French and American colleagues, to hold together the Argentine Republic at a time when powerful forces both internal and external were working for its break-up into smaller political units. Perhaps his greatest single contribution to the shaping of Anglo-Argentine relations was the bias he gave to British policy in the direction of the landed interests of Argentina. Parish and Canning had believed that the liberal bourgeoisie of Buenos Aires were the bearers of

[1] F.O. 59/2, Hotham to Malmesbury, 20 Feb. 1852.

progress and the best friends of Britain. The worst follies of
Rivadavia had not shaken their confidence in this class. Rosas
had been accepted as a *pis aller*. Hotham, however, reversed
the scale of values established in the mind of the British Foreign
Office. The politicians of Buenos Aires he stigmatized as men
without honour or understanding, capable only of bribery and
deceit. 'Whilst dealing thus severely with the Province of
Buenos Aires', he wrote in his last dispatch, 'justice requires
that I should exempt the remaining parts of the Confederation;
I believe that seeds for good are there to be found, and I hope
that commerce and contact with civilized Nations will bring
them to maturity.'[1]

The news of Rosas's overthrow brought not only Sir Charles
Hotham to the Foreign Office. Letters came from the Committee of Bondholders of Buenos Aires asking for assistance, and in
March Sir Thomas Baring wrote seeking some assistance for
the agent whom he proposed to send to Buenos Aires for the
purpose of negotiating a settlement of the debt question. What
to do? Malmesbury seized the opportunity of the new condition of affairs in Buenos Aires to lay down a policy which assigned an order of precedence for the questions which required
settlement.

Malmesbury accepted Hotham's argument that the opening
of the rivers to international commerce was the most important
object of policy. The collection of debts, he decided, was a
secondary matter. Hotham was appointed a special envoy to
negotiate a treaty of free navigation, and Baring Brothers were
told that 'Her Majesty's Government consider it inadmissible
to instruct Captain Gore to urge the claims of the Bondholders
as long as the English and French special ministers are negotiating the opening of the great rivers'.[2]

Malmesbury's instructions to Hotham were conceived in
a liberal spirit of international generosity and co-operation.
Britain, he declared, had 'no selfish or exclusive objects in
view, and . . . [her] desire is to obtain for all Commercial States
advantages which, however great to them will be repaid tenfold
to the Argentines themselves'.[3] Hotham was instructed to act

---

[1] F.O. 59/8, Hotham to Clarendon, 3 Aug. 1853, from Montevideo on his way
home.   [2] *B.P.*, Addington to Baring Bros., 5 Apr. 1852.
[3] F.O. 59/1, Malmesbury to Hotham, 30 Apr. 1852.

in the closest co-operation with the French Special Envoy, the Chevalier de St. Georges, with whom he was to work 'without any reserve'. He was ordered, likewise, to co-operate to the fullest degree possible with the representative of the United States. Furthermore, the object of his negotiation was not just to secure free navigation to Britain and France but 'to the commerce of the whole world'. Malmesbury, like everyone else at that time, was too uncertain about the events in Buenos Aires to instruct Hotham in a course of action in relation to Argentine domestic affairs, but he did express one fear about the River Plate and ordered one particular course to be followed there. That concerned the activities of Brazil in the area and particularly in Uruguay. 'The point is the preservation of the independence of Monte Video . . . it is one on which you . . . must employ if necessary the firmest language and admit of no compromise.' Finally, Malmesbury ordered Hotham to give his whole attention to the question of free navigation and 'not [to] interfere with other subjects relative to the slave trade, loans or personal claims'.

By the time Hotham arrived in Buenos Aires in August 1852 the principal object of his mission was the least of his worries. The determination of Urquiza to improve Argentine relations with the neighbouring states by abandoning pretensions to control or undue influence had been given concrete expression in the recognition of Paraguayan independence in July. A private informant told the agent of Baring Brothers as early as June that Urquiza was determined to open the rivers to free navigation of his own accord and that his Government 'wished to show that it had done this act of its own proper will and not by any extraneous influence or fear or persuasion'.[1] The decree of the provisional Government opening the rivers was promulgated a few weeks after Hotham's arrival. Apart from securing, by treaty, rights already accorded by Argentine legislation, there was nothing for Hotham and St. Georges to do.

And yet there was everything to do, for there was no certainty about the course which Urquiza might take finally, nor was there certainty about the resolution of the tensions quickened with the breaking of the dictatorship. When Urquiza had recovered from his momentary pique at the escape of Rosas

[1] B.P., *White's Diary*, p. 76.

through British help and had manifested a friendly spirit to the British chargé d'affaires, Gore responded by giving to his Government a steady support. The Foreign Office approved of this 'determination to afford General Urquiza all . . . moral support . . . so long as he pursues his present satisfactory course of Government'.[1] Hotham's appointment, however, changed the attitude of the provisional Government. The appearance of an admiral who had fought against Argentina in the character of a special envoy was interpreted as an act of potential hostility by some of Urquiza's entourage. It was reported to the General from Montevideo that the Admiral intended to travel to Buenos Aires and hence to Paraguay in a ship of war. Immediately two Argentine war vessels were posted at Martín García to bar the way. Gore hastily repaired to the Fort and explained that a mistake had been made; that Sir Charles Hotham was coming as a friendly envoy in a packet boat.[2] Urquiza explained that the war vessels at Martín García had been posted there for some time before Sir Charles's arrival. When Sir Charles landed, Urquiza sent his carriage to convey him to his residence, but within a few days the Argentine leader was making difficulties about the inadequate and erroneous contents of the letter of credence of the envoys.

Once Hotham had been received, he put Urquiza's apprehensions to rest. Hotham was a stiff and arrogant man who spoke loftily of 'these people' when discussing the inhabitants of Argentina, but he was very intelligent and quick, not merely in a narrow naval way, but socially and politically. He had the additional merit of knowing something about Argentina both as a community and as a nation of individuals with characters and capacities of their own. He appreciated their pride and he knew that, if offended or molested in their independence, the Argentine leaders and the people would fight and knew how to fight. Hotham told Urquiza in one of his first interviews that he did not wish to interfere, or appear to interfere, in Argentine affairs. In writing to the Foreign Secretary, he said that it was his policy to show 'the utmost deference to the national honour'.[3] Repeatedly, when British assistance was sought by one or other

---

[1] F.O. 6/166, Malmesbury to Gore, 28 Sept. 1852.
[2] F.O. 6/169, Gore to Malmesbury, 1 Aug. 1852.
[3] F.O. 59/2, Hotham to Malmesbury, 26 Aug. 1852.

of the Argentine factions, Hotham insisted that Britain had a duty of non-interference and that the policies of Argentina and the fate of Argentine political leaders was a matter for the Argentine nation itself to decide.

Hotham further won the heart of Urquiza's Government by commending warmly their liberal policies in the sphere of commerce, international relations, and economic development. 'Encourage immigration', he told the Foreign Minister, 'let the immigrants be of all classes and nations, give the preference to Germans, neutralize the contentious spirit of your Countrymen, and you will have done wonders.'[1] The Foreign Minister agreed. An interest in commerce, he said, would cause the Argentine people 'to forget ambition'. Urquiza improved on this by saying, 'We shall advance, Sir; we shall do well. I intend to do so; this shall be a commercial country and there shall be free navigation.'

Henceforward Hotham supported Urquiza. In spite of his self-denying ordinance on the subject of Argentine internal affairs, Sir Charles contrived a policy of neutrality distinctly advantageous to Urquiza and favourable to the unity of Argentina under one Government in which the rural and provincial interests had a prominent place. He saved Urquiza from himself on more than one occasion. When Buenos Aires threw off Urquiza's control in September 1852 and declared itself independent of the Confederation and of the Constituent Congress at Santa Fé, Urquiza in despair began to sound the British Government through his son, the Argentine chargé in Montevideo, about its attitude towards breaking up the Confederation into small republics of which his own Province of Entre Rios united with Corrientes would be one. Hotham spoke out strongly against such a course of action. 'We . . . are . . . interested in maintaining the Argentine Confederation on its present basis', he reported himself as saying, 'and in opposing by all the means which our moral influence can give, its disruption and separation'.[2] Brazil might welcome the break-up of Argentina; Britain would not. The creation of a number of petty landlord republics would be bad for trade, he argued, and he wished to encourage a representative landlord like

---

[1] F.O. 59/2, Hotham to Malmesbury, 26 Aug. 1852.
[2] F.O. 59/4, Hotham to Malmesbury, 25 Oct. 1852.

Urguiza to see that the creation of a great state controlled by landlords would be preferable to a number of small ones.

When Urquiza established the provisional capital at Paraná, Hotham and St. Georges remained in Buenos Aires. Urquiza interpreted this as an act of disloyalty to himself and his Government, and he reproached Hotham. Hotham was able effectively to demonstrate that by remaining in Buenos Aires he had rendered great assistance to Urquiza. This was certainly so. When the army of General Hornos began to move against Urquiza in late October, Hotham prevailed upon the French and United States agents to join him in visiting Alsina, the Governor of Buenos Aires, to 'express . . . the alarm and anxiety which pervaded the commercial body, [and] request . . . [that] he would . . . in plain language declare whether or not it was the intention of the Provisional Government to commence a Civil war against General Urquiza'.[1] Alsina was put on the defensive, and lamely tried to excuse himself. A few days later, when it was learned that General Paz had failed to arouse the Province of Córdoba against Urquiza, Hotham again waited on Alsina, and pressed him to stop. 'Peace, Peace, no matter how',[2] was Hotham's plea.

Hotham was not deceived by Alsina's fair words of agreement. The Province of Buenos Aires must be deprived of all means of resisting Urquiza, Hotham argued. 'My Lord, I have been too long dealing with these people', he wrote, 'not to know what all this means. If the time shall arrive when the Government of Buenos Aires shall find itself without a shadow of hope, they may perhaps listen to counsel; but so long as they think they have a reed to lean upon, they will deceive themselves, buoy up others, and prolong a crisis perilous to the country and disastrous to European Commerce.'[3]

Once it was clear that Urquiza could not be overthrown, at least for the time being, Hotham boarded H.M.S. *Locust*, and sailed away for Paraguay, but not before he had explained that his conveyance on a ship of war was no act of defiance on his part, but a necessity owing to the draught of the vessel and its speed. He offered both Urquiza and Alsina its use as a means of

---

[1] F.O. 59/4, Hotham to Malmesbury, 4 Nov. 1852.
[2] F.O. 59/4, Hotham to Malmesbury, 7 Nov. 1852.
[3] F.O. 59/4, Hotham to Malmesbury, 4 Nov. 1852.

conveying official mail to Paraguay. In this spirit both leaders agreed to see it steam along the watercourse of Argentina open to mercantile vessels but not to ships of war. A few days later Captain Gore also removed from Buenos Aires to Paraná, and Britain thus severed its connexions with the Province.

Hotham's policy of supporting Urquiza was strongly criticized by some at least of the British community in Buenos Aires and by the mercantile interests in Liverpool. Major Ferdinand White, the agent of Baring Brothers in Buenos Aires, declared himself in his diary bitter about the 'decided and to my mind very questionable part the British authorities are taking in the internal dissensions going on here'.[1] Like many others connected with business, White's view was circumscribed by his immediate interests. Because the townsmen of Buenos Aires shared the same enthusiasm as the British business class they thought they not only ought, but could, govern Argentina. On the other hand, British business men wanted peace and quiet for the purpose of trade and investment. The result was that, in the absence of leadership, they encouraged the Government of Buenos Aires and yet served to deter them, chopping and changing their views and in some cases becoming a means employed by the Buenos Aires Government of exerting pressure on the British Government.

From December 1852 until March 1853 Hotham and St. Georges were away in Asunción practising diplomacy with the First Consul of Paraguay and his irascible son, General López, whose punctilious notions of the art were derived from a study of an edition of Vattel published before the Congress of Vienna. When the Admiral returned down the river he found Urquiza's army arrayed to assault Buenos Aires, his fleet preparing to lay down a close blockade, and the British community in despair. The Committee of British Merchants had already written to Hotham urging him to intervene and restore peace. Hotham declared that foreign interference could only make matters worse, but he suggested that the mercantile community should draw up a petition urging him and St. Georges to mediate. All the British merchants except one and great numbers of other foreign merchants signed the petition. Hotham and his colleagues waited on the Government of Buenos Aires, and to

[1] *B.P., White's Diary*, p. 187.

Hotham's great relief learned that Bolivia and Brazil had already promised to conduct talks between the opposing forces.

Hotham was, in fact, anxious to see Urquiza victorious. When Urquiza notified the powers of his intention to blockade Buenos Aires, Hotham agreed that he had the forces to do this and that the blockade should be recognized by the British Government. Simultaneously he urged Urquiza to sign a treaty of free navigation. At this stage the British community in Buenos Aires began to split. A Society of Foreigners was formed under the chairmanship of a British merchant, Wilfrid Latham, for the purpose of advocating a lifting of the blockade. The Chairman of the Committee of British Merchants refused to join the Society of Foreigners. Hotham himself claimed that the Society was a put-up job engineered by the *Ministro de Gobierno* of Buenos Aires, Señor Torres.[1] But he took it seriously enough to counter its activity by organizing in collaboration with his French colleague a relief scheme for distressed British, French, and other foreign residents. This scheme involved using British and French war vessels to transport unemployed foreign workmen and other distressed persons to Uruguay or to the territory under General Urquiza's control, where they were promised employment and where they could not enlist in the army of Buenos Aires.

It was at this stage that the Government of Buenos Aires scored their tremendous coup of buying the fleet blockading the city. The price was high. Hotham understood it amounted to £100,000. The Admiral, an American, was able to retire from the strenuous life of a mercenary. Very soon General Flores, the Buenos Airean commander, moved against Urquiza's forces. 'He came, not with an Army', Hotham reported indignantly, 'but with a sort of portable Bank, drawing letters of credit on the City of Buenos Aires to all who joined him.'[2] In the presence of this formidable armament Urquiza retired, and it now looked as if the offensive belonged to Buenos Aires.

The circumstances of Urquiza were not, however, desperate. He still had space and gaucho savagery on his side. All he lacked was the means of buying armies and navies. He appealed to Hotham to come to his assistance, 'even [with] the arms

---

[1] F.O. 59/7, Hotham to Clarendon, 11 June 1853.
[2] F.O. 59/8, Hotham to Clarendon, 15 July 1853.

which your Government has at its disposal in the Rio de la Plata, towards preventing those possible hostilities made in the name of Authorities whom Your Excellency neither does, nor can recognize'.[1] Hotham avoided this application, but suggested something quite as good and in line with the objects of his mission, namely, the signature of a treaty of free navigation making Britain and France as well as the Argentine Confederation the guarantors of the free movement of commercial ships in the rivers. Thus, Britain and France would have a treaty right and an interest to prevent the blockading of the rivers by Buenos Aires. In two days Hotham and St. Georges had their treaty. Within a year the United States, Chile, Bolivia, Paraguay, Brazil, Prussia, Sardinia, and Belgium had obtained equivalent rights by treaty. The Government of Buenos Aires would now have to defy a formidable array of powers if its cruisers commenced interfering with river traffic proceeding to the ports of the Confederation.

Hotham departed almost at once, but his policy of supporting the rural, federalist forces remained. Immediately the question of the Loan of 1824 was taken up not with Urquiza, whose Government could not have paid anything, but with Buenos Aires, which officially Britain did not recognize. Legally the debt was an obligation of the Province of Buenos Aires, but it had been contracted for national purposes and it had been expended largely for the prosecution of the war against Brazil. The agent of Baring Brothers, who had arrived in Buenos Aires some weeks before Hotham, had explored the possibility of an arrangement for repayment with Urquiza's Government, but he had come to the conclusion, particularly after the separation of Buenos Aires from the Confederation that only Buenos Aires possessed the resources necessary for repayment.[2] As soon as the stalemate between Buenos Aires and the Confederation began to assume an aspect of permanency late in 1853, Baring Brothers decided to send out a new agent. When they applied for assistance to the Foreign Office this time the Foreign Secretary himself provided their agent with a letter of introduction.[3]

[1] F.O. 59/8, Note signed by Angel Elias, 23 June 1853.
[2] B.P., *White's Diary*, p. 161.
[3] F.O. 6/187, Parish to Clarendon, 31 Jan. 1854, referring to Clarendon's letter of introduction, 22 Nov. 1853.

This adoption of a positive policy towards the collection of Buenos Aires's debts to British bondholders and its relationship to the British alignment with the political groupings in Argentina can best be understood in the light of general British policy concerning the collection of foreign debts and its application in the River Plate area. The policy of giving complete political and military support to financial interests bent on maintaining and expanding their investments in foreign states, which finds its finest example in the Egyptian invasion of 1882, was by no means characteristic of British policy of the 1840's and 1850's. The Don Pacifico incident was not concerned with protecting and expanding investment opportunities, and the assault in China was concerned with trade not capital accumulation. Palmerston liked to affect the style of a grand bum-bailiff, and he is alleged to have once advised the Chairman of the Buenos Aires Bondholders' Committee to put 'plenty of pepper and mustard into your despatches'.[1] When he came to instruct a Minister, at least in Buenos Aires, Palmerston was much more restrained. We have already observed him reproving a chargé for presenting a note on the subject of the defaulted debt of Buenos Aires. A note was going too far in Palmerston's view. There is no evidence that he ever wished to do more than remind the Argentine authorities that they owed money in London. During Aberdeen's tenure of the Foreign Office the Bondholders' Committee opposed the intervention in the River Plate. When Palmerston returned to office in 1846 he encountered considerable criticism of the uncertain character of the Government's policy on the subject of collecting defaulted debts abroad, but this only produced finally his circular instruction of 1849 to Ministers and agents abroad, in which he reserved the general right of the British Government to act against defaulters, but denied the intention of doing anything in particular instances on the grounds that British capitalists ought to invest at home, and if they invested abroad, they ought to bear the risks of doing so themselves. The Buenos Aires Bondholders did not object to this policy. At a meeting in the London Tavern in May 1851 they 'lament[ed] that the wise example of England has not at once been followed by other countries'[2] in adopting a policy of non-intervention.

[1] *B.P., White's Diary*, p. 166.   [2] Third resolution, *B.P., White's Diary*, p. 20]

Malmesbury's refusal to give debt collection priority over a treaty of free navigation suggests that the influence of the Baring Brothers at the Foreign Office did not measure up to the popular notion that they had dictated the British Government's attitude towards Rosas.[1] Malmesbury, like Palmerston, was willing to take the initiative in employing British power to advance the cause of free trade but he was much more reserved on the matter of securing investment. The bondholders, however, were full of 'bursting expectation'. There was no mourning for Rosas on the London Stock Exchange. The bonds of Buenos Aires gained on the news of his overthrow, and when it was learned that an agent of Baring Brothers was on his way to Buenos Aires they jumped from 70 to 77. Thomas Baring did not himself share the expectations of the bondholders for whom his house was commissioned to act in negotiating a settlement. He told his agent, Major Ferdinand White, that 'however great might be our regret, we shall feel that no blame will attach to you if adverse circumstances frustrate your exertions'.[2] When White arrived in Buenos Aires, Gore, whom he discovered to be an old friend from his Bombay days, frankly told him his mission was ill timed, and that it might be several years before a settlement could be usefully discussed.

The various doubts about a settlement were well founded. There were two favourable factors in the situation; firstly, that Chile had lately set an example by making a very favourable debt settlement and, secondly, that popular sentiment was increasingly friendly to economic development and the importation of capital and immigrants. But the difficulties of translating these favourable factors into an actual settlement were formidable. A great many people wanted the advantages which might flow from a settlement, but no interest in Argentina was concerned particularly in the settlement itself. The creditors resided abroad, and had no influence in Argentina itself. Something more than homilies on the importance and virtue of justice and the sacred character of bonds was required to effect a redistribution of public funds on the scale sufficient to pay

---

[1] *B.P., White's Diary*, p. 193, remarks on the widespread character of this belief.

[2] *B.P.*, Baring to White, 7 Apr. 1852.

the British bondholders. White found that the revenues of
Buenos Aires were roughly 3¼ million hard pesos annually;
public indebtedness was roughly 30 million hard pesos and
that more than one-third of this debt could be accounted for
by the Loan of 1824 plus its defaulted interest. To reach a
settlement in full would require the public authorities either to
divert nearly one-quarter of the public revenues towards London or else increase taxes directly or indirectly to that extent.
The politics of such a change presented some problems for the
agent of Baring Brothers.

He first encountered the problem in Rio de Janeiro where he
met Henry Southern, then the British Minister at the Court of
Brazil. Southern was astonished to learn that Buenos Aires
bonds stood at 70. This was optimism without any foundations
in his view. Urquiza was a villain, he argued, and the fall of
Rosas had dissipated all hope of repayment. Southern conceded
that Urquiza might make a settlement to win foreign support
for his régime, but that he was not likely to last and that his
liberal and progressive legislation was but window-dressing.
Southern, however, explained to White that the new Foreign
Minister, Dr. Peña, was a man of much influence and that he,
Southern, had a close friend, Señor Beláustigue, who was in his
turn very intimate with Dr. Peña. Beláustigue understood the
Loan question, and had worked so hard to assist Falconnet in
effecting a settlement that Southern had recommended him to
Baring Brothers as their agent for receiving the money paid by
Rosas. Southern gave White letters of introduction to Beláus-
tigue and Peña who were both in Montevideo on official
business.

White's relations with Beláustigue led him into some rather
unsavoury blind alleys, but they taught him much about what
to do and what not to do in reaching his objectives. Beláustigue
did indeed possess some influence with Peña. He was also the
means of putting White in touch with his own nephew, Dr.
Ensilade, who understood the need and the technique for
managing the press. Beláustigue was, however, an adventurer
and, it was alleged, a pander whose relations with Mr. Southern
were not entirely concerned with the bonds of Buenos Aires.[1]
White was at first impressed by Beláustigue for he talked

[1] B.P., *White's Diary*, p. 146.

intelligently and he possessed documentary proofs of having tried to induce Rosas to make a settlement in full with the bondholders. After the first introduction to Peña was effected and the way was opened for a sympathetic reception from Urquiza, Beláustigue revealed that further progress would require that he be made the agent for collecting the money. White was shocked by this frankly interested attitude on the part of Beláustigue and he was disturbed by the gossip concerning some of Beláustigue's business activities, but he was persuaded that he needed Beláustigue's assistance. He prayed daily for guidance[1] with the result that he recommended Baring Brothers to appoint Beláustigue as their agent, and they agreed to pay him 1 per cent. on all sums transmitted to them once a settlement was reached. They also agreed to pay Dr. Ensilade for his press relations work.[2]

Facts which emerged later suggest that Beláustigue could never have promoted a satisfactory settlement. His notion of effecting his purpose was to persuade Baring Brothers to raise a fresh loan to pay the old one. In entertaining such a scheme Beláustigue was no more cynical than the Chairman of the Buenos Aires Bondholders' Committee, who was quite willing to promote a new loan before it was demonstrated that Argentina could support an old one.[3] Baring Brothers, needless to say, would have nothing to do with such a proposal no matter whence it emanated or whose interest it served.

The revolution of September 1852 which separated Buenos Aires from the Confederation put an end to all immediate hope of a settlement. Although he felt obliged to resort to prayer for guidance, White appears to have had little difficulty in abandoning all idea of seeking a settlement with Urquiza. His personal inclination was towards the men of Buenos Aires, and when it became apparent that they alone possessed the means of settlement, White broke off his connexion with Beláustigue and addressed himself to Governor Alsina. Alsina was civil and verbally encouraging, but his resources were so taxed with buying over his opponents and arming himself, that with the best will in the world he could not have undertaken

---

[1] Ibid., p. 151.
[2] B.P., Baring Brothers to White, 7 Aug. 1852.
[3] B.P., Robertson to George White, 13 Apr. 1852.

repayment of Buenos Aires's foreign debts. White soon decided that his mission would come to nothing, and in March 1853 he prepared to leave.

Before his departure several British business men in Buenos Aires came forward with ideas for a settlement. Samuel Lafone, the romantic hide merchant and land speculator, produced a grand scheme for land settlement, the revenues from which could pay the bondholders. Edward Lumb, a wealthy merchant and landed proprietor, who helped the Government of Buenos Aires Province float several internal loans and who later negotiated the Buenos Ayres Great Southern Railway concession, let it be known that he had a solution, the disclosure of which depended upon the character of the deal he would make with Baring Brothers. Daniel Gowland, a prominent figure in mercantile circles from revolutionary times, advised White to deal only with the Province of Buenos Aires on the basis of straightforward repayment. Another proposal related to the guano deposits in Patagonia. White with Gore's assistance investigated this last possibility and advised against its acceptance.

All these proposals, save Gowland's, had a common characteristic of requiring a further investment of British money for their implementation. All of them avoided the central problem of establishing the accumulative process in Argentina. Although they did not formulate the problem exactly in these terms, the directors of Baring Brothers and White himself saw clearly that further investment by foreigners in Argentina depended upon the willingness of the Argentine state authorities themselves to undertake the skimming-off process which is the essential characteristic of capital accumulation. In the absence of such willingness and without the protection and finally the exercise of political power of their own governments, foreigners cannot become the agents of capital accumulation. Baring Brothers were unwilling to become the means of inducing one set of British capitalists to compensate another set of British capitalists (this was the essence of the proposal to float a new loan to repay the old one), nor were they willing to induce investors to create enterprises in a community whose authorities did not regard the accumulative process as sacred and beyond violation. White and his principals thought of the problem not as one of social process as we tend to see it now, but as one of morals. The

Argentine state authorities and the community itself were being put to a test. If they honoured their bond they could expect the benefits which came from a good name in the world of commerce and finance; if not, they could expect the contrary. Baring Brothers considered it their duty to determine the character of Argentina by an accounting calculation. This distinguished them from those who were seeking some other less rigorous arrangement.

There were, of course, dangers in the too continuous use of moral analysis. Before he left the River Plate in April 1853 White had begun to question the morality of the Loan itself. Baring Brothers, he thought, were blameless, but the original promoters, Robertson and Castro, had 'realized pretty pickings'.[1] But, he concluded, 'a bargain is a bargain' and Buenos Aires ought in justice to pay up.

What had White accomplished? He had decided, and he so reported to Baring Brothers, that British investors could expect satisfaction only from a government which drew its revenues from the community of Buenos Aires—the city and its hinterland. The implication of this recommendation was that investment would be linked with repayment, and both with a political settlement which gave mercantile and financial interests in Buenos Aires at least as much power as the landed interests. Thus, White saw an aspect of the problem only imperfectly discerned by Hotham. The future justified one as much as the other. After Mitre's victory at Pavón in 1861 and Urquiza's retirement from politics a balance was struck between the interests, and capital at once began to flow to Argentina.

White, further, reported that an atmosphere of enterprise existed. White's reports were less glowing than Woodbine Parish's had been twenty-eight years previously, but they were more concerned with what human beings were actually doing to advance production and communication. Parish had been enraptured by the vastness of the pampas, the immensity of the rivers, and the richness of the soil. He had had little to say about people. White observed that Samuel Lafone was trying to promote a railway from Córdoba to Santa Fé in order to bring the produce of the interior to the markets of the world.

[1] *B.P., White's Diary,* p. 218.

A Frenchman was negotiating to bring in 15,000 immigrants. White, indeed, asserted that it would be better for Argentina to import 50,000 men capable of work than £5 millions of capital,[1] and he was able to say that immigrants were beginning to come.

White and the business class reasoned that, Buenos Aires being the richest and economically the most important province of Argentina, British policy should be directed to its support against Urquiza and the Confederation.[2] The Foreign Office reasoned otherwise. The Foreign Secretary agreed to send a Vice-Consul to Buenos Aires in the person of Frank Parish, the son of Sir Woodbine, but resolutely resisted the suggestion of recognizing the independence of Buenos Aires or falling in with its pretensions to represent the Argentine Republic in the international community. It was explicitly acknowledged inside the diplomatic service that Britain's object was to force Buenos Aires into the Confederation.[3]

In the ensuing contest between the rival forces of Argentine politics Urquiza and his Minister in London, Juan Alberdi, tried hard to identify foreign investors, and particularly British investors, with their régime and to obtain assistance for development from the British Government. The Treaty of Free Navigation was quickly ratified. In 1855 José Buschenthal, a Spanish promoter, was granted a concession on generous terms to build a railway from Rosario across the northern pampas to Córdoba,[4] and he commenced upon a campaign to interest British investors and contractors. An official application was made to the British Government to subsidize the Royal Mail Steam Packet Company in order that it could operate a direct service between Europe, Rosario, and the river ports.[5] A French statistician and geographer, Martin de Moussy, was invited to prepare a careful and detailed description of the Republic for the better understanding of the possibilities of the area.[6] Alberdi in London argued with Clarendon that it was

[1] In a letter from White's clerk, George White, 8 Jan. 1853, *B.P.*, *White's Diary*, p. 233.

[2] Several letters from Liverpool merchants during 1855 in F.O. 6/191.

[3] Comments in F.O. 6/196.

[4] *Registro Oficial de la Republica Argentina*, 3441, iii, pp. 207–8.

[5] F.O. 6/189, Parish to the Foreign Office, 29 Oct. 1855.

[6] Published in 1860–1 in Paris, V. Martin de Moussy, *Description géographique et statistique de la Confédération Argentine*.

in the British interest to assist the development in South America of a republic of ample proportions based on a progressive economy as a guarantee 'against the threatening ascendancy of the United States'.[1] He wished the British Government to demonstrate their interest concretely by surveying a railway route across the Andes and to assist in building an inter-oceanic railway.

In the first stages of the contest to break the stalemate the Government of Buenos Aires pursued a contrary policy of isolation and of independence of foreign capitalists. Being very much richer than the Confederation, the Province attempted a course of independent development based upon local supplies of capital. In 1853 the first railway in Argentina, the *Ferrocarril al Oeste*,[2] was undertaken by an Argentine company, the president and secretary of which were Argentinos and the vice-president, Daniel Gowland, the chairman of the Committee of British Merchants. The Government subscribed one-third of the capital, and undertook to forgo dividends until the private investors were making 9 per cent. It also undertook to provide the land for the right of way and to exempt all capital equipment from customs duties.

Simultaneously, road building, harbour improvements, and land settlement schemes were undertaken by the Government. The public accounts for 1854–5 indicated that slightly more than 4 per cent. of expenditure was directed to roads and public works; about 40 per cent. to servicing the internal debt and about 36 per cent. to the armed forces. The percentage of expenditure directly on public works was not impressive, but the fact that money was being spent at all alarmed Parish, the Vice-Consul, who thought the revenues should be applied to the 'liquidation of this just Debt',[3] the Loan of 1824. Parish regarded expenditure by the state authorities on development schemes as useless.[4] He seems to have been hostile even to private enterprise under local auspices, for he warned the Foreign Office about Gowland, the vice-president of the *Oeste*, and his close association with the Buenos Aires Government,

---

[1] F.O. 6/196. In a memorandum submitted by Alberdi during an interview with Lord Clarendon at the Foreign Office, 11 Aug. 1856.

[2] Hereafter the *Oeste*.

[3] F.O. 6/189, Parish to the Foreign Office, 30 Jan. 1855.

[4] Ibid., 25 May 1855.

declaring him to be a 'porteño by birth, residence, and connexions'[1] even though he was the chairman of the Committee of
British Merchants.

The determination of the British Government to ally itself
politically with the Confederation and to apply pressure to
Buenos Aires Province both for the purpose of altering its
independent course in the direction of incorporation in the
Republic and for the collection of the Loan of 1824 may be
properly regarded as one of the critical events in the history of
the Argentine community. Had Buenos Aires succeeded in
maintaining its political independence it would have been
obliged, at least in the formative stages, to undertake its own
capital accumulation. The social, political, and economic
consequences of this would have been profound, for it would
have been the means of creating in the richest and most com-
pact productive area of Argentina a class of financiers and
entrepreneurs dominant in their own community and independent of others. On a smaller scale there would have been
created a class of similar character to that which existed in the
United States. Whether the Province of Buenos Aires was well
enough peopled and sufficiently knowledgeable in the arts and
technology of production to sustain the accumulative process
independently is not entirely a profitless or an impossible
speculation. The *Oeste* was a very small enterprise—in its first
stages simply a suburban transit system of Buenos Aires—but
it was profitable from the start. There is no reason to suppose
that it would not have duplicated without foreign investment
the financial feats of a railway like the Buenos Ayres Great
Southern, begun with British capital but expanded very largely
by its own internal financial resources. Likewise with other
public works which required heavy capital expenditure. The
use made of the harbour of Buenos Aires and of the city's
facilities was sufficiently heavy to warrant the supposition that
internal capital accumulation either by the public authorities
or by private concessionaires would lead to expansion of physical
equipment through reinvestment.

As it was, the eventual integration of Buenos Aires Province
in the Republic placed the financial resources of the richest
area at the disposal of the whole Republic, and made these

[1] F.O. 6/187, 1 May 1854.

resources the means of financing vast railway schemes of continental dimensions which were run at heavy losses for many years, and some permanently. These vast railways running through areas of a low population density and low productivity were built with foreign capital for the very good reason that they were beyond the capacities of the Argentine community. This investment was encouraged to enter the country by the dominant landed interest, which saw in the process advantages to themselves both in economic benefits and political power. But the cost of rapid and grandiose expansion beyond the frontiers of settlement and into economically marginal areas was enormous. The burden for the Argentine people and the immigrants who swelled their numbers with the passage of time was heavy. A geographically more concentrated development confined to the Province of Buenos Aires and the southern pampas, where railway building costs are low and distances relatively short, would have been not only less burdensome but might have led to a more balanced economic and industrial development. As it was, saddled with a vast foreign investment, Argentina was obliged to export or go bankrupt, and this meant concentration upon a limited range of exportable staple products with all the social and political, not to mention moral and intellectual consequences of intense specialization in an agricultural and pastoral setting.

The purpose in speculating upon the alternatives open to the various interests existing in the Argentine community in the middle of the nineteenth century is not to impose an interpretation upon events but to illuminate in some intelligible way the anxieties and conflicts which men like Parish encountered. The Foreign Minister of Buenos Aires 'has a very bad spirit personally towards me' Frank Parish reported early in 1856. Repeatedly he was depressed by the hostility around him, while at the same time excited by the evidence of change and advance. Argentine society was at a point of crisis, but it was a crisis which lacked the dramatic quality which the sieges, blockades, massacres, and upsets had hitherto imparted to the movement of its history. This was a more sophisticated crisis of economics, clearer in its character, perhaps, to those who know how it was resolved than to those who determined its resolution.

The new agent of the bondholders sent out in 1854 with a

letter of introduction from the Foreign Secretary, Lord Clarendon, was Mr. James Giro. The letter may have borne an
exalted signature, but it cut no ice. In the message to the
Provincial Assembly in May 1854 the Governor never mentioned the defaulted Loan. After twelve months of futile
manœuvring on the part of Giro and Parish, the Vice-Consul
reported that the money would never be collected as long as
the Government of Buenos Aires believed 'that Her Majesty's
Government will deal with the claim as a Commercial Speculation'. He complained that the Assembly was able, however, to
vote money 'for purposes which cannot be classified as coming
within the absolute Necessities of the Country'.[1]

Early in 1855 a change took place in the Ministry of Finance.
The new Minister was Norberto de la Riestra, who up to the
time of his acceptance of office, had been a partner in the
Liverpool firm of Nicolson, Green & Co. Parish advised Clarendon not to expect anything from the change in spite of the
'liberal and correct commercial principles Señor Riestra may
have learned from his connection with an English mercantile
house'. At first Parish's pessimism seemed justified. Giro published the terms of the original bonds in the press, expecting that
a statement of information might assist him. Instead, he was
greeted with an outburst of indignation directed at the Loan.
Almost simultaneously, however, the Governor in his message
to the Assembly stated that his Government 'did not ignore the
justice attending the claims of the Bondholders', but he added
the old formula of Rosas, that payment was not practical at the
moment. When the public accounts were published in May
the budget was in a balanced state in spite of expenditure on
public works and the disbursement of more than 40 per cent. of
the revenue on the service of the internal debt. There was a
plan broached to put the currency on a gold basis through the
sale of public land.

Parish continued pessimistic. In June he reported that nothing could be done about the defaulted Loan, and Clarendon
agreed. Quite unexpectedly in August the monthly payments
agreed to in Rosas's time were doubled. Parish declared that
this simply indicated that the Buenos Aires Government planned
never to settle, but to fob off the creditors at the lowest price

[1] F.O. 6/189, Parish to the Foreign Office, 30 Jan. 1855.

possible. He complained about 'useless expenditure' on public works, and he wanted to publish his entire correspondence with the Government. Clarendon pencilled in the margin of his dispatch, 'This would never do'.

In fact, however, the situation was changing in a way favourable to foreign investors. The news that Urquiza's Government had granted a railway concession to the promoter, Buschenthal, seems to have shaken the resolution of the Buenos Aires Government to deal harshly with foreign interests. In September 1855 Urquiza applied for assistance to enable the steam-packets to sail directly to the ports of the Confederation. Within a few weeks the Government of Buenos Aires further increased its payments to the bondholders by £1,000 a month.

With this change in the atmosphere both Parish and Giro began to press the Buenos Aires authorities hard. Giro formally declared that the increased monthly payments were not a settlement and he protested against the sale of public land, which, he argued, had been declared by law a security for the public debt. The formal protest about the sale of land he entered in the official register of the Consulate, but he could find no notary in Buenos Aires who would affix an official seal to the documents, and Parish was obliged to enter the document over his own signature. At the same time Parish sent a note to the Government declaring that Britain had not taken stronger action than she had so far only because the British Government believed that Buenos Aires intended to honour its bonds.

As the Buenos Aires Government began to yield behind a smoke screen of public abuse of the bondholders, other claimants began to appear upon the scene. In 1836 General Rosas had closed the National Bank of Buenos Aires when its bankruptcy was apparent. Some of its shareholders were British. These appointed a certain Lord de Manley to place their case before the Foreign Secretary and to ask for the support of the British Government. But Parish had reported adversely on these claims. Clarendon told Lord de Manley that the Bank had a history of paying dividends out of capital, and that the shareholders' remedy, if there was any, lay in legal action in the courts of Buenos Aires.[1] Some months later these shareholders

---

[1] F.O. 6/191, Clarendon to Lord de Manley, 4 Jan. 1855. There is no record of a peer of this name.

were still grumbling about the way in which Parish had allowed himself to be imposed upon, but it did them no good.

There could be no mistake, however, about the pressure being applied to Buenos Aires for other and larger purposes. Early in 1856 it was decided to send a Minister to Paraná, the first resident British Minister to be accredited to the Argentine Confederation since Southern's departure in 1851. At the same time France and Brazil decided to send Ministers. When the new British representative, W. D. Christie, arrived in Montevideo he decided to proceed from there to Paraná by warship, avoiding all contact with Buenos Aires. On his first official visit to General Urquiza he plainly stated Her Majesty's Government's 'hope in the general interests of humanity and civilization, to see the various states which border on the Plata and its great tributary streams all bound to one another in firm friendship'. These words were uttered in June. At the end of July Christie told Urquiza's Foreign Minister that 'the Confederation should consider [that] the present anomalous position of Buenos Ayres, really independent but nominally a part of the Confederation, is one in which Foreign Powers having important interests there cannot be expected to acquiesce for ever'.[1] This was ominous talk. In Buenos Aires there were rumours of British intervention, which Christie instructed Parish to deny. None the less in October he wrote to Clarendon suggesting 'without urging it, that, if Her Majesty's government would at any time interfere with a naval force to insist on an equitable adjustment of this Loan question by Buenos Aires, the present is a favourable moment for doing so, and that a demonstration of force now might not only gain the immediate object, but bring about the union of Buenos Aires with the Confederation. Your Lordship would have the sympathy of the National Government.'[2]

Fortunately His Lordship did not hearken to this suggestion. Indeed, Clarendon appears to have been more anxious for the politicians in Buenos Aires and Paraná to settle the questions in which he was interested than to do anything very positive himself. And the history of half a century demonstrated his wisdom in this. Alberdi was plying him with schemes for the construction

[1] F.O. 6/194, Christie to Clarendon, 30 July 1856.
[2] F.O. 6/195, Christie to Clarendon, 29 Oct. 1856.

of an interoceanic railway across the Andes and for subsidizing a steam-packet service to Paraná. Clarendon was prepared to inquire about the subsidy which the Royal Mail would require to run directly to Paraná, but he was unwilling to do more than 'co-operate indirectly with the promoters'[1] of a railway as far as Córdoba, and he pronounced the survey of a route across the Andes impractical.

The pressure upon Buenos Aires which Christie, Alberdi, and Clarendon were building up was already beginning to produce some unpleasant inconvenience for British merchants. As a measure of economic warfare Urquiza's Government decreed differential duties on all goods entering the Republic through Buenos Aires. The object of this decree was to give advantages to traders importing goods directly through river ports outside the territory of Buenos Aires Province. But there was no market of sufficient size in the river ports to take full cargoes, and costs would have been raised by the operation of the decree. One of Christie's first pieces of business in Paraná was to ask for a suspension of the decree 'to afford a reasonable chance of a reconciliation with Buenos Aires'.[2] This underlined the dilemma. Even mild pressure created difficulties. What would happen if stronger measures were taken? Whether Clarendon ever reflected on the experience of Aberdeen we cannot say, but he appears to have accepted the proposition that one cannot run a commercial and financial empire with gunboats and bayonets.

Mild pressure was, however, yielding favourable results. In March 1856 the Finance Minister of Buenos Aires came forward with a plan to satisfy the bondholders. He proposed to increase interest payments progressively until full interest and sinking fund payments were resumed in 1860. The defaulted interest he proposed to meet with non-interest bearing bonds chargeable on the land revenues and exchangeable for land at the rate of 5 pesos to the pound.

Giro rejected de la Riestra's proposal, and Parish supported him in this. Giro appears, however, to have overplayed his hand. In August he decided to return home, but he was first obliged to withdraw a letter to the Governor of Buenos Aires which His Excellency declared insulting. At the same time the

[1] F.O. 6/196, Clarendon to Alberdi, 8 Dec. 1856.
[2] F.O. 6/194, Christie to Clarendon, 30 July 1856.

Government of Buenos Aires announced that they would deal privately and directly with Baring Brothers. Parish advised that this new negotiation be given time to yield results before any further action at the diplomatic level was taken. The Foreign Office agreed, but at the same time prepared stronger instructions than any yet sent to Buenos Aires. 'Her Majesty's Government', the instructions read, 'would be perfectly justified in proceeding at once to the adoption of other and stronger measures for supporting and enforcing the rights of H.M.'s subjects.'[1] In a private note to Parish there was a reference to coercion, but Parish was recommended to speak privately to the authorities in Buenos Aires in the hope that a Note would not have to be presented.

The public statements of the Buenos Aires Government concerning their finances in the early part of 1857 revealed a further marked improvement in their revenues. Parish appears to have worked upon the Minister of Finance in private and to good effect. In June de la Riestra promised that he would produce a new proposal. In the meantime there had arrived in Buenos Aires a new emissary of Baring Brothers, George White, who had accompanied his namesake, the Major, in 1852. de la Riestra admitted the principle that the bonds for the defaulted interest should themselves bear interest. Baring Brothers therefore gave White a free hand to settle on the best terms he could obtain. These turned out to be better than White had expected. In a letter to Christie he described how de la Riestra had been moved by very large increases in the state revenues to make a proposal very like that which the Bondholders' Committee regarded as satisfactory. de la Riestra proposed to deal with the defaulted interest by issuing bonds payable in sterling, bearing interest at 1 per cent. from 1861 to 1865, at 2 per cent. from 1866 to 1870, and 3 per cent. from 1871 until amortized. This meant a payment of only £7,000 less than the demand of the Bondholders' Committee. 'I have therefore thought it advisable to close with them at once, and I trust the affair may now be considered as virtually settled', White informed Christie.[2]

The successful conclusion of this negotiation and the establishment of an accumulative flow into the pool of British capital

[1] F.O. 6/193, Clarendon to Parish, 8 Nov. 1856.
[2] F.O. 6/201, White to Christie, 27 Sept. 1857.

reinforced the British determination to assist in bringing about a compromise between the Confederation and the Province of Buenos Aires. Christie worked hard in Paraná to put off the impending economic warfare, but to no purpose. A tariff war broke out in 1858 which turned into an armed conflict in the spring of 1859. Urquiza's forces moved upon Buenos Aires. This time they were proof not only against the cannon but also the letters of credit of Buenos Aires. At Cepeda they conquered. At once powerful forces both domestic and international went to work urging forbearance and compromise. The politicians of Buenos Aires agreed to enter the Confederation if some modification in the Constitution of 1853 were made to ensure their survival. These changes were agreed to. Buenos Aires became once more part of the Republic.

In 1860 Urquiza's term as constitutional President of the Republic came to an end. He was succeeded by his Minister of Interior, Derqui, who not only was his political ally but a kinsman and a provincial landlord. This was too much for the politicians of Buenos Aires. General Bartolomé Mitre, the Governor of Buenos Aires, took the field. At Pavón in September 1861 an inconclusive engagement was fought. If the forces of Buenos Aires did not break the army of Urquiza, they broke Urquiza's will. He announced his retirement from politics. Derqui resigned the Presidency. The Federal Congress dissolved itself, and new elections were held in May 1862.

Bartolomé Mitre was a new type of Argentine leader: not a very good soldier, but an excellent and literate politician; a city man who was willing to overlook provincial manners and political methods; a man of ideas who was willing to modify them in the light of immediate circumstances. Mitre was unmistakably Argentine in his private and public personality, and yet there was something almost English in his flexibility. Perhaps this was something more universal—the temperament of the mid-nineteenth century colonizing the heart of an Argentine patriot.

Mitre wished to revive the constitutional notions of Rivadavia in the matter of Buenos Aires's place in the Republic. He wished to do away with the Province and merge it in the Republic, leaving provincial governments to function only in the provinces and to operate under constant threat of intervention by the central government. When he saw that this plan would only lead to further war, he accepted the Constitution of 1853; acknowledged the independent character of the provinces, and agreed that Buenos Aires Province should retain its separate character—an idea very acceptable to the rural interests of the Province itself. It was agreed that the National Government and the Provincial Government of Buenos Aires should exist side by side in Buenos Aires, a living proof that the powerful interests of the community had ceased to seek dominance one over the other. When Mitre entered upon his office as constitutional president of the Argentine Republic the basic compromise or general will of the Argentine community had been expressed in a social form. At the same time one of the objectives of British policy had been achieved.

XI

THE BEGINNINGS OF BRITISH
CAPITAL INVESTMENT

IN an account of Anglo-Argentine relations running from
the invasion of the River Plate in 1806 to the outbreak of
World War I the year of General Mitre's inauguration as
President of the Republic is the half-way mark in time. By
a coincidence, it is also the dividing point of this history. Its
character changes at this stage. Diplomats, generals, admirals,
extraordinary envoys now cease to figure so prominently in the
flow of events. Personalities become less conspicuous and social
processes occupy our attention in increasing measure. Prices,
commodities, and investment techniques are henceforward
more the subject matter of the story than the *pronunciamientos* of
caudillos. The whistles of railway locomotives sounding across
the sub-Andean deserts assume a greater significance than the
gritos of revolutionary soldiers summoning the gauchos to
battle.

The transformation of Anglo-Argentine relations at this point
is well illustrated by the attention paid in London to the Paraguayan War. This terrible tragedy of the Paraguayan people,
which engulfed in death approximately 75 per cent. of the male
population of that country, lasted for five years. It absorbed
a substantial proportion of the Argentine national revenues at
a time when Argentina was beginning to borrow large sums in
Europe. One would have supposed that a social disaster of the
magnitude of this war would at least have gravely disturbed the
Foreign Office and stimulated a disposition there to mediate
and to bring hostilities to a close. For five years the British
Ministers in Buenos Aires sustained themselves with the belief
that the war would soon be over. They limited themselves to
commenting bitterly upon the savagery of the Paraguayan
dictator and the incompetence of the Argentine and Brazilian
commanders. The reasons for this aloof impassivity in the
presence of a prolonged and savage struggle are not difficult to

discover. The war was far away from the scene of trade and investment. Unlike all the previous wars, civil and international, in which the Buenos Aires Government had been involved, the Paraguayan war did not lead to a cessation of trade or a destruction of life and property in the Argentine centres of production. On the contrary, trade and investment were expanding, and Argentina was being transformed into something more acceptable to European ideas of civilization. Immigrants were flowing in from Europe and spreading out across the pampas, while in the great forests of Paraguay a military machine was gobbling up and destroying the turbulent gauchos. In 1867 the British Minister attributed the political disturbances in Mendoza Province to the last efforts of the gauchos to resist service in the Paraguayan War.

Wherever railroads have penetrated through this Republic [he reported to Lord Stanley] civilisation and business have followed, and the former political disturbances and pronunciamientos have ceased, but it is yet easy in the more distant states, for the older partisan leaders to collect a body of followers upon any cause of discontent. For this the question of the Paraguayan War, in clever hands, has afforded full opportunity, for while the idle gaucho is ever ready for a plundering foray, the discipline of regular military service is abhorrent to him, and the greater part of those who were obliged to serve have already deserted.[1]

Mathew might well have added 'or been killed', for the losses in battle and through disease were very great. Furthermore, the Argentine Government did not clothe, pay, or feed its troops adequately.[2]

Dark and bitter dispatches about the war in Paraguay were relieved by reports of economic progress. 'There is no doubt whatever', one Minister informed the Foreign Secretary, 'that the material progress of Buenos Aires and the rest of the Republic has much increased of late years particularly since General Mitre's accession to power.'[3] Year by year the tale was told to London of increasing exports and the expansion of immigration—doubling themselves in five years.

The fact is that General Mitre's inauguration as President

[1] F.O. 6/267, Mathew to Stanley, 27 Jan. 1867.
[2] F.O. 6/267, Mathew to Stanley, 23 Apr. 1867.
[3] F.O. 6/262, Ford to Aberdeen, 24 Mar. 1866.

marked the making of a fundamental political decision through-out the whole society. The primary political decision having been made in favour of economic expansion and integration into the international commodity and capital markets, a multi-plicity of secondary decisions in the field of economic activity was now possible. The significant decisions of the community now became *ipso facto* decentralized, so that we are obliged to look at them as components of a process and not as solely the acts of individuals and public bodies. Both the nature of our information and the magnitude of the task make impossible so personal an account as could be given when General Rosas manœuvred to baffle the Earl of Aberdeen.

The new age ushered in by General Mitre's victorious entry into the presidential office was planned as an epoch of capital investment and free trade. Thus it responded to and accelerated the rhythm of development across the Atlantic. Free trade was fully and firmly established in Britain. Belgium and Holland had lately adopted liberal commercial policies. France had agreed by treaties to free the flow of trade among herself, Britain, and Belgium. The river Scheldt, so long denied its natural commercial advantages, was freed to international trade in 1863. In Britain the Companies Act of 1862 established on a firm legal basis a simple procedure for the formation of joint-stock companies, the indispensable agencies for pooling capital and spreading risks.

While business expansion was being thus encouraged by the policies of *laissez-faire* in western Europe, in Argentina the new authorities planned by state action to encourage foreign enter-prise with guarantees. The particulars of the guarantees and the encouragement were soon exhibited in the register of laws. The Law of 5 September 1862 set forth a new set of terms under which railway concessions would be granted.[1] The concession granted by Urquiza to Buschenthal had reflected the poverty of the national treasury and the wealth of land, for under its terms land was the endowment granted the promoter. Mitre's law was evidence of the advantages of tapping the financial re-sources of Buenos Aires Province. It guaranteed investors in a railway built from Rosario to Córdoba a dividend of 7 per cent. on a capital of £6,400 per mile. It provided land necessary for

[1] *Registro Oficial de la Republica Argentina*, 5668, iv, pp. 473–4.

building lines, stations, marshalling yards, and docks. Furthermore, the law provided liberal tax exemptions and a guarantee
against rate fixing until 15 per cent. was being earned on the
capital stock. Almost simultaneously the Province of Buenos
Aires granted a concession on even more favourable terms,
guaranteeing 7 per cent. on a capital of £10,000 a mile for
a line running 72½ miles from Buenos Aires to Chascomús
together with many ancillary benefits such as free land, tax
exemptions, and guarantees against rate fixing.

Within a year of this initial railway legislation a general law
governing the public debt was placed in the official register.
The Law of 16 November 1863[1] established a public record of
all debts of the state entitled *Del Gran Libro de Rentas y Fondos
Públicos*. All debts were declared to be a charge on all revenues
of the state. A *Caja de Amortización* was set up. All public debts,
unless otherwise stated, were declared payable in London at
the rate of 65½ shillings per ounce of gold.

In the sphere of commercial policy Mitre may be said to
have completed the process first begun during the revolution a
half century earlier of creating in Argentina a free exchange of
goods and services within the territories of the Republic and of
providing for the admission of men and goods into the community from foreign states on the freest possible terms compatible
with the collection of revenue by a system of indirect taxes.
Legally the system of free commerce was established by the
Constitution of 1853, but the system only became a practical
reality under the régime of Mitre. The policy of Mitre made
possible the abolition of provincial tariffs, exactions, and privileges by providing the provincial authorities with financial
means in the shape of grants from the national treasury, which
were in fact a share in the receipts of the Buenos Aires customs
house. This political compromise was rendered increasingly less
necessary as economic expansion set in, for the expansion itself
created new sources of revenue in the provinces and new roads
to wealth for individuals, thus increasing the public revenues
while diminishing relatively, if not absolutely, the numbers
living at the public expense in the traditional manner.

The response to General Mitre's policy of encouraging foreign
investment was almost instantaneous. Within three years British

[1] *Registro Oficial de la Republica Argentina*, 6043, v, pp. 108–9.

business men and engineers had established banks and railway and tramway companies operating in Argentina, followed shortly by public utilities such as gas-works, water-works, and sewerage systems. This first phase of capital investment lasted from 1862 to 1875 when depression briefly brought the process to a halt. A rough contemporary estimate of the British capital investment in Argentina in 1875 suggests a total of £23,060,000 exclusive of capital invested in land and in the traditional commercial enterprises devoted to the export and import of raw material and manufactured goods. This £23,060,000 was distributed approximately as follows:[1]

	Amount invested	Proportion of total
	£	per cent.
Government loans .	12,970,000	56·2
Railways . . .	6,610,000	28·6
Banks	1,600,000	6·4
Tramways . . .	800,000	3·2
Meat factories . .	530,000	2·3
Mines	200,000	0·8
Gas works . . .	200,000	0·8
Telegraphs . . .	150,000	0·6
	23,060,000	100·0

An examination of this investment impresses one at once with the enormous importance of state power in ensuring the functioning of the process by which funds in Britain were made available for the purchase of goods and services contributing directly or indirectly to Argentine economic development and by which a portion of the new income created was in turn transferred to the owners of the original funds. The state was responsible for the capital and interest of the state loans—more than 55 per cent. of the total—and was the guarantor of a minimum profit on a railway capital amounting roughly to £4,250,000 in 1875. Thus, a proportion in the neighbourhood of 80 per cent. of the investment made by British capitalists or through the agency of the London money market was dependent directly or indirectly in this early phase of investment upon the ability and willingness of the political authorities in

[1] M. G. Mulhall, *The English in South America* (Buenos Aires, 1878), p. 529.

Argentina to levy taxes with one hand and with the other to transfer an appropriate proportion of the public revenues to private investors.

In the Argentine Republic in the 1860's and, indeed, for at least three decades thereafter, an acute scarcity existed both of capital and of labour capable of the sustained and disciplined work indispensable for the functioning of a complex commercial and industrial economy. By scarcity we mean a paucity compared with that prevailing in the communities of western Europe and the Atlantic seaboard of the United States. This scarcity manifested itself in high interest rates and high wages for skilled and semi-skilled labour. The interest on loans secured by first-class readily saleable real property was never below 12 per cent. when General Mitre came to power,[1] and short-term loans, well secured, earned 18 per cent. As late as 1874 short-term loans could be procured at only 12 per cent. to 18 per cent. depending on the credit rating of the borrowers.[2] Furthermore, local capital was strongly attracted to investment in land, for capital gains in this sphere of investment were enormous once economic expansion seriously commenced. The *Buenos Aires Standard* estimated in 1872 that land in the immediate vicinity of the Argentine capital had increased fiftyfold in market value during the years 1850–70.[3]

Our knowledge of wage levels in the 1860's and 1870's is not as concrete as that of interest rates and the profits of land speculation. The social position enjoyed by skilled men such as telegraph clerks, locomotive drivers, and draughtsmen suggests that wages were high compared with European standards and vastly superior to those commanded by the peons and gauchos engaged in the traditional rural pursuits.

Railway construction labourers were sufficiently well paid to induce Basque and Italian peasants, shopkeepers, and craftsmen to borrow money in order to travel across the Atlantic, to live in the Argentine Republic and, in many instances, to return to Spain or Italy with the means of strengthening their places in Spanish or Italian society through the possession of

[1] de Moussy, *Description géographique et statistique de la Confédération Argentine*, ii, p. 375.

[2] *Bankers' Magazine*, xxxiv, 1874, p. 44.

[3] The British chargé d'affaires estimated that land values in Buenos Aires had doubled between 1860 and 1865. F.O. 6/262, Ford to Clarendon, 24 Mar. 1866.

additional capital. Some articles of popular consumption were fantastically cheap by European standards. Meat was so abundant in the Buenos Aires market during the 1860's that it was not sold by weight but by the piece. A leg of lamb sold for 10*d.* or 1*s.* and beef was cheaper.[1] On the other hand, wine, house room, and clothing were expensive by European standards, and this serves to explain at least in part why many European immigrants were birds of passage and why the European immigrant worker was at the same time so vastly different from the gauchos and peons, who still consumed very few articles of European manufacture, still lived abundantly on meat, drank mate, lived in the open air or in a mud hut, and wore the cotton trousers and woollen ponchos of their ancestors. When the first spate of railway building was getting under way the British chargé d'affaires observed that 'the supply [of labour] falls very far short of the demand, and unlimited employment can be procured without difficulty at most remunerative wages, as in this country artisans and labourers are greatly needed'.[2]

The economic significance of the victory of General Mitre consisted in the recognition at the centre of authority of the advantages to the mercantile and landowning class of securing capital and labour from Europe, both of which were cheap by comparison with the capital and labour available in Argentina itself. It was assumed correctly that both would flow to the River Plate if security were offered, and security was a matter of political action. Once Argentina had demonstrated a capacity to protect the lives of foreign immigrants and to pay a fixed rate of interest and debt service charges, both workers and investors, the first mainly in Spain and Italy, the second mainly in Britain, were willing to try their luck in the Argentine Republic.

The history of Anglo-Argentine relations in this period of development is concerned more with capital investment than with immigration. A study of this investment impresses one, firstly, with the large total sums invested, and, secondly, with the smallness of the individual contributions. The investment of capital anywhere under any auspices is a co-operative social process involving a variety of decisions and judgements about

---

[1] F.O. 6/263, Ford to Clarendon, 26 June 1866.
[2] F.O. 6/262, Ford to Clarendon, 24 Mar. 1866.

the disposition of spendable funds. In the Anglo-Argentine case the process established by the policies of General Mitre and participated in by the English investing class involved three general classes of decisions harmonized and made practical through the agency of the state. The individuals possessing investable funds in Britain were required to make only one decision: whether to transfer their funds or not. The purpose of this class was to secure an income from their capital, and they were governed solely by expectation based on experience that an abstraction called Argentina was good for a return on capital. The investors in Argentine bonds did not know and could not know how the money they lent would be spent. Judging from some of their letters addressed to the public press, to the Foreign Office, and to the various committees established to handle the interests of investors, their level of information was extremely low. Some of them confused Argentina with Chile and even Mexico. The distinction between the Province of Buenos Aires and the Argentine Republic was too subtle for most. One dissatisfied investor in Argentine railways appears to have believed that the Buenos Ayres Great Southern Railway, of which he owned a small part, was in Brazil.[1] Indeed, the name of a banking firm like that of Baring Brothers or Murietta & Company meant more to investors than the names Argentina or Buenos Aires. Their decision to handle Argentine business was a certificate of reliability and a substitute for knowledge, initiative, and enterprise. From the evidence of the few reports of Baring Brothers' agents available, it would appear that the bankers themselves made their decisions to market loans on fairly reliable information and a reasonably acute appreciation of the real capacity of the Argentine community not only to pay but to use what was lent. George White, the Barings' agent, and E. Zimmerman, the Barings' correspondent in Buenos Aires and Montevideo, were alert, competent, and shrewd in their observations, but one cannot escape the conclusion from the behaviour of the investment bankers that their understanding and judgement deteriorated in the 1880's and their irresponsibility and ignorance were factors in the Baring Crisis of 1890–1. During this initial period of development, however, the banking firms responsible for more than 50 per cent. of the British public

---

[1] *Herapath's Railway Magazine*, xxx, 1868, p. 353.

investment were cautious without being prohibitory, and their judgement was vindicated by events.

The decision to lend having been made in Britain by investment houses and possessors of capital, decisions concerning use were left entirely to the Argentine public authorities. What came of the investment depended, therefore, on the capacity of the Argentine Governments, both national and provincial, to contribute directly and indirectly to that economic development which alone could support the debt incurred. At first the decisions of the National Government concerning the use of borrowed funds seemed ominously like the decisions taken in 1825 and 1826. This seems to have been a factor in the reluctance of the public to take up the Loan of 1866. Only 50 per cent. of the offering was purchased and the proceeds were spent largely for military purposes. A change in the character of spending decisions came as the Paraguayan War drew to a conclusion. The great £6,000,000 loan of the 1870's floated on behalf of the National Government was employed almost entirely as a means of building railways to Tucumán and Río Cuarto and harbour works at Buenos Aires and Rosario.[1] As an economic proposition judged by the criterion of profit the railway to Tucumán was an act of near madness, but as a contribution to building the Argentine nation and settling its character as a peaceful and developing community it was a heroic enterprise having a significance for Argentine life similar to that of the Canadian Pacific Railway in Canadian life. Some of the public investment of the Province of Buenos Aires in this period before 1875 was actually self-liquidating. The funds spent on the *Oeste* yielded a positive return to the state strengthening the provincial revenues rather than otherwise. In general, however, Argentine public investment at this time was non-self-liquidating, and hence a burden on the community income. Although unprofitable in the short run, and often so even in the long, it tended in this period, unlike the public expenditure of the 1820's, to strengthen the economy as a whole by

---

[1] *Herapath's*, xxxii, 1870, p. 976, gives the disposition of the Loan as follows: repayment of loan to National Government from Provincial Bank of Buenos Aires—£560,000; railway from Villa Nueva to Río Cuarto—£430,000; railway from Córdoba to Tucumán—£2,800,000; harbour works and warehouses at Buenos Aires—£800,000; public works at Rosario—£10,000; remainder unappropriated.

contributing to social peace, by making continuous productive work possible, and, above all, by opening ways of communication with remote areas where transport costs in the pre-railway age were an absolute barrier to participation in the international division of labour. It must be recognized, however, that investment through the agency of the state was, and remained, an exceedingly blunt and inexact device for effecting the purposes of the investors and more particularly of the British economy as a whole. Even so, the British investor was well rewarded, having regard for his ignorant and passive contribution to the process of development.

Investment through the agency of joint-stock companies in railways, banks, public utilities, and industrial enterprises constituted the most significant contribution of the British community to Argentine economic development at this stage. This investment involved not only a contribution of purchasing power by investors but also a contribution of creative decision-making, organizing ability, continuous administrative responsibility, and technical knowledge. The investors in joint-stock companies like the investors in Argentine loans were primarily interested in profit, but the institutional devices for obtaining profit were units of precise accountability whose functioning depended in the long run upon an ability to sell goods or services and to cover costs out of revenue. In the matter of railway enterprise it was considered necessary for the state to guarantee a minimum profit in order to induce investment. The consequences of the guarantees of profit were thoroughly bad, and several of the railway companies themselves, notably the Buenos Ayres Great Southern Railway, preferred independence of the state and reliance upon their capacity to provide a service to produce the profits the investors sought. Although they operated under laws and agreements prescribed by the public authorities, the banks, tramway companies, gas companies, and industrial enterprises set up by British business men were independent of the state and operated as truly free enterprises liable to the harsh discipline of bankruptcy for failure to cover their costs out of revenues derived from the sale of goods and services to the public.

The joint-stock part of the British investment in Argentina required not only capital but men to organize, administer, and build. Two kinds of knowledge and capacity were needed: firstly, technical and business knowledge such as how to build and operate a railway and secondly, knowledge of the Argentine community—its politics, its needs, its resources, and its people. The British community, and particularly that part of the British community living in Argentina, were uniquely endowed during this early stage of development to provide this knowledge.

The British contribution to the transformation of the Argentine economy in this phase grew naturally out of the commercial phase of British enterprise in the Republic, for the British mercantile class in Buenos Aires contributed the men with knowledge both of business and of Argentina to organize and direct nearly all the great enterprises which came into being at this time. Edward Lumb, who obtained the original concession for the building of the Buenos Ayres Great Southern Railway, was a leading figure of thirty years' experience in Buenos Aires commercial circles. William Wheelwright, the concessionaire of the Central Argentine Railway, was an American with thirty years' experience in steam navigation on the west coast of South America. One of the leading directors of the Central, Thomas Armstrong, had a long life-time of experience in commercial banking reaching back before the dictatorship of General Rosas. Frank Parish, for many years chairman of the Buenos Ayres Great Southern, was the son of Sir Woodbine Parish, and his sons in turn were on the boards of a wide variety of Argentine enterprises. Thomas Fair, a director of railways, land companies, banks, and public utilities, was a River Plate merchant, whose father had established himself in Buenos Aires in the year of the revolution, 1810. Perhaps the ablest and most effective British business man of this period was G. W. Drabble, the chairman of the Bank of London and the River Plate, a member of the board of several railway companies and a pioneer of the frozen- and chilled-meat business. Drabble had come to Buenos Aires in 1848 as a salesman for his family's firm of Manchester cotton goods exporters. In the 1850's he had added ranch management to his cotton business. He invested a small sum in the Central Argentine Railway, when it was first formed, but not in any of the other enterprises being planned at this time. However, he was elected to join the board of the

Bank of London and the River Plate. He became a modest investor in the company and soon its chairman. From this central position Drabble's influence ramified through all the principal enterprises and into the field of Argentine politics, tightening up administration, converting poorly run railways into profitable concerns, and promoting amalgamations, always insisting that enterprises must be made to pay their own way, that performance must live up to promise, and that the art of management consists principally in making ends meet.

It seems reasonably clear that at this time the Argentine community, as distinct from the British mercantile community in Argentina, was not equipped to undertake alone the economic expansion which had become acceptable to the ruling groups and particularly to General Mitre and his following. The religion of the Argentine community, the educational system, the social stratification, and the traditional scale of values originating in Spain predisposed the articulate elements to base their power upon landowning, political and military offices, the professions, and a limited number of commercial activities. At this stage of Argentine history the ownership and management of complicated financial, transport, and industrial enterprise was of little interest to the dominant native groups. The Central Argentine Railway, for example, sought to interest Argentinos as investors and participants in the affairs of the company. They opened a special South American list of shareholders and arranged meetings in Buenos Aires. The response was disappointing. The Anchorenas, perhaps the most powerful and certainly at this time the richest family in Argentina, invested £200 and they never increased their holdings. A few individuals in Argentina had as many as 40 shares, but an overwhelming majority of the 540 shareholders listed in 1871 as resident in Argentina held less than 10 shares each.[1] On the other hand, the Argentine Government was the largest single shareholder in the company, being possessed of 17,000 out of 65,000 shares and the Province of Buenos Aires owned 350. In fact, an inspection of the share lists of the Central Argentine Railway, or of any of the many companies formed at this time, suggests that Argentine interests were not concerned either to invest in or to gain control of such undertakings, no matter how

[1] Bush House, Companies Registration Office (henceforward C.R.O.), file 14352.

freely they might criticize their activities in the newspapers and in the halls of the Congress.

The initiative in organizing the enterprises which came into being during the 1860's as well as the capital which made them possible came very largely from mercantile interests in the city of London. Twenty-two names appeared on the applications to form the Buenos Ayres Great Southern Railway, the Central Argentine Railway, and the Bank of London and the River Plate. Of these thirteen were described as merchants of the city of London. Two were bankers; two were gentlemen; two were Members of Parliament; one was a railway contractor; and one was an army officer and one a civil engineer. One name, that of a merchant, appeared on two of the applications. The big initial contributions of capital came from the mercantile group and from railway contractors. William Wheelwright, the concessionaire of the Central Argentine Railway, originally possessed 7,931 £20 shares (£158,620) of the railway company, but, apart from Wheelwright, no investor put up more than £100,000, and the amounts called were, of course, much less than the nominal shares. Sir Samuel Morton Peto, a contractor, held 5,000 shares of the Buenos Ayres Great Southern. The core group of investors, who put up sums ranging between £10,000 and £100,000, were very largely merchants and railway contractors, although a certain lady in Derbyshire named Sandars held 5,000 £20 shares of the Central Argentine. Henry Bruce, the first chairman of the Bank of London and the River Plate, for example, made himself liable for £36,000 if the full amount of his shares was called.[1]

The big investors—those with holdings in the £4,000 to £100,000 range—contributed roughly half the initial capital for these enterprises. The rest was supplied by a much more numerous group of men investing sums ranging from £100 to £1,000. These investors were drawn predominantly from the ranks of merchants, manufacturers, and craftsmen. Of the 411 original shareholders in the Central Argentine 83 were gentlemen, 14 were widows or spinsters, 40 were professional men, civil servants, officers of the armed forces, and Members of Parliament, and the rest were merchants, tailors, farmers, upholsterers, glass manufacturers, and so on. Noble names were

[1] C.R.O., file 2854.

noticeably absent from the list. Investors were nearly all residents of the British Isles, and predominantly London men. Only forty-three shareholders in the Central Argentine lived in the Midlands and the north, and most of these in Liverpool and Halifax. There were 6 shareholders in Manchester, 5 in Glasgow, and only 2 in Birmingham. The same was generally true of the Buenos Ayres Great Southern, except that Birmingham men figured more prominently among its shareholders. Another notable feature of this period of initiation was the very small scale of institutional investment. The London Financial Association put £60,000 into the Central Argentine and the General Credit Company held a few shares, but these were the sole institutional investors, although the Argentine Government was a large shareholder for some years and a nunnery in Córdoba very early became a holder of Central Argentine stock. There were no institutions among the original shareholders of the Buenos Ayres Great Southern or of the Bank of London and the River Plate.

The men who initiated this new phase of British enterprise characterized by investments of capital in joint-stock companies operating in Argentina may be divided into two groups: the core group of investors who had some knowledge of what they were doing and who made a larger investment than the average shareholder, and the more numerous passive investors who contributed nothing but money. These groups were interdependent, and, if we may judge by the leading enterprises, the dependence of the first group upon the second for the means of expansion tended to grow as the enterprises grew. In the case of the Buenos Ayres Great Southern, for example, there were 198 shareholders in the company at the time of its foundation in 1862, when the authorized capital was £750,000 and the number of shares sold was 27,500 representing a paid-up investment of £82,500 and a potential investment of £550,000. In 1914, when the authorized share capital was £40 millions and the paid-up capital was £37 millions, there were approximately 36,000 shareholders.[1] During this period capital grew 67 times but the number of shareholders 180 times.

Thus it appears that, just as the investment banking firms

---

[1] Based upon a rough estimate of lists in the files of the Companies Registration Office.

served as intermediaries between a numerous body of British investors and the public authorities in Argentina which borrowed money, so these core groups of capitalists served as intermediaries between working enterprises in Argentina and the great body of individual British investors. These core groups initiated the enterprises, attracted the capital required, managed and administered the enterprises in Argentina. Their motives or incentives are not easy to determine. To say that they were seeking profits is not to say anything very meaningful. Indeed, if we take the term to imply that these core groups were financiers and speculators the notion is seriously misleading. Some years later, when the main fields of British capital investment had been firmly marked out, the British Minister in Argentina expressed the belief that British business men operated there because they made greater profits there than they could do at home.[1] But the possibility of a higher rate of profit than they could make at home does not seem to have galvanized the original organizers of the great enterprises. Their principal purpose in organizing railway enterprises seems to have been the sale of manufactures and of services. When the British Minister applied to the Foreign Office in 1862 for permission to allow the Consul-General in Buenos Aires to serve on the local committee of the Buenos Ayres Great Southern Railway, he argued that the enterprise would open up a new market for British manufactures, and Lord John Russell consented for this reason.[2]

This motive seems to have operated powerfully in the formation of the companies in England. The railway contracting firm of Brassey & Wythes were the principal English promoters and the largest investors in the Central Argentine. The firm of contractors, Peto and Betts, were likewise among the initiators and the largest investors in the Buenos Ayres Great Southern. Another principal organizer of the Southern was Thomas Rumball, a civil engineer, who obtained the first contract of the company for surveying the route from Buenos Aires to Chascomús. Likewise, the merchants who participated either as organizers or investors seem to have regarded investment not as an end in itself but as a means of improving commercial opportunities which were their main source of income. There is no direct

[1] F.O. 6/360, Egerton to the Foreign Secretary, 29 June 1880.
[2] F.O. 6/240, Thornton to Russell, 19 Aug. 1862.

evidence on this point available at the present time, but there seems to be little other explanation for the relatively large investments of Manchester merchants like William Ashworth, which, when once made, were never increased. Their investments seem to have been made on the principle of using a sprat to catch a mackerel.

In Argentina itself the landed interests likewise pressed for the building of railways not because they wanted to profit from them as investors but because railways increased land values and made produce more saleable. As soon as the Buenos Ayres Great Southern reached Chascomús the landowners beyond the Río Salado began to agitate for an extension to and beyond the river[1] and the Provincial Government began to apply pressure on the Company to extend its line as far as Dolores. When it was finally decided to build farther into the southern pampas the rejoicing among the *estancieros* was reported to be very great.[2] But it should be added that the Argentine landed interest never felt impelled to invest in railways. A few shares, perhaps, but it was easier to kick the companies through the agency of the government and more profitable to speculate in land, sell cattle and wool, and institute share-cropping, all of which railways greatly stimulated by opening a way to the markets first of Buenos Aires and then the world.

In the several other fields of enterprise—public utilities and food processing in particular—the same pattern of initiative may be discerned. Great enterprises were not formed as the means of making great profits for the investor, but as a means of stimulating capital gains and enlarging market opportunities for existing interests: some of them Argentine, some of them British or European. The rewards of investors tended to be just sufficient to induce investment—never much greater than the 7 per cent. guaranteed by the Argentine Government and frequently much less. Great fortunes were not made by British investors in the Argentine Republic either in the first phase or later. The great fortunes accrued to the landed interest, to the investment bankers who marketed securities, and to commercial interests which trafficked in Argentine produce, supplied fuel and equipment for railways, and manufactured goods for the community as a whole.

[1] *Herapath's*, xxx, 1868, p. 1159.   [2] Ibid., xxxii, 1870, pp. 456–7.

While it may be argued with some justice that foreign investors in Argentina were not the principal beneficiaries of contributions to the Argentine economy, it must be noticed that some enterprises were very profitable and some, not so dramatically profitable, were very stable and secure sources of investment income. The fact that a small number of great enterprises like the Bank of London and the River Plate (profitable and secure), the Buenos Ayres Great Southern Railway (modestly but steadily profitable), and the Buenos Ayres Tramways (extremely profitable) were very successful from the investors' point of view created a climate of opinion concerning the Argentine Republic which unfroze the funds of the investing classes in Britain and established a flow of money and credit irrigating the pampas of the River Plate.

As we have already observed, Argentine state loans absorbed more than 50 per cent. of all British investments handled on the London money market during the period 1862–75. Argentine bonds paid 6 per cent., although certain 7 per cent. bonds of the provinces were offered between 1872 and 1875. These bonds appeared on the market when the yield on Consols was declining[1] and the percentage yield from investments in the securities of the major European states was falling. No 6 per cent. Argentine bonds were marketed above 89½ before 1875. The National Government's Loan of 1866 was offered by Baring Brothers at 75 for one half and 72½ for the other. In 1870 Murietta & Company offered £1 million at 6 per cent. on behalf of the Province of Buenos Aires at 88, and £6 millions at 6 per cent. on behalf of the National Government at 88½. Two years later the National Government employed the services of the Anglo-Argentine firm of Wanklyn & Company to market a loan, but they could not move the bonds at better than 76. But this was in the year 1874. In 1873 the city of Buenos Aires placed £500,000 at 6 per cent. at the unprecedented figure of 89½. Hitherto no Argentine province except Buenos Aires had attempted to borrow in the London market, but in 1874 and 1875 Entre Rios sold an issue of £225,000 at 7 per cent. at 90, and Santa Fé a 7 per cent. issue of £300,000 at 92.[2]

By 1875 interest and amortization charges on sterling loans

[1] W. W. Rostow, *British Economy of the Nineteenth Century* (Oxford, 1948), p. 8.
[2] J. B. Peña, *La Deuda Argentina* (Buenos Aires, 1907), pp. 349–53.

were absorbing 25 per cent. of the revenues of the National
Government. At first sight such a sudden expansion of financial
obligations might seem dangerous. And it was. The National
Government came close to bankruptcy in 1875, but the débâcle
of 1827 did not repeat itself. The Paraguayan War and the two
small civil wars in Entre Rios and Corrientes absorbed a substantial part of the Loan of 1866, but military expenses began
to decline both relatively and absolutely after the overthrow of
the Paraguayan dictator. Indeed, the military forces became so
inadequate that Indian incursions from the south threatened
the town of Bahia Blanca with destruction in 1871, and insecurity on the frontier had become a major national problem
by the late 1870's and a serious check to economic development.

More important than the relative diminution of military
expenditure was the expansion of taxable capacity which
accompanied the expansion of the economy. More people
working, more productive work, and improved techniques explain the ability of Argentina to bear an increasing weight of
public debt. In the 1850's approximately 30,000 immigrants
entered the country, but during the sixties and seventies nearly
400,000 immigrants entered the Republic through the ports of
Buenos Aires and Rosario. In terms of quality they were probably the best body of men and women ever to immigrate to
Argentina: young, strong, healthy, and habituated to hard
work and saving. Only such people could survive, for at this
period no government offered more than encouragement and
only the morally toughest and physically strongest could endure.
Mainly they were Basque and northern Italians; some Irish and
Scots; some French; some Germans and a few English of the
managerial and clerical class.

With this labour force the Argentine economy became more
productive. The production of hides and wool increased. These
were already established lines of production. The newcomers
helped to add cereal production, so that by the mid-seventies
Argentina had become once more self-supporting in cereals
with a steady export surplus of maize and occasional surpluses
of wheat. The railway to Tucumán stimulated the sugar industry. Timber harvesting in Misiones and Chaco expanded.

Not only did productivity increase during these years but the
terms of trade in the international market tended to move

slightly in favour of Argentina. Until 1871 the prices of manufactured goods and fuel imported into Argentina tended to decline while the prices of hides and wool tended to improve somewhat. Tallow, a big item in Argentine exports before 1875, underwent a continuous decline leading to the eventual extinction of the trade, but in this speciality the Argentine economy exhibited for a time what came to be a characteristic feature of resilience, namely, a capacity to expand production in the face of falling prices.

The Argentine system of taxation continued to be based primarily upon indirect taxes levied on exports and imports. Certain heavy import items were exempt from tax under agreements with the railway companies, but duties on consumer goods and on exports swelled the public revenues so long as economic expansion continued and was oriented towards the world market. The system of taxation, however, had its weaknesses, and these manifested themselves when the pace of expansion slackened and the volume of trade declined.

While Argentine public investment absorbed the largest proportion of British capital during this initial period, the investment in transport and industrial enterprises, though smaller in amount, deserves closer attention as a contribution to the process of development. At the stage reached in the 1860's improved transport was the critical element in the situation. The limitations of rivers as a key to expansion of markets had been demonstrated in the years following the Treaty of Free Navigation. In the railways across the treeless plains there now existed the means of breaking through the immemorial obstacles to civilization and to a high rate of production. Railways required not only capital but a new order of social and technical knowledge which was not abundantly available in Argentina and which the educational system and the habits of mind of the community were not adapted quickly to create. The determination of Mitre and his followers to delay no longer a transformation which could match that of the United States implied that European resources of experience and wealth must be relied upon. Sarmiento urged that the Argentine people must educate themselves universally and along new lines, but the ruling group were determined not to wait for education to do its work. Perhaps they did not wish to have it accomplish its unsettling tasks. And so a quick means was found to make effective the knowledge and experience as well as the capital to create railways.

During this initial period of development six British joint-stock railways[1] were formed to operate in the Argentine Republic under agreements reached either with the National Government or the Provincial Government of Buenos Aires. Two of these—the Central Argentine and the Buenos Ayres Great Southern—came to occupy the first rank among Argentine railways, and they grew into major transport systems. Another two of them—the Northern of Buenos Ayres and the Buenos Ayres and Ensenada—were lines in the suburbs of Buenos Aires, a combination of tramway and rapid transit systems. The remaining two—the Campaña and the East Argentine—were small, local lines unfortunately fated to lives of financial misery, popular criticism, ineffectiveness, self-pity, and finally absorption into other systems.

The Central and the Southern[2] were essentially different enterprises in their character, purposes, and early history. The Central was a pioneer railway built not to meet an existing demand for railway services but to create it. The Southern was built through territory well populated by Argentine standards, whose inhabitants were eager to use the service provided. The Central was planned from the start on an ample scale and its success or failure depended upon its effectiveness as a complete system. The Southern was built in little pieces, each piece planned as a means of competing effectively with existing transport facilities and of feeding traffic into the lines already built. The economic, financial, and political problems of these lines stemmed from these peculiarities of circumstance.

The Central emerged first as a dream in the minds of General Urquiza and his followers, whose political problems prompted them to find some means of uniting the provinces effectively in order to ensure their equality with and perhaps predominance over the Province of Buenos Aires. The concession they gave to

---

[1] A British railway in Argentina is defined as one whose head office was in the British Isles and the capital of which was subscribed in the British market.

[2] For the sake of convenience we shall use the names Central and Southern, which are the English equivalents of the popular Argentine names. Their registered legal names in the United Kingdom were the Central Argentine Railway Limited and the Buenos Ayres Great Southern Railway Company Limited.

the promoter Buschenthal produced nothing. General Mitre, however, found in William Wheelwright a man who could give substance to an idea. Wheelwright was one of the great business men of the nineteenth century. His imagination encompassed the oceans and his ambition embraced whole continents. An American from Newburyport in Massachusetts, he came first to South America as a sailing skipper. When he first conceived of linking up the coast ports of South America with steam vessels, he was introduced to the city of London by a British diplomat with South American experience, the Hon. Peter Campbell Scarlett. With the assistance of London merchants and bankers Wheelwright had launched the Pacific Steam Navigation Company, and he had developed it into a successful transport system. Not content with this, he conceived of penetrating the interior continent of South America with steam power and crossing the Andes. General Mitre gave him a concession to build a railway from Rosario to Córdoba: from a mean river port in Santa Fé Province to the conservative, old colonial town in the shelter of the foothills of the Andes. The territory through which the line was to run was largely uninhabited and uninviting. Herdsmen drove scrawny cattle over the plains. Hardly any sheep farms existed in these parts. No cereals were produced except in the immediate vicinity of Córdoba, and many people argued that cereal farming was impossible because of the high winds, drought, and locusts.[1] On the other hand, there were some advantages and a great potential which Wheelwright could see. Rosario may have amounted to nothing in 1862, but it was well located for the purposes of development. Steam vessels had a sheltered, easy passage, which eventually made Rosario a favourite destination of tramp steamers. Loading and unloading problems and harbour construction presented fewer difficulties than at Buenos Aires. The terrain between Rosario and Córdoba presented no serious engineering difficulties. And in spite of wind, insects, and the absence of men the land was rich. Much of it required only fencing and breaking before being ready for cereal production. Admittedly there was no prospect of heavy traffic in the immediate future, but the National Government was prepared to guarantee a

[1] *Parliamentary Papers*, 1872, lxx, Report on Immigration to the Argentine Confederation.

profit of 7 per cent. on a capital cost of £6,400 per mile; and the Government had control of the principal revenues of the community including those of the Province of Buenos Aires.

Wheelwright's concession,[1] dated 26 May 1863, gave a guarantee of profits; a grant of land amounting to one league on each side of the line together with three square leagues in Rosario and Córdoba, freedom from import duties on equipment and tools for forty years, a guarantee of freedom from military service for all servants of the company, and the right to build churches and schools on the company's lands. The company undertook to complete the line in five years, to carry the mails free, and to carry troops at half fare. The concession required the company to have a legal domicile in the Argentine Republic, and an article of the company exempted the directors from the requirement of notifying shareholders of a meeting if they were residents of the United Kingdom. But in spite of the terms of the concession the effective legal domicile was the United Kingdom, and no circumstance ever developed which put the conflict to a test. Conceivably the shareholders of the Central could not have claimed, however, the protection of the Treaty of 1825.

The authorized capital of the Central Argentine was £1,600,000 divided into 80,000 £20 shares. Fifty thousand shares only were issued, and one year after the application to form the company (22 March 1865) the 50,000 shares had been taken up and £6. 10s. had been called on each share. There were 407 shareholders originally, of whom 111 sold their holdings during the first year.

Before the line was complete in 1870 the full amount of the shares was called and an additional 15,000 were issued. The invested capital was thus £1,300,000 by the time the railway was completed from Rosario to Córdoba. This was in fact the amount covered by the government guarantee. In adding to the capital an effort was made to secure money in Argentina. In 1871 there were actually more shareholders resident in Argentina than in Britain, but their individual holdings were very small, and none except the Argentine Government held more than ten shares.

---

[1] C.R.O., file 14352, vol. i, gives the concession as a schedule to the application to form a company.

The building of the Central commenced in 1865, and the line reached Córdoba in 1870. The first fifteen years of the Central's history can only be described as unhappy. The shareholders were disappointed. The Argentine Government was dissatisfied and frequently unwilling to pay the guaranteed profits. The public were critical of the infrequent and costly service. Minor politicians repeatedly demanded expropriation and state ownership. This unhappiness derived partly from the fact that the railway was bound to operate at a loss until the country through which it passed developed to the point of contributing a traffic sufficiently heavy to pay all expenses, depreciation, and provide a surplus. It derived partly, too, from the character of the investing public in Britain and of the directors of the enterprise.

From the beginning the Central was under-capitalized, but neither the directors nor the investors were willing to venture the sums necessary to bring the line to the point of profitable operation. Only once in the first fifteen years were the revenues sufficient to pay 7 per cent. without recourse to the state under the guarantee clauses. The Government protested that the rolling stock was insufficient to handle the traffic, and the directors retorted that the rolling stock was unavailable because they could not attract capital. In order to provide the capital necessary to complete the last section to Córdoba, the Government bought 17,000 shares, which they declared free of dividend until the private shareholders had received 7 per cent., thus providing a quarter of the capital themselves without right of dividend.

The Central was in reality a railway and a land company, and sufficient capital was required to build a railway and develop the land holdings of the company. If both these developments were undertaken one development would stimulate the other. But the directors of the Central raised less than enough capital to build the railway, and spent nothing on colonizing their lands. In 1872 the Central Argentine Land Company was formed to purchase the lands held by the railway company. Thus for small sums amounting to only £100,000 the lands measuring over 500 square leagues intended as a subsidy for the railway were transferred to a private company, whose shareholders benefited from the appreciation of land values which came as the community developed.

When the Central was launched Wheelwright was an old

man and a busy one. He never seems to have come really to grips with the problem of the Central, and the directors soon became subject to the fears and the greed of the investors. They themselves were not too confident of their enterprise, for they reduced their holdings of shares, and they did not seek to raise new capital on the assumption that good service would do more to improve profits and encourage development than petty agitation and complaint directed at the Argentine Government on account of guarantees. It must be borne in mind, however, that in the 1860's and early 1870's joint-stock investment was much more of a novelty than it is at present, and curates, widows, and solicitors were in that age more ready to trust their surplus funds to a government than to a railway company, particularly one overseas. Investors are not bold risk takers in any age, and least of all were they so in the 1860's and 1870's. They appear to be dominated as a class by the sentiments of greed and fear, and these feelings were so nicely balanced in the case of the Argentine Republic that the majority preferred to lend their capital to the Argentine Government at 6 per cent. for purposes of extending a railway line to Tucumán or to Río Cuarto than to give it to the Central Argentine Railway for a similar purpose. Indeed, private-risk capital only began to predominate in Argentina when there were no longer any risks. So long as there were real uncertainties the Argentine Government was expected by the investors to bear them.

After all has been said about the unhappy character of the Central Argentine Railway in its childhood, it is necessary to observe that it was born to an important inheritance. It occupied a key position across the northern pampas. By 1875 the traffic of two government lines was obliged to run over the Central in order to reach the world markets or even the best domestic markets. The Central was strategically located to branch out north, south, and west into potentially rich agricultural and pastoral lands. It is suggestive of the low horizon of expectations prevalent in the investing classes and even among business leaders in the 1860's and 1870's that they were so reluctant to acquire shares in so valuable a property. But, perhaps, hindsight is more abundantly given to all of us than foresight.

The early history of the Southern differs greatly from that of the Central. From the beginning there was a strong River Plate interest associated with its affairs: men with long mercantile experience in Buenos Aires. The concessionaire was Edward Lumb, reputed to be the wealthiest British merchant in Buenos Aires in the 1850's, and a man intimately connected with the political leaders of Buenos Aires Province in the days of Rosas. By 1862, when he obtained the concession from the Government of Buenos Aires Province, he was an old man and he never played a great part in the active management of the company, but he seems to have brought in his leading associates in the British mercantile community in Buenos Aires. Thomas Duguid, who had advised Aberdeen and Palmerston against intervention in 1846, was one of the original shareholders; so was David Robertson, whose kinsmen had half a century of experience in Argentina; so were the Fair family; and the Parishes. On the railway side the contractor, Sir Samuel Morton Peto, and his partner Betts were, with Lumb, the largest investors, possessing 5,000 shares each. George Glyn, the banker, was an initiator of the enterprise and its banker. Thomas Rumball, a civil engineer and its surveyor, was a proprietor. William Scholefield, a Member of Parliament for Birmingham, was on the first board of directors. The Anglo-Argentine firm of Wanklyn & Company were the auditors.

The original authorized capital was £750,000 in shares of £20. Lumb's concession provided for a guarantee of 7 per cent. on a capital of £10,000 per mile for forty years. But the Government retained the right to fix rates during the life of the guarantee and to expropriate the company for the capital plus 20 per cent. No land was granted except the right of way itself. The gauge must be the same as that of the government-owned *Oeste*. Lumb sold his concession to the company for £21,500, but he took 5,000 shares which, £3 being paid up on application, left him with a net profit of £6,500. Before this second call for capital in 1865, Lumb sold his holdings, apparently to Peto, who increased the holding of his firm to 10,000 shares.

Apart from Peto and Lumb there were at first no large shareholders in the Southern; 27,500 shares were taken by 198 persons one year after the application for incorporation. Only one man except Peto and Lumb had more than 500 shares; 88 had less than 100 shares, and only 30 had 200 or more shares. London shareholders predominated, but Birmingham,

Liverpool, and Manchester were reasonably well represented by comparison with some of the other early Anglo-Argentine enterprises. Very early in the company's history the Drabble family of Buenos Aires, Liverpool, and Manchester acquired a substantial holding of 2,300 shares, and a partner of Nicholson, Green & Co. (another of whose partners was Noberto de la Riestra, the Finance Minister of Buenos Aires Province) became a large shareholder.

During the early period, and indeed at any time, ownership of the Southern was not concentrated. The directors always had modest holdings. In 1868 a rule was made that directors must possess at least 200 shares. This rule in fact established the pattern of power which persisted for many years in the direction of the Southern: widely dispersed ownership coupled with direction by men with a moderate financial stake in the company's prosperity; and direction, too, by men with strong local and hereditary connexions with the River Plate whose concern was not just for the prosperity of the Southern but for that of many other enterprises and of the community of which the Southern was an indispensable part.

Another characteristic of the Southern company was its 'Englishness'. The first share list displays predominantly English names and English addresses: a few Scots, a few Irish, and a few Argentinos; but no Germans, no French, no Belgians, no Jews, no Austrians. A rule of the company was, that in future share allotments, a first choice should be given to existing shareholders. The number of shareholders grew year by year: over 200 in 1864; 1,000 by 1875; 2,000 by 1880; 14,000 by 1900; and approximately 36,000 by 1914. But, as one turns over the pages of the increasingly fat volumes of share lists, the impression of 'Englishness' remains and of ownership by individual Englishmen, for there were few institutional investors and no evidence of ownership by syndicates, financial groups, or speculators. The sons and grandsons and more often daughters and granddaughters of men who owned the original shares were frequently still shareholders fifty years after the foundation of the company. Southern shares were quoted on the London Stock Exchange but they were never easy to buy. They had, it seems, the character of heirlooms, carefully guarded by Parishes, Barings, and the spirits of those shrewd, resilient men who had witnessed the overthrow of Spanish power, had lived through the civil wars, had counselled Rosas and opposed Aberdeen; who had always believed, like the first British Consul-General there, that Argentina is one of the treasure-houses of the world.

It is hard to determine whether the prosperity of the Southern owes most to intelligent management or fortunate circumstances. The first line ran from Buenos Aires in a south-easterly direction to Chascomús seventy miles away. It ran through settled country where sheep farming, hay harvesting, and tallow rendering were long established. When the Southern came to this part of the pampas there was already in existence a considerable ox- and horse-drawn transport system moving wool, hay, tallow, and hides to the markets in Buenos Aires. When the line was only partially open over forty-eight miles in 1866 the directors estimated that the railway was carrying only 13 per cent. of the produce of the area, but when the line was completed the next year the estimated percentage jumped to 28·8 per cent.[1] In the first half of 1868 they estimated they were carrying 28 per cent. of the wool and hair produced in the area, 48 per cent. of the hides, and 89 per cent. of the tallow and grease. Indeed, the sheepmasters found that the railway enabled them to switch from wool to tallow when wool prices dropped, and the building of tallow-rendering plants followed the construction of the railway.

Thus the demand for the services of the Southern was quite different to that which the Central encountered on the much less developed pampas of Santa Fé. The directors of the Southern could see traffic potential everywhere around them. To the west of their line the produce of the region about Azul and Las Flores was still moved entirely by cattle-drawn wagons. They observed, too, that wool loaded on wagons beyond the Río Salado continued to the Buenos Aires markets along the route of the railway, because once the drivers had made the difficult fords of the Salado it was not worth while unloading and paying railway charges to complete the journey by rail.

In spite of the ability of the line to pay 5 per cent. on the paid-up capital from the opening of the first forty-eight miles of road, in spite too of the readiness of the Government of Buenos Aires to make up the company's surpluses in order to

[1] *Herapath's*, xxx, 1868, p. 1158.

pay 7 per cent., and in spite of the great traffic potential, the investing public remained extremely cautious and critical and even the existing shareholders were full of fears. In order to complete the line an additional £100,000 was required over and above the £650,000 of paid-up share capital. The directors could not find takers for the unissued shares, and were obliged to issue 8 per cent. debenture bonds to secure the last £100,000 required. And these bonds were taken up largely by the existing shareholders! When the directors decided to extend the line beyond the Salado they could only get the capital by issuing special Salado Extension shares, the dividends on which would be paid out of the earnings of the extension, and thus would not prejudice the earnings of the original line. It became a fixed principle of the company that new lines and new shareholders must not prejudice the benefits of old-established shareholders, and that extension shareholders must undergo, as it were, a probationary period before their shares were incorporated in the ordinary or preference share structure of the company. Even as late as 1914 there were issues of 4 per cent. extension shares at a time when the ordinary shares were paying 7 per cent. or better and the preference 5 per cent.

The directors themselves do not seem to have altogether shared the fears of the investors, whose nervousness complicated the accounts of the company and was wholly irrational. They seem to have believed in educating the investing public, for they gave a very great deal of information about the company's affairs at semi-annual meetings and in the press. After two extensions had been made they published a very impressive demonstration of the economics and common sense from the investors' point of view of building new lines and adding to investments. They demonstrated that extensions increased receipts faster than expenses per train mile and thus increased profit as shown in Table 1.

But the investors remained cautious and conservative, and the Southern was obliged always to grow only in response to a proved demand for the services it could provide. In this caution we must recognize a social wisdom of some value; for, if they were not the stuff of which pioneers are made, neither were the proprietors of the Southern the dupes of speculators or the agents of useless and often dishonest enterprise which so frequently wasted the substance of both the Argentine and British people to build railways through swamps, across deserts, and over mountains for no purpose except the profit of contractors and promoters.

A factor of great importance in the history of the Southern was its low capital cost. Nature had provided a terrain over which it was comparatively easy to build railways, but flat land is not necessarily the only element in keeping capital costs low.

TABLE I[1]

	1867	1869	1871	1873	1875
Miles of railroad .	71	71	88½	146	202
Gross traffic revenue as a percentage of capital invested . .	11·37	16·19	16·40	17·21	18·75
Receipts per train mile in sterling .	11s. 2½d.	12s. 11¾d.	14s. 4½d.	13s. 3¼d.	16s. 3d.
Expenses per train mile in sterling .	6s. 6½d.	6s. 8¼d.	7s. 8¼d.	7s. 3¼d.	8s. 4d.
Profit per train mile in sterling . .	4s. 8d.	6s. 3¼d.	6s. 8¼d.	5s. 11¾d.	7s. 11d.

The line to Chascomús was built by Messrs. Peto and Betts on a contract basis. They completed the work within the limits set by the government guarantee, i.e. for less than £725,000 (or £10,000 a mile). Although there is no direct evidence on this point, the directors seem to have had capital in hand when the first line was completed for they were able to meet the demand for wool and tallow warehouses, and part of the large increase in their traffic appears to have been due in the case of tallow to the warehousing facilities they offered. Not only did the directors complete the line for £10,000 a mile, but they seem to have always possessed rolling stock adequate to the traffic.

Shortly after the completion of the original line Peto and Betts went bankrupt. After Peto's disappearance from the scene (his shares were sold by a special arrangement which kept them off the market) the Southern directors adopted a policy of building their own lines, thus keeping the profits of contracting within the company. The extension beyond the Salado was built for £7,000 a mile, which included an increase in rolling

[1] *Herapath's*, xxxviii, 1876, p. 584, abbreviated.

stock, an improvement in the station and marshalling yards in Buenos Aires, and the purchase of land for the right of way. This last was offset by a government subsidy of £500 a mile in lieu of a land grant.[1] One short extension in the 1870's was built for £5,000 a mile, another in the 1880's for £4,000 a mile. These costs were low both by Argentine and world standards. The Central Argentine was inadequately equipped at £6,400 a mile. The average cost of all mileage in Argentina in 1875 was £8,000 per mile.[2] Some lines, built later, such as the Buenos Ayres and Rosario, cost £18,000 a mile. £12,000 a mile was a common average in other South American countries, and contemporary Indian railways cost £18,000 a mile.[3]

Alert direction and careful management were factors of some importance in the Southern's good start. Both the kind and the abundance of information which the Southern's directors gave the shareholders semi-annually indicate that they knew what the real problems of railway management were. The absence of petty complaints and wrangles about the government guarantee suggest, not that the Southern did not have a problem of a sort in this matter, but that they saw clearly that the way to make a railway pay is to induce people to use it, and that this can best be done by providing service at prices people are willing and able to pay. The concern of the directors to provide warehousing facilities for customers and the steady inroads made by the railway on existing transport business indicate a 'customer consciousness' on the part of the Southern which helps to explain its progress. The reports of the meetings of the Southern shareholders always suggest, when compared with the bad temper and self-pity of Central and East Argentine meetings, the presence of knowledge and common sense among the directors. The directors not only had a financial stake in the company which prompted them to run it well, but they were personally interested in the details of its operation. In 1883 one of the directors, John Fair, rode over 200 miles on the cowcatcher of a locomotive in order to report to the directors on the state of the road bed and lines of the company.[4]

One of the tests of good railway management applied in the

---

[1] *Herapath's*, xxxv, 1873, p. 96.   [2] Mulhall, *The English in South America*, p. 497.
[3] L. H. Jenks, *The Migration of British Capital to 1875* (London, 1938), p. 222.
[4] *Herapath's*, xlv, 1883, p. 469.

1870's was the ratio of working expenses to receipts. By this test the Southern was better managed than the best British railway, the Taff Vale, whose gross receipts and capital structure happen to resemble closely those of the Southern. In 1873 the Southern's working expenses were 54·3 per cent. of receipts, compared with 56·6 per cent. for the Taff Vale.[1] This record was achieved in the face of difficulties such as the high price of imported coal and repair parts and high labour costs, at least for skilled men such as locomotive drivers, signalmen, and machinists. On the other hand the Southern paid no taxes, unskilled labour was cheap, and rates tended to be what the traffic would bear. But circumstances alone do not account for the low expense ratio nor high rates for the company's success. The directors knew how to cut costs. Coal, for example, sold at prices from 18*s.* to 23*s.* a ton in the Buenos Aires market during the late 1860's and 1870's, but by 1875 the Southern had reduced their coal costs to 10*s.* 3*d.* a ton.[2]

One evidence of the shrewd and far-sighted character of the Southern's management was its decision to rid itself of the Government guarantee. During the first four years of the company's operations it was obliged to ask the Province of Buenos Aires for subsidies sufficient to pay the guaranteed profit of 7 per cent. It soon became evident not only that the annual request for a subsidy was a troublesome business, but that the guarantee was not worth the risk to freedom of action involved in the power to fix rates conferred upon the Government by the terms of the guarantee agreement. In 1869 the company re-negotiated this agreement, by the terms of which it accepted a subvention of £500 a mile for every extension made along a route approved by the Government in lieu of land and guarantees. Bit by bit the original agreement was abandoned until by 1875 the Southern operated without a guarantee, without the threat of rate fixing, and on the understanding that the Government would pay the stock exchange value of the company plus 20 per cent. should it decide to expropriate the company.

The Southern's relations with the Government of Buenos Aires were not embowered in roses. As profit-seekers they preferred to build extensions where the traffic was likely to be the heaviest. The Government and the landed interests, however,

---

[1] Ibid. xxxvi, 1874, p. 508.   [2] Ibid. xxxviii, 1876, p. 15.

were bent on having extensions made towards the frontier so
that people could flow into vacant spaces and produce would
begin to flow out. The company would have liked to build its
first extension from Chascomús at right angles to the existing
line, so that the Southern would begin to make a perimeter
around Buenos Aires, and be the means of preventing the
penetration of the Government-owned *Oeste* into the southern
pampas. The Government, however, wished to see the line
pushed beyond the Río Salado towards Dolores and eventually
to Bahia Blanca. In the controversy, threats of expropriation
were uttered. In the end something was arranged. The Southern
agreed to build an extension to Dolores beyond the Río Salado
and the Government agreed to permit an extension to the west
into the region of Las Flores, Tandil, and Azul as a means of
keeping out the *Oesete*. The compromise agreement reached
with the Government at this time was of the highest importance
for the company's future, for it ensured the Southern's hold
over the eastern half of Buenos Aires Province, thus providing
the foundation for the substantial railway system which the
Southern eventually became.

If the Southern company exhibited shrewd common sense in
management, the Northern Railway Company of Buenos Ayres
provided a demonstration of something quite the opposite. In
1862 a group of British capitalists, of which a Member of Parliament, E. H. S. Crawford, was the leading figure, obtained a
concession with a guarantee from the Government of Buenos
Aires Province to build a railway from Buenos Aires to San
Fernando, where the Río Maldonado flows into the Paraná.
Here ships could unload from deep water close to the shore, and
it was expected that, with the construction of docks, the great
disadvantages of Buenos Aires as a port could be overcome.
The company intended eventually to extend their line parallel
with the Paraná to Rosario. Commercially and naturally everything seemed in the company's favour. They had permission to
build a tramway into the centre of Buenos Aires and to build
a steam railway through well-settled territory to a spot where
it was possible to create an expanding freight traffic. Furthermore, the distance, twenty miles, was such that a modest capital
well within the capacities of the investors could accomplish the
purpose of the company.

Nothing turned out as intended. Irresponsible management and, it was charged, nepotism blighted the enterprise from the beginning. The Government had guaranteed a capital of £150,000; £250,000 was spent, and still there was an inadequacy of rolling stock. The chairman did not know what had been paid for locomotives. At a special meeting in 1864 the shareholders were surprised to learn that the contractor had presented a bill for £60,000 in spite of the fact that they had been informed at all previous meetings that the contracts were being paid in full as work progressed. Although the capital guaranteed was only £150,000, the directors thought that the Government would certainly pay 7 per cent. on £250,000; but they did not know. In fact dividends were being paid out of capital, and working expenses exceeded revenue during the first two years.

One explanation of these deficits emerged when a great shake-up of the company's management came in 1866. It was discovered that a group of the company's employees had set up a ticket office of their own outside the Northern's station in Buenos Aires where they sold tickets 33 per cent. cheaper than the standard fares. It likewise emerged that useless surveys had been made; that an extension had been made to Tigre where there was no deep water where ships could dock; that coal bought through dealers in Buenos Aires was two to three times as costly as coal bought on contract in Great Britain. As a result of the shake-up a new board of directors and a new manager in Argentina were appointed, the permanent staff was reduced from 129 to 70, and coal was purchased in Great Britain. Money was borrowed at 12½ to 15 per cent. interest, and one unknown lender put up £25,000, half of which he was willing to secure on debentures of the company. The company's property in Liverpool was mortgaged. The Government paid up its guarantee on £150,000 faithfully. More rolling stock was purchased. The situation began to improve. Working expenses were cut to 79 per cent. of revenue by 1869. But the shareholders clamoured for 7 per cent., and the directors did not have the courage to put them off. In spite of the bad shape in which the company found itself, the directors paid 7 per cent. in 1869 instead of employing surpluses to buy much-needed

---

[1] *Herapath's*, xxviii, 1866, pp. 568 and 617.

equipment. In 1870 the Government of Buenos Aires told the company bluntly that it would not pay the guarantee unless there was a considerable improvement in the service it provided. Reluctantly they added a few carriages, wagons, and locomotives. The history of the Northern leaves one with an impression of incompetence, greed, and stupidity, which were eventually rewarded on an ample scale when the company sold its command over the access to a central position in Buenos Aires to the Central Argentine Railway for an immense sum.

Three of the British railways in Argentina operated tramlines into the centre of Buenos Aires in the 1860's, but these were conceived of as feeders to their railway lines, and their final purpose emerged as a means of giving access to central positions where railway stations were built. It was not until 1870 that a tramway company having the sole purpose of providing surface transport in Buenos Aires was projected by British business men. The initiator was George Drabble. The City of Buenos Ayres Tramways Company was established with a capital of £75,000.[1] Drabble anticipated a profit of 40 per cent. a year. He was not far wrong. The trams began to run on 18 October 1870. By the end of the year the company had a surplus of £5,660 available for dividend. The capital of the company steadily increased until it was £450,000 by 1874 with a reserve of £12,000. The dividend that year was 12 per cent. The only cloud on this enterprise's horizon was a municipal ordinance which made it obligatory that each tram be preceded by a trumpeter on horseback. The directors estimated that this requirement increased costs by 20 per cent., even though the trumpeters served the additional purpose of hauling the trams out of mud holes and ditches. Such was the passion for progress in Buenos Aires that in 1873 the ordinance was repealed.

The City of Buenos Ayres Tramways Company was no miracle, producing automatic increases in capital plus a 12 per cent. dividend. Absence of effective management was demonstrated by the experience of another British tramway company which began with a capital of £138,000. The Buenos Aires National Tramways Company invested its capital in trams, lines, horse farms, and meadows for the provision of fuel for its hay-burning motive power. The City of Buenos Ayres Tramways'

[1] *Herapath's*, xxxiii, 1871, p. 239.

policy of buying horses and hay in the open market was the most economical. The National Tramways Company had too much capital tied up in horse farms and not enough in trams. The National sold some of its lines to the City of Buenos Ayres Tramways in order to buy more trams. The shareholders quarrelled with the directors. In 1877 the company leased its property and franchises to an Argentine firm at a figure which yielded 0·5 per cent. on the invested capital. This firm failed to make the enterprise go. A new British company was formed which took over the properties, exchanging stock in the new company for stock in the old at a substantial loss to the original shareholders.

Commercial banking was a field into which British capitalists entered with enthusiasm and success during this period. After the liquidation of the *Banco Nacional* in 1836, banking facilities, apart from those offered privately by mercantile houses, ceased to exist in Argentina. The Government's *Casa de Moneda* issued currency, but it made no loans to business men nor did it discount bills or receive deposits. The Government's own borrowing operations were committed to the hands of private merchants many of them British. Shortly after the overthrow of Rosas the Province of Buenos Aires established a state bank with the sole right of note issue in the Province. In 1858 a Brazilian enterprise, the Mauá Bank, opened an office in Buenos Aires and rapidly extended its operation over the whole country through a system of branches. The Mauá Bank undertook all kinds of business; invested in real estate and industrial enterprises, discounted commercial paper, and made short-term loans on security. Except in the Province of Buenos Aires, where it was forbidden to do so, the Mauá Bank issued notes, and in the Uruguayan Republic it provided for a time the principal medium of exchange. The success of this bank encouraged others, and at the same time created in the mind of the Argentine authorities a fear of Brazilian influence.[1] A private English bank, Wanklyn and Company, was opened on the ground floor of Mr. Edward Lumb's mansion. Mr. Henry, who was considered 'one of the best judges of city paper', conducted another private bank in the Calle San Martín.

[1] A. S. J. Baster, *The International Banks* (London, 1935), p. 129. Also N. Piñero, *La Moneda, el crédito y los bancos en la Argentina* (Buenos Aires, 1921).

In the summer of 1862 a notice appeared in the *Bankers'*
Magazine.

An enterprise, to be called the London, Buenos Ayres and River
Plate Bank (Limited) with a capital of £500,000 in 5,000 shares of
£100 each, and a power to increase, has been announced. The
deposit is to be £2 on application and £2 on allotment . . . the
promoters say that 'they have the assurance of the representatives of
these states that their respective governments would regard with
favour the establishment of such an institution as a powerful means of
contributing to the advancement of commercial relations with
Great Britain'.

The promoters were a group of London merchants headed by
Henry Bruce, John Septimo Rivolta, and George Alexander
Holt. Rivolta and Holt were also connected with the foundation
of the Buenos Ayres Great Southern Railway. Each of the
applicants and each of the first directors had at least fifty shares,
of which £40 a share was paid up when business operations
commenced. Bruce, the chairman, had shares worth £18,700
at par fully paid up and he invested another £18,700 in the
second year of the bank's operation. Altogether there were 190
original shareholders. Average shareholdings were small, but
the core group invested more heavily than they had in railway
enterprises. Bruce was liable for 2½ times as much as the largest
single shareholder of any railway enterprise. There were a
substantial proportion of holdings of from £5,000 to £15,000.
A member of the Guinness family invested £40,000, and two
of the proprietors of the *Manchester Guardian* held shares. The
rank and file of the shareholders resembled that of the railway
companies in its social composition: a few professional men,
clergymen, and army officers, a phalanx of gentlemen, but a
majority of merchants and manufacturers.

In the second year of the bank's life the authorized capital
was doubled by the issue of £500,000 in £25 shares on which
£10 was immediately called. A voting procedure was adopted
which gave votes only to possessors of £200 worth of stock and
up, the number of votes increasing with each £500 held up to
£5,000, and one vote for all holdings over £5,000.

The management in Buenos Aires had a long experience of
the River Plate and good connexions both commercial and
political. The resident director was Norberto de la Riestra, who

retired from the post of Minister of Finance of the Province of Buenos Aires a few months before becoming a shareholder in the new banking company. A former business colleague of de la Riestra's, J. H. Green, who had traded in Buenos Aires for many years, became the manager. From the moment of opening the London and River Plate prospered. No dividends were paid the first year, but the scale of the bank's operations prompted the directors to increase the authorized capital to £1,000,000, much of which was taken up by the original shareholders. At the end of the second year the dividend was 11¼ per cent. and £10,000 were placed in the reserve. In 1865 the dividend was 15 per cent. and London and River Plate shares were unobtainable on the London Stock Exchange.[1] Overend Gurney failed, and the Argentine Government permitted the banks to refuse all transactions in gold, but the London and River Plate ignored this decree and continued to pay in sterling. They declared a dividend of 15 per cent. in this crisis year. Branches were opened in Montevideo, Rosario, and Córdoba. The premises in the Calle Piedad, the old street of the British shopkeepers, proved insufficient for their thriving affairs. The directors purchased a site in the Calle Florida, but seeing a chance for a windfall profit, they sold this property and bought something less expensive at the corner of Piedad and Reconquista, where they created a Roman-Corinthian structure usefully ornamented with a clock imported from London. It was a matter of marvel that the roof was constructed of light metal of the latest invention and design specially imported from Britain. The floor was paved with Winton's tiles, and a firm of furnishers in St. Paul's Churchyard sent out a cashier's counter with 'a sweep of 60 feet in length'. In 1870 the directors reported that in under seven years the London and River Plate had placed £100,000 in the reserve and had paid 87¼ per cent. on the capital in dividends and bonuses.[2]

The explanation of this success is to be found partly in circumstances and partly in policy. Interest rates on short-term loans were high—as high as 18 per cent.—and remained high until after the crisis of 1876–7. This was the money-lenders' paradise into which the London and River Plate entered. Another favourable circumstance was the state of the Argentine

[1] *Bankers' Magazine*, xxvi, 1866, p. 38. [2] Ibid. xxx, 1870, p. 34.

currency. In spite of many resolutions to adhere to the principles of hard currency, the Argentine public authorities still operated on a paper standard domestically. The London and River Plate early demonstrated that it would pay all claims in sterling. Thus Argentine citizens, as well as foreigners, were provided with the means of depositing assets in a form which had a relatively more stable value than the local currency. Furthermore, a sterling deposit in the London and River Plate was spendable in the world market and the person who possessed sterling was relieved of the risks inherent in changes in monetary conditions as well as in price changes in commodity markets. The London and River Plate's policy of paying interest on the daily balance of depositors together with the policy of paying in sterling on assets converted to that currency attracted deposits from all classes, and their willingness to redeem their notes in gold or its sterling equivalent in fact created a hard currency circulating in the presence of a soft one. This created difficulties, as we shall see, but it also attracted business.

Although Argentina was a money-lenders' paradise, it was also a place abounding in serpents capable both of tempting and stinging the innocent. But the directors of the London and River Plate were anything but innocent. Argentine banking laws imposed few restrictions on the type of business a bank could do, and the kind of business a bank undertook and the form of its investments was largely a matter for the judgement of the directors. The London and River Plate's directors adopted a policy of investing their assets almost entirely in bills and secured overdrafts. In 1870 the directors discharged the manager in Buenos Aires for contracting several bad debts. The London and River Plate refused to invest in long-term securities, shares, or real estate. In the crisis year 1876 their accounts showed their current assets distributed as follows:

	£
Cash in hand, at branches and on deposit	977,756
Bills discountable and receivable, current accounts and securities . . .	2,781,889
Bank premises	48,682
Bank furniture	8,517
Undistributed dividends . . .	30,000
	£3,846,845[1]

[1] *Bankers' Magazine*, xxxvi, 1876, p. 449.

Admittedly the second item is not very revealing, but in the context in which it is quoted together with other items of information about the general policies of the bank it is possible to infer that bills and current account overdrafts did in fact make up a substantial part of the £2,781,889, and that securities in the form of shares, stocks, and real estate were a small proportion of the assets.

The policy of the London and River Plate in the matter of investments insured high liquidity, a close adjustment to the movement of the main productive activities of the Argentine economy, and participation in the most profitable activity of the community, save perhaps land speculation, commerce.

As in the case of railways and tramways, British bank directors likewise demonstrated how not to make profits as well as how to make them. The Mercantile Bank of the River Plate provided an example of a failure. This company was formed in 1872 with the original name, soon changed, of the Commercial Bank of the River Plate Ltd. There were twenty-seven founders who possessed special founders' shares of £1 each—in fact 33,360 of the 50,750 £1 shares issued. The authorized capital was £1,500,000 in £20 shares, but only slightly more than £1,000,000 was actually raised. The twenty-seven founders were mostly professional financiers and not merchants turned bankers in the manner of the London and River Plate founders. Both the Banque de Paris et des Pays-Bas and the London Banking Association were founders and large shareholders. So were the financiers, Baron Louis d'Erlanger, Henry Oppenheim, L. de Laski, Raphael and Louis Beer. A Viennese bank was a large shareholder but not a founder. William Ashworth, a Manchester merchant and a moderately heavy investor in other Argentine enterprises, was another founder, and so also were Edward Lumb and two Wanklyns. Indeed, the firm was founded 'to acquire the good will of the banking and general monetary business heretofore carried on at Buenos Aires and Montevideo under the firm of Wanklyn and Company'.[1]

In spite of a heavy capital, a local connexion, and a body of founders from among the most experienced financiers, the Mercantile Bank of the River Plate was only a temporary success. In 1873 this bank paid 15 per cent. and put £50,000 to

[1] Public Record Office, Board of Trade (henceforward B.T.), 31/1736–6406.

reserve, and it paid 10 per cent. in 1874 adding nothing to its reserve. When depression hit Argentina in 1876, a committee was set up to examine the Mercantile's affairs. The bank staggered along, hardly breathing, until the necessity of raising more capital decided the directors and shareholders to seek voluntary liquidation in 1881. This revealed that the Mercantile held a controlling interest in the Montevideo Waterworks. An account from the year 1876 shows that bank premises, real estate, shares, and stocks constituted nearly one-third of all assets, including the Bank's reserve funds. Cash on hand did not constitute 5 per cent. of their assets, and bills and overdrafts constituted only 63 per cent. of assets compared with 73 per cent. in the case of the London and River Plate. What else was wrong with the Mercantile's management it is not possible to determine, but its fate foreshadowed that of many later efforts on the part of large-scale speculators to move into Argentina without a clear idea of what they were trying to do.

Although British capitalists controlled the surface transport business in Buenos Aires they did not dominate the public utility field. In 1863 an English firm proposed to provide Buenos Aires with a water-supply system at an estimated cost of £100,000. Municipal politics being what they were, nothing was decided, and the English firm abandoned the proposal. In January 1868 there was a terrifying outbreak of cholera in the city. At last it was realized that the dirty water-carts of colonial times were no longer equal to the task of watering a rapidly growing city reputed to contain a quarter of a million people.[1] The Provincial Government dispatched an engineer to England to purchase equipment, and in September 1869 the machinery arrived and work was commenced on a system designed to deliver 2,500,000 gallons per day through twelve miles of mains.[2] Financing was provided by the London money market through the means of a loan to the Province, and thereafter Buenos Aires depended heavily upon London for the financing of municipal development. Indeed, the greatest financial crisis in Argentine history—and one of the most perilous in

[1] In 1866 the British chargé d'affaires estimated the population of Buenos Aires at 160,000, and Latham, a student of Argentine conditions with considerable mercantile experience, estimated 200,000. See W. Latham, *The States of the River Plate* (London, 1866), p. 5.

[2] M. G. Mulhall, *Handbook of the River Plate* (Buenos Aires, 1869), i, p. 113.

British history—was precipitated by a Buenos Aires waterworks loan.

Gas lighting was undertaken by Argentine capitalists in 1856. Lest it be supposed that only foreigners made profits in Argentina, it is well to relate that this company charged £1. 3s. per 1,000 cubic feet for gas when coking coal could be bought for £1 a ton or less, and its dividends were from 20 to 30 per cent. per annum. An English merchant in Montevideo, James Bell, proposed the establishment of a company on the principle of mutuality which would permit shareholders to enjoy substantial reductions in charges. He organized The Buenos Aires Mutual Gas Company with a capital of £200,000 part of which was raised in London.

Very little capital, foreign or native, was invested in industrial enterprises in this stage of Argentine development. With the disappearance of local crafts under the impact of competition by the sellers of machine-made products from abroad the comparative advantages of industrial activity were non-existent at this stage. The shortage of labour, the absence of organizing, administrative, and commercial experience in the industrial field, and the smallness of the market all militated against industrial growth. Only one industry of any consequence flourished in Argentina at this time: meat packing for export. In 1866 the British chargé d'affaires estimated the export of jerked meat at 72 million lb. a year. The jerked-meat industry was largely in Argentine hands, although there were some French-owned *saladeros*. The capital investment in this industry was low, for the techniques of killing, drying, salting, and packing had changed hardly at all from colonial times. The market was still mainly in the slave centres in Brazil and in the West Indies. Europeans had never been induced to eat jerked meat in spite of the growing scarcity of meat supplies in western Europe in the 1860's.

European business men were, however, beginning to explore the possibilities of transforming the meat-packing industry of Argentina at this time, and the shortages of meat were sufficient to provoke the British Foreign Secretary to inquire what were the opportunities of securing increased supplies from Argentina.[1]

[1] F.O. 6/263, Ford's report of 26 June 1866, suggests that he had been requested to supply information on this subject. At a time of declining prices of

Several plans of transformation were projected, each backed by a small capital investment. Morgan's method amounted to a system of embalming carcasses. The Morgan Patent Meat Preserving Company marketed beef in Liverpool at 4*d*. a pound in the 1860's, but the method had so many disadvantages that it never became the basis of an established trade. The Germans were pioneers of a successful method of using meat to produce a product saleable in Europe. Baron Liebig devised a technique for manufacturing beef extract by vacuum boiling which was admirably adapted to the utilization of the tough, stringy range cattle of the pampas. Liebig's *extractum carnis* brought to the consumer a suggestion of beef. Advertising endowed it with magical properties. These enabled it to perform miracles of physical restoration which ordinary cooks equipped with stock pots had never been able to equal. An English company was formed to use Liebig's patents, and the foundations were laid of the beef-extract industry.

A third method tried out was Sloper's method of canning meat in tins. Great secrecy surrounded this method, for Sloper was believed to have discovered rare gases which, injected into the cans, prevented oxidation. In spite of his scientific powers and his patents, Sloper had to contend with the tough carcasses of cows and bulls which had spent their lives running over vast prairies in search of food and to escape from men. His method, too, represented a stage in progress towards a new meat trade, but it was not the agency of an immediate transformation.

At this time a fourth suggestion was made. Argentina needed people and Europe needed cattle. A group of imaginative projectors proposed to build steamships which would carry men and women swiftly to the River Plate and bring back cows and bulls for the slaughterhouses of Liverpool and Antwerp.[1] A scheme so rational and dispassionate as this deserved to succeed, but it did not. Why we cannot say, but it is proper to observe that this system of commerce would have encountered the difficulty which contributed to the failure of all but Liebig's system: the unsatisfactory character of Argentine cattle. When, some twenty years on, the development of specialized

consumer goods and increased living standards, meat prices remained more stable and meat became relatively more expensive. S. G. Hanson, *Argentine Meat and the British Market* (New York, 1937), p. 27.   [1] Mulhall, *Handbook*, 1869, i, p. 114.

steamships and refrigeration made possible a large-scale trade both in slaughtered and live animals, a great transformation of the pastoral industry itself was required. Beef animals had to be bred; alfalfa feeding was developed in closed meadows and pens; finishing on coarse grains was undertaken; and for all of these things heavy investments of capital were required. But in the 1860's none of these things was considered, and the focus of development was sheep-breeding and the wool and tallow harvests.

The fundamental alteration in the structure of Argentine production and the expansion of commodity sales which it involved was in fact centred upon the transformation of the pastoral industry from an emphasis primarily on cattle to an emphasis primarily on sheep. This transformation and expansion supported all the other developments we have described—and it was made possible by them. In 1854 hides, horsehair, buoes, horns and hooves, and jerked meat comprised more than half of Argentine exports. Wool, sheep-skins, and tallow accounted for a little more than one-third of exports. On balance Argentina was an importer of cereals at that time. Between 1850 and 1870 Argentine wool production increased from 21,000,000 to 137,000,000 lb., and productivity was improved from an average of 3 lb. per sheep to 3·3 lb.[1] The big increase came in the 1860's when production more than tripled in volume.

In the seventies the signs of another revolution in the Argentine countryside began to emerge. In 1875 the manager of the Southern Railway reported that grain and hay were the two most rapidly growing freight items on its lines.[2] In 1876 Britain imported 37,000 cwt. of Argentine maize, and already Argentine cereals, fulfilling home demand, were beginning to enter the Brazilian market.

The question for us is this: What was the part played by British capital and British people in these revolutions in the most important of all fields of Argentine production? The need for capital was great. Only capital could provide the means for barbed-wire fencing, well-drilling, the provision of shearing

[1] H. Gibson, *The History and Present State of the Sheep-Breeding Industry in the Argentine Republic* (Buenos Aires, 1893), p. 50. Also F. Latzina, *L'Agriculture et l'élevage dans la république argentine* (Paris, 1889). [2] *Herapath's*, xxxviii, 1875, p. 500.

and baling equipment and tallow-rendering plant, and the purchase of breeding-stock. Investment in pastoral enterprise was not as simple, particularly for foreigners, as investment in railways, banks, and public funds. A high percentage of good land readily accessible to the coastal markets had been privately appropriated in the century previous to the fall of Rosas. Latifundia were characteristic, the inheritance of the pastoral age now passing away. The developing fields of production—sheep-farming, grain-growing, and the raising of beef cattle—required smaller units of production than the old estancias of noble proportions: and they required more invested capital. Unappropriated land was relatively scarce. Even land along the pioneer railways was either already in private hands or was being rapidly transferred thence in large blocks.[1] The would-be sheep- or grain-farmer could normally expect that he would have either to buy or to rent land. The newcomer in the Argentine countryside was thus obliged to have sufficient capital not only to equip a farm but to purchase it, unless he was prepared to share the profits of enterprise by the payment of an economic rent. In either case the landowners of the Republic were in a position to effect, through the existing institutional arrangements governing resource use, a transfer of capital from the newcomer to themselves.

In the period under review, British subjects continued to go into sheep-farming. In the sixties they could expect to buy and stock a sheep farm at a cost of £6,500 per square league for land in a possible but not highly favourable location.[2] Land in the best parts of Buenos Aires Province would cost as much as £10,000 a square league, while land in the remote interior could be had for £300 a league. How much British capital went into sheep-farming in this period is a matter of guesswork and conjecture. Mulhall estimated that there were 1,100 sheep farms owned by British subjects, and he guessed they were worth £2,500,000 in 1875.[3] The average value of this estimate seems low, but an allowance for rented farms probably makes an average value of £2,250 reasonable. Mulhall's figures tell

---

[1] Zimmerman, *H.A.H.R.* xxv, 1945, pp. 22–30. Between 1876 and 1899, 229 concessionaires obtained 15,539,000 hectares of unsurveyed land, while in the same period colonies of smallholders obtained only 172 square leagues (about 500,000 hectares).   [2] Latham, *The States of the River Plate*, pp. 179, 186, and 199.

[3] Mulhall, *The English in South America*, p. 529.

nothing about the actual import of capital involved. Some sheep-farmers came to the Argentine with nothing except knowledge, and sometimes not much of that, and, by working on shares, achieved an independent position. Hannah, one of the most successful sheep-masters of the earlier generation, did this. In such cases there was a migration of technical knowledge and labour power, not capital. Others brought capital as well as knowledge and the capacity to labour. All we can definitely say is that British capital was invested in pastoral enterprise, especially in sheep-farming. In 1871 the British Consul reported this to be the case, and he estimated that, of 10,533 British subjects known to be in the Argentine, 5,971 were resident in the rural parts of Buenos Aires Province.[1] Working from the census figures a decade later, Latzina came to the conclusion that 1·68 per cent. of the landed proprietors of the Argentine were British subjects.[2] At the same time Mulhall estimated that these proprietors owned 26·4 per cent. of the sheep and 4·6 per cent. of the cattle and horses of the Republic[3] These are figures of a later period, and in any case they need to be received with caution. They point, however, to something characteristic of British pastoral enterprise in Argentina from late revolutionary times, namely, British proprietors were not numerous but they were prosperous and well established in the finest province and in the most progressive sector of the economy at this time.

In the sixties strenuous efforts were devoted to making the British residents of the Republic not only prosperous but numerous. The Argentine Government, the Central Argentine Land Company, various public-spirited men in Britain, and a number of entrepreneurs were all anxious to foster colonization. The notion was widely entertained that the Argentine might become the scene of a mass migration of both people and capital for the purpose of establishing colonies of farmers located in communities which would preserve for the inhabitants an adequate framework of life in the wild environment of the pampas. In 1863 on behalf of the Welsh Emigration Society, G. H. Whalley, M.P., David Williams, the High

[1] *Parliamentary Papers*, 1872, lxx, p. 31.
[2] Latzina, *L'Agriculture et l'élevage dans la république argentine*, pp. 373–93.
[3] Mulhall, *Handbook*, 1885, p. 22.

Sheriff of Carnarvon, and R. J. Parry, Esq., signed a contract with the Argentine Government by the terms of which they undertook to establish colonies in Patagonia at the rate of 300 to 500 families annually for ten years. The Government promised land, subsidies, tax exemptions, and protection. The banking firm of Thomson, Bonar & Company acquired a similar concession in Santa Fé Province. The Central Argentine Land Company under the direction of its immigration agent, William Perkins, a Canadian, planted several colonies along the line of the railway in Santa Fé.[1] A spate of books appeared in the late sixties describing the Argentine and providing advice about how to survive and prosper there.

But a substantial British emigration to the Argentine never developed. In 1871 the British Government asked the Consul-General to report on 'the Subject of Immigration to the Argentine Confederation'. Mr. Macdonell's report was printed in the *Parliamentary Papers* of 1872 for all the world to read. Its sober conclusions and frank comment were supported by a lively correspondence, presented to Parliament at the same time, concerning the murder of British subjects in Santa Fé and Buenos Aires Provinces. It would be hard to find anything more calculated to discourage emigration to Argentina than Consul-General Macdonell's report.

The Consul-General was very sceptical about the possibilities of agricultural development, the only kind of development which could support a numerous population from the rural parts of Britain. He founded this judgement upon the high cost of transport, the climate, the frequency of insect plagues, and the danger of Indian raids. He accused Messrs. Thomson, Bonar & Company of misrepresentation in advertising the advantages of Argentina as a field for colonists. He asserted that there was no instance of a successful British colony in Argentina, although he agreed that the colony on the Central Argentine Railway at Frayle Muerto was surviving and the one at Bahia Blanca would probably do likewise if the Indians did not succeed in murdering the inhabitants.

The Consul-General could see little prospect of the British community's growing. He did not believe that Englishmen,

[1] J. J. Gschwind, *Guillermo Perkins, su contribución al progreso económico Argentino* (Rosario, 1936).

especially if they lacked capital, would find the Argentine community congenial or up to their hopes as emigrants. Religion, he said, is nominally free, 'but no possible sympathy between the Protestant and the Catholic natives on the subject' is possible. Of the Argentinos he expressed this ambiguous opinion: 'The urban dwellers have yielded in some degree, and notably so in the capital, to the advancing civilization introduced by the foreign element of the population and are urbane, polished and intelligent; but, as a rule, idle, corrupt and very jealous of foreign, especially English, innovations and enterprise.'[1]

Mr. Macdonell's concluding advice was quite in accord with the facts of Argentine life as we have so far described them. A man with some capital and a knowledge of pastoral or mercantile pursuits could expect to do reasonably well. Macdonell added the cautionary note that he would have to avoid the temptations of alcohol and be prepared to work hard as a day-labourer until he learned his way around. Some men of no capital might find opportunities in commerce and on the railways, where special knowledge was needed. For the rest, the Argentine had little to offer but sorrow to the Englishman expecting to improve himself by emigration.

The Consul-General's analysis was deficient in several particulars, but his general conclusions were sound. The English worker could scarcely hope to improve his lot in Argentina, and he was unlikely to find the Mediterranean community growing up there to his liking. Unskilled labour and the older skilled trades were performed by Italians, Spanish Basques, and Frenchmen. They tended to work for wages lower than Englishmen expected, and the English workman could not generally hope to find Buenos Aires a better place than Birmingham. The absence of industrial development offered little opportunity for the kind of skills possessed by English industrial workers, and the United States was a better destination for them. For the English agricultural worker the hope of acquiring an independence in a land where there was no homestead law was insubstantial. English telegraph clerks might be the swells of Buenos Aires, but the penniless Englishman who did not know the Morse code was better advised to go to Canada, Australia, or the United States.

[1] *Parliamentary Papers*, 1872, lxx, p. 25.

A wholly new channel for the flow of British capital into Argentine pastoral and agricultural enterprise began to develop just at the moment when projects of colonization were being hit on the head. In 1872 the Government of the Province of Buenos Aires organized the *Banco Hipotecario Provincial*. This bank was authorized to lend money up to one half of the value of land offered for security. The system of lending was rather complicated, and some explanation is required in order to understand how the *Banco Hipotecario* became a channel for the flow of foreign capital into the Argentine economy.

The *Banco Hipotecario* did not lend money directly. To the borrower it issued *cédulas*. These were in fixed denominations bearing a fixed rate of interest and having maturity provisions common to the series in which the *cédula* was issued. The total amount of a series and all the terms connected with it were public knowledge. The *cédula* was a promise of the *Banco Hipotecario* to pay both the interest and the principal named in the *cédula*. The bank was, thus, the general debtor of those holding *cédulas*. It was in its turn creditor of the persons who pledged property in return for *cédulas*. The borrower, having received *cédulas*, sold them in the open market, and his receipts from their sale represented his borrowing. He was bound to repay the bank principal and interest on the terms stated in his agreement with the bank. He could pay either in the national currency or in *cédulas*; *cédulas* payable in gold were issued, but these amounted to only a small proportion of the total. *Cédulas* could be secured by any kind of real property, and a good deal was borrowed on city property as well as on the security of rural lands.

It is easy to see how open this type of security was to abuse, to the stimulation of speculation and to the promotion of inflation. Once a large number of *cédulas* were in circulation the advantages of an inflated paper currency to the borrowing classes were very great. And in the Argentine the landed interest, the borrowing interest, was all-powerful politically. Borrowing made it possible for the borrowers to buy more land to offer as security for more debts. Fresh land purchases drove land prices upward, and, as land values increased, the capacity of landowners to borrow automatically increased. No more successful instrument of inflationary speculation has probably ever been invented than a *cédula*. As the time approached for the repayment of loans, borrowers had the most powerful of incentives to drive down the price of *cédulas* so that they might be purchased as a means of satisfying the Bank. The curious thing about *cédulas* is that they flowed abroad. Most probably Argentinos understood them too well, and foreigners not well enough. Before 1875, however, they did not appear in the English market, and it is hardly proper to describe them as a channel for the flow of British capital into pastoral enterprise and urban building in this early period. Indeed, the quantity of *cédulas* issued before 1875 was small; the entire quantity issued between 1875 and 1886 was only 76,500,000 paper pesos.[1]

No account of Anglo-Argentine intercourse during these years would be complete which does not notice the effects upon Anglo-Argentine trade of the developments which we have described. In 1861, which we may consider to be the last year of the pre-investment era, Britain exported commodities worth £1,383,529, and bought from Argentine commodities worth £1,471,649. There is no reason why in a multilateral trading system the commodity accounts of any two countries should approximately coincide, but the Anglo-Argentine commodity accounts had tended to do so for many years. The investment of capital and the economic development which followed these investments greatly changed the character of Anglo-Argentine trade. Britain began to sell more to Argentina than she bought. British exports to Argentina had for many years expanded less rapidly than her exports to the world as a whole, but this began to change. In 1872 and 1873 the rate of expansion of British sales to Argentina was considerably above the rate of expansion to the world as a whole. The character of British commodity sales, too, began to change. In the years immediately preceding the beginning of capital investment 75 per cent. of all British exports to Argentina were textiles, and fuel and manufactures of metal accounted for only 11 per cent. of the trade. By 1875 textiles accounted for only 42 per cent. of all exports and fuel and manufactures of metal for nearly 25 per cent.[2]

[1] Council of the Corporation of Foreign Bondholders, *Nineteenth Annual Report* (London), 1891, p. 33.

[2] Based on figures from *Parliamentary Papers*. For a detailed examination see the author's 'Investment and Trade Between Britain and Argentina in the Nineteenth Century', *Economic History Review*, 2nd series, vol. iii, no. 2, 1950, pp. 203 ff.

By 1875 the main patterns of British participation in Argentine economic development had been established. British investment was destined to increase fifteenfold before World War I, and its character was growing bolder and less dependent upon the Argentine state, but the main fields of investment and enterprise had been marked out by 1875.

A remarkable feature of this development was the absence of political factors in the day-to-day and year-to-year course of development. There was a harmony of purpose on the part of the politically dominant groups in Argentina and the governing body in Britain which reduced political tension to a minimum and gave to diplomatic intercourse a humdrum character. In the Foreign Office there developed an absence of mind about Argentina which bespoke both satisfaction and indifference. On the Argentine side there developed a well-founded belief that it was more important to please the City of London than the inhabitants of Whitehall. In 1866 General Balcarce, Mitre's Minister in London, protested to Lord Clarendon about the adverse publicity in certain English newspapers concerning Argentina. So little did Clarendon know about Argentina that he wrote to the British chargé d'affaires to ask him what was happening on the banks of the River Plate and whether the economic transformation of which Balcarce spoke was actually taking place. Of course he could not do anything, the press being free, &c., &c., but he wished to be fair, and so on and so forth. The chargé d'affaires replied with a long report,[1] detailing the progress of the country and assuring the Foreign Secretary with some impressive statistics that a revolution in wool exports was taking place and immigrants were flowing into the country from Italy in an unprecedented volume.

Without any large conscious purposes the British authorities were willing to help along the process of change. In 1867 the British Consul protested about the condition of the Buenos Aires harbour and implored the Argentine Government to do something about the means of unloading ships quickly and cheaply.[2] As we have already related, the British Vice-Consul was given official permission to serve on the local committee of the Buenos

---

[1] F.O. 6/262, Ford to Clarendon, 24 Mar. 1866.
[2] F.O. 6/269, Mathew to Rufino de Elizalde, 9 Feb., enclosed with Mathew to Stanley, 23 Feb. 1867.

Ayres Great Southern Railway, a move which carried him not to the top of the consular service but eventually to the chairmanship of the railway company. Late in 1866, when a British company was undertaking to lay a submarine cable from the Uruguayan shore to Buenos Aires, the chargé did not hesitate to order H.M.S. *Dotterel*, a gunboat on the River Plate station, to assist the cable-laying operations.

The British Government's policy concerning immigration to Argentina was founded on no deeply considered view of the movement of British people. Facts were facts, and the Foreign Office wished to discourage mass immigration and thus to reduce the number of difficulties which could arise from conflicts about the rights of British subjects. When a few malcontents attempted to make out a case against the treatment of the first Welsh colonists at Chubut, the British chargé declared plainly that the Argentine authorities had behaved in the most generous and fair fashion to overcome the mistakes made by the Welsh organizers of the colony and that the Argentine Government, far from behaving unjustly, had provided the means for the colony's solid foundation.[1]

[1] F.O. 6/263, Ford to Clarendon, 14 July 1866.

XII

THE FIRST DEPRESSION

THE period 1875–82 in the history of Anglo-Argentine relations may be described as one of depression and recovery or of political tension and relaxation. It is not possible in any full account to make a choice between the two, for the course of economic and political developments was unusually inter-connected in this part of the world at this time. The years 1862–75 had witnessed a transformation in the character of the British interest in Argentina and of Argentine interest in their own country no less. When the pace of development slackened, tensions developed in the economic and financial sphere which projected themselves into political life, calling for a reconsideration briefly of British policy in relation to the Argentine Republic. In 1876 a direct threat was offered to part of the British joint-stock investment in Argentina, and in 1880 the outbreak of a brief civil war endangered generally the political stability of the River Plate, provoking on the part of British interests an agitation for direct British political intervention to protect British property interests. These developments obliged the Foreign Office to consider once again the principles of policy.

In order to understand the parallel and interconnected developments of this period, it is necessary to give first some account of the economic, financial, and commercial experience of Argentina in its relations with Britain. It must be noted that the economic depression, the full import of which was first felt in 1873, was by no means a uniform experience of all branches of the Argentine economy or of the British interest in Argentina. Some branches of commerce suffered more than others and at different times. Some investors likewise suffered more than others and at different times. Furthermore, some enterprises were harder hit by depression than others. All banks, for example, experienced a decline in profits, but all banks were not forced into liquidation. Similarly in the case of railways. Indeed, the unevenness of the impact of economic events upon British interests seems to have imparted a lack of uniformity to their political responses. In the days now gone by a blockade or a civil war or a sharp price decline in the commodity market afflicted the River Plate interest in a fairly uniform way generating a fairly uniform demand for political and diplomatic action; but in the new circumstances there was a complexity of events which tended to mute and make more difficult any kind of political action apart from that which Castlereagh had originally prescribed, namely, *laissez-faire, laissez-aller.*

From 1862 to 1872 British exports to the Argentine had continued to rise steadily and at an increasing rate. In 1867 and 1868 the rise had been more rapid than the general rise in British exports. In 1872 the progress exceeded anything hitherto experienced. In the succeeding year exports fell slightly. In 1874 they fell still more, and the index of exports to Argentina dropped below the index of total British exports.[1] The year 1875 was bad, but the succeeding one was much worse. Between 1872 and 1876 the index of British exports to the Argentine fell from 308·7 to 122·0. A halting recovery developed in 1877. There was a set-back in 1879. By 1881 the gross value of British exports to Argentina had increased substantially. In 1882 the index surpassed that of 1872. From that time forward the tide of expansion flowed again strongly and surely.

The passing of the peak in 1872 revealed itself first in textile exports. Iron and steel and coal were only reaching the peak, when textiles were already in sharp decline. But iron and steel and coal experienced sharper declines and their recovery came later. See Table 1.

Gross receipts dropped even more sharply than the quantity indexes would indicate. The index for gross receipts from the sale of iron and steel in Argentina stood at 451·5 in 1877 compared with a quantity index of 506·1. The value index for textiles and haberdashery fell from 231·0 in 1872 to 86·5 in 1875, and gross receipts never moved ahead of quantity in the

---

[1] 100 = £1,267,125, i.e. the figure for 1854. However, 1872 was a peak year. Total exports to Argentina on the same base were:

1870	185·0	1872	308·7	1874	245·5
1871	194·4	1873	294·5	1875	188·5

TABLE I. *Quantity Indexes*

1854=100

Year	Textiles	Iron and steel	Coal, coke, and fuel
1872	183·8	935·6	816·4
1873	145·9	1,000·4	904·6
1874	110·1	1,927·2	1,074·4
1875	93·0	1,396·3	626·8
1876	78·6	782·1	618·2
1877	173·5	506·1	734·2
1878	173·5	566·1	639·2
1879	138·6	889·1	927·6

textile field until 1885, and then only briefly. The years 1872, 1873, and 1874 were years of unusually high coal prices. A sharp break came in 1875. The value and quantity indexes moved as follows:

TABLE 2

1854 = 100

Year	Coal, value	Coal, quantity
1872	1,329·0	816·4
1873	1,957·8	904·6
1874	2,056·6	1,074·4
1875	764·6	626·8
1876	889·0	618·2
1877	853·0	734·2
1878	628·5	639·2
1879	974·0	927·6

The statistics of imports of Argentine produce into Great Britain do not tell a complete story. They suggest trends, however, and are worthy of examination. The year 1873 was the best in history, and remained so until 1888. In 1873 the gross receipts from the sale of Argentine wool and hides in Britain were very good; in the case of wool they had never been better. The quantity of tallow sold was almost up to the level of 1871, but the market for this commodity was beginning to go to pieces as petroleum and its derivatives invaded and conquered one part of the market. But agricultural production was beginning to

develop. The British customs houses began to list cereals from
Argentina in a separate category in 1878. Although Britain
failed to absorb Argentine produce in ever-increasing amounts
and the trade to Britain appears, from the indexes, severely
depressed from 1873 until 1888, the hard dollar value of Argentine exports mounted with few set-backs from 1872 onward.
Indeed, depression in Argentina took the form of a decline in
imports and an increase in exports.[1]

The slackening pace of development began to be felt in the
mercantile sphere in the last quarter of 1874. Exports from the
Argentine fell slightly this year compared with the two previous
years. Imports into Argentina dropped sharply, and consumer
goods were particularly hard-hit. Confidence was still considerable, however. The Mercantile Bank of the River Plate acknowledged that there was a crisis both in commerce and politics,
but the directors ordered a dividend of 10 per cent.[2] The London and River Plate Bank paid 12½ per cent. and increased
their reserve funds the same year. In spite of a rising volume of
exports and only a slight decline in imports 1875 proved to be
a bad year. Failures during the last three months of the year
exceeded £10 millions.[3] The London and River Plate paid
10 per cent., but the directors could afford to place nothing in
their reserve. The Mercantile Bank paid nothing, and a committee of stockholders was appointed to assess the value of the
assets of the Bank.[4] Tension between native and foreign enterprises began to grow as calamity appeared to approach. In
Santa Fé Province the Rosario branch of the London and the
River Plate was forbidden to issue notes, and the rival *Banco
Provincial* of Santa Fé was given the privilege exclusively. In
Buenos Aires the London and River Plate had to endure sharp
criticism in the press much to the advantage of the *Banco Provincial* of that Province.

The year 1876 was regarded as the worst on record. The
Argentine Government decreed the suspension of convertibility
of the notes of the *Banco Provincial* of Buenos Aires.[5] In May the
Government of Santa Fé Province decreed the liquidation of

[1] See Table 1 in Appendix.
[2] *Bankers' Magazine*, xxxv, 1875, p. 496.
[3] Ibid. xxxvi, 1876, p. 43.
[4] Ibid. xxxvi, 1876, p. 449.
[5] Ibid. xxxvii, 1877, p. 48.

the Rosario branch of the London and River Plate Bank and jailed the manager.[1] The Mercantile Bank was forced to call up more capital, and it wrote off £700,000 in bad debts. The directors had reduced advances on current accounts to £300,000 and the Bank was headed for liquidation.[2] From the bankers' point of view 1877 was also a bad year. The Bank of London and the River Plate was reduced to paying a dividend of 4 per cent. The Mercantile Bank cut its bills receivable to £37,573 and was ready to quit. It was not until 1878 that the London and River Plate could report a turn in the tide. As a result of operations that year £10,000 was put in the reserve and a dividend of 6½ per cent. was declared.

The buoyancy of Argentine production and exports saved the railways from the experience of the banks. More and more goods were flowing to the ports, and the reports of the railway directors might be describing another world to that inhabited by the bankers. Not a hint of depression is heard in the shareholders' meetings of 1874. In 1875 both the Southern and the Central reported increased traffic and increased revenues. In July the directors of the Southern decided to pay 10 per cent. and to put £350,000 into an extension of the line to Azul.[3] The lesser lines made a good showing in 1875. The Buenos Ayres and Ensenada paid 7 per cent. and put some money in the reserve. The stock of the Northern was at a premium, and the line had to claim only £2,071 from the Government on guarantee account in order to pay 7 per cent.[4] The Central Argentine paid 5½ per cent. out of its revenues and claimed £23,002 from the Government on guarantee account. The City of Buenos Ayres Tramways paid 9 per cent. In 1877 the editor of *Herapath's* attacked the 'bears' who had been blackguarding the Argentine on the Stock Exchange, and he accused *The Times* of deliberately endeavouring to drive down Argentine stocks and shares in order to enable its backers to buy advantageously into the Argentine Eldorado.[5]

Herapath's spoke a little too confidently. In 1877 the railways

[1] F.O. 6/345, A. E. Smithers, manager of the Bank of London and the River Plate, to Derby, 25 May 1876.
[2] *Bankers' Magazine*, xxxvii, 1877, p. 491.
[3] *Herapath's*, xxxvii, 1875, p. 456.
[4] Ibid. xxxvii, 1875, p. 528.
[5] Ibid. xxxix, 1877, p. 14.

began to feel the pinch. This was not so much in their revenue departments in the Argentine, but in their head office in London, where the conversion of receipts into sterling from depreciated paper presented a problem. Although the rate structure of the railways was flexible and the practice of changing the rates frequently was well established, it was not always possible to follow exactly the rise in the gold premium. The Southern paid 8 per cent. per annum for the first half of 1877, but the directors reported a loss of £7,632 on the exchange.[1] In the last half of 1877 floods as well as economic conditions affected the revenues of this line, and the dividend was reduced to 5 per cent.[2] The revenues of the Central fell £100,000.[3]

The year 1878 may be described as the depression year from the railways' point of view. Prices on the world market were falling, nature was unkind, and the continued rise in the gold premium made the conversion of receipts into sterling the occasion of loss. The Southern lost £22,000 on the exchange in the first half of 1878, and £42,900 during the year.[4] Dividends were cut to 6 per cent. for the year. The Government's debt to the East Argentine on guarantee account rose to over £100,000.[5]

The distress of 1878 was only momentary. Production increased in 1879 and 1880, and exports began to climb after the set-back of 1878. Monetary inflation began to operate favourably to the railways; costs were apparently not rising as rapidly as rates. Although losses on exchange were being sustained, working expenses were being cut drastically. In the last half of 1880 the Southern reported a loss of £48,076 on exchange but a reduction of working expenses, which had been above 50 per cent. in 1874, to 38·2 per cent. of total revenue. Even after the loss on exchange a dividend at the rate of 12 per cent. per annum was paid on the half-year.[6] In 1879 gross profits of the Southern were up 27·4 per cent. The directors authorized an investment of £340,000 in an extension of the line, and began laying steel rails.[7]

What of the public funds of Argentina, its provinces and its municipalities? The Argentine public revenues, particularly

---

[1] Ibid. xxxix, 1877, pp. 505, 518. [2] Ibid. xxxix, 1877, p. 1182.
[3] Ibid. xl, 1878, p. 59. [4] Ibid. xl, 1878, p. 1158.
[5] Ibid. xl, 1878, p. 677. [6] Ibid. xliii, 1881, p. 452.
[7] Ibid. xlii, 1880, pp. 461 and 1245.

those of the National Government, were susceptible in an unusual degree to the influence of a depression such as that experienced from 1874 to 1879. The principal source of revenue was still in the 1870's the same as it had been in the 1820's, namely, the customs house. Large imports made for buoyant revenues and optimistic policies of guaranteeing railways and making public investments; falling imports meant sharply contracting revenues. The sharp drop in imports in 1876 precipitated a crisis. Specie payments were suspended in June. The National Government could not pay the coupons for the last quarter of 1876 in gold, and the holders accepted paper pesos at the average rate for the quarter.[1] The next coupons due were paid in paper pesos at their June value. Individual protests were made but no concerted action was undertaken. It was revealed later that the interest on the public debt for 1876 was only paid by a short-term loan from Baring Brothers.[2] In order to save the credit of the nation the national and provincial financial resources had to be pooled by a series of inter-governmental loans, the Province of Buenos Aires lending to the National Government and the National Government to some of the poorer provinces in order to maintain the credit of the nation. Suggestions were made in the press (*Herapath's* argued that they were inspired by interested speculators) that sinking-fund payments should be suspended.

The cessation of Government borrowing and the increase in exports in 1877 and 1878 were favourable factors. The threat to the public funds began to disappear. Argentine 6 per cent. stock, which had fallen to 30 in 1877 under the pressure of rumour and the suspension of specie payments, began to climb once more on the exchange. Early in 1880 this stock stood at 90, and the Government was considering a refunding operation with a view to cutting interest to 5 per cent.[3] By 1881 the principal guaranteed railway accounts were settled.

Without wishing to labour the obvious, one is obliged to examine briefly the way in which economic maladjustment bred political tension between native and foreign elements. From 1874 to 1881 British banks and railway enterprises were under attack

[1] Corporation of Foreign Bondholders, *Seventeenth Annual Report*, 1889, p. 20.
[2] *Bankers' Magazine*, l, 1890, p. 1261.
[3] *Herapath's*, xlii, 1880, p. 110.

in the press and in Congress. Resentment was felt against foreign competition with native enterprise, high railway rates, and the payment of government guarantees to railways which provided poor service. The belief was cherished that native enterprise or government enterprise could do the job to the public satisfaction. The test came in 1876 when the Government of the Province of Santa Fé took direct action against the Bank of London and the River Plate, first suspending some of the charter rights of its branch in Rosario and finally closing the branch and jailing the manager.[1]

The background of the dispute about the Rosario branch of the Bank of London and the River Plate is interesting. In 1867 the Bank opened its branch in Rosario, the first banking establishment in Santa Fé Province with an extensive European connexion and a sterling capital. The business of the branch expanded as the city developed in its capacity of port and terminus of the Central Argentine Railway. In 1874 the Government of Santa Fé borrowed £300,000 in London, giving sterling bonds bearing 7 per cent. Part of this loan was used to finance the establishment of the *Banco Provincial* of Santa Fé. This bank was a joint-stock enterprise, but the Provincial Government was a major stockholder.

The year 1874 was a bad one in which to start a bank, particularly a bank sponsored by a Government and susceptible to political influence. Within a year the *Banco Provincial* began to experience a heavy drain on its specie reserves. In the winter of 1875 a large volume of its notes was presented for redemption as the liquidity preference began to develop strongly. Among those who presented a large volume of notes for payment was the Rosario branch of the Bank of London and the River Plate. At the same time the notes of the English Bank (as it was commonly called) remained acceptable to the general public. On 22 June 1875 the Provincial Government issued a decree suspending the English Bank's right of note issue.[2] The bank commenced a legal action for infringement of its charter, and

---

[1] Baster, *The International Banks*, pp. 131–7, presents a careful account of this episode, but Baster tends to emphasize the part played by gunboats and 'severe language' on the part of the British Minister and to neglect the strength of the Argentine political forces seeking a reasonable settlement.

[2] F.O. 6/345, G. E. Maschwitz, manager of the Bank of London and the River Plate, to L. Sackville West, H. B. M.'s Minister in Buenos Aires, 25 Nov. 1875.

took the precaution of applying to the British Government for assistance. The British Minister in Buenos Aires received the application, remarking that 'the interested parties are fully aware that no interference on the part of H.M. Government can be expected'.[1]

Early in 1876 it was clear that the Government of Santa Fé were anxious either to compel the Bank of London and the River Plate to help the *Banco Provincial* in its difficulties or to drive it out of the Province. The English bank was, curiously enough, a stockholder of the *Banco Provincial*, but it was refused the privilege of paying its taxes with dividend coupons of the *Banco Provincial*. In February 1876 the Federal Supreme Court declared that the Government of Sante Fé had acted within its constitutional right in denying the note-issuing privilege to the English bank, and that the London and River Plate had no case.

As winter was drawing on and heavy purchases outside the Province were being made, the *Banco Provincial* found itself in increasing difficulty. The granting of an exclusive note-issuing privilege to the *Banco Provincial* had back-fired. The public was turning towards the English bank because of its strength and its willingness to do business in gold on demand. The English bank threatened to engross the banking business of the Province.[2] This is not surprising. In a year like 1876 even the Mercantile Bank of the River Plate with a capital five times as great as the *Banco Provincial* of Santa Fé, and that in sterling, was in difficulties. On 19 May 1876 the Government of Santa Fé issued a decree ordering the Bank of London and the River Plate to liquidate its Rosario branch since 'it had become an institution ruinous to the public interests and hostile and dangerous, in the present circumstances, to the interior and exterior credit of the Province'. The commercial community in Rosario were put in a panic. A meeting was 'spontaneously' called in the Olimpo Theatre, and a petition urging the Government to withdraw the decree was drawn up. This was on a Saturday. On Sunday the provincial Finance Minister came to town from the provincial capital. A committee from the Olimpo Theatre meeting arranged for a meeting of the

[1] F.O. 6/345, Sackville West to the Foreign Office, 25 Nov. 1876.
[2] F.O. 6/345, Baron Holleben to the German Foreign Office, 26 May 1876.

Finance Minister, the directors of the *Banco Provincial*, and the
manager of the Bank of London and the River Plate. It was the
Finance Minister who applied pressure to the English bank. He
proposed that 'the London Bank should lend the Provincial
Bank the sum of $500,000 silver (say, £80,000 sterling) for a
period of six months, provided the Government at once revoked
the decree of the 19th instant which ordered the Bank to go
into liquidation'.[1] An alternative proposal was that the London
and River Plate should open a current account up to £90,000
sterling for the *Banco Provincial*. The manager of the Rosario
branch asked leave to consult the manager in Buenos Aires.

The next morning the *Jefe Politico* of Rosario presented himself at the offices of the English bank, stating that he was there
to liquidate the bank. The manager protested, but the doors
were closed and the books sealed. The next day the *Jefe Politico*
appeared again with a detachment of soldiers and demanded
that gold be deposited in the *Banco Provincial* up to the amount
of the notes in the tills of the London and River Plate. The
manager was arrested and the gold stocks of the branch were
removed. While this was happening the Buenos Aires office of
the bank forwarded £40,000 to Rosario, which it deposited
with the British Vice-Consul; but it refused to consider a loan
to the *Banco Provincial* until the gold seized by force was returned.

The Foreign Office heard of these events with indignation but
inaction. So did the German Foreign Office, for the manager in
Rosario was a German. The British chargé d'affaires in Buenos
Aires was told that the proceedings were unjust, but the
damage would have to be remedied by recourse to the Argentine Law Courts.[2] The chargé d'affaires, St. John, was no man
for legal obfuscation. He had already called for a gunboat from
Montevideo. As H.M.S. *Beacon* proceeded up the river to
Rosario, St. John and Dr. Quintana, the legal adviser of the
Bank of London and the River Plate, waited upon Dr. Irigoyen,
the Argentine Foreign Minister. St. John very tactfully left
it for Dr. Quintana to tell the Foreign Minister about the
gunboat.

Dr. Irigoyen hereupon turned to me and said he regretted I had
taken such a step, as the effect would be to render a settlement with

[1] F.O. 6/345, St. John to Derby, 1 June 1876.
[2] F.O. 6/345, Note of 1 June 1876.

the Provincial authorities more difficult. I at once explained to His Excellency that this step on my part was not a menace, but simply a measure of precaution taken in consequence of the representations which had been made to me by the London and River Plate Bank on the necessity for the same in view of apprehended disturbances and the convenience which would thus be afforded for the consignment to a safe place of a large amount of British property.[1]

Powerful forces beside gunboats were making for a solution. The press in Buenos Aires was by no means burned up with 'patriotism'. *La Nación* declared that it would be necessary 'to make echo in Europe' the protests of the nation against authorities which behaved in such a fashion.[2] Too many Argentine interests were by 1876 enmeshed in the process of development dependent upon foreign capital to welcome an exhibition of gaucho public finance. Prosperity had created a nation of boosters, and the *porteños* looked on the Governor of Santa Fé as Pierpont Morgan might have regarded William Jennings Bryan. At first Irigoyen, probably thinking about the gunboat, was either not available to the British chargé d'affaires or disposed to engage in abstruse legal speculation upon the fine point of whether a joint-stock company, not being an individual, could legitimately be a subject of diplomatic protection.[3] In July George Drabble, the chairman of the board of the Bank of London and the River Plate, arrived in Buenos Aires. This had a solvent effect.

It is not impossible [St. John informed the Foreign Office] ... that the arrival of Mr. Drabble who in the midst of the general monetary crisis in this country is looked upon as the harbinger of better times, may enable the National Government to exercise that influence upon an insolvent and recalcitrant province which the prospect of a money loan at such a moment is sure to give.[4]

In England the Law Officers of the Crown recommended strong and forceful action. The Earl of Derby kept calm. 'We need not resort to extreme measures till all others have failed',[5] he wrote on the margin of a dispatch. In Buenos Aires the chargé d'affaires hinted that right might not be entirely on one

[1] F.O. 6/345, St. John to Derby, 1 June 1876.
[2] *La Nación*, 6 June 1876.
[3] F.O. 6/345, St. John to Derby, 23 June 1876.
[4] F.O. 6/345, St. John to Derby, 14 July 1876.
[5] F.O. 6/345, St. John to Derby, 14 Aug. 1876.

side: 'I stated to Mr. Drabble that I much regretted the existence of the rumours that the English Bank had more than once gone out of its way to collect a large amount of Provincial notes for the purpose of suddenly presenting them for redemption, without any previous notice, to this rival and native establishment, which was known to be in difficulties.'[1]

Drabble more or less took over the negotiations. He saw his 'intimate friend' the Foreign Minister. He travelled to Santa Fé where he saw the local officials and conferred with Captain Dunlop of H.M.S. *Beacon*. Things began to mend. The criminal charges against the manager of the Rosario branch were dismissed by a local judge. St. John visited Dr. Irigoyen and suggested to him that the commercial dislocation in Rosario had so reduced traffic on the Central Argentine Railway that the National Government would probably have to pay the Railway as much as £100,000 on guarantee account. This affected Irigoyen as a gunboat could not. He telegraphed the Governor of Santa Fé urging him to settle the matter.[2] The Province of Buenos Aires lent the National Government £110,000 and the National Government lent the Santa Fé Government £25,000.[3] The Government of Santa Fé returned the bullion seized in May. Drabble agreed to forgo all claims for compensation in return for the right of the Bank of London and the River Plate to carry on banking operations in the Province of Santa Fé.[4] The bank's manager at Montevideo was sent to Rosario because he was a personal friend of the Governor of Santa Fé. At an evening party the chargé d'affaires saw the President of the Republic, Dr. Avellaneda, and the President of the Lower House of Congress. He pointed out to them that the English bank, were it allowed to operate in Rosario, would accept the notes of the *Banco Provincial* and would thus enhance their value. The President nodded, and turned to the Congressman saying, 'We must really settle this question'.[5] The decree of liquidation was revoked. For some months the Bank of London and the River Plate stood on its dignity asserting that not only a revocation of the decree was required, but a confirmation of their

[1] Ibid., St. John to Derby, 27 July, 1876.
[2] Ibid., St. John to Derby, 12 Sept. 1876.
[3] Ibid., St. John to Derby, 30 Aug. 1876.
[4] Ibid., St. John to the commander of H.M.S. *Beacon*, 11 Sept. 1876.
[5] Ibid. St. John to Derby, 19 Sept. 1876.

charter. But finally the branch at Rosario was reopened. H.M.S. *Beacon* was withdrawn in spite of the Rosario manager's desire that it should remain 'in view of the effect which a war vessel has on these people'.[1]

As prosperity returned tension died away. The chorus of cries for the expropriation of the Buenos Ayres Great Southern Railway continued unabated until the chairman of the board, Frank Parish, visited Buenos Aires in the later part of 1881. He went into conference with the provincial officials and emerged, not with an agreement for expropriation, but for an extension to Bahia Blanca. When the news was released 'there were three cheers on the Bolsa for the Governor and Mr. Parish'.[2] The shareholders of the East Argentine Railway adopted a resolution 'that in the opinion of this meeting, it is desirable that the directors should take immediate steps to record the protest of the company, not only in London but also in Paris and elsewhere, against the introduction or quotation of any new loan on behalf of the Argentine Confederation until the guarantee upon this company's capital has been discharged or satisfactorily arranged'.[3] But neither London nor Paris listened. Baring Brothers advanced £200,000 to the National Government to enable it to extend the *Oeste* to Pergamino,[4] and in Paris the Comptoir d'Escompte, the Banque de Paris et des Pays-Bas, and Messrs. Cohen and Company of Antwerp joined forces to lend the Argentine 12 million hard pesos.[5] Nobody sympathized with the holders of the 9 per cent. Argentine Treasury Bonds when the Argentine Government commenced to call them in and exchange them for cash or bonds at a lower rate of interest. The Foreign Office brushed them off with a promise to 'commend (these representations) unofficially to the favourable consideration of the Argentine Government'.[6]

The role of the Argentine political authorities in constructing the basis of recovery was not a passive one. Indeed, action in the political sphere was a factor of, perhaps, decisive

---

[1] F.O. 6/345, Drabble to St. John, 9 Sept. 1876.
[2] *South American Journal*, 13 Oct. 1881.
[3] Ibid., 6 Jan. 1881.
[4] Ibid., 12 May 1881.
[5] Ibid., 28 Apr. 1881.
[6] Tenterden to the Committee of 9 per cent. Bondholders, 25 Mar. 1882, printed in *South American Journal*, 30 Mar. 1882.

importance. Between 1878 and 1881 three lines of policy were carried to a successful conclusion, and these produced the greatest effect in the economic sphere. The first was the determined and successful action of the National Government in defeating the Indians and pushing the frontier beyond the Río Negro. Between 1820 and 1870 the Indians had stolen 11 million cattle, 2 million horses, 2 million sheep, killed 50,000 people, destroyed 3,000 houses, and stolen $20 millions' worth of property.[1] Both in the north and the south they had set effective limits to the use of land resources and to settlement. In 1872 Bahia Blanca was almost lost to the savages. In economic terms the Indian control of southern Buenos Aires Province and western and northern Santa Fé meant the preservation of a primitive form of production, and the siphoning off of primitive productive surpluses to Chile. In 1878–9 General Roca put an end to this situation. The *Salidas de Roca* penetrated deep into Indian territory, villages were destroyed, many of the young men and women were massacred, and the remainder were dispersed throughout society or driven into the distant wilds of farther Patagonia. The defeat of the Indians had a secondary effect of reducing to nothing the declining power of the gauchos in politics. In 1874 the British Consul reported that 'the wielder of the long knife and lasso has almost ceased to play a prominent part in the political history of the country, and the gaucho of the Pampas must needs give way before authority, supported by the disciplined soldier and his breech loading rifle'.[2] After the conquest of the Indians the gaucho became finally and for ever a picturesque farm labourer. Thus land and men were made available, and the frontier of enterprise was widened.

General Roca likewise played a significant role in the reorganization of the political life of the Republic, but not without provoking a civil war which for a space of weeks threatened to raise a number of perilous problems of diplomacy. At the time when Roca's Indian campaigns were drawing to a successful close, the term of Nicolás Avellaneda as constitutional President of the Republic was coming to an end. General Roca was closely identified with the régime of Avellaneda and a popular soldier of provincial origins who had helped to grant away

[1] *Parliamentary Papers*, 1872, lxx, p. 39.
[2] Ibid., 1876, lxxiii, p. 179.

large tracts of frontier lands to the friends of the Government.
To the provincial interests and the rural landed class he seemed
to be the logical man to carry on the policy of making available
for the development of the whole Republic the resources of the
rich Province of Buenos Aires. Furthermore, he commanded
the army, a factor of no small importance in winning elections. Early in 1880 it was clear beyond a doubt that as a result
of the elections to the Chamber of Deputies the representatives of all the provinces except Buenos Aires and Corrientes
would support Julio Roca when the Chamber met to elect a new
President.

The Province of Buenos Aires was determined to oppose by
all possible means the man who was regarded as responsible for
keeping part of the vast new frontier regions out of the hands of
the politicians of Buenos Aires. The Governor of Buenos Aires
Province, Carlos Tejedor, became a candidate for the Presidency. Knowing they could not win the 'election' in the
Chamber of Deputies, Tejedor's supporters began to arm in the
hope of intimidating the Chamber which met in Buenos Aires,
since the presidency of Mitre the capital both of the Republic
and the Province.

In May 1880 Argentine naval vessels stopped the Lamport
and Holt steamer *Plato* in the estuary of Río de la Plata, seized
it, and searched it for arms allegedly ordered by the Province of
Buenos Aires. Submarine cables brought the news to London
within a matter of hours, and questions were asked in the
House of Commons. Twenty years previously an incident of
this kind would have been settled on the spot and become a
matter of no account by the time the news reached London.
Now there was an outcry. Was British property being respected?
Egerton, the British Minister, wrote privately to the Foreign
Office warning them not to make too much of the incident.
'To bully this cocky little rising American Republic into
legality may be possible', he wrote, 'but is it the best policy?
You can't, and this is the truth of it—entirely protect the
property of British subjects in these countries; as regards per-
sonal safety—you can do a little more.'[1]

In spite of the seizure and release of European steamships,
arms were landed for the provincial forces. A great national

[1] F.O. 6/359, Egerton to the Foreign Office, 22 May 1880.

celebration in memory of Rivadavia and the return from France of San Martín's remains and their reburial in Buenos Aires failed to distract the political activists in Buenos Aires from their determination to intimidate the National Government and influence the election in favour of Tejedor. The national forces drew back when the police of Buenos Aires assembled to protect the landing of 5,000 Remington repeating rifles. This failure so frightened the deputies that they fled from the city.

Avellaneda was no soldier, but he was a man of courage and guile. He at once ordered the national forces in Buenos Aires, the Chamber, and the offices of the Government to withdraw to Belgrano outside the city. There, under the protection of the army of the Republic, Avellaneda decreed an intervention in the Province of Buenos Aires. In Buenos Aires the provincial guards were given repeating rifles, and clerks and working men began to drill under officers of the provincial militia. Out in the camp a deserter from the national army, Colonel Arias, began to raise a gaucho militia in the style of General Rosas. The customs houses were occupied by provincial officers. On 7 June Avellaneda replied to this move by proclaiming the blockade of Buenos Aires harbour, and the Argentine naval forces stood in the outer roads to stop all merchant vessels endeavouring to pass into the inner roads or to reach the docks at Boca or San Fernando. Only fighting could now settle the antagonism.

'Such, my Lord', wrote the British Minister, 'is the position to which a want of respect for legality on the part of the lawyer statesmen of this Republic has reduced its affairs.'[1]

The British were the most seriously affected of all foreign interests by this situation of blockade and the threatened destruction by military operations of much physical capital. Egerton, however, counselled no separate action by Britain nor threats or loud talk of any description. On the day of the proclamation of the blockade he and his French colleague, M. Rouvier, jointly went to the German Minister, and the three of them went out of the city to call upon the President. The next day a joint delegation made up of the Ministers of Germany, Brazil, Austria-Hungary, France, Spain, the United

[1] F.O. 6/360, Egerton to Granville, 4 June 1880.

States, and Britain presented themselves to Avellaneda, and he decreed ten days' grace to permit the unloading and loading of existing cargoes before the full blockade would go into effect.

On 10 June the Papal Delegate to the Republic invited the foreign representatives to meet at his house, as a result of which meeting 'a sort of committee [was set up] to act together in questions affecting the interests of their Subjects'.[1] Only the United States Minister refused to participate. Egerton declared that he was 'most anxious' to co-operate with the American representative but he was put off with the curious excuse that the American Minister did not speak French or Spanish.

Egerton observed that the British naval forces available in the River Plate were smaller than they had ever been, and that for the first time the Argentine Navy was superior to the European naval forces in the river and coastal waters of the Republic. The Argentine Navy could and would close Buenos Aires. Furthermore, the national forces held Buenos Aires in a vice on the landward side. Fresh from Indian campaigns and officered by men with the bitter experience of the Paraguayan War, they were superior both to the militia of Buenos Aires and the gaucho levies of Colonel Arias. They possessed artillery and disciplined cavalry. Likewise the navy in the outer roads possessed guns which could shell the city in a way which Popham or Hotham could never have done. There only remained the question of whether the superior forces of the National Government could be bribed.[2]

Here again the National Government demonstrated the changed relationship of forces. The feats of bribery executed twenty-seven years earlier when General Urquiza was driven from Buenos Aires in a storm of bills of exchange were not repeated, nor could they be. The National Government had had its hands on the customs too long for the Province of Buenos Aires to outbid its rivals. Their troops had been regularly paid. The officers clearly saw that the General, under whom they had fought serious engagements, for which the nation honoured them, was shortly to become President of the Republic.

[1] F.O. 6/360, Egerton to Granville, 11 June 1880.
[2] The rate offered was $1,000 per man and $2,000 per man with rifle. Ibid., Egerton to Granville, 14 June 1880.

Colonel Arias's force of gauchos penetrated through the siege lines of the National Government and entered Buenos Aires, but Arias was not Rosas and the gauchos were not what they were. Or, perhaps, they were; for they looted the meat markets of the city, depleted the food supplies, and spread terror in the streets. When the National forces advanced to seize the bridges over the Riachuelo giving access to the city the fighting fell to 'the provincial troops composed in great part of clerks and townspeople ill supplied with arms and ammunition [who showed] a self sacrifice and a quiet courage'. On the third Sunday and Monday in June there was heavy fighting on the perimeter of the city, and several thousand men fell—ten times as many as fell when Rosas was overthrown. The British Minister discerned something new politically in the struggle— something of the revolutionary fighting of sixty years ago in the past and something of Perónismo sixty years in the future. On one side he saw the trained troops of the Government; on the other 'ardent, earnest and educated young men'. 'This earnestness in fighting', Egerton told the Foreign Secretary, 'is perhaps a greater sign of true progress here (the word progress is never out of an Argentine mouth) than all their adoptions of foreign inventions.'[1]

As soon as the fighting had died away in the suburbs and National troops had secured the bridges, discussions were opened at the suggestion of the 'Trading Community' and the 'Diplomatic Body'. General Mitre emerged from retirement to take command of the forces of Buenos Aires. The Papal Delegate plied his trade as a mediator. The horses of Colonel Arias' force were dying in the streets for want of fodder while the negotiations went on. Governor Tejedor resigned from the Governorship of Buenos Aires. In October 1880 General Roca was installed as President of the Republic.

As a consequence of Roca's rise to authority a drastic settlement of the relationship between the Province of Buenos Aires and the rest of the Republic was dictated by the National Government. The city of Buenos Aires was separated from the Province, and the Province was given a new capital, La Plata, a metropolis as yet unbuilt and uninhabited. Buenos Aires city became the national capital and a federal territory. The debts

[1] F.O. 6/360, Egerton to Granville, 24 June 1880.

of the Province of Buenos Aires were taken over by the National Government, but it was allowed to keep its property, such as the *Oeste* railway and its unappropriated lands. This settlement, more or less dictated to the Province by force, ended the conflict between the Province and the nation as a whole and prepared the way for the modern antitheses of Argentine political life. Henceforth the financial resources of the whole Republic were indisputably controlled by the National Government, and the sovereign authority belonged to a single government residing in its own capital city—in fact as well as in law.

During the anxious month of June when gauchos roamed the streets of Buenos Aires and National gunboats were shelling the city, the pressure of the British business community upon the British Minister to protect British lives and property with armed force was very great. Egerton, however, refused to yield to this pressure or to act without the closest support and co-operation of other foreign missions in Buenos Aires. He reported his decision on this matter but he did not ask for instructions and did not seem to think he needed any. 'My opinion', he declared, 'is that Her Majesty's subjects who are domiciled in foreign states for their pleasure or for the purpose of earning a larger percentage of profit in business, are not exactly in the same category as British subjects at Ramsgate, Margate, Manchester, Sheffield or other pleasure or business resorts within Her Majesty's dominions, or on board vessels carrying the British flag.'[1] To ask for the assistance of the Royal Navy and to land marines would do far more harm than good, Egerton asserted, and would be 'illegal in the first instance and besides offensive to the national pride'. The German Minister sounded Egerton on one occasion about landing armed forces to protect foreign interests, but Egerton told him that only in the most extreme necessity would he agree to ask for twenty marines to be posted in the British Consulate and the offices of the Bank of London and the River Plate and then only if other foreign representatives agreed similarly to land marines from their own warships.[2]

The Foreign Office never questioned Egerton's policy. Indeed, the principal worry at the Foreign Office was the cost of

[1] F.O. 6/360, Egerton to Granville, 29 June 1880.
[2] Ibid.

Egerton's telegrams. A dispatch was addressed to him to ask why he had felt it necessary to write out the name and address of the Foreign Secretary in full when cabling him about Avellaneda's proclamation of a blockade, and he was instructed to inquire by what mode of reckoning the cable company had calculated £150 as the proper charge for a cypher cablegram from Buenos Aires to London.[1] The Foreign Office appears to have been so concerned with the economical principles of Gladstone that they had little time for contemplating the diplomatic principles of Castlereagh. In any event, the crisis passed so swiftly that no serious questioning of policy was provoked. Egerton closed the incident by explaining the cost of his cables and by sending a gunboat to Rosario to put heart into the British subjects residing there.[2]

By the end of 1880 there were more heartening things for British subjects in Rosario than gunboats, and in fact everywhere in the Republic. Recovery was in full swing. As soon as the fighting in the suburbs of Buenos Aires was over, the gold premium began to decline. Railway profits began to soar. One Liverpool firm bought an estancia of 72 square leagues in December 1880, broke up the whole into sheep farms, and resold them for £72,000 within four months making roughly 350 per cent. per annum on their money. 'This transaction goes to show', wrote the editor of *The South American Journal*, 'that we have been guilty of no exaggeration in asserting, as we have done so frequently, that no country in the world offers greater advantages to foreign capital than the Argentine Republic.'[3] Out on the camp fences were going up in every direction as a means of converting the open range into sheep farms or into wheat or corn fields. British manufacturers were selling the wire fencing—of 9,688,574 kilogrammes of fencing imported in 1880, 6,205,574 kilogrammes came from Britain and 2,160,945 from Belgium.[4] Immigrants were pouring into the River Plate from Italy and Spain: more than 6,000 a month in the early part of 1881.

Part of the explanation of this recovery centres around the

[1] F.O. 6/360, numerous minutes and dispatches, June and July 1880.
[2] Ibid., Egerton to Granville, 1 Aug. 1880.
[3] *South American Journal*, 14 Apr. 1881.
[4] *Parliamentary Papers*, 1881, lxxxix, Report of Mr. Egerton on the Navigation and Commerce of the Argentine Republic, p. 111.

preservation of political stability, both domestic and international. During five difficult years from 1875 to 1879 disruptive
forces had emerged, some characteristic of the old Argentina
now passing away, some foreshadowing the Argentina of the
future, but none had proved strong enough seriously to challenge the ruling landed interest, and that interest in its turn was
determined to maintain cordial relations with the investing and
business class of Europe and particularly Great Britain. Both
the tone of the press and the action of the Government in the
matter of the Rosario branch of the Bank of London and the
River Plate had demonstrated that, whatever the differences
between Argentine interests and foreign enterprise might be,
the Argentine interests wanted to maintain the flow of capital
into the country from abroad.

It must be noted, too, that Britain helped also to preserve
political stability by keeping the temperature of international
intercourse between the River Plate and Europe low. Britain
pressed nothing upon Argentina, and, indeed, discouraged
enterprises like immigration which might involve Great Britain
too much, knowing that it has always been easier, in spite of
certain popular beliefs to the contrary, to involve the British
Government in political expansion on account of people than
on account of property and money.

More of the explanation of the recovery which came in 1880
and 1881 can be found in the character of the Argentine
economy itself. A fluid and highly competitive economy characterized by a low level of fixed capital in the units of production
(at this stage even in the railways) made rapid adjustment to
price changes possible. The absence of all organization among
labour, the rapid influx of immigrants from the low-wage areas
of Europe, the relatively small demand in an agricultural and
pastoral economy for workers with industrial skills, and the
existence of a paper currency were all factors contributing to
keeping the wages bill low. The frontier, expanding rapidly as
railways branched out, tended to keep land prices low relatively
to their productivity, in spite of great capital gains from land
speculation. Technological innovation not only in transport but
also in the agricultural and pastoral industries was a price-
reducing factor. Thus, Argentina was able to increase production and increase gross receipts in a period when prices were

declining. In these circumstances a renewal of capital investment was possible. Such an opportunity came at a very fortunate time for Great Britain, for such investment helped to improve sales of British industrial products while at the same time stimulating a flow of cheap industrial raw materials and some cheap food into the markets of Europe.

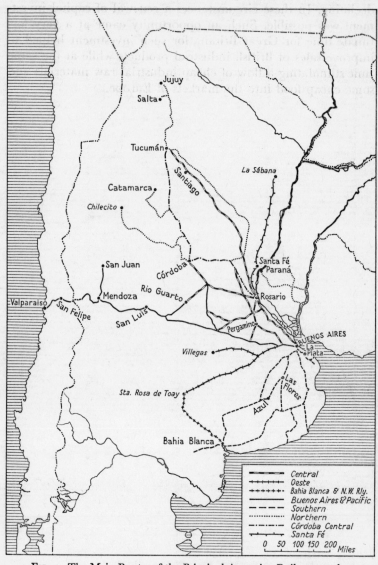

	Central
	Oeste
	Bahia Blanca & N.W. Rly.
	Buenos Aires & Pacific
	Southern
	Northern
	Córdoba Central
	Santa Fé

0 50 100 150 200 Miles

FIG. 4. The Main Routes of the Principal Argentine Railways at the
end of the Nineteenth Century.

XIII

A DECADE OF RAPID EXPANSION

ONCE recovery set in with the passing of civil conflict during the winter (June–July) of 1880, Argentina embarked upon a decade in which economic expansion accelerated so greatly that its culmination and collapse in 1890–1 shook the financial world of London to its foundations. In terms of gross capital investment the 1880's exceeded all other decades as far as Britain was concerned. Before the inauguration of President Roca the British investment in joint-stock enterprise in Argentina amounted to a sum in the neighbourhood of £25 millions. By 1885 this sum had increased to £45 millions.[1] When the Baring Crisis came to a head in 1890 the British investment was something like £150 millions. Some observers placed the investment much higher: the Commercial Secretary to the British Legation in Buenos Aires at a figure in excess of £200 millions[2] and the President of the Republic at something like £250 millions. Even if we reject figures like £200 millions (and there are strong reasons for doing so) and keep to the lowest estimate which careful calculation will permit, the British investment during the 1880's expanded at a rate astonishing by the standards of that age and greater than during any subsequent decade. The year 1889 was, indeed, an *annus mirabilis* when Argentina absorbed between 40 and 50 per cent. of all British funds invested outside the United Kingdom.

While this large expansion of investment was under way, a number of changes were taking place in its character. The wish for security still dominated the minds of a substantial part of the British investing public, but notions of what constituted security were being revised. By 1890 a much smaller percentage of British investments were in stocks of the Argentine Govern-

[1] *The Economist*, 23 Jan. 1886, p. 105, estimated £45,602,000 as the book value and the market value at £45,997,000.
[2] Herbert in *Parliamentary Papers*, 1892, lxxxi, pp. 92–93.

ments, national, provincial and municipal, and a smaller percentage were likewise in enterprises whose profits were guaranteed by the state. The percentage of investment in Government stocks during the eighties fell from something near 50 per cent. to about 30 per cent. In spite of the frequent public discussion of the railway guarantees and the abuses of the guarantee system about 28 per cent. of British investment in railways was in lines which had abandoned guarantee agreements. On the other hand, a new field for the fixed-interest investor seeking security rather than high profits or capital gains was opened up in the form of railway debentures.

If the quest for security in investment still dominated an important portion of the investment public, a speculative spirit also began to manifest itself. Every new enterprise financed by share capital was, of course, speculative, and the quest for capital gains through land and property deals increased, but these were established modes of speculative investment. The new medium was *cédulas*. It probably never will be possible to calculate with any exactness the gross amount invested by the British public in these land-mortgage bonds during this period, but there is sufficient evidence to suggest that by 1890 considerably more money was invested in *cédulas* than in urban utilities and public services or in industrial enterprises or in banking.

The greatly increased volume and the changing pattern of investment did little to change the character of the Argentine economy. The Argentine economy grew in strength and weight as a child grows before puberty, but the range of its activities changed very little. The years before the Baring Crisis are less interesting from the point of view of volume and variety of Argentine work and production than the years after. Whatever the form of investment, the physical capital which grew most and had the most effect during the eighties was railway plant. Investment in land-mortgage bonds was of some assistance, however, to the transformation of land use from pastoral to agricultural production. The emphasis must be placed on the word *some*, because the proceeds of land-mortgage bonds could be, and frequently were, used to finance simple land speculation, to provide consumer goods (such as palaces on the pampas and in Paris) for landowners, and the construction of urban housing, warehouses, and shop space. Although meat-freezing plants were in the experimental stage in the 1880's and the production of electrical power and telephone services were projected, these new fields of production did not add significantly to the volume and variety of Argentine production before the Baring Crisis. The great expansion of food cereals and flax-seed production and the increased timber harvesting of the 1880's contributed more to domestic consumption than to the international markets. In short, capital investment tended to run ahead of productive capacity in the 1880's.

A large-scale flow of investment, like other great social processes, seems always to require some great, galvanic public pronouncement or political *démarche* to set it in motion. The great first flow of capital which began in the 1860's and ended in 1875 had followed the victory of General Mitre and his laws concerning railway guarantees and public-debt payments in sterling. Avellaneda's victory over Buenos Aires and General Roca's inauguration in November 1880, followed by his currency reforms initiated in 1881 and brought to completion in 1883, constituted the stimulus of the 1880's: the symbolic confession and declaration which prepares communities of men for action along a particular line. The significance of the victory over Buenos Aires is easy enough to understand, for it simply meant social peace for an indeterminate period of time and the possibility of mobilizing the whole resources of the Argentine community for the policy of borrowing and guaranteeing capital. The monetary reforms are less easy to understand. President Roca regarded them as second only to his Indian campaigns as a civilizing act capable of changing the destiny of his country. He once declared that he would rather sell Government House than decree a *curso forzoso*. In fact, his attempt to establish a currency freely convertible into gold or silver lasted only eighteen months, and from the very moment of its inauguration the notes of the National Bank were at a discount of 3 per cent. in terms of the gold coins in circulation.[1] Many of the principal supporters of the régime were opposed to a hard currency and became increasingly so as the sale of *cédulas* increased. Admittedly, the reforms removed the commercial inconvenience of a multiple currency and a variety of foreign coinage in circulation, but it is difficult to see any

[1] *South American Journal*, 1 Mar. 1883.

overwhelming advantage to the domestic economy of the Republic in the reforms. Their main point seems to have been the confidence which they inspired in European investors that some disciplinary agency existed in Argentina which could ensure long-term stability and a clearly discernible horizon of expectations. All this is rather metaphysical, but the metaphysics of investment is not without its significance.

The expansion of the 1880's was no smooth process characterized by a steady and increasing flow of funds. The decade divides itself into two halves, split by the crisis year of 1885-6. The first half may be conveniently referred to as the currency-reform period; the second half as the controlled-investment period. The terms are scandalous misnomers. The currency reforms failed in the first period and the control of investments broke down completely in the second. But the terms are properly applied because they represent what the leading actors in the drama sought to do in the presence of forces which they could not control and in their heart of hearts, perhaps, did not wish to control.

The first period of expansion began cautiously in 1880 in the form of extensions by already existing railways. At the time of Roca's inauguration late that year the editor of the leading British railway journal, *Herapath's*, referred to the belief that 'there are £200,000,000 burning in Mr. John Bull's inexhaustible pockets, and waiting to be employed in enterprises of some kind, good, bad and indifferent'.[1] By 1882 some of this inexhaustible fund was flowing strongly to the River Plate. The effect on Argentine trade was immediate. In 1880 the value of Argentine exports was nearly 13 million hard pesos in excess of imports. In 1881 the excess dropped to 2 million and by the end of 1882 a deficit on commodity account had emerged which grew steadily larger until the Baring Crisis supervened.[2] The pace of development began to act as a brake upon exports. Population was expanding rapidly as immigrants flowed in, and the internal market was expanding so rapidly that cereal production could hardly keep pace with domestic needs.[3] In 1881 and 1882 no Argentine wheat entered the British market,

---

[1] *Herapath's*, xlii, 1880, p. 1026.
[2] See Table 1 in Appendix.
[3] *South American Journal*, 1 Sept. 1881.

although in 1882 maize sales reached the highest figure yet attained. Simultaneously British iron and steel exports to Argentina began to expand rapidly, and volume was expanding much more rapidly than total receipts from sales.[1] It is possible to suppose from these figures that physical equipment—railways, wire fences, threshing machines, and steel ploughs—was expanding more rapidly than the claims and even expectations of the owners of capital, but, even if the prices of capital equipment were falling relatively to the price of the products of this equipment, this advantage was still insufficient to avert the crisis whose first signs manifest themselves in September 1884.

During the years 1883 and 1884 the gap between Argentine commodity exports and imports widened enormously by the standards of previous experience, even though exports were growing in volume. Part of this widening of the gap may be attributed to a decline in price of exports,[2] but mainly it arose from the investments of capital taking place and the heavy purchases of capital equipment which the investment made possible. So long as Europeans continued to invest and thus make available credits or gold to cover the gap between Argentine income from produce sales and Argentine outlays on foreign manufactures, services, and other requirements, the process could continue. In 1884 something happened, however, to dry up the supply of gold or its equivalent, and the *Banco Provincial de Buenos Aires* was obliged to suspend specie payments in September. President Roca tried hard to maintain the convertibility of the notes of the National Bank, but in January 1885 he was obliged to decree a suspension of convertibility for two years.

A crisis of this kind invites theorizing, but the invitation must be declined in favour of recording what the participants in the situation thought was happening. Their thoughts provided the basis of the decisions made and the actions taken to resolve the crisis. For this reason opinion was perhaps as important as the impersonal forces which a theory may teach us to suppose existed.

One contemporary view attributed the crisis to the floods of

---

[1] See Table 2 in Appendix.
[2] A. G. Ford, 'Export Price Indices for the Argentine Republic, 1881–1914', *Inter-American Economic Affairs*, vol. ix, no. 2, autumn 1955.

1884, to the decline in the demand for the dried and salted
beef, and to the diversion of cattle ordinarily available for
export to the stocking of frontier lands.[1] It was also charged
that inadequacy of rolling stock on the Central Argentine Railway was hampering production for export.[2] Taken together,
these observations suggested that the expansion of production
for export was not so great as it might have been, and that the
Argentine capacity to pay interest, profit, and depreciation was
approaching a point of exhaustion which was impairing the
confidence of the investing classes. Whether investors reasoned
in these terms or whether they were shaken by the immediate
symptom of distress presented by the suspension of specie payments by the *Banco Provincial de Buenos Aires*, they reacted adversely to an £8 millions loan by the National Government to
finance harbour and sanitary works in Buenos Aires. Less than
£3 millions was subscribed, and by the end of 1884 the agents
were unable to move the securities. A press campaign against
Argentine investments developed at this time. Labouchère in
particular had begun a campaign in 1883 in the pages of *Truth*,
and when the harbour public-works loans were proposed, he
denounced them as swindles, alleging that no real investment
proportionate to the outlay of the investors would take place.

The belief in a crisis in productivity and hence in the capacity
to pay was important, for it provoked measures designed to
restore confidence in the investing classes. Early in 1885 Dr.
Carlos Pellegrini, a former Minister of Finance, was sent to
Europe to make some arrangement to this end. Pellegrini was
a remarkable figure in Argentine public life. He was a kinsman
on his mother's side of John Bright, and he had been educated
at Harrow. Apart from a quick business sense and an intelligent
interest in the life of the community, Pellegrini little resembled
el viejo Quakero. While still a very young man he ran through the
considerable fortune which his father, an Italian immigrant
engineer, had made during the first wave of Argentine expansion in the 1860's. Having spent one fortune, Pellegrini made
another as quickly as he had lost its predecessor. A tall, attractive man, he was famous for his feats of gallantry, for his daring
as a gambler, for his love of horse racing, and for his skill as

[1] *South American Journal*, 24 Jan. 1885.
[2] *Herapath's*, xlvi, 1884, p. 263.

a political manipulator. His *Escritos y Discursos* contain many shrewd and sensitive observations about political and social problems in South America, Europe, and the United States, which call to mind the great intellectual figures of Argentine political life such as Moreno or Sarmiento. But Pellegrini was, perhaps, too intelligent and too variable for continuous success as a political leader, and his record is that of a brilliant substitute player—an interim Finance Minister, an interim diplomat, and finally an interim President.

The loan agreement which Pellegrini made with the European bankers had the character of a treaty. The introductory clauses of the agreement are in the language of international law:

Dr. Carlos Pellegrini, representative of the Argentine Government with full powers on the one hand [here follows the document of the Argentine Government conferring full powers on its commissioner] and the Banque de Paris et des Pays-Bas, the Comptoir d'Escompte de Paris, Messrs. A. and B. Cohen d'Anvers, the Société Générale de Commerce et Industrie, Messrs. Baring Bros. & Co., and J. S. Morgan & Co., as the others agree . . . .[1]

What he agreed to is simple enough. In return for a loan of £8,400,000 he gave the bankers a first mortgage on the customs houses, and promised that the Argentine Government would not borrow any more money without the consent of the bankers. The Argentine Government undertook to allocate daily a portion of the customs house revenues sufficient to pay the interest and sinking-fund charges on the loan. Monthly the accumulated sums were to be paid into the Banque de Paris et des Pays-Bas in sterling. The Argentine Government agreed to establish a legal domicile in the Argentine legation in Paris. In return the bankers promised to float a loan of £8,400,000 at 5 per cent. guaranteeing the borrowers 75, and 55 per cent. of everything over 75, less a commission of 2½ per cent. and all legal and advertising costs.

Pellegrini's agreement encountered the most strenuous opposition in Buenos Aires. The repudiation of Pellegrini would surely have won the approval of Congress and part of the press. Roca wanted further capital investment, however, and so did his supporters. In November 1885 the agreement was ratified,

[1] The agreement was printed in the *South American Journal*, 6 Feb. 1886.

and money for harbour works and sanitary systems began to flow once more. As a means of stimulating a renewed flow of capital there is probably something to be said for the Pellegrini agreement. As a means of introducing some government into the investment process it can only be described as a total failure. It was designed to put some check upon borrowing by the National Government, but it could not operate to influence borrowing by the Argentine provinces or by private enterprises. Some of the parties to the agreement, such as Baring Brothers, actually floated large loans to provincial Governments without any consideration for the principle of making investment depend upon an estimation by professional bankers of capacity to pay. By comparison with the Pellegrini agreement the Roca monetary reforms were a far more honest and effective method of economic discipline, for under their operation there at least existed a mechanism, in the convertibility requirement, for registering before the public eye the evidence that the sales of output were or were not meeting the costs of inputs. The Pellegrini agreement, on the other hand, left the impression with the public that the investment process was under the supervision of institutions which understood the investment process and its necessities, whereas in fact it was not a general scheme for control at all, but simply a means of ensuring a narrow group of bankers and their clients a first claim on the public revenues of the Argentine Republic.

The Pellegrini agreement was only one of a number of agreements made during 1885 which restarted and then accelerated the investment process. From 1883 to 1885 an undeclared war between the Central Argentine Railway and the National Government was in progress, which impeded the flow of freight and at the same time stopped all further investments of capital in this important arterial route across the northern pampas. The reason for the trouble was the guarantee clauses of the contract under which the railway had been originally built. The prosperity of the early 1880's together with a number of extensions had pushed up the earnings of the Central to the point where the Government could begin to reclaim the payments which it had made in previous years in order to bring the profits of the Central up to the guaranteed level of 7 per cent. In 1882 the Central paid the shareholders 6 per cent., but the directors could have paid 12 per cent. had they not been obliged to meet the Government's claims under the guarantee clauses.[1] With the hard selfishness which always seemed to distinguish the Central's directors they determined to break the guarantee agreement and secure complete control of their income, and also to enlarge their freedom in fixing rates.

The Argentine Government undoubtedly had a case against the Central, and so did the public who used the line. The generous land subsidy given with the original concession had been turned over to another company for a meagre sum. This company was now paying 15 per cent. per annum.[2] During the hard years the Argentine Government had not only paid under the guarantee clauses but had bought large blocks of stock on which it had claimed no dividend. An elementary sense of justice would have suggested that with the advent of prosperity and a good revenue the Argentine Government should be reimbursed or at least that surpluses should be reinvested in equipment capable of providing a good, cheap service for the public. The directors of the Central, unlike the directors of the Southern, were determined neither to do justice nor to provide good service.

The demand for expropriation was loud. It must be stated, however, that Argentine opinion was divided on this question. Certain doctrinaire liberals were opposed to all forms of public ownership on the ground that public and political bodies could not operate public utilities efficiently. These doctrinaires were always careful not to mention the *Oeste*, which was successful both financially and as a public service, but they always called attention to the *Entreriano*, which proved their point. More important than the doctrinaires, however, was the large body of business and landed men whose views found expression in newspapers like *La Nación*. These men believed that no action should ever be taken which might impede the flow of capital from abroad. Giving railway directors a free hand was like paying the interest on bonded indebtedness—not a moral obligation or necessarily the most efficient way of doing business, but simply a condition for sustaining a flow of funds for investment purposes. Expropriation, like repudiation, would dry up the flow of

[1] *Herapath's*, xlv, 1883, p. 782.
[2] Ibid., p. 698.

capital, and these interests were not convinced that the Argentine community could itself do the job which foreign capital was doing. It must be borne in mind that the decisive local opinion was that of the commercial and landed class which benefited from appreciating land values and the increased flow of goods to and from the international markets. They may have had the resources to finance railways and buy government bonds, but neither railways nor public securities were profitable enough to attract the attention of these men who possessed the effective economic and political power in Argentina itself.

The directors of the Central judged the circumstances of the moment ruthlessly and correctly. Early in 1885 their pressure yielded results. The Government agreed to settle all outstanding claims under the guarantee clauses for a payment of £283,000, to abolish the guarantee system, to give the company a free hand in fixing passenger and freight rates so long as dividends did not exceed 12 per cent., and to permit the calculation of dividends from working expenses, fixed at 50 per cent. of gross receipts. The company for its part agreed to increase its capital by £2 millions. In this way the investing public were encouraged to hope for 12 per cent. rather than to believe in a guaranteed 7 per cent.

While the way was thus being opened for large new investment in an already established railway network, a new investment opportunity was being created by the reorganization of the Campaña Railway Company.[1] Under the direction of George Drabble, who took over the chairmanship of the reorganized company, it was decided to build from Buenos Aires to Rosario and to branch out from there. The capital was doubled. Drabble's first aim was to transform the most highly capitalized railway line in the country (£18,000 a mile) into a company with a much lower capital per mile by the device of building a low-cost extension to Rosario. His second aim was to occupy the strategic position between Buenos Aires and the northern pampas.

In addition to the integration and extension of existing lines and the linking up of the centres of population along the littoral a bold plan for crossing the Andes was beginning to take shape. In 1882 the Buenos Ayres and Pacific Railway Company was

[1] Renamed the Buenos Ayres and Rosario.

formed in London. The very magnitude of the plan seems at first to have frightened the investors, but when a modest capital of £1 million was proposed with the object of constructing a commercially feasible line from Mercedes on the *Oeste* railway through hitherto unserved territory to a point in San Luis Province, the investing public responded with more enthusiasm. By 1885 this project, too, was absorbing capital in increasing amounts.

There was nothing accidental about the creation of these new investment opportunities.[1] The demand for railway service was there. Agricultural prices might be falling, but Argentine producers were operating under conditions of decreasing costs, and were revealing a capacity to absorb price falls by expanding production. The Central had already used the pressing demand for railway service as a lever against the Government. Drabble and his Rosario Company planned to transform a highly capitalized, small suburban railway by meeting that same demand for quick, cheap transport to tidewater and hence to world markets for wool and cereals. While it is not perhaps possible to demonstrate the fact statistically, there are strong reasons for supposing that in 1885 a million pounds invested in railway plant in Argentina contributed to the production of more saleable commodities than a million pounds invested anywhere else in the world at that moment in history.

A favourable factor, too, in the opportunities of the Argentine economy at this time was the decline in ocean freight rates taking place as a result of technical improvements in the construction and working of ocean-going vessels, particularly steam-driven vessels of steel construction. The price of new tonnage fell in 1885 to what was regarded as a new low of £7–8 per ton for iron and £7. 15s.–£9 per ton for steel ships.[2] Rates to and from River Plate ports were not yet quoted in London, but grain rates from American, Canadian, and Russian ports were very low in 1885 and 1886 compared with previous years. This fall in ocean grain-freight rates came just

[1] As A. K. Cairncross suggests, *Home and Foreign Investment, 1870–1913* (Cambridge, 1953), p. 194.

[2] E. A. V. Angier, *Fifty Years of Freights, 1869–1919* (London, 1920), p. 64. See also G. S. Graham, 'The Ascendancy of the Sailing Ship, 1850–85', *Economic History Review*, 2nd series, vol. ix, no. 1, 1956, for an account of the revolution in shipping.

at the moment when Argentine grain exports were beginning to grow rapidly.

If we wish to grasp why an almost fanatical enthusiasm in Britain for Argentina infected the investing classes with growing intensity between 1886 and 1889 we must keep in mind these favourable commercial facts. The outlook for investors in other parts of the world might be bleak, but there was a glow in the southern hemisphere which was not just a mirage. Investment was leading to production and production to sales, which, in 1886, 1887, and 1888, were sufficient in the receipts they yielded to cover outlays on capital and wages and to provide a surplus attractive to investors and speculators. A happy conjunction of factors, some technological, some commercial, some relating to the character of resources, and all of them real, provided the solid foundation for what in the end became wanton fancies.

The year 1886 started poorly. There was an epidemic of suicides in commercial circles in Buenos Aires in January 1886.[1] The polvillo, a blight affecting locally grown seed, struck the flax crop. But investors were confident. *The Economist*, looking at the whole South American investment picture, estimated British investments in Argentina at £45,602,000 of authorized capital and £45,997,000[2] market value. It is doubtful whether so fine a calculation can be made, but there is no doubt that joint-stock enterprises in Argentina were favourably regarded. The shares and debentures of Argentine railway companies were nearly £4 millions above their par value. The great increases in traffic on the Central Argentine owing to the rapid expansion of acreage under wheat, flax, and maize had pushed Central Argentine ordinary shares to 168–170 by the end of 1885.[3] Of nineteen Anglo-Argentine railways quoted on the London Stock Exchange only three were quoted at a discount when the year 1886 opened. Profits were good even though heavy losses were being made on exchange owing to the suspension of convertibility and to the premium on gold. The Central Argentine paid 10 per cent. in 1885 in spite of losing £80,000 on exchange. The Central Argentine Land Company paid 15 per cent.; the London and River Plate Bank, 11 per cent.; City of Buenos

---

[1] *South American Journal*, 7 Jan. 1886.
[2] *The Economist*, 23 Jan. 1886, p. 105.
[3] *Herapath's*, xlvii, 1885, p. 1076.

Ayres Tramways, 10 per cent. Even the pitiful East Argentine, whose trains never ran on time and whose locomotives had to pause for breath, was beginning to show faint signs of profitability independent of the government guarantee.

Something like 65–70 per cent. of all British capital invested in Argentina during the four boom years 1886–9 was employed to finance railways directly through the joint-stock companies or indirectly through the medium of government borrowing. The acts of investment and the growth of the capital claims (e.g. interest on government stocks or railway debentures and guaranteed shares) preceded by something like two years the physical growth of the railways themselves and by something like four years the effective use of the railways. During the period of heavy investment the total mileage of railways in the Republic grew from approximately 2,800 miles at the end of 1885 to 4,783 miles at the end of 1889. During the peak year of capital movement, 1889, the physical increase in mileage was only 364 miles, but after new investment had virtually ceased in 1890 the mileage of working railway increased from 4,783 miles at the end of 1889 to 7,270 at the end of 1891 and 8,376 at the end of 1893. In 1885 the railways carried 4,145,117 tons of freight. In 1886, 1888, and 1889 they actually carried less than this amount and it was not until 1892 that freight traffic was significantly (28 per cent.) above the level of 1885. In 1893 it was 52 per cent. above 1885, and thereafter continued to grow.[1] Passenger traffic, however, grew faster than mileage, but varied according to economic and financial condition, declining noticeably when the boom exploded.

The fact that investment growth preceded physical and productive growth by a considerable space of time helps to explain in part the sudden arrest of the flow of capital which precipitated the Baring Crisis in 1890.[2] But other factors leading towards difficulty began to emerge as the pace of investment quickened. These were political, and they had serious economic consequences.

In 1886 the term of General Roca as constitutional President

[1] Calculated from *Parliamentary Papers*, Foreign Office, Diplomatic and Consular Reports on Trade and Finance, Argentine Republic, Report for the year 1894, No. 1495, C. 7581–35, p. 39.

[2] A. G. Ford, 'Argentina and the Baring Crisis of 1890', *Oxford Economic Papers*, N.S., viii, no. 2, 1956, develops this argument in precise detail.

of the Republic came to an end. He was succeeded by a kinsman, Dr. Miguel Juárez Celman, a liberal lawyer of Córdoba.
Like Roca, Celman was the nominee and agent of the landed
interest, and particularly of the provincial landed class in the
poorer sub-Andean provinces of the west and north-west. His
warmest supporters, or rather managers, were those most determined to use the credit and the resources of the state to
build railways into the interior. A policy which, under the
direction of Mitre and Sarmiento and even under Roca, had
been rationally conceived as a measure for uniting politically
and developing economically the Argentine community became under Juárez Celman an excuse for authorizing railway
building wherever the friends of the administration wanted
them built. As a result Argentina rapidly became a railway
inferno where no fewer than twenty-one private railway companies and three state railways were struggling for the business
of approximately 4 million people. The struggle might have
had some beneficent consequences if the railway companies had
seriously fought for the right to provide service, but too often
they neglected investment in such elementary essentials as
locomotives and goods wagons in favour of miles of line laid
down either to keep out a rival company or to get a guaranteed
profit from a Government anxious to please its friends by promoting railways into areas where those friends had land.[1] It is
not possible to argue that too much was invested in railways *in
the long run*, for Argentina more than doubled its mileage during
the next twenty years and made profitable use of it; but, in
relation to existing need and in relation to labour supplies, the
productivity of farms, and the return on the produce of the
nation *at that time*, too many miles of railway were being undertaken in response to the stimulus offered by the Government or
in response to the competitive necessity for existing lines of
keeping open access to the new frontiers of settlement.

A high proportion of the British capital invested in private
railway companies at this time went into non-guaranteed enterprises like the Southern, the Central, and the Buenos Ayres and

[1] It was reported in the *South American Journal*, 27 Nov. 1886, that land values in
parts of Corrientes rose over 200 per cent. in a month following the granting of the
Buenos Aires and Valparaiso railway concession to the British railway contractor,
J. D. Clark.

Rosario. Although this investment was not directly a response
to the Government's policy of guaranteeing dividends, it was in
many instances an indirect response. As a result of a Government guarantee two companies were launched to build railways
from Bahia Blanca across the Province of Buenos Aires. Although
the directors of the Southern were faced with expenses amounting more rapidly than revenue, they decided in 1889 to do
nothing less than double their mileage in order to meet this
competition and anticipate the local pressure for new extensions.[1] The establishment of new companies like the Buenos
Ayres and Pacific and the Córdoba Central provoked the older
companies not only to build extensions but to think about ways
and means of sealing off access to Buenos Aires and Rosario.

This seemed to spell amalgamation. When Drabble launched
the Buenos Ayres and Rosario it was popularly supposed that
he planned eventually to effect an amalgamation of that line
with the Central, in which he was a shareholder—at one time
the largest single shareholder, having bought the 17,000 shares
held by the Argentine Government. It was even supposed that
the Central, the Buenos Ayres and Rosario, and the Southern
might eventually form one system. Frank Parish, the chairman
of the Southern, was a member of the boards of the Buenos
Ayres and Rosario and of the Central. In his view[2] the old-
established companies could do nothing to stop the building of
competitive lines either by new companies or by the Government. For this reason they were obliged to consider temporary
sacrifices in order to consolidate their position and avoid
antagonizing the Government or public opinion. Judging from
his policies as chairman of the Southern, sacrifice meant reductions in freight and passenger rates, the building of extensions,
and the amalgamation of existing lines to cut overheads. He
and his fellow directors were criticized by the shareholders for
not declaring bigger dividends, but he held to this policy, with
the result that Southern shares were quoted below Central
Argentine shares from 1884 to 1889. In 1885–6 Parish seems to
have been working hard at the first step towards amalgamation,
i.e. the union of the Central and the Buenos Ayres and Rosario.

[1] *Herapath's*, li, 1889, p. 1070.
[2] Stated in his letter of resignation from the Board of the Central Argentine,
printed in *South American Journal*, 23 July 1887.

No evidence is at present available to reveal what conceptions of interest or personal animosities caused the endeavours of Parish to fail. The directors of the Central refused to come to terms with the Buenos Ayres and Rosario. Parish resigned from the Central's board in 1887, and the chairman of the Central accepted the resignation with scant courtesy. The Buenos Ayres and Rosario decided to build into the north-west towards Tucumán. The Central pushed an extension south to Pergamino on the *Oeste* line, running into Buenos Aires. Their next step consisted of a deal with the Northern of Buenos Ayres, which possessed those lines into the central part of Buenos Aires over which the trains of the *Oeste* ran into the city. Northern shares had seldom returned more than 2 or 3 per cent. and the company was grossly over-capitalized. As a result of the deal with the Central the Northern shareholders were guaranteed 12 per cent. in gold, and Northern shares, which were quoted at less than 6 per cent. of their issue price in 1880, rose to a point 140 per cent. above that price. One of the Central shareholders protested against the directors' policy, arguing that the Central should improve its services and cut its charges instead of engaging in railway warfare. The chairman replied: 'The question you have to consider is what sum it is worth our while to give in order to get possession of the neck of the bottle leading into the Central Station at Buenos Aires.'[1]

Virile realism of this kind may have won the hearts of the shareholders in London, but it was spreading dismay in Argentina. In spite of continuous rate increases during part of 1887 and the first half of 1888 the Central's management increased freight rates by 36 per cent. in the month of July. Settlers in the Cañada de Gomez complained that it cost more to ship a ton of grain to Rosario than it did to ship it from Rosario to Liverpool. In his Presidential message to Congress Juárez Celman had already described the rates of the railway companies as 'criminal and iniquitous exactions', and he had declared that the shortages of rolling-stock threatened to cause the loss of millions of tons of export produce. Since his arrival in Buenos Aires George Jenner, the new British chargé d'affaires, had been worried by the foolishness and greed of some of the companies. As soon as he received the text of President

[1] *South American Journal*, 11 Aug. 1888.

Juárez Celman's speech, he wrote to the Marquis of Salisbury saying:

There is a passage in the message . . . which appears to me well calculated to give rise to serious reflections in the minds of the Directors of English Companies engaged in working Railways in the Argentine Republic. . . . Even to one who has had so little opportunity of becoming acquainted with the facts as myself, they point to a state of things which, to say the least of it, is highly discreditable to British enterprise. I have thought it my duty to call Your Lordship's attention to the matter as I have every reason to believe that it is only by immediate and energetic action that we shall be able to maintain our present prominent position in the construction and working of the Railways of this country. French and German capitalists are beginning to compete with us. . . . We should have nothing to fear from them if our Railways were conducted on the sound and honourable principles which have always distinguished our trade; but if every consideration of the future development of traffic and the extension of lines, to say nothing of the well-being of the Public, be set aside for the sake of showing a heavy dividend on the Shares, we shall lose ground in this country as we have already done in some others for much the same reason.[1]

Not content with uttering this warning, Jenner commissioned a British business man with long experience in railway enterprise in Argentina to report on the validity of Juárez Celman's charges. This business man found for the plaintiff. His memorandum on the subject revealed an extraordinary situation. With one or two exceptions the railway companies preferred to keep their capital investment low and their rates high. It was the belief of Jenner's adviser that if capital in the shape of rolling-stock was increased and rates were reduced the companies would make so much money that the agitation for expropriation would get out of hand. Paradoxically capital was lacking in the railways at the very time when capital was flowing into the country, and at a time of high profits railway directors feared higher profits. Jenner's adviser further reported that, in the case of guaranteed lines, the Argentine Government was obliged to foot the bill for irresponsible management and for the payment of 'fat' salaries to officials who 'keep right with their Board'. '"Sufficient unto the day is the evil (on guaranteed interest)

[1] F.O. 6/399, Jenner to Salisbury, 27 May 1888.

thereof" should be the heading of the prospectuses of some of these guaranteed Railways.'[1]

It is not clear whether Jenner's adviser was on the right track in attributing the poor equipment on railways like the Central to fear of high profits. The reason for the inadequacy of rolling-stock and freight-handling facilities seems to have been the disproportionate amount of capital being sunk in new building designed to secure territory from competitors. It is difficult to credit the argument that reduced freight rates leading to higher profits would have stimulated the demand for expropriation. On the contrary, the existing practice of increasing rates at monthly and even weekly intervals in order to compensate for losses due to monetary and credit inflation was generating an extremely dangerous head of public criticism of the railways. The public complaint in Argentina centred around the fact of ever-increasing freight and passenger charges, whereas the more sophisticated and abstract objection to profits was seldom heard. Even the most ardent exponents of expropriation and public ownership argued principally on the political ground that the Argentine community ought to own its own railways and on the economic ground that public properties would better serve the public, but little criticism was directed either at profits or at their level.

Whatever may have been the merits of Jenner's adviser's view of the situation, what he reported was enough to stir the Marquis of Salisbury to take a prompt and unusual step. Copies of Jenner's dispatch, suitably edited, were sent with a covering letter from the Foreign Office to the directors of the British railway companies operating in Argentina. Men who had completely ignored the President of Argentina hearkened to the voice of the British Foreign Secretary. The Railway Council invited 'all the managers in the Argentine Republic . . . to hear a lecture by the President of that body on "Duties of Railway Managers and the Rights of the Public"'.[2] The Buenos Ayres and Pacific purchased 150 additional goods wagons. 'They might well have bought 1,500', commented the *Buenos Aires Standard*. The Southern hired an American expert on grain handling to advise them about grain elevators, loading, and

---

[1] F.O. 6/399, enclosed with Jenner to Salisbury, 27 May 1888.
[2] *South American Journal*, 4 Aug. 1888.

storage problems. By December 1888 it was reported that 'large orders for cars are being executed by the Birmingham Carriage and Wagon Company, the Gloucester and Bristol Wagon Company, the Ashbury Carriage Company. Messrs. Beyers and Peacock have several locomotive orders.'[1] By the end of 1890 the number of railway carriages and goods wagons shipped to Argentina from Britain was almost three times as great as it had been in 1887.

In spite of the cautionary action of the Marquis of Salisbury the mania for expansion had become uncontrollable by the end of 1888. By the end of 1887 Argentina possessed 3,848 miles of railway. During that year the National Government and the Congress had authorized projects which would double that mileage, and if the Congress passed all the railway bills on the agenda in the session of 1888 it would still further increase the length of lines by 150 per cent.[2] The whole process had become thoroughly corrupt and irrational. When Senator del Valle rose in the Congress to question the wisdom of guaranteeing a railway in the jungles of the Chaco, he was openly offered £10,000 for his vote by a colleague interested in the project.[3] Those who could not be corrupted were intimidated. Jenner, the chargé d'affaires, had pressure applied to him on account of his scepticism about the course of developments. When his report for 1887 on commercial conditions in Argentina was published in 1888, the Argentine Minister in London presented a note of protest in which he argued that Mr. Jenner was hostile to Argentina.[4]

While capital was freely, and indeed turbulently, flowing into railway enterprise, funds for the development of the meat industry were difficult to obtain, and the transformation of cattle marketing was proceeding only slowly. What eventually became a profitable and socially useful field of enterprise was in its prolonged first stage of development beset by serious difficulties, some of them technological, some of them commercial, but all of them unfamiliar and none susceptible of quick solutions. For more than a decade profits were low or

[1] Ibid., 15 Dec. 1888.
[2] F.O. 6/399, Jenner to Salisbury, 26 June 1888.
[3] *South American Journal*, 17 Nov. 1888.
[4] F.O. 6/400, Dominguez to Salisbury, 29 Sept. 1888.

non-existent in the overseas meat-and-cattle trade. Those conditions of sure and automatic returns on capital outlays did not exist, and hence funds for development were hard to come by.

By 1880 progress in the construction of ocean-going steam vessels and in the techniques of refrigeration had reached a point where it was becoming commercially feasible to transport frozen meat from the southern hemisphere to the consuming centres in western Europe. This development came at a fortunate moment for the Argentine cattlemen and meat packers, for the old-fashioned *saladeros* supplying the domestic market with fresh meat and foreign markets with dried and salted meat were faced with severe difficulties. In 1882 Eugenio Terrason converted his *saladero* into a *frigorifico* on the Australian pattern. In the same year George Drabble launched The River Plate Fresh Meat Company Ltd. with a capital of £100,000, a substantial proportion of which was subscribed by himself and his fellow directors. Both firms concentrated on freezing mutton, but Terrason did not concentrate all his capital in this new field, whereas The River Plate Fresh Meat Company did. Terrason continued to supply the Buenos Aires market with fresh meat, and with him freezing, if not a sideline, was at least not an indispensable condition of business survival. Drabble, on the other hand, located his *frigorificos* close to the source of supply at Campaña on the Paraná and at Colonia across the river in Uruguay. He concentrated entirely on the English market for frozen mutton. This specialization involved several initial difficulties. Argentine sheep generally were not so large and heavily fleeced as Australian sheep nor such good animals for butchery as those in New Zealand. Breeding, however, was well understood and widely practised in Argentina, and the adaptation of existing stock to the needs of the meat market was comparatively simple. Merinos and Lincolns were commonly crossed to secure a carcass fit for freezing.[1] Even so the change-over presented some difficulty. Drabble was obliged to close the plant at Colonia for lack of a sufficient supply of satisfactory carcasses.[2]

In England frozen mutton did not flow instantly into the kitchens of consumers. A certain Mr. Tallerman, a London

[1] *South American Journal*, 24 Jan. 1885.
[2] Hanson, *Argentine Meat and the British Market*, p. 53.

wholesale dealer, encountered serious opposition from the butchers of Manchester when he tried to break into the market there. They offered to handle Argentine frozen mutton at 3*d.* a pound, which, of course, was only a way of saying 'no'. Tallerman decided to circumvent the butchers by setting up a stall of his own in the Knot Hill Market. When he applied for space the superintendent of the market appears to have hesitated, for he referred the application to the chairman of the Markets Committee of the Council. The chairman, Councillor J. F. Roberts, not only granted permission to establish a stall, but he even consented to eat some Argentine meat. He declared it to be 'quite as good as the hot-pot he had got at the Reform Club'.[1] Alderman Worthington thought so too. Londoners were eating Argentine meat, he declared, and 'he thought many people would rejoice to learn that good sweet meat could be bought at prices ranging from 8d. to 4d. per pound . . . those who could afford a higher price would be glad to know that their poorer brethren could obtain good, sweet meat at such low prices'.

Tallerman's stall was a success. At first he had no customers, but he cheered up when at last 'he saw one or two poor women going away with a pound or half a pound, and return shortly afterwards accompanied by several other women who came to purchase'. The year that Tallerman beat the butchers of Manchester saw 17,165 frozen carcasses exported from Argentina to Britain. The trade grew to 873,460 carcasses[2] in 1888. With experience of the new techniques spoilage declined from 10 per cent. of all cargoes in 1883 to 4 per cent. five years later.[3] By the time this state of efficiency was achieved frozen mutton in Britain was cheaper than fresh mutton in Buenos Aires.

In 1884 the Sansinena brothers converted their *saladero* to a *frigorifico*, and they too were organized to supply the local markets as well as the overseas trade. In 1886 the landowners' society of Buenos Aires Province, *La Sociedad Rural*, initiated a company *La Congeladora Argentina* with a plant at San Nicolás. Inexperience in management, technical inefficiency, and insufficiency of capital caused this enterprise to fail very quickly.

---

[1] *South American Journal*, 3 Jan. 1884.
[2] F.O. 6/405, enclosure in Jenner to Salisbury, 18 Mar. 1889.
[3] Hanson, *Argentine Meat*, p. 57.

The same year an English firm, James Nelson & Company, sent out one of their proprietors, Hugh Nelson, to establish a plant at Zarate. Nelson diversified his operations, undertaking to freeze meat, but also to export live animals for butchery in England.

In spite of these vigorous first steps, the frozen-meat industry remained a tough, competitive business, which required commercial and managerial skill together with a willingness to take repeated losses during the long period of establishment. As volume grew, prices fell steadily in Britain. Drabble's firm lost £37,500 in 1886, and reduced the nominal value of its shares from £8 to £5 in order to attract more capital. Simultaneously he induced *La Sociedad Rural* to help get the export duty on frozen meat eliminated and to interest itself in securing subsidies for beef freezing. In 1887 Congress passed a law guaranteeing 5 per cent. on the capital invested in freezing establishments, provided 20 per cent. of the capital was Argentine-owned. An export bounty of 12*s.* a head was established for cattle. When asked to inquire into the effectiveness of bounties, the British chargé d'affaires expressed the view that the depreciation of the currency was a far more generous bounty than that paid by the Government.

> For the producers and purchaser of meat [he wrote] the paper dollar has scarcely lost value at all. It continues to be accepted in payment of rent and wages at its par value long after it has become depreciated abroad. An English pound sterling worth about eight paper dollars at the present exchange, can, roughly speaking be purchased with meat that has cost the seller five paper dollars. The exporter is thus in the enjoyment of a bounty of 60%, the withdrawal of which by the resumption of specie payments would not fail to have a serious effect upon the trade.[1]

In 1887 the three big freezing firms in Argentina, The River Plate Fresh Meat, Sansinena Brothers, and Nelson & Company, began meeting to plan market strategy. They could not control the situation, for Australia and New Zealand together sold two to three times as much as the River Plate. But they agreed to cut production if over-stocking threatened price collapse. Many years later (in 1898) the big three leased Terrason's

---

[1] F.O. 6/405, enclosure in Jenner to Salisbury, 18 Mar. 1889.

plants and shut them down.[1] Taking a leaf out of the Manchester butchers' book, the Argentine exporters also tried in their turn to keep Australian and New Zealand mutton out of the Manchester market.

Bounties, guarantees, and agreements between producers were only palliatives. Meat freezing was a complex and highly capitalized business which required enormous volume for success. Terrason and Sansinena partially solved this problem by supplying the local market, where meat consumption on a great scale was part of the national character. In the end all freezers came to rely on the Argentine market for that extension of operations which permitted full use of capital equipment. Argentine plants achieved an average operation of 60 per cent. of capacity compared with only 40 per cent. in Australia.[2] Another solution of the problem of volume was the addition of beef to mutton as a raw material. Bounties might help, but beef freezing required an almost complete reorganization of the Argentine cattle industry which in turn required large investments of capital by the landowning class. A meat packer unlike a poet cannot say that a cow is a cow, is a cow, is a cow. For a meat packer a cow is not a skeleton covered with hide, but an animal covered with meat, and the production of such a creature required fenced estates, planted alfalfa pastures, careful breeding, and fattening and finishing close to the place of slaughter. The reformation of Argentine cattle for the purpose of meat packing was almost as difficult and prolonged a process as the reformation of Argentine people for the purpose of capital investment. The landed class, however, wanted one as much as the other, and from 1885 onward *La Sociedad Rural* bent its energies to this reformation. Until that reformation came, the investors in meat-freezing plants received very little. The River Plate Fresh Meat ordinary shareholders received no dividends until 1896. James Nelson's shareholders always received something, but their trading profits only began to expand after 1892. Terrason was eventually bought out. Sansinena did not fail in 1890–1, but was taken over by the Argentine banking house of Tornquist & Company, reorganized and supplied with fresh capital, whereupon it began to pay profits, which reached 25 per

[1] Hanson, *Argentine Meat*, p. 67.
[2] Ibid., p. 57.

cent. on the ordinary shares during the Boer War and 50 per
cent. in the year 1903.[1]

Perhaps, if the meat packers had invented something like a
cédula, they might have attracted more capital. *Cédulas* together
with bank credit constituted the principal means by which the
landed proprietors financed themselves during the 1880's. The
general tendency of the 1880's was in the direction of cutting
down the size of the vast estancias of Rosas's time by selling or
renting out parts of the great estates. At the same time the
estancieros were pouring capital into the physical equipment of
the retained parts, the working of which they undertook themselves or through the medium of estate managers (many of them
British). A contemporary description of the estancia of Señor
Roberto Cano, situated 180 miles north-west of Buenos Aires,
suggests the character of this development and the kind and
quantity of capital which was being absorbed:

> The entire property consists of 90 square miles of land and is not
> only a pleasant resort in summer for Señor Cano, his family and his
> friends (for he entertains largely), but also a source of enormous
> profit, as can be readily seen by calculating the value of wool pro-
> duced and the sale of cattle. . . . The buildings are almost too
> numerous to mention; it is like a small city. Among them you can
> find large stables; machine shops containing various kinds of
> machinery necessary such as corn shellers, chaff cutters, corn
> crushers, revolving saws etc. all driven by an English engine manu-
> factured by Messrs. Richard Garret & Co.
> An immense building is devoted to sheep shearing, and has the
> railroad tracks running right into it, thus saving the cost and
> trouble of carting the wool to the station to ship it. Here is also a
> very fine press for baling wool of which 400,000 to 450,000 pounds
> are baled annually. At the *estancia* there are 100,000 sheep, 40,000
> cattle and about 12,000 horses. The annual sale of cattle alone is
> about 10,000 head.[2]

It was also observed that Señor Roberto Cano had installed
on his estate a supply of piped water better than that available
in any Argentine city except Buenos Aires.

In order to create estates of this description the landed class
were heavily dependent upon foreign capital. The principal
direct agency for its acquisition was the *cédulas* of the Provincial

[1] Hanson, *Argentine Meat*, p. 137.
[2] *South American Journal*, 5 Feb. 1887.

Hypothecary Bank of Buenos Aires and the National Hypothecary Bank of Buenos Aires. Unfortunately the very nature of
the *cédula* as an instrument for borrowing and lending money
creates a difficulty in measuring the amount lent or the amount
borrowed, and furthermore, makes it hard to know how in fact
the proceeds were employed. A possessor of landed property
who obtained *cédulas* with a face value of, say, 100,000 paper
dollars bearing interest at 8 per cent. might sell them for
75,000 paper dollars, which in their turn might be worth at the
moment of sale in London about £11,000 in sterling. Such a
borrower would thus be borrowing about £11,000 but would
be contracting a debt of £20,000 bearing 8 per cent. interest,
if he were obliged to pay in sterling. But he was not obliged to pay
in sterling. He was only obliged to repay the bank issuing the
cédulas the amount on the face of the *cédulas* plus interest in
paper currency or in *cédulas* of an equivalent face value to his
original loan. Suppose our landowner sold his *cédulas* in London
at 75 in September 1886, when the gold premium was only 10 per
cent. He would have obtained $67,500,[1] or a sterling balance
of £13,500, less brokerage fees, with which he could order
corn-shellers, chaff-cutters, one of Richard Garret's engines,
a few hundred miles of barbed wire, a few miles of water-pipe,
and, perhaps, a half-dozen of Messrs. MacWilliams's 'Ivy' water-
closets 'designed for the South American market'. Less than five
years later, as a result of the depreciation of the paper peso,
our landowner could sell wool for sterling and buy 100,000
paper dollars for approximately £6,100, or he could do even
better by buying *cédulas* at 35 and offering them to the Hypothecary Bank in discharge of his debt.

Somewhere someone suffered a severe loss, but it was not the
Argentine borrower. The debts contracted by the Argentine
public authorities, the debentures of the railway companies, and
the railway guarantees were all sterling obligations both by the
terms of the contracts establishing them and by the domestic
laws of the Argentine Republic. These obligations were chargeable to the whole community and were paid either out of
taxes or railway charges payable by the whole community. The
direct borrowings of the politically dominant landed class were,

[1] *Cédulas* of face value $100,000 paper sold at 75 for $75,000 paper less 10 per
cent. for gold premium = $67,500, which, converted into sterling = £13,500.

however, obligations written in terms of paper currency. Except for a small proportion of gold *cédulas* (and these were made payable in paper by a special law passed in 1891), the borrowings of the landed class could be written down by the complex strategy of currency and credit manipulation. Nothing in the domestic laws of Argentina or in the contracts themselves could protect the investor in *cédulas*.

How much British money went to Argentina by way of *cédulas* is extremely difficult to estimate. What proportion went to finance agricultural and pastoral production is even more difficult to guess. The Commercial Secretary of the British Legation in Buenos Aires, Arthur Herbert, fixed upon a figure of £28,625,745 to describe the total sterling value of the *cédulas* issued by the hypothecary banks of Argentina by the end of 1892.[1] Except to indicate that the investment was many times larger than the investment in, say, meat-packing plants, and considerably smaller than the investment in railways, this figure is quite meaningless. Herbert made the calculation by adding up the face value of all the series of *cédulas* listed and dividing by 20 to state the amount in sterling. Herbert himself believed that the amount outstanding in 1890 was £4·5 millions less than this total. But the total can tell very little about the amount actually invested by British capitalists. In the first place *cédulas* were never bought above 90 per cent. of their redemption value, and they were often much lower during the period of heavy investment between 1886 and 1889. Furthermore, the sterling investment depended upon the rate of exchange. The gold premium in 1886, for example, fluctuated between a high of 59·9 and a low of 9·8.[2] It was 131 by December 1889. The amount of sterling realized—and this was the investment by the British capitalist—by the sale of a particular *cédula* could vary enormously. Our hypothetical landowner managed to get £13,500, less brokerage charges, for $100,000 of *cédulas* when he sold on a good day in September 1886. If he had sold in April 1886, when the gold premium was nearly 60, he could have received as little as £9,375. On the other hand, if the price of *cédulas* rose as the gold premium rose—and this usually happened during the boom year 1889—the rise tended to offset

---

[1] *Parliamentary Papers*, 1892, lxxxi.
[2] *South American Journal*, 8 Jan. 1887.

the gold premium, but in spite of this the amount of sterling which went to Argentina through the sale of *cédulas* in London was probably well in excess of Herbert's figure, which was calculated on a gold premium of 400.

If the task of calculating the amount of real purchasing power borrowed by means of *cédulas* is difficult or impossible, the determination of the extent to which British investors supplied this purchasing power is even more beset with hazards and obstacles. *Cédulas* were marketed by borrowers in Buenos Aires and thence they found their way to the money markets of Europe. They were never listed securities on the London Stock Exchange, and in Berlin the manager of the Deutsche Bank informed the manager of the Hypothecary Bank of Buenos Aires that his (the Berlin) market would consider only gold *cédulas* whose coupons were payable in Europe.[1] In a sense *cédulas* circulated in the financial *demi-monde* of Europe. The editors of *The Economist*, who uttered stern and repeated warnings against *cédulas*, believed that the British investment was substantial and in 1888 they described *cédulas* as 'well known' in London, but they never ventured to estimate how much money in sum had actually been invested.

The purchasing power obtained by the sale of *cédulas* was spent generally in four ways, and it is not easy to determine how much flowed into each of these several forms of expenditure. The purchase of physical capital for agricultural and pastoral purposes seems to have absorbed a fairly large part of the borrowing if we may judge from the amount of physical transformation taking place in the Argentine countryside. Ancillary to this development was the growth of conspicuous waste among the landowning class. In the old days, before the railways, only great *caudillos* like General Urquiza affected a baronial style of living. The average *estanciero* tended to live more like those described by Hudson in *The Purple Land*. In the 1880's, however, structures imitative of French châteaux and English country mansions began to sprout upon the pampas. Argentine magnates began to congregate in Paris and their children to go to English public schools.[2] How much of this

---

[1] H. Wallich to Dr. Paulino Llambi Campbell, 10 Aug. 1886, printed in *South American Journal*, 16 Oct. 1886.

[2] The sons of both Roca and Juárez Celman were at public schools.

opulence was financed by *cédulas* is beyond calculation, but the simultaneous existence of *cédulas* and conspicuous waste was not a random occurrence.

A third channel of expenditure of borrowings was land speculation. Landowners borrowed on land to buy more land to borrow on in order to buy more land. The profits to the man who bought and sold at the right time and had the sense to convert his profits into gold or sterling were enormous. There is much evidence to suggest that land values appreciated by something like 1,000 per cent. between 1883 and 1887 in Buenos Aires Province; 420 per cent. in Santa Fé, 750 per cent. in Córdoba, and 370 per cent. in Entre Rios.[1] The directors of the Central Argentine Land Company were embarrassed by their profits from land sales. The most evil feature of *cédulas* and the lax personal-credit policy of the Argentine banks was the insane stimulus they gave to the appreciation of land values, for it enabled speculators freely supplied with paper dollars to push up land values far in excess of the productive possibilities of the land. A situation was created where either the final holder at the moment of the crash had to take a severe loss or he had to face the future with an enormous debt burden. If this final owner was a speculator, he was merely ruined, but if he was a working farmer he became a debt slave. There were reports of armed men employed to keep farmers on their debt-burdened property, and there is also the indubitable fact of a heavy net loss of emigrants when the crash came.

The fourth channel for expending the purchasing power made available by *cédulas* was urban building. The I and J series issued by the National Hypothecary Bank of Buenos Aires were devoted almost entirely to the building of a new capital city for the Province of Buenos Aires. There may be much to be said for Roca's solution of the political difficulty, which was achieved by federalizing the city of Buenos Aires and establishing the Government of the Province at La Plata. From an economic point of view the building of a new capital city was a dubious proceeding. At a time when the National Government was building a Hall of Congress which was described as 'one of the most magnificent constructed in the nineteenth

---

[1] Based on a calculation in *The Economist*, 5 May 1888, p. 570, which only bears out other evidence in Foreign Office papers and in journalists' observations.

century', a community of a mere 4 million people was undertaking to construct another whole city for the purpose of
governing a portion of this community. If such a city produced
anything saleable, such expenditure could, of course, be justified. But it did not. La Plata was almost entirely an item of
consumption expenditure, and yet it was financed on the
assumption of growing productivity. La Plata, like the great
Hall of Congress, which cost £2,500,000, was an instance of
conspicuous public waste. All young pioneer communities seem
prone to this type of expenditure. It happened in Texas,
Nebraska, and Manitoba, as well as in the Province of Buenos
Aires. It is argued that such opulence is a by-product of the
connivance of politicians, contractors, and land speculators.
Perhaps. But the photographic evidence[1] from Outer Mongolia
in 1956 suggests that without the assistance of contractors and
land speculators the same phenomenon is developing there as
we see in Buenos Aires in 1888. Perhaps such building is a
psychological necessity of young communities.

Whatever the reason for such expenditure, it took place, increasing the obligations of the debtors to the creditors. It would
require much research and more mathematical ingenuity to
assess the amount of these obligations in terms of real purchasing power. Whether it will ever be worth anyone's while to do
this would be difficult to say. For the purpose of this history it
is sufficient for us to notice that the debts were written in terms
of a currency whose management was in the hands ultimately
of the debtor class. As a result of this management, European
investors lost large sums of money. But it must be observed that
the sums lost to individuals were a part of the total process of
development, serving much the same purpose as the 'foreign
aid' doled out by the Great Powers after World War II. The
money invested in *cédulas* was substantially lost, but it served
several purposes: to sweeten the ruling groups in Argentina;
to assist in the increase in productivity (but not nearly to
the amount of the investment); to stimulate the sales of the
manufactured goods of the leading countries; to stimulate land
speculation; and finally to satisfy the psychological needs of
a young community which required some visible evidence of
opulence in order to become so.

[1] Kindly supplied to me by Mr. W. J. Pringle of Birmingham.

Just as today an amalgam of fear, ignorance, and generosity creates the popular impulse enabling governments to grant 'foreign aid', so in the 1880's a mixture of greed, recklessness, and enthusiasm for progress impelled a vast number of investors to provide some of the necessities and luxuries of development in Argentina. A more experienced and sober body of investors, however, began in the late eighties to explore the possibilities of reaping some of the benefits of land speculation and large-scale agricultural and pastoral production by investing through the orthodox channels of joint-stock enterprise. Schemes for selling land, of course, dated back to early revolutionary times. These schemes had all had common features: the land grant by the state; the financing of colonization by the investors; and the recovery of the investment and the making of profit by renting and selling land to the colonists. Invariably these schemes had failed. When the lands of the Central Argentine Railway were sold to the Central Argentine Land Company in 1872, the intention was to utilize the capital of the company, partly to pay the purchase price of the land and partly to settle colonists. Colonization was set on foot under the direction of William Perkins,[1] and he was responsible for several settlements along the line of the railway in Santa Fé Province. As immigrants began to flow in increasing numbers seeking land, the directors of the company saw great commercial advantages in abandoning colonization in favour of selling or renting land without the expensive business of collecting colonists and assuming the social costs of establishing communities. By the mid-1880's the Central Argentine Land Company had demonstrated the profitability of land sales in a rising land market. By the late 1880's the directors were distributing dividends above 20 per cent. per annum, and in 1888 they hinted that only the danger of public scandal restrained them from paying 40 per cent., and that they, therefore, would have to limit themselves to a mere 22 per cent.[2] From 1885 onward their £1 shares fluctuated between £3 and £3. 10s. on the London Stock Exchange.

It was in these circumstances of profits and enthusiasm that a number of land companies began to appeal for investment funds. In 1888, for example, the Santa Fé and Cordova Great

---

[1] Gschwind, *Guillermo Perkins.*
[2] *South American Journal,* 9 June 1888.

Southern Land Company Limited was formed with a proposed capital of £400,000 from 20,000 £20 shares on which £16 was to be called before the end of the year. This company proposed to buy up sheep and cattle lands along the line of a projected railway from Villa Constitución on the Paraná south of Rosario to La Carlota in the southern point of the Province of Córdoba. The proposition was a simple one. The company would buy land at present producing 50 tons of wool, hides, and grease per square league (6,672 acres), and they would resell the land in small farms of 332 acres each to settlers who they estimated could produce after the railway arrived 900 tons of cereals per half square league, after allowance was made for seed, fallowing, and fodder crops, leaving the remainder for grazing purposes.[1]

Such projects became numerous by the late eighties. The directors of the Buenos Ayres and Enseñada Railway and the Central Argentine Railway were interested in the Argentine Land and Investment Company Limited with a capital $2\frac{1}{2}$ times as large as that of the Santa Fé and Cordova Land Company.[2] Indeed, one is sometimes prompted to wonder whether or not the promoters of railway companies really had land companies in mind when they projected a line.

Another type of enterprise which came to occupy the attention of investors at this time was the estancia company, the purpose of which was pastoral and agricultural production. The best example of this type was the Curamalam Land Company Ltd. The land which gave its name to the company was an estancia of 600,000 acres in the southern part of Buenos Aires Province. Originally it had been a horse ranch granted to an Argentine capitalist for the purpose of raising cavalry remounts for the army, but the Argentine proprietor, either failing or tiring, sold his holding to Edward Carey, an Anglo-Argentine business man. Carey formed a company to raise capital in England to equip the estancia for the production of wool, cereals, and meat. By 1888 the company employed 500 men who, with their families, made the population of the estancia 2,000. No fewer than four stations of the Buenos Ayres Great Southern Railway were located within the estancia's boundaries. The cereals

---

[1] From a condensed prospectus printed in *The Economist*, 2 June 1888, p. 720.
[2] *South American Journal*, 21 July 1888.

marketed amounted to £120,000 in value in 1887 and the company milled part of this for sale as flour. There were 175,000 sheep on the estate, 36,000 cattle, and 13,500 horses. The estimated value of the land was £930,000. In 1889 Baring Brothers undertook to market £500,000 of First Mortgage Bonds bearing interest at 7 per cent., from the proceeds of which the company proposed to expand production and to increase the work force to 10,000 within fifteen years. The £200 bonds were quoted at a 5 per cent. premium as soon as offered.[1]

The investment during the years 1886–90, some features of which we have described, amounted to a figure in the neighbourhood of £100–110 millions. So large an investment of capital was bound, one would expect, to have an effect upon trade between Britain and Argentina. And so it did. Britain was still an industrial and exporting community and not primarily a capital-accumulating and capital-exporting one. There were some signs that finance was attracting more attention and receiving more consideration than physical production, but the advantages of investment in terms of the export opportunities of industry were not lost sight of. As British capital investment in Argentina increased, British exports to the Republic increased, but not to the same extent or even at the same rate. While the British community was investing £100–110 millions in Argentina, they sold there commodities valued at slightly more than £38 millions before loading at British ports (i.e. during the years 1886–90 inclusive). Delivered at Argentine ports, these commodities had a value in excess of £40 millions. The proportion of fuel and manufactures of iron and steel grew as investment expanded. Not only did the absolute volume of commodities grow, but the proportion of British goods in the total imports of the Argentine Republic grew.[2] In 1880 Britain supplied 27·6 per cent. of Argentine imports; in 1886, 35 per cent.; in 1890, 40·6 per cent. Germany and Belgium gained ground during this period. France, the United States, and Italy tended to maintain their proportionate

[1] *South American Journal*, 20 Oct. 1889.
[2] *Parliamentary Papers*, Statistical Abstract for the principal and foreign Countries for relevant years. These statistics also indicate that this was not true for Argentine exports, whose principal destination was France; Belgium and Germany, with Great Britain, were next in importance.

position, and countries like Brazil lost ground. It is interesting
to observe that even after capital ceased to flow in 1890, Britain
continued to gain ground in the sale of goods in Argentina, as
credits created by investment were spent in order to bring projects like railways to completion.

The competitive position of Great Britain during the 1880's
was very much in the minds of both the British Government
and British business interests. In the past revolutionary days
during the 1820's and early 1830's the competitor which Britain
noticed most had been the United States. In the 1840's and
1850's France had appeared as the most formidable trade rival,
but in the early decades of capital investment in the sixties and
seventies we hear little of competition by other European
powers or by the United States. Britain was then the bank,
stockbroker, railway builder, and supplier of the Argentine
Republic. This condition of primacy began to change in the
1880's, or rather British business men and the Government
began to think it was changing. According to a familiar formula
business men blamed the consular service for failing to assist
the commercial classes, and the consular service described the
commercial classes as bumptious, conservative, and lacking in
energy and adaptability.[1]

Just as an energetic and successful man may from time to
time experience fits of critical self-depreciation when he considers himself a failure doomed to a gloomy end, so feelings of
inferiority may darken for a time the temper of a community.
The anxieties about foreign competition in Argentina which betrayed themselves at this time were indicative of something, if
not exactly of what the worried men thought. In the early days
of the century British trade in Argentina was predominantly a
trade in consumer goods. British success had been dependent
upon three main factors: low prices compared with the prices
of goods supplied by domestic and foreign competitors; abundant credit; and the existence in Argentina of a British community proportionately and numerically larger than any other
foreign community. Low prices and generous credit were much
reinforced by the third factor, for the British community in the
Río de la Plata not only itself provided a market, but helped to
communicate to the native population English conceptions of

[1] *South American Journal*, 25 Dec. 1886.

taste and utility which became favourable factors in the sale of commodities. In the 1880's, however, the British community was not nearly so important proportionately as it had been earlier. Immigration had converted Buenos Aires and Rosario into cities with a very large Italian population, so that by 1885 Buenos Aires was a bigger Italian city than Parma or Pisa. And it was a German city, too, and a Spanish Basque city. In the higher ranges of society France was the other *patrie* of the rich and well-to-do. At the same time Belgian, German, French, and American consumer goods were competitively priced. In his report for 1888 the British chargé d'affaires urged that British manufacturers should make a closer and more detailed study of the Argentine market. The Germans and French were outdistancing the British in the sale of haberdashery. The Belgians were coming to dominate the market for building steel, and so on.

None the less the volume of British trade was growing. The British community in the River Plate may have been declining in its proportionate position in terms of numbers, but those British who were there were coming to occupy an increasingly strategic position in the Argentine economy. This fact arose from the investment of capital and the organization of business enterprises, and this fact was important in the increased sales of fuel, engineering products, and capital equipment and the provision of services such as insurance, banking facilities, and ocean shipping. No laws existed which obliged companies owned by British capitalists to buy British capital goods, British coal, or British repair parts. There is no evidence that British manufacturers of railway equipment, refrigeration equipment, or any other kind of machinery used in Argentina had any control over British enterprises in Argentina or that they were able in any way to oblige them to buy British. But they tended to do so. American and Belgian locomotives were seen on government-owned lines, but not on British lines. Why not? Did the directors of British railways in Argentina buy the best and/or cheapest equipment they could get, or did they buy in Britain for reasons of patriotism or profit obtained in some other way than by managing a railway on the basis of buying cheap?

We have already told how the railway companies were so devoted to what they conceived to be their own interests that they did not buy enough equipment, British or foreign, to operate effectively. A severe reproof from the British Government was required in order to make them buy more equipment. This could hardly suggest that the manufacturers of railway equipment called the tune or instructed the railway companies when to play. There is evidence that some at least of the companies were governed strictly by circumstances in purchasing equipment. The Southern, for example, went to the United States for grain-handling equipment. There is considerable evidence, too, that in competing for the custom of non-British enterprises, British steel-rail manufacturers, or gas-equipment manufacturers could underbid German, Belgian, and French competitors. In 1886 a Sheffield firm, for example, underbid all its German competitors for the supply of steels rails for the Chilean railways.[1] Another Sheffield firm outbid German competitors for the supply of gas-works equipment to *La Sociedad Cooperativa de Alumbrado à Gas de Buenos Aires.*[2] A Gainsborough engineering firm, abandoning the agency system in favour of direct salesmanship, was reported to be successfully meeting American competition for farm machinery.[3]

The fact of the matter seems to be that capacity for price competition was part of the explanation—but only a part—of the growth of British trade with Argentina at this time. A sale is a social transaction of a complicated sort, and what determines a sale is only in part price. A sale takes place within a cobweb of relationships, some administrative, some historic, some convivial and emotional, some scientific and severely technical. Without the cobweb, sales are hard to make anywhere and low prices alone will not enable them to be made. All this was clearly understood by the financial, commercial, and diplomatic men interested in the River Plate. Jenner explained to Salisbury that if British railway companies misbehaved themselves and German and French capitalists came to the fore the consequences would be serious far beyond the interest of the railway investors themselves.[4] The Germans saw this, too. A German merchant in Buenos Aires writing to the

---

[1] *South American Journal,* 8 Jan. 1887.
[2] Ibid., 24 Nov. 1888.
[3] Ibid., 25 Mar. 1887.
[4] F.O. 6/399, Jenner to Salisbury, 27 May 1888.

President of the Society for the Promotion of German Industry Abroad argued that the progress of German trade was slow because Germans were not investing and organizing businesses in the way the British were.[1]

In the light of the evidence at present available, it appears that the expansion of British exports to Argentina in the 1880's was the result of a combination of four principal factors: a capacity for price competition and/or a capacity to supply goods adapted technically to existing needs; a capacity to grant short-term credit and to provide an abundance of long-term investment funds; a capacity to organize new enterprises and effectively manage existing ones; a capacity to avoid political conflicts with Argentina and to maintain impartiality with respect to the internal political forces of the country. But the expansion which British investment stimulated opened opportunities for others as well as for Britain. How the others took advantage of the opportunities, of course, depended upon the character of the economy of each.

The French with an abundance of investment funds and a willingness to bid for risky business in the loan markets made some headway in finance. Except in luxury consumer goods and in certain lines of industrial equipment like sugar-refining machinery, however, French business men were unable to consolidate and advance their position in the competition with British business. France seems to have lacked the supply of organizing talent on the one hand and the output of heavy industry on the other to create and supply an important part of the Argentine economy. A French firm, Erlanger et Compagnie, outbid Baring Brothers for the $12 million railway loan of 1881, and by 1889 French bankers were beginning to take a very large part in the financing of the smaller Argentine provinces. But there was only one French railway enterprise. Although French ships were carrying some frozen meat, the French were not active in the growing meat business, nor in any of the new fields opening up, such as telephones and electricity.

The Germans by contrast revealed a spirit of determination and they were organized. They were inhibited, however, at this stage by a lack of men capable of organizing enterprises and by

[1] Quoted in *South American Journal*, 31 Mar. 1888.

the caution of German investors and the hostility of the German Government to investment abroad. When a German firm secured the contract to lend the Province of Buenos Aires £2,500,000 in 1886, it was reported that Prince Bismarck was much disgusted by the operation.[1] As we have already noticed, Berlin would only look at gold *cédulas*. In 1887 the German attitude to investment in Argentina began to change. The Deutsche Übersee Bank opened an office in Buenos Aires in that year, and became the first successful German bank in Argentina. A fresh loan of the Province of Buenos Aires was launched successfully, and a National Government loan was being discussed. In 1888 ex-President Roca paid a short visit to Berlin where he was cordially received. When Russo-German relations started to go sour, Argentina began to replace Russia in the affections and interest of German financiers. Shortly after the Tsar's cold reception in Berlin in the autumn of 1889, *The Economist*'s correspondent in Berlin reported great efforts to boost the Argentine Republic as a field of investment. Unfortunately the boom was near bursting, and the German investing public, cautious as usual, seemed to know this.

Farther down the scale of economic activity the Germans were very busy at this time. German immigration to Argentina was substantial. In 1884 a leader of the German anti-Semitic movement, Dr. Forster, led a migration to Argentina. Generally speaking, however, the German immigrants were Social Democrats. One of the first industrial strikes in Argentine history was organized by the German carpenters in Buenos Aires in 1887. Whatever their political views a German community in the 1880's was building up a repository of knowledge of Argentina and a base for commercial operations. Commercial advance itself was being carefully studied. One British observer believed that German sales organization was superior to the British and that German commercial men were better educated and of a social class superior to that of their British counterparts.[2] One American observer believed there were actually more German mercantile houses in Buenos Aires than British in 1888.[3] Krupps were supplying the artillery for arming the island of Martín

---

[1] *South American Journal*, 8 Jan. 1887.
[2] Ibid., 25 Dec. 1886.
[3] Ibid., 18 Aug. 1888.

García, although Britain supplied nearly everything in the naval line. Krupps were also supplying steel to government-owned railways. But despite all this activity, the Germans still lacked that essential element which consisted of organizing business enterprises.

The position of the United States was weak, although in terms of American sales in Argentina the United States was in a position comparable with that of Belgium and little below that of Germany. Little or no American money went directly into Argentine public funds during the 1880's. Commercially the United States was in a weak position, having few outlets for goods and no regular shipping connexions with the River Plate. In 1890 the Argentine connexion with the United States was still further weakened by the McKinley Tariff which raised a high duty on wool. The American wool tariff remained for some years a sore grievance in Argentine governing circles. This is understandable, for the United States was, next to France, Argentina's best market for wool, and had been for many years. Furthermore there was no American immigration to Argentina. There was some talk of inviting American cow-punchers to migrate to Argentina, but a gentleman from Wyoming who toured the country in 1887 expressed the view that Argentina was a rich man's country and the average American cow-puncher could not improve his lot on the pampas.

There were, however, elements of strength in the American position. The Argentine pampas resembled the American West in its productive circumstances. Techniques were being developed in the United States on a massive scale which were well adapted to Argentine conditions. In farm machinery the Americans were already well in the lead. They sold windmills in large numbers to the farmers and sewing-machines to their wives. They had not yet entered the field of meat packing, but the possibility was there that the experience of Chicago would prove as valuable to the Argentinos as Australian experience was proving to the British. The American Consul in Buenos Aires believed that American locomotives were superior to those manufactured in Britain and Belgium,[1] but he suggested that only the government lines would buy them. Perhaps the United States needed to build some railways under American control.

[1] From his report printed in *South American Journal*, 19 Sept. 1884.

Such a project indeed was being talked about just before the boom collapsed.

By the end of 1888 Argentina had become one of the wonders of the world: the dream of the South Sea adventurers come to life. But early that year the editor of the *Bankers' Magazine* had written: 'The Confederation is piling up liabilities after much too wholesale a fashion, and great as are its resources, it cannot stand such a strain as this threatens to be.'[1] A few months later the British chargé d'affaires warned the Marquis of Salisbury against 'the reckless spirit in which it is sought to embark the country in speculative undertakings'.[2] Unfortunately these were not the voices which could be heard above the cries of the hucksters. As the speed of expansion grew, so did the satisfaction with it. In 1889 the delirium was beyond control. An estimated 40 per cent. of available British investment funds flowed to the Argentine Republic that year. As the rich grew richer, the poor grew poorer. 'Let the people of Buenos Aires look out,' wrote the editor of the *Buenos Aires Standard* as the year drew to a close, 'for some fine morning we may wake up in the midst of a general strike.' Before that happened the house of Baring Brothers fell.

[1] *Bankers' Magazine*, xlviii, 1888, p. 382.
[2] F.O. 6/399, Jenner to Salisbury, 26 June 1888.

XIV

THE BARING CRISIS

THE events of the year 1890 which temporarily brought the flow of foreign capital to Argentina to an end and reduced that flow to a trickle for nearly ten years are commonly described as the Baring Crisis. On 14 November 1890 the British Government agreed secretly with the Governor of the Bank of England to bear half of any loss which might be incurred by continuing to honour the signature of Baring Brothers on bills presented for payment.[1] The purpose of so radical a departure from the accepted rules of a *laissez-faire* economy was to avoid a financial collapse compared to which that of 1866 would, in the opinion of the Chancellor of the Exchequer, 'be a trifle'. Another South Sea Bubble had burst. The damage which the explosion threatened to do demanded nothing less than the mobilization of the entire resources of the British community in order to bring it under control.

The Baring Crisis is, perhaps, the best known event of Anglo-Argentine history. It has attracted the attention particularly of economists, who have discovered in its complexities an opportunity to test or to justify their theories. Certainly theories are a help in the difficult task of organizing a coherent account of the many things which happened at that time, but no theory can alone explain what happened; for one theory can be proved as well as another by the events of 1890 and 1891. And many theories have been advanced both by contemporary observers and by students after the event. All are useful, and each has contributed to a description of the elephant which no single eye can completely see.

As we approach the scene of confusion and hysteria which shook the Argentine Republic and the City of London, we would do well to bear certain facts in mind. Firstly, we must keep before us the general terms on which Argentina had been

[1] J. H. Clapham, *The Bank of England* (Cambridge, 1944), ii, p. 332.

financed. Without exception the investing classes of western Europe, like the investing class in Argentina itself, had advanced sums of money—purchasing power—for the purpose of economic development on the understanding that these sums would be repaid plus some addition out of the production of the country. If the investment was made in a railway, it was expected that the earnings of that railway from its freight and passenger traffic would pay the cost of the railway sooner or later and would give the investor something in addition which might take the form of a dividend or the return on a debenture. If the investment was made in a government loan, it was expected that the investor would sooner or later receive back the money lent plus interest. So in the case of *cédulas*; so in the case of a meat-freezing establishment; or a lighterage company; or a gas-works. In short, the underlying assumption of all investors was that their money would be returned to them sooner or later with some addition. A failure to make a return in individual instances might not affect the process of investment as a whole, but any large-scale failure would bring the process to an end. In the case of a government loan the investor expected the literal return of his money over a period of years, secured in the form of payments into a sinking fund. In the case of a joint-stock company he expected the property created by his investment to be renewed and kept in being by depreciation reserves. In every case output had to exceed input plus something, or the investment process would cease.

All this seems obvious enough, but it was not obvious to the parties playing this game. The rules were strict, but very few seemed to know them, or if they knew them they had by 1889 ceased to take them very seriously. Lord Revelstoke, the head of the firm of Baring Brothers, did not seem to know the rules or at least how to apply them. President Juárez Celman did not seem to know them. Even the cautious Mr. Frank Parish of the Buenos Ayres and Great Southern Railway, who knew the rules, allowed the heady optimism of the year before the crash to affect his judgement.

No doubt the pace is rapid [he told his shareholders in September 1888] and no doubt the country's engagements and indebtedness are increasing to an enormous amount, but, on the other hand, recollect that you are dealing with a country possessed of enormous resources

of national wealth. . . . So far we may say that the Argentine credit
has stood the test in the London market, and although some of us
older ones may question the practical utility of some of the projects
in which money has been invested, still I may say this . . . that any
English investor exercising a proper amount of judgement and discretion, will find ample means in the Argentine for investing his
money to advantage.[1]

Given the rules of the process—the absolute conditions which
had to be met if the process were to operate—the hazards were
enormous. Suppose some outlays were made on projects which
could not contribute, or contribute sufficiently, to the volume
of saleable products. Suppose some outlays were made on projects which could not contribute to production *in time* to meet
the demands of investors. Suppose the weather reduced the
volume of saleable products (a real hazard in an economy
producing almost exclusively agricultural and pastoral products). Suppose some outlays were made on projects incapable
of producing anything saleable, such as a Hall of Congress.
Suppose some outlays were made on consumer not producer
goods. Suppose the receipts from saleable goods were reduced
by declines in prices due to factors over which Argentina
had no control. Suppose that the wage workers demanded
and could enforce the demand for more food, clothing, and
house-room.

Each of these suppositions can be inflated to the dimensions
of a theory. Each would be relevant, for such suppositions are
rooted in an observation of the events of the late 1880's. Our
purpose, however, is to give an account of these events which
does not depend upon or illustrate any particular theory; for
it seems to us that there existed at this time a kind of schizophrenia among the parties concerned—investors, bankers, promoters, immigrants, and Argentine leaders—which drove them
into incompatible and contradictory courses.

This schizophrenia is best illustrated among the investing
classes. Argentina had become a golden dream by the year
1888, and yet the investing classes were predominantly cautious.
A high percentage of investment funds had flowed and were
still flowing as late as 1889 into fixed-interest securities or into
shares the profits on which were guaranteed by the public

authorities. As we have already noticed, capitalists willing to take risks in new fields of enterprise, such as meat packing, were difficult to find, and the state was invited to provide security in this field. In railways—the biggest field of investment —the favourite form of investment was the debenture and the mortgage bond. One student has calculated that 60 per cent. of new investment in railways in the years 1885–90 was in fixed-interest securities.[1] *Cédulas*, too, were fixed-interest securities. In short, the investment in Argentina was predominantly in a form which required the Argentine economy to produce and pay *at once*. Not only did the Argentine economy have to produce and pay at once, but it had to produce sufficiently to pay in gold or in sterling. The only large block of securities not written in sterling or gold were the *cédulas*. These were predominantly payable in paper currency.

The next important characteristic of the Argentine investment was its relation to the state. The Argentine public authorities were committed to paying directly or indirectly a considerable part of the obligations undertaken. This meant that payment was directly related to the capacity of the Argentine public authorities to collect revenue in a sufficient volume to pay in gold or in sterling. Again, the only large exceptions were the *cédulas* and the obligations of the privately owned unguaranteed railways. In the case of the latter their freedom from state control enabled them so to alter their charges that they tended to maintain their incomes in terms of sterling. The Southern, for example, linked its freight rates directly to the gold premium, exciting much popular indignation among all classes on account of the rapid increases this involved.[2]

The capacity of the Argentine public authorities to collect the revenues necessary to meet their contractual obligations to investors depended upon two factors: firstly, the total production of saleable commodities and services, and secondly, the efficiency of the taxing system in taking a proportion of these goods and services sufficiently large to meet the requirements of the contracts with investors.

Let us examine the second of these factors first. The Argentine public authorities depended primarily upon indirect taxes

[1] Ford, *Oxford Economic Papers*, viii, 1956, p. 135.
[2] F.O. 6/399, Jenner to Salisbury, 19 Aug. 1888.

for their revenue and secondarily upon the profits of state enterprises and the sale of public lands. The principal source of revenue of the National Government was the excise taxes and customs duties levied on imported and exported commodities. The provincial Governments relied upon the sale of lands and the profits of railway, banking, and other public enterprises, such as docks. They possessed an additional source of revenue in the form of grants made to them by the National Government, which meant in fact that the provincial Governments, too, received part of their revenue from the customs and excise duties.

This revenue system depended for its efficiency to a very large extent upon the degree to which the levies were a real and not a fictitious proportion of the saleable goods and services of the community. The degree to which these levies were real or fictitious was bound up with the currency and credit policies of the Government. Both President Roca and his successor, Juárez Celman, professed to believe in the necessity of a gold-based currency and in a banking policy which closely related the volume of notes and credit to the gold assets of the banks. Roca had attempted but failed to establish a currency freely convertible into gold at par. Juárez Celman fostered the Law of National Guaranteed Banks in 1887, the object of which was to tie the note issue firmly to the holdings of gold or gold bonds of the banks. The legislation of Juárez Celman failed in exactly the same way and for the same reasons as that of Roca. The consequence was that Argentina's domestic economy operated under a system of inconvertible paper money and a loose credit policy at a time when a high proportion of Argentina's obligations on capital account were payable in gold or gold-backed currencies, principally sterling.

The consequence of the abundant issue of paper currency and the loose credit policies of the Argentine public banks was an increase in domestic purchasing power which rapidly but unevenly pushed up domestic prices. Generally speaking, wages, rents, taxes, and debt service charges on loan agreements written in national currency did not rise as fast as prices of commodities. This suited the rural interests very well—large and small, owners and share croppers alike. They had never taken kindly to Roca's currency reforms, and their pressure was responsible for the ineffective character of the Law of National Guaranteed Banks. They wanted paper money—in the rural districts its scarcity was a cause for complaint—and easy credit. When the crash came an attempt was made to blame the credit policies on rings of political favourites who received enormous loans on inadequate backing. These charges were justified, but the landed interest as a whole, and not favoured individuals alone, compelled the Governments, both national and provincial, to deny their own legislation and the policies in which they professed to believe.

One of the consequences of the monetary and credit policies forced upon the Argentine Government by the class having the most weight and influence in the community was the disorganization of the taxing system. At a time when the direct and indirect sterling and gold obligations of the Argentine public authorities were growing rapidly, the amount of gold or sterling which could be purchased with the bales of paper collected in the custom houses declined. The real incidence of fixed duties diminished with every increase in the gold premium, and even *ad valorem* duties showed a loss of real value between the moment of receipt and expenditure. Before the proclamation of 50 per cent. gold duties in June 1890 the burden of converting a revenue collected in paper into gold or sterling grew steadily. The calculations of one student suggest that in 1889 the 'cost' of conversion from paper to gold increased the obligation of the Argentine Government to its sterling and gold creditors by something approaching 45 per cent.[1] Any Government at any time would find it difficult to increase taxes sufficiently rapidly to fill such a gap. The Government of Juárez Celman was, perhaps, the least qualified imaginable to undertake measures of the severity required and the Argentine community of 1888–9 the least likely to endure them. The Southern might be able to execute such a policy of linking its charges to the gold premium, but the Argentine Government in 1889 had neither the inclination nor the determination to gear taxes directly to gold. When it took a half-step, a revolution followed within a matter of days.

The provincial revenues were in an even more serious plight

[1] J. H. Williams, *Argentine International Trade under Inconvertible Paper Money, 1880–1900* (Cambridge, Mass., 1920), pp. 94–97.

than those of the National Government. That Government at least had its hands upon a well-organized system of levying tolls on the principal commercial flow of the nation, but the provincial governments, traditionally ill equipped with the means of collecting revenue, were plainly unequal to the tasks of finance which they undertook. Even the Government of the rich and relatively densely populated Province of Buenos Aires was poor. Having no longer direct access to the customs revenues, the Government of Buenos Aires was, like its poorer brethren, dependent to a considerable degree on grants from the National Government. These grants, never large, were much reduced in real value by the rapid rise in domestic prices. The provincial public lands, which always seemed such a sure security to investors, were not the means of revenue which they might have been. The provincial governments were first sellers and thus not the beneficiaries of the rapid rise in land values. Moreover, the lands were alienated in large blocks at nominal prices. This is understandable because the lands available for sale were undeveloped and largely uninhabited. The business enterprises of the provinces—the banks and railways—might have yielded a profit, but both the banks and the railways were financed by foreign borrowing. In the case of the railways it was always a reasonable inference that if a provincial government built a railway it was not at this stage a commercial proposition. The exception was the *Oeste* owned by the Province of Buenos Aires, but by 1889 what had once been a profitable enterprise was badly run down and not a sure source of revenue. In the case of the banks all without exception pursued such lax policies of lending that their bad debts made impossible the payment of any surplus into the provincial treasuries. Indeed, clandestine issues of bank notes as a result of connivance between the provincial authorities and the bank directors contributed to the inflationary situation,[1] and only marked the inadequacy of the real revenues of the provinces. In August 1891 the British chargé d'affaires in Buenos Aires informed a colleague in the Foreign Office privately that his study indicated that the revenue of the provincial Governments 'does not come up to the service required for their public debt!',[2] and he

---

[1] Notably so in Catamarca and Buenos Aires Provinces.
[2] F.O. 6/418, Herbert to Currie, privately, 31 Aug. 1891.

believed the situation so serious that it did not bear public discussion.

The disorganization of the public revenues by the credit and monetary policies of the Argentine Government must be treated separately from the problem of production. A substantial percentage of the money advanced by British and European investors had been, and was being, employed to buy tools with which the Argentine community were exploiting the natural resources of the pampas and converting them into products saleable in the world market. Whether or not the Argentine public authorities were willing and able to lay hands on a portion of these saleable products and transfer them to the creditors of Argentina was a matter of politics. Whether the investment in tools—railways, port works, freezing plants, and farm machinery—was yielding what was expected of it was a matter of management, organization, the willingness of people to work, and the weather. With the advantage of hindsight it can be said that the investment in general was made with sufficient intelligence to produce in the long run a sufficient volume of commodities to pay for the investment and to absorb a good part of the corruption, misjudgement, and conspicuous waste which were rampant at the time. But in the short run there were real productive difficulties which contributed to the breakdown in 1890 and 1891. Furthermore, the monetary and credit policies of the Argentine public authorities contributed to the short-run difficulties.

There was no evidence of substantial over-building of railways in the years 1885–90, but there was some over-building in relation to immediate use. This is a phenomenon usual in expanding communities of the frontier type where the peopling of lands is indispensable to the success of railways. Argentina 'grew into' the railway mileage projected in the late 1880's and completed by 1892, but the growing process was slower than the building process. As a result the railway capital was growing faster than railway earnings at the moment when the financial breakdown occurred. A study made by the Corporation of Foreign Bondholders[1] revealed, for example, the relationship between railway capital, earnings, and profits, shown in the Table, p. 444.

[1] Corporation of Foreign Bondholders: *Twentieth Annual Report*, 1892, p. 34.

In 1892 this trend changed. Traffic, receipts, and earnings began to grow faster than capital invested, and continued to do so with very little interruption for many years thereafter.[1]

As we have already observed, over-building in relation to immediate use was not only a frontier phenomenon but an aspect of the competitive scramble of the railways for control of areas of potential traffic. There was some duplication of lines, but this was not a serious burden to the community, because Argentine lines were cheap to build, and of light construction for low-speed operation. Duplication did not, therefore, present the same problem as it did in countries like Canada, where high construction costs and long hauls meant large capital investment in relation to use.

Year	Capital	Earnings	Net profits
	£	£	£
1887	40,710,000	3,276,000	1,461,000
1888	43,592,000	3,580,000	1,484,000
1889	49,584,000	3,885,000	1,193,000
1890	68,748,000	3,305,000	1,074,000
1891	74,710,000	2,983,000	943,000

One aspect of the arrest of development which characterized the Baring Crisis has been insufficiently noticed. Few students have studied the effect of the monetary and credit policies of Argentina upon the immigration so essential to the peopling of vacant land. Generally speaking, direct colonization, that is, the transfer of agricultural labourers and farmers directly from Europe to agricultural enterprises in Argentina, was a failure. Free immigration, which was responsible for an overwhelming proportion of all immigration at this period and later, was a two- or three-stage process. The immigrant moved from Italy, Spain, Greece, Ireland, or Germany his own volition but with the advantage of a small travel subsidy from the Argentine Government. Upon arrival the great majority became wage workers, some permanently: but for a great many this was a step in the direction of becoming farmers, on shares or as

[1] A. B. Martínez and M. Lewandowski, *The Argentine in the Twentieth Century* (London, 1911), p. 94. This work shows a less drastic decline in receipts and profits than the study by the Corporation of Foreign Bondholders, but it confirms the trend.

owners of land purchased outright or with the assistance of a mortgage loan. For all but a small minority with some capital wage work was an essential stage in entering the agricultural industry, for it was the stage wherein immigrants accumulated the capital or part of the capital to commence wheat growing.[1] The effectiveness of this system of free immigration as a means of peopling the wilderness and bringing the pampas into production depended upon whether or not the immigrants could pass from stage one to stage two. Any event which hindered the accumulation of capital by immigrants tended to slow up the process or stop it, and this was exactly the effect of the monetary and credit policies of the Argentine Government.

Argentine wage-workers were not well organized to bargain with their employers, but a large majority of them, being immigrants, were not obliged to come or to stay in Argentina. A sharp cut in real wages had the effect of checking immigration and of reversing the flow of people from one side of the Atlantic to the other. Furthermore, it had the effect at first of checking the flow from the cities to the countryside and from the ranks of wage labour to the ranks of working farmers. In the year 1891, when the gold premium reached its highest point and real wages were at their lowest, there was an emigration of 30,000 people from the Argentine Republic compared with an immigration of 220,000 in the year 1889.[2]

As early as 1886 the effect of rising prices upon real incomes was beginning to be noticed, but the only official action taken was legislation in September of that year to double the paper salaries of judges and generals of the Army. Generals of division got a 50 per cent. increase, and so did generals of brigade. From colonel downward no notice was taken of falling real incomes. This was the policy of the Government, and it ramified through the whole community: for the privileged few an adjustment upward, for the rest a submission to the iron laws of a rubber currency. By the winter of 1887 a wave of discontent was beginning to rise among the wage-workers. 'They begin to feel sore', reported the *South American Journal*. 'For more than

---

[1] A share-cropper working 250 acres required an estimated £320 worth of equipment in the years before World War I. See Martínez and Lewandowski, *The Argentine*, p. 148.

[2] From *Extracto Estadistico, 1915*, quoted in Williams, *Argentine International Trade*, p. 207.

two years . . . their wages have been going down, down! The rents of their houses and prices of their clothing have been going up, up! Between two or three years ago these skilled workmen could save—aye, and did save money sufficient to buy their own houses and ground. . . . Ya no se puede, señor. It is now almost impossible.'[1] In spite of the fall in real wages attempts were made to cut money wages. The Anglo-Argentine Tramways Company cut the wages of their drivers and conductors, and the English-language *Buenos Aires Standard* cried out against the injustice. 'Living in this city is now so dear that the smallest reduction of wages presses terribly on the humble classes; but London shareholders must have their fat dividends made fatter no doubt.'

The tram-workers went on strike. In November 1887 the German carpenters issued an invitation to a meeting to form a workers' committee to consider the reduction in real wages and the prolongation of hours which was coming about as a result of the installation of electric lighting in workshops and factories. Some enterprises began to make partial adjustments in wages in accordance with the gold premium. The Southern, for example, undertook to pay 50 per cent. of the wages of permanent staff in gold or the equivalent. Measures such as these mitigated the discontent in some degree. The wages of seasonal workers in the harvest fields could not be kept unduly low, for they had to rise sufficiently high to attract men. Throughout 1887 and 1888 a combination of measures and circumstances contrived to maintain a rate of real wages which could still attract immigrants and enable them to flow into the countryside.

In 1889, however, the gold premium began to climb rapidly. In 1887 it had been on average only 35 per cent. and in 1888 48 per cent., but in 1889 the average was 94 per cent., getting progressively higher as the year passed. In October 1889 the British Minister in Buenos Aires warned Salisbury of the 'grave depreciation of the paper currency',[2] and he told of a growing wave of strikes which happily were not yet beyond the control of the police. Immigrants were still pouring into Buenos Aires, and the Argentine agents in Europe were intensifying their

[1] 23 July 1887.
[2] F.O. 6/404 Pakenham to Salisbury, 15 Oct. 1889.

immigration propaganda, particularly in northern Europe.[1]
The condition of the immigrants was, however, deteriorating
rapidly. The only large immigrant groups from Britain were
Irish. Both the immigrants themselves, their priests, and the
British authorities in Buenos Aires were reporting back that
unemployment, low wages, and inadequate accommodation
were spreading misery among them. As early as February 1889
the hierarchy of the Roman Catholic Church in Ireland had
become so alarmed at the fate of their people that the Archbishop of Cashel published a pastoral letter advising Irishmen
not to emigrate to Argentina. In April a protest came from
a less ecclesiastical quarter when Mr. Bradlaugh asked the
Government whether or not only 9,536 out of 22,749 immigrants landed in Buenos Aires in November 1888 had been
able to obtain work. The Government itself would do nothing
to check the flow of immigrants. The Foreign Office conducted
a prolonged negotiation with the Treasury lasting a twelve-
month to obtain an additional Vice-Consul in Buenos Aires to
protect immigrants and straighten out their troubles, but at the
same time turned down flatly a proposal by one of its own
members that immigrants be advised publicly to settle in
British possessions and 'certainly not [to go] to more or less
unsettled Spanish countries'. In dismissing the suggestion the
Under Secretary remarked: 'We have no ground whatever for
such a statement'.[2]

By July 1890 the flow of immigration had come to a stop, and
more people were leaving Argentina than were entering.[3] Thus,
as the financial crisis mounted in intensity and the gap between
obligation and ability to pay widened, the labour force began
to diminish. The effect of this upon production is not easy to
determine. The diminution of immigration was offset from
mid-1889 onward by the growing unemployment which accompanied the check in capital investment. In spite of a net emigration from Argentina in the last half of 1890 and throughout
1891, the labour market was glutted. Living conditions in the
towns were very bad. During March and April 1891 the British

[1] F.O. 6/406, papers printed by the so-called 'Information Office of the Argentine Republic', contained in Bridgett to Fergusson, 9 May 1889.
[2] F.O. 6/408, Paper of 27 Mar. 1889, on Emigration to Argentine Republic.
[3] F.O. 6/410, Bland to Salisbury, 15 July 1890.

Minister reported discontent, unemployment, and gross poverty owing to the 'enormous cost of the commonest necessaries of life'.[1] Only the lucky or the prudent had the means of returning to Europe. Even prudence meant little as inflation destroyed the purchasing power of bank deposits. The unemployed were forced to migrate to the countryside and accept the work which was offered. In his report for the year 1891 Vice-Consul Bridgett told of low wages and abundant labour available in the wheatfields of Santa Fé. As railway building came to an end and new investment ceased, labour turned to the production of saleable goods in the countryside—and at low cost to the producers. In July 1891 the Commercial Secretary of the British Legation reported wages of labourers in towns as the equivalent of 2s. 6d. a day, and in the countryside peons were working for 8d. to 1s. a day with maté, meat, maize, and huts provided. Railway wage-bills were coming down, too. Even men working on the Transandine Railway at an altitude of 10,000 feet were earning only 1s. 10d. to 2s. 6d. a day and were deeply in debt at the food stores run by the contractors.[2]

In any attempt to understand the Baring Crisis it must be borne constantly in mind that extremely hard work at very low real rewards for those who laboured in the wheatfields, corrals, slaughterhouses, and railway yards of Argentina was the foundation of its resolution. This labour produced the saleable products which in the end enabled the Argentine Government and the railway companies to satisfy the investing classes—or a decisive part of them. The labour became available at low cost at a time when nature was kind. Although the year 1888–9 was one of bad weather and drought, the crop harvested in 1890 was reasonably good. That of 1891 was somewhat better in wheat, but the maize and linseed crops failed. Then followed a period of good years when wheat and flax flourished, and maize did very well some seasons. Simultaneously labour was abundant and cheap. Total receipts from exports for the years 1890–5, inclusive, were nearly £21 millions greater than in the years 1884–9, inclusive. If one wants an 'explanation' of why Baring Brothers did not finally break and why a settlement was reached with the creditors of Argentina, there it is.

---

[1] F.O. 6/415, Pakenham to Salisbury, 4 Mar. 1891.
[2] F.O. 6/418, Herbert to Pakenham, 4 July 1891.

But is it? Such a generalization assumes the omnipotence of the social forces which were evidently in operation grinding the helpless in order that the strong might escape the consequences of their ignorance and folly. But the story can be told in another way, and this reveals the part played by individuals.

Early in 1889 the optimism of the previous years began to wane. The prospect of a poor crop worried the speculators on the Bolsa, and the premium on gold began to rise. Juárez Celman's Finance Minister began to realize that the time was fast approaching when it might be difficult for the Government to pay what it owed in Europe. In February he decreed the prohibition of gold sales on the Bolsa, as if he could exorcise the spectre of the gold premium by an administrative act. This measure, of course, solved nothing. Gold or its equivalent still had to be found to meet the claims of the creditors. Finance Minister Varela commenced drawing on the stocks of gold which were the reserve funds of the Guaranteed Banks. Simultaneously he began to look round for a new set of creditors who would lend at a lower rate of interest and require a smaller annual repayment of capital. Various newspapers told of plans to convert the Argentine public debt by operations in Berlin and Paris. Unfortunately the bankers in Berlin and Paris were rather stricter than those in London concerning the terms on which advances might be made.[1]

Signs of difficulty emerged above the surface of events when the Government proposed to pay the Hard Dollar Loan of 1872 in paper dollars. In plain language this was a proposal to break the terms of their bond with a particular group of creditors by a verbal ingenuity which shook confidence. By September 1889 the faith of the investing classes was thoroughly shaken, and the crash might have come then had not there existed the intermediaries between the individual investors and the Argentine public authorities, namely the underwriters, such as Baring Brothers, whose judgement was still trusted by the people with investment funds. The bankers and underwriters were working desperately to keep capital flowing, but they could see clearly

---

[1] M. Ewald of the Banque Russe et Française declared that Argentine credit was unquestionable, *provided* there were no further emissions of paper money or *cédulas*, customs duties were collected in gold, and the administration of the finances and landed property of the provinces was improved. *South American Journal*, 4 Jan. 1890.

by the end of 1889 that some alteration in the existing distribution of Argentine production would have to be made if the existing interest of investors was to be maintained.

The best suggestion which the bankers could make was a more drastic version of the Pellegrini agreement of 1886, which involved supervision of the disposition of a refunding loan; a standstill on fresh loans for ten years; an undertaking to stop issuing paper money; and a severe pruning of government expenditure. Proposals of this kind were no better than total bankruptcy as far as Juárez Celman's Government was concerned. The people who made up his immediate entourage, those who consistently supported him in Congress, and his protagonists in the provinces were 'a collection of persons, some of whom were said to draw salaries from the Nation, and all, or nearly all, of whom have, it [was] alleged, within a comparatively recent period emerged from positions of obscurity and even almost of indigence, to the possession of great wealth'.[1] Economy in government expenditure and deflationary monetary and credit policies meant the end of the men then in the saddle. The Government, therefore, had no hesitation in rejecting the terms of the European bankers.

These *nouveaux riches* were not the only people of authority in Argentina. If the German carpenters of Buenos Aires cried out against the relaxed monetary and credit policies of the Government, they were not alone. Some of the older and well-entrenched landed class were as unhappy as the carpenters, but for different reasons. Senator Aristóbulo del Valle was one of these. He had spent nearly ten years denouncing the rackets and the financial and commercial immorality of Argentine public life. Vice-President Pellegrini, whose lack of morals never clouded his judgement, had decided that the time had come to stop. In another quarter, too, a force was forming against the Government. Leandro Além, the radical idealist who had played a leading part in the uprising of 1880 against General Roca, was galvanized into more intense action. In September 1889 an alliance was formed which took the name of the *Unión Cívica Radical* and declared its determination to turn out the *Partido Autonomista Nacional* of Juárez Celman.

The formation of the *Unión Cívica* only served to intensify the

[1] F.O. 6/404, Pakenham to Salisbury, 15 Oct. 1889.

contradictions of the Government's policy. In September Juárez Celman suspended the operation of the Law of National Guaranteed Banks, which meant a further round of credit and currency expansion, but in October his supporters in the Congress started cutting public expenditure and giving consideration to sharp increases in the tariff on luxury products. Simultaneously, efforts appear to have been made to distract public attention from the crisis in politics by circulating rumours that Britain was planning some sort of forcible interference in Argentine affairs. When he heard the rumours of a British naval concentration in the waters of the River Plate, Pakenham at once waited on the Foreign Minister to deny them.[1]

As the year 1889 drew to a close, the opposition began to focus their attention upon the moral and legal aspects of the monetary and credit policies of the National Government. It was alleged, and much solid evidence was produced in support of the charges, that the directors of the various Guaranteed Banks had, with the connivance of the Government, systematically and repeatedly broken the laws by clandestinely emitting large sums of paper currency and, further, that the friends of the Government and the bank directors had received large unsecured loans. This corruption was already well known in commercial circles and among speculators and was a factor in the continuous rise in the gold premium, reflecting the determination of those with knowledge to protect themselves against the consequences of a further domestic price rise by acquiring assets written in terms of stable currencies.

As prices rose and unemployment increased, the temperature of popular discontent mounted in Buenos Aires. The European bankers were unwilling to promote a vast conversion operation unless the Government of Juárez Celman adopted a course of action which would destroy its *raison d'être* and most of its supporters. In March 1890 the great Madero Port Works were opened, but no ship could enter the docks with any confidence because the channels were improperly planned and dredged. This fiasco seemed to reveal the character of Juárez Celman's administration—a vast expenditure on something which was needed but would not work. A few days after the opening of the docks it was learned that the Hon. John Baring had been in

[1] F.O. 6/404, Pakenham to Salisbury, 15 Oct. 1889.

Buenos Aires for several weeks. Why? Something surely was wrong. Such was popular rumour.

Meanwhile, Juárez Celman and his ministers were endeavouring to effect some alteration in policy which might satisfy the bankers and bring some order into the affairs of the Republic. Late in March the President sent a number of decrees to the Congress for approval, the purposes of which were to cut public expenditure; to cease all further guarantees of railways; to levy gold customs duties; to regulate speculation in gold on the Bolsa; and to inquire into the operation of all joint-stock companies. There is little doubt that Juárez Celman wished to bring inflation under control and to eradicate the worst evils of corrupt credit policies. These is no doubt that he had some idea of what was required in the circumstances. But he was not a strong man personally nor did he have the character to rally to him the men who wished to end the privileges and rackets of the *nouveaux riches*.

While these events were in progress, some indication of the desperate condition of the finances of the Province of Buenos Aires began to emerge. Early in March the greatest asset of the Province, the *Oeste*, was put up for sale. A firm acting for Baring Brothers offered $35 millions gold (£7,000,000), and were refused, but a month later the Bank of London and the River Plate, acting for an unnamed group of capitalists, secured the property for £8,200,000. Even this sum could not save the Province of Buenos Aires.

On 10, 11, and 12 April there were great popular demonstrations in the streets of Buenos Aires under the leadership of the *Unión Cívica*. On the 12th the Cabinet resigned, and on the 16th President Juárez Celman named a new Cabinet with a critic of the Government, Roque Sáenz Peña, at the Foreign Office, and a leader of the established landed interest, Dr. José E. Uriburu, in the Ministry of Finance. The history of the following three months turns around the efforts of Uriburu to find a compromise which would keep Juárez Celman in office, win the support of the European bankers and hence a refunding loan, and save as much of the inflationary policy as would benefit the interests with which he was connected. It must be said at once that Uriburu failed.

The British Minister reported that Uriburu was 'well known

and much trusted, both here and . . . in financial circles in Europe, especially in England'.[1] Negotiations for a refunding loan in London took on a new life, but this life depended upon what Uriburu could do in Argentina. He was exceedingly cautious in his public utterances, but he seems to have been determined to bring into the open the scandalous administration of the Guaranteed Banks. A letter which Uriburu had received from the President of the *Comisión Inspectora de Bancos* was made public. This official letter drew attention 'to certain alarming facts and proceedings which affect the system of Banking laws'. It was revealed that the Provincial Banks of Catamarca and Santa Fé had illegally increased the volume of their notes. But Uriburu did not seek to break the banks. On the contrary he secured a decree which enabled him to lend money to the Provincial Bank of Buenos Aires and the National Bank in order, presumably, to keep them from shutting their doors. In return for the loan, however, he demanded the resignation of the President of the National Bank and his assignment to a sinecure in Europe. Simultaneously, Uriburu decreed a 15 per cent. increase in customs duties and the collection of 50 per cent. of the duties in gold.

Given this kind of policy, Juárez Celman was obliged to choose between Uriburu and his own supporters; between deflation with increased real taxes and the *status quo*. Juárez Celman chose his supporters. He refused to remove the President of the National Bank. Uriburu resigned. In one day the gold premium jumped from 118 to 165. The President of the National Bank was obliged to inform Baring Brothers that Argentina could not pay the quarterly dividends due on the bonds of the Republic.

Argentina had now reached a crisis in her history. For nearly thirty years the landed magnates of Argentina, the men with great social and economic power, had committed themselves to a course of economic development in agreement with the investing classes of Great Britain and western Europe. Were they now to break the great general contract within which all the particular legal contracts were comprehended? Were they by great acts of repudiation to cut themselves off once more and, perhaps, for ever from the source of credit in the great industrialized

[1] F.O. 6/409, Pakenham to Salisbury, 27 Apr. 1890.

nations? Were they to say, as General Rosas had so often said, 'We stand alone'?

In the answer given, Dr. Miguel Juárez Celman had little voice. With Uriburu's departure the negotiations with the bankers in London soon came to an end. The new Finance Minister, Señor García, began to lead the nation farther along the path to total inflation and repudiation. A bill was presented to Congress in July authorizing the National Hypothecary Bank to issue $100 millions in mortgage notes, and another bill authorized an issue of $6 millions in notes of a fraction of a peso. Juárez Celman seemed to be bent on repudiation.

While Uriburu was still in office, the British Minister in Buenos Aires had advised the Foreign Secretary that the Argentine Government would soon be more solidly based than for some years past. Even after Uriburu resigned Pakenham took a complacent view of the situation. He refused to postpone his visit to Paraguay, and on 28 June 1890 he set out for Asunción. The suspension of the quarterly dividends on the Argentine loans did not seem to worry him. Indeed, the suspension appears to have been regarded as so temporary an expedient that it was not mentioned in Pakenham's dispatches, and he may not even have known of the fact. During July the chargé d'affaires, Bland, reported on the failure of the conversion loan project, but the explosive possibilities of the situation did not communicate themselves to him either. On 21 July he reported to Salisbury that there was a rumour of a conspiracy to overthrow the Government, but in his view the concentration of troops around the Government buildings was more an inconvenience to street traffic than anything else. He doubted whether there was any real danger to the Government.[1]

At 5.30 p.m. on 26 July the chargé sent a telegram to the Foreign Office *en clair*: 'Military and civil revolution broken out here this morning. Fighting going on all day. Result hitherto uncertain. Godfrey Bland.' At 6.45 p.m. on the 27th he telegraphed again. 'Revolution still proceeding. Heavy firing this morning. Four men of war declared for insurgents and bombarded position belonging to Government troops. President left Buenos Ayres yesterday; Vice-President remains. Hostilities have temporarily ceased,—armistice until ten tomorrow

[1] F.O. 6/410, Bland to Salisbury, 21 July 1890.

morning having been agreed to. Success of revolutionary party seems probable. H.M. ships *Beagle* and *Bramble* here. Town tolerably quiet, for the moment.'[1]

On the 28th Bland telegraphed news of negotiations. On the 29th he reported agreement and an amnesty for the insurgents. At 7 p.m. on 30 July he telegraphed: 'Everything settled; town quiet; street traffic resumed.'[2]

What was settled? On the surface very little, or so it seemed. It is possible, however, to argue that the revolution of 26 July preserved that connexion with the centres of European capital and established the political foundation of the solution which was finally found for Argentina's economic difficulties. There were two possible courses for Argentina at this time. Juárez Celman's course was one of repudiation and further inflation; Pellegrini's course was one of compromise with the bankers and underwriters in London and Paris. As a result of the rising of 26 July Pellegrini won power, and the way was opened for a settlement.

When the firing ceased, Juárez Celman attempted to retain control. He proposed that the existing Cabinet, which still contained members of the anti-Celman opposition, should remain in office. When this was proposed Sáenz Peña and, surprisingly, García, who had succeeded Uriburu in the Finance Ministry, resigned. Juárez Celman's next move was a proposal that he, Pellegrini, and General Roca, who had lately joined the Cabinet as Minister of the Interior, should resign *en bloc*. An appreciation of this manœuvre is, perhaps, an acquired taste which many may not feel it worth while to learn. It meant simply that Juárez Celman wished to deprive of office and authority Pellegrini, who had an alternative policy, and the strong man of the *Partido Autonomista Nacional*, General Roca, in the hope and expectation that he, Juárez Celman, would afterwards be invited to reassume the Presidential Office with a free hand to choose a new Cabinet. But Juárez Celman had misjudged the situation. There was in fact no hope for him. General Roca, like Pellegrini, seems to have come to the conclusion that Argentina could not break with the European bankers and underwriters. He sided with Pellegrini, and refused to join Juárez Celman in

[1] F.O. 6/409, Bland to Salisbury, 26 and 27 July 1890.
[2] F.O. 6/409, Bland to Salisbury, 30 July 1890.

resigning. Juárez Celman then withdrew his resignation, but a deputation of Senators and Congressmen waited on him and advised him to quit. On 6 August he departed from the office of President of the Republic. On the same day Dr. Carlos Pellegrini was sworn in as provisional President.[1]

Pellegrini chose as his Minister of Finance a man from the ranks of the *Unión Cívica*, Vicente López. In the succeeding years the men who re-established the Argentine connexion with the financiers of the European capitals were also drawn from the *Unión Cívica*: J. J. Romero and Victorino de la Plaza. On the other hand, the men who fixed the political limits to agreement were drawn from the landed class. When in 1892 there was a fear that something more than a financial compromise might be required of Argentina, the man called briefly to the office of Foreign Minister was Tomás de Anchorena, the greatest landlord of them all. Anchorena spoke no European language but Spanish. He had never travelled outside the Argentine Republic. His forebears were the kinsmen of General Rosas. He said very little to foreign diplomats, and that little amounted always to 'No!'

Such was the combination of forces over which Pellegrini presided. López soon announced his financial programme. The real public revenues, he stated, had been reduced 50 per cent. by inflation. He proposed to cancel the emission of $100 millions paper decided upon by his predecessor, and to issue instead $60 millions which would be lent to the National Hypothecary Bank, to the National Bank, and to the municipality of Buenos Aires to meet their urgent current obligations. He proposed further to sell 4½ per cent. bonds locally, and to borrow $20 millions gold abroad at 5 per cent. for refunding the public debt at a lower rate of interest. Simultaneously he expressed the determination to inquire into the debts of the municipality of Buenos Aires in order to throw out all fraudulent claims, or claims tainted with corruption. Real pressure was applied to the Guaranteed Banks to sort out their creditors and discover their real position. In October López announced a plan for the National Government to take over all municipal and provincial debts, and to serve warning on all investors that in future any loans to provincial and municipal Governments would be

[1] This account is based upon F.O. 6/409, Bland to Salisbury, 7 Aug. 1890.

entirely at the risk of the investors, and that borrowings by the provinces and municipalities would be invalid by national law. Finally, López announced the end of all further railway guarantees.

In October the customs duties on imported tobacco, clothing, food, carriages, and works of art were increased to 60 per cent., and the duties on productive machinery and equipment were cut to 10 per cent. and 5 per cent., and some items were put on the free list.[1] One hundred per cent. gold customs were announced and by January 1891 they were being collected.

Thus it is plain that the 'solution' of the crisis in Argentine affairs designed to win the confidence of European financial interests was projected *before* the Baring Crisis shook the City of London in November 1890. López's policy was not, of course, implemented overnight. Pellegrini's determination to spring clean the banks required much preparation and a thorough public revelation before they could be reorganized and a rational credit-granting system established. López's proposal to take over the provincial debts, and to prohibit in effect any further borrowing by the provinces, was strongly resisted because this meant striking from the hands of the *nouveaux riches* and the would-be *nouveaux riches* the principal means of making fortunes out of land deals, government contracting, and railway promotion. Nor could plans, no matter how drastic, reverse at once the trend in domestic prices and the quick increase in the gold premiums, which amounted to 250 per cent. by the end of 1890. Likewise nothing could be done immediately to straighten out the finances of the provinces. Nothing existed in the provincial treasuries with which to pay either the bondholders or the school teachers.

The overthrow of Juárez Celman may be described as having created the possibility of a settlement with the European financial interests rather than a settlement itself. If anything, the political difficulties of Pellegrini's Government increased rather than diminished. Pakenham described it as 'a strong and a sincerely upright and capable Government',[2] but gravely handicapped by the discontent bred of the poverty of the working people and the intrigues and jealousy of the disappointed

[1] F.O. 6/410, 16 Oct. 1890, enclosed with Pakenham to Salisbury, 27 Oct. 1890.
[2] F.O. 6/410, Pakenham to Salisbury, 25 Nov. 1890.

careerists and political adventurers. The poor, however, were
not well organized politically or economically, and they presented no real danger either to the régime or to the economic
course which it was planning. The political adventurers, on the
other hand, were a real threat, the only guarantee against whose
actions were the possession of armed forces by the Government and the presence of the ablest opposition elements in the
Government itself.

Such was the position of affairs in November 1890, when
Baring Brothers and Company were forced to look bankruptcy
in the face. The embarrassment of Baring Brothers derived from
the refusal of the investing public to buy Argentine securities.
In 1888 Baring Brothers underwrote the Buenos Ayres Water
Supply and Drainage Loan of $25 millions gold. In return for $25
millions' worth of gold bonds they promised to pay $21 millions
in three instalments. By the end of 1889, however, the high
bank rate in London, the mounting gold premium in Buenos
Aires, the tales of distress among immigrants, bankruptcy of
several large enterprises, such as the *Banco Constructor*, and the
well-founded rumours about attempts to pay the Hard Dollar
Loan in paper—all these things had combined to undermine
seriously the willingness of the investing public to buy more
Argentine securities even when recommended by Baring
Brothers. Under the terms of this contract Baring Brothers
found themselves in the position in the autumn of 1890 of having
to pay out more than they were able to collect from the sale of
securities. A portfolio overloaded with unsaleable Argentine
securities now threatened their entire business, creating doubt
about every piece of paper bearing their name. In October
Baring Brothers had borrowed substantial sums in order to
meet their obligations currently coming due, but this was not
enough and other banking firms would no longer lend to them.
If the Bank of England, too, joined the ranks of those who
would no longer lend to Baring Brothers they were finished.
If Baring Brothers fell, it was certain to the Governor of the
Bank of England that the rush of creditors to obtain gold might
even bring down the Bank of England. In the event of Baring
Brothers' insolvency the Bank's reserve of £10,815,000 would
be 'entirely inadequate'.[1]

[1] Clapham, *Bank of England*, ii, p. 329.

According to the account of Sir John Clapham, the Chancellor of the Exchequer and the Governor of the Bank of England agreed that the British Government and the Bank would act as joint guarantors of a fund to be raised by the private and joint-stock banking firms which was to be used for the support of Baring Brothers until their affairs were put in order, i.e. to meet the claims of their creditors while they liquidated their assets. Liquidating the assets of Baring Brothers meant in considerable part obtaining from Argentina good money in sufficient volume to make Argentine securities saleable. The Chancellor of the Exchequer, Viscount Goschen, undertook to 'work on the Argentine Government'[1] with this end in view.

Once the Government undertook to share any possible losses occasioned in the liquidation of Baring Brothers, the Bank of England took the initiative in raising a guarantee fund. Altogether the private and joint-stock banks put up £17 millions, and on the strength of this the Bank of England continued to accept Baring Brothers' bills.

The success of this manœuvre from the bankers' point of view depended upon a settlement with the Argentine Government which would sustain the market value of Argentine securities and thus enable Baring Brothers to liquidate their holdings without too severe a loss. Early in November 1890 an emissary from the Argentine Ministry of Finance appeared in London in the person of Dr. Victorino de la Plaza. The bankers appointed an international committee under the chairmanship of Lord Rothschild for the purpose of reaching an agreement with Dr. de la Plaza on behalf of the holders of Argentine National securities and the bonds of the Buenos Ayres Waterworks. The Corporation of Foreign Bondholders appointed another committee under the direction of Sir John Lubbock and Lord Eustace Cecil to look after the interests of Argentine investors generally. Eventually a Guaranteed Railway Committee was also formed. On the fringes of outer darkness, with small help from the big men, a *cédula* committee operated with little hope except that provided by an affiliation with the Corporation of Foreign Bondholders granted in 1893.

Dr. de la Plaza made it plain to the Rothschild Committee that the Argentine Government could not go on paying its

[1] Ibid.

obligations by purchasing bills in the open market. Such a procedure had already driven up the gold premium to dangerous heights, and a continuation would 'make living unbearable except for the richer classes, and might even cause a revolution'.[1] The Rothschild Committee were willing to concede that this was so, and that a solution consisted of lending the Argentine Government more money in order to pay their current obligations. It was, of course, argued[2] that this proposal was only postponing the day of reckoning. Three views emerged. One group took the strict view that Argentina ought immediately to make the reforms necessary to pay without a loan. The German and French members of the Rothschild Committee argued for a small loan of approximately £1,500,000 to pay current obligations on the understanding that the Argentine Government contracted its currency and reformed its banks, levied 100 per cent. gold duties, imposed a severe land tax, and cut public expenditure.[3] Lord Rothschild and the English members advocated a large loan of £12–15 millions, the effect of which would bring down the gold premium considerably and ease the position of the railways, whose sterling profits were now being hit severely by the high gold premium. Rothschild argued sensibly that new investment projects had come to an end, Argentine imports were falling, exports were rising, and Argentina would grow into her capital structure so that the additional obligations of £15 millions used to pay current obligations could be borne. It was, of course, widely suspected that the real point of Rothschild's 'liberal' solution was to maintain the market value of Argentine securities for the time being and thus assist Baring Brothers to unload their holdings on a wider public.[4] No agreement was reached inside the committee, the German and French bankers eventually withdrew, and Rothschild and his English colleagues reached an agreement with de la Plaza in March 1891.

Politically the Rothschild Loan Agreement was very liberal. It bound the Argentine Government to nothing except the reduction of the volume of its currency in circulation by $15

---

[1] *The Economist*, 6 Dec. 1890, p. 1535.
[2] Ibid., 20 Dec. 1890, pp. 1598–9.
[3] Ibid., 13 Dec. 1890, p. 1568.
[4] Ibid., 7 Mar. 1891, pp. 301–2.

millions a year for three years; the acceptance of the coupons of the bonds of the loan in payment of gold customs duties; and the use of the bonds to pay current obligations, including railway guarantees.[1] Unfortunately the Rothschild Loan Agreement was so liberal that it did not achieve its main purpose, i.e. to maintain the market value of Argentine securities. *The Economist's* narrow view was the view of the investing public. The day of reckoning was being postponed, they said, and therefore confidence was gone.

Until the crisis in the affairs of Baring Brothers, established Argentine securities had maintained their market value surprisingly well, having regard for the real difficulties of the Argentine Government and the fact of revolutionary violence in July. Stocks of Buenos Aires City, which had stood at 96·8 in January 1890, had only declined to 87–90 by 1 November. Argentine 6 per cents, which had been selling at 100–2 in January, were going at 98 in November. Central Argentine shares had fallen from 178 to 104 between January and November, and Buenos Ayres Great Southern from 184–7 to 160–3. With the news of Baring Brothers' embarrassments a decline set in, which grew in severity until August 1891. Between January 1890 and June 1891, *The Economist* estimated, the total market value of Argentine National Government securities fell from £26,157,000 to £13,379,000 and provincial and municipal Government securities from £29,903,000 to £9,218,000.[2] A large part of this decline took place between November 1890 and August 1891.

It is a simple matter to explain theoretically the failure of the Rothschild Loan Agreement as a measure for arresting the collapse of Argentine securities. Not quite so simple, however, is an explanation of the behaviour of the Argentine Government during the months following Baring Brothers' difficulties. The Rothschild Agreement was exactly what Pellegrini and his followers had been seeking. In the absence from the agreement of any categorical prohibition of foreign borrowing it was far more liberal than the Argentine Government had any right to expect and many of the bankers had any disposition to concede. None the less, the Pellegrini Government, which had already

---

[1] Based on the text of the agreement from *La Nación* in F.O. 6/418, 4 Jan. 1891.
[2] *The Economist*, 6 June 1891, p. 725.

indicated a determination to clean up the Guaranteed Banks, now moved in the direction of attacking the foreign-owned banks in order, as they imagined, to assist the Argentine Guaranteed Banks. In November the British Minister reported that Pellegrini had accused the foreign banks of 'locking up gold in their vaults and catering to unhealthy speculation'. He accused them, too, of distributing large dividends at a time of crisis.[1] Gold sales on the Bolsa were prohibited and the circulation of foreign gold coins was made illegal. These measures were followed in December by a 2 per cent. tax on all deposits in foreign-owned banks. The object of this decree was candidly stated to be not an increase in the public revenues but a diminution of deposits in foreign banks and an increase in deposits in the Guaranteed Banks.

The tax on deposits in foreign banks was the beginning of a campaign directed at foreign-owned enterprise. In January a 7 per cent. tax on the profits of foreign joint-stock companies was imposed. Heavy increases in the licence fees of foreign insurance companies were levied. Tramway companies and gas companies were prohibited by the municipal authorities from increasing their charges and were subjected to serious harassment, such as orders to remove tracks or mains from certain streets. Subsequently railway and meat-packing companies were exempted from the 7 per cent. profits tax.

When news of these measures reached London, the Marquis of Salisbury asked the Law Officers of the Crown to consider whether or not the Argentine Government and the provincial and municipal authorities were breaking the terms of the Treaty of 1825. While these questions were being studied, the political situation in Argentina did not improve. The good harvest in progress seemed to stimulate rather than diminish the disposition to violence. In Entre Rios, San Juan, and Mendoza there were outbreaks of revolutionary action. The Government was able to keep the upper hand, but in February an attempt was made on the life of General Roca, now serving as Minister of the Interior. Pakenham attributed the attempt to the influence of trashy novels on the youth of Buenos Aires. It is possible, however, to suppose that someone was seeking in Roca's death an opportunity for a new combination of political

[1] F.O. 6/410, Pakenham to Salisbury, 25 Nov. 1890.

forces, for Roca was the agency of the existing compromises. In response to the effort to kill Roca, the Government did not ban trashy novels, but it did impose a state of siege in Buenos Aires, which 'produced a feeling of security and comfort to which the residents therein have long been strangers'.[1] Pakenham was happy to add that the British community continued to play outdoor games 'just as though no such exceptional state of things existed'.

Whether the exceptional powers conferred upon the Government by a state of siege emboldened them or not is difficult to determine, but Pellegrini began at this time to shift his fire from foreign enterprises towards the Guaranteed Banks as the true agencies of the inflationary difficulties. In April he ordered the liquidation of the *Banco Nacional*. This measure may have chagrined the recipients of unsecured loans, but it brought joy to the commercial classes in Buenos Aires. The British Minister declared that he had never before witnessed the spectacle of men praising God for a bankruptcy. Once the decree of liquidation was published, the gold premium fell from 363 to 343 and finally to 324, and there was a procession in the streets.[2]

The annual Presidential Message delivered to Congress in May made a point of attacking the state banks, which Pellegrini declared had played a leading part in bringing on the crisis by lending money without security. He expressed the view that these banks ought to be replaced by private banks operated on strictly commercial principles. Pellegrini confessed to a desire to see a gold or fairly rigid silver standard established, but he admitted that a rigid metal-based currency was next to impossible at the moment.

In the Message the President announced a number of economies in the public service. He proposed to discharge 1,500 postal employees and to cut the expenditure of the Ministry of Foreign Affairs by half. He cancelled a number of fraudulent land sales, abrogated a number of guaranteed railway concessions, and closed down a number of expensive public works. Optimistically Pellegrini announced the expectation of the Government's being able to pay its way within a year's time.

These measures suggested a new quality of resolution in the

[1] F.O. 6/415, Pakenham to Salisbury, 24 Feb. 1891.
[2] F.O. 6/418, Pakenham to Salisbury, 14 Apr. 1891.

Government, but there was still a considerable gap between what the Government proposed and what it could in fact do. The Presidential election was only a year away. The temptation to seek the support and co-operation of the rascals feeding on loans from the Guaranteed Banks was very great, and the willingness to create a broad electoral front against foreigners was correspondingly evident. In June Pakenham reported intense anti-English feeling. The Commercial Secretary, Herbert, doubted whether he could remain in Argentina, and he reported that social intercourse between Englishmen and Argentinos was coming to an end.[1] A run on the English-owned banks was organized. This manœuvre back-fired. The run spread to all the banks. As a result, the strength of all but one of the English banks was demonstrated, for they continued to pay all claims throughout the run, while four other foreign banks and one Argentine bank were forced to close their doors. The wave of disquiet, generated by the attempt to break the English banks, alarmed the Minister of Finance. He offered to declare a moratorium. The Bank of London and the River Plate courteously but publicly declined to take advantage of the offer, declaring that there was nothing in the state of its resources which required a suspension of its contractual obligations.[2]

This outward calm on the part of the Bank of London and the River Plate concealed an inner disturbance. Jenner, who was in London in June 1891, estimated for the Foreign Office that the 2 per cent. tax on deposits and the 7 per cent. tax on dividends would reduce the Bank's surplus for the year from £269,000 to £55,000. In July the manager of one of the banks in Buenos Aires returned to England, and he sought an interview with the Marquis of Salisbury. Salisbury instructed the Under Secretary, Sir James Fergusson, to see him. Fergusson described the interview to Salisbury thus:

According to your message through Mr. Barrington I saw Messrs. Pritchard and Burnet to-day. The former is Manager of the London and River Plate Bank at Buenos Ayres now on leave.

As he proposed to make a representation of British interests in the Argentine I asked him if he spoke with the authority of any considerable body. He said only informally with the concurrence of a

---

[1] F.O. 6/420, Herbert's private letter to Barrington, 4 June 1891.
[2] F.O. 6/415, Pakenham to Salisbury, 9 June 1891.

few persons, and by no means with that of the Bank Directors, and he desired not to be quoted for what he wished to say

The condition of the country is such that only the intervention of other Powers can produce good Government, and it would be most effective, if by agreement with others some Power could intervene and set up a Provisional Government. No one was so much interested as Great Britain, for British subjects had 200 millions sterling embarked in the country. The United States should be asked but would probably be unable to undertake it. The interest of the debt was provided for by a loan for the next year and a half; but then would come a terrible collapse

I pointed out some of the manifest difficulties or impossibilities of the course suggested

He was an earnest and respectable man; but had only looked at the matter from one point of view

J. F. 24.7.91.[1]

Salisbury read Fergusson's report, and scrawled across the bottom of it in red ink 'Dreams!' Five days later Salisbury seized the opportunity of a speech in the Mansion House to head off the growing demand in the City of London for political intervention both in Argentina and in Chile, where a civil war had broken out and a danger of armed conflict with the United States existed. Salisbury declared that were Canning to experience a reincarnation, he would doubtless be disappointed by what he would see in South America. But Britain ought to stick to Canning's policy of non-intervention in the affairs of the South American states.

We have no intention of constituting ourselves a Providence in any South American quarrel, [Salisbury said]. We have been pressed, earnestly pressed, to undertake the part of arbitrator, of compulsory arbitrator in quarrels in the west of South America. . . . We have been earnestly pressed, also . . . to undertake the regeneration of Argentine finance. On neither of these subjects are Her Majesty's Government in the least degree disposed to encroach on the function of Providence. (Laughter and cheers.)[2]

The bankers did not abandon hope of intervention, however. A few days after the Mansion House speech the firm of Morton, Rose & Company wrote to Salisbury suggesting a modified plan of interference by the terms of which a special British envoy to

[1] F.O. 6/420, Fergusson to Salisbury, privately, 24 July 1891.
[2] *The Times*, 30 July 1891.

Argentina would be appointed to survey the economy of the country and to advise the Argentine Government about the policies it should pursue. Sir Philip Currie's reply to Morton, Rose & Company was carefully corrected by Salisbury. It amounted to a flat refusal. 'His Lordship . . . cannot think that it would be advisable that any such steps should be taken by H.M. Govt.' Currie offered, however, to introduce to the Argentine Government any representative the financial interests might themselves appoint to carry on discussion with the Argentine Government.[1]

Complaints from various interests continued to reach the Foreign Office, but Salisbury had thus brought to a standstill the movement for intervention. The evidence which might enable one to assess Salisbury's motives in strengthening the policy of Castlereagh and Canning is not abundant. When the demand for intervention manifested itself in July 1891 the weight of legal opinion in the Foreign Office was already heavily against positive action in Argentina. Sir Ernest Hertslet argued that 'there is nothing in our Treaty with the Argentine Republic of 2 February, 1825 . . . relating expressly to Joint Stock, Insurance, or other companies'.[2] Both France and Greece had taxed British insurance companies as the Argentine Government was doing, but Britain had never protested. Hertslet thought, however, that if the United States protested and got satisfaction, Britain could claim like treatment under the most-favoured-nation clause of the Treaty of 1825. The Law Officers of the Crown had been as strict as Sir Ernest Hertslet in their interpretation of the Treaty. 'Where the persons acting as agents are Argentine citizens, or foreigners, the fact that they represent a British Company does not entitle them or the Company, to invoke the assistance of Her Majesty's Government in asserting for them the right to the privilege given by the Treaty.'[3] The Law Officers were likewise of the opinion that the 2 per cent. tax on bank deposits would not justify a protest by the British Government.[4] Concerning the grievances of the tramways companies, one Foreign Office man expressed

[1] F.O. 6/420, letter of 6 Aug. 1891, and reply of 11 Aug. 1891.
[2] F.O. 6/421, several memos.
[3] F.O. 6/421, opinion of 16 Mar. 1891, by Webster and Clarke.
[4] F.O. 6/421, opinion of 17 Mar. 1891, by Webster and Clarke.

the view that the British Government would not interfere with the right of the London County Council to regulate the fares on trams owned by foreigners, and he could see no reason why Britain should object to the municipal authorities of Buenos Aires regulating the fares on trams owned by British companies.[1] British capitalists had invested in Argentina on their own responsibility, and they ought to accept the consequences of their own judgement and, likewise, of the municipal authorities of Buenos Aires.

These legal and moral foundations of policy do not appear to have been strengthened or elaborated by a consideration of economic conditions as they existed in 1891. In fact Salisbury's refusal to play the part of Providence, which seems to have been based consciously on legal opinion and political calculation, was well justified by changes in the position of the Argentine economy. True, Argentina was paying its obligations not out of current revenues but out of the proceeds of the Rothschild Funding Loan, but on the other hand the production of marketable commodities was growing, the number of projects requiring fresh capital had been drastically reduced, the gold revenues of the state were increasing, and the unemployed of the towns were being absorbed into the agricultural and pastoral labour force. New railway mileage was being completed, and the provision of rolling-stock on existing lines was improving. The germ centres of speculative insanity had been cauterized with the closing of the *Banco Nacional* and the exposure of its corruption by the publication, in June 1891, of the report on its activities. Although there were still ample grounds for misgivings on the part of foreign investors, we can see now that a favourable turn in the direction of stability had already been made by the mid-winter (July) of 1891. Pellegrini's policy of maintaining an intimate connexion with the centres of investment capital was being implemented in spite of many deviations and much lip-service to the favourite slogans of the *nouveaux riches*.

Salisbury's determination not to yield to a movement for intervention came at a moment when the United States was embarking on a forward policy in the southern part of South America. At the Pan-American Conference in March 1890 the

[1] F.O. 6/421, note on the back of private letter, Voules to Langley, 31 Mar. 1891.

Americans had spoken about the small amount of trade between the United States and Argentina, and suggested the need for an American zollverein. The Argentine delegates had criticized the American proposals and asserted their determination to maintain their sovereign independence and their connexions with Europe, which provided Argentina with immigrants, capital, and markets. When the Baring crisis came in November 1890, the Americans remained passive in Argentina. As the crisis became more acute, their chief concern in this part of the world seems to have been focused mainly on Chile, where they allowed themselves to become involved in local party strife. As a result of an assault by a Chilean mob upon sailors of the U.S.S. *Baltimore* the United States sent an ultimatum to Chile in January 1892.

It was in this circumstance of antagonism with Chile that the United States began early in 1892 to attempt to draw Argentina into the orbit of American influence. In March 1892 Pakenham reported to Salisbury 'in the strictest confidence' that 'the United States Minister, Mr. Pitkin has made two or more distinct offers to supply the Argentine Government with silver up to one hundred million (100,000,000) dollars'.[1] While these proposals were being made, a U.S. Fleet visited Buenos Aires. Pakenham went on leave at this moment. On 29 March the British Legation's most trusted source of information came with a report of American-Argentine negotiations. This so shook the chargé d'affaires that he sent to the Foreign Office the longest cipher telegram in the history of the British Legation. According to Herbert's informant the proposed American loan had been rejected because the Americans required the establishment by special legislation of an American-owned bank. The Argentine authorities would only consent to the establishment of such a bank if it operated under existing legislation such as that which governed the operations of the Bank of London and the River Plate. The Americans, however, had proposed a political agreement with Argentina by the terms of which the United States would support Argentina in any disputes which

---

[1] F.O. 6/423, Pakenham to Salisbury, 28 Mar. 1892. T. F. McGann, *Argentina, the United States and the Inter-American System, 1880–1914* (Cambridge, Mass., 1957), p. 166, presents evidence that the initiative in this matter came from Pellegrini some months before Pakenham heard about the proposal.

might develop with Chile and Brazil. The American officer conducting the negotiation had stated that the object of injuring Chile was 'to destroy British influence in Pacific'. Herbert stated that he believed what he was reporting was absolutely correct. He further stated that it was a matter of public discussion that the 'U.S. Government will agree to prevent foreign interference here in case of difficulties arising from Argentine foreign debt'.[1]

At this stage the British Legation's sources of information appear to have dried up; perhaps because of the coming of a new Minister. During April 1892 the chargé d'affaires was obliged to rely upon reading between the lines of the press. *La Nación* published a leader which implied that the Argentine-American negotiations were at an end. 'Some cherish the idea of substituting the United States for Europe', the editor of *La Nación* admitted, but he argued that the European creditors of Argentina were meeting Argentina half-way and it would not be in the national interest to effect a radical alteration in the course of policy. A few days after this editorial comment appeared *The Times* published a brief account of American attempts to obtain a naval base in the River Plate. The American Minister reacted at once. He sent a telegram to the London *Standard*, denying this and at the same time the rumour of an Argentine-American alliance. To the British chargé d'affaires the American Minister declared that he had done nothing more than propose to act as an arbitrator in disputes between South American states. Herbert admitted that the Argentine Foreign Minister may have inferred more than the Americans intended, and that the American Minister himself may not have proposed an alliance. According to Herbert's source of information the proposals concerning an alliance were made by the Admiral of the visiting American Fleet. The French Minister was satisfied that such discussions had taken place. Both the French and Uruguayan Ministers were agreed that the Americans had endeavoured to buy a naval base from either Argentina or Uruguay.[2]

The alarming spectre of an American-Argentine alliance soon dissolved. Before a month was out the Americans and the

---

[1] F.O. 6/425, Secret and Confidential telegram from Herbert, 29 Mar. 1892.
[2] F.O. 6/423, Herbert to Salisbury, 3 May 1892.

Argentinos were about to embark on a tariff war touched off by an interpretation of the McKinley tariff which affected Argentine hides. The prospect of a 1½ cent per pound gold duty on hides provoked the Argentine Government to threaten an absolute prohibition on American petroleum, timber, and machinery. So ended the dream of a partition of the Americas. Within another month the Russians were reported to be seeking a coaling station at Staten Island.[1] When the new British Minister officially inquired about the proposed American-Argentine treaty in July, he was told that nothing was fixed but that 'any advantages or concessions which might be made to the United States would be equally enjoyed by Great Britain in view of the Treaty now existing between the two countries'.[2]

While the Americans were thus coming and going in the River Plate, the settlement with the Europeans was in a state of suspended animation. Dividends were still being paid in bonds issued under the Rothschild Loan Agreement. The loans of the provinces were still in default. New capital investment had ceased. The hope and confidence which could induce a flow of money from the accounts of investing classes as distinct from the bankers and underwriters was buried in the tomb. How to roll the stone from the door? Pellegrini had no answer, nor could he be expected to have one so long as an election was impending.

The revolution of July 1890 had ensured that the followers of Juárez Celman could not hope for power. Pellegrini had further undermined them by exposing the banking rackets and by closing the *Banco Nacional*. But Pellegrini had acted as a block to the ambitions of the Radical authors of the putsch which had driven Juárez Celman from office. Pellegrini represented the authority and possessed the power of the established landed interest determined officially to sacrifice the *nouveaux riches* and to keep out the middle and working classes of the city of Buenos Aires, whose political instrument was the *Unión Cívica*. The man picked to succeed Pellegrini was Dr. Luis Sáenz Peña, whose principal assets were age, personal honesty, and the confidence of the established interests. He had the added merit of being able by the exercise of his patriarchal prerogative to exclude

---

[1] F.O. 6/423, Herbert to Salisbury, 7 June 1892.
[2] F.O. 6/425, Welby to Salisbury, 12 July 1892.

from politics his son Roque, whom the conservatives regarded
as a menace to the established order. The merit of Sáenz Peña
as a candidate consisted in his capacity partially to blunt the
hatred of the *Unión Cívica* and the people who supported Leandro
Além. The hard core of the *Unión Cívica* was as willing to attempt
assassination or a *coup d'état* against Sáenz Peña as against Roca
or Juárez Celman, but the people as a whole were less likely to
support them in such an enterprise when the object of violence
was the old and honourable jurist, Luis Sáenz Peña.

The elections were held in two stages: the first in February
was concerned with the election of the Senate and the Chamber
of Deputies; the second in April with the election of the President and Vice-President. The Congressional elections were
relatively peaceful. 'In [Buenos Aires] . . . itself the list of killed
and wounded was comparatively small', Pakenham reported,
'about fifteen or sixteen all told.' The Government was firmly
in control, and the *Unión Cívica* were kept out of the Congress.
Indeed, the new Congress was so like the old one that the
British Minister warned the Foreign Office not to expect much
change on this account.[1] In the interval between the Congressional and the Presidential elections the Government organized
an assault on the *Unión Cívica* with the object of disrupting it. A
few days before the Presidential election a conspiracy was discovered. The leaders of the *Unión Cívica* were arrested and their
headquarters occupied. Artillery and cavalry were moved into
Buenos Aires. Pellegrini established himself in the Central Police
Station to prepare for the election. The *Unión Cívica* announced
a boycott. In these circumstances the nation went to the polls
on 10 April, and Dr. Luis Sáenz Peña was elected President
and Dr. José E. Uriburu Vice-President.

The significance of the election in the relations between
Argentina and her creditors centred around the appointment
of Dr. J. J. Romero as Minister of Finance and Don Tomás de
Anchorena as Minister of Foreign Affairs. Romero's appointment 'caused much satisfaction among the mercantile community', the British Minister reported, for he was regarded 'as a
sure guarantee towards a sound and honest administration of
the Ministry of Finance'.[2] Anchorena's appointment excited

---

[1] F.O. 6/423, Welby to Rosebery, 20 Dec. 1892.
[2] F.O. 6/423, Welby to Rosebery, 14 Sept. 1892.

little public comment, but privately the British Minister was apprehensive of the consequences of finding a man so conservative and so little acquainted with world politics at the Foreign Ministry.[1] Romero and Anchorena were two sides of the same coin. One was determined to drive a harder and better bargain with the creditors of the Republic; the other was determined to maintain Argentine political independence.

Of all the men who handled the economic troubles of Argentina at this time, Romero stands out as the ablest and most sensible. He had been Roca's Finance Minister when Roca was endeavouring to stabilize the currency in 1883–4. Romero saw the need for further capital investment and he saw that the principal obstacle to further investment was the practice of paying debt service out of borrowings. He was completely opposed to the ostrich policy of trying to conceal the size of the debt of the Republic and to obscure the real capacity of Argentina to pay. On 20 November 1892 he sent a long letter to *La Nación* stating the position of the Republic and his determination to end the system of paying obligations with funding bonds. Romero's letter revealed that, given the current revenues of the Republic, Argentina could not pay its debt service charge and railway guarantees in full. This bit of realism shook the exchanges. The gold premium which had been falling for some months jumped up again, and the prices of Argentine securities sagged from their already low levels. Romero's next step was to remove Dr. de la Plaza from the post of financial agent in London on the ground that Plaza was 'too much in the hands of the firm of Messrs. Morgan'.[2] He then proposed to the Rothschild Committee in London that Argentina should begin paying her obligations in accordance with her capacity. Romero suggested that the bondholders accept a reduced rate of interest for five years; that the amortization charges be suspended for a rather longer period; and that the payments be made out of revenue. There is no evidence at present available on the subject, but it can be inferred that Romero's agent in London informally promised that if a settlement in accordance with Romero's ideas were made he would undertake to have the National Government do something about defaulted provincial

---

[1] F.O. 6/423, privately, Welby to Clarke-Jervoise, 14 Oct. 1892.
[2] F.O. 6/429, privately, Welby to Clarke-Jervoise, 15 Feb. 1893.

securities. Romero's proposals were so honest and realistic that one would like to use a less-abused epithet than statesmanlike to describe them.

The Arreglo Romero was signed by the Argentine Minister in London and by Lord Rothschild on 3 July 1893.[1] The Rothschild Committee was, of course, greatly interested in the liquidation of Baring Brothers and in order to meet the Committee the Argentine Government agreed to release the Buenos Ayres Water Supply and Drainage Company from all obligations to the public authorities of Argentina. This out of the way, the parties reached a compromise. For five years the interest on various Argentine national securities would be reduced—on some from 6 per cent. to 5 per cent., on some from 6 per cent. to 4 per cent. (this in the case of the waterworks loan), and on some by a flat 40 per cent. The overall reduction was by slightly under 30 per cent. During the period of reduced interest, the Argentine Government would pay annually a round sum of £1,565,000 to the Bank of England for distribution to the bondholders. After one year of full debt service, i.e. at the end of the sixth year, Argentina would deal directly with the issuing houses. Sinking Funds were suspended until 1 January 1901.

The principal merit of the Arreglo Romero, apart from its realism and honesty, was the way in which it directed the growing revenue surpluses of the Argentine Government into the channels of investment. The supreme defect of the Rothschild Loan Agreement had been the opportunity it presented to the Government to spend revenues on current needs, for the simple reason that debt service was being taken care of by the Funding Loan. The pressure to spend money on current projects is strong in any community, and was not least in Argentina in the 1890's. The effect of the Arreglo Romero was to divert a substantial part of the revenue to the investing classes and to provide for an increase in this diversion as time passed. If it is acknowledged that investment was desirable, this was the only way both to make it possible and to induce it.

Dr. Romero did not last long as Finance Minister. Sáenz

---

[1] Its terms can be found in detail in *Memoria de hacienda*, 1893, vol. i, pp. 146–72, and in *Exposición sobre el estado financiero y economico de la República Argentina*, 1893, pp. 79 ff., and in Corporation of Foreign Bondholders, *Twenty-first Annual Report*, 1893. There is a full summary in Williams, *Argentine International Trade*, p. 128.

Peña rid himself of Romero as quickly as he could because Romero was too much of a Rocista to suit the President. But Romero's policy was firmly established before he left the Ministry of Finance. Perhaps no Argentine Finance Minister ever did so much positive good in so short a time as Dr. Romero, and perhaps that is why his official life was so short. The British Minister once observed that Sáenz Peña was an honest man and the state of the Argentine Treasury was likely to keep him so. It could well be added that the Arreglo Romero preserved the purity of the President to the end, for it ensured that the gold revenues of the state flowed substantially into the investment channel and not into the pockets of pensioners and armament contractors.[1]

The part played by the British Government in the negotiation of the Arreglo Romero is a matter of some interest. Salisbury left the Foreign Office just before Romero took up the portfolio of Finance in Buenos Aires. The Liberals, always considered rather more susceptible to the influence of financiers than the Conservatives, came into office in August 1892, and Rosebery was at the Foreign Office when Romero was seeking to come to terms with the creditors of Argentina. Romero wanted a general settlement, but the bankers and underwriters represented by the Rothschild Committee were primarily interested in a much narrower question, viz. the bonds of the Buenos Ayres Water Supply and Drainage Company, Ltd. The Argentine Government alleged that the works built by this company were in some respects unsatisfactory, and there is little doubt that the capital cost of the waterworks exceeded the original and reasonable estimates for the work done. The money had, however, been spent, but the Argentine Government delayed the issue of the bonds to the amount of £6 millions from the sale of which the underwriters, Messrs. Baring Brothers & Company, were to recover their advances to the contractors. On the delivery and sale of these bonds turned in very large part the liquidation of Baring Brothers and the security of the guarantee fund raised

---

[1] Judging by the communications of the Argentine Minister with the Foreign Office during the period of the Baring Crisis, one would imagine Señor Dominguez to have been almost exclusively concerned with the delivery of naval vessels, gunnery trials, visits to arsenals, &c. This impression coincides with a popular belief that some Argentine politicians would have liked to solve all difficulties *à l'Américaine*, i.e. by attacking Chile or Brazil or both.

in November 1890 by the Bank of England, the joint-stock banks, and the private bankers of London. The waterworks bonds were thus a matter of great importance to the Rothschild Committee.

Some time in January 1893 Lord Rothschild went to Rosebery to ask for his help in obtaining the bonds from the Argentine Government. On 27 January Rosebery sent a telegram to the British Minister in Buenos Aires, the cost of which, £52. 2s. 2d., was paid by the Rothschild Committee. The telegram was as follows:

Buenos Ayres Water Supply and Drainage Company ask for our intervention to obtain more equitable and considerate treatment from the Argentine Govt. . . . Do what you can. The matter involves large interests, and on it depends in great measure the issue of the Baring liquidation. A want of good faith on the part of the Argentine Govt will have the worst possible effect.[1]

Welby, the Minister, does not appear to have detected the ambiguities or dangers in this telegram. Was this an instruction to intervene on the Egyptian pattern, or an instruction to use his good offices on behalf of some bankers negotiating directly with the Argentine Government? Welby interpreted the telegram in the latter sense, as, indeed, he was almost bound to do in the light of all the precedents. But the word intervention had come to mean something different by 1893 from what it meant in the days of Sir Woodbine Parish. Upon receiving the telegram Welby composed a note which he presented to Anchorena on 30 January. It was harmless enough:

I have been instructed by Lord Rosebery to bring this matter to Your Excellency's notice, and I trust that I may count on Your Excellency's good offices to obtain the necessary order for the delivery of these bonds as any further delay would greatly affect the position of Argentine credit in London which it is the interest of both countries so much to uphold.[2]

Anchorena was 'most considerate' and stated that the Argentine Minister in London had already been instructed to deliver the bonds.[3] Within a few days, however, one of the bankers in

---

[1] F.O. 6/431, Foreign Office to Welby, 27 Jan. 1893.
[2] F.O. 6/429, 30 Jan. 1893, enclosed with Welby to Rosebery, 21 Feb. 1893.
[3] F.O. 6/429, privately, Welby to Clarke-Jervoise, 15 Feb. 1893.

London either thoughtlessly or deliberately let it be known to the press that the British Government had undertaken to intervene in Argentina on behalf of the creditors. On 8 February 1892 *La Prensa* published 'news of the most serious nature' under the heading, 'Muy grave de Londres'. Welby hastily wrote to the Foreign Office privately asking for instructions.[1] On 17 February Anchorena called Welby to the Foreign Ministry and handed him a note which read:

I must inform you that both the Ministry for Foreign Affairs and the Ministry of Finance have considered themselves bound not to admit any intervention in matters connected with the Public Debt except that of the bondholders or the Firms chosen and recognised by the Government as Intermediaries, as it is thought that no foreign official action can be admitted by the Argentine Government, and still less that of other Agents not the private representatives of the Creditors themselves.[2]

When Welby's letter arrived at the Foreign Office, the permanent officials were in favour of sticking to traditional policy. 'I think he might be told that our general line is to confine ourselves entirely to giving the representatives of the Bondholders such unofficial assistance as seems judicious, and he might have a copy of Lord Palmerston's celebrated circular', Sir Thomas Sanderson minuted. By the time the matter got to Rosebery he was prepared to do nothing more than ask the Argentine Government to hurry up. The Minister in Buenos Aires was asked whether he kept his important papers properly locked up.

At this time the press was making trouble in another quarter. A new Don Pacifico threatened to be born in the person of a naturalized British subject named Edelman. This man claimed to have been arrested by the police in Mendoza and robbed of 47 rubies and £243 in cash. His case was taken up by the *Western Courier*, an English language newspaper in Valparaiso, which described him as an 'aged and learned gentleman of over seventy years of age, travelling in pursuit of scientific knowledge'.[3] The British Minister reported that Dr. Edelman was

---

[1] F.O. 6/429, privately, Welby to Clarke-Jervoise, 15 Feb. 1893.

[2] F.O. 6/429, Anchorena to Welby, 17 Feb. 1893, enclosed in Welby to Rosebery, 21 Feb. 1893.

[3] F.O. 6/429, 1 Apr. 1893, enclosed with Edelman to the British Minister, in turn enclosed with Pakenham to Rosebery, 18 Apr. 1893.

engaged in selling a cure for venereal disease, and that he had been mistaken for 'Jack the Ripper'. But Pakenham was alarmed by the fuss in the English language press, and dreaded lest the hysteria be communicated to the press at home. He called upon Dr. Bunge, the legal adviser of the British Legation and a former Minister of Foreign Affairs, to ask for suggestions. Bunge advised that Edelman be urged to bring his case to the notice of the Governor of Mendoza. When it was learned that the British Minister had recommended this course to Edelman, the *Western Courier* quoted Bret Harte: 'Is our civilization a failure, or is the Caucasian played out?'[1] Fortunately it was not necessary to mobilize the British Fleet on behalf of Dr. Edelman. The Governor of Mendoza was as satisfied as the British Minister that Edelman was a swindler and that his fate was hardly a test of Caucasian virility.

With the signature of the Arreglo Romero the way was opened for settlement of the remaining questions between the creditors of Argentina and the Republic: the defaulted provincial loans and the dividends of the guaranteed railways. It would be tedious to record the details of the negotiations on these subjects. A general account of the settlement is, however, of some interest.

The first important factor in the settlement was the assumption of the financial responsibility for the indebtedness of the provinces by the National Government. This was the last blow struck at the federal structure of Argentine politics: more deadly than the interventions and military thrusts of the past. The creditors of the Provinces of Buenos Aires, Córdoba, and Santa Fé, for example, finally accepted a settlement which consisted of receiving $34 millions gold dollar bonds of the National Government bearing $4\frac{1}{2}$ per cent. interest in place of the defaulted securities of the provinces. The creditors received thus £83 in National bonds for every £100 of provincial bonds, they accepted a lower rate of interest, and they recovered defaulted interest.[2] Another form of settlement was reached in 1898 with the creditors of the Province of Tucumán. They accepted £110 in National bonds for every £100 of provincial bonds, but received no defaulted interest.

[1] Ibid.
[2] Corporation of Foreign Bondholders, *Twenty-fifth Annual Report*, 1897, p. 8.

These settlements were achieved within the framework of Anchorena's Note of February 1893; i.e. the negotiations were carried on by the agents of the creditors.[1] The system worked out for negotiation consisted of the appointment by a Committee of the Corporation of Foreign Bondholders of an agent in Argentina, usually a banking firm such as the River Plate Trust, Loan and Agency Company, O. Bemburg & Company, or L. Cohen and Sons. These agents then negotiated a settlement which was referred to the Corporation of Foreign Bondholders for approval. The Committee of the Corporation in London generally drove a hard bargain, but accepted the fact that interest rates on Argentine loans had generally been high compared with those of the securities of comparable states and were willing to reduce interest and take a capital loss in return for the greater security offered by the National Government of the Republic. Non-British creditors were sometimes softer. The German creditors, for example, accepted £74 in National bonds as a settlement of claims for £100 from the Province of Buenos Aires, a figure well below the £83 which the British creditors obtained.

One of the most worth-while reforms to come out of the Baring Crisis was the ending of railway guarantees. The evidence that the guarantee of dividends by the public authorities was at the heart of the bad management, bad financing, and bad planning of Argentine railways is overwhelming. One guaranteed line achieved the remarkable average working speed of 3 miles an hour! The subject on which Sáenz Peña's Government achieved unanimity and won popular support was the policy of ending guarantees. Although the legislation to end the system was passed after his resignation in 1895, the ground for the reform was prepared by his Ministers. In January 1896 the National Congress authorized the issue of 50 millions gold dollar bonds bearing interest at 4 per cent. with amortization of ½ per cent. for the purpose of paying all outstanding guarantees and the extinction by negotiation of as many guarantee contracts as possible. As a result of negotiation, five

[1] The Corporation of Foreign Bondholders approached the Foreign Office for help in the matter of provincial bonds on several occasions, but the Foreign Office always stood firm on Lord Palmerston's Circular, e.g. F.O. 6/450, Memorandum on the Bonds of Buenos Aires, by Oakes, 24 Dec. 1896, which also contains a copy of Palmerston's Circular of 1849.

companies accepted lump sums in lieu of guarantees and two companies were bought outright.[1] As a result possible guarantee claims were reduced by 50 per cent. After 1905 no guarantee or subsidy of any kind was ever given to an Argentine railway company.

Of all the creditors of Argentina the holders of *cédulas* fared worst. It must be borne in mind that *cédulas*, with the exception of a few gold series of the National Hypothecary Bank, were written in terms of the national currency. Furthermore, they were not obligations of the Argentine public authorities but of the hypothecary banks. There were neither legal nor practical reasons for considering *cédulas* in the same category as state securities or railway guarantees. The Argentine authorities exhibited no intention of meeting the claims of the holders of *cédulas*, and the holders themselves seem to have been conscious of the fact that, whatever their disappointments may have been, they had no legal claims upon the Argentine authorities nor even upon the hypothecary banks so long as those banks paid in currency or the equivalent. The Foreign Office commissioned a certain Mr. Findlay to report on *cédulas* for the Council of the Corporation of Foreign Bondholders, and Rosebery personally read the report. Pakenham, however, made the point that the Council of Foreign Bondholders had not troubled to name an agent to negotiate about *cédulas* and appeared generally to treat the claims of *cédula* holders as not of the first consequence.[2]

In fact the holders of *cédulas* were exposed to the full effect of every device the landed interests of Argentina could invent to avoid the real discharge of their obligations. These debtors could pay off their debts in actual *cédulas*, which they could buy whenever the price seemed right to them. They could pay in currency. Findlay found that debtors in Buenos Aires Province were being allowed to discharge current obligations with unsecured IOU's and by fresh loans, and that in some instances mortgage agreements were torn up. This last device had a certain straightforward simplicity about it. Generally, however, more complicated devices for relieving landowners were employed. By the law of 18 April 1891 the Hypothecary Bank of

---

[1] J. S. Duncan, 'British Railways in Argentina', *Political Science Quarterly*, lii, 1937, p. 567.

[2] F.O. 6/430, Pakenham to Rosebery, 5 July 1893; Findlay's report enclosed with this, dated 29 June 1893.

Buenos Aires was authorized to pay interest on *cédulas* in *certificados al portador* which were a species of open promissory note. The holders of *cédulas* were forced to sell their *certificados al portador* in a market dominated by inflated currency, and the mortgagors could purchase them to discharge their debts to the Hypothecary Bank. Thus even paper currency ceased to figure in the accounting of the Bank. The face value of outstanding *cédulas* of the Bank had been reduced from $374,846,326 in 1889 to $156,794,437 in 1899.[1] What the loss of the original purchasers had been is incalculable.

Thus far we have described the fate of the creditors who had lent money either to the public authorities or invested it in enterprises guaranteed or sponsored by them. How did the investors in private enterprises fare in the troublous period of the Baring Crisis?

The privately owned unguaranteed railways fared relatively well in the crisis. The year 1891 was a bad one. The heavy decline in exports in 1890 and the even heavier decline in imports in 1891 affected traffic revenues, while the sharp increase in the premium on gold together with the threat of a general strike made it difficult to remit profits to London and to keep down paper dollar costs in the Argentine sufficiently to offset falling revenues, losses on exchange, and the high paper price of coal and repair parts. In 1891 the Southern could pay only 4 per cent., the *Oeste* 3 per cent., the Buenos Ayres and Rosario 2½ per cent., the Buenos Ayres and Enseñada 2½ per cent., and the Central Argentine ¾ per cent. The remaining unguaranteed lines took collectively a loss of £30,000.[2] Recovery came quickly for the unguaranteed lines, however. The increase in both imports and exports, the levelling off of the gold premium, and sharp reductions in staff enabled the companies to show profits which were again good but below those of the 1880's. In 1893 *The Economist* called attention[3] to a strange phenomenon brought about by the general atmosphere of uncertainty surrounding Argentina: no British line paid profits like the Argentine railways and yet the stock of every British line was selling at a premium of from 22 per cent. to 41 per cent., whereas all

[1] *Anuario Pillado*, 1899, p. 68.
[2] Corporation of Foreign Bondholders, *Twentieth Annual Report*, 1892, p. 34.
[3] *The Economist*, 10 June 1893, p. 693.

Argentine stocks except those of the Southern were selling at a discount. Total railway profits had gained 47 per cent. in 1892 over the previous year.[1]

The experience of British banks during the crisis duplicated in many ways the experience of the depressed years 1874–9. The London and River Plate Bank, which continued to specialize in financing the movement of goods, hardly felt the crisis in so far as profits were concerned. Between October 1889 and September 1890 the London and River Plate made a gross profit of £395,578 on an invested capital of £750,000.[2] A dividend of 15 per cent. was declared: £100,000 was put in the reserve and the remainder was put in a 'profits in suspense' account. One can understand the jealousy felt for the London and River Plate when it could do this at a time when native banks were being threatened with bankruptcy. In 1891 10 per cent. was paid in dividends; £50,000 was put in the reserve; a branch was opened in Rio de Janeiro; and the capital was raised to £900,000. In 1892 the dividend was 12½ per cent.; £50,000 was put in the reserve and £10,000 was put in an employees' pensions and benevolent fund. And so went the affairs of the London and River Plate. In 1896 the directors distributed 16 per cent.

In the 1880's two new British banking enterprises were started: the Anglo-Argentine Bank and the English Bank of the River Plate. Both did well until the years of crisis. In 1891 and 1892 the Anglo-Argentine had to cut its dividend to 2½ per cent. In 1893 it paid 3 per cent. and in 1896 6 per cent. The English Bank paid 10 per cent. in 1890, but when the crisis came it ceased to make public its position. In 1896 it was liquidated in bankruptcy.

In the public utility field—tramways and gas companies particularly—there were acute and continuing difficulties throughout the 1890's. The opposition of the municipal authorities to increased charges at a time when the paper prices of imports necessary for operation were seriously inflated left these enterprises generally in a position where they could not pay profits and could not attract new capital. Equipment deteriorated and so did the services provided. Had there been

[1] Ibid., 17 June 1893, p. 726.
[2] *Bankers' Magazine*, li, 1891, p. 120.

any grand strategy of British enterprise in Argentina, the public utility field might well have been abandoned and the losses written off. As it was, the directors and shareholders of these enterprises were reluctant to abandon their property, and so the struggle for 'justice' went on. Shareholders and directors continued to lay their complaints before the Foreign Office. The British Minister continued to call the attention of the Argentine authorities to the effect of municipal action upon the investment process, and the Argentine authorities continued to acknowledge that there was a difficulty. But nothing effective ever happened to alter the situation.

The estimate of the British investment in Argentina made by the Commercial Secretary of the British Legation in 1890 suggested that the total British investment in miscellaneous enterprises including public utilities was roughly £20 millions. An estimate made ten years later by the Argentine banking firm of Tornquist y Compañía fixed miscellaneous investment at a similar figure.[1] A factor in the static character of miscellaneous investment seems to have been the difficulties in the public utility field. Indeed, small British firms providing public services appear to have been pulling out of Argentina in the 1890's. The Argentine Steam Lighterage Company, for example, which started in 1885 with an authorized capital of £50,000 and an issued capital of £21,225, began to reduce its capital in 1895 by returning money to shareholders. By 1900 the company was wound up.[2]

Big firms in the fields which the Argentine Government was determined not to obstruct continued to expand during the 1890's once the worst difficulties were over. This was the case with the well-established railways. Tornquist y Compañía's estimate of capital suggested a British investment of approximately £95 millions in 1900. This is a figure more than 40 per cent. greater than Herbert's estimate of railway capital in 1890.[3] The paid-up capital of the Buenos Ayres Great Southern in 1890 was £8 millions and there were approximately 6,500 shareholders. By 1895 the paid-up capital was £12 millions and there were something like 9,000 shareholders. By 1900 the capital had grown to £13,775,000 and the authorized capital

---

[1] Quoted in Williams, *Argentine International Trade*, p. 150.
[2] B.T., 31/3382–202B.   [3] *Parliamentary Papers*, 1892, lxxxi.

to £16 millions, indicating a serious intention to expand. The number of shareholders grew faster than the capital. There were roughly 14,000 shareholders by 1900.[1] Similarly the capital of the Central Argentine grew from £6,750,000 in 1890 to £8 millions in 1900 in spite of the low returns earned by the Central during the years of crisis.[2]

This expansion accompanied and was a factor in the enormous increase in Argentine production which is the most impressive feature of the 1890's. Cereals (particularly wheat and linseed), wool, mutton, beef, and live-cattle exports, all expanded enormously, and the British market absorbed an increasing tide of Argentine produce.[3]

These exports were achieved under difficult conditions of falling prices during the first part of the decade. In 1893, 1894, 1895, and 1896 the terms of trade were unfavourable to Argentina. Only in 1897 did the terms begin to shift in a direction favourable to Argentina,[4] but even so the golden years of favourable terms lay beyond the Boer War. The principal factors in the Argentine achievement were low labour costs and the abundance of virgin land. Some attention began to be paid to scientific and technical progress in agriculture and stock raising, but progress in this side of production does not appear to have been a substantial factor in productivity at this stage. Indeed, blight and animal diseases increased their incidence rather than otherwise, but they could not stay the energy of expansion.

When the terms of the Arreglo Romero were announced they met a cool or hostile reception both in Buenos Aires and London: in Buenos Aires because they were considered too favourable to the possessors of badly depreciated securities; in London because the settlement was regarded as piecemeal. By 1897, however, the Argentine Government was able to resume full interest payments one year ahead of schedule. This was the proof of soundness that created the confidence upon which the investment process in that age depended.

Our story closes when Argentina faced the abundant opportunities of the Boer War. Horses, hides, beef, mutton, wheat, wool,

---

[1] Companies' Registration Office, file 2864.
[2] Ibid., 14352.
[3] See Tables in Appendix.
[4] Ford, *Inter-American Economic Affairs*, vol. ix, 1955, p. 51.

were in demand. Commodore Sir Home Popham had thought the River Plate country important as a means of provisioning the Cape. He had been wrong then; but he was right ninety-three years later. The possibilities about which Sir Woodbine Parish had enthused, and in which he never ceased to believe during his long life, were now realities.

If our story ends happily, at least for some, it also ends on a note of comedy. The Welshmen settled in the Chubut had become Argentine citizens. As such they were obliged to serve fifteen days a year in the militia. Unfortunately the Argentine Government regarded Sundays as appropriate days for the performance of military duties. Two imaginative and perhaps ambitious inhabitants of the colony thought the solution of Sunday drilling was incorporation in the British Empire. They went to Britain to spread the gospel of annexation of Patagonia. The Argentine Government charged them with high treason. A Welsh member asked a question in the House. The President of the Republic visited the Chubut. All was put right. The Welsh-speaking citizens of the Republic resident in Patagonia would drill for fifteen days in December, Sundays excluded. H.M.S. *Pegasus* visited the colony. The Captain reported all quiet, and all residents loyal to the Argentine Republic. Away in the countryside a retired Admiral named Brent complained to the Foreign Office about the miseries and injustices of the Welshmen in Patagonia. The Foreign Office gave the Admiral the facts gathered by the best of authorities—a senior officer in the Royal Navy. The old Admiral replied that he thanked God for the prosperity which was reported to him, but he still thought a Welsh Republic under Argentine sovereignty might constitute a suitable compromise.[1]

[1] Mostly in F.O. 6/459 and 6/462, 1899.

XV

CONCLUSION—RENEWED EXPANSION
SOME QUESTIONS AND ANSWERS

THE developments described in these pages were the foundations of the golden age of the Anglo-Argentine connexion which lasted from the Boer War to World War I. During those years Britain was Argentina's best customer and Britain occupied very much the first place as a supplier of the Argentine market. The danger of repeated breakdown and crisis seemed to have passed. In the years before the Baring Crisis Argentina had on balance sold much less to Britain than she had bought from Britain. This was no longer the case. During the years 1901–14 the Argentine export of commodities to Britain consistently exceeded by a large margin the Argentine import of British goods. In 1913, for example, Britain absorbed Argentine commodities worth £40,726,496 and exported to Argentina goods worth £18,589,272.[1] Likewise Argentina in her trade with the world as a whole had a surplus on commodity account. Hence Argentina possessed the means of avoiding financial crises such as that which had assailed her in 1890–1. She possessed the surplus sufficient to cover the claims of investors abroad and to pay for the many services she was purchasing from foreigners.

The principal factors in this happy state of affairs were the enormous expansion in Argentine productivity and the favourable terms on which she sold her produce in the international market. Cereal production increased three to four times. There was no dramatic increase in the number of cattle raised and the number of sheep even declined, but the weight of meat, wool, and butter produced increased as the techniques of production improved. This great increase in productivity came at a singularly favourable period in the movement of food prices in relation to the price of manufactured goods and services like ocean shipping. In some years the terms of trade were fantastically

[1] *Parliamentary Papers*, 1914–16, lxv.

favourable to Argentina. In 1895, for example, when Argentina was struggling with the problem of recurring payments on capital account, the terms of trade were an estimated number of 86 (1900 = 100). In 1909 the terms of trade were 155 and in 1910, 146.[1]

Commercial and productive developments of this description were, of course, extremely favourable to capital investments. The same banking firm which had estimated British investments in Argentina at approximately £190 millions in 1900 placed the figure at approximately £290 millions in a statement published in 1911.[2] In terms of total volume of investment this was an expansion within a decade which rivalled the 1880's. But it was an expansion from a broader base and it was too much, it may be argued, along established lines. Indeed, there is evidence that the willingness to enter new and risky fields of enterprise was on the decline among the British, and that the initiative was passing to the Germans and Americans by World War I.

These prosperous years witnessed a considerable relaxation of political tension within Argentina. The armed forces as a factor in politics appeared to be fading out and the institutions and political habits of representative democracy to be gaining in strength. There was little direct political tension between Britain and Argentina, but indirectly Argentina eyed Britain with suspicion. The pressure of the financial interests to use force in the collection of debts and other claims, which Salisbury had resisted during the Baring Crisis, was successful in 1902 in the case of Venezuela, and Britain joined with Germany and Italy in blockading Venezuelan ports. Argentina reacted sharply to this unwise proceeding. The Drago Doctrine was given to the world by the Argentine Foreign Minister. For the first time since the brief romance of 1846 the United States and Argentina found themselves effectively on the same side politically. But even the Venezuelan contretemps was obliterated from the public conscience by the flood of prosperity.

The long-standing ambivalence of the Argentine community to foreign enterprise was not effaced by an age of abundance nor by favourable terms of trade. Professor Eteocle Lorini, in his study of the Argentine public debt, voiced a very common

---

[1] Ford, *Inter-American Economic Affairs*, vol. ix, no. 2, 1955, p. 51.
[2] Martínez and Lewandowski, *The Argentine*, p. 358.

view: 'All the industrial, commercial, agricultural, and mining companies which furnish our Argentine statistics bear the foreign mark *limited*; so that one ends by getting the impression that one is studying a purely English colony, for one finds *limited* upon all species of manufactures; *limited* after the statement of capitals; all undertakings are *limited*; insurance is *limited*; the circulation and distribution of Argentine wealth is *limited*.'[1] Lorini acknowledged that capital investment increased employment, raised land values, and increased production, but he advised his countrymen to save and invest on their own account in order to create a 'national capital' which would reduce dependence upon international finance. Thoughts of this kind take us back to the 1850's when the business men and politicians of Buenos Aires Province were projecting a development based on their own accumulation and forward to the 1950's when Perón was seeking to emancipate Argentina from foreign influences. Were they worth uttering then and are they worth examining now?

Speculation on the subject of British enterprise in Argentina carries us to the heart of Anglo-Argentine relationship both as it has existed historically and as it exists at the present time. The term 'imperialism' is widely used in Argentina and elsewhere in discussing the connexion between the two countries. Argentina has never belonged to the British Empire, of course; but Argentina is, or was, part of Britain's informal empire.[2] Argentina is within a British sphere of influence. Britain exercises great influence in Argentina. Britain exploits Argentina. So the argument runs, and the argument is widely believed, and attitudes affecting action derive from it.

There is a case for the large British investment in Argentina, and there is one against it. The evidence suggests, however, that neither case has been sufficiently related to the facts.

Can the term imperialism be applied to Anglo-Argentine relations? If we accept the proposition that imperialism embraces the fact of control through the use of political power, then the verdict for Britain is unquestionably 'Not Guilty'. The only complete attempt made by Britain to establish political power in the River Plate failed, and out of that failure developed

[1] Quoted in Martínez and Lewandowski, *The Argentine*, p. 359.
[2] As the present author suggested in *Past and Present*, Nov. 1953, no. 4.

a policy which specifically recognized that political power exercised in and over Argentina or any other country in South America was an ineffective means of achieving the British objective of a beneficial commercial and financial relationship. The Anglo-Argentine political equation, which recognized Britain and Argentina as independent variables, was not derived from the liberal idealism of Canning, but from the material facts learned on the field of battle and discernible to anyone familiar with the character of the terrain and people of Argentina. During the nineteenth century there was no alteration in the Anglo-Argentine equation, and there is no reason for supposing it is any different today than it was a century and a half ago.

This political equation is the equation from which all equations in the sphere of economics have been derived. The Argentine Government has always possessed the power to forbid, to encourage, or to shape the economic relations of Argentina with other communities including the British community. The British Government has never had the power to oblige Argentina to pay a debt, to pay a dividend, or to export or import any commodity whatever. The only occasion when the British Government went beyond talk in dealing with Argentina, during the troubled time of General Rosas, they were defeated and they formally admitted that they were defeated. When powerful financial interests urged the use of political power to influence Argentine economic policy in 1891, the British Foreign Secretary privately and publicly repudiated such a suggestion. Every crisis in the economic and financial relations of Britain and Argentina has been resolved in economic and financial terms—by a weighing of advantages and disadvantages by both parties—and not by the intrusion of political power. Of course, British commercial and financial interests have exercised great influence in Argentina; but so have Argentine interests exercised great influence in Britain. Any agricultural landlord or farmer in Britain between the years 1890 and 1939 could argue that Argentina was a factor in their fate, and a very adverse one. Derelict fields in Cambridgeshire existed in part because fields in the Argentine Republic were heavy with cheap cereals, and Argentine *estancieros* have wintered on the Riviera while herdsmen in Shropshire went bankrupt. These are facts which make nonsense of myths about British imperialism and Argentina as a semi-colony of a great and powerful state.

One may deplore the consequences for Argentina, and likewise the consequences for Britain, of the kind of relationship worked out by the Argentine landed and commercial interests in conjunction with the financial, industrial, and commercial interests of Great Britain, but when one starts deploring let no one blame an abstraction called Britain or another one called Argentina. If, over a long span of time, Argentina has possessed a weak and narrowly based industrial structure compared with that of the United States or even Canada, this has been due to the concentration of effort in Argentina upon agricultural and pastoral enterprise and upon the production of pastoral and agricultural commodities. Political power and/or decisive influence upon policy in Argentina has belonged until recent times to the interests with most to gain by such a concentration.

The dominant interests in Argentina sought out the foreign capitalists in the first instance; the foreign capitalists did not invade Argentina, and in the beginning and for many years after the investment process commenced European investors were reluctant to supply Argentina with as much purchasing power as the Argentine Government required. That the European investors invested anything depended partly upon the guarantees given by the Argentine authorities, partly upon the direct responsibility for payment undertaken by the state, and partly upon the existence in Argentina of a British business community capable of organizing in a practical way enterprises like railways and meat-freezing plants. Contrary to common belief the British investor received help and protection from the Argentine Government not the British Government. When the British Government finally felt obliged to assist British investors in Argentina, it did so not by sending an expeditionary force to the River Plate, but by underwriting the Bank of England, which in turn underwrote the private and joint-stock banks, which in their turn underwrote the firm of Baring Brothers.

There is still much work to be done before any convincing answer can be given to the question: who benefited most from economic development in Argentina? The evidence in hand, however, suggests some tentative answers. Some foreign interests benefited greatly; for example, the shareholders of some of the banks; some railway shareholders and investors in meat-processing and cold-storage enterprises and some mercantile establishments. But the overall profits of British investors were sufficiently low to prompt the hypothesis that the great interests of Argentina did not dominate the fields occupied so largely by British enterprise because the returns were greater in the fields dominated by Argentinos. The appreciation of land values and the profits of pastoral enterprise, commercial agriculture, and share-cropping seem to have been the best sources of wealth in the years from 1860 to 1914. The political power, the social knowledge, the entrenched position of native Argentinos gave them a tremendous advantage in this field. The system of education, handicapped in its scope by niggardly state expenditure and in its content by the influence of the Roman Catholic Church, further ordained that native Argentinos were ill equipped to take control of enterprises requiring great technical knowledge and habits of exact application to managerial responsibilities. Thus foreigners, and particularly the British, dominated in the less rewarding and more demanding fields of endeavour.

There seems to be considerable evidence during the period we have studied that the permanent wage worker both urban and rural benefited least from the developments we have described. If this is so, why was immigration so abundant? Economic opportunities not wage rates seem to be the predominant inducement to immigrants. Argentine wages in the long run seem to have been rather better than wages in Italy and Spain, from whence the majority of immigrants came, but much inferior to wage rates in the United States, Canada, or Australia. But economic opportunities seem to have been roughly alike. Indeed, in Argentina the prizes open to people possessed of peasant shrewdness in buying and selling were, perhaps, greater than elsewhere. For a man with only a strong back and a willingness to work, Argentina was, perhaps, a slight improvement on his homeland, but not a place of rich rewards.

Among the beneficiaries of Argentine expansion before 1914 we must not neglect mention of the English wage working class. Some benefited from employment opportunities created by manufacturing for the Argentine market. A much wider mass benefited as consumers from the cheap food products flowing in increasing flood from the River Plate. If the Englishman of that age was the biggest meat eater in Europe it was partly due to the fact that Argentina was the cheapest producer of beef in the world.

The Anglo-Argentine connexion, with the benefits and disadvantages which we have described as they existed in the years between the Boer War and World War I, was a phase in the life of growing communities and not a system which can be recreated. The passage of time and the changing social composition of the Argentine community revealed weaknesses and altered the objectives of economic activity. One of the leading staples of Argentine international trade—cereals—was marketed under conditions of nearly perfect competition. So long as the overall factors in the world market kept up cereal prices in relation to the prices of manufactured goods, the Argentine economy functioned without crippling frustrations. When the overall factors in the world market began to alter this relationship between cereal prices and the prices of manufactured goods, Argentina began to discover the limitations and defects of concentration on food production.

Changes in world-market conditions ran parallel after World War I with changes in the social composition of the Argentine community. So long as Argentina possessed an open frontier where new land was continuously being brought into production, the flow of immigrants and the growth of great commercial metropolises like Buenos Aires and Rosario did not seriously disturb the rural-urban balance either in politics or policy making. When the land frontier closed, as it did in the golden age at the beginning of this century, the urban masses began to assert themselves, and the better educated began to question the wisdom of placing all Argentina's eggs in the well-worn basket of agricultural and pastoral production. Why not make more jobs and more opportunities for native Argentinos? The popular pressure for industrialization began to develop even before World War I. Perhaps rich land is Argentina's best resource, but Argentina is also a people, and a growing number of them after World War I began rightly to doubt whether the life of a farm labourer, a cold-storage worker, or a grain clerk was good enough. When the Great Depression of 1928 struck down cereal and meat prices, the bell began to toll for the old Anglo-Argentine relationship whose birth and growth is the subject of this book.

STATISTICAL APPENDIX

TABLE I. *Anglo-Argentine Trade and Investment*

Year	ARGENTINE TRADE[1] (£000's)		UNITED KINGDOM TRADE[2] with Argentina (£000's)		UNITED KINGDOM CAPITAL in Argentina (£000's)
	Imports	Exports	Imports	Exports	
1854	..	..	1,285	1,267	..
1855	..	..	1,052	742	..
1856	..	..	981	998	..
1857	..	..	1,574	1,287	2,605[3]
1858	..	..	1,195	1,009	..
1859	..	..	1,664	959	..
1860	..	..	1,098	1,782	..
1861	..	..	1,472	1,384	..
1862	..	..	1,133	854	..
1863	..	..	1,240	1,331	..
1864	..	..	1,186	1,757	..
1865	..	..	1,014	1,951	5,375[4]
1866	..	..	1,073	2,841	..
1867	..	..	912	2,837	..
1868	..	..	1,496	1,927	..
1869	..	..	1,268	2,271	..
1870	9,904	6,093	1,486	2,346	..
1871	9,199	5,449	1,989	2,464	..
1872	12,416	9,530	1,903	3,911	..
1873	14,805	9,556	2,604	3,729	..
1874	11,685	8,980	1,271	3,128	23,060[5]
1875	11,628	10,486	1,360	2,386	..
1876	7,273	9,695	1,664	1,544	..
1877	8,154	9,026	1,699	2,092	..
1878	8,822	7,565	1,100	2,318	..
1879	9,347	9,951	828	2,063	..
1880	9,181	11,770	887	2,451	..
1881	11,141	11,588	585	3,341	..

[1] *Parliamentary Papers*, Statistical Abstract for the principal and other Foreign Countries for relevant years.

[2] W. Page, editor, *Commerce and Industry, Tables of Statistics for the British Empire from 1815* (London, 1919), pp. 110–11.

[3] This is the debt of the Province of Buenos Aires acknowledged by the law of October 1857, consisting of approximately £1,000,000 on account of the Loan of 1824 bearing interest at 6 per cent. and £1,641,000 in 3 per cent. bonds issued on account of defaulted interest on the capital sum.

[4] This is made up of the unrepaid portion of the Loan of 1824 plus unrepaid defaulted interest plus the authorized capital of two railways and one bank.

[5] Compiled from data in M. G. Mulhall, *The English in South America* (Buenos Aires, 1878), p. 529.

TABLE I *(cont.)*

	ARGENTINE TRADE[1] (£000's)		UNITED KINGDOM TRADE[2] *with Argentina* (£000's)		UNITED KINGDOM CAPITAL *in Argentina* (£000's)
Year	*Imports*	*Exports*	*Imports*	*Exports*	
1882	12,249	12,078	1,234	4,167	..
1883	16,087	12,042	946	4,904	..
1884	18,811	13,606	1,159	5,811	..
1885	18,444	16,776	1,879	4,660	45,602[3]
1886	19,082	13,967	1,646	5,191	..
1887	23,470	16,884	2,177	6,230	..
1888	25,682	20,022	2,659	7,657	..
1889	32,914	24,563	2,016	10,683	..
1890	28,448	20,164	4,130	8,416	174,768[4]
1891	13,442	20,644	3,451	4,247	..
1892	18,296	22,674	4,540	5,652	..
1893	19,245	18,818	4,837	5,536	..
1894	18,558	20,338	6,169	4,515	..
1895	19,019	24,014	9,084	5,351	..
1896	22,433	23,360	8,974	6,621	..
1897	19,658	20,234	5,754	4,801	..
1898	21,486	26,766	7,788	5,587	..
1899	23,370	36,984	10,942	6,211	..
1900	22,697	30,920	13,080	7,143	189,040[5]
1901	22,792	33,543	12,415	6,752	..
1902	20,608	35,897	14,022	5,871	..
1903	26,241	44,197	19,144	8,011	..
1904	37,461	52,832	23,035	10,847	..
1905	41,031	64,569	25,034	13,003	..
1906	53,994	58,451	23,803	19,429	..
1907	57,172	59,241	26,480	17,817	..
1908	54,595	73,201	35,728	16,421	..
1909	60,551	79,470	32,528	18,698	..
1910	70,354	74,525	28,933	19,120	291,110[6]

[1,2] *See footnotes 1 and 2 opposite.*

[3] *The Economist*, 23 Jan. 1886, p. 105.

[4] This estimate is based, after considerable revision and correction, upon an estimate made by Arthur Herbert, Commercial Secretary in Buenos Aires, and printed in *Parliamentary Papers*, 1892, lxxxi, pp. 92–93. Herbert's total was £204 millions. Two modern estimates are J. F. Rippy, 'The British investment Boom of the 1880's in Latin America', *H.A.H.R.* xxix, 1949, pp. 282 ff.; and J. H. Williams, *Argentine International Trade Under Inconvertible Paper Money, 1880–1900* (Cambridge, Mass., 1920), p. 103. Rippy's total is £154,338,385 and Williams, for all foreign investments on 1 Jan. 1892, is £184,500,000.

[5] Estimate by the Argentine banking firm of Tornquist y Compañía quoted in Williams, *Argentine International Trade*, p. 150, n. 3.

[6] Estimate also by Tornquist y Compañia quoted in A. B. Martinez and M. Lewandowski, *The Argentine*, p. 358.

TABLE 2. *Content of United Kingdom Trade with Argentina (£000's)*

	Total exports	Textiles	Coal	Iron and steel	Hardware	Railway carriages	Tools and machinery
1818	1 yr. 731	626	1	8	19	··	··
1854	1 yr. 1,267	··	··	··	··	··	··
1850–4	5 yrs. ··	3,154	14	142	247	··	41
1858–62	5 yrs. 5,988	4,501	56	325	252	··	181
1863–7	5 yrs. 10,717	7,475	120	1,096	379	··	481
1870–4	5 yrs. 15,578	7,747	370	2,714	770	··	242
1875–9	5 yrs. 10,403	5,758	204	1,655	407	··	··
1886–90	5 yrs. 38,177	11,095	1,603	9,604	707	3,008	3,851
1891–5	5 yrs. 25,301	10,343	2,285	3,243	207	885	2,476

	Total imports	Hides and skins	Wool	Tallow	Cereals	Meat and animals	Flax
1818	··	··	··	··	··	··	··
1854	1 yr. 1,285	448	107	415	··	··	··
1850–4	5 yrs. ··	··	··	··	··	··	··
1858–62	5 yrs. 6,562	2,849	985	1,261	··	··	··
1863–7	5 yrs. 5,425	2,071	1,060	1,125	··	··	··
1870–4	5 yrs. 9,253	3,898	1,181	2,941	··	5	··
1875–9	5 yrs. 6,651	2,990	578	1,577	148	26	··
1886–90	5 yrs. 12,628	1,020	539	415	5,486	3,145	1,140
1891–5	5 yrs. 28,081	1,230	1,019	418	14,446	7,376	2,286

Source: 1818, R. A. Humphreys, *British Consular Reports on the Trade and Politics of Latin America, 1824–1826* (London, 1940), pp. 56, 345. Remainder calculated from *Parliamentary Papers* for relevant years, quoted in H. S. Ferns, 'Investment and Trade between Britain and Argentina in the Nineteenth Century', *Economic History Review*, second series, vol. iii, no. 2, 1950.

INDEX

PRINTED IN GREAT BRITAIN
AT THE UNIVERSITY PRESS, OXFORD
BY VIVIAN RIDLER
PRINTER TO THE UNIVERSITY